TRIUMPHUS

TRIUMPHUS

AN INQUIRY INTO THE ORIGIN, DEVELOPMENT
AND MEANING OF THE ROMAN TRIUMPH

BY

H. S. VERSNEL

LEIDEN
E. J. BRILL
1970

This book was printed with the financial support of the
Netherlands Organization for the Advancement of Pure Research
(Z.W.O.)

Homines enim ad deos nulla re propius accedunt quam salutem hominibus dando.

Cicero

CONTENTS

PREFACE

According to one of the many Leyden *mores* the author of a thesis is not allowed to mention by name those persons who are in any way connected with the University. This means that many people who by their moral support, their warm interest, their advice or suggestions contributed to the writing of this book, will unfortunately have to remain anonymous. I am greatly indebted to them and to the friends who were kind enough to read the proofs of the various chapters, and thereby took a great deal of work off my hands.

However, those who undertook the most onerous tasks, may be mentioned by name. Mrs. M. H. Boomsma-Huisman translated the thesis in the shortest possible time. Unfortunately, the possibilities for communication between author and translator were so limited that there was no opportunity for them to discuss some problems of translation. Therefore Mr. E. M. H. van Gendt and Mr. F. Lettinga each read a large part of the translation, amended the text where it seemed necessary and made many useful suggestions for improvement. I am very grateful to them for giving so much of their valuable time and energy.

For a number of years my wife had to share her husband with a demanding and unco-operative member of the family: the triumph. Not only did she bear with this intruder, but she also typed the entire manuscript, including the footnotes, with two fingers. It is hard to say which of these two achievements deserves more admiration.

My mother-in-law, Mrs. E. A. Hoogvliet-Smelik, made an important contribution to the thesis by reading all the proofs with admirable accuracy and patience, thus eliminating countless errors.

Drs. A. V. van Stekelenburg undertook the unrewarding and time-consuming task of compiling an index, a task which he performed with great scrupulousness, for which I owe him many thanks.

The Netherlands Organization for the Advancement of Pure Research (Z.W.O.) not only encouraged the publication of the book, but also enabled the author to devote himself completely to his studies for a full year by granting him a stipend. But for this highly valued support this thesis would in all probability never have been completed.

ABBREVIATIONS

A.J.P.	American Journal of Philology.
Act. Or.	Acta Orientalia.
Arch. Jahrb.	Jahrbuch des deutschen archäologischen Instituts.
Arctos	Arctos. Acta philologica Fennica.
A.R.W.	Archiv für Religionswissenschaft.
Athen. Mitt.	Mitteilungen des deutschen archäologischen Instituts. Athen. Abt.
B.C.H.	Bulletin de Correspondance Hellénique.
Bibl. Or.	Bibliotheca Orientalis.
Bonner Jahrb.	Bonner Jahrbücher des Rheinischen Landesmuseums in Bonn.
B.S.L.	Bulletin de la Société de linguistique de Paris.
Bull. Com.	Bullettino della Commissione Archeologica comunale in Roma.
Class. Phil.	Classical Philology.
Class. Quart.	Classical Quarterly.
Class. Rev.	Classical Review.
Emerita	Emerita. Boletín de Lingüística y Filologia Clásica.
Eranos	Eranos. Acta philologica Suecana.
Ét. Class.	Les Études Classiques.
Glotta	Glotta. Zeitschrift für griech. und lat. Sprache.
Gnomon	Gnomon. Kritische Zeitschrift für die gesamte klassische Altertumswissenschaft.
Gött. Gel. Anz.	Göttingische Gelehrte Anzeigen.
Gymnasium	Gymnasium. Zeitschrift für Kultur der Antike und Humanistische Bildung.
Harv. Theol. Rev.	Harvard Theological Review.
Hermes	Hermes. Zeitschrift für klassische Philologie.
Historia	Historia. Zeitschrift für alte Geschichte.
I.F.	Indogermanische Forschungen.
J.E.A.	Journal of Egyptian Archaeology.
J.S.S.	Journal of Semitic Studies.
Latomus	Latomus. Revue d'Études Latines.
Lingua	Lingua. International Review of general Linguistics.
M.A.A.R.	Memoirs of the American Academy in Rome.
Maia.	Maia. Rivista di Letterature classiche.
Mél. Éc. Rom.	Mélanges d'Archéologie et d'Histoire de l'École Française de Rome.
Mnemos.	Mnemosyne. Bibliotheca Classica Batava.
M.R.K.	Myth, Ritual and Kingship. Essays on the Theory and Practice of Kingship in the Ancient Near East and in Israel, Oxford, 1958. Ed. by S. H. Hooke.
Mus. Helv.	Museum Helveticum.
Orbis	Orbis. Bulletin international de documentation linguistique.
Philol.	Philologus. Zeitschrift für das klassische Altertum.
R.E.	Pauly-Wissowa, Real-Encyclopädie der classischen Altertumswissenschaft.

R.E.A.	Revue des Études Anciennes.
R.E.L.	Revue des Études Latines.
Rend. Ist. Lomb.	Rendiconti dell'Istituto Lombardo. Classi di Lettere, Scienze morali e storichi.
Rev. Arch.	Revue Archéologique.
Rev. Hist.	Revue Historique.
Rev. Phil.	Revue de Philologie.
Rhein. Mus.	Rheinisches Museum für Philologie.
R.H.R.	Revue de l'Histoire des Religions.
Röm. Mitt.	Mitteilungen des deutschen archäologischen Instituts. Röm. Abt.
R.V.V.	Religionsgeschichtliche Versuche und Vorarbeiten.
S.E.	Studi Etruschi.
S.M.S.R.	Studi e Materiali di Storia delle Religioni.
Studi class. e or.	Studi classici e orientali.
Symb. Osl.	Symbolae Osloenses.
Vig. Christ.	Vigiliae Christianae.
Wien. Stud.	Wiener Studien. Zeitschrift für klassische Philologie.
Z.A.	Zeitschrift für Assyriologie und verwandte Gebiete.
Z.S.S.	Zeitschrift der Savigny-Stiftung für Rechtsgeschichte. Romanistische Abteilung.

INTRODUCTION

Certamente si tratta sempre di ipotesi; ma, come
sempre, nella scienza importa scegliere quella che
spiega il maggior numero di fenomeni.

P. de Francisci

According to Orosius [1] no fewer than 320 triumphs were celebrated during the period between the founding of Rome and the
reign of Vespasian. Nor was this all; also in subsequent years
triumphs were held, be it at increasingly long intervals, until
Honorius in 403 A.D. combined his accession to the consulate with
the last official triumph known to us [2]. The entire history of Rome
has thus been marked by a ceremony which testified to the power of
Rome, its mission of conquest and domination, and to the courage
of its soldiers. Primarily, however, the triumph characterized the
greatness of Rome as being due, on the one hand, to the excellence
of the victorious general, and, on the other, to the favour of the
supreme god, who, *optimus maximus*, ensured the continuance and the
prosperity of the Roman empire. In no other Roman ceremony do
god and man approach each other as closely as they do in the
triumph. Not only is the triumphal procession directed towards
the Capitolium, where the triumphator presents a solemn offering
to Iuppiter O.M., but the triumphator himself has a status which
appears to raise him to the rank of the gods. Amidst the cheers of
io triumpe he enters the city via the Porta Triumphalis, standing on
a triumphal chariot, which is drawn by four horses. He is clothed
in a purple *toga* and a *tunica* stitched with palm-motifs, together
called *ornatus Iovis*, and in his hand he carries a scepter crowned by
an eagle. His face has been red-leaded. It seems as if Iuppiter
himself, incarnated in the triumphator, makes his solemn entry
into Rome.

What did this remarkable ceremony stand for? If the Romans
themselves are asked this question, the answer received is highly
unsatisfactory. The triumph is a *honos*, for gods as well as for men,
we are told by Livy, 45, 39, 10, *diis quoque ... non solum hominibus*

---

[1] Hist. 7, 9, 8.

[2] Claudian. 28, 543 ff. See Ehlers, R. E. 2e Reihe 7, 1939, 500, s.v.
Triumphus.

debetur triumphus. The triumph, which is looked upon as a special homage to Iuppiter—Tacitus, hist. 4, 58, 6, *Iuppiter optime maxime, quem...tot triumphis coluimus*—, was to the Roman citizen the highest mark of honour that could be conferred upon him: Liv. 30, 15, 12, *neque magnificentius quicquam triumpho apud Romanos...esse*. The great sacrifices generals were prepared to make in order to attain this distinction, and the strict requirements victor and victory had to meet, testify to the honorific character of this ceremony. Beyond this characterization the ancient authors do not supply any information, and we find to our regret that it does not throw any light on the many problems the ceremony evokes.

It was not before the end of the nineteenth century that questions were raised as to the nature and meaning of the triumph, and in the course of years many theories have been put forward without any agreement having been reached on the main issues. When, however, the existing theories are surveyed, one thing stands out: practically without exception they deal with only one aspect of the triumph, but often pretend that this particular aspect discloses the essential character of the ceremony. This may be the reason why so far no monograph has been devoted to the triumph, and why the only summarizing study which might pretend to bear this name, the R. E. paper by Ehlers [1], arrives at an explanation of the triumph which proves to be nothing but the sum total of the various partial interpretations furnished by other authors: "Er ist in historischer Zeit in erster Linie eine Ehrung des siegreichen Feldherrn und eine Schaustellung des errungenen Sieges... Aber der Triumph ist ursprünglich weniger ein politischer als ein religiöser Akt: sakralrechtlich bedeutet die Feier auf dem Capitol die Einlösung der beim Auszug in den Krieg gegebenen Gelübde, rituell dient die Prozession der Reinigung des Heeres vom Unsegen des Krieges". (495)

In itself it is, of course, neither impossible nor *a priori* improbable that various aspects of the triumph had specific meanings of their own, but there are grounds for scepsis when it is found that the interpretations of the various aspects of the triumph adopted by Ehlers are each of them based on investigations of one detail which neglect the other facets of the ceremony, as if the detail in question were given *in vacuo*. This procedure is to be observed with respect to each of the following essential aspects of the triumph.

---

[1] R.E. 2e Reihe 7, 1939, 493 ff., s.v. *Triumphus*.

The name triumphus and the cry triumpe have so far almost exclusively been dealt with by linguists. It is at present generally acknowledged that they are to be traced back to Gr. θρίαμβος, but apart from a few dogmatic and unverified statements no information has as yet been supplied on the semantic aspects of this evolution.

The figure of the triumphator has for the past fifty years commanded a widespread interest. This is quite understandable, as it is closely linked up with fundamental questions concerning the Roman religion. Did the triumphator represent the god Iuppiter? Wissowa [1] thought he did, and his view carried so much weight that the voices of those few who pointed out that such a phenomenon is contrary to everything we know about the genuinely Roman religion, were scarcely heard. The first author who did evoke some reactions, though not all of them positive ones, was Deubner [2], who defended the thesis that the triumphator represented not Iuppiter, but the former *rex*. A remarkable fact is that none of the antagonists pays any attention to the name *triumphus*. More recent scholars restrict themselves to an often scarcely reasoned acceptance of one of the views. No general agreement has been reached, and the problem remains unsolved.

The relation between the ludi Romani and the triumph, which are both characterized by a *pompa*, is the only facet of the triumph on which there is nearly full agreement. Only one dissident, A. Piganiol [3], opposes the generally accepted theory of Mommsen [4] that the *ludi Romani* originally formed part of the triumphal ceremony, gradually detached themselves from it, and finally began to lead an existence of their own. No further thought has as yet been given to the consequences of the undoubtedly Etruscan origin of the *ludi* and the *pompa circensis* in connection with the origin and the fundamental meaning of the triumph.

Since the rise of the ethnological branch of the study of religions the *passage through the Porta Triumphalis* has been explained as a lustration or expiation rite. It was thought that the army, on returning home, had to be purified of the stains of war, death and blood. This forms a very clear example of how the isolation of one detail of the triumph inevitably leads to myopia: no one considered

---

[1] R.u.K. 1st ed. 111, 2nd ed. 127.
[2] Hermes, 69, 1934, 316 ff.
[3] Recherches sur les jeux romains, Paris, 1923, 75 ff.
[4] Röm. Forsch. II, 42 ff.

the—obvious—question of why a victorious army did need a purification whereas a losing one did not. Wagenvoort [1] was the first to recognize the significance of this question, and answered it on the basis of his dynamistic theory. Even his solution, however, does not satisfactorily account for the specific character of the triumph as compared with the celebration of victories generally.

The ius triumphandi was the first aspect of the triumph to draw the scholars' attention. On this subject we find two diametrically opposed views. Mommsen [2] thinks that the condition that the triumphator should have *imperium* formed the central requirement for the triumph, whereas Laqueur [3], in a paper he entitled "Über das Wesen des Römischen Triumphs", put forward *auspicium* as being the prime requisite. The latter theory, which interpreted the triumph as a *voti solutio*, is still mentioned as the correct interpretation of the sacral aspects of the triumph. What seems surprising is that this theory about the essential character of the triumph was established without any attention having been given to the other aspects of the ceremony—the name is not discussed any more than is the Porta Triumphalis, the relation with the *ludi Romani* is referred to in passing, the figure of the triumphator dismissed in a foot-note—and that such a procedure has not aroused any protest among later scholars.

This, then, is the present state of affairs: there are several studies about details of the triumph, and conflicting theories about each of them. In addition it should be borne in mind that many of the interpretations have been proposed as part or against the background of phenomenological or theological studies and theories which are not restricted to Roman phenomena and in which the triumph is used only in so far as it may serve as an argument or illustration. Van Windekens [4], e.g., uses the evolution of θρίαμβος into *triumphus* to support his Pelasgian theory, Frazer [5] employs the divine status of the triumphator as proof of an ancient Roman/Italian divine kingship, and the Porta Triumphalis is found to give admittance to van Gennep's "Rites de passage" [6] as well as to Wagenvoort's

---

[1] Roman Dynamism, Oxford, 1947, 168.
[2] Röm. Staatsrecht I³, 126 ff.
[3] Hermes, 44, 1909, 215 ff.
[4] Orbis, 2, 1953, 489 ff.
[5] Golden Bough I³, 2, 174 ff.
[6] Les rites de passage, Paris, 1909, 28.

"Roman Dynamism" [1]. To these examples many could be added. Far from denying anyone the right to this manner of approach I nevertheless hold the view that interpretations of this kind should never be used as a basis if we try to explain the triumph as an independent phenomenon. In too many instances they overemphasize the data that fit in with the theory concerned, whilst leaving out those that do not.

The above remarks largely determine the task of anyone who proposes to investigate the origin, development and meaning of the triumph. First of all he has to evaluate and sift the existing theories about the various details of the ceremony, and to go *ad fontes* in each case. It will be found that many sources which were tapped long ago, have not dried up yet. Like his predecessors—in fact, even more so—the investigator will have to deal with the major aspects of the triumph separately, so as to prevent a *petitio principii*. Unlike his predecessors, however, he will have to avoid making the mistake of thinking that his conclusions concerning *one* aspect furnish an explanation of the essence of the triumph. Finally, he will have to let himself be influenced as little as possible, in this part of his investigation, by preconceived views on the nature of *the* Roman religion and by the dynamistic, animistic and polydaemonistic theories about it, even though everyone is bound to base his conclusions on a point of view he is unable and unwilling to disavow.

The above principles are to guide us in the analytical part of this study, which deals with the five most important elements of the problem presented by the triumph. Not until the building-stones have been cleaned of the dust and the dirt they have collected in the course of generations, and have subsequently been cut into shape or remodelled, can a start be made with the constructive work, the synthesis. In trying to interpret the collective material and the results attained in the first five chapters, it will time and again be impossible not to show one's colours. Philological and historical research will now be replaced by the drafting of a concept, a plan in which the elements are arranged in such a way that they should automatically fall into place and together form a harmonious and well-balanced construction. Such a concept should be based on a theoretical fundament, about which I wish to make a few preliminary remarks, although it will have to prove its value and right of existence by the manner in which it functions.

---

[1] Roman Dynamism, 154 ff.

In the study of Roman religion there are several branches and schools, whose representatives have occasionally made valuable contributions to science by open and honest discussions. In many instances, however, their implacable attitudes did not only preclude a fruitful "choc des opinions", but, as it were, implicitly required of a third party to take sides. Absolutizing viewpoints to such an extent will, in my opinion, lead to a deadlock, and have in many instances even proved catastrophic, particularly where the problem of the triumph is concerned. For this reason I have refused to let myself be persuaded to choose one entire school or theory on which to base an explanation of the triumph.

Any scholar—particularly any Netherlands scholar—writing about an important phenomenon of Roman religion, is sure to come into contact with, and almost as sure to fall under the spell of the views Wagenvoort defends in his "Roman Dynamism", a book to which Bömer in 1949 [1] accorded "die volle Anerkennung dieser seit Altheims Arbeiten fraglos bedeutendsten Erscheinung auf dem Gebiet der altrömischen Religion". This, however, does not preclude a recognition of the value of the arguments and theories of his—in every sense—fiercest opponent, Dumézil [2], even by a person who cannot possibly regard the well-known tripartition theory of this French scholar as the *non plus ultra* in the science of Roman religion. Taking sides in the discussion between Nilsson and W. Otto —which the former [3] himself characterizes as offering very little perspective—would equally lead to a sterilization of the investigation if it were to imply a disregarding of all interpretations and results of either scholar. Taking a concrete example which will be dealt with in the present study, I think that no student of the Dionysiac religion will make any headway if he refuses to put the views of Nilsson and Otto opposite each other, and compare them in every single detail. *Mutatis mutandis* the same applies to the fundamentally different theories and methods of Wissowa and Latte on the one hand, and those of Altheim and Koch on the other.

Finally, I am of the opinion that the investigator of a Roman ceremony which owes so much to Etruscan, Hellenic and possibly

---

[1] Gnomon, 21, 1949, 344.

[2] See his controversy with the "primitivists" in Rev. Phil. 26, 1952, 7 ff.; Rev. Phil. 28, 1954, 19 f.; La religion romaine archaïque, Paris, 1966, 33 ff.

[3] G.G.R. I², 374; 564 n.1.

other cultures, should not hesitate to go *extra pomerium*. The scholar who wants to explain the triumph with the aid of Roman data only, resembles the *flamen Dialis*, who, however venerable he might have been, was nevertheless rendered completely powerless by his many taboos, one of which forbade a stay of more than one night outside Rome. However, also outside Italy the investigator encounters unsuspected *bella, horrida bella*, such as the conflict between the advocates and the opponents of the "Myth and Ritual school". Also in this field, where the classicist fears to tread, I found it impossible unconditionally to take sides with either of the parties. Here again this eclectic point of view is not based on theoretical considerations, but on purely practical experience, which has taught that explaining all facts from one angle puts a strain on these facts which affects their relevance and value. Moreover, the triumph is found to be a phenomenon of such complexity that not one single theory can possibly be assumed to explain all its aspects. It has become increasingly clear to me that here, too, the truth, though rarely midway, lies never entirely on one side.

In connection with the term synthesis I may point out that the proper meaning of the substantives ending in -σις was an activity, not the result of an action. One of the principal theses of the present study is that the triumph is not an originally Roman phenomenon, but an ancient sacral ceremony which was introduced into Rome via Etruria. If this development is to be traced step by step, it is necessary, if only for methodical reasons, to distinguish two phases: the pre-Roman triumph and the *interpretatio Romana* of this ceremony. When, therefore, the data and conclusions of the first five chapters are summarized, the result will not be a simple explanation of one triumphal ceremony, but an elucidation of a historical development. This may also serve as an answer to the reader who, to quote Cicero [1], might think: *interdum ut in herbis rustici solent dicere in summa ubertate inest luxuries quaedam quae stilo depascenda est.* The chapters VI and VIII, in particular, might give rise to this thought. My decision of not pruning them more drastically was based on the consideration that in a study of this kind the reader should be enabled to follow closely the author's train of thought, especially in those sections which serve as the fundament of the final interpretation of the subject investigated.

---

[1] De orat. 2, 96.

Chapter VI contains the religious-historical material by which it is endeavoured to explain the Etruscan triumph, whereas in Chapter VIII the *binomium "imperium auspiciumque"* is to form the background against which the Roman triumph stands out in relief.

To conclude: the amount of literature studied is always too small when a subject as complicated as the present one is dealt with. It will undoubtedly be possible to point to *lacunae* in each section. I only hope I did not overlook too many essential works.

PART ONE

ANALYSIS

Der Fortschritt in unserem Wissen geschieht durch die Untersuchung, also die analytische Kritik der Überlieferung, die zur Feststellung einer Wahrheit führt. Es bleibt analytische Untersuchung, auch wenn neue Faktoren in die Rechnung eingestellt werden; die Vermehrung des Materials ändert das Ergebnis, nicht die Methode.

U. von Wilamowitz-Moellendorff

CHAPTER ONE

ΘΡΙΑΜΒΟΣ AND *TRIUMPHUS*

οὐ δεῖ γὰρ ἐπὶ τῶν κυρίων ἐτυμολογίας λαμβάνειν

Herodianus

1. *Introduction*

Sic triumphare appellatum, quod cum imperatore milites redeuntes clamitant per Urbem in Capitolium eunti "<i>o triumphe"; id a Θριάμβῳ *ac Graeco Liberi cognomento potest dictum*, thus reads the oldest, and, as is now generally assumed, correct explanation of the word *triumphus* in Varro [1]. In spite of this scholar's authority other etymologies have been suggested, in ancient [2] as well as in modern [3] times. None of these suggestions, however, appears convincing. In favour of Varro's hypothesis is not merely the striking formal similarity between the Latin word and the Greek one, but also the fact that, in spite of imaginative constructions, *triumphus* or the older *triumpe* cannot be connected with any other Latin word, and may therefore be surmised to be of foreign origin. Also as far as meaning is concerned, a relationship between Θρίαμβος and *triumphus* can be demonstrated; a relationship which, as I hope to prove, differs from, but is no less clear than the one so far supposed to exist. Finally, the decisive argument is the fact that historiographers writing in Greek translate the Latin *triumphus* by Θρίαμβος. The Greek term in this meaning is already used by Polybius [4], which proves that the relation Θρίαμβος-*triumphus* was already known before Varro. Apart from a few linguists cited by Walde-Hofmann, there is, consequently, no one who still doubts the correctness of the derivation put forward by Varro [5], and in the present stage

---

[1] l.l. 6, 68. This etymology is in ancient literature also found in Serv. ad Aen. 10, 775; Gramm. Lat. ed. Keil, 2, 20, 19; 5, 239, 15.

[2] A survey of these is found in Ehlers, R.E. 2e Reihe, 7, 1939, 493, s.v. *Triumphus*.

[3] See Walde-Hofmann, L.E.W.³, s.v. *Triumphus*.

[4] Polyb. 6, 15, 8.

[5] Sceptical is von Wilamowitz, Euripides Herakles I, 1889, 63 n. 25: "*Triumpe* im Arvallied kann man nicht leicht als entlehnt ansehen. Eher dürfte es Interjektion sein wie τήνελλα und das ursprüngliche enthalten." Bruhl, Mél. Éc. Rome, 46, 1929, 87, thinks that *triumpe* is a truly Latin word, and that it was only later on connected with Θρίαμβος.

of our investigation there are no reasons for re-opening the discussions on the subject.

In addition to providing us with our starting-point, Varro furnishes the briefest formulation [1] of the questions which should be asked in dealing with a subject as is here discussed, viz. *a qua re et in qua re vocabulum sit impositum*. If we add: *qua via*, these questions may serve as the framework for this chapter.

The investigation of θρίαμβος and *triumphus*, and the derivation of the one from the other should cover two fields, viz. that which *Graeci vocant* ἐτυμολογίαν and that περὶ σημαινομένων. The ideal procedure in which the sciences of etymology and semasiology [2] are applied in co-ordination and—once again to quote Varro—*promiscue*, presents difficulties as to method. Though it is necessary, for ease of survey, to approach the formal and semantic aspects of a linguistic problem separately, and though both sciences are for the time being awarded equal rights, this does not mean that the order of treatment has become arbitrary. In a paper in which one of the subjects dealt with is θρίαμβος, C. Theander [3] points out in this connection: "...scheint es doch vielmehr selbstverständlich dass eine besonnene Erklärung einer beliebigen sprachlichen Erscheinung sich jedesmal vor allem mit derjenigen Sprache, der diese angehört, zu beschäftigen hat, indem es dem Forscher obliegt, dort alles das auf zu lesen, was mit derselben in Zusammenhang gebracht werden und zu ihrer Aufhellung dienen kann; nur wer diese Bedingung sorgfältig erfüllt, erwirbt das Recht die Grenze zu überschreiten, um auch auf fremdem Boden Anknüpfungen zu suchen". This warning, levelled at the *rabies etymologorum* which, though particularly characteristic of the 19th century, still has not been completely eradicated, has by now become common property. If in this chapter we, too,grant the investigation on the function of the word in its own language priority over formal-etymological comparisons with other languages [4], this is done for yet another reason.

The object of our study is the origin and the essence of the

---

[1] 1.l.5,2.
[2] In the meaning indicated in Varro, 1.l.5,2.
[3] C. Theander, Eranos, 15, 1915, 99.
[4] I start from the derivation "*triumphus a* θριάμβῳ" on the basis of its unquestionable and generally recognized evidence, which, I hope, will be confirmed by my argumentation.

Roman triumph. In this study formal linguistic data can and should be used, but only in so far as they further the investigation on the meaning of the word. Now it is found that for the word θρίαμβος the number of etymological explanations suggested exceeds that of the testimonia of this term to be found in the Greek language [1]. If, on the other hand, the well-known dictionaries are consulted on the *meaning* of the word, it is found that there is no agreement on this matter either. "Cortège religieux accompagné de chants inspirés et de danse" [2], e.g., is not the same thing as "hymn to Dionysos" [3]. In view of this uncertainty as to meaning it will be obvious that etymological derivations from Lydian or Phrygian—in themselves not improbable—hardly contribute to our inquiry in this stage. Of paramount importance to us is the question of what the Greeks meant by θρίαμβος and in order to find this out it is necessary to re-evaluate the Greek data.

It is to be expected that this investigation will also throw a new light on the Latin word *triumphus*. It would, however, not be correct to apply the result of the investigation on the word θρίαμβος to the Latin term without first having examined, as far as possible, the meaning of *triumphus* in the oldest stage of Latin available. The history of this investigation may serve as a warning. Because it was a universally established fact that *triumphus* was derived from θρίαμβος, and Kretschmer [4] had convincingly demonstrated that in that case a direct derivation was linguistically impossible, and, therefore, looked for an intermediate phase, so much attention was given to the formal-etymological aspects of this problem that a few very obvious semasiological questions were not asked or scarcely heard. The oldest form we find in Latin is not *triumphus* but *triumpe*. Besides during the procession of the victorious general this cry is repeated five times in one of the oldest fragments of Latin that have survived: the *carmen arvale*. Having established the fact that the earliest stage of the Latin term is not the nominativus *triumphus*, but an exclamation *triumpe*, we are faced with a number of questions.

---

[1] Not counting θρίαμβος as the translation of *triumphus*.

[2] E. Boisacq, Dict. Étym²., s.v. θρίαμβος; cf. J. B. Hofmann, Etym. Wörterb., s.v. θρίαμβος: "religiöser Aufzug mit Gesang und Tanz."

[3] Liddell and Scott, Greek-English Lex., s.v. θρίαμβος; cf. Frisk, Griech. Etym. Wörterb., s.v. θρίαμβος: "Name eines bei den Dionysosfesten gesungenen Liedes."

[4] P. Kretschmer in Gercke-Norden, Einleitung in die Altertumswissenschaft, I³, 1927, abt. 6, 112. *Vide infra* p. 48.

How is one to imagine that an appellativum θρίαμβος meaning
"ceremonial procession of Dionysos" should have developed into the
exclamation *triumpe*? Why does a characteristic triumphal cheer
figure in a song linked up with a rural cult? These questions are
obvious, but have not yet been asked, as far as I know. Most of the
studies on the *carmen arvale* do not attempt to give *triumpe* in this
song any meaning. A few authors, Norden [1] among them, explain the
exclamation as being the triumphal cry, a most unlikely solution,
as will appear. Also concerning the function of the Latin term
triumphus, therefore, a new investigation is needed, which should
start from the oldest testimonium in Latin: *triumpe* in the *carmen
arvale*; it should be endeavoured to deduce the meaning of the exclamation first of all from the context of this song only. Not before the
starting-point (θρίαμβος) and the final stage (*triumpe/triumphus*)
of the development have been closely investigated and defined as to
function and meaning, can any statements concerning the development itself be made. Remarks such as : "Geht das Wort (viz.
triumpe) auf griech. θρίαμβος zurück, das nur im Zusammenhang mit
dem Dionysoskult erscheint, so muss der Ruf seine Bedeutung
völlig geändert haben" [2] are, therefore, premature.

Not until after this investigation has been carried out can we hope
to find an answer to the questions which are linked up with the
third task we set ourselves: that of trying to find the way along
which θρίαμβος came to Rome. More so than in the preceding we can
here be guided by the formal-linguistic data. Besides, we have
someone to show us the way. As was stated above, no less a person
than Kretschmer has demonstrated that the Latin word cannot
have been derived directly from Greek, but that the derivation
must have taken place via a third language. Supported by historical
and archaeological data he looked for this intermediate phase in
Etruscan. There are several reasons why we have to present a
detailed discussion of Kretschmer's theory, which has met with
general recognition [3]. Proving the existence of an Etruscan intermediate phase is, first of all, not the end but the beginning of the
real problems. What we should like to know, for example, is what

---

[1] E. Norden, Aus altrömischen Priesterbüchern, Lund, 1939, 228.

[2] K. Latte, R.R.G. 152 n. 2.

[3] M. Leumann-Hofmann, Lat. Gramm. I, 130; F. Altheim, Geschichte d.
Lat. Sprache, 235; Ehlers, o.c. 493; Walde-Hofmann, L.E.W.³, s.v. *Triumphus*; E. Fiesel, Namen, 63; 85.

function the term *triumpe* (?) had in Etruria, in what kind of ceremony it figured, how the derivation from Greece should be imagined.
All these and similar questions will be dealt with in a later chapter.
The reason why Kretschmer's views will have to be judged on their
linguistic merits in the present chapter is a different one: the theory
that the triumphal ceremony and, in consequence, the name, have
their origin in Etruria was recently attacked by two scholars, partly
on the basis of linguistic arguments.

The German Wallisch [1] and the Italian Durante [2] have independently made attempts to show that the Roman triumph did develop directly from a Greek θρίαμβος-ceremony. To do so they have to
eliminate a number of statements made by ancient authors, who
explicitly indicate Etruria as the country of origin of the triumph
and the *insignia triumphalia*[3]. Durante is of the opinion that the
triumph originally formed part of the Campanian Dionysos-cult,
which came to Rome in the sixth century B.C. In Wallisch's view
the triumph is an imitation of the Hellenistic processions of the
Ptolemies, which were not introduced until the third century B.C.
Remarks such as [4]: "Wir haben es hier in dieser Einzelfrage wie im
gesamten Phänomen des Triumphes bei den Annalisten mit einer
bewussten Hinaufdatierung zu tun", stamp his approach as an
after-blossoming of historical hypercriticism. The fact that to-day's
historians [5] have abandoned this method, and are inclined to attach
a greater value to literary tradition, should not induce us to accept
frenis remissis everything that the *fasti*, Livy, Dionysius and
Plutarch report about the triumph as right, against scholars such as
Wallisch. The result would be a pointless firing between two firmly
held fortifications, by which neither the research on the triumph,
nor the science of history would benefit. It is for this reason that I
restrict myself in this chapter to a critical comparison of the linguistic
arguments. If the linguistic argumentation of Wallisch and Durante appears to be right or, at any rate plausible, it is necessary

---

[1] E. Wallisch, Name und Herkunft des römischen Triumphes. Philol.
98, 1954/55, 254 ff.

[2] M. Durante, *Triumpe* e *triumphus*. Un capitolo del più antico culto
dionisiaco latino. Maia, 4, 1951, 138 ff.

[3] For the testimonia *vide infra* p. 83.

[4] Wallisch, o.c. 256.

[5] I may here refer to the studies of H. Last and H. Stuart Jones in the
seventh volume of C.A.H. and to the thorough paper of A. Momigliano:
An interim report on the origins of Rome. J.R.S. 53, 1963, 95 ff.

for their entire theories to be discussed in more detail; if it is not acceptable it follows that their historical arguments are at the same time robbed of a large part of their value.

2. Θρίαμβος

In the sphere in which the term is used, as well as in form Θρίαμβος has points of contact with ἴαμβος and διθύραμβος. Ancient testimonia which will be discussed further on, bear witness of a relation of Θρίαμβος and διθύραμβος with the cult of Dionysos. Although such a testimonium is lacking as far as ἴαμβος is concerned, it may be assumed on the basis of indirect data that this term, too, is linked up with the cult of Dionysos. The satirical character of the oldest iambs recalls the σκώμματα, which are typical of the Dionysiac cult. In a gloss to be referred to further on Hesychius explains Θρίαμβος... Διονυσιακὸς ὕμνος, ἴαμβος, by which ἴαμβος is connected with Dionysos. It is not a coincidence that the woman whose jests cheered the sad Demeter was called Ἰάμβη [1]. It is especially in the ritual, aeschrological, satirical and abusive songs that the cults of Demeter and Dionysos overlap.

The common element -αμβος, which hardly occurs anywhere else in Greek, and whose consonantism is found in pre-Greek, particularly Asia Minor names [2], as well as the relation with Dionysos justify the thesis defended by several scholars that the three terms came from Asia Minor, together with the god [3]. In an investigation of the meaning of Θρίαμβος the data about the other two related terms are, therefore, not to be neglected, even though we realize that the iambic verse and the dithyrambic song are final stages of a development whose beginning lies beyond our scope.

By way of introduction and orientation we first present a survey of the linguistic literature about Θρίαμβος, published after 1900. The literature on ἴαμβος and διθύραμβος is included as far as it is relevant here [4].

---

[1] Homer. hymn to Demeter I, 201 ff.; Proclus, Chrestomath. p. 242. 28 (W).

[2] Theander, o.c. 130 f., mentions: Σάραμβος, Σαλάμβω, Ἀρύμβας, Τορύμβας, Κόρυμβος, Ὄλυμπος. See A. J. van Windekens, Le pélasgique. Essai sur une langue indo-européenne préhellénique. I, Louvain, 1952, 42 f., 106 f., 111 ff.

[3] About Asia Minor as Dionysos' country of origin *vide infra* p. 292ff.

[4] I do not aim at completeness. Numerous scholars, while writing about the most widely different subjects, in passing give their views about the meaning or origin of one or more of the terms. For older literature see Boisacq, Dict. Étym.², s.v. Θρίαμβος, ἴαμβος, διθύραμβος.

The first important interpretation is that of Sommer [1], who starts from the point of view that θρίαμβος belongs to an IE language. The element θρι- is supposed to have developed from τρισ-, and -αμβος is connected with Skr. *anga* = "Glied", as a result of which a meaning "Tanz im Dreischritt" emerges. In his review of the work in which this theory was published, Kretschmer [2] points out that a stem αμβ- with the meaning "Glied" is non-existent in Greek, and suggests to connect the element —αμβος with Λυκάμβης = "Wolfgang". θρίαμβος would, according to this theory, have developed from τρισ- and the substantivum verbale belonging to ἀναβαίνειν. Unlike Sommer's theory this suggestion did not meet with any response in later literature. It is not at all certain that Λυκάμβης does indeed mean "Wolfgang". The term ἀναβαίνειν for "dancing"—for Kretschmer does accept the meaning Sommer suggested—is baffling, and it is difficult to see how a substantive ending in -βος could be formed side by side with the verbal stem βη/βᾰ.

Sturtevant [3] looked for a new line of approach. In a lexicological investigation on words ending in -βα, -βη, -βος etc. he found a large group of terms whose meaning, in one way or another, implied the notion "sound". Following this train of thought he connects ἴαμβος with ἰαίνειν "to cheer" [4], and θρίαμβος with *θριαίνειν (= θριάζειν) "to be rapt, possessed" [5], and arrives at the meanings "song of cheer" and "song of rapture", respectively. As regards the word διθύραμβος, he follows a suggestion made by von Wilamowitz [6], who thinks that -θύραμβος has developed from θρίαμβος by metathesis. This theory was modified by Theander [7] to the effect that he considered the three words to be not IE, but what Kretschmer later on called 'protindogermanisch', and stressed their having been derived from a pre-Greek language. As the verb belonging to ἴαμβος he replaced ἰαίνειν, which in view of its meaning does appear rather doubtful, by ἰάζειν, a verb occurring once and meaning "to cry aloud".

---

[1] F. Sommer, Griechische Lautstudien, Straszburg, 1905, 59 f.; -αμβος = *anga* already in Fröhde: see Boisacq, s.v. θρίαμβος.

[2] P. Kretschmer, Berliner Wochenschrift, 26, 1906, 54 f.

[3] E. H. Sturtevant, Studies in Greek Noun-formation. Class. Phil. 5, 1910, 326 ff.

[4] So already W. Prellwitz, Etym. Wörterb. der griech. Sprache², Göttingen, 1905, s.v. ἴαμβος.

[5] Etym. Magn. 455. 55: θριάζειν· ἐνθουσιάζειν.

[6] Euripides Herakles I, 1889, 63.

[7] o.c. 130 ff.

2

In spite of the scepsis as to the possibility of explaining the words formulated by Boisacq [1]: "nombreuses étymologies anciennes et modernes dont aucune ne satisfait" and Chantraine [2]: "...un groupe de mots dont l'origine n'est évidemment pas indoeuropéenne", and in spite of the undoubtedly justified opposition of Nehring [3] against Sommer and Kretschmer:"...aber zweifellos ist -αμβος nur suffixal wie ἴθυμβος mit abweichendem Vokal deutlich lehrt", Brandenstein [4] in 1936 followed in Sommer's tracks and made a fresh attempt to bring not only θρίαμβος, but also ἴαμβος and διθύραμβος as "two-step" and "four-step" respectively, within the sphere of the dance, and to explain them via IE. This theory is not convincing [5]. The transition from the hypothetical form *τιτυρ- "deren Vokalismus mit der Homerischen Form πίσυρες, deren Konsonantismus aber mit der böotischen Form τέτορες gegeben ist" (!) to διθυρ- Brandenstein can explain only by assuming that there has been a 'Tyrrhenian-Aegean' intermediate phase. This phase is first of all supposed to effect a transition *τιτυρ- > *θιθυρ-; after this, dissimilation is said to produce *τιθυρ-, which again in the Tyrrhenian-Aegean language should have developed into διθυρ-. Hofmann [6] still considers this theory tenable, but Frisk [7] counts it among the many unsuccessful attempts.

In 1966 O. Haas [8] nevertheless bases his theory of the Phrygian origin of these terms ending in -αμβος on the papers of Sommer and Brandenstein, but he is of the opinion that ἴαμβος means "one-step" (< *ιο = "one"). He even uses this theory to confirm linguistic laws he thinks he has discovered, such as the one according to which the labiovelar becomes a labial in N. E. Phrygian. Highly complicated and in my view unacceptable is his derivation of διθυρ from *θιδρα "four" (p. 164 f.)

---

[1] s.v. θρίαμβος.

[2] P. Chantraine, La formation des noms en Grec ancien, Paris, 1933, 260.

[3] A. Nehring, Glotta, 14, 1925, 153 f., who, for that matter, does think that θρίαμβος etc. are terms denoting orgiastic dances.

[4] W. Brandenstein, ἴαμβος, θρίαμβος, διθύραμβος. I.F. 54, 1936, 34 ff.; cf. Puhvel, Glotta, 34, 1955, 37 ff.

[5] See P. Kretschmer, Glotta, 27, 1939, 219.

[6] Etym. Wörterb., s.v. θρίαμβος.

[7] Griech. Etym. Wörterb. ,s.v. θρίαμβος; cf. E. Schwyzer, Griech. Gramm. I, 458: "Fremdwörter wie ... ἴαμβος, θρίαμβος"; and 591 about Brandenstein's theory: "fraglich".

[8] O. Haas, Die phrygischen Sprachdenkmäler, Sophia, 1966, 150; 158; passim.

The above synopsis, which might be considerably added to,[1] sufficiently illustrates the major controversies. In the field of linguistic history we find two opposing theories: some authors are of the opinion that the terms ending in -αμβος belong to a non-IE language and cannot be explained, whereas others hold the view that they belong to IE, Protindoeuropean or Pelasgian, and try to give them meanings with the aid of IE stems. Also as far as meaning is concerned, however, there are striking differences. Some authors, Sturtevant among them, choose a meaning "song", others, among whom there are a few compilers of etymological dictionaries [2], translate it by "religious procession (accompanied by singing and dancing)", whereas, finally, there is a large number of scholars who base the etymological derivation of the word on a meaning "dance" or "dance step".

Too often when a great scholar has presented his view "schwört man auf des Meisters Worte", uncritically accepting his theory and premises. The translation "dance" is thus generally justified by referring to Sommer, who, as was stated in the preceding, was the first to interpret θρίαμβος as "Tanz im Dreischritt". Precisely in this case, however, prudence was called for and scepsis justified, since neither Sommer nor any of his epigones [3] confirm the meaning postulated by a single ancient testimonium. This is only too understandable since, as will be seen, it is impossible to point out a single instance in which θρίαμβος means "dance" or "procession" in either the literature of the flourishing period of Greece, or in the later lexicography [4].

There is one scholar who often soundly criticized prevailing views, but who, at the same time, illustrates how a dictum posed by a man of authority fifty years ago is still uncritically accepted as a dogma—with deplorable consequences. With a rendering of the view of this scholar, A. J. van Windekens, as it was laid down in the paper

---

[1] A theory as fantastic and unsupported as that of Th. Fitzhugh: *Triumpus-*θρίαμβος. The Indoeuropean or Pyrrhic Stress Accent in Antiquity. Univ. of Verginia. Bulletin of the School of Latin, 2nd ser. no 1-2, Oct. 1930, I cannot possibly discuss in any detail here.

[2] i.a. in Boisacq, Chantraine, Hofmann, in the works mentioned.

[3] Brandenstein, o.c. 34, for example, writes: "die Bedeutung (the one given by Sommer) passt gut, da wir ja Termini der Tanzkunst (und lyrische Dichtung) vor uns haben", without making this credible.

[4] A seeming exception in Hesychius is explained below.

"Gr. θρίαμβος et lat. *triumphus*" [1] this introductory section will be concluded.

Van Windekens shares Georgiev's [2] view that the terms ἴαμβος, θρίαμβος and διθύραμβος belong to a pre-Hellenic, but Indoeuropean language, which he calls Pelasgian. He also follows Georgiev and Nehring, who consider the element -αμβος suffixal and who for this reason—and in my opinion rightly so—deny any connection with Skr. *aṅga*. A meaning "dance(step)" is, therefore, not to be looked for in this part of the words. Against the interpretation given by Georgiev and others of ι-, θρι-, διθυρ- as "two-, three-, four-" respectively, van Windekens argues that this "est une pure hypothèse, qui, d'ailleurs, ne résiste pas à un examen approfondi". Here, too, his arguments [3] are, in my view, convincing. Moreover, van Windekens, is one of the very few to point out that θρίαμβος—according to Liddell and Scott—means "hymn to Dionysus, epithet of Dionysus, Lat. *triumphus*", and that the meaning "cortège..... repose sur une contamination avec lat. *triumphus*". Now it is this *triumphus* which van Windekens takes as the starting-point for his further considerations.

According to van Windekens *triumphus* (< *triumpus*) did not, as is generally assumed, develop from Greek θρίαμβος via Etruscan, but was directly derived from "Pelasgian"—a view which will be dealt with further on. From this it follows that the Latin meaning of *triumphus* is the original one and that it is not connected with Dionysos. Van Windekens continues as follows[4]: "Le 'triomphe', c'est essentiellement le 'défilé d'un général victorieux': il faut donc (!) partir de l'idée de "± marcher, s'avancer, etc. en vainqueur". On songera à skr. tárati "traverser, franchir, vaincre, surmonter, sauver" (some more words follow, all of them having the stem *ter "passer par-dessus ou à travers, franchir etc. (...) dont pélasg. *tr <*thr serait le degré zéro.")

(Gr) θρίαμβος aussi a dû désigner à l'origine un défilé en l'honneur d'un vainqueur. (!) Le terme a été employé pour les défilés dans lesquels on célébrait l'action libératrice de Dionysos (...) Mais ensuite l'accent a été mis sur les hymnes qui accompagnaient ces défilés,

---

[1] in: Orbis. Bulletin international de documentation linguistique, 2, 1953, 489 ff.

[2] V. Georgiev, Vorgriechische Sprachwissenschaft, Sophia, 1941-1945, I, 86 f.

[3] o.c. 490.

[4] o.c. 492.

et aussi sur l'objet de ces défilés et de ces hymnes, c.à.d. sur Dionysos lui-même. De là θρίαμβος dans le sens de "hymne en l'honneur
de Dionysos" et θρίαμβος épithète de Dionysos".

It is impossible and unnecessary to refute this argumentation in
detail here. It is, to use van Windekens own words, "une pure
hypothèse, qui, d'ailleurs, ne résiste pas à un examen approfondi" [1].
The point at issue, and this is the reason for this long quotation, is
that of getting an insight into the causes which up to the present
stood in the way of a simple interpretation of θρίαμβος and the
relation between this word and Lat. *triumphus*. The argumentation
of van Windekens quoted above may lead to this insight: although
θρίαμβος means "hymn to Dionysos", and although the suffix
-αμβος has nothing to do with "dance", the author—after a long and
difficult detour, during which θρίαμβος is in passing defined as
"défilé en l'honneur de Dionysos" (a meaning not found in Liddell
and Scott!)—manages to introduce the notion "movement" into
the term; this time not in the element -αμβος, however, but in the
element θρι-. All this as a result of an unfounded theory advanced
more than fifty years ago [2].

The great discrepancy between the various theories, and the
arbitrariness they testify to would appear to warrant a renewed
inquiry into what the Greeks really meant by θρίαμβος.

The first time θρίαμβος appears in a fragment of Pratinas [3], a
contemporary of Aeschylus. In a song which is called ὑπόρχημα by
Athenaeus [4], and which is characterized as a *dithyrambus* by von
Wilamowitz and as a chorus song of a satyr-drama by others [5],
Pratinas makes the chorus call to Dionysos: θριαμβοδιθύραμβε. In
addition to showing that this term is used as an *epiclesis* of Dionysos,
the fragment makes it clear that in the early fifth century B.C.
θρίαμβος and διθύραμβος were felt to be related, a fact to which the
composition owes its existence [6]. The text does not furnish an

---

[1] Frisk, Griech. Etym. Wörterb., s.v. θρίαμβος: "eine ganz willkürliche
idg. Etymologie".

[2] The legacy of Sommer and Brandenstein is also clearly apparent in
van W's proposal to recognize the notion 'movement' in the element -ι-
of ἴαμβος and ἴθυμβος (which latter word "contient l'idée de 'danse' ").
(< *vei, cf. ἴεμαι).

[3] Athen. 14, 617 B. ff.

[4] *ibid.*

[5] See A. Pickard-Cambridge, Dithyramb, Tragedy and Comedy², Oxford,
1962, 17 ff.

[6] I fail to understand how Sturtevant, o.c. 330, can think that precisely

explanation of either of these components. As by-names of Dionysos we find θρίαμβος in Diodorus Siculus (4, 5) θρίαμβον δ'αὐτὸν ὀνομασθῆναι φασιν, Arrian (Anab. 6,28,2) καὶ Θρίαμβον τε αὐτὸν ἐπικληθῆναι τὸν Διόνυσον , Suda (s.v. θρίαμβος) λέγεται δὲ καὶ Διόνυσος θρίαμβος and indirectly in Athenaeus (1,30 B) Τιμᾶται δὲ παρὰ Λαμψακηνοῖς ὁ Πρίηπος, ὁ αὐτὸς ὢν τῷ Διονύσῳ ἐξ ἐπιθέτου καλούμενος οὕτως, ὡς Θρίαμβος καὶ Διθύραμβος.

Also in the last-mentioned fragment we find the parallelism of the two names.

A different function the word is given in a fragment of the writer of comedies Cratinus [1]: Ὅτε σὺ τοὺς καλοὺς θριάμβους ἀναρύτους' ἀπηχθάνου. Here θρίαμβος is used appellatively. If we have to choose between the meanings "song" and "dance", the former undoubtedly fits better into the metaphor, since ἀναρύτειν means "to draw from a well" [2]. A passus in Plato is illuminating in this respect. In the Ion (534AB) he makes Socrates say: λέγουσι γὰρ δήπουθεν πρὸς ἡμᾶς οἱ ποιηταὶ ὅτι ἀπὸ κρηνῶν μελιρρύτων (....) δρεπόμενοι τὰ μέλη ἡμῖν φέρουσι....

There is no room for doubt here: ποιηταί and μέλη belong in the sphere of the song, not primarily in that of the dance. Noteworthy is that a little earlier Plato compared this poetical inspiration with Bacchic ecstasy: ὥσπερ αἱ Βάκχαι ἀρύονται ἐκ τῶν ποταμῶν μέλι καὶ γάλα, in which ἀρύω is related to (ἀν)αρύτειν mentioned in Cratinus[3]. Furthermore, it is difficult to imagine how one can make oneself hated by means of a dance—David and Hippokleides are in fact unique—, whereas it seems easy to do so by means of a song, particularly if this θρίαμβος—song had the character of a satirical poem. That this was indeed the case is confirmed by two authors.

A fragment from Conon [4] reads: τέμνει τὴν αὐτῆς γλῶσσαν δεδιὼς

---

this compositum should have yielded the two separate elements θρίαμβος and διθύραμβος. His translation "whose διθύραμβος is a θρίαμβος" is also mysterious.

[1] The Suda, s.v. ἀναρύτειν.

[2] The Suda explains: ἀναρύτειν· ἀναντλεῖν ἀπὸ τοῦ ἀρύεσθαι. ἀρύω also means "to draw from". Hesychius gives:

ἀρύει· ἀντὶ τοῦ λέγει, βοᾷ
ἀρύουσαι· λέγουσαι, κελεύουσαι
ἀρύσασθαι· ἐπικαλέσασθαι

Is the last-mentioned ἀρύειν a metaphoric use of the first?

[3] Frisk, Griech. Etym. Wörterb., s.v. ἀρύω; cf. preceding note.

[4] Conon 31, 1. ed. F. Jacoby. F. Gr.H. I, 190.

τὸν ἐκ λόγων θρίαμβον, in which θρίαμβος is sure to mean "contumely, scorn". Photius says: θριάμβους· τοὺς ἰάμβους ἔνιοι ἔλεγον.

One of the meanings of ἴαμβος often encountered is "satire, squib". The meaning of θρίαμβος "song" has thus become certain, confirmed definitively by Pollux [1], who counts the θρίαμβος with the ἴαμβος and the διθύραμβος among the ποιήματα καὶ ᾠδαὶ καὶ ᾄσματα καὶ μέτρα καὶ λόγοι ἔμμετροι and Hesychius: θρίαμβος· .... Διονυσιακὸς ὕμνος, ἴαμβος.

So far we ascertained two meanings of θρίαμβος: 1. epithet of Dionysos 2. song. Photius further states: θρίαμβος· ἐπίδειξις νίκης, πομπὴ καὶ τὸ σεμνύνεσθαι, which is literally found again in the Suda [2]. Here, I think, lies the *fons et origo malorum* which has caused the misunderstandings concerning the meanings of θρίαμβος. It is true that the meaning "dance" has still not been attested, but the translation by "cortège" now seems warranted. However, is this meaning the original Greek one? This question has to be answered in the negative.

Both statements found in Photius are almost certain to go back to Hesychius or to a common source, since in Hesychius one finds: θρίαμβος· πομπή, ἐπίδειξις νίκης ἢ Διονυσιακὸς ὕμνος, ἴαμβος. Even if it were, *prima specie*, to be concluded that θρίαμβος had the double meaning "procession" and "song", it is shown by the following considerations that only one of them is the old-Greek meaning. The disjunctive ἢ separates the statement into two parts, of which each has a meaning of its own, which differs from that of the other. Each part again is made up of two elements, which, however, belong together mutually, and are merely a double definition of one phenomenon. Διονυσιακὸς ὕμνος, ἴαμβος may be paraphrased as "a Dionysiac song, a kind of (or: such as the) *iambus*". The fact that Hesychius does not attribute the predicate Διονυσιακός to πομπή, as well as the definition ἐπίδειξις νίκης clearly show which phenomenon he refers to in this part of his definition: the Roman triumph, which was in fact the exposition of a victory characterized by a procession. There is no doubt that Hesychius or his source combined the two meanings of θρίαμβος he knew: Dionysiac song, the old-Greek meaning, and triumph, a meaning which did not develop until the Roman period [3].

---

[1] Pollux, Onomasticon, 4, 53.
[2] The Suda, s.v. θρίαμβος.
[3] This, as we saw, was rightly pointed out by van Windekens.

All other meanings found in the dictionaries of later Greek [1] have developed from the late meaning of θρίαμβος = *triumphus* (θριαμβεύειν = *triumphare*). A meaning furnished by Hesychius may form an exception: θριαμβεῦσαι· θορυβῆσαι, βοῆσαι, since this meaning does not go with the Roman triumph. In Greek authors of the Roman and Byzantine periods θριαμβεύειν means [2]: 1. to triumph (abs.) 2. to lead in triumph (as a captive) 3. to lead in triumph (as a general his victorious army) 4. to publish, divulge, manifest, expose, etc. These are all of them activities of the general. The triumph was accompanied by shouting, but this was done by the people and the soldiers. It is, for this reason, difficult to assume that θριαμβεύειν = *triumphare* developed into θορυβεῖν, βοᾶν. In θορυβεῖν, βοᾶν the old-Greek meaning may, therefore, have survived, which fits in very well with some noisy customs inherent to the Dionysiac cult.

These are all the testimonia of θρίαμβος we have. We may conclude that neither the meaning "procession", nor the meaning "dance" has been attested for classical Greek.

Our knowledge of διθύραμβος, dithyramb, now enables us to give this conclusion, which was based on scanty data, a sounder foundation. Not only do the terms show an outward similarity but, as we saw above, they also have already one function in common, viz. that of being used as an epithet of Dionysos [3]. In the case of διθύραμβος its meaning as an appellativum which is, e.g., given by the Suda: διθύραμβος· ὕμνος εἰς Διόνυσον, is unequivocally supported by the many places in literature in which the word is found in combination with ᾄδειν or φθέγγεσθαι. Archilochus' well-known verses: Ὡς Διωνύσοι' ἄνακτος καλὸν ἐξάρξαι μέλος οἶδα διθύραμβον, οἴνῳ συγκεραυνωθεὶς φρένας, do not leave room for any doubt: even in the earliest literary period the *dithyrambos* was a song. The same holds good for the third term ἴαμβος, which is not used as a name of a god [4],

---

[1] Lampe, A patristic Greek Lexicon; E. A. Sophocles, Greek Lexicon of the Roman and Byzantine Periods; G. Kittel, Theologisches Wörterbuch zum neuen Testament.

[2] See the works referred to in the preceding note.

[3] Euripides, Bacchae, 526; Philodam. Scarpheus, ed. J. U. Powell, Coll. Alex. 165,=H. Weil, B.C.H., 19, 1895, 401; Athen. 1, 30 B; Pratinas, θριαμβοδιθύραμβε; Etym. Magn. 274.44. In an isolated position Διθύραμφος is further found as the name of a satyr on a fragment of an Attic red-figured crater (see Pickard-Cambridge, o.c. 5). Διθύραμβος as a proper name: Herod. 7, 227.

[4] An attempt made by Ch. Picard, R.H.R. 45, 1927, 220 ff. to reconstruct a male god Ἴαμβος (= Proshymnos = Baubon) is, in my opinion, successful, but cannot, of course, be used as evidence.

and which has the meaning "metrical foot, kind of poetry", as well as "iambic song, satire" [1].

Summarizing, we may conclude that none of the three terms investigated had in Hellas the choreutic meaning of "dance" or "procession". This conclusion might, however, be contested by an argumentation as the one found in the paper of M. Durante [2]: "θρίαμβος invero non è attestato nel senso di "festa" o "πομπή", quale è l'accezione del lat. *triumphus*, sebbene di "inno" (...) Ma ciò non fa nessuna difficoltà: e perchè *triumphus* risale, come si è detto, a una variante dialettale di θρίαμβος della quale non conosciamo il senso preciso; e, soprattutto, perchè, tra l'inno-danza greco preletterario e la cerimonia nella quale esso veniva eseguito non ci doveva essere distinzione netta".

The fact that *triumphus* did not develop from a dialectal form at all will be shown later; here I only wish to draw attention to an inadmissible method the author appears to have followed without being aware of it. What is first called "inno" is called a little further on "inno-danza", which, of course, gets the author closer to the meaning πομπή he desires. One might, however, go still further and defend Durante's procedure by pointing out that singing was in Hellas practically always accompanied by dancing, and that these two forms of expression were felt to be inseparable. An example is found in the Homeric μέλπεσθαι, which, as is generally known, expresses both "dancing" and "singing". However true this may be, it is nevertheless to be observed that terminologically the Greeks did make a distinction between the two forms of art. If, as we have seen, Pollux [3] includes the ἴαμβος, the θρίαμβος and the διθύραμβος among the ποιήματα καὶ ᾠδαὶ καὶ ἄσματα καὶ μέτρα καὶ λόγοι ἔμμετροι, as clearly distinct from an endless series of terms denoting dancing and kinds of dances which he enumerates a little further on [4], if everywhere in Greek lexicography and literature the terms ἴαμβος, θρίαμβος and διθύραμβος are defined as ὕμνος, ᾠδή and ἄσμα etc., whereas χόρευμα, χορός, ὄρχημα and ὑπόρχημα are never used; if, moreover, examples of iambic and dithyrambic songs have come down to us, there is no justification for anyone to start from a meaning "song", to arrive, via "song-dance", at a fundamental

---

[1] See Liddell and Scott, s.v. ἴαμβος.
[2] o.c. 140 n. 3.
[3] Onomasticon 4, 53.
[4] *ibid.* 4, 95 ff.

meaning "dance" and to begin etymologizing on the basis of this meaning.

This is not meant to imply that the *iambos*, the *triambos* and the *dithyrambos* were never accompanied by choric dances [1], but it does mean that in our further considerations concerning θρίαμβος only two fundamental functions will have to be reckoned with, viz. 1.the by-name of Dionysos; 2. the name of a song.

The fact that θρίαμβος never had the meaning "procession" in Hellas receives extra confirmation from Varro's explanation quoted above. He derives *triumphus*, via *triumpe*, from θρίαμβος, *Graecum Liberi cognomentum*. Why didn't Varro, as did his colleagues two millennia later, derive the Latin name of the triumphal procession directly from the Greek name of a Dionysiac procession? The answer has already been given: because such a "cortège religieux accompagné de chants inspirés et de danse" was not called θρίαμβος in Hellas!

Now that we have found the two meanings of θρίαμβος, we are faced with two questions: how did these meanings develop and which of the two was the original one. The data concerning θρίαμβος and διθύραμβος are of no great help in this investigation. Among the by-names of Dionysos, however, there are a few which, like θρίαμβος, have several meanings whose origins do prove traceable with certainty or a high degree of probability. These will have to show us the way.

---

[1] In one instance we are told about a chorus of ἰαμβισταί at Syracuse (Athen. 5, 181 C). A dithyrambic dance has been attested in Pollux, Onomasticon 4, 105: τυρβασίαν δ'ἐκάλουν τὸ ὄρχημα τὸ διθυραμβικόν. Hesychius: τυρβασία· χορῶν ἀγωγή τις διθυραμβικῶν. Although it may not have been one originally, the dithyramb, during its flourishing period, was decidedly a chorus song. The detailed discussion of the dithyramb in Pickard-Cambridge, o.c. 1 ff. does not leave room for any doubt that its vocal significance was primary, its choreutical one secundary. Neither is ἴθυμβος simply to be termed a "Bacchischer Tanz" (O. Haas, o.c. 165). At best it may be said with van Windekens that the word "contient l'idée de danse". ἴθυμβος is in Photius ᾠδὴ μακρὰ καὶ ὑπόσκαιος. In Hesychius we find the same, and moreover: γελοιαστὴς καὶ τὸ σκῶμμα ἀπὸ τῶν ἰθύμβων, ἄτινα ποιήματα ἦν ἐπὶ χλεύῃ καὶ γέλωτι συγκείμενα. The meanings are therefore: 1. song, 2. products (verses or objects?) which provoke laughter, 3. buffoon. Pollux, Onomasticon, 4, 104, finally, gives: ἦν δέ τινα καὶ Λακωνικὰ ὀρχήματα, διὰ Μαλέας· Σειληνοὶ δ'ἦσαν, καὶ ὑπ' αὐτοῖς Σάτυροι ὑπότρομα ὀρχούμενοι. καὶ ἴθυμβοι ἐπὶ Διονύσῳ καὶ καρυάτιδες ἐπ' Ἀρτέμιδι. Wouldn't it be the most natural thing to recognize in these ἴθυμβοι the γελοιαστής of Hesychius, equated with Silenes, Satyrs and Karyatides?

The god Dionysos has an extensive collection of epithets—πολυώνυ-μος he is called by Sophocles [1]—.Kern [2] has collected these names under the denominator of "Cultnamen", but this does not mean that they are all of the same kind. There are topographical epithets (e.g. Ἐλευθερεύς) and others, sometimes of a ritual, sometimes of a poetical origin, which refer to a typical quality or function of the god (e.g. μειλίχιος, δενδρίτης). A third group stands more or less by itself. The names which belong to this group, and which include those multivocal epithets we have in mind, are neither topographical nor functional determinatives. Among them are the following:

Ἴακχος
Βάκχος (Βακχεύς, Βακχεῖος, Βάκχιος, Βακχέβακχος, Ἀρχεβάκχος,
Σαβός (Σαβάζιος)   Ἰοβάκχος)

Ἐλελεύς
Εὔας (Εὔιος)
Ἰήιος
Ἰυγγίης

The first three terms, in particular, require our attention, whereas the others will help to find an explanation.

According to the lexicographers Ἴακχος had several meanings:

Hesychius: Ἴακχον· τὸν Διόνυσον (...) ἢ μίαν ἡμέραν τῶν μυστηρίων, ἐν ᾗ τὸν Ἴακχον ἐξάγουσιν, καὶ ἡ ᾠδή, ἣν οἱ μεμυημένοι ᾄδουσιν (......) τινὲς δὲ καὶ αὐτὸν τὸν Διόνυσον οὕτως ἔλεγον.

Hesychius: Ἴακχα· στεφάνωμα εὐῶδες ἐν Σικυῶνι.

Photius: Ἴακχος· Διόνυσος ἐπὶ τῷ μαστῷ. καὶ ἥρως τις·καὶ ἡ ἐπ' αὐτῷ ᾠδή· καὶ ἡ ἡμέρα καθ' ἣν εἰς αὐτὸν ἡ πανήγυρις· ἔνιοι δὲ καὶ θόρυβος.

Suda: Ἴακχος· ὕμνος εἰς Διόνυσον.

Among the many functions of this term there are two of special interest to us: 1. the by-name of the god, 2. the name of a song, since these functions are the same as those of θρίαμβος and διθύραμβος.

Similar shades as to meaning are found in Βάκχος.

Hesychius: Βακχέβακχος· ὁ Διόνυσος οὕτως ἐκαλεῖτο ἐν ταῖς θυσίαις.

Suda: Βάκχος· οὕτως οὐ μόνον τὸν Διόνυσον ἐκάλει, ἀλλὰ καὶ πάντας τοὺς τελοῦντας τὰ ὄργια. οὐ μὴν καὶ τοὺς κλάδους <οὓς> οἱ μύσται φέρουσιν. ἔστι δὲ καὶ στεφάνου εἶδος.

---

[1] Antigone, 1115.
[2] R.E. 5, 1905, 1026 ff., s.v. Dionysos.

Suda: Βακχέβακχον ἆσαι· ἀντὶ τοῦ εὐφημῆσαι τὸν Διόνυσον· Βάκχαν γὰρ ὁ Διόνυσος.

This time the meaning "song" is not given *disertis verbis*. It can, however, be directly deduced from the expression βακχέβακχον ἆσαι, which may mean two things: 1. 'singing' the cry βακχέβακχε, 2. singing the song entitled βακχέβακχος. In exactly the same way Ἰόβακχος is an epithet of Dionysos [1], but also, and this time explicitly defined as such, a song; Archilochus wrote *Iobakchoi* [2].

Σαβός, lengthened to Σαβάζιος, finally, is an epithet of Dionysos, but at the same time of the βακχεύοντες, and in this respect, therefore, corresponds with Βάκχος.

Photius: Σαβοὺς καὶ Σαβὰς καὶ Σαβαζίους· τοὺς βακχεύοντας τῷ Σαβαζίῳ· τὸ γὰρ σαβάζειν τῷ θεῷ τοῦτο· ὑπὸ δέ τινων ὁ Διόνυσος Σαβὸς καλεῖται [3].

This is the first instance in which we can trace the origin of the name with a fairly high degree of certainty. Σαβός and Σαβάζιος have developed from a ritual exclamation (εὐοῖ) σαβοῖ [4], which was heard during orgiastic rites in the cult of this Thracian-Phrygian god. On this subject all ancient sources agree. The origin of the other ἐπικλήσεις mentioned by us is also abundantly clear. Ἐλελεύς is to be traced back directly to the exclamation ἐλελεῦ, just as Εὔας and Εὔιος correspond with εὐα or εὐοῖ, Ἰήιος with ἰή and Ἰυγγιής with ἰύ (ἰύζω).

We see, therefore, that Dionysos had several by-names which have developed from ritual exclamations. One of these, Σαβός, has a few meanings in common with Βάκχος, which, in its turn, corresponds with Ἴακχος. Now it has long since been generally agreed that the god Ἴακχος is nothing but "die Personifikation der Ἴακχος-Rufe der jubelnden Menge, einer Gestalt Hymenaios vergleichbar, der in analoger Weise letzten Endes aus dem Hochzeitsrufe erwachsen

---

[1] Hesychius Ἰόβακχος· ὁ Διόνυσος, ἀπὸ τῆς βακχείας.

[2] Hephaestion ed. Consbruck p. 53; Menander in Walz, Rhett. Gr., vol. 9, 129 (speaking of ὕμνοι): Διθυράμβους καὶ Ἰοβάκχους καὶ ὅσα τοιαῦτα εἴρηται Διονύσου; Procl. *apud* Photius, Biblioth. p. 320.31.

[3] Further: Harpocration, s.v. σαβοῖ; Eustath. ad Hom. Od. 1431.

[4] The ancient sources are unanimous about this. All modern attempts to fit this exclamation into an etymological development start from the wrong idea that σαβοῖ as an exclamation must have an exact meaning. About this matter see: Schaefer, R.E. 2e Reihe 1, 1920, 1540 ff.; Eisele, Roscher Lex. 4, 232 ff. Cf. Perdrizet, Cultes et mythes du Pangée, Paris, 1910, 78 ff.

ist" [1]. In the Etymologicum Magnum we already find: Ἴακχος·
αὐτὸς ὁ Διόνυσος, ἢ ἑορτή. παρὰ τὴν ἰαχὴν τὴν ἐν ταῖς χορείαις γενομένην,
τουτέστι τὴν βοήν, γίνεται ἰάχος, καὶ πλεονασμῷ τοῦ κ, ἴακχος. When
Photius gives θόρυβος as one of the meanings of ἴακχος, he means the
same thing. Kern [2] even thinks that in Herodotus (8, 65) the process
of the god's "birth" has not yet been completed: ἴακχος is here
merely a φθεγγόμενον, of which it is said: καὶ τὴν φωνὴν τὴν ἀκούεις ἐν
ταύτῃ τῇ ὁρτῇ ἰακχάζουσιν.

What is certain in the case of Ἴακχος, is by Miss Harrison [3]—
without any argumentation, however,—also assumed to apply to
Βάκχος: "Some names like Ἴακχος and probably Βάκχος itself, though
they ultimately became proper names, were originally only cries".
This is, in fact, highly probable. Βακχέβακχος as the name of a god
and as the title of a cult-song undoubtedly developed from the cry
βακχέβακχε, whose iteration is characteristic of the sacral exclamation [4]. When, in addition, Hesychius s.v. Βαβάκτης gives κραύγασος
ὅθεν καὶ Βάκχος, this shows a close resemblance to Photius Ἴακχος...
θόρυβος, by which he also meant the noisy Ἴακχος -cry. The solid
combination ἰόβακχος, developed from ἰὼ βάκχε, in which ἰώ is exclamatory, is also in favour of this point of view. Highly illuminating,
finally, is a statement by Eustathius [5], who gives various names
for those possessed by a god. In addition to Σαβός and Σαβάζιος
he gives Βάκχος καὶ Βαβάκτης καὶ Βάβαξ. Certain is that Βαβάκτης
and Βάβαξ have the meaning "chatterer", i.e. originally "someone
saying 'βᾶ' or 'βαβάι' " [6] cf. βάζω, βαβάζω, βαβαιάξ. In view of this
it may safely be assumed that Βάκχος is also based on such a

---

[1] L. Deubner, Attische Feste, 73. A similar view is found, for example,
in von Wilamowitz, Glaube II, 159 ff.; Kern, R.E. 9, 1914, 614, s.v. Iakchos;
Frisk, Griech. Etym. Wörterb., s.v. ἴακχος; Mylonas, Eleusis and the Eleu-
sinian Mysteries, London, 1961, 238; A. W. Persson, The religion of Greece
in prehistoric times, Berkley, 1942, 151; C. Theander, o.c. 121 ff.; Nilsson,
G.G.R. I², 664; W. K. C. Guthrie, The Greeks and their Gods, 288; H.
Jeanmaire, Dionysos, 93; 437. The view that ἴακχε is an exclamation precludes its formation from ἰαχή/ἰάχος after expressive gemination, as is proposed by the Etymol. Magn., and still thought by modern scholars. The
point to start from must, in that case, be a cheer ἰα, which develops into
the cheer ἴακχε.
[2] R.E. 9, 1914, 614, s.v. Iakchos. I do not consider this view to be correct.
[3] J. Harrison, Prolegomena, 413; cf. Themis, 48; also Theander, o.c. 121.
[4] About the sacral iteration: E. Norden, Comment. Verg. Aen. VI³,
Leipzig-Berlin, 1934, 136 f.
[5] ad Hom. Od. 1431.
[6] Thes. L. Gr., s.v.

meaning. Just as an expressive cry ἴακχε developed side by side with ἰά, βάκχε developed from an exclamation βᾶ. This is not meant to imply that both cries are to be traced back to one and the same culture [1], or that they should be etymologically related [2].

It is not difficult to understand how the meaning ὕμνος or ᾠδή could develop from an exclamation. Not only did ἴακχε and βάκχε, repeated as a refrain, figure in ritual songs, as e.g. Ἴακχ’ ὦ Ἴακχε in Aristophanes, Ranae, 315 ff., and a three times repeated refrain of a *paean* [3] found in Delphi: Εὐοῖ ὦ ἰὸ Βάκχ’ ὦ ἰ[ὲ παι]άν, but it seems probable that the exclamations also formed the start of the song. It is not exceptional for the exclamation with which a song starts to be turned into the name of the song, as is shown by titles such as *te Deum, Io vivat, Halleluja* etc.

The evolution into the name of a god is also clear now. Kern [4] calls it "charakteristisch für die griechische Religion, dass aus dem Refrain des Hymnos manches Mal ein neuer Gott oder auch der Beiname eines schon verehrten Gottes entstanden ist". As examples he mentions: Hymen, developed from the exclamation Ὑμὴν ὦ Ὑμεναῖε; Linos, developed from the exclamation αἴλινον, αἴλινον; Ἰουλώ, by-name of Demeter from πλεῖστον οὖλον ἵει, ἴουλον ἵει; Apollo's epithet Παιάν from the hail ἰήιε παιάν [5]; whereas the cry εὖα or εὐοῖ gave rise to Dionysos' epithet Εὖας and the cry ἴακχε to the god Iakchos.

Summarizing, we may draw the following conclusions:

1. At the start of the development we find a ritual exclamation. In later times this exclamation was interpreted as the vocative of the name of a god. In the case of Ἐλελεύς <ἐλελεῦ and Εὖας <εὖα

---

[1] According to Kern, Die Religion der Griechen I, 227, both Bacchos and Iacchos have come from Thracia.

[2] This had been written when my attention was drawn to a paper by van Windekens: Βάκχος. Beiträge zur Namenforschung, 4, 1953, 126. He is found to arrive at the same conclusion. He strikingly cites: Cornutus, Theologiae graecae compendium, c. 30 about Dionysos: Βρόμιος δὲ καὶ Βάκχος καὶ Ἴακχος καὶ Εὔιος καὶ Βαβάκτης καὶ Ἰόβακχος καλεῖται διὰ τὸ πολλὰς τοιαύτας φωνὰς τοὺς πατοῦντας αὐτὸν πρῶτον, εἶτα τοὺς ἕως μέθης μετὰ ταῦτα χρωμένους ἀφιέναι. For the rejection of a theory of H. Grégoire in Rev. Arch. 6e ser. tome 29/30, 1949, = Mélanges Charles Picard I, 401 ff. see this paper.

[3] Ed. Weil, B. C. H. 19, 1895, 392; Vollgraff, *ibid.* 49, 1925, 104; 50, 1926, 263; 51, 1927, 423.

[4] Die Religion der Griechen I, 153.

[5] In view of a Knossos tablet with the god's name pa-ja-wo-ne (KN V 52, Documents, 208) the last-mentioned example has become less probable.

this will be readily seen. The same holds good for Ἴακχος. In poetry
this name is so often encountered in the vocative that mere chance
is out of the question. ἴακχε was the original exclamation "höchste
Ausdruck der Freude" [1]. Owing to the form with its "vocativus"-
ending and in view of the occasion at which the cry was heard, it
was thought that by this exclamation a god Ἴακχος was invoked:
a new god came into being. At the time of Aristophanes the personification had been completed. In spite of this, it is hard to avoid
the impression that Ἴακχ' ὦ Ἴακχε [2], repeated again and again,
constitutes the stereotyped form of the old sacral exclamation. In
exactly the same way Βάκχος developed from an exclamation
βάκχε, sometimes doubled to βακχέβακχε or extended to ἰόβακχε.
Here, too, a god was born from an invocation.

2. The names which came into being in this way are sometimes
affixed as epithets to existing names of gods: Ἐλελεύς, Εὔας,
Ἰήιος, Παιάν, Ἰουλώ, or developed into independent gods: Ὑμήν,
Λίνος.

A third possibility is that first a new god is created, who is subsequently identified with an existing god. An example is Σαβός,
Σαβάζιος. This god, whose origin appears to have been in Thracia,
was worshipped in Phrygia and identified with Dionysos, undoubtedly owing to a fundamental mutual relationship [3] manifesting itself,
among other things, in the orgiastic character of their cults.

Originally Ἴακχος had nothing to do with Dionysos [4]. He was the
personification of the cry ἴακχε, which was uttered at the 19th of
Boedromion, when the procession of the mysts headed for Eleusis.
He became the divine leader of this procession and not, as it is
often formulated, the personification of this procession [5]. Occasion-

---

[1] Kern, R.E. 9, 1914, 614.

[2] Ranae, 315 ff.

[3] Nilsson, G.G.R. I², 579: "Die Verwantschaft, ja Identität des Sabazios
mit Dionysos ist offenbar".

[4] Nilsson, G.G.R. I², 664; Kern, R.E. 9, 1914, 615.

[5] Nilsson, G.G.R. I², 599: "Personifikation des Iakchoszuges"; H. Jeanmaire, Dionysos, 437: "Iacchos ... qui était en quelque sorte, l'âme collective ... de la foule en marche"; P. Foucart, Les mystères d'Eleusis, Paris,
1914, III: "Un génie qui personnifia et le chant mystique et la procession
tout entière". In my view this is a misunderstanding, which is to be traced
back to expressions such as ἐξελαύνειν τὸν Ἴακχον (Plut. Alc. 34, 3); τὸν
μυστικὸν Ἴακχον ἐξάγουσιν (Plut. Cam. 19, 15); τὸν Ἴακχον ἐξ ἄστεος Ἐλευ-
σινάδε πέμπειν (Plut. Phoc. 28); προπέμπειν τὸν Ἴακχον (C.I.A. 2, 467 and 471).
ἐξελαύνω or πέμπω (πομπήν) may indeed mean "to lead a procession out
(of town)"; as far as I could ascertain, however, προπέμπω and ἐξάγω never

ally identified with the Ploutos boy, he was, finally, definitively identified with Dionysos, a process which was, of course, furthered by the resemblance between the names of Βάκχος and Ἴακχος. It is no longer possible to ascertain whether or not Βάκχος was originally also an independent god.

3. The names do not have the same place of origin. Σαβάζιος was Thracian-Phrygian, Ἴακχος was an Athenian creation, even though the exclamation ἴακχε may also have occurred elsewhere, Βάκχος is by many thought to be Lydian [1].

Neither the difference as to origin, nor the differentiation as to development of these by-names are of direct importance in connection with the object we aim at. What is important, however, is the fact that large numbers of these epithets, which are to be traced back to exclamations, are centred round the god Dionysos. This matter will have to be dealt with in more detail later on.

In view of their double function, that of being the name of a god as well as a song, θρίαμβος and διθύραμβος belong to the series of ἐπικλήσεις of Dionysos discussed above. Now that it has been made plausible that Ἴακχος, Βάκχος and Σαβός originally were exclamations, and that only this origin explains their later development, I wish to go one step further by suggesting a similar origin for θρίαμβος [2] and διθύραμβος [3].

---

have this meaning. If Aristophanes, Ranae 404, 410, 416, writes Ἴακχε φιλοχορευτὰ συμπρόπεμπέ με and the scholiast interprets verse 399: ὁδεύουσι . . . προπέμποντες τὸν Διόνυσον, the only inference possible is that ἐξάγω τὸν Ἴακχον means: "to take out the statue of Ἴακχος (a wooden image has been attested: I.G. III, 1,5). For this purpose a special priest, the Ἰακχαγωγός, had been appointed. This view is found in Thes. L.Gr., s.v. ἴακχος; Kern, R.E. 9, 1914, 616; E. Pfuhl, De Atheniensium pompis sacris, Berolini, 1900, 40.

[1] In this case the Lydian bilinguis (Sardis, 6, 1, 38): Διονυσικλῆς ΒακιϜαλι is always referred to; contra: Jeanmaire, Dionysos, 58, who thinks that βακι < βάκχος was taken over from the Greeks by the Lydians; slightly different: Otto, Dionysos, 58.

[2] Indirect also for ἴαμβος.

[3] This suggestion can already be found in von Wilamowitz, Griechische Verskunst, Berlin, 1921, 28, for θρίαμβος. H. Jeanmaire, Dionysos, 234, sees in dithyrambos a "répétition de thriambos". He points out that triumpe in the carmen arvale must have developed from θρίαμβε "et vu le caractère incantatoire du texte, justifierait l'idée qu'il s'agit d'une formule d'invocation, plus exactement même d'une acclamation rituelle". A highly important statement, as we shall see. A detailed study on the development from cheer to god: K. Marót, S.M.S.R. 8, 1932, 189 ff., who also suggests that Διθύραμβος belongs to these "Urschöpfungen" which "mittels direkter Benützung der . . . primären Erregungslauten . . . entstanden sind" (p. 192 f.).

The first time the words are found is in the form θριαμβοδιθύραμβε mentioned above. In Euripides, Bacchae, 526, we find Διθύραμβος for the first time by itself: ἴθι, Διθύραμβε, ἐμὰν ἄρσενα τάνδε βᾶθι νηδύν. In both cases we find the "vocativus". The similarity as to rhyme pattern between βάκχε, ἴακχε on the one hand, and θρίαμβε, διθύραμβε on the other, the resemblance between the composite forms βακχέβακχε and θριαμβοδιθύραμβε, peculiar to the sacral cry, strengthen my opinion that these are all ritual exclamations. We also see these acclamations combined in different ways. Dionysius of Halicarnassus [1] gives us the first line of a song: Ἴακχε διθύραμβε, σὺ τῶνδε χοραγέ.

The song from Delphi quoted earlier in this chapter begins as follows: [Δεῦρ' ἄνα Δ]ιθύραμβε Βάκχ'....

This leads us to the assumption that an acclamation ἰα, *θρια, *διθυρα [2] was extended to ἴαμβε, θρίαμβε, διθύραμβε.

In favour of this theory pleads the fact that the element -μβ- was preferably used in onomatopoeic words such as βόμβος, ῥόμβος, στέμβος. If Schulze's[3] theory that the name Εὐαμβεύς (in Diodorus 5,172) conceals a non-attested name of Dionysos *Εὔαμβος is correct, it strongly supports our view: θρίαμβος might via θρίαμβε have developed from *θρια in the same way as *Εὔαμβος developed via *εὔαμβε from εὖα.

We can now draw parallels between the following series:

Cry	After expressive lengthening	Verb	Noun
ἰά	ἴαμβε ἴακχε	ἰάζω cry ἰακχάζω shout "ἴακχε"	Ἴακχος name of a god / name of a song
βᾶ	*βαμβα(ι) [4] βάκχε	βάζω speak βαβάζω shout	Βάκχος name of a god / name of a song
		βακχάω ⎫ shout „βάκχε" βακχεύω ⎬ βακχιάζω ⎭ be in frenzy	βάκχος ⎫ possessed βάβαξ ⎬ βαβάκτης ⎭ reveller
*θριά θρίαμβε		θριάζω [5] be possessed	Θριαί [6] nymphs; nurses of Apollo

[1] Συνθεσ. Ὀνομάτων, 72.
[2] Von Wilamowitz' suggestion that διθυρ- should have developed from *διθρι- as a result of metathesis then remains attractive.
[3] Gött. Gel. Anz. 1896, 240.
[4] Cf. βαμβαίνω 'rattle together (of teeth), stutter'; βαμβακύζω 'chatter with cold'; βαμβάλειν· τρέμειν, ψοφεῖν τοῖς χείλεσιν (Hesych.)
[5] Hesychius: θριάζειν· ἐνθουσιάζειν.
The Suda: λέγουσι γὰρ θρίασιν τὴν τῶν ποιητῶν μανίαν.
[6] Philoch. Müller, F.H.G. I, 196, p. 416.

Miss Harrison [1] has made it clear that these Θριαί were originally not the nurses of Apollo, but the Θυιάδες, frenzied followers of Dionysos. If the meanings of θριάζω and Θριαί are compared with those of the words mentioned above, a fundamental meaning "to call θριά", "woman calling θριά" is here also possible.

So far our arguments were based on hypotheses. There is, however, one datum which can confirm with a probability bordering on certainty that θρίαμβε was in fact originally an exclamation: the Latin *triumpe*, which functioned as a cry in the *carmen arvale* and in the triumph. This leads to a highly important consequence: contrary to what was generally assumed so far, it was not a (non-attested) θρίαμβος-ceremony that was taken over by Rome, but first and foremost a ritual exclamation! If this is indeed the case, the mystery of how an appellativum θρίαμβος could change into a cry *triumpe* has been solved, only to make room for new questions: what did the Greeks aim at by this exclamation, what was its religious meaning, and at what kind of occasions was it used? When trying to answer these questions, we can start from the data found so far: the exclamation formed part of the Dionysiac cult and it is comparable with other exclamations such as σαβοῖ, ἴακχε, βάκχε, etc.

When I shall now try and describe the aspect of the Dionysiac worship in which a ritual exclamation has an understandable function and has actually been attested, I have to make drastic restrictions. Not only are both the subject-matter and the amount of literature published about it of overwhelming proportions, but it is this very aspect of the Dionysiac religion which will have to be dealt with in more detail further on. A more extensive statement of the major facts and problems, as well as an ampler treatment of testimonia and literature may, therefore, be found elsewhere in the present study [2].

In spite of the great diversity of opinion obtaining among the experts on religious history as regards the origin, the descent and the character of the god Dionysos, there are a few characteristic features by which Dionysos distinguishes himself from the other gods in the Greek pantheon, and about which there is no disagreement in the world of learning: Dionysos is the god of the mask, of the μανία, of the wine. His cult and his mythos speak of death and

---

[1] Prolegomena, 442.
[2] *Vide infra* p. 235 ff.

resurrection. His presence reveals itself, among other things, in the ἐνθουσιασμός of his followers.

One of the principal characteristics of the Dionysiac worship is the epiphany. Dionysos is pre-eminently a god who manifests himself, an aspect to which W. Otto in particular, in the chapter "Der kommende Gott" of his well-known book about Dionysos [1], paid a great deal of attention. "Die Kultformen . . . . . zeigen ihn als den Kommenden, den Epiphaniengott, dessen Erscheinung viel dringender und zwingender ist als die irgend eines anderen Gottes" he states [2]. It is this facet of Dionysos' personality that concerns us.

Although the epiphany of the god constitutes a standard feature of myth and cult, it varies as to place and form. In Boeotia [3] women in a Bacchic trance looked for the god on mount Helicon during the spring month of *Agrionios* [4], but on their return reported that he had gone into hiding among the Muses. The inhabitants of Argos thought that the god was hidden in the depths of the lake of Lerna [5], into which, according to a myth, he had been thrown by Perseus [6], and called him up with a flourish of trumpets. In Migonion in Arcadia women found the god in the spring in the shape of a beautiful bunch of grapes [7]. In Elis it was a chorus of sixteen women which asked the god to appear. Their request was couched in an ancient song [8]:

Ἐλθεῖν ἥρω Διόνυσε
Ἀλείων ἐς ναόν·
ἁγνὸν σὺν Χαρίτεσσι
ἐς ναὸν τῷ βοέῳ ποδὶ θύων
ἄξιε ταῦρε, ἄξιε ταῦρε

In Athens during the *Lenaia* the *dadouchos* orders: καλεῖτε θεόν, after which those present call Σεμελήι' Ἴακχε πλουτοδότα [9]. In

---

[1] Dionysos. Mythos und Kultus, Frankfurt, 1933, 75 ff.

[2] *ibid.*

[3] Plut. quaest. symp. 717 A.

[4] Agrionios as spring month: Nilsson, G.G.R. I², 598 n. 2; Griech. Feste, 274.

[5] Plut. de Iside et Osiride, 364 F; cf. Pausanias, 2, 36, 7 ff.

[6] Schol. T. Ilias 14, 319.

[7] Paus., 3, 22, 2.

[8] Plut. quaest. graec. 299 A.

[9] Schol. Arist. Ranae, 479; in exactly the same way we find in Ranae 395 the *coryphaeus* calling the chorus: νῦν καὶ τὸν ὡραῖον θεὸν παρακαλεῖτε δεῦρο ᾠδαῖσι, τὸν ξυνέμπορον τῆσδε τῆς χορείας, after which the chorus begins: Ἴακχε πολυτίμητε.

Delphi the choruses of the Thyiads every other winter climbed Parnassus to rouse the newly-born Dionysos Liknites from his sleep [1]. In Athens and other, particularly Ionian, towns the god's return from overseas was celebrated [2].

These examples do not by any means exhaust the material on this subject. However, they adequately illustrate the central motif, which returns again and again in various forms: Dionysos has disappeared and is to come back. Whether the god has to rise from the dead, returns from far-away places, is re-born as a child, or is roused from his sleep, his epiphany never takes place ἀπὸ τοῦ αὐτομάτου. The initiative always rests with man, who by the action of the καλεῖν, παρακαλεῖν, ἀνακαλεῖν or ἐγείρειν, which was throughout accompanied by a great deal of noise and the sound of instruments [3], invited the god to manifest himself.

The way in which the god reveals himself, whether in the shape of a bull, as an idol or statue, occasionally represented by a human being, but always tangible and concrete [4], his triumphal entry into the city and the celebration of his παρουσία, are all subjects to be dealt with further on. What should be pointed out here is that the frenzy, the crying and singing, the rejoicing do not come to an end after the appearance of the god, but rather reach a climax. The ἐνθουσιασμός of the Maenads, Thyiads, Bacchantes or whatever their names may be, the exultation at the god's manifestation among the people finds an outlet in new cheers. On the *Choes*, the day on which Dionysos makes his entry into Athens on his *carrus navalis*, the people on the chariots which joined the procession sang loud songs of a satirical and perhaps aeschrological nature [5].

In order to arrive at a conclusion, we now summarize the data and arrange the facts. Dionysos had many epithets, one category of which drew our special attention: the group of names of which some also had the meaning "song", and whose origin we have traced back to the ritual exclamation. These names, in particular, are

---

[1] Plut. de Iside et Osiride, 365 A.

[2] *Anthesteria* at Athens: Deubner, Attische Feste, 93 ff.; in Ionian cities: Nilsson, Griech. Feste, 267 ff.

[3] During the imperial period on Rhodos even by means of a water organ: Oesterr. Jahresh. 7, 1904, 92 f.

[4] Otto, o.c. 78, rightly stresses the "Unmittelbarkeit seines Erscheinens".

[5] Photius in the Suda: τὰ ἐκ τῶν ἁμαξῶν . . . ᾿Αθήνησι γὰρ ἐν τῇ τῶν χοῶν ἑορτῇ οἱ κωμάζοντες ἐπὶ τῶν ἁμαξῶν τοὺς ἀπαντῶντας ἔσκωπτόν τε καὶ ἐλοιδόρουν.

specific to Dionysos. A second characteristic of the Dionysiac worship is the fact that the god is periodically called up from death, exile or sleep to reveal himself amongst his followers. The connection between these two data is now obvious. The exclamations εὐοῖ, εὖα, ἐλελεῦ, βάκχε, ἴακχε, θρίαμβε, διθύραμβε were the cries by which the god was called to epiphany, and which as orgiastic shouts of joy accompanied his appearance. There are numerous reminiscences of this original connection between calling and appearing: in the verses of Aristophanes already mentioned νῦν καὶ τὸν ὡραῖον θεὸν παρακαλεῖτε δεῦρο .... Ἴακχε πολυτίμητε and in the subsequent refrain repeated over and over again Ἴακχ' ὦ Ἴακχε; in the summons of the *dadouchos* already quoted καλεῖτε θεόν with the reply Σεμελήι' Ἴακχε πλουτοδότα. "Bakchos ist der Name, der den Gott als den orgiastischen bezeichnet", says Nilsson [1]. The orgies are exactly the occasions on which the god is summoned to manifest himself. In the name Βακχέβακχος the invocation which was heard ἐν ταῖς θυσίαις survived. Διθύραμβε is found side by side with βάκχε in the opening words of the Delphic hymn in which Dionysos is asked to reveal himself, now that spring has come. Also in Euripides' Bacchae, 525 ff., Διθύραμβε is used to denote an order to appear: Ἴθι, Διθύραμβ', ἐμὰν ἄρσενα τάνδε βᾶθι νηδύν [2]. From the context we see that Euripides uses the word Διθύραμβε here to allude to Dionysos' double birth, following the ancient derivation of the word from δι- and θύρα: "(the god) who entered life through a double door" [3]. Miss Harrison [4], however, has pointed out that behind this incorrect interpretation a real relation between the dithyramb and Dionysos' birth did exist. Plato [5] refers to an ἄλλο εἶδος ᾠδῆς Διονύσου γένεσις, οἶμαι, διθύραμβος λεγόμενος. The Delphic hymn is a birth-song. Plutarch in Περὶ τοῦ Ει τοῦ ἐν Δελφοῖς (388 F) mentions the difference in character between Apollo and Dionysos [6]. The latter is the god of change, of metamorphosis. In his myths one finds πάθημα and διασπασμόν, φθοράς and ἀφανισμοὺς but also ἀνα-

---

[1] Griech. Feste, 305.

[2] Cf. Euripides, Bacchae, 1020: ἴθ', ὦ Βάκχε.

[3] E. R. Dodds, Commentary on Euripides, Bacchae, verse 526; J. Harrison, Prolegomena, 436; Pickard-Cambridge, Dithyramb, Tragedy and Comedy, 14 ff.

[4] Prolegomena, 436 ff.

[5] Leges III, 700 B. This and other testimonia are extensively discussed by Pickard-Cambridge, o.c. 1 ff.

[6] By this time Dionysos has, however, already been identified with Zagreus, so that Orphic ideas are discernible everywhere.

βιώσεις καὶ παλιγγενεσίας. About these events they sing διθυραμβικὰ
μέλη and it is this dithyramb which is sung in winter at Dionysos'
awakening: ἀρχομένου δὲ χειμῶνος ἐπεγείραντες τὸν διθύραμβον... [1].
Finally, Miss Harrison, points to the fact that the dithyramb is
especially connected with Dionysos as the bull-god [2], the shape in
which he preferably manifests himself [3].

Dionysos is not the only god who is invited by man to manifest
himself. The raising of a dead or sleeping god which, though not
in all, yet in many instances represents the death and re-birth of
nature, is found—as is generally known after the works of Mannhardt
and Frazer—as a magico-religious act among many peoples [4]. Such
rites in the cult of "dying and rising gods" are found to be centred
particularly in Asia Minor. It is also in this country that we have to
look for the origin of some of the epithets of Dionysos, of the gods
who were originally called up by these names, and possibly also of
Dionysos himself [5]. In view of their non-Greek character, it is,
therefore, at least probable that ἴαμβος, θρίαμβος, διθύραμβος, which
are closely linked up with the cult of Dionysos, also originated in
Asia Minor.

In very guarded terms the conclusion of this paragraph may
therefore be formulated as follows: θρίαμβος as an *epiclesis* and as
the name of a song developed from an exclamation θρίαμβε. By this
exclamation a god of the Dionysiac type, at one time identified
with Dionysos, was summoned to epiphany. It appears probable
that, like the god to whom it was addressed, this exclamation is to
be traced back to Asia Minor.

3. *Triumpe*

The word *triumphus* [6] goes back to an older form *triumpe*, which,
five times repeated, forms the conclusion of the *carmen arvale*, "das

---

[1] Plut., o.c. 389 C.

[2] Pindar, Ol. 13, 18: ταὶ Διωνύσου πόθεν ἐξέφανεν σὺν βοηλάτᾳ Χάριτες
διθυράμβῳ; Pickard-Cambridge, however, with the scholiast on Plato Rep.
394 C, explains βοηλάτης from the custom that the winner of the dithyramb
competition was given a bull. Cf., however, the hymn from Elis: ἄξιε ταῦρε.

[3] Nilsson, Griech. Feste, 261 ff.

[4] A similar origin of the god's name Yahweh has been proposed by K.
Müller, Kartellzeitung der Akad. theol. Vereine, Nov. 1921, on the basis
of which R. Otto, Das Heilige⁹, 1922, 263, defines the short form Jah or
Jahu as "numinöser Urlaut". About god's name and ritual exclamation:
Th. H. Gaster, Thespis, 31-32.   [5] *vide infra* p. 292 ff.

[6] Quintilian, inst. orat. 1, 5, 20, records an older *triumpus*; so does Cicero,
orator, 160.

einzige zusammenhängende Stück, das wir besitzen im ältesten Latein" (Mommsen [1]). The flood of publications about this cryptic song has not diminished [2] even after Norden's epochal work [3], although his invitation to future scholars his "Ergebnisse zu verbessern und zu ergänzen" [4], has only in a few instances been accepted. Too often it has been attempted on inadequate grounds to force the issue by giving an entirely new interpretation, while dismissing Norden's well-considered explanation without any argumentation. That this cannot be done with impunity is illustrated by a theory published by García Calvo [5] in 1957, which interprets the *carmen arvale* as a song accompanying a war-dance(!) [6]. Another view, that of S. Ferri [7], who finds all kinds of misunderstood abbreviations in the inscription, opens the door for the most arbitrary versions. *Fere*, for instance,—"che non dice nulla" (!)— should be read *ferc*, an abbreviation of *fercto*. The same author dates the *carmen* to before 1000 B.C.—no less!—from which it follows: "Naturalmente non c'entra *Triumpus* Bacco che non poteva essere in discussione nel II millennio". The fact is that, according to Ferri, *triumpe* is either an imperativus of **triumpere*, or an abbreviation of an equally non-existing verbum **triumpedare*.

More than anything else these and similar theories testify to the truth of Birt's words quoted by Norden [8]: "Wir müssen Anschluss an die übliche Sprechweise suchen, und je mehr dies erreicht wird,

---

[1] Th. Mommsen, Ueber die römischen Ackerbrüder. Reden und Aufsätze, 275, quoted by Norden, o.c. 115.

[2] E. Bickel, *Carmen Arvale*. Rhein. Mus. 89, 1940, 28 ff.; F. Dornseiff, Buchglossen I. Altitalisches. Rhein. Mus. 89, 1940, 228 f.; F. Mentz, Zum *carmen arvale*. Zeitschr. f. vergl. Sprachforsch. 70, 1952, 209 ff.; L. Bernardini, Osservazioni ad alcune parti della III e IV strofa del *Carmen Arvalium*. Studi Class. e Orient. 5, 1956, 79 ff.; R. G. Tanner, The arval hymn and early Latin verse. Class. Quart. 11, 1961, 209 ff. For older literature see: M. Nacinovich, *Carmen Arvale* I, II, Roma, 1933/34. Cf. also notes 5 and 7.

[3] E. Norden, Aus altrömischen Priesterbüchern, Lund, 1939.

[4] o.c. 111.

[5] A. García Calvo. Una interpretación del *carmen arvale*. Emerita, 25, 1957, 387 ff.

[6] The idea is not new. R. Meringer, Wört. und Sache, 7, 1921, 33 ff., saw in the *carmen* a war song. Refuted by A. Nehring, Glotta, 13, 1919, 302 ff. and Nacinovich, o.c. I, 21.

[7] S. Ferri. Metodo archeologico e *Carmen Fratrum Arvalium*. Studi Class. e Orient. 5, 1956, 87 ff.; *idem*, Il *Carmen Fratrum Arvalium* e il metodo archeologico. Latomus, 13, 1954, 390 ff.

[8] o.c. 110.

je richtiger ist die Auslegung". The interpretation of Norden, who based his method on this statement, will form the starting point of our inquiry into the meaning of *triumpe* in the *carmen arvale*. The *aporia* as to the separation of the words, which for years stood in the way of an explanation, does not apply to the last verse. No misunderstanding is possible here: the exclamation *triumpe* concludes the *carmen* and is repeated five times, "weil fünf *triumpe* einen richtigen Vers geben" (F. Leo [1]). This oldest form developed into *triumphus*, via *triumpus*, as formulated by Walde-Hofmann: *"triumphus* entstanden aus dem dreimal wiederholten Ruf *io triumpe*, also zunächst im Vokativ". What these authors exactly mean is not quite clear. If "Vokativ" is only meant to denote a *form*, this formulation is in no way objectionable. If, however, they also have a *function* in mind, caution is called for. Was this vocativus, after all, based on an ancient nominativus *triumpus* which has not come down to us? If so, who was addressed by this vocativus? This kind of confusion had perhaps better be precluded by slightly modifying the formulation: *triumphus* evolved from *triumpe*, a form which resembles a vocativus formally, and which at one time was taken as such by the Romans. Whether or not such an interpretation was already current at the time when the *carmen* came into being [2], is a question which cannot be solved. As is apparent from other examples the word need not have been a vocativus —semantically as well as formally—when it was introduced into Rome. *Hercle*, interpreted by the Romans as a vocativus, was in all probability a nominativus [3] in Etruscan; *talassio*, an exclamation of unknown, perhaps Etruscan origin [4], was by the Romans interpreted as a nominativus [5], but, in addition, a nominativus *Talassius* was formed. Anyhow, the position of *triumpe* at the end of the *carmen*, its repetition as well as its use in the triumph determine its function: in the oldest stage

---

[1] Quoted by Norden, o.c. 232.

[2] About this date nothing can be stated with certainty. Guesses range from the second millennium B.C. (Ferri) to the 6/5th century B.C. (Norden). See: G. Pasquali, Preistoria della poesia Romana, 60 ff.

[3] Walde-Hofmann, L.E.W³., s.v. *Hercules*, see a vocativus in it of an Italic o-stem *Herclo-*. I prefer the view of Devoto, S.E. 2, 1928, 317 ff., as given in the text. Cf. E. Fiesel, Namen, 87; Altheim, R.R.G. II, 1931, 33; A. Ernout, Philologica, I, Paris, 1946, 25 n. 5. Cf. the traditional first name of Persius: Aule.

[4] A. Ernout, B.S.L. 30, 1930, 112.

[5] Walde-Hofmann, L.E.W.³, s.v. *Talassio*.

of Latin accessible to us *triumpe* is an exclamation. But what did it signify?

There is no denying that so far this question has not been answered [1]. Von Grienberger [2] writes in 1906: "Wenn *triumpus*...eine Entlehnung aus griech. θρίαμβος ist, ..., so liegt es doch nahe für das griechische Wort, das ein Beiname des Dionysos ist, ursprünglich adjektivischen Charakter zu behaupten und in demselben ein *Epitheton ornans* zu erkennen, das in gleicher Weise, wie an Dionysos, so auch an Mars, oder an den im Triumphe einziehenden Sieger gerichtet werden könnte". On two points this scholar is already far ahead of many who came after him. In the first place, he does not refer to a θρίαμβος—ceremony which should have survived in Rome as a triumphal ceremony, but rightly stresses the function of the word as an *epiclesis* of Dionysos. Secondly, he is, as far as I know, the only scholar who identifies the *triumpe* of the *carmen arvale* with that of the triumph without, however, explaining the former from the latter. This positive result stands, even if we criticize certain details of his theory. Von Grienberger did not know that θρίαμβος was not originally an *epitheton*. Nor did *triumpus* have this function in Latin, since no *Mars triumphus* or *victor triumphus*, which would be expected in that case, exist. Other problems—why is it the god Mars who inherited this *epitheton* from Dionysos? What is the resemblance between Mars (decidedly not a war-god in the *carmen arvale*) and the triumphator?—von Grienberger also leaves undiscussed.

Norden [3] proceeds along different lines. His explanation reads as follows: "Die das Lied beherrschende Spannung löst sich in einem sakralen Ruf: Der Erfolg des Gebets, die Rettung aus Not und Gefahr, ist gesichert." Norden, therefore, gives *triumpe* of the *carmen arvale* the meaning of the cry *io triumpe* heard during the triumph [4]. This view is contestable. In the first place, it would have to be proved that the cheer of the triumph had the character of a triumphal cry *ab origine*. This is by no means certain. The second

---

[1] "Eine Deutung des "*io triumpe*" ist noch nicht geglückt". G. Radke, Gymnasium, 77, 1970, 44.

[2] Von Grienberger, Das *carmen arvale*. I.F. 19, 1906, 140 ff.

[3] o.c. 228.

[4] Cf. A. Ernout, Recueil de textes Latins archaïques[2], Paris, 1957, 109: "*triumpe*: sorte d'exclamation triomphale". V. Pisani, Testi Latini arcaici e volgari[2], Torino, 1960, 2: "*triumpe* è il noto grido, probabilmente il gr. θρίαμβος, passato attraverso l'etrusco".

objection is that *triumpe* as a shout of triumph *in* the *carmen* would be slightly premature. The song aims at warding off disaster and imploring the god's blessing—so much is certain—, not at celebrating the granting of the prayer. Now it would be possible to resort to the following line of reasoning: *triumpe* is a magic pression by means of which man, by representing the success as having been achieved, forces the god to give his sanction. It should, however, be realized that such an explanation does not follow logically from the trend of the song, but would have been introduced only with a view to giving *triumpe* the character of a cry of triumph, also in the *carmen arvale*. In any case, it is methodically more correct to try and explain the oldest testimony of *triumpe* from its context [1].

I first of all give the text of the *carmen*, followed by a translation based on Norden's interpretation:

> *Enos Lases iuvate*
> *neve lue rue Marmar sins incurrere in pleoris*
> *satur fu, fere Mars, limen sali, sta berber*
> *Semunis alternei advocapit conctos,*
> *enos Marmor iuvato,*
> *triumpe triumpe triumpe triumpe triumpe.*

> Lares, help us,
> Prevent pestilence and corruption, Mars, from rushing at several (?)
> be satisfied, wild Mars, jump on the threshold, remain standing there,
> the Semones you in turn shall call, all of them,
> Help us, Mars.
> *triumpe, triumpe, triumpe, triumpe, triumpe* [2].

---

[1] A sentence such as "das abschliessende fünfmalige *triumpe* entspricht den Schlussschritten des kultischen Tanzes" (F. Mentz, o.c. 227) is, of course, not an explanation.

[2] Of other possibilities only those relating to the fourth line will be found to be of interest to us. For this see below. For the rest, there are interpretations which differ from that of Norden as to details: *sins < sinās* remains difficult. Perhaps better: Thurneysen, Zeitschr. f. vergl. Sprach. 27, 1879, 173, who takes it to be an "Injunktivform" such as gr. δός, θές. *Pleores* hardly = *plures*; not *flores* either, as many think; see Mentz, o.c. 219; perhaps < *ploro- 'Boden, Flur'? (Mentz, o.c. 220). In nearly hundred pages (o.c. I, 18-115) of his book, Nacinovich has not succeeded in making plausible that *fere Mars* should be an un-Roman phrase. The explanation of Norden of *limen sali sta berber*, in which only *berber* remains doubtful (Latte, Philol. 97, 1948, 152 n. 1), is in my view greatly to be preferred to older suggestions: "Sprudel, springe, stehe Halm", defended by Mentz, o.c. 222 ff., linguistically as well as because Mars lacks the character of a sun-god required in that case.

The song furnishes, as will be seen, a very early example of an anthropomorphic representation of the god Mars. Norden[1] reminds us that Mommsen[2] already considered Mars "das Vorbild des Wehrmannes und den ältesten Hauptgott der italischen Bürgergemeinden", and pointed out that Mars, whose name is the only one recognizable in Roman proper names, was already very early represented in human shape[3]. In the *carmen arvale* the god is asked to jump on the threshold and to remain standing there, in other words, he is in the most literal sense "herbeigerufen". In the text we find this verb in *advocapit*, which in any case—upon that point everyone agrees—must have *Semunis conctos* as its object. As regards the form *advocapit*, however, the final word has not yet been spoken. At present it is generally agreed that it is a futurum form of *advocare*, in which the change $b > p$ is due to Oscan-Umbrian or Sabine influences[4]. As to the ending, however, opinions differ.

At first sight *advocapit* would appear to be 3rd ps. sg. fut.: "he will call". In the *carmen*, however, this does not make sense: that Mars should call the Semones seems highly improbable and is not defended by anyone. Hammarström[5] sees in this line stage directions to the priest on duty, which have landed in the text of the *carmen*. Mentz and others follow him in this respect. The consequence is, however, that *alternei*—by most of the scholars considered to be an adverb—has to be translated by "der Reihe nach", since it is impossible for one priest to take turns in calling the Semones. However, *alternei* decidedly does not have the meaning of "der Reihe nach", as is pointed out by Norden (p. 180). An attempt made by Mentz to get out of the difficulties is equally desperate. According to him[6] *alternei* refers to *Semunis conctos*. He states: "Also der diensttuende Priester .... soll die Saatgötter *conctos*, insgesamt, aber unter Namensnennung jedes einzelnen.... herbeirufen. Dies ist ohne Zweifel der Sinn von *alternei*....". Apart from the fact that this does not mean any improvement on Hammarström's theory, Mentz is guilty of a contradiction: the meaning of *conctos* "ins-

---

[1] o.c. 157.

[2] Römische Geschichte, I, 51.

[3] Cf. *Mars, vigila*, which is comparable with *vigilasne deum gens*? (Serv. ad Aen. 2, 148) said by the *pontifex maximus* to the gods, who were present and visible during the *lectisternium*.

[4] See Norden, o.c. 178 ff.; Mentz, o.c. 223 f.

[5] Arctos, 1, 1930, 242.

[6] o.c. 225.

gesamt" is wholly inconsistent with a "Namensnennung jedes einzelnen", which Mentz (wrongly) deduces from *alternei*. A place in Suetonius [1] mentioned by Mentz directly refutes his theory instead of corroborating it.

If, therefore, *alternei* cannot be combined with *conctos*, the inevitable conclusion is that *advocapit* must be a plural, a conclusion already drawn by scholars such as Grotefend, von Blumenthal, Bergk, Bücheler, and defended by Norden. The explanation that *advocapit* developed from *advocabite* (an older form of *advocabitis*, just as *loquere* was not until late replaced by *loqueris*), the only solution which, in my view, appears acceptable, involves a problem which did not escape Norden's attention [2]. How is one to explain that an explicitly announced calling of the Semones is not followed by this *advocatio* itself? Norden [3], rejecting older suggestions, says: "eine Handlung, die in der Zukunft erfolgen soll, wird von den Chorsängern nur angekündigt; ihr Vollzug liegt ausserhalb des Liedes." By means of examples from the Greek tragedies he tries to prove that such a procedure was not unusual. He thinks, for example, that the last line of Aeschylus' Persians, πέμψω τοί σε δυσθρόοις γόοις, will actually be followed by the lamentation as soon as the chorus has entered the palace.

This view was rightly opposed by F. Dornseiff [4]. He pointed out that neither in Greek, nor in Latin literature phrases like these are meant literally. Notably in Pindar, for instance, the invitation to sing a song is a *topos*. "Es ist eines der ersten Dinge die der Pindarleser in sich aufnehmen muss, dass dies nicht bedeutet: Diese Hauptgesangsleistung wird nächstens noch kommen, sondern dass das Besingen mit dieser Aufforderung geleistet und abgegeltet ist". Also in the psalm "Sing unto the Lord a new song" the exhortation is responded to on the spot. These remarks are stringent, the more so if we consider the manner in which Norden manipulates his testimonia in order to attain his end [5].

---

[1] Aug. 6o, quoted by Mentz: *reges in suo quisque regno . . . et cuncti simul.* The complete text reads: *Reges amici atque socii èt singuli in suo quisque regno Caesareas urbes condiderunt èt cuncti simul aedem Iovis Olympii Athenis . . . perficere . . . destinaverunt.* Comment is superfluous.

[2] This problem does not exist for V. Pisani, o.c. 2 ff., who reads this verse as follows: *O, Semones, alternei, ad vos capite conctos (nos).*

[3] o.c. 199.

[4] o.c. 230.

[5] In Sophocl. Trachiniae, 220 ff., the chorus calls: ἀνολολυξάτω . . . ἀ μελλόνυμφος· ἐν δὲ κοινὸς ἀρσένων ἴτω κλαγγὰ τὸν εὐφαρέτραν Ἀπόλλωνα

Norden's method is open to criticism of a more fundamental nature. Although there are certain formal resemblances between Greek lyrical turns and the diction of the *carmen arvale*, the essential differences should not be lost sight of. The examples from the Greek tragedies furnished by Norden have all been taken from lyrical passages expressing personal emotions. A possibly deliberate inaccuracy or inconsistency might be expected there. How great, however, is the difference between this elaborate, artistic form developed in a sophisticated civilization and the uncomplicated, primitive directness of the *carmen arvale*! Instead of a personal, spontaneous outpour, we find in the *carmen* a primitive prayer-formula, handed down by oral tradition and copied by one generation after another: the first example of this typically Roman, juridically-balanced formulation also applied throughout sacral liturgy. It is extremely hard to imagine that the Roman, who in sacral texts says too much rather than too little, would in the *carmen arvale* confine himself to the announcing of an *advocatio* which, without any demonstrable reason, is not to be put into words until later, outside the *carmen*.

If, as Norden suggests [1], this invocation were of the type: *adesto Tiberine cum tuis undis*, and if such an *indigitamentum* were addressed to each of the (12?) Semones, it would, *a fortiori*, be expected that stereotyped formulae, like the *carmen* itself, would have been recorded. However, the use of such *indigitamenta* for the Semones is fully out of the question, for the same reason why also Mentz' theory had to be rejected. *Cuncti significat quidem omnes, sed coiuncti et congregati* we learn from Paulus ex Festo [2]. This is confirmed by literature in which *cuncti* always means "gesamt, sämtlich, vollständig, alle" [3]. Not until Statius does this meaning

---

προστάταν, ὁμοῦ δὲ παιᾶνα παιᾶν' ἀνάγετ' ὦ παρθένοι, βοᾶτε τὰν ὁμόσπορον Ἄρτε-μιν κ.τ.λ. This is followed by (verse 216) ἀείρομ' οὐδ' ἀπώσομαι τὸν αὐλόν κ.τ.λ. Finally the call (verse 221) ἰὼ ἰὼ Παιάν. With respect to the exhortation in the first verses Norden speaks of "Lieder auf Apollon, Artemis und die Nymphen", although it is clearly an exhortation to a παιάν; with reference to the *futura* in verse 216 he mentions a "Paian auf Dionysos", although precisely here the word παιάν is not used. The promise expressed in the *futura* is, according to Norden, fulfilled by the cheer in verse 221: ἰὼ ἰὼ Παιάν. All this in order to prove that the hymn to Apollo will be sung later (outside the song), and that the invocation to Dionysos is made now, within the song.

[1] o.c. 207.
[2] p. 44 (L).
[3] Walde-Hofmann, L.E.W.³, s.v. *cunctus*.

gradually weaken and may *cunctus* mean "each", like *omnis* [1].
The original meaning of *cunctus*—most probably developed from
concitus—was, therefore, preserved in Latin for a very long time.
This forms all the more reason for attributing the meaning "all
together" to *conctos* in the *carmen arvale*. *Advocapit Semunis conctos*
is, therefore, the opposite of *advocapit Semunis singulos*. *Indigitamenta* for each of the Semones are, consequently, out of the question
here, whilst moreover, it is highly doubtful whether each of them
had a separate identity [2]. Lares and Penates are not given individual
names either. If, therefore, we are looking for an evocatory formula, the one quoted by Norden *divi veteresque novique...cuncti
adeste* [3] is as an example greatly to be preferred to the one mentioned
above.

In view of this argumentation it is *in* the *carmen* that we expect
the *advocatio* announced by *advocapit*. Of this *advocatio* we know
that it does not call the Semones *nominatim*, but that it "herbeiruft"
all Semones together, as a group. Well, in the song we find a call
which satisfies all requirements: *triumpe*. This means abandoning
the wholly unproved premise which up till now was generally used
as a starting-point, viz. that *triumpe* was *ab origine* a triumphal cry.
We are interested in what the context of the *carmen arvale* presents
and what it requires. We find a self-exhortation to invoke the
Semones, i.e. to invoke them collectively. This invocation should
be sung *alternei*, in turns. In the *carmen* itself we find a call *triumpe*,
which, since it is an exclamation, may be addressed to several gods
at once, and, because it is repeated five times, may be sung *alternei*.

Our interpretation is admittedly a hypothetical one, as large
parts of the *carmen* allow of only hypothetical explanations. If
Norden is followed, however,—and I consider him the best guide
up to the present—the meaning of *triumpe*, as we have deduced it
from the *carmen*, is less hypothetical than that of triumphal cry [4].
In addition, however, there is an extra-textual datum we found
earlier on, and which strongly supports the above argumentation.
At the end of the previous paragraph we concluded that θρίαμβε

---

[1] Quite impossible, therefore, is the proposal of Marx, ad Lucilium, 1322,
II, 424, to take *conctos* as nomin. sg.: *divos alternei advocabit quisque*.

[2] Nor does Norden get further than two, who do not even have a right
to this 'name': Semo Sancus Dius Fidius and Salus Semonia.

[3] Ovid, Ibis, 83 f.

[4] This also holds for the large majority of the other interpretations by
which the fourth line is given the meaning of summoning the *Semones*.

was the cry by which the Greeks and the pre-Greek peoples of Asia Minor called a god of the Dionysiac type to epiphany. In Latin *triumpe* is found as the oldest form, just as in Greek an exclamation. From this it follows that θρίαμβε, as an exclamation, without an appellative intermediate phase θρίαμβος, therefore, developed into the Latin cry *triumpe*. But in that case they may be expected to be akin as to function and meaning! As a matter of fact, we see that the meaning of the (pre-) Greek θρίαμβε we deduced from the Greek data, is largely similar to the meaning we found for the Latin *triumpe* solely on the basis of the text of the *carmen arvale*. The only difference is that the *advocatio* in the *carmen arvale* is not linked up with the cult of Dionysos or Liber, but addressed to the Sowing-gods [1], and perhaps also to Mars, who in the *carmen* is most emphatically invited to manifest himself. However, this is not the place to discuss this divergence in any great detail. Suffice it to state for the time being that the generally accepted view—of which Latte's formulation was already quoted—that the cry *triumpe* must have acquired quite a different meaning than θρίαμβος originally had, is incorrect. On the contrary, the meaning has, remarkably enough, remained the same [2].

Now that we have recognized in the *triumpe* of the *carmen arvale* an exclamation by which a god or gods are called and asked to reveal themselves and render aid, the question which remains is whether the same applies to the cheer which accompanies the triumph and which in historic times was definitely a triumphal cry.

First of all it should be noted that *io triump(h)e* is never found as a shout of joy immediately after a victory, but was used only during the solemn entry of the general into Rome, which in many cases did not take place until several months after the victory proper. It is therefore definitely incorrect, or at least insufficient, to define *triumpe* as a mere cheer of victory. It is possible to express a more positive opinion, but in order to do so it will be necessary briefly to anticipate matters which will be dealt with in more detail further on.

Not merely was the cheer reserved for the entry of the victorious general into the city, but even as such it was subject to restrictions:

---

[1] G. Radke, Die Götter Altitaliens, 286.

[2] The resemblance is even closer when it is found in Norden, o.c. 177: "Wer *advocare* als 'anrufen', also synonym mit *invocare* auffasst, verschliesst sich von vornherein das Verständnis des Verses: es bedeutet in genauer sakraler Sprache das 'Herbeirufen' einer Gottheit".

it was confined to the entry of the commander who by his insignia distinguished himself from the normal successful general, i.e. to the entry of the triumphator. The fundamental difference between triumph and *ovatio* is given concrete form by the difference in name —in both cases developed from an exclamation [1]—in insignia and in importance. The insignia of the triumphator in themselves make it clear that the triumph is much more than the joyous homecoming of a victorious general. In the next chapter we shall have to try and find an answer to the question whether, during the triumph, the triumphator represented the god Iuppiter, as many scholars think, or the *rex*, as is thought by a few great authorities on Roman religion. The fact that, outwardly, the triumphator resembled the god Iuppiter in many—according to some scholars all—respects can hardly be denied, however exceptional such a phenomenon may be in Roman religion. From this fact it may at least be concluded that the meaning which *triumpe* had in the *carmen arvale* may also be appropriate in the triumph. If it will subsequently be demonstrated that the triumph shows the specific aspects of an epiphany, this possibility will become a certainty.

4. *From* θρίαμβε *to triumpe*

When, in 1923, P. Kretschmer [2] postulated an Etruscan intermediate phase in the linguistic development of θρίαμβος into *triumphus*, he could refer to the Etruscan origin of the triumph, which had long since been recognized by archeologists and historians[3]. Kretschmer's theory met with general acknowledgment. However, the attacks made on it by Durante and Wallisch compel us once again to examine critically both Kretschmer's theory and the arguments of his opponents.

If θρίαμβος is placed side by side with *triumphus* (<*triumpus*), explanations are required for: 1. $\theta > t$; 2. $\alpha > u$; 3. $\beta > p > ph$. The change under 1. is of no interest to us: aspirates in Greek words sometimes change into *tenues* in Etruscan: Σθένελος > *Stenule*; Θράσω > *Tarsu*, whereas in other cases the aspiration is retained: Φοιβή > *Φuipa*; Χάρων > Χ*arun*. Both Etruscan and Greek aspirates, however, yield a *tenuis* in Latin. For this reason it is no longer

---

[1] See for the difference between triumph and *ovatio* p. 166 ff.

[2] In Gercke-Norden, Einl. I[3], 6, 112.

[3] Good survey in Müller-Deecke, Die Etrusker, I, 346 ff.; II, 198 ff.; cf. below p. 83.

possible for us to ascertain whether the word began in Etruscan with a *tenuis* or with an aspirate, nor is it of any importance in connection with our inquiry. As regards 3, we find in Kretschmer: "So erklärt sich nun auch das bisher rätselhafte lautliche Verhältnis von *triumpus, triumphus* zu Θρίαμβος: der im Etruskischen erklärliche Ersatz von β durch *p* (Φυίρα <Φοιβή), sowie die Aspiration in der Form *triumphus*, weisen auf etruskische Vermittlung".

It should be pointed out right away that the first part of this motivation is sound, whereas the second is not, for various reasons. In the first place one cannot possibly use an aspiration which does not take place until the second century B.C. in Latin [1] as an argument for a much older Etruscan origin. Secondly, it is by no means certain that this aspiration is due to Etruscan influences. Thirdly, we have in *triumpe* of the *carmen arvale* the oldest, unaspirated Latin form. The aspiration of the *p* should therefore not be used as an argument when the origin of the word is discussed.

This leaves 2. α > *u*. Like the change β > *p* this development can only be explained by resorting to Etruscan, and not by means of Latin linguistic laws. Eva Fiesel [2] gives the following examples: Πρίαμος > *Priumne*; Ἄρταμις > *Artumes*, in which α before *m* changes into *u*.

In his attack on the prevailing theories, of which he first of all tries to refute the linguistic arguments, Wallisch [3] refers to a statement he received from H. Krahe "dass es durchaus den altlat. Lautgesetzen entspräche, wenn *a* vor Labialen zu *u* sich wandle, wenn θ dem *t* weiche, und auch die Schwankung zwischen β und *p* sei durchaus nicht auf etruskischen Einfluss zurück zu führen".

It is highly regrettable that Wallisch does not quote his source more completely, since Krahe cannot be supposed to consider the rule "-*a*- before labial changes into -*u*-" applicable to Θρίαμβος > *triumpus*. As every handbook tells us, this rule holds only for -*a*- in open syllables [4]: Ἑκάβη > *Hecuba*; σησάμη > *sesuma*, etc. In closed syllables, however, -*a*- nearly without exception changes into

---

[1] Leumann-Hofmann, Lat. Gramm. I, 131; Sommer, Handb. d. Lat. Laut- und Formenlehre, 199 ff.; F. Stolz, A. Debrunner, W. P. Schmid, Gesch. d. Lat. Sprache, 53; 62.

[2] E. Fiesel, Namen, 63; 85. One may add: Gr. ἄφλαστον (α- before two consonants) becomes-via Etr.-Lat. *aplustre*. Cf. A. Ernout, B.S.L. 30, 1930, 121 = Philologica I, Paris, 1946, 49.

[3] o.c. 245 n. 1.

[4] Leumann-Hofmann, o.c. I, 85; Sommer, o.c. 100.

-e-[1], in originally Latin words: *effectus, anceps, ineptus, condemno*, as well as in loan words: *talentum, Tarentum*. The remark about β > p also stands in need of further elucidation. In the case of direct derivations the -b- in Greek loan words is throughout retained in Latin: κυβερνᾶν > *gubernare*[2].

Our conclusion must be that, so far, Wallisch failed to advance a single sound argument against Kretschmer's theories, and this conclusion is in no way modified by Wallisch' remaining arguments[3]. "Die jüngste Forschung führt das Wort auf eine ägäisch-tyrrhenische Vermittlung zurück, welche nicht notwendig über das Etruskische führen musste[4], zumal wir im Etruskischen das Wort nicht kennen, ein immerhin auffallendes Moment wenn wir an die Bedeutung der Einrichtung denken. Wir nähern uns damit der griechischen Mittelmeerwelt, so dass die bisherige Auffassung von der etruskischen Vermittlung des Wortes wegfallen muss". Leaving aside the vagueness of this formulation, we still may point out that a possible "ägäisch-tyrrhenische" origin does not by any means cancel an Etruscan intermediate phase. On the contrary, as an intermediate language between the "griechische Mittelmeerwelt" and Rome Etruscan could hardly be improved upon[5]. Wallisch does not, for that matter, incorporate his linguistic considerations into his theory as a whole. He takes the view that the triumph is the imitation of the Dionysiac processions of Hellenism, as we know them from the Ptolemies[6]. The name *triumphus* is supposed to constitute an argument in favour of this theory, even though *triumpe* is already found in the *carmen arvale* without any Dionysiac reminiscences.

The method followed by Durante, who also sets out to derive *triumphus* directly from Θρίαμβος, is more scientific. He concedes that -α- in closed syllables changes into -e-, but adds[7] that: "un

---

[1] Leumann-Hofmann, o.c. 82; Sommer, o.c. 97 ff. Only *a*- before l + cons. >*u*-: *insulsus, conculco*. About a few exceptions, *vide infra*.

[2] Leumann-Hofmann, o.c. 130, in which also the necessity is pointed out of an Etruscan intermediary phase in the development Θρίαμβος > *triumpus*.

[3] o.c. 245.

[4] A note contains a reference to Brandenstein, I.F. 54, 1936, 34 ff.

[5] That the word has not come down to us in Etruscan is due not only to the scarcity of the material, but chiefly to the nature of the word as we got to know it.

[6] o.c. 258.

[7] o.c. 139.

antico -a- avanti -m- o altro suono labiale, più altra consonante, dà sporadicamente -u-: *condumnari* accanto a *condemnari* (C.I.L. 1,² 582), *surruptus* (da *surripio*) accanto a *surreptus*". The term "sporadicamente" speaks for itself. These examples are indeed the only exceptions to the rule. As an explanation of *condumnatus* Sommer [1] suggests: "Einfluss des dumpfen Präfix-vokals", and *surruptus* is by Leumann-Hofmann [2] explained as having been formed on the analogy of *surrupui*. In any case, it seems rather risky to explain the -u- of *triumphus* by pointing to two exceptions. If, on top of this, it is found that, in order to explain β > p, Durante once again has to resort to an exception, his theory has also lost all cogency. On the strength of Διθύραμφος on the fragment of a vase [3], and occurring only once, he assumes that, side by side with Θρίαμβος, a form *τριαμφος has existed < *Θρίαμφος, "la quale rende pienamente conto dal consonantismo latino". *Obscurum per obscurius*! As is observed more often in the study of antiquity, a whole castle is built on one potsherd.

The choice between a development via Etruscan which explains all difficulties effortlessly [4], and a direct derivation from Greek which calls for repeated appeal to exceptions, is not a difficult one [5]. Our conclusion, which is based on purely linguistic considerations, is that the derivation of the word must have taken place via Etruscan, as was proposed by Kretschmer.

Latin has derived many words from Greek via Etruscan: *sporta*, *groma*, *cisterna*, *lanterna*, *Catamitus*, *Hercules* are some of the well-known examples [6]. There are other words, found in both Latin and

---

[1] o.c. 107.

[2] o.c. 85. It is to be noted that *condemnatus* and *surripui* are the normal forms.

[3] Kretschmer, Vaseninschriften, 152; Pickard-Cambridge, o.c. 11.

[4] That this is the case can be proved by the above examples; see further the lists in Pallottino, Elementi di lingua etrusca, Florence, 1936, and Devoto, Tendenze fonetiche etrusche. S.E. 1, 1927, 255 ff.

[5] The remaining arguments or conclusions of Durante will in the following be refuted implicitly. The remark that the doublet Θρίαμβος/Θρίαμβε would in Etruscan develop into a single form ending in -e, is indeed true, but not relevant; that *triumpe* should have been formed during the influence of the initial accent is unprovable in view of the Etruscan origin. That the triumph, like the *carmen arvale* had an apotropaeic-cathartic character is incorrect. It is, therefore, by accident that Durante is close to the truth when he writes: "(*triumpe*) è il nome del dio che si invoca, a che venga e allontani, con la sua stessa presenza, il male che incombe".

[6] A. Ernout, Les éléments étrusques du vocabulaire latin. Philologica I, 2 ff.; E. Fiesel, Namen, *passim*. A good summary now to be found in C.

Greek, whose relations are less obvious. The Latin *cupressus*, for instance, is by some assumed to have been derived from Greek via Etruscan, but by others it is thought to be one of the words from a Mediterranean substratal language which along various channels have found their way into Greek and into Latin without any intermediate phase [1]. This development is assumed for *vinum*, οἶνος; *oleum*, ἔλαιον [2], and many others, of which the majority relate to plants, fruit, agricultural products or handicrafts [3].

Van Windekens [4] thinks that the Latin *triumpus* (as the Greek θρίαμβος)was in this way directly, without any Etruscan intermediary, taken over from a basic language, which he, as is generally known, calls Pelasgian. On earlier occasions he postulated a similar development for the words: *culleus, cuturnium, calendrium, calendae, columba, plumbum* [5], the majority of which have, for that matter, long since been attributed to a pre-Greek language. To quote van Windekens: "A mon avis il faut partir de pélasg. *triumph-*, une variante de θρίαμβος. Ce *triumph-* présenterait le suffixe à voyelle *u* : cf. ἴθυμβος en face de διθύραμβος, θρίαμβος, ἴαμβος; voir aussi les mots pélasgiques κόρυμβος et κόλυμβος cités ci-dessus, et, en latin même, *columba* et *plumbum* que je viens de mentionner. Dans pélasg. *triumph-*, -mph- remonterait directement à i.-e. *-np.* comme le suffixe -νθ-, dont le parallélisme avec -μβ- a été souligné ci-dessus, a i.-e. *-nt-* comme origine immédiate. Donc -μβ- (de θρίαμβος) serait à-mph- ce que -νδ- (Asie Mineure) est à -νθ- (.........) En d'autres termes pélasg. *triumph-* constituerait une trace d'un dialect pélasgique, dans lequel une sourde aspirée remontant à une sourde simple indo-européenne et se trouvant après nasale, n'aurait pas abouti à la sonore correspondante, comme dans κόρυμβος, κόλυμβος, διθύραμβος, ἴαμβος, θρίαμβος, mots pélasgiques empruntés par le grec, et comme dans *columba* et *plumbum*, qui ont été empruntés par le latin. Pélasg. *triumph-* lui-même aurait dissimulé de *thriumph-*: pour le rapport *triumph-*: θρίαμβος, cf. celui qui existe entre pélasg. τάφος "stupeur" et θάμβος "effroi, étonnement, etc.".

---

de Simone, Die griechischen Entlehnungen im Etruskischen I-II, Wiesbaden, 1968-1970.

[1] Ernout, o.c. 36; Walde-Hofmann, L.E.W.[3], s.v. *cupressus*.

[2] A. Meillet, Linguistique historique et linguistique générale, Paris, 1921, 301 ff.

[3] A. Ernout, Aspects du vocabulaire latin, Paris, 1954, 17 ff.

[4] o.c. 491 f.

[5] Le pélasgique, 101 ff.

It might be argued that I should leave the criticism of linguistic details to the specialists, who have spared themselves no pains [1]. However, I think there are a few crumbs of criticism left for non-specialists such as the present author. We are asked to believe that *triumph-* is a variant of θρίαμβος. Where else do we find a variation of -*amb*/-*umb*- within one and the same stem? Van Windekens does not give a single parallel; nor is there any, as far as I know. Owing to dialectal differences, the one stem is supposed to have developed into two directions: into θρίαμβος and into *triumphus*. This, however, leads to the consequence that Latin has direct derivations from two different Pelasgian dialects (colu*mb*a side by side with triu*mp*us). How is one to imagine this; where and when were these dialects spoken, and when did the derivation take place? The vast majority of the words Latin derived from a Mediterranean substratal language are *concreta*, whereas *triumphus* is a word of a totally different nature. This holds all the more if the term did not originally mean a dance or procession, as van Windekens still thought it did, but was an exclamation, as we concluded. Consequently I cannot but support Hester [2], who, when criticizing the theory of the Pelasgianists, in connection with the words ending in—αμβος, concludes by saying: "Once again, the Pelasgianists have cast darkness on a dark subject". The fact that van Windekens is conspicuously silent on the subject of the historical data connecting the triumph with Etruria is one more argument for rejecting his theory.

So far we have defended Kretschmer's view, according to which the Greek θρίαμβος, via Etruscan, had developed into the Latin *triumpus*. There is yet another possibility, which linguistically need not entail any changes in Kretschmer's theory, but which, in view of the pre-Greek origin of θρίαμβος, suggests a different way along which the derivation took place. A number of words which originated in a pre-Greek language, and of which some were attested in an Asia Minor language, are found again—obviously with variations—in Greek and Etruscan, occasionally also in a latinized form. From the examples generally considered certain I here give a few [3].

---

[1] See particularly: D. A. Hester, "Pelasgian"-a new Indo-European language?". Lingua, 13, 1965, specially 354 f.

[2] *ibidem.*

[3] Cf. A. Kannegieser, Aegaeïsche, besonders kretische Namen bei den Etruskern. Klio, 11, 1911, 26 ff.; G. Herbig, Kleinasiatisch-etruskische Namengleichungen. Sitz. Ber. kön. Bayer. Ak. d. Wiss. Phil.-Hist. Kl.

Asia Minor	Greek	Etruscan	Latin
	ὀπυίω	*puia*	
	νηδύς	*netsvis*	
		(= *haruspex*)	
Τύραννος [1]	τύραννος	*Turan*	
Lyd. Τύρσα	τύρσις	Τυρσηνοί	*Etrusci; turris*
Artimus			
Artimmes	Ἄρτεμις	*Aritimi* [2]	
		Artumes	
Lyc. *epriti*	πρύτανυις	*purθne*	*Porsenna*(?)
		eprθne	

It does not appear probable that these pre-Greek words have, via
Greek, ended up in Etruscan. It is generally thought that words
from a pre-Greek (occasionally Asia Minor) language have been
taken over in Greek and, independently, in Etruscan before the
Etruscans left their native country in Asia Minor. If θρίαμβε, just
as ἴαμβε and διθύραμβε, derived from a non-Greek, Asia Minor language, as is indicated by the element -μβ-, the place in the orgiastic
rites and the connection with Dionysos, a possibility which should
at any rate be taken into account now is that a non-Greek *t(h)riam-
be—the -a- is sure to be original, as it is in ἴαμβος and διθύραμβος—
was taken over as θρίαμβε in Greek, and in Etruscan, which also
derived it, developed along the lines indicated by Kretschmer and
Eva Fiesel into *triumpe*, which in turn was inherited by the Romans.
This is, of course, no more than a possibility, but a possibility which
deserves serious consideration, because, if true, it provides a solution
to many insuperable problems the current view presents, the most
important of which is how to find an explanation for the fact that
the Etruscan-Latin *triumpe*, and hence also the triumph, has lost
practically all reminiscences of Dionysos. I believe that the answer
to this question and to many others can be given only if we con-

---

1914, 13. E. Fiesel, Namen, *passim*; E. Schwyzer, Griech. Gramm. 60 ff.;
H. Krahe, Sprache und Vorzeit, 153 ff.; A. Heubeck, Praegraeca. Sprach-
liche Untersuchungen zum vorgriechisch-indogermanischen Substrat. Erlanger Forsch. A 12, 1961.

[1] Name of an Asia Minor goddess in Herondas, 5, 77.

[2] That Aritimi is the Asia Minor name, which the Etruscans brought
with them from that country, was proposed by E. Fiesel, o.c. 85. Although
Aritimi can also be explained on the basis of Etruscan phonetic laws (G.
Devoto, S.E. 1, 1927, 276; 269; 272.), there are sound arguments which
make this proposal probable: see F. Altheim, S.M.S.R. 8, 1932, 149 ff. and
Griech. Götter, 170; Clemen, Die Religion der Etrusker, 33.

sider the development described above to be correct. This, however, is a subject to be dealt with in more detail further on.

The conclusion to be drawn from the present chapter may be formulated as follows: An exclamation derived from a pre-Greek language has in Greek developed into θρίαμβε, in Latin into *triumpe*. In both cases its function is that of invoking a god or gods and inviting them to manifest themselves. Etruria is the link connecting θρίαμβε and *triumpe*, it being possible that a pre-Greek word was taken over by Etruscan and, independently, by Greek.

CHAPTER TWO

THE TRIUMPHATOR

Zoo schijnt de vorst een Godt,
geen sterflijck mensch.

Vondel

1. *Introduction* [1]

The victorious general whom the senate had granted the right to a triumph, entered Rome standing on a high, two-wheeled chariot, the *currus triumphalis*, which was drawn by four horses. Under the chariot, which was decorated with laurel-branches, a phallos had been fastened, whilst reports moreover speak of bells and whips being tied to the chariot. The triumphator is clothed in the *vestis triumphalis*: the *tunica palmata*—thus called after the palm-branches embroidered on it — and the *toga picta*, a name it owed to its rich embroidery, according to Appian[2] in the form of gold stars. Both garments were purple, and there is reason to assume that originally the toga was purple all over [3] and that the gold-coloured ornaments were a later addition. On his head the triumphator, and his military suite, wore the *corona laurea*, the symbol of the triumph, and for this reason often called *corona triumphalis*. In one place, however, Livy [4] uses the term not for the laurel-wreath but for the heavy gold

---

[1] I do not by any means intend to add another detailed description of the triumph and the triumphator to the many already existing. For testimonia and details I refer to the following works: W. Ehlers, R. E. 2e Reihe, 7, 1939, 493 ff., s.v. *Triumphus*; Aust, Roscher Lexikon, 2, 1890-94, 725 ff., s.v. *Iuppiter*; R. Cagnat, Daremberg-Saglio, 5, 1917-19, 488 ff., s.v. *triumphus*. For the *insignia triumphalia* see also: J. Marquardt, Römische Staatsverwaltung, II², 1884, 582 ff.; Th. Mommsen, Römisches Staatsrecht, I³, 1887, 126 ff.

[2] Lib. 66, in which he describes Scipio's triumph.

[3] Festus, 228 (L); Liv. 27, 4, 8; 31, 11, 11.

[4] Liv. 10, 7, 9. There is great confusion about the various kinds of wreaths called *triumphales*. I think the best *exposé* of the matter is given by Alföldi, Insignien, 38 ff., who distinguishes four kinds: 1. The gold wreaths which *imperatoribus ob honorem triumphi mittuntur* by the subjugated cities (Gellius, 5, 6, 5.). 2. The gigantic gold wreath which was held by a slave over the head of the triumphator (testimonia see p. 58 ff.). 3. The *corona laurea* (see the numerous testimonia in Ehlers, o.c. 505 f. The place in Liv. 23, 11, 5, cited by Alföldi, does not belong to this category). 4. The gold wreath which, during the late republic, was given as a mark of honour to Pompey, Caesar,

wreath, elsewhere called *corona Etrusca*, which is held over the head of the triumphator by a *servus publicus*. It is also this slave who speaks the well-known words: *Respice post te, hominem te esse memento*. In his right hand the triumphator carries a laurel-branch, in his left an ivory sceptre surmounted by the eagle; in addition he wore the *bulla*, whilst his face was, in ancient times at any rate, red-leaded. Pliny, to whom we owe many data, further reports that both the triumphator and the slave wore iron rings. The triumphal *ornatus* was also worn by the magistrates leading the *ludi Romani* and other games.

As regards their interpretation of the figure of the triumphator and the meaning and origin of his insignia the protagonists of the study of Roman religion hold diametrically opposed views. Within the range of opinions, which differ as to details, there are two contrasting theories to be distinguished: one which sees in the triumphator the personation and embodiment of the god Iuppiter, and the other which traces back the *insignia triumphalia* to the regal robes and consequently recognizes the former *rex* in the triumphator.

The absence of an unequivocal, recorded interpretation by the Romans themselves is one of the factors which have led to this difference of opinion. Another is that many scholars have let themselves be guided in their investigations by what they considered possible *in religiosis* in Rome. Everything not fitting into the generally accepted picture was too quickly dismissed as incompatible with Roman usage. "Unroman and unitalic"is a phrase encountered again and again in many variations among the opponents of the Iuppiter-theory [1].

On the other hand we find that the defenders of this theory sometimes allow themselves to be guided by what they want to, rather than by what they are able to prove. Frazer [2], e.g., used the identification of triumphator and Iuppiter to prove that in primitive times the Roman and Italic kings were looked upon as gods.

Augustus, and which was worn at the games (Pompey) and later on at all ceremonies (Caesar). Unlike Alföldi I agree with K. Kraft (Der goldene Kranz Caesars, 22 n. 84) that this wreath cannot possibly be the same as the triumphal wreath referred to under 2. A discussion of these problems is to be found on p. 74 ff.

[1] Reid, p. 182, and Deubner, p. 318, of the papers mentioned below. More guarded: Warde Fowler, p. 153, of the treatise mentioned below. Cf. Burck, Gymnasium, 58, 1951, 168 n. 11.

[2] The golden Bough, I[3], vol. 2, 175 ff.

What does appear time and again is how little value such generalizing a prioris have when used as arguments. Yet it should be borne in mind that they are on both sides supported by sound arguments based on factual data. In a difference of opinion between scholars such as Wissowa, Koch and Latte—to mention only a few—on the one hand, and Warde Fowler, Deubner and Wagenvoort on the other, it is, moreover, not to be expected that one group will be absolutely right and the other wrong. The curious thing is that very many have, with or without motivation, joined one of the two parties, but that, to my knowledge, no serious attempt has ever been made to select the positive elements of both views and to try and find out whether the theories in question are really as irreconcilable as they would appear to be.

In the present chapter I intend to summarize the two views, to subject them to a critical examination and, on the basis of the results of this examination, to draw a carefully considered conclusion which is not influenced by presuppositions.

2. *The two theories*

A. The triumphator as a personation of Iuppiter

The view that the triumphator represented the god Iuppiter is one not found explicitly formulated in ancient sources. It was inferred by modern scholars from data the most important of which, quoted *in extenso*, will follow here.

1. Testimonia in which the triumphal garb is called *ornatus Iovis* or is in some other way connected with Iuppiter.

I. Liv. 10, 7, 10 (about the triumphator)

> *qui Iovis optimi maximi ornatu decoratus curru aurato per urbem vectus in Capitolium ascenderit.*

II. Juven. Sat. 10, 36 ff. (about the praetor who leads the games)

> *Quid si vidisset praetorem curribus altis*
> *extantem et medii sublimem pulvere circi*
> *in tunica Iovis et pictae Sarrana ferentem*
> *ex umeris aulaea togae magnaeque coronae*
> *tantum orbem, quanto cervix non sufficit ulla?*

Quippe tenet sudans hanc publicus et, sibi consul [1]
ne placeat, curru servus portatur eodem.
Da nunc et volucrem, sceptro quae surgit eburno . . . . .

III. Suet. Aug. 94 (dream of Octavius about his son)

. . . . . *videre visus est filium mortali specie ampliorem, cum fulmine et sceptro exuviisque Iovis optimi maximi ac radiata corona, super laureatum currum, bis senis equis candore eximio trahentibus.*

IV. Tertull. coron. 13, 1 [2]

Coronant et publicos ordines laureis publicae causae, magistratus vero insuper aureis, ut Athenis, ut Romae. Superferuntur enim [3] *illis Etruscae. Hoc vocabulum est coronarum, quas gemmis et foliis ex auro quercinis ab Iove insignes* [4] *ad deducendas tensas cum palmatis togis sumunt.*

V. Servius ad. Verg. Ecl. 10, 27

. . . . . *triumphantes qui habent omnia Iovis insignia, sceptrum, palmatam — unde ait Iuvenalis in tunica Iovis — faciem quoque de rubrica inlinunt instar coloris aetherii.*

2. Testimonia according to which the triumphator's face was red-leaded, as is also reported of the statue of Iuppiter.

VI. Plin. n.h. 33, 111

Enumerat auctores Verrius, quibus credere necesse sit Iovis ipsius simulacri faciem diebus festis minio inlini solitam triumphantiumque corpora; sic Camillum triumphasse; hac religione etiamnum addi in unguenta cenae triumphalis et a censoribus in primis Iovem miniandum locari [5].

---

[1] The scene shifts from the praetor leading the games to the consul in the *processus consularis*, which imitates the triumph. See below p. 302 f.

[2] About the testimonium cf. below p. 73 f.

[3] Other mss. *etiam.*

[4] According to the best ms., the Agobardinus; other mss. have the unintelligible and decidedly corrupt *ob Iovem insignis.* Deubner, Hermes, 69, 1934, 319 n. 4, reads: *insignes ab Iove,* which reading is, in my view, the only intelligible one. A. Kroymann, in his edition in the Corpus Christianorum, Tertulliani Opera, II, 1954, 1060, retains the original sequence, but does consider it *satis quidem coactus.*

[5] Latte's remark (R.R.G. 152 n. 3): "Verrius gibt an, auch die Iuppiterstatue wäre so gefärbt gewesen, was sich höchstens auf eine spätere Marmorstatue beziehen kann" is incorrect, since Plin., n.h. 35, 157, says about this statue: *fictilem eum fuisse et ideo miniari solitum.*

VII. Serv. ad. Verg. Ecl. 6, 22

.....*quod robeus color deorum sit*: *unde et triumphantes facie
miniata, et in Capitolio Iuppiter in quadrigis miniatus* [1].
idem cf. V

VIII. Isidorus, Orig. 18, 2, 6 (about triumphators)

*Inde et colore rufo perliniebantur quasi imitarentur divini
ignis effigiem.*

IX. Tzetzes, Epist. 97 (after Cassius Dio)

Εἰς δίφρον τὸν θριαμβονίκην ἀναβιβάσαντες σινωπιδίῳ ἢ κινναβάρει
τὸ πρόσωπον ἀντὶ αἵματος ὡς μὴ ἐρυθριᾶ περιχρίουσι . . .
idem, Chil. 13, 43 ff.

About the red lead of the statue of Iuppiter see the testimonia given
below (p. 80).

There are a few additional *insignia triumphalia* which are by many
scholars reckoned among the attributes of Iuppiter, although there
are no ancient testimonia by which they are unequivocally defined
as such. They are the following:

3. The *scipio eburneus* surmounted by the eagle [2]. Alföldi [3] here
makes a distinction between the short staff of the triumph, later on
also carried by emperors, and a longer *sceptrum* taken over from
Greece [4]. In a picture from the republican period [5], however, we already see a triumphator carrying a long, eagle-crowned staff. There
are two testimonia in which the sceptre of the triumphator is connected with Iuppiter, viz. III and V, of which III in particular has
to be used with great caution, as will be seen later on.

Other arguments were advanced here [6]. The first is that Iuppiter

---

[1] As Thilo has it in his edition; *in quadrigas miniatas*, mss.
[2] Dion. Hal. 4, 74, 1; 5, 47, 3; Val. Max. 4, 4, 5; Iuven. 10, 43; App.
Lib. 66; Cass. Dio, Zonaras, 7,8,7; Serv. ad Ecl. 10, 27; Isidor. Orig. 18, 2,
5; Liv. 30, 15, 11.
[3] Insignien, 112 ff.
[4] The name *sceptrum* is, however, also generally used for the short triumphal staff; see e.g. Iuven. 10, 43.
[5] A *cista* from Praeneste of the third century B.C. Reproductions: Annali
dell' Istituto, 1876, 105 ff.; Mon. Inedita, 10, 1876, tav. 28; I. Scott Ryberg,
M.A.A.R. 22, 1955, 20 ff.
[6] See Aust, Roscher Lex. 2, 726; Hug, R.E. 2e Reihe, 2, 1923, 368 ff.,
s.v. *Sceptrum*; Mommsen, Staatsrecht, I³, 425; Müller-Deecke, Die Etrusker,
I², 348.

himself is depicted in works of art with the eagle-crowned staff; the second that the eagle is the bird of Iuppiter and consequently the sceptre surmounted by an eagle an attribute of Iuppiter, just as in Greece the sceptre of the kings is supposed to have belonged to Zeus.

4. The *quadriga* of the triumphator is thought to be the counterpart of Iuppiter's four-in-hand, one of his ancient attributes, which, together with the statue of the god, has come from Etruria, according to Pliny (n.h. 35, 157):

> *Vulcam Veis accitum cui locaret Tarquinius Priscus Iovis effigiem in Capitolio dicandam; fictilem eum fuisse et ideo miniari solitum; fictiles in fastigio templi eius quadrigas, de quibus saepe diximus.*

Cf. also testimonium VII [1].

The only texts in which the *currus triumphalis* is connected with the *quadriga* of Iuppiter refer to the exceptional triumph of Camillus, who harnessed greys to his chariot:

X. Liv. 5, 23, 5

> *Maxime conspectus ipse est curru equis albis iuncto urbem invectus; parumque id non civile modo sed humanum etiam visum. Iovis Solisque equis aequiperatum dictatorem in religionem trahebant, triumphusque ob eam unam maxime rem clarior quam gratior fuit.*

XI. Plut. Cam. 7

> τά τε ἄλλα σοβαρῶς ἐθριάμβευσε καὶ τέθριππον ὑποζευξάμενος λευκόπωλον ἐπέβη καὶ διεξήλασε τῆς Ῥώμης, οὐδενὸς τοῦτο ποιήσαντος ἡγεμόνος πρότερον οὐδ᾽ ὕστερον. ἱερὸν γὰρ ἡγοῦνται τὸ τοιοῦτον ὄχημα τῷ βασιλεῖ καὶ πατρὶ τῶν θεῶν ἐπιπεφημισμένον

The conclusions, if any, drawn from these passages will be discussed further on.

Finally, the following data are considered [2] to be indicative of the close relationship between triumphator and Iuppiter: the ultimate destination of the triumphal procession is the temple of Iuppiter;

---

[1] Further: Plin. n.h. 28, 16; Festus, 340 (L); Plut. Public. 13; Plaut. Trin. 83 ff.

[2] See e.g. Wissowa, R.u.K.[2] 127.

it is to Iuppiter that the triumphator sacrifices white bulls [1]; it is
in gremio Iovis that the laurel-wreath of the triumphator is deposited.[2]

On the basis of these data Preller-Jordan already saw in the
triumphator "ein lebendes Bild des capitolinischen Iuppiter" [3], a
view which in Wissowa's formulation [4]: "der triumphierende Feldherr ist in allen Stücken ein menschliches Abbild des Iuppiter O.M.",
became widely known and found general favour. In his paper, which
will be discussed presently, Deubner mentions a number of scholars
who support the Iuppiter-theory: Koch, v. Wilamowitz, Bailey,
Huth, Weinreich, Bruhl and Latte [5]. This list may be extended ad
lib. by a large number of names of scholars who at that time held,
and/or at present still hold, the same view: Frazer [6], Lily Ross
Taylor [7], Gagé[8], M. A. Levi [9], Alföldi [10], Altheim [11], R. Bloch [12],
Bömer [13], Grenier [14], Rose [15], Dumézil [16] are only a few of them.

It goes without saying—Deubner points this out[17]—that the
communis opinio concerning the triumphator as the representation
of Iuppiter does not imply that there is also general agreement as
regards the interpretation of this remarkable phenomenon. On the
contrary, fundamental contrasts become apparent here. Mrs. S.
Arthur Strong[18] thinks that in the eyes of the Romans the triumphator actually *was* the god, von Wilamowitz[19] believes that the
triumphator "acted" the part of Iuppiter, Altheim[20] writes: "Er
trägt die Tracht des Iuppiter O.M., ohne doch mit ihm identisch zu
sein. Er ist es nur in einem einzigen Akt....."

---

[1] Serv. ad Verg. Georg. 2, 146.
[2] Plin. n.h. 15, 134; Sil. Ital. 15, 118 ff. and others.
[3] Römische Mythologie, I[3], 230.
[4] R.u.K., 1st ed. p. 111, 2nd. ed. 127.
[5] For titles of the works cf. the paper cited p. 316 f.
[6] The golden Bough, I[3], vol. 2, 175 ff.
[7] The Divinity of the Roman Emperor, Middleton, 1931, 44.
[8] Rev. Hist. 171, 1933, 1 ff.
[9] Reale Ist. Lomb. Rend. Classe di lettere, 71, 1938, 110.
[10] Insignien, 28 n. 6.
[11] Die Welt als Geschichte, 1, 1935, 434.
[12] Tite-Live et les premiers siècles de Rome, Paris, 1965, 111.
[13] Gnomon, 21, 1949, 344 f.
[14] Les religions étrusque et romaine. Mana III, 73.
[15] The Roman Questions of Plutarch, 1924, 90.
[16] La religion romaine archaïque, Paris, 1966, 286.
[17] o.c. 316 f.
[18] Apotheosis and Afterlife, 1915, 64.
[19] Glaube der Hellenen, 2, 1932, 429 n. 3.
[20] Welt als Geschichte, 1, 1935, 434.

However, before it has been ascertained that the triumphator does in fact represent Iuppiter, there is no point in explaining this phenomenon. The above, generally accepted view has been attacked, and it is to this dissenting view that we first have to give our attention.

B. The triumphator as the representative of the *rex*

Independently of each other two English scholars in 1916 opposed the prevailing view: J. S. Reid [1] and W. Warde Fowler [2]. Their arguments are complementary to each other and may be summarized as follows:

If the triumphator were to represent Iuppiter, this would be reflected in ancient literature. However, this appears not to be the case. Even Tertullian, when dealing with the triumph, nowhere refers to a representation of this kind, which, if it had existed, he would undoubtedly have made the most of for propaganda purposes. The idea that the triumphator should be the image of Iuppiter is so alien to the Romans that Camillus, when he used white horses at his triumph, aroused *invidia* and was reproached with attempting to put himself on a level with Iuppiter or Sol [3]. This supposed representation of Iuppiter by the triumphator is "unroman and unitalic" and moreover leads to an absurdity: in the *pompa circensis*, which is led by a magistrate in triumphal attire, statues of gods are carried, including that of Iuppiter. How then could the triumphator, originally one and the same person as the magistrate leading the *pompa circensis* [4], represent Iuppiter? How could the triumphator redeem the *votum* he made when going to war to the god he himself represented? The triumphator moreover lacks an important *insigne* of Iuppiter: the thunderbolt. He could hardly carry it anyway, Warde Fowler adds practically, since he already has both his hands full. How much value this scholar attaches to this argument is clear from one of the last sentences of his paper [5]: "But if anyone can produce a coin or other work of art on which he (i.e. the triumphator) is represented as holding the thunderbolt, I should at once reconsider the whole question".

---

[1] Roman Ideas of Deity. J.R.S. 6, 1916, 177 ff.

[2] Iuppiter and the Triumphator. Class. Rev. 30, 1916, 153 ff.

[3] Cf. testimonia X and XI.

[4] According to the theory of Mommsen, which will be discussed in Chapter III.

[5] p. 157.

The two main arguments in favour of the Juppiter theory, viz. the term *ornatus Iovis* and the red lead, are refuted as follows: the *vestis triumphalis* is only rarely called *ornatus Iovis*. If it is, the name does not mean "the robes taken from the statue of Iuppiter", but merely indicates that the robes were kept in the temple of Iuppiter and were therefore "of Iuppiter". As telling in favour of this theory is taken the fact that Livy and others in those passages in which it is reported that foreign princes are given the *toga picta* and *tunica palmata*, never call these garments *ornatus Iovis* [1]. On the contrary, in the passus in which it is described how this honour was bestowed on Masinissa [2], the words *Ibi Masinissam, primum regem appellatum* .... do not leave room for any doubt: "it was the *ornatus* of the Rex to which that of the triumph was a reversion".[3]

Red lead is in ancient as well as in modern times widely used as a cosmetic for both men and images of gods. Warde Fowler explains the red colour of the statue as an "expression of more intense life". That of the triumphator he tries to explain, independent of this, as "war-paint". Finally, the *quadriga* was originally the chariot of the king, which in the process of the anthropomorphization of Iuppiter was also given to the supreme god. The same holds good for the sceptre, of which Warde Fowler admits that the eagle at least points to Iuppiter. He thinks that 'The "rex" might carry it as the symbol of Iuppiter without claiming to be the god himself, and so too the triumphator'. (157)

In 1934 L. Deubner writes a paper "Die Tracht des römischen Triumphators"[4], in which the theory of the two English scholars, which in his opinion had found too little appreciation, is emphatically endorsed, amended and corroborated by new arguments. He, too, interprets *ornatus Iovis* as robes belonging to the temple of Iuppiter, "dessen Statue wahrscheinlich nie ein Gewand getragen hat" (319). He elaborates the idea of Warde Fowler that the triumphator has retained certain aspects of the figure of the king, pointing out that already in ancient sources triumphal insignia were attributed to the former *rex*. Those elements the triumphator and

---

[1] Dion. Hal. 5, 35; Liv. 27, 4, 8; 30, 15, 11; Tac. Ann. 4, 26.

[2] Liv. 30, 15.

[3] Warde Fowler, o.c. 154. Reid, o.c. 180, on the other hand, writes: "I can find nothing in the evidence which will support a notion which has been often held, that the insignia of the *triumphator* were once royal and descended to the *imperator* from the monarchical period."

[4] Hermes, 69, 1934, 316 ff.

Iuppiter have in common: eagle-crowned sceptre, red lead and *quadriga* (Deubner, as we saw, does *not* include the *ornatus Iovis* in this category), they both derive from the *rex*, for "was dem irdischen Herrscher zustand, wurde naturgemäss auch auf den höchsten unter den Göttern übertragen". (320). More consistent than Warde Fowler, Deubner thinks this also applies to the red lead. This red colour, which intended "den König blühend, strahlend und kraft-voll erscheinen zu lassen" (321) the king has also given to the god.

The triumph and the *insignia triumphalia* have come from Etruria. From this it follows that the royal robes worn by the triumphator must also have been the robes of the Etruscan kings. This is proved by a datum which until then had been overlooked: during the *ludi Capitolini* an old man dressed up in *toga praetexta* and *bulla* was jeeringly offered for sale [1]. Festus [2] says about this: *senex cum toga praetexta bullaque aurea....quo cultu reges soliti sunt esse Etruscorum.* Now this *bulla*, which is practically certain to be Etrus-can [3] and which also elsewhere is connected with the kingship, is found again with the triumphator: Macrob. Sat. 1, 6, 9: *bulla gestamen erat triumphantium, quam in triumphum prae se gerebant.*

Like the phallos under the chariot—and perhaps the red colour—this *bulla* had an apotropaeic purpose: it had to protect originally the *rex* and later on the triumphator. "Der Triumphator aber hätte keinerlei Apotropaia—weder Bulla noch Phallos—nötig gehabt wenn er Iuppiter O.M. gewesen wäre" (323), Deubner states by way of conclusion.

Only few scholars have later on endorsed this theory [4]. The most important of them are Ehlers[5], Wagenvoort[6], de Francisci[7], Burck[8]. Wagenvoort proposes a new interpretation of the red colour, which will be dealt with in the next paragraph.

---

[1] Plut. Rom. 25, 7; Quaest. Rom. 53; Festus 428 (L).

[2] 428 (L).

[3] *aurum Etruscum*, Iuven. 5, 164; cf. Plin. n.h. 33, 10; Mau, R.E. 3, 1899, 1048, s.v. *Bulla.*

[4] For earlier suggestions for an identification of triumphator and *rex* see Deubner, o.c. 320 n. 7.

[5] R.E., s.v. *Triumphus*, 494.

[6] Imperium, 72, elaborated in Roman Dynamism, 167.

[7] S.E. 24, 1955/56, 31 f., who supports Wagenvoort's theory which will be discussed further on.

[8] Gymnasium, 58, 1951, 168, who, like Warde Fowler, considers it possible that an identification of the triumphator (king) with Iuppiter did take place in Etruria.

3. *The triumphator*: *Iuppiter or rex?*

The vast majority of the later scholars writing about subjects connected with the triumph appear not to have accepted the views of
Reid, Warde Fowler and Deubner. It is to be regretted that no
attempts have been made to subject the theory described above to a
thorough examination. It is in most cases briefly dismissed: "Dass
Iovis O.M. ornatus bei Liv. 10, 7, 10, den Ornat des Gottes selbst
bedeutet, hätte niemals bezweifelt werden sollen" [1], or is considered
to require not more than one counter argument: "Dem (viz.
Deubner's argumentation) widerspricht, dass der Triumphator sich
mit Mennige rot färbte, was nur als Nachahmung der Tonstatue zu
erklären ist" .[2] But after an objective examination even the most
sceptical reader will have to admit that the paper by Deubner in
particular presents a sufficient number of plausible arguments to
warrant a critical consideration of all his arguments.

In discussing these arguments I shall retain the order followed by
the three scholars:

1. general arguments,
2. the *ornatus Iovis*, with which, for ease of survey, I also include
   corona, *quadriga* and sceptre,
3. the red colour.

General arguments

As we saw, the three scholars formulated their objections to the
prevailing views by representing their consequences as absurd. Of
most of these objections it can be demonstrated that they are incorrect themselves or based on incorrect premises.

That literature should not furnish any examples of a representation of the triumphator as identified with Iuppiter is not quite
true. In this connection we may refer the reader to testim. III, the
dream of Octavius. Warde Fowler is undoubtedly right when he
argues that this passage does not give anyone the right to claim the
thunderbolt as an attribute of the triumphator, but decidedly
incorrect, or at any rate too undifferentiated, is his conclusion,
which was formulated by Deubner as follows[3]: "Allein der Traum
des Octavius, in dem Octavianus u.a. den Blitz hält, meint nicht den

---

[1] Altheim, Welt als Geschichte, 1, 1935, 434 n. 77.
[2] Latte, R.R.G. 152 n. 3, to which Dumézil refers.
[3] o.c. 321, followed by Ehlers, o.c. 494.

Triumphator, sondern den Gott". It is not to be denied that in this passage we have an "apothéose avant la lettre", and that Octavianus appears in the shape of Iuppiter. He is *mortali specie amplior*, he carries thunderbolt and *corona radiata*, neither of them attributes of the triumphator. But it is equally true that there is one element by which the scene is, to the Roman reader, unequivocally characterized as a triumph: the *laureatus currus*, the characteristic *par excellence* of the triumph generally. No one who realizes this can be compelled to choose between the triumphator and Iuppiter. Starting from what is given, one finds that elements of the triumph, enlarged to divine proportions—twelve greys!—have here been used as the material to represent the scene of an apotheosis. This could be done because the triumph by nature carried the germs of deification, and showed its outward features.

The same can be remarked with respect to the triumph of Camillus. This story (cf. testim. X, XI) is by some thought to be a projection of the *invidia* Caesar aroused by his chariot drawn by greys [1]. Modern science has restored it to its original place amongst the legends around Camillus [2]. Warde Fowler has stated that this story should never have been used as an argument in favour of the theory that the triumphator is Iuppiter, because it proves exactly the opposite. Here, too, I think a more careful formulation is called for. Camillus aroused the people's indignation because he put himself on a level with Iuppiter or Sol by using white horses. This indicates that to the Romans of his time, or of the time to which this legend dated, an identification of Iuppiter with the triumphator either did not exist or was not acknowledged. On the other hand it shows how little it took to turn the triumphator into a god, also in the eyes of the Romans: only the use of white horses! [3] Here, too, it has there-

---

[1] On this subject: F. Münzer, R.E. 7, 1912, 324 ff., s.v. *Furius Camillus*; O. Hirschfeld, Festschrift Friedländer, Leipzig, 1895, 125 ff.; F. Pais, Storia di Roma, III, 345 n.1.

[2] J. Bayet, Tite-Live, édit. Budé, V, Paris, 1954, 140 ff.; J. Hubaux, Rome et Véies, Paris, 1958, see index; F. Bömer, Ovidius, Fasten, ad 6, 724. *Contra*, but not convincing: C. J. Classen, Gymnasium, 70, 1963, 312 ff.

[3] Not only is there no foundation whatever for the view of J. Bayet, Tite-Live, V, p. 147, followed by R. Combès, Imperator, 47, that Camillus introduced the Etruscan form of the triumph, but against it tells, apart from the entire tradition, chiefly the improbability that a form of triumph which aroused so much indignation nevertheless became the usual one in Rome. For further details about the triumph of Camillus: J. Hubaux, Rome et Véies, 149 ff.

fore to be concluded that the triumph carried such strong elements
of a deification [1] that any small modification or extension of one or
more of its details inspired the Romans to this—to them inadmissible
—thought.

One does have to grant Warde Fowler this: the Romans of the
literary republican period did not express the thought that the
triumphator was to represent Iuppiter, and even consciously rejected the idea, as we see from the Camillus legend. In the late republic, however, as well as during the imperial period, the triumph,
impregnated by Greek and Oriental-Hellenistic thought, forms the
purely Roman component of the emperor cult [2]. But if this germ lay
concealed in the triumph, latent during the republic, coming to life
during the later years of the *libera res publica*, we are left with the
question of when, where and how this germ found its way into the
triumph. As long as it has not been ascertained where the triumph
originated, from what period it dates, when it was introduced into
Rome, and what were the religious possibilities of that period and
that people, terms such as "unroman and unitalic" should not be used.
In short, we have to reckon with the possibility that the royal
period, unlike the republic, or the Etruscan culture, unlike the Roman, realized a temporal identification of Iuppiter and the triumphator, which was unacceptable to the later Romans.

With this restriction the first argument of Warde Fowler and his
supporters can for the rest be fully endorsed. The curious thing is
that Warde Fowler [3] himself makes this restriction: "it is not impossible that the oriental idea of the divine king and the embodiment
of a god in him, may have trickled as a survival through an Etruscan
channel into Roman times". He fails, however, to draw the obvious
conclusion that in that case it is not necessary to reject every feature
of the triumphator which is reminiscent of Iuppiter as a delusion or
misinterpretation. The following, directly refutable argument, in
particular, could have been left out.

In the *pompa circensis*, which, after Mommsen, is looked upon as
an original part of the triumph, two "*Ioves*" take part: the magistrate leading the games, a replica of the triumphator, and the statue
of Iuppiter, which is carried in the procession, a situation which,

---

[1] Lily Ross Taylor, o.c. 57: "the triumph was the closest thing in Roman
state ceremony to deification."

[2] See Lily Ross Taylor, o.c. 57; Alföldi, Insignien, 25 ff.; 95 ff.

[3] o.c. 153.

according to Warde Fowler, is "impossible" and according to Deubner "undenkbar". Parallels will show that primitive man from widely different periods and regions either failed to notice inconsistencies of this kind, or was unable or unwilling to lay them open to the criticism of logic.

Philippus II of Macedonia, the man who made a slave admonish him every day "Philippus, you are a human!" [1], on the day on which he was to be murdered, ordered his statue to be carried among those of the twelve great gods [2]. This made him the τρισκαιδέκατος θεός [3]. His death is probably due to the indignation this *hubris* gave rise to, just as Caesar's may have been, who, just like Philippus, had his statue carried in the *pompa* of the gods [4].

More remarkable still is a representation of Hadrian surrounded by the twelve gods, because he impersonates Zeus [5]. Whereas in the first two instances a man confronts his deified image, Hadrianus here stands in the shape of Zeus side by side with the image of Iuppiter/Zeus himself. In the triumphal procession of Ptolemaeus Philadelphus [6], Dionysos was represented several times, once in his old shape, once as the returning conqueror of India, as he was often represented since Alexander, once as a suppliant at the altar of Rhea with Priapos holding a gold ivy-wreath over his head. But the images of Alexander and Ptolemaeus Soter are also represented in Dionysiac shape.

In ancient Egypt it was not unusual for the pharao, king and god, to appear before the face of the god Horus, whose name he bore [7]. We must simply state the fact that such scenes, which are impossible

---

[1] Aelian. Var. Hist. 8, 15.

[2] Diod. Sic. 16, 92, 5 and 95, 1; Neoptolemos in Stobaeus, 4, 34, 70.

[3] O. Weinreich, Roscher Lex. 6, 787, s.v. Zwölfgötter.

[4] Cass. Dio, 43, 45, 2; Suet. Div. Iul. 76; Florus, 4, 2; Val. Max. 1, 6, 13. Reactions of the people: Cic. ad Att. 13, 44, 1; ad Fam. 12, 18, 2; Philipp. 2, 43.

[5] Reproduction in O. Weinreich, Lykische Zwölfgötterreliefs, Sitz. Berichte Heidelberg, 1913, 8; *idem*, Roscher Lex. 6, 795, s.v. Zwölfgötter.

[6] Kallixenos in Athen. 5, 25 ff.

[7] S. Morentz, Aegyptische Religion (Die Religionen der Menschheit 8), Stuttgart, 1960, 42: "Das Paradoxon, das eine solche Mittlerstellung zwischen Gott und Mensch in sich trägt, springt dann besonders in die Augen, wenn (im N.R.) der König, teilweise als Priester, seinem eigenen Bild als Gott gegenübergestellt ist". Reproductions of such situations: Bonnet, Reallexikon der ägyptischen Religionsgeschichte, Berlin, 1952, 387, fig. 97; D. H. Haas, Bilderatlas zur Religionsgeschichte, ägyptische Religion, 1924, fig. 92.

by modern standards, were possible in antiquity, not merely in
ancient Egypt, the Macedonia of Philippus II, Hellenism or the
period of the emperors, but also, for example, during the flourishing
period of Greece: did the Athenians refuse to believe that Athena
personally brought Peisistratus back because they already saw
the statue of Athena in the city, on the Acropolis?[1] It will have to be
acknowledged that the belief in god or gods is bound to lead man to
"undenkbare" consequences, that religious belief and logical reflection are two completely different things, a thought which reached
its ultimate consequence in the famous *credo quia absurdum.*

This is the place to point out that none of the apotropaeic elements: the motto *hominem te esse memento,* the phallos under the
triumphal chariot, the *bulla,* the satirical songs of the soldiers [2],
have any bearing on the problem of whether the triumphator is a
man or a god. Both parties have tried to make use of these elements.
Mrs. Strong [3] thinks that the warning of the slave proves that the
triumphator is "entinctured with divinity", in Deubner's opinion
it is precisely the proof of his humanity. Levi [4] holds the view that
the triumphator acts the part of the god and is just for this reason
to be protected against *superbia.* If it is borne in mind that the
Etruscans often depicted gods with the *bulla,* and that the Egyptian
god-king was at certain ceremonies protected by evil-averting
charms [5], it will be readily understood that there is no point in using
the *apotropaea* in the triumph as arguments.

For various reasons Deubner's remark: "es ist undenkbar, dass
Iuppiter zu sich selbst hinauffährt, um die Gelübde darzubringen,
und damit in zwei Personen gespalten erscheint" also loses its
demonstrative force. It is impossible here to enter into a detailed
discussion of this problem, which would prematurely lead us *in
medias res.* I have to confine myself to the suggestion that the
triumphator lays aside his divine status at the moment of his
confrontation with the statue of Iuppiter. We know that the triumphator deposits his laurel-wreath *in gremio Iovis,* and also that,

---

[1] Herod. I, 60, 3.

[2] The apotropaeic character of these elements of the triumph is on the
whole agreed upon. Cf. Ehlers, o.c.; *contra*: Bömer, R.E. 21, 1952, 1978,
s.v. *Pompa,* who assigns a Greek origin to the motto and rejects an apotropaeic meaning.

[3] Mrs. S. Arthur Strong, J.R.S. 6, 1916, 45.

[4] M. A. Levi, o.c. 109 n. 40, as well as others.

[5] G. Foucart, Histoire des religions et méthode comparative, 1912, 228,
referred to by Deubner.

after the ceremony at the Capitol, he was no longer entitled to wear the *insignia triumphalia*. Marius, at any rate, gave offence when, immediately after the ceremony, he appeared in the senate wearing the triumphal garb.[1] Would not the logical inference from this be that the *insignia triumphalia* were returned to Iuppiter together with the laurel-wreath?[2] This calls to mind a widely followed practice in which the king (for a short time) gives his *insignia regalia* to the god, or at any rate appears before the god without these insignia. This usage has been attested for Egypt[3], Babylon[4], but is also found in the Middle Ages[5]. No such custom is known from republican Rome, but this tells us nothing about the character of the triumph during the regal period. Our tentative conclusion must therefore be that all these things Warde Fowler and Deubner considered impossible and absurd, did exist in various cultures and periods and should therefore not *a limine* be denied.

The absence of the thunderbolt is to Warde Fowler a factor of major importance. On this subject the following remarks may be made. The triumph is inextricably linked up with Iuppiter O.M. as the state-god. In his well-known book "Der römische Iuppiter", C. Koch[6] has made it clear how, amongst the many Italic *Ioves* this central Roman god could come into being, and how he had to lay aside many other and older functions in the process. One of these functions which, although it never quite disappeared, yet fell into the background, was that of being the god of weather and thunder. This does not mean that his attribute, the thunderbolt, disappeared, but it does mean that Iuppiter is often depicted without it. The sceptre, on the other hand, is the attribute *par excellence* of the

---

[1] Liv. perioch. 67; Plut. Marius, 12; C.I.L. I, I², p. 195.

[2] Cf. F. Noack, Triumph und Triumphbogen. Vorträge der Bibliothek Warburg, 1925/26, 157: "Dort (viz. on the Capitol) legte der Triumphator jenen Lorbeerzweig dem Gotte, dem er gebührte für den Sieg, in den Schoss und gab damit die Göttlichkeit die ihm an diesem Tag innewohnte, zurück um alsdann, nun wieder nur Mensch und Feldherr, die Opfer zu vollziehen." On the famous goblet of the Boscoreale the triumphator does not during the sacrifice wear the *toga picta*, with which he is depicted on the other side, in the procession: I. Scott Ryberg, M.A.A.R. 22, 1955, 143.

[3] J. Vandier, La religion égyptienne, Mana I, Paris, 1949, 201, with a remarkable parallel with the triumph.

[4] S. Langdon, The Babylonian Epic of Creation, Oxford, 1923, 26: "He (the king) had received his authority from Bêl and to Bêl it had returned". Cf. about these instances p. 222ff.

[5] R. Eisler, Weltenmantel, 18 n.1; 20 n. 5; 22 n. 1; 26 n. 2.

[6] Der römische Iuppiter, Frankfurter Studien zur Religion und Kultur der Antike 14, Frankfurt, 1937.

great god, particularly when he is represented as the protector and ruler of the Roman state. In my opinion it is, therefore, by no means accidental that the only representation of a confrontation of Iuppiter with the triumphator [1] dating back to the republic shows the god without his thunderbolt. It is obvious that the triumphator, if he borrowed his attire from Iuppiter, was given precisely those insignia which characterized Iuppiter as the state-god. Add to this a practical consideration: many of the insignia the triumphator received from Iuppiter—assuming that he did—belonged to the paraphernalia of the statue: *corona, toga, tunica, (sceptrum)*. They could simply—as Tertullian expresses it—be taken from the statue. If, however, the oldest statue of Iuppiter of the temple on the Capitolinus had a *fulmen* in his hand [2], it seems fairly certain that this thunderbolt formed part of the statue and, unlike other insignia, could not be removed.

All these counter-arguments are—I wish to state this emphatically — mere possibilities. We have to keep reminding ourselves that the triumph as we know it from the literary period, had a development of centuries behind it, during which it was subjected to strong Greek-Hellenistic influences [3]. For this reason it is very difficult to recognize its original form. I hope I shall be able to prove that the triumph and its *apparatus* have evolved from another ceremony, and that this opens up new possibilities of explaining the subject-matter discussed so far. For the time being I strictly confine myself to the framework set up by the scholars referred to, and start from the data supplied by the Roman sources. It is precisely the discussion of the concrete data which clearly forms the weakest point of the *rex*-theory.

The *ornatus Iovis*

The attire of the triumphator is described as: *Iovis O.M. ornatus* (test. I), *tunica Iovis* (test. II), *exuviae Iovis* (test. III) [4], *Iovis*

---

[1] On a *cista* from Praeneste of the third century B.C. See above p. 60 n. 5.

[2] This is as good as certain: in the Villa Giulia there are fragments of a terracotta thunderbolt from this period. Helbig, Führer II³, 354; A. della Seta, Museo di Villa Giulia, I, 276. Ovid, Fasti, 1, 201, who refers to a *fictile fulmen* of the image of Iuppiter, cannot, of course, be taken as evidence. See Bömer *ad loc.*

[3] See Bruhl, o.c.; Piganiol, Recherches sur les jeux romains, Strasbourg, 1923, 29 ff.

[4] In view of what was argued above, I think these *exuviae Iovis* also represent the triumphal robes.

insignia (test. V). We have seen that Deubner and his predecessors rejected the obvious translation of "garments etc. of Iuppiter", and gave as their interpretation "garments etc. forming part of the property of the temple of Iuppiter". This interpretation might be accepted if *ornatus Iovis* were a ἅπαξ λεγόμενον, from poetry, for instance, in which a complicated idea is expressed in a serried form. However, the expression (with variations) is found four times, and, what is even more important, in four different authors. To believe that Livy, Iuvenal, Suetonius and Servius [1] should, independently of each other, have used the genitivus *Iovis* to express *templi Iovis* or *e templo Iovis* [2] is too great a tax on our credulity, the more so because the defenders of this theory do not supply a single Latin parallel.

In this connection it is interesting, even though it does not directly prove anything, that in later antiquity anti-emperors often had themselves adorned at their proclamation with the robes of the statue of a god [3].

That *ornatus Iovis* was indeed the robes of Juppiter is, moreover, in my view indisputably, confirmed by Tertullian (test. IV), of which Deubner's version reads: .... *coronarum, quas gemmis et*

---

[1] Servius, who refers to *insignia Iovis*, is, in fact, still more explicit. He is not to be dismissed as a witness because his interpretation is based on combination (as is done by Warde Fowler, o.c. 155 n. 1; Deubner, o.c. 319 n. 7). If the testimonium is read carefully, it is found that Servius *knows* that the triumphator had all insignia of Iuppiter (and he is sure not to have known this only from Iuvenal, since the latter does not refer to the triumphator but to the magistrate leading the games) and thus explains the red colour.

[2] The translation "robes as worn by Iuppiter" is rightly dismissed by Deubner, o.c. 319 n. 5. The expression *de Iovis templo* is found in the Vita Alex. Severi, 40, 8: *praetextam* (!) *et pictam togam numquam nisi consul accepit, et eam quidem, quam de Iovis templo sumptam alii quoque accipiebant aut praetores aut consules.* About Gordianus I (vita Gord. 4, 4), for example, we are told: *palmatam tunicam et togam pictam primus Romanorum privatus suam propriam habuit, cum ante imperatores etiam vel de Capitolio acciperent vel de Palatio.* Stress is here laid on the place in which the triumphal *ornatus* was kept. Alföldi, Insignien, 28 f., has shown that these texts contain inaccuracies. However, neither in Cass. Dio, 55, 10, 3, nor in Suet. Aug. 29, 2, I read with him, that the triumphal *ornatus* was since Augustus kept in the temple of Mars Ultor. An expression *togam pictam . . . de templo Iovis sumptam* does, for that matter, obviously not prove that this attire did not belong to the statue.

[3] Hist. aug. Trig. Tyr. 29, 1; vita Probi, 10, 5; Quadr. Tyr. 9, 3. Libanius, or. 11, 159. See Alföldi, Insignien, 29 n. 3; Eisler, Weltenmantel, 44 n. 1.

*foliis ex auro quercinis insignes ab Iove ad deducendas tensas cum
palmatis togis sumunt.*

This can only mean that the magistrates leading the games (and
therefore also the triumphators) literally took both *corona* and *toga*
from the statue of Iuppiter, that, therefore, they wear Iuppiter's
attire! [1]

The fact that the *vestis triumphalis* is really the *vestis Iovis* is
corroborated rather than disproved by Warde Fowler's argument
that the robes given as a mark of honour to a foreign prince are
never called *ornatus Iovis*.

I think the explanation is, quite simply, this: on the day of the
triumph the triumphator is given the *ornatus Iovis*, which he has to
return after the ceremony. This attire was used only at the triumph
and the *ludi*, which implies that it could not, as a mark of honour, be
given to foreign princes. The *ornatus triumphalis* which is given to
Masinissa, and which is explicitly called by that name [2], is at best a
copy of the *ornatus Iovis*. The same applies to the garments which
in later times *viri triumphales* were allowed to wear at the *ludi* [3]
or during their last journey to the grave [4]. The term *ornatus Iovis* [5]
was deliberately avoided here because it was not appropriate. Livy
and others use it only where it is called for: for the triumphator and
the leader of the *ludi*.

With the testimonium of Tertullian the *corona Etrusca* was also
introduced into our argumentation. According to Tertullian this
wreath was made of gold oak-leaves. The *corona Etrusca* is in
addition twice referred to by Pliny. In n.h. 33,11 we find: *sic
triumphabant, et cum corona ex auro Etrusca sustineretur a tergo,
anulus tamen in digito ferreus erat aeque triumphantis et servi fortasse
coronam sustinentis.* In n.h. 21,6 it is repeated that the *corona
Etrusca* was made of gold leaves. Tertullian is, therefore, the

---

[1] I fail to understand how Deubner, o.c. 319 n. 4, can think that this
testimonium fits in well with his view.

[2] This is rightly argued by Deubner, o.c. 318, against Warde Fowler.

[3] Recorded for L. Aemilius Paullus (Vir. Ill. 56, 5), Pompey (Cic. ad
Att. 1, 18, 6; Vell. Paterc. 2, 40, 4; Cass. Dio 37, 21, 4), Caesar (Cass. Dio
43, 43, 1).

[4] Polyb. 6, 53, 7; Ovid, Fasti, 6, 363 f.; Mommsen, Staatsrecht I³, 441.

[5] That the statue of Iuppiter did wear robes is precisely proved by terms
such as *ornatus Iovis*. There were more images of gods in Rome which
wore robes; see A. W. Persson, Staat und Manufakturen im römischen Reiche,
1923, Exkurs, Angezogene Götterstatuen, p. 117. Cf. I. Scott Ryberg,
o.c. 20 n. 5.

only author mentioning gold *oak*-leaves, and his testimony has been attacked by K. Kraft [1], to whose argumentation we have to devote some attention here. He argues as follows: the wreath with which Caesar is depicted on coins is neither the *corona laurea*, as was assumed so far, nor the diadem, as is supposed by some scholars, but an artificial product with gold leaves, pictures and specimens of which have been found in Etruscan tombs. The wreath of Caesar is for this reason called a *corona Etrusca* by Kraft. This *corona* of Caesar is most definitely not an oak-wreath. So far his argumentation is, in my opinion, sound [2]. He then proceeds to try and prove that the wreath of Caesar (= *corona Etrusca*) is identical with the large *corona triumphalis*, which the slave holds over the head of the triumphator. However, his defence of this thesis, as well as his refutation of ancient data which are incompatible with his theory fail to convince me.

From Iuvenal 10,40 (test. II) it does not follow, according to Kraft, that the wreath was too large, but that it was too heavy. He specially emphasizes the word *cervix*, which is supposed to corroborate this. Against it might, however, be argued, that *tantus orbis* unmistakably refers to the size: the wreath (of Iuppiter) was simply too large (and too heavy) for a human head.

As far as the description of the oak-leaves is concerned, Kraft suspects Tertullian of confusing the Roman Iuppiter with African versions of Iuppiter. The African apologist is thought to be insufficiently familiar with the Roman situation. However, as Kraft himself concedes, Tertullian uses a treatise about the wreath written by Claudius Saturninus [3], who had probably borrowed fairly extensively from Varro. And there is no doubt about these two being familiar with Roman conditions! So far there is, therefore, not a single reason to doubt the fact that the *corona triumphalis*, which is called *corona Etrusca*, was a large wreath of gold oak-leaves, an attribute of Iuppiter.

This last-mentioned fact, however, Kraft also denies. He finds that Iuppiter is on coins only rarely depicted with an oak-wreath,

---

[1] K. Kraft, Der goldene Kranz Caesars und der Kampf um die "Entlarvung des Tyrannen". Jahrbuch für Numismatik und Geldgeschichte, 3/4, 1952/53, 7 ff.

[2] See also the concurring view of H. Volkmann, Gymnasium, 64, 1957, 303 ff. = Das Staatsdenken der Römer, Darmstadt, 1966, 587 ff.

[3] Tertull. de coron. 7.

but very often with a laurel-wreath [1]. The *corona Etrusca*, therefore,
—although also according to Kraft a wreath of Iuppiter—is supposed to be not an oak-, but a gold laurel-wreath. In connection with
this it may be pointed out that the laurel-wreath of Iuppiter had
been imported from Greece, and that it gradually gained ground
since the third century B.C., particularly in the ideology of the
victory. However, this does not tell us anything about the originally
Roman or Etruscan wreath of Iuppiter. That this was definitely an
oak-wreath shows, Kraft notwithstanding (29), Ovid, Tristia
3,1,35 ff. Additional proof is furnished by an argument not previously mentioned, viz. that the victors of the *agon* which in 86 A.D.
was instituted by Domitian in honour of Iuppiter Capitolinus,
were the only persons given an oak-wreath [2]. The Etruscan pictures
showing Iuppiter with a laurel-wreath, to which Kraft (30) refers,
are just as much subject to Greek influence as are the Roman representations.

Summing up, I think the following view may be considered best
to do justice to the factual data:

1. There existed in Rome a *genus coronarum Etruscarum*, of which
   the characteristic feature was that it consisted of gold leaves.
2. The enormous gold wreath over the head of the triumphator had
   for centuries been the only wreath of this *genus* and was for this
   reason *the corona Etrusca*. It was made up of gold oak-leaves.
3. One may call Caesar's gold laurel-wreath a *corona Etrusca* without necessarily identifying it with the gold oak-wreath.
4. These gold laurel-wreaths, which for the first time were given to
   Pompey, and later on to Caesar and Augustus, are nothing but
   sumptuous and durable versions of the triumphal laurel-wreath.
5. The only wreath the triumphator ever wore, apart from the
   corona Etrusca of gold oak-leaves, is the green laurel-wreath.
6. The gold wreaths which, together with the triumphal *ornatus*
   and *sella currulis* and other gifts not belonging to the triumph,
   were given to foreign princes, are neither the original royal
   wreath (Deubner) nor a *corona triumphalis*. This is proved by

---

[1] The monumental statues of emperors wearing the robes of Iuppiter
—or Zeus, rather—with wreaths of oak-leaves, are indeed not to be brought
into the discussion. The wreath worn here is unquestionably the *corona
civica* (Kraft, o.c. 28 ff.; H. G. Niemeyer, Studien zur statuarischen Dar-
stellung der römischen Kaiser, Berlin, Monumenta Artis Romanae VII,
104 ff.)

[2] R.E. 4, 1901, 1642, s.v. *Corona*.

the fact that, during the same ceremony at which Masinissa is presented with the *aurea corona*, the Roman C. Laelius—neither king nor triumphator—is given a gold wreath [1].

Our conclusion may therefore be that, next to the *ornatus Iovis*, the *corona triumphalis*, which "was taken from Iuppiter" and was too large for a human being [2], furnishes a second proof of the theory that the triumphator represented Iuppiter. Against an identification of this wreath with the regal wreath pleads not primarily the weak attestation of a *corona regalis*, which is clearly based on combination [3], but chiefly the fact that the gold wreath is not worn on the head, not even on the occasion on which the absence of the laurel-wreath would render this theoretically possible, viz. at the *ludi* (cf. note 2) [4].

There is no point in dealing with the meaning of the sceptre and the *quadriga* at any great length. Both parties have claimed these attributes as supports for their theories and, if viewed by themselves, with equal rights. The sceptre is attributed to both the king and Iuppiter [5]. It may be true that, in accordance with Mommsen's often quoted words [6], the oldest and best stories do not attribute the sceptre to the king. However, the staff is so widely encountered as the *insigne* of princes, judges, priests, etc. that it would be most surprising if the Italic king did not have a sceptre. The sceptre surmounted by an eagle, on the other hand, is the attribute of Zeus/

---

[1] Liv. 30, 15; gold wreaths were often presented for courageous actions; for testimonia see P. Steiner, Bonner Jahrb. 114, 1906, 31 ff.

[2] That this was the reason why it was held by the slave, and not, e.g., because the triumphator already wore a laurel wreath on his head, is proved by the fact that the gold wreath was also held by a slave over the head of the magistrate leading the games, who did not wear a laurel wreath.

[3] Dion. Hal. 3, 62; Serv. ad Aen. 1, 276. Florus, 1, 1, 5 does not mention the wreath when enumerating *omnia insignia quibus imperii dignitas eminet*. See Mommsen, Staatsrecht I³, 427 n. 2.

[4] Specialistic works about the wreath do not as a rule discuss this problem: Egger, Fournier, Daremberg-Saglio I, 1887, 1522, s.v. *Corona*; Fiebiger, R.E. 4, 1901, 1638, s.v. *Corona*; Köchling, *De coronarum apud antiquos vi atque usu*, R.V.V. 14, 1913/14; K. Baus, Der Kranz in Antike und Christentum, Inauguraldissertation, Bonn, 1940; L. Deubner, Die Bedeutung des Kranzes im klassischen Altertum, A.R.W. 30, 1933, 70 ff.

[5] See: Hug, R.E. 2e Reihe, 2, 1923, 370 ff., s.v. *Sceptrum*; Dorigny, Daremberg-Saglio, 4, 1908, 1115 ff., s.v. *Sceptrum*; F. J. M. de Waele, The magic Staff or Rod in graeco-italian Antiquity. Diss. Nijmegen, 1927, 114 ff.; H. Diels, Die Scepter der Universität. Rektoratsrede, Berlin, 1905.

[6] Staatsrecht I³, 424 n. 6.

Iuppiter [1], but is also carried by humans without any apparent reference to a god or gods [2]. Viewed by itself this datum leads to a *non liquet*, just as the *quadriga*, which since Helbig's paper "Le *currus* du roi romain" [3] may be looked upon as the old chariot of the Italic king, but may with equal justification be defined as an imitation of the *quadriga* of Iuppiter as seen on the Capitol.

At first sight the same might be said to apply to the red-leading of the triumphator. However, a closer inspection of data and backgrounds of this much-disputed problem may lead to better results.

The red colour

Everyone at all familiar with the problems involved in the interpretation of sacral objects and symbols knows that in the cult objects such as the wreath, the staff, the phallos, the wool, etc, usages such as aeschrology, the touching of altar, earth or *sacrum*, the application of colours, red, white, black, etc. etc. are capable of more than one interpretation. A sanctifying, strengthening effect is often inextricably interwoven with a cathartic or apotropaeic motive. The red colour can moreover be interpreted in a number of other ways: as an imitation of blood, as a psychological stimulant with a view to inspiring fear (war-paint) or respect (the royal purple), as an imitation of sunlight, etc. That it is difficult, often even impossible to trace the original intention of the red colour is shown by Eva Wunderlich's well-known book [4], in which author and reader repeatedly come to the conclusion that a given meaning might just as well be replaced by any other. From her discussions with other scholars it becomes apparent that the interpretation of the red colour changes with the angle from which it is viewed. Concrete examples of this will be given further on.

In our case the problem is even more complicated because we have to deal with two wearers of the red lead: a man and a god, so that three possibilities present themselves: 1. there is no interdependence, 2. the red colour of the human being is an imitation of that of the statue of the god, 3. the human being has given the red colour to the statue of the god.

---

[1] See particularly Dorigny, o.c. 1118.

[2] Herodot. 1, 195.

[3] Mélanges Perrot, 1903, 167 f. Cf. Ernst Meyer, Röm. Staat und Staatsgedanke[2], 41 f.; D. van Berchem, Mélanges d'Archéologie et d'Histoire offerts à A. Piganiol, Paris, 1966, 742 ff.

[4] Eva Wunderlich, Die Bedeutung der roten Farbe im Kultus der Griechen und Römer. R.V.V. 20, 1925.

The first possiblity has, as we saw, been defended by Warde Fowler. Nor does Eva Wunderlich see any correlation. The red leading of Iuppiter's statue serves, in her opinion (63), the practical purpose mentioned by Pliny of keeping the loam statue presentable. The red lead of the triumphator serves as an apotropaeic agent to keep the spirits of the slain enemies at bay (86). Deubner [1] quite rightly objected to this theory by arguing that, in view of the many features the triumphator and Iuppiter have in common, the red colour used for both cannot be accidental.

The vast majority of scholars are in favour of the second possibility. In addition to those referred to above (p. 62), we must here mention von Duhn and Bömer. The former [2] explains the red colour found in the tombs, on urns, coffins and skeletons, particularly skulls, as a means to suggest life continued after death. Statues of gods are also painted red with a view to expressing a "pulsierendes kraftvolles Leben" (20). The triumphator painted himself with the red lead of Iuppiter "um als lebendiger Repräsentant des höchsten Gottes, dessen Epiphanie seinen Mitbürgern darzustellen er berufen war, von der Jugendkraft derselben eine möglichst augenfällige Vorstellung zu geben" (20).

Bömer [3] refers to the pompa funebris, in which the dead ancestors are represented as di parentes, the resemblance mainly being achieved by means of imagines. He concludes (p. 358): "Es besteht kein Grund, in der Gesichtsfarbe etwas anderes zu sehen als, parallel zur Maske, das Zeichen für die Identität mit Iuppiter".[4]

Deubner is one of the few who insist that the third possibility is the correct one and that the colour, just as the other insignia, was given by the triumphator (= the rex) to the statue of the god. His choice is to be rejected for various reasons. The practice of painting statues or parts of them red is a wide-spread one [5]. So is that of

---

[1] o.c. 321.

[2] F. von Duhn, Rot und Tot. A.R.W. 9, 1906, 1 ff.

[3] Gnomon, 21, 1949, 354 ff.

[4] Cf. idem, R.E. 21, 1952, 1980, s.v. Pompa: "Rote Farbe bedeutet gesteigerte Kraft, eine Kraft die man den Toten ins Grab mitgab und die der Triumphator als Gott von sich aus besass."

[5] On this subject see: W. Nestle, Philol. 50, 1891, 500 ff.; W. Wrede, Athen. Mitt. 53, 1928, 89 f. In Hellas specially statues of Dionysos: Paus. 2, 2, 6; 8, 39, 6; 7, 26, 11. On this subject see Frazer, Comm. Pausanias, 2, 2, 6; Altheim, Terra Mater. R.V.V. 22, 2, 1931, 80 f. About the Etruscan custom of painting statues red: Poulsen, Etruscan Tomb Paintings, Oxford, 1922, 18.

painting people, or their faces, red. [1] That in these cases the painting
of the statue of a god should be the imitation of the red colour of the
human being is something I have not been able to find anywhere.
Of the reverse process[2], however, there is an example which so closely
resembles that of Iuppiter and the triumphator that we shall have to
discuss it in more detail later on. Klearchus, tyrant of Herakleia
from 366-353[3], called himself son of Zeus and adorned himself with
several attributes of the supreme god, one of these being that he had
his face painted red! The great similarity between the ceremony in
which Klearchus played a part and the triumph indicates that also
in the triumph the red colour originally belonged to the statue of
the god.

The same conclusion is reached in the following way: in our testimonium VI Pliny reports that on festive days (*diebus festis*) the
face of Iuppiter was red-leaded and that taking care of this constituted the first task of the censors. The same is recorded by Plutarch[4]:
Διὰ τί οἱ τιμηταὶ τὴν ἀρχὴν παραλαβόντες οὐδὲν ἄλλο πράττουσι πρῶτον
ἢ τὴν τροφὴν ἀπομισθοῦσι τῶν ἱερῶν χηνῶν καὶ τὴν γάνωσιν τοῦ ἀγάλματος; (............) Ἡ δὲ γάνωσις τοῦ ἀγάλματος ἀναγκαία· ταχὺ
γὰρ ἐξανθεῖ τὸ μίλτινον, ᾧ τὰ παλαιὰ τῶν ἀγαλμάτων ἔχρωζον.
This prosaic reason for this practice, which, in another place [5], is also
given by Pliny: *fictilem eum fuisse et ideo miniari solitum*, may be a
rationalization of later times. It is possible to insist with von Duhn
that the actual object was that of giving the statue of Iuppiter an
appearance of energetic, youthful life. A comparison with another
Roman custom is illuminating.

About the boundary stones from which the god Terminus sprang,
Siculus Flaccus [6] says that in former days the Romans: *unguento*

---

[1] See particularly: Berkusky, Zeitschrift des Vereins für Volkskunde, 23,
1913, 146 ff., especially 253 ff.
[2] Prof. B. Hartmann draws my attention to a remarkable Semitic parallel.
In the Ugaritic epic Aqhat the Hero's sister paints herself red with a view
to disguising herself as the goddess Anat, who is characterized by this
colour. See: J. C. de Moor, Orientalia, 37, 1968, 212 ff.; G. R. Driver, Canaanite Myths and Legends, Edinburgh, 1956, 67. Cf. Driver, o.c. 29, about
Keret painting himself red. For the red face of the god Marduk see: Reallexikon der Assyriologie, 3, 1957, 25, s.v. *Farben*.
[3] Memnon in Photius, p. 222 ed. Bekker; Plut. Fort. Alex. 2, 5; Suda, s.v.
Klearchos; Justin. 16, 5. Literature see p. 87 n. 1.
[4] Quaest. Rom. 98.
[5] n.h. 35, 157, accepted by J. H. Rose, The Roman Questions of Plutarch,
209; cf. *idem*, S.M.S.R. 5, 1929, 235.
[6] De cond. agr. ed. Lachmann, p. 140.

velaminibusque et coronis eos coronabant. In the *acta fratrum arvalium*[1] notes are found: *"deam Diam unguentaverunt"*; *"signis unctis"*; *"deas unguentaverunt"*. The most obvious explanation of this anointment is that it served as a means by which to increase the strength[2] of the boundary stones, a pure *mactatio*. The fact that the painting of the statue of Iuppiter should also be looked upon as an increasing of strength is made plausible by the second primary task of the censors: the care of the feeding of the geese. The reason for this is undoubtedly that the life of the geese was magico-sympathetically bound up with the continuance of the *imperium Romanum*[3]; they formed a *pignus imperii*. In the same way I think that the *mactatio* of the statue of Iuppiter entrusted to the care of the censors has to be looked upon as a magic act which was to ensure the *salus publica*[4]. This testifies to the autonomous character of this rite.

Finally, the following should be considered: even Deubner does not believe that the *rex*, as the example of the triumphator, had his face covered with red lead all the year round. His remark[5]: "der König hat den Ornat offenbar insbesondere beim Triumph getragen", *a fortiori*, of course, holds for the red colour. In that case, however, it is highly improbable that the red colour of the *rex*, which was seen only at the triumph, was transferred to the statue of Iuppiter, on which it was periodically (*diebus festis*) renewed and therefore always visible. The reverse appears much more plausible.

For the same and other reasons we have to reject the theory that the red colour of the triumphator symbolized the blood of the enemies that had been slain. This theory is found in "Roman Dynamism" by H. Wagenvoort[6]. The author points to the condition that a commander was not entitled to a triumph unless a certain number of enemies had been killed in battle and continues: "There can hardly, therefore, be any more question why the triumphant war-lord

---

[1] ed. Hentzen, p. CXIX; CXXIII; CCIV; CCVIII. See Wagenvoort, Roman Dynamism, 44.

[2] See H. Bolkestein, Theophrastos' Charakter der Deisidaimonia. R.V.V. 21, 2, 1929, 21 ff.

[3] By way of comparison one might here consider the position of the monkeys in Gibraltar.

[4] It is quite unnecessary, and even uncalled for, to take the red lead as the substitute for an original blood-sacrifice, as does Frazer, The golden Bough, I³, 2, 175.

[5] o.c. 320 n. 7.

[6] Oxford, 1947, 167. His view is, as was stated above (see p. 65 n. 7), shared by de Francisci.

affected this flaming red complexion. The answer forces itself upon us: it was not red paint at all originally, but blood". (167) However, this answer is less obvious than is here suggested.The condition that blood had to be shed [1] has been transmitted to us by various authors, although reports as to the number of dead required differ [2].

This, however, does not imply that this blood should actually be visible on the face of the triumphator, the less so since Verrius Flaccus (test. VI) says that, according to *older* writers, it was the custom to use red lead, and in this connection refers to Camillus [3]. Already in very ancient times, therefore, red lead should have replaced blood, whereas in other rites in Rome blood has retained its place [4]. Parallels of the use of blood by "Brazilian tribes" mean little or nothing in this connection, since there are at least as many examples to be found in which "war-paint" is used to deter enemies, or, after the victory, demons [5].

Finally, it appears impossible to reconcile the motive of covering the face with blood ("the king used to daub his face with the blood of the slain to appropriate their mana") (167) with Wagenvoort's interpretation of the *Porta Triumphalis*, which precisely had the function of purifying the commander and his army from "the mana from the blood of thousands slain in battle"! (164) [6] To this contradiction I shall return later. Wagenvoort's proposal does not induce us to modify our argumentation. The triumphator took his insignia from the statue of Iuppiter and represented, for whatever reason, the god.

---

[1] Plin. n.h. 15, 125; Val. Max. 2, 8, 1; Gellius, 5, 6, 21; Serv. ad Aen. 10, 775; 11, 6 and 790.

[2] Some scholars think this should be looked upon as a republican measure against too large a number of triumphs.

[3] The use of the red colour during the procession has, in fact, been kept up for a very long period, as is apparent from the description of Gordianus (Hist. aug. vita Gord. 6, 1): *pompali vultu, ruber magis quam candidus* (pointed out by Bömer, R.E. 21, 1952, 1980, s.v. *Pompa*). What Pliny takes from older authors is, therefore, rather the usage of the red-leading of the Iuppiter image and perhaps the legend that Camillus did not merely paint his face red, but his whole body.

[4] During the *Lupercalia* and in curing epileptics; see Wagenvoort, o.c. 148 n. 2. It goes without saying that the phrase of Tzetzes (test. IX) ἀντὶ αἵματος ὡς μὴ ἐρυθριᾷ is just as much a theory of this Byzantine, as is *instar coloris aetherii* of Servius (test. V).

[5] Cf. Frazer, ad Pausan. 2, 2, 6: "The red paint with which savages often stain their bodies may sometimes be a substitute for blood, though more often perhaps it is merely ornamental."

[6] Cf. p. 168.

The moment has now come to add to the most important arguments which led to this conclusion: the *ornatus Iovis*, the *corona*, which *ab Iove sumitur*, and the red lead, a new argument, viz. the function of the exclamation *triumpe* discussed in the first chapter. In that chapter we concluded that *triumpe* was an exclamation causing and accompanying the epiphany of a god, a function which, already prominent in θρίαμβε, could also be observed in the *carmen arvale*. The question was whether this also held good for the exclamation *triumpe* heard during the Roman triumph. The answer can now be an unconditional yes—it may even be said that our interpretation of the cry *triumpe* forms the key-stone of the argumentation by which it is demonstrated that the god Iuppiter manifested himself in the shape of the triumphator, even though it has to be conceded that during the republic such an epiphany was not recognized or acknowledged.

This does not mean that everything argued by Warde Fowler and Deubner should be rejected. Their conclusion that many insignia of the triumphator are to be traced back to the regal attire is correct and important. No more than there are ancient testimonia identifying the triumphator with Iuppiter are there testimonia for the thesis that the triumphator really represents the *rex*. Of the *insignia triumphalia*, however, many are, in ancient reports, traced back to the regal robes [1], just as is done with the insignia of the magistrates, which were also attributed to the *rex* or, what comes to the same thing, were looked upon as Etruscan imports. This holds, among other things, for the *lictors*, the *fasces*, the *sella currulis*, the *quadriga*, the sceptre, the *toga praetexta*, the *toga picta*, the *corona*, the *bulla* [2]. This may in part be due to combinations and deductions made by later authors, but the brilliant archaeological confirmation

---

[1] Epiced. Drusi 333; Dion. Hal. 2, 34, 2; 3, 61 and 62; 4, 74; 5, 35; 6, 95; Cass. Dio frg. 6, 1a; 7, 8, 7; 9, 28, 3; 44, 6, 1; 44, 11, 2; 46, 17, 5; Verg. Aen. 12, 161 f.; Serv. ad Aen. 7, 612; Plin. n.h. 9, 136; 33, 63; Flor. 1, 1, 5, 6. See Ehlers, o.c. 494; Alföldi, Insignien, 30 n. 1; Mommsen, Staatsrecht I³, 411 ff.

[2] The subject has often been dealt with. Testimonia will be found in Mommsen, o.c. 372 ff.; Alföldi, Der frührömische Reiteradel und seine Ehrenabzeichen. Deutsche Beiträge zur Altertumswissenschaft, Baden-Baden, 1952, *passim*; R. Bloch, Tite-Live et les premiers siècles de Rome, Paris, 1965, 102 f.; R. Lambrechts, Essai sur les magistratures des républiques étrusques, Bruxelles-Rome, 1959, 29 ff.; about their Etruscan origin in particular: P. de Francisci, S.E. 24, 1955/56, 19 ff.; Müller-Deecke, Die Etrusker, I, 344 ff.; J. Heurgon, La vie quotidienne chez les Étrusques, Paris, 1961, 59 ff.

of Silius' statement [1] that the *fasces* had come from Vetulonia shows that too great a scepsis is uncalled for. For who could have been the original wearers of the insignia but the kings, the last three of whom were probably, the Tarquinii certainly, Etruscans? We may therefore safely follow Alföldi when he briefly states [2]: "In Rom wusste man nicht nur, dass das Triumphalkleid der *ornatus Iovis O.M.* gewesen ist, sondern man war überzeugt, dass es einst auch die Tracht der eigenen alten Könige war".

In this representation Warde Fowler and Deubner saw a contradiction, and they tried to remove it by eliminating one of the parts. The defenders of the Iuppiter theory, on the other hand, have neglected the royal character of the triumphal *ornatus*. It is our task in the last paragraph of this chapter to find a solution for what appears to be generally felt as an inconsistency.

4. *The triumphator: Iuppiter and rex*

The insight that the anthropomorphic gods, together with their human shape, had also assumed the qualities and external characteristics of men was 2500 years ago for the first time put into words by Xenophanes, the father of the projection idea, in the verses ascribed to him: [3] ἀλλ' οἱ βροτοὶ δοκοῦσι γεννᾶσθαι θεοὺς τὴν σφετέρην δ' ἐσθῆτα ἔχειν φωνήν τε δέμας τε.

Clothing, voices and figures of the gods were in the Homeric epic modelled after the human pattern. Cult took over and converted them into visible reality: Athena wore the outfit of the warrior, Poseidon carried the trident of the fisherman, Hephaistos the hammer of the smith, Zeus the sceptre of the king. Already in Homer [4] we see Hecabe offering her most beautiful robe to Athena, and the priestess putting this garment on the knees of the statue of the god. The presenting of robes to gods is, particularly in Greek cultus, universally known [5].

The *peplos* of Athena in the *Panathenaia* is the best-known example [6], but reports about such *peploi* have also come to us from

---

[1] Pun. 8, 483.

[2] Insignien, 29.

[3] In Clemens, strom. 5, 110. Diels, Fragmente der Vorsokratiker, I[6], 1951, 132.

[4] Z. 86 ff., 286 ff.

[5] About the clothing of statues: Eisler, Weltenmantel, 52 ff.; Frazer, ad Paus. vol. 2, p. 574 f.; F. Willemsen, Frühe griechische Kultbilder, Diss. München, 1939, 36 ff.

[6] See Deubner, Attische Feste, 29 ff.

elsewhere: that of Athena at Tegea [1], Doto at Gabala [2], Hera in Elis [3], Apollo at Amyclae [4]. Euripides [5] gives a detailed description of the robes of the Delphic Apollo. Eisler [6] has connected this with an Attic inscription [7]: ἀμφιεννύουσι ἐν ἑορταῖς τὸν πέπλον Διὶ Μοιραγέτει Ἀπόλλωνι. So, on festive days the statues of the gods were given new garments or wore on those occasions the festive attire they already possessed. The fact that these robes gradually assumed "divine" proportions and also as regards motifs—often stars, sun and moon— differed from garments worn by human beings may be noted without denying that they had originally come from "Hecabe's store-room". Following in Xenophanes' tracks, we can, therefore, endorse Warde Fowler's remark [8]: "And indeed common sense must reject the notion that a particular kind of chariot should be invented for a god in the first place, and then transferred to the use of man", and Deubner's [9]: "Was aber dem irdischen Herrscher zustand, wurde naturgemäss auch auf den höchsten unter den Göttern übertragen". This, however, is only part of the truth.

The need to visualize the gods as corporeal and tangible might lead to the wish to invite the god to manifest himself, not as a statue, but alive and identifiable as a god. If the god did not come to man of his own accord, as in the ancient epic, or in legendary times in which Hermes with a ram on his shoulders still manifested himself to the inhabitants of Tanagra when they were in distress[10], man, i.c. king or priest, had to impersonate the god. In order to do so he wore on this occasion the garments and attributes of the god. Examples from Egypt, Babylonia and other cultures will engage our attention later on. Here we may first of all point to some Greek examples[11]. In Pellene Athena's priestess—ἡ καλλίστη καὶ μεγίστη τῶν παρθένων— manifested herself armed and with a helmet on her head[12], the

---

[1] Paus. 8, 5, 3.
[2] Paus. 2, 1, 8.
[3] Paus. 5, 16, 2.
[4] Paus. 3, 16, 2.
[5] Ion, 1141 ff.
[6] Weltenmantel, 59.
[7] C.I.A. I, 93, 12.
[8] o.c. 156.
[9] o.c. 320.
[10] Paus. 9, 22, 1.
[11] Collected by Back, *De graecorum caeremoniis, in quibus homines deorum vice funguntur*, Diss. Berlin, 1883; Eitrem, Symb. Osl. 10, 1932, 31 ff.
[12] Polyaen. 8, 59. See Nilsson, Griech. Feste, 91.

priestess of Artemis Laphria at Patrai rode in a chariot drawn by
deer [1], a priest of Demeter at Pheneos wore the mask of the goddess [2],
in the Dionysiac cult not only satyrs etc., but also Dionysos, Palai-
mon, Kore, Aphrodite were represented by human beings [3]. Such
scenes were also enacted for less sacred purposes, as is apparent from
the story of Herodotus referred to above, about the return of
Peisistratos under the escort of a woman who was dressed up like
Athena and for this reason identified with her.

Nor do the following examples of man identifying himself with a
god by borrowing the divine attributes, deserve to be called instances of a *"pia* fraus". Here the identification with the god no
longer had a function in the religious belief of the community, but
had been made subservient to the *hubris* of one man. The examples
nevertheless clearly illustrate the development and the meaning of
the triumphal *ornatus* in Rome.

Menekrates, the famous hypomanic physician from the 4th century
B.C., called himself Zeus [4] and was accompanied by a *chorus* of
followers, his δοῦλοι, who represented various gods. He not only
calls himself Zeus, but also dresses himself as such, and—I now
deliberately quote the description given by Weinreich[5] — "wir
dürfen sagen als Zeus Basileus! Er trägt ein Purpurgewand (wie
sonst Götterstatuen, Könige, Feldherrn, geistliche Würdenträger),
er hat im Haar einen goldenen Kranz (das Zeichen des Sieges und
der Götterwürde), er hat das Szepter in der Hand (das Symbol der
Könige, des Götterkönigs, des Richters über Leben und Tod) und
an den Füssen die sandalenartigen Riemenschuhe (jene κρηπῖδες,
die wir an so mancher hellenistischen Götter- und Herrscherstatue
sehen)." It is, Weinreich remarks, exactly the costume Domitian,
dominus et deus, wore at the games referred to above, held in the
honour of Iuppiter Capitolinus. It is by his comments between
brackets that Weinreich's description has a direct bearing on the
subject under discussion. The fact is that, if only the description of

---

[1] Paus. 7, 18, 11. Nilsson, Griech. Feste, 219: "sie stellt die Göttin selbst
in ihrer Epiphanie dar."

[2] Paus. 8, 15, 1. Nilsson, o.c. 343 f.

[3] During the *Iobakcheia*; see Deubner, Att. Feste, 149 f. and Eitrem, o.c.
31 ff., who furnishes additional examples.

[4] Chief testimonia: Athen. 7, 289; further: Clem. Alex. Protrept. 4, 54;
Suda, s.v. *Menekrates*; Aelian. var. hist. 12, 51; Plut. Ages. 21; Ps. Plut.
apophth. Lac. 213 A; reg. apophth. 191 A.

[5] Menekrates Zeus, 9.

Menekrates' attire had come down to us, it might, just as in the case of the triumph, have given rise to a discussion: did Menekrates consider himself Zeus or king? But here the answer has come to us from at least six sides and does not leave room for any doubt. Menekrates called and felt himself Zeus.

Another instance, still more relevant to the triumph, is the behaviour, already referred to in passing, of Klearchus, tyrant of Heraklea 366-353 [1]. He called himself son of Zeus, and had an altar. On the occasion of a victory he wore a purple robe, a gold wreath, a thunderbolt: on his feet he wore *cothurni*. He had the golden eagle of Zeus carried ahead of him, and in addition painted his face red! He called his son Keraunos. Now this outfit in every respect corresponds with that of the triumphator, and also in the case of Klearchos his object has been explicitly stated. By means of these attributes he wanted to present himself as a son of Zeus [2].

Far from following Wallisch [3] and seeing in the ceremony of Klearchus one of the first examples of what was to develop into the triumph in Rome —the establishing of historical relations is not in order now—I have merely described these instances with a view to disclosing a process which, by a term rather freely adapted from van der Leeuw [4], might be termed a "Kreislauf der Macht". Zeus as the highest of the gods has been given the attributes of the human king. If, for whatever reason, it is desirable that a human being should assume the shape of the supreme god, this is achieved by his —temporarily—taking "back" the attributes, which have now become divine. In this procedure it is fundamentally immaterial whether these attributes are taken from the statue of the god, or are imitated on the basis of literary patterns.

In exactly the same way the victorious commander was in Rome for one day given the attributes of the supreme god, which Iuppiter had at one time been given by the king. This, however, creates a new problem. If Deubner and his followers were right, and the trium-

---

[1] Testimonia see above p. 80 n. 3. Literature: H. Apel, Die Tyrannis von Heraklea, Diss. Halle, 1910, 35; Lenk, Mitt. d. Vereins d. klass. Philol. in Wien, 4, 1927, 32; Weinreich, Menekrates Zeus, 17; L. Cerfaux et J. Tondriau, Le Culte des Souverains, 470; Cook, Zeus II, 11 ff.

[2] Eisler, o.c. 56 n. 3, suggests that the stories of the plundering of the temple by Dionysius the Elder, tyrant of Syracuse, are a misinterpretation of a similar investiture by means of the robes of the temple image.

[3] o.c. 250.

[4] Phaenomenologie der Religion², Tübingen, 1956, 402.

phator were, during the republic, nothing but a short-lived revival of the king in a triumphal procession, the situation would be quite simple. The royal robes were in that case worn not only during a ceremony which already existed during the regal period, but also at the triumph during the republic. Our way of representing the matter, however, entails a complication: the triumphator wore the *ornatus Iovis*, a practice which cannot date from the period of the republic, and must therefore go back to the regal period. At that time the king was the triumphator, as we know from traditional sources [1]. On the day of the triumph the king wore the *ornatus* of the god, the *ornatus* the god had at one time received from the king. Here the following questions arise: 1. what did the king wear when he did not triumph; did he also wear these royal robes then? 2. which kings are we talking about: the old-Roman kings or the kings of the Etruscan period? 3. during what period is the representation of Iuppiter by the king to be expected or possible? We shall begin with the last question.

Many attempts have been made to demonstrate a sacral or even divine character for the old-Roman kings. The well-known theory of Frazer [2] has long since been rejected. The great British scholar used data about Roman, Latin and Etruscan rites promiscuously in order to demonstrate a divine kingship for Rome. Altheim [3], who carefully confined himself to what must have been genuinely Roman, was more cautious. However, his conclusion: "Gewiss ist der *rex sacrificulus* kein Gottkönig. Aber in seinem Tun kündet sich eine kosmische und damit göttliche Ordnung, ein göttliches Sein an" [4] is based on a tendentious interpretation of the mysterious *Regifugium*; the author leaving the *Poplifugia* out of account. A treatise by Koch about "die Person des Königs [5]" is weakened by the writer's not strictly maintaining the difference between Roman

---

[1] Fasti triumphales; Dion. Hal. 2, 34; 2, 54; 3, 22; 3, 31; 3, 41; 3, 54; 3, 59; 4, 27; Plut. Rom. 25; Liv. 1, 38, 3.

[2] The golden Bough, I, 1 and 2.

[3] 'Altrömisches Königtum', in: Die Welt als Geschichte, 1, 1935, 413 ff.

[4] o.c. 434. When, however, he advances the triumph as evidence, he loses sight of the distinction between the primitive Roman range of ideas and the Etruscan one.

[5] C. Koch, Gottheit und Mensch im Wandel der römischen Staatsform. Religio, 1960, 94 ff. In this treatise Koch has nevertheless as it were intuitively seen what we now try to infer from the data, not only with respect to the relation between the king and Iuppiter, but also, as we shall see, as regards the correspondence between θρίαμβος and *triumphus*.

and Etruscan kingship. One can follow Coli [1], who sees in the *rex* a priest, but "non nel senso etimologico di celebratore di sacra, bensì nel senso più ampio di intermediario fra gli dèi e gli uomini del suo gruppo, ai quali egli soltanto poteva assicurare la protezione divina". However, how great is the difference between the status of an "intermediario" and that of a *rex divinus* who, either permanently or periodically, represents the god? If the triumphator, once the *rex*, represented the god by wearing the *insignia Iovis*, we cannot think of the old-Roman kings of the pre-Etruscan period.

This leaves the kingship of the Etruscans at Rome: the Tarquinii, perhaps Servius Tullius [2].

All positive data about the triumph point that way. The name, as we have seen, came to Rome via Etruria. Ancient tradition indicates Etruria as the cradle of the triumph or the *insignia triumphalia* [3]. It is true that the *fasti triumphales* mention triumphs from the time of Romulus, but it is nevertheless remarkable that, unlike Dionysius and Plutarch, Livy [4] for the first time refers to a triumph in connection with Tarquinius Priscus. An archaeological datum corroborates Livy's point of view. The triumphal ceremony supposes the presence of a statue of Iuppiter [5]. Ancient tradition [6], according to which no statues of gods existed in Rome prior to the Etruscan period, is fully borne out by the archaeologists. The first statue— that of Iuppiter—was made by the Vejentan sculptor Vulca by order of the Tarquinii [7]. Prior to the period of the Tarquinii no triumph, as we know it, can therefore have been celebrated. Worth

---

[1] U. Coli, Regnum, 1958, 77.

[2] About the possible Etruscan origin of Servius Tullius and his identification with Mastarna see the extensive literature mentioned by de Francisci, Primordia Civitatis, 639 n. 85, and Alföldi, Early Rome and the Latins, 213 ff.

[3] See the testimonia and literature referred to above (p. 83), particularly Florus, epit. 1, 5, 6; Strabo, 5, 220.

[4] Liv. 1, 38, 3; hence Eutropius, 1, 6, about Tarquinius Priscus; *primus triumphans urbem intravit*.

[5] See K. Latte, R.R.G. 150 ff.; recently stated explicitly by E. Gjerstad, The origins of the roman republic. Entretiens Hardt, 13, 1966, 13, and in the subsequent discussion, *ibid.* p. 31 ff., defended by Hanell and Heurgon. (About the triumph *in monte Albano vide infra* p. 281 ff.) See further F. Bömer, Rom und Troia, 94 ff.; 51 n. 1; Ahnenkult und Ahnenglaube, 114 ff. and literature referred to there.

[6] Varro in Augustinus, civ. dei, 4, 31: *antiquos Romanos plus annos centum et septuaginta deos sine simulacro coluisse.* See: P. Boyancé, R.E.A. 57, 1955, 65 ff.

[7] Plin. n.h. 35, 157.

noticing is further that not only the statue of Iuppiter, but also a
statue of Hercules was made by Vulca [1], and that there was in Rome
a Hercules *triumphalis* [2]; the statue of Hercules was on the day of a
triumph decorated with the triumphal *ornatus*. An Etruscan origin
of the triumph is moreover indicated by the name *corona Etrusca* and
by the *pompa triumphalis*, which bears a strongly Etruscan character
not because Appian (Lib. 66) says so, but because the outward
features prove this, as we shall see in chapter III [3].

There are indications that the representation of divine beings by
humans, which was inacceptable to the Romans, was normal to the
Etruscans. K. Latte [4] stresses this difference between primitive
Roman and Etruscan religions. The *hirpi Sorani* (priests of Suri)
represented wolf-demons, the *pompa funebris* shows the spirits of
the dead in the shapes of masked men. In this category Latte also
includes the triumphator as Iuppiter. We can add here that during
the games of the gladiators the dead bodies were taken away by
people who, by having a hammer as an attribute, unmistakably represented the Etruscan demon Charun [5], a custom which, together
with the gladiatorial games, had its origin in Etruria. There is,
therefore, a sufficient number of examples available to show that in

---

[1] Plin. n.h. *ibid.*

[2] Plin. n.h. 34, 33.

[3] Wallisch has not succeeded in refuting all these arguments. In his paper
referred to he suppresses the historic testimonia or speaks of "Hinaufdatierung". About his justified objections against an equation of the triumph
and the *pompa* on Etruscan urns, see Chapter III. That the *corona Etrusca*
in Rome should not be old, is a wrong conclusion from Plin. n.h. 21, 6. It is
not possible to deal with each of his arguments here, nor is it necessary,
since the untenability of his thesis is obvious. Wallisch looks upon the triumph
as an imitation of the Hellenistic *pompa*, as that of Ptolemaeus Philadelphus,
in which Dionysos forms the centre. The state god Iuppiter is in Rome
supposed to have replaced Dionysos. The implications of this view should
be realized: The Hellenistic *pompa* does not enter its flourishing period in
Egypt until the beginning of the third century B.C. The *pompa* of Philadelphus took place in 274 B.C. During the same period the first official
contacts were established between Rome and Egypt. The introduction of
the ceremony in Rome can, therefore, not have taken place much before
the second quarter of the third century B.C. Now tradition does not mention
this at all, although the historiographers know exactly that the first *triumphus
navalis* was held in 259 B.C. by Duillius! (Liv. perioch. 17; Valer. Max.
3, 6, 4; Plin. n.h. 34, 20; Sil. Ital. 6, 664; Tac. ann. 2, 49.) This inconsistency
added to other arguments- the presence of the cheer *triumpe* in the *carmen
arvale*, the series of triumphs starting in the regal period (Camillus!), linguistic data, etc.—make a further discussion of Wallisch' theory superfluous.

[4] R.R.G. 148 f.

[5] Tertull. ad nation. 1, 10; cf. Bömer, Ahnenkult und Ahnenglaube, 111.

Etruria a human being acting the part of a god did not give offence [1]. Further on we shall discuss a legend which, in my view, was inspired by such a custom. In this legend it is an Etruscan king who acts the part of Iuppiter: Mezentius, the *contemptor deum*.

There is, therefore, every indication that the triumph is an Etruscan ceremony, which was introduced into Rome by the dynasty of the Etruscan kings. The task now remaining is that of defining the difference between the regal robes in which the *rex* usually appeared in public, and the equally regal Iuppiter-*ornatus* he wore on the day of the triumph. Was there any difference at all ?

After having explained that there are two kinds of togas, the purple and the *praetexta*, Mommsen [2] states: "Selbst den römischen Königen legt, wenigstens nachdem sie aufgehört haben das Kriegsgewand immer und überall zu tragen, die bessere Überlieferung nur die Prätexta bei". He explains this by suggesting that the annalists reconstructed the royal attire after the consular costume. He himself holds the view that the purple toga—the real official garb of the king—*odio regni* was reduced to the *praetexta* with a purple band for the magistrates. We have here entered a field in which even the Roman annalists had to resort to hypotheses. Certainty is out of our reach. Yet it would seem to me that our knowledge warrants a view which differs from that of Mommsen, and which moreover is more in keeping with tradition.

Livy 1, 8, and Pliny, n.h. 8, 195, state that the *toga praetexta* came from Etruria. Pliny [3] elsewhere says: *nam toga praetexta et latiore clavo Tullum Hostilium e regibus primum usum Etruscis devictis satis constat*, thus joining the ranks of those who consider the *praetexta* to be the royal robes introduced in connection with a victory over the Etruscans. Pictures from Etruria do not make it clear whether, and in how far, garments with a *clavus* may be compared with the *toga praetexta* [4], but there is one report which is significant in this regard: the place in Festus mentioned by Deubner. Deubner failed to notice

---

[1] See F. Taeger, Charisma, II, Stuttgart, 1960, 13.

[2] Staatsrecht I[3], 410, and the testimonia there.

[3] n.h. 9, 136.

[4] Daremberg-Saglio, V, 348 fig. 6998; Müller-Deecke, Die Etrusker, I, 248 n. 54; Martha, L'Art étrusque, fig. 219, 221 etc.; Giglioli, L'Arte etrusca, pl. 187. Compare the well-known picture from Caere of a king seated on the *sella curulis* with a sceptre in front of the image of a goddess. He wears a white *tunica* and, on top of it, a purple robe, which Heurgon, La vie quotidienne chez les Étrusques, Paris, 1961, 219, calls a *tebenna*.

that this text, which depicts an Etruscan king with *bulla* and *prae-texta* [1], only partly supports his theory. The *bulla* is an attribute the triumphator and the Etruscan *rex* have in common, but the *toga praetexta* is not worn by the triumphator.

The fact that both the *praetexta* and the *purpurea* [2] have been attested for the king can be explained by assuming that one was the normal, and the other the official attire which was worn only on high-days. In itself it appears unlikely that the kings always wore their costly, heavy, official robes, and also the *mutatio vestis* at the crossing of the *pomerium* [3], a practice which definitely goes back to the royal period, tells against this. It is not only in modern times that a king has state-robes which he wears only on certain occasions, as, e.g., at his accession to the throne. We shall come across ancient examples of this. If we assume this, it will be found that the confusion about the *toga picta* and *praetexta* has ceased to exist. It goes without saying that the statue of Iuppiter was arrayed with the official robes, not with the *praetexta*.

The conclusion of this chapter is the following:

By wearing the *ornatus Iovis*, the *corona Etrusca*, the red lead, the triumphator is characterized as the representative of Iuppiter. The exclamation *triumpe* proves that he was looked upon as the god manifesting himself. This idea, however, was no longer alive during the time of the Roman republic. It had its origin in Etruscan kingship, and can be explained only against the background of Etruscan religion. In the case of some of the insignia, e.g. the *corona*, it can no longer be ascertained whether originally they belonged to Iuppiter or to the *rex*; as far as the *ornatus Iovis* is concerned, it is clear that these robes—originally the state robes of the king—were, when they had turned into *ornatus Iovis*, on the day of the triumph taken back from the god by the king, together with other character-istics of Iuppiter, such as the red lead.

Briefly stated: On the day of the triumph the *rex* wore robes by which he was characterized as both Iuppiter and king. Our investi-gations will, in the second part of this study, be focussed on this "coincidence".

---

[1] Plutarch, Rom. 25, when describing the same rite, also reports that the old man is dressed ἐν περιπορφύρῳ.

[2] Dionysius, 3, 62, 2, gives as one of the reasons for the reduction of purple *toga* to *toga praetexta* that the gold-embroidered royal *toga* was too heavy for every-day use, but this is, of course, theory.

[3] About the *mutatio vestis* see p. 353.

The triumph was not the only ceremony during which the triumphal *ornatus* was worn. There was yet another ceremony, the *ludi Romani*, which will now have to be discussed in connection with the triumph.

CHAPTER THREE

THE *POMPA TRIUMPHALIS*

Heil diesem lachenden zug:
Herrlichsten gutes verweser
Maasslosen glückes erleser!
Schaltend mit göttlichem fug . . .
Stephan George

1. *The three great pompae of Rome* [1]

The development of the ancient *pompa* [2] extends from the profane escort in Homer, via the great Attic festive processions and the
religious-political processions which were kept up throughout Roman
history, into Christianity. During the last-mentioned period it was,
apart from the rarely mentioned *pompa Christi*, particularly the
pompa Diaboli [3]—the denominator to which all things of the devil,
temptation, pomposity, lust, were reduced—which became well-
known. In spite of its Greek name it is not Hellas to which the
Roman *pompa* owes its essential features, but Etruria, where, in all
probability, Greek elements were grafted upon an originally
Etruscan ceremonial. "Griechische P. sind im wesentlichen grie-
chisch, römische sind nicht so sehr römisch wie etruskisch", as it is
formulated by Bömer [4], to whose impressive R. E. paper I am
greatly indebted. In Rome three *pompae*, all showing Etruscan
elements, greatly flourished: the *pompa triumphalis*, the *pompa*

---

[1] This chapter had been written when I set eyes on two papers by W. K.
Quinn-Schofield: *"Ludi, Romani magnique varie appellati"*, Latomus 26,
1967, 96 ff., and "Observations upon the *Ludi plebei"*, *ibid.* 677 ff. It was
no longer possible to incorporate the views of this author into my argumentation. In as far as he thinks that the *ludi Romani* are an imitation of
the *feriae Latinae* and that the *ludi plebei* have taken over elements of
the triumph, I cannot possibly share his views in this form.

[2] A survey of all *pompae* is given by F. Bömer, R.E. 21, 1952, 1878 ff.,
s.v. *Pompa*; see also Encicl. dell' Arte Antica, 6, 307 ff., and literature cited
there.

[3] The most recent publication about the *pompa Diaboli* is that of J. H.
Waszink, Vig. Christ. 1, 1947, 13 ff. The reader is referred to the literature
cited there. The view defended in this paper, that the *pompa Diaboli* is to be
traced back, not to the ancient triumph, but rather to the *pompa circensis*,
I consider so convincing that it is not necessary further to include the
pompa Diaboli in our discussions.

[4] o.c. 1976.

circensis and the *pompa funebris*. Since pairs of these *pompae* or the ceremonies of which they form part have recently been related in various ways, and the theories in question are closely linked up with our investigations, I shall first of all give a short description of each of these processions.

A. The *pompa triumphalis* [1]

The part of the procession which entered the city ahead of the triumphator's chariot gave the spectators an idea of the victory. Not only were spoils of war carried along—weapons, gold, silver and jewellery—, but also pictures of battle-scenes, of towns conquered, and boards with the names of the peoples subjugated. Here we find the famous *veni, vidi, vici* [2]. The gifts of honour presented by the conquered peoples, originally laurel-wreaths, later on gold wreaths, were shown. White oxen, to be sacrificed to Iuppiter, were brought along. The procession marched to a flourish of trumpets. Appian [3], when writing about the triumph of Scipio over Carthage, speaks of a χορὸς κιθαριστῶν τε καὶ τιτυριστῶν ἐς μίμημα Τυρρηνικῆς πομπῆς. Aromatic substances were also carried. The chained prisoners, the most prominent of whom were as a rule killed in the dungeon before the sacrifice was made to Iuppiter, walked right in front of the *currus triumphalis*. The triumphator was preceded by the lictors in red war dress with laureate *fasces*. The magistrates and the senate also walked ahead of the chariot with the triumphator and his small children. Older boys accompanied the triumphator on horseback, as did his officers. The chariot was followed by the Romans who had been liberated from slavery, wearing the *pileus* of the *liberti*. The soldiers, wearing laurel-wreaths on their heads and singing songs deriding their commander, brought up the rear.

Plutarch [4] reports that in the triumph: γέροντα μὲν ἄγουσι δι' ἀγορᾶς εἰς καπιτώλιον ἐν περιπορφύρῳ, βοῦλλαν αὐτῷ παιδικὴν ἅψαντες, κηρύττει δ' ὁ κῆρυξ· Σαρδιανοὺς ὠνίους. Elsewhere [5], however, he connects this custom with the *ludi Capitolini*, which in turn are

---

[1] The extensive and amply documented descriptions of R. Cagnat in Daremberg-Saglio, 5, 488, s.v. *Triumphus*, W. Ehlers in R.E. 2e Reihe 7, 1939, 501 ff. and J. Marquardt, Röm. Staatsverwaltung, 2², 1884, 582 ff., render it superfluous to mention the testimonia.

[2] Suet. Div. Iul. 37, 2.

[3] Appian. Lib. 66.

[4] Rom. 25.

[5] Quaest. Rom. 53.

linked up with a victory of Romulus over the Veientes. Festus [1] appears to hold the same view. The custom is of great interest, because it shows a striking similarity to the description of Scipio's triumph by Appian, which follows his reference to the chorus of satyrs, of which he says: λυδοὺς αὐτοὺς καλοῦσιν, ὅτι, οἶμαι, Τυρρηνοὶ Λυδῶν ἄποικοι. τούτων δέ τις ἐν μέσῳ πορφύραν ποδήρη περικείμενος καὶ ψέλια καὶ στρεπτὰ ἀπὸ χρυσοῦ, σχηματίζεται ποικίλως ἐς γέλωτα ὡς ἐπορχούμενος τοῖς πολεμίοις.

B. The *pompa circensis* [2]

Of this *pompa* we have a detailed description, given by Dionysius of Hal [3]. In order to prove that the founders of Rome were Greek colonizers and not, as some thought, barbaric fortune-hunters, he sets out to demonstrate that the *pompa circensis* and also the *ludi* themselves betray a distinctly Greek origin. He employs a more critical method than is usual for historians of his period and certainly for Dionysius himself. So as to forestall the counter-argument that certain Greek features are due to recent influencing, he promises to base his argumentation exclusively on Fabius Pictor's description of the famous *ludi votivi* of Aulus Postumius after the battle on Lacus Regillus. He did not keep this promise. It is true that he was not allowed much scope for any too wide deviations, since, as Büdinger [4] rightly points out, his contemporaries could check his statements by means of his source, and by their own observation of the contemporary *pompa*. Piganiol [5] nevertheless manages to prove that "Dénys ..... intervient à chaque instant, commente, annote, confirme, et sans doute fait des retouches". Dionysius himself repeatedly informs his readers of additions or comments. In spite of all this, it is possible to see, through his account, what in all likelihood was the text of Fabius Pictor. Quite a different question, however, is whether Pictor had data going back to before the decemvirate at his disposal. It is a question Piganiol rightly brought up, and answered in the negative. Piganol [6] thinks that Pictor gives

---

[1] 428 (L).
[2] Detailed descriptions to be found in: Bussemaker-Saglio in Daremberg-Saglio, I, 2, 1887, 1187 ff., s.v. *Circus*; Habel, R. E. Suppl. 5, 1931, 608 ff.; Regner, R.E. Suppl. 7, 1940, 1627 ff.; Piganiol, Jeux, 15 ff.
[3] 7, 70 ff.
[4] Die römischen Spiele und der Patriciat. Sitzungsber. der Phil.-hist. Cl. der Kais. Ak. der Wissensch. 123, 1890, abh. 3, 37 ff.
[5] Recherches sur les jeux romains, Paris, 1923, 15.
[6] o.c. 31.

the programme of the *ludi saeculares* celebrated in 249 B.C., a programme drawn up "peut-être par quelque Grec, copiant, non sans fantaisie—sur les ordres d'un grand pontife romain—les détails d'une antique fête étrusque". The learned scholar has not succeeded in convincing me. I think causes can be indicated for the amalgamating of Greek, Roman and Etruscan elements, other than the creation of a Roman ceremony by a Greek from Etruscan material. All this does not detract from the fact that Dionysius' description greatly contributes to our knowledge of the *pompa circensis*.

The *pompa* is described as follows: [1] At the head of the procession were boys from the Roman nobility riding on horseback. They were arranged κατ' ἴλας τε καὶ κατὰ λόχους, and were followed by the boys who were to join the infantry later on, who went on foot. After them came the charioteers and athletes who were to take part in the games, and the groups of dancers, divided in men, youths and children, who, to the accompaniment of flute and lyre, and following the example of a leader, performed war dances which resembled the Cretan πυρρίχη. They wore purple tunics, and carried swords and short spears. The men in addition wore helmets. Here Dionysius is sure to have followed Pictor, since elsewhere [2] he reports having seen *ludiones* in the circusprocession who were indeed dressed like the group just described, but no longer danced. In this instance, therefore, his source differs from what he himself had observed as an eyewitness. The dancers were followed by a chorus of Satyrs and Silenes. This chorus, which imitated and ridiculed the serious weapon dance, reminds Dionysius of the triumph, which also gives considerable prominence to mockery and derision. Here he also refers to the procession of chariots at Athens. Dionysius himself, on the other hand, watched the performances of similar groups of Satyrs in the funeral-processions of great men. The entire passage [3] is of great significance to our investigation: ἐφεῖται γὰρ τοῖς κατάγουσι τὰς νίκας ἰαμβίζειν τε καὶ κατασκώπτειν τοὺς ἐπιφανεστάτους ἄνδρας αὐτοῖς στρατηλάταις, ὡς Ἀθήνησι τοῖς πομπευταῖς τοῖς ἐπὶ τῶν ἁμαξῶν, πρότερον ἀμέτροις σκώμμασι παρορχουμένοις, νῦν δὲ ποιήματα ᾄδουσιν αὐτοσχέδια. εἶδον δὲ καὶ ἐν ἀνδρῶν ἐπισήμων ταφαῖς ἅμα ταῖς ἄλλαις πομπαῖς προηγουμένους τῆς κλίνης τοὺς σατυριστῶν

---

[1] Cf. Iuven. 11, 194 ff.; Tertull. de spect. 6; Columella, de re rust. 3, 8, 2.
[2] 2, 71.
[3] 7, 72.

χοροὺς κινουμένους τὴν σίκιννιν ὄρχησιν, μάλιστα δ'ἐν τοῖς τῶν εὐδαι-
μόνων κήδεσιν.

Following a group of men carrying gold bowls and perfumes, the
procession of the gods concluded the *pompa*. In his description of
this part of the procession Dionysius is not accurate [1]. He reports that
the statues of the gods were carried on the shoulders. From other
sources we know that *fercula* [2] (litters) were used for this purpose
and that the *exuviae* (attributes) of the gods were transported in
tensae or *thensae* [3] (high, closed carriages) drawn along by *pueri
patrimi et matrimi* [4].

Finally, mention should be made of the fact that the magistrate who leads the games rides in a *currus*, and wears the same
insignia as the triumphator in the *pompa triumphalis* [5]. This detail,
too, is wanting from Dionysius' account, although elsewhere [6] he
reports that the *aediles*,when leading games, wore the purple robe
and the other insignia of the king. This testimony will be dealt
with further on.

C. The *pompa funebris* [7]

In the past it was thought that funerals or cremations in Rome
originally took place at night, by the light of torches, as was still
attested for later times for the funerals of children, and people without means, as well as for the *translatio cadaveris* [8]. This was thought
to have changed when the love of display, which manifested itself in
the funeral rites at such an early state that the laws of the twelve
tables had to set bounds to it [9], called for a *funus* in daylight. Rose[10],
however, demonstrated in 1923 that there is no reason whatever to

---

[1] See Latte, R.R.G. 249 n. 1; cf. Macrob. saturn. 1, 23, 13; Ovid, Amor.
3, 2, 45.

[2] Suet. Div. Iul. 76; Macrob. saturn. 1, 23, 13.

[3] Festus, 500 (L); see A. L. Abaecherli, *Fercula, carpenta* and *tensae* in the
Roman procession. Bollettino arch. dell' Associazione degli Studi Mediterr.
6, 1935/36, 1 ff.

[4] Cicero, de har. 11, 23.

[5] On this matter see p. 130 f.

[6] 6, 95.

[7] Detailed descriptions found in: J. Marquardt, Das Privatleben der
Römer, 1, 1886, 340 ff.; Mau, R.E. 3, 1899, 350 ff., s.v. Bestattung; Blümner,
R.E. 9, 1916, 1097 ff., s.v. *Imagines maiorum*; Bömer, Ahnenkult und Ahnen-
glaube, A.R.W. Beiheft 1, 1943, 104 ff.

[8] Serv. ad Aen. 11, 143; Donat. ad Terent. Andria 108, 115.

[9] Cicero, de leg. 2, 23, 59.

[10] Nocturnal funerals in Rome. Class. Quart. 17, 1923, 191 ff.

defend such a hypothesis, which is not corroborated by a single ancient testimonium. The practice of burying children at night had a meaning quite its own, from which no conclusions may be drawn with respect to funerals in general. According to Rose[1] the torches were: "magical protectors as they were at marriages and births, the latter of which, at least, certainly were not confined to the hours of darkness".

Our knowledge is largely confined to the *funus indictivum*, the funeral of the person of high rank, which was proclaimed by heralds. When, after the death of a prominent person, the first rites, viz. the *conclamatio*[2], the washing, the embalming[3], had been completed, the dead man was dressed in the *toga*[4] and, if he had held an office, adorned with the insignia belonging to it[5]. The wreaths acquired in battle were put on the bier[6]. During his last journey the magistrate wore the insignia of the highest office he had held, whilst the magistrate who had at one time triumphed, also wore the *insignia triumphalia*[7].

After a summons of the herald to join the procession, the *pompa* was drawn up by the *dissignator*. At its head we find a group of musicians, the *siticines*, blowing a special *tuba longa*[8], followed by groups with *tubae*, *tibiae*, sometimes also *cornua*[9], and wailing-women—in older times, at least-singing *neniae* (funeral songs)[10]. They were followed by mimic dancers[11], one of whom, during the imperial period anyway, imitated the deceased. In his imitation he was allowed all sorts of jests and mockeries[12]. The characteristic part of the *pompa* was the group which now followed, and which was made up of ancestors of the deceased, impersonated by actors, who wore not only the *imagines* (wax-masks), but also the official insignia of the *maiores*, and who were preceded by lictors[13]. During

---

[1] p. 194.
[2] Serv. ad Aen. 6, 218; Terent. Eun. 348; Liv. 4, 40, 3.
[3] Stat. Silv. 2, 1, 160; Pers. 3, 104; Lucian. de luctu, 11.
[4] Iuven. 3, 172; Mart. 9, 57, 8; Dig. 15, 3, 19.
[5] Liv. 34, 7, 3.
[6] Cicero, de leg. 2, 60; Plin. n.h. 21, 7; Serv. ad Aen. 11, 80.
[7] Polyb. 6, 53, 7.
[8] Ateius Capito in Gellius, 20, 2; Ovid, Amor. 2, 6, 6.
[9] Hor. sat. 1, 6, 44; Petron. 78.
[10] Varro, l.l. 7, 70; Festus, 154 (L)
[11] Dionys. 7, 72; Suet. Div. Iul. 84.
[12] Diod. exc. 31, 25, 2; Suet. Vespas. 19.
[13] Polyb. 6, 53, 6; Diod. exc. 31, 25, 2; Cass. Dio, 56, 34, 2; Tac. ann. 3, 76.

the period of the emperors the group of the deceased was preceded
by pictures of his war-feats, *spolia* [1], and by lictors and torch
bearers. The dead man was lying on a high bed of state or was
represented by an *effigies* in wax, sometimes in a seated position [2].
Relatives and friends followed the bier. The *pompa funebris* may
be said largely to illustrate the *laudatio funebris*, which was pronounced on the *forum*.

The fact that the *pompae* described show a number of striking
similarities was observed long ago. Dionysius, as we have seen,
discovered the element of mockery they have in common. The
presence of groups of dancers, whether Satyrs, weapon-dancers, or
both, in the three *pompae* also drew Dionysius' attention. He used
these common features of the *pompae* to demonstrate that they had
originally come from Greece. Modern investigations adopt a different course here. In a detailed discussion of the musical and choreutical aspects of the Roman *pompae* Müller-Deecke [3] have demonstrated
an Etruscan origin for many details, and, in view of this, for this
type of *pompa* generally. The similarity of the *pompa circensis* and
the *pompa triumphalis* in particular was once again strongly emphasized. Even though Piganiol in his thorough study on the *pompa
circensis* [4] devotes more attention to later, Greek-Hellenistic influences, he fully acknowledges its Etruscan character, just like
Bömer [5], as we have seen. Given the fact that the three *pompae*
are essentially Etruscan, it now appears obvious to explain their
common characteristics from one basic type of *pompa*, from which
the three *pompae* known to us have developed along diverging
lines. It is found, however, that this explanation is implicitly rejected by two scholars, who explain the similarities between the

---

[1] Cass. Dio, 56, 34, 3; Tac. ann. 1, 8.

[2] Tac. ann. 3, 5, concerns the case of Germanicus, who had died abroad;
the same applies to Severus (Herodian. 4, 2, 2); Pertinax (Cass. Dio epit. 74,
4, 2). About Augustus we are told that his body lay in a coffin, and that
his wax image had been placed upon it (Cass. Dio, 56, 34, 1). About the
meaning of the wax image at the *funus imperatorium*: E. Bickermann,
A.R.W. 27, 1929, 1 ff.

[3] Die Etrusker II, 1877, 196 ff. They deal with the Greek influence on the
Etruscan customs.

[4] o.c. 1976. See also Weinreich, Roscher Lex. 6, 806, who wonders whether
statues of gods are carried in the *pompa triumphalis*, as is done in the *pompa
circensis*. Nothing is known about this.

pompae from a fundamental relationship between the ceremonies of which they form part.

Th. Mommsen, in a paper which has become famous, "Die *ludi magni* und *Romani*" [1], advanced the theory that originally the *pompa circensis* was nothing but an extension of the *pompa triumphalis*, or, in other words, that the two *pompae* were identical as to origin, and formed part of one ceremony, viz. the triumph, to which the *ludi* were attached. A. Brelich, on the other hand, in a paper "Trionfo e morte" [2], aimed at demonstrating a "vasta corrispondenza fra l'ideologia trionfale e funeraria", which, among other things, should be apparent from the *pompae* connected with these two ceremonies. These theories evidently do much more than demonstrating typological similarities of *pompae*. They concern the essential character of the *pompa funebris* and the *funus*, of the *pompa circensis* and the *ludi*, and —of direct significance to us— of the *pompa triumphalis* and the triumph. A critical examination of the views of Mommsen and Brelich is, therefore, indispensable here.

2. The pompa triumphalis and the pompa circensis; the relation between triumph and ludi Romani

A. Mommsen's theory

In his paper already referred to Mommsen set out to give a new description of the meaning and the development of the *ludi magni, maximi, Romani* [3]. His conclusion, which was based on historical, rather than phenomenological considerations, that the *ludi* originally formed part of the triumph, gradually detached themselves from it and probably became *feriae statae* in 367 B.C., has at present been generally accepted [4], partly thanks to the enthusiastic support of

---

[1] Rhein. Mus. f. Philol. 14, 1859, 79 ff. = Römische Forschungen II, 1879, 42 ff. In the references the pagination of the latter work is followed.

[2] S.M.S.R. 14, 1938, 189 ff.

[3] These terms are interchangeable: Liv. 1, 35, *Mansere ludi Romani magnique varie appellati.* Cicero, de rep. 2, 20, 35, *eundem primum ludos maximos, qui Romani dicti sunt, fecisse accepimus.* Paul ex. Festo, 109 (L), *Magnos ludos Romanos ludos appellabant, quos in honorem Iovis, quem principem deorum putabant, faciebant.* Pseudo Ascon. p. 142., *Romani ludi sub regibus instituti sunt magnique appellati sunt, quod magnis impensis dati.* See further below.

[4] Latte is sceptical. He shares Mommsen's view that the *ludi* were originally *ludi votivi* (R.R.G. 250), but advances against a connection between triumph and *ludi* a number of arguments, which in view of the nature of his work are brief, but, on the other hand, also fail to convince (o.c. 153). Note

Mommsen's pupil, Wissowa[1], whose influence is perceptible up till now.

The nucleus of Mommsen's argumentation lies in the answer to the question: were the *ludi Romani* from the outset *ludi annui*, or were they at one time *ludi votivi* like the ones we know from subsequent periods, and did they become annual games only later on? An answer in the affirmative to the first question virtually disposes of any relation between triumph and *ludi*, since the natural irregularity of the triumph is irreconcilable with the regularity of annual games. An affirmative answer to the second question, however, admits of an original interconnection between triumph and *ludi*.

Among all the passages from ancient literature dealing with the *ludi Romani* there is only one which makes a statement on the problem concerned. Livy concludes a report on games instituted by Tarquinius Priscus with the sentence [2]: *sollemnes deinde annui mansere ludi Romani magnique varie appellati*, the obvious translation of which is: "Dès lors, chaque année revinrent ces jeux solennels qu'on appelle tantôt Jeux Romains, tantôt Grands Jeux" [3]. Mommsen, however, interpunctuates after *sollemnes* and arrives at quite a different translation: "diese Feier wurde gebräuchlich und späterhin jährlich" (p. 45). This interpretation, from which it should follow that the games were originally not annual, Mommsen defends by the arguments outlined here:

1. The condition that the magistrate leading the *pompa circensis* had to hold the *imperium* required for the triumph, his wearing the triumphal robes, and the fact that this *pompa* begins where the *pompa triumphalis* ends, viz. at the Capitol, prove that the *pompa circensis*, "Triumphalprozession ohne Triumph", must originally have been part of the triumph. This is corroborated by the tradition that Tarquinius Priscus instituted the *ludi* after a victory over the Latini (Livy, I, 35) or over the Etrusci (Dion. 6, 95), so that the *ludi* have to be looked upon as "durch besondere Gelübde motivirte

---

1 on p. 153 "Mommsen gibt selbst zu, dass die *Ludi* die im ältesten Kalender fehlen, jünger sein müssen", is based on a misunderstanding. According to Mommsen the *ludi* are not younger than the calendar, but have only later on become *feriae statae*. R. M. Ogilvie, comm. Liv. p. 149: "It is, therefore, better to follow Mommsen and believe that the annual *ludi magni* evolved out of the sporadic celebration of votive games, akin to but distinct from the triumphal *ludi Capitolini*", also gives an incorrect rendering of Mommsen's argumentation.

1 Gesamm. Abhandl., 1904, 281; R.u.K.² 452.

2 I, 35.

3 Translation of G. Baillet in the edition of J. Bayet, Budé, Paris, 1958.

Sieges- und Dankfeste, unzweifelhaft eben diejenigen, welche die Fasten als den ersten und zweiten der tarquinischen Triumphe aufzählen." (p. 46)

2. The thesis that the *ludi* did not until later on become annual ones, is proved by their absence from the oldest calendar of festivals, whose recording Mommsen dates at the period of the decemvirate [1].

3. In his discussion of the historical data Mommsen argues that the extension of the festival, which originally lasted one day, to two days after the expulsion of the kings, and subsequently to three days after the battle on Lacus Regillus [2] does not decide the question of the games being or not being held regularly. From the fact that the games to which the well-known vision of T. Latinius refers, are given the character of *ludi votivi* just as decidedly as that of *ludi sollemnes* by Cicero, Livy and Dionysius [3], it is clear that the historiographers thought that during that period the games were not yet held annually. Now Ritschl [4] observed that Livy, even though he declared *ludi Romani* and *ludi magni* identical, uses the term *ludi magni* to denote *ludi votivi* and the term *ludi Romani* for *ludi annui*. In Livy's work the term *ludi Romani* occurs for the first time in the year 322 B.C. This gives us a *terminus post quem* for the institution of the annual festivals: the decemvirate, and a *terminus ante quem*: 322 B.C. Hence the supposition that the year 367 B.C., the year in which the office of the *aediles curules* was created, was the one in which the *ludi* became *feriae statae* [5].

B. Criticism

The only scholar who, to my knowledge, raised a number of well-founded objections against Mommsen's theory, is Piganiol [6]. His criticism, which was levelled exclusively at the historical aspects of Mommsen's argumentation, has met with little response. The un-

---

[1] Die römische Chronologie bis auf Caesar[2], 1859, 30.

[2] About the addition of the third day there is great confusion. According to Dionys. (6, 95) the day is added on the occasion of the return of the *plebs* in 494 B.C.; here he confuses moreover the *feriae Latinae* with the *ludi Romani*. In 5, 57 Dionys. already refers to three-day games after the discovery of the conspiracy of the followers of Tarquin (500 B.C.). For a different tradition, according to which the games were instituted after the battle on Lacus Regillus, see below.

[3] Cicero, de div. 1, 26, 55; Liv. 2, 36; Dionys. 7, 71.

[4] Ritschl, Parerga Plautina Terentianaque, Lipsiae, 1845, 1, 290.

[5] The same view found in de Sanctis, Storia dei Romani II, 1907, 533.

[6] Jeux, 75 ff.

tenability of his final conclusion that the *ludi Romani* in 367 B.C. replaced a plebeian Ceres festival, and his equally contestable views, linked up with this conclusion, on the *plebs* as an ethnic unity [1], have distracted the attention from his well-considered judgment: [2] "que l'évolution n'a pas été aussi simple que Mommsen l'a décrite, et, en particulier, que les jeux triomphaux, les jeux votifs, les grands jeux annuels ne doivent pas être considérés comme les termes successifs d'une seule série, mais plutôt comme trois séries distinctes".

However, if a theory as influential as Mommsen's is considered contestable, it merits criticism on each of its arguments. When I venture to subject it to this treatment, —Piganiol's argumentation will be dealt with in due time—I shall provisionally isolate one detail: the triumphal garb of the leading magistrate. There is no doubt that this remarkable phenomenon did not only constitute the principal argument for the identification of *pompa triumphalis* and *pompa circensis*, but was used as the starting-point for the entire theory. If it could be proved that all Mommsen's arguments are refutable, and if it could moreover be made plausible that it is historically impossible for the *ludi* ever to have formed part of the triumphal ceremony, the double function of the triumphal robes would cease to be an argument, but would, on the contrary, become the central problem. The discussion of this problem is, however, beyond the scope of this chapter and will have to wait.

Mommsen's interpretation of the sentence: *sollemnes deinde annui mansere ludi Romani magnique varie appellati*, however ingenious, is to be rejected for various reasons. In the first place, it should be pointed out that the distinction postulated by Mommsen [3]: "*sollemnis* bezeichnet die häufige, durch den Gebrauch geheiligte, *annuus* die rechtlich festgestellte Wiederholung" is definitely not a distinction between mutually exclusive, opposing concepts. On the contrary, the original meaning of *sollemnis* is 'yearly' [4]: Festus [5] defines the concept *sollemne sacrum* as *quod omnibus annis praestari debet*. That *sollemnis*, gradually acquiring the meaning "established,

---

[1] Essay sur les Origines de Rome, Paris, 1917. For criticism on the view defended here see Rose, J.R.S. 12, 1922, 106 ff. and literature mentioned by E. Meyer, Staat, 475 n. 50.

[2] o.c. 76.

[3] o.c. 44.

[4] Walde-Hofmann, L.E.W.³, s.v. *sollemnis*.

[5] Festus 384 (L).

stated"—but not in the strictly legal meaning of Mommsen—in later times did not develop into an opposite of *annuus* either, is clear from a phrase such as *sollemne in singulos annos*, in Livy [1]. No objections can, therefore, be raised against the translation: "since that time these solemn games continued to be held annually (as annual ones)". A meaning "diese Feier *wurde* gebräuchlich und späterhin jährlich" could, moreover, hardly read "sollemnes deinde annui *mansere* ludi ..." in Latin, whilst in this case we would certainly have expected a clarifying *primum* as against *deinde* [2]. Eutropius [3], in fact, does not hesitate to say: *Tarquinius .... ludos Romanos instituit, qui ad nostram memoriam permanent.* Finally, the context also suggests that here we are dealing with games that were *ludi annui ab origine.* In the same *caput* Livy, following in Varro's tracks, states that Tarquin was the first to give the games a regular place—before him Rome also had games, the *Consualia*, for example—, that the space for the audience was subdivided and that stands were erected. All this presupposes recurrent games, at least —and this is what matters here—in Livy's line of thought.

The first argument in favour of an interrelation between *ludi* and triumph was that Tarquin instituted the games on the occasion of a victory. It is worth our while to subject the passages in question to a closer inspection. Livy [4] connects the games with the spoils seized at the capture of Apiola during the war against the Latini. In relation to this victory Livy knows nothing about a triumph. He makes Tarquin triumph for the first time after his third war, the one against the Sabini [5]. But with this triumph the games have,

---

[1] 3, 15, 4, to which refers a note of Weissenborn-Müller: "*Sollemne* von regelmässig wiederkehrenden religiösen Feierlichkeiten entlehnt, ist noch genauer durch *in singulos annos*: für jedes Jahr, jährlich, bestimmt". Walde-Hofmann, l.c. speak of "Abundanzen wie *sollemne in singulos annos.*"

[2] This translation and interpretation are consequently rejected by Ogilvie, o.c. 150: "*deinde* is conclusive against this. *Deinde* must be used here as at 27, 23, 7, *is dies deinde sollemnis servatus*. Heurgon, Comm. Liv. I, 36 (Érasme, Collection de textes latins commentés, Paris, 1963), rejects Mommsen's punctuation.

[3] brev. 1, 6.

[4] 1, 35.

[5] 1, 38. This is the very first time Livy refers to a triumph, a fact from which Eutropius (brev. 1, 6) has inferred that Tarquinius Priscus *primus triumphans urbem intravit*. According to unanimous reports of Cicero, de rep. 2, 20, Dionys. 3, 69, Liv. 1, 38, Tac. hist. 3, 72, Plut. Public. 14, Serv. ad Aen. 9, 446, Tarquinius Priscus did vow the Capitolinian temple during this war.

in Livy, nothing to do! Dionysius on his part, in conformity with the *fasti triumphales*, attributes one or more triumphs to all kings, except the peace-loving Numa, Tarquin being given three. In 6, 95 he reports that Tarquin dedicated the first day of the games καθ'ὃν χρόνον ἐνίκησε Τυρρηνούς. Here again, the *ludi* are not directly connected with the triumph. The absence of any interrelation between *ludi* and triumph is all the more remarkable because it was, as it were, forced on the spectators of the *pompa circensis*, and Livy elsewhere [1], in the phrase: *quae augustissima vestis est tensas ducentibus triumphantibusve* places the two wearers of the triumphal robes side by side.

Now it might be said with some justification that during the regal period, during the Etruscan period at least, every victory was celebrated by a triumph. Although Livy obviously holds a different view, I shall not use this as an argument. I prefer to show by means of a list of *ludi votivi* from the early-republican period [2] that also during that time there is no connection whatever between triumph and *ludi*.

1. The first *ludi votivi* were vowed during the war which is concluded by the battle on Lacus Regillus. Cicero, de div. 1, 26, 55: *Omnes hoc historici, Fabii, Gellii, sed proxime Caelius: cum bello Latino ludi votivi maximi primum fierent, civitas ad arma repente est excitata. Itaque ludis intermissis instaurativi constituti sunt.....* These must have been the games the dictator Postumius vowed in 499 B.C. according to the computation of Dionysius, 6, 10: καὶ ὁ Ποστόμιος .... τοῖς θεοῖς εὐξάμενος, ἐὰν εὐτυχὲς καὶ καλὸν τέλος ἀκολουθήσῃ τῇ μάχῃ, θυσίας τε μεγάλας .... καὶ ἀγῶνας καταστήσεσθαι πολυτελεῖς, οὓς ἄξει ὁ Ῥωμαίων δῆμος ἀνὰ πᾶν ἔτος..... The *instauratio*, the immediate cause of which Cicero says, was a sudden alarm, was according to most reports made necessary by the anger of Iuppiter about the indecorous *praesultator*. This well-known anecdote is by Dionysius (7, 69) dated to 490 B.C. Livy (2, 36), who in this connection speaks of *ludi magni*, by which he always means *ludi votivi*, but who fails to report by whom the games were vowed, gives as their date 491 B.C. The triumph of Postumius is by Livy (2, 20) dated to 496 B.C.

---

[1] 5, 41.

[2] A list of *ludi votivi* is found in Piganiol, o.c. 78. He is mistaken when he thinks that Livy does not make any further mention of the games which were vowed by Camillus in 396 B.C. According to Livy, 5, 31, they were held in 392 B.C.

2. Games held in 441 B.C. Livy, 4, 12, 2: *ludi ab decemviris per secessionem plebis a patribus ex senatus consulto voti eo anno facti sunt.* The year of the *votum* is not known.

3. Games vowed by the dictator Postumius in 431, held in 424 B.C. Livy, 4, 27, 1: *Dictator praeeunte A. Cornelio pontifice maximo ludos magnos tumultus causa vovit, profectusque ab urbe.....* Livy, 4, 35, 3: *Annum insequentem* (424) *... ludi bello voti celebrem et tribunorum militum apparatu et finitimorum concursu fecere.* This Postumius triumphed in 431 (Liv. 4, 29, 4).

4. Games vowed by Camillus in 396, held in 392. Liv. 5, 19, 6,: *dictator...ludos magnos ex senatus consulto vovit Veis captis se facturum aedemque Matutae Matris refectam dedicaturum, iam ante ab rege Servio Tullio dedicatam.* Liv. 5, 31, 2: *Hi consules magnos ludos fecere, quos M. Furius Camillus dictator voverat Veienti bello.* Camillus triumphs over Veii in 396 (Liv. 5, 23).

5. Games held according to Diodorus Siculus (14, 106, 4) in 388 (= Livy 392) after the capture of Λιφοίχουα [1]. No further details are known.

6. Games vowed in 360 by the dictator Servilius. Liv. 7, 11, 4: *creatus Q. Servilius Ahala T. Quinctium magistrum equitum dixit et ex auctoritate patrum si prospere id bellum evenisset ludos magnos vovit.* Whether the games were held is not known.

7. Games held in 358, in accordance with a *votum* of Camillus. Liv. 7,15, 12: *ludi votivi, quos M. Furius dictator voverat, facti.* The year of the *votum* is not known. The games were held after the death of Camillus (365).

However lacunary this list may be, it nevertheless provides valuable information about the problems we are dealing with, and it is for this reason that I quoted the most important passages in more detail than may at first sight seem necessary. We are, first of all, struck by the significant fact that—in so far as the data admit of a conclusion—there was not a single instance in which the *ludi* were held in combination with the triumph, or were as much as celebrated in the same year. Intervals of several years are not exceptional, and tradition does not furnish any evidence of a gradual splitting up of *ludi* and triumph. We may moreover ask why, if triumph and *ludi* originally formed a unity, they were separated, not by one or more days, but by years. Why is it that a triumph can, and the votive

---

[1] According to Mommsen, o.c. 51 n. 16, these are identical with those of Camillus, no. 4.

games cannot be held in the year of the victory? And how are we to imagine the gradual separation to have taken place? The two ceremonies, which, according to Mommsen, still formed a unity during the rule of Tarquinius Priscus—which, for that matter, is not recorded in literature anywhere—are found to have already been separated in the beginning of the republic! However, there are more arguments which tell against Mommsen's theory.

The games held in 441 B.C. were not vowed with a view to imploring a victory, but *per secessionem plebis*, and were held after the return of the *plebs*. That it was indeed this return the *votum* aimed at, is made plausible by the statement of Dionysius [1] that the third day of the *ludi Romani* was added on account of the return of the *plebs*. Also in other instances it is found that what appears to be an indication of the time of the *votum*, is at the same time the reason for the vow. That, generally speaking, the wish laid down in a *votum publicum* need not be a military success, is clearly demonstrated by the vota *quinquennalia* or *decennalia* reported elsewhere by Livy [2], which were made on the occasion of epidemics, failure of crops, etc., and by which "man gewissermassen eine göttliche Garantie für den Fortbestand des Staates zu erreichen sucht" [3]. But also in the cases in which the *votum* does relate to a war, its conditions differ from those of the triumph.

Entitled to a triumph was the general who had gained a victory which had to meet certain requirements[4]. These requirements did not, however, include the termination of the war—as is apparent from the numerous triumphs held during the Punic wars—the capture of a town, etc. The games held in 431 were *tumultus causa*, the games vowed in 396 concerned the capture of Veii, and in 360 the formula read: *si prospere id bellum evenisset*; all reasons which may collectively be defined as: *pro salute rei publicae*, such as the return of the *plebs*, but none of which were among the conditions for the triumph. Even though this is not explicitly stated, they were obviously *vota* extending over a longer period of time, and were redeemed either after the war, or the emergency generally, or, as became customary in later years, after a number of years stated in the *votum*.

---

[1] 6, 95.

[2] Liv. 31, 9, 9; 22, 10, 2.

[3] Wissowa, R. u. K.[2] 383. On this subject also Piganiol, o.c. 83.

[4] For a description of the conditions for a triumph see chapter **V.**

Mommsen's theory leads to the consequence that, since the oldest *ludi* were votive games, and formed part of the triumph, the entire triumphal ceremony was a votive ceremony. Other scholars, too, argued something to this effect, and with just as little justification, as I hope to be able to prove in chapter V. Here I only wish to single out one characteristic of the *votum* in general and votive games in particular which is incompatible with an essential feature of the triumph. In 191 B.C. the consul M' Acilius vowes great games with the words (Liv. 36, 2, 3): *si duellum quod cum rege Antiocho sumi populus iussit, id ex sententia senatus populique Romani confectum erit, tum tibi, Iuppiter, populus Romanus ludos magnos dies decem continuos faciet, donaque ad omnia pulvinaria dabuntur de pecunia, quantam senatus decreverit. Quisquis magistratus eos ludos, quando ubique faxit, hi ludi recte facti donaque data recte sunto.* Similar arrangements hold for the *ver sacrum* (Liv. 22, 10) and, as appears from tradition, also for the temple *votum* [1]. From the passages quoted it is clear that, also as far as the *votum* of games is concerned, the arrangement of 191 B.C. was not a novum. Already in the early republic votive games were given, not merely years after the *votum*, but sometimes by someone other than the *vovens*, in a few cases even after his death. This is fully in agreement with what may be expected of a *votum*. Once the gods have satisfied the conditions laid down in the *votum*-formula, the *votum* has to be redeemed, irrespective of the fact whether this is done by the *vovens* himself or, in case of illness or death of the *vovens*, by someone else. This in itself already proves that the *ludi votivi* can never have formed part of the triumph, one of the fundamental characteristics of the triumph being that it was celebrated by the commander under whose *imperium* and *auspicium* the victory was gained, and not by a deputy. No exception to this rule was made in the whole of Roman history. The fact that the triumph, in contradistinction to *ludi votivi*, or, in fact, to any official *votum*, was non-transferable proves that the triumph can never have been part of a *votum*.

Finally, the following might be considered: in addition to the games, Postumius, during the Latin war, also vowed a temple to Ceres, Liber and Libera, whilst Camillus vowed to dedicate the temple of Mater Matuta. Next to the games, the temple is, according

---

[1] The best-known example is that of the *dedicatio* performed by the consul Horatius.

to Wissowa [1], the most common votive offering. In fact, Livy [2] makes Tullus Hostilius vow *fana* for Pallor and Pavor prior to the introduction of the Etruscan type of temple. G. Rohde in an important paper: "Die Bedeutung der Tempelgründungen im Staatsleben der Römer" [3] has already pointed out the specifically Roman character of the temple *votum*, which was responsible for the founding of the large majority of the temples.

"Die römischen Staatstempel sind Symbole der Erweiterung des Herrschaftraumes der Römer oder Denkmäler von Siegen". (p. 192). This is why the dates of dedication of most of the temples are known to us [4]. The temple *votum* and the founding of temples are in this way directly connected with war and victory. In some cases they were even related to the triumph: Macrobius [5] writes: *Tullum Hostilium, cum bis de Albanis, de Sabinis tertio triumphasset, invenio fanum Saturno ex voto consecravisse et Saturnalia tunc primum Romae instituta.* In the same war which was concluded by his triumph, Tarquin vowed the temple on the Capitol. If, therefore, the majority of the Roman temples were vowed for a victory, and are for this reason far more closely connected with war and victory than are the *ludi votivi*, and if some temples are even associated with triumphs, the conclusion to be reached via Mommsen's way of reasoning would be that the triumph is linked up with the founding of temples rather than with *ludi votivi*. It is quite unnecessary to prove the non-existence of such an interrelationship, which, for that matter, is not defended by anyone. But in that case we have to conclude that any interrelatedness between triumph and *ludi*—games which from the point of view of sacral law fully correspond with the votive temple— is equally improbable.

We have seen that tradition is not aware of any original interconnection between triumph and *ludi*, that during the early republic the *ludi* were not even once held in combination with a triumph, but often after an interval of several years, that the *ludi votivi* often had an object which differed demonstrably from that of the triumph,

---

[1] R. u. K.[2] 385; cf. the *devotio* formula in Macrobius, sat. 3, 9, 8: *Si ita feceritis, voveo vobis templa ludosque facturum.* Cf. E. Pais, Fasti Triumphales Populi Romani II, 1920, 491 ff.

[2] I, 27, 7.

[3] Antrittsvorlesung, Marburg, 1932 = Studien und Interpretationen zur antiken Literatur, Religion und Geschichte, Berlin, 1963, 189 ff.

[4] Dates of founding collected in Wissowa, R.u.K.[2] Anh. II.

[5] Sat. 1, 8, 1.

occasionally were not connected with a military action at all, and that the requirements as to sacral law differed fundamentally in both ceremonies. Finally, we concluded that *vota* of *ludi* on the one hand, and *vota* of temples on the other, the latter of which can definitely not be associated with a triumph, are essentially of the same type. Taking all this into consideration, I think the conclusion is warranted that the *ludi* in Rome never formed part of the triumph, either originally or in later times.

This conclusion is historically confirmed by the fact that over thirty triumphs were recorded for the period 509-350 B.C., but only seven *ludi votivi* [1].

Now that the supposed interrelation between triumph and *ludi* has been proved to be non-existent, we may go one step further, and wonder whether the *ludi Romani* were originally votive games at all, a hypothesis which, as we saw, was *conditio sine qua non* for Mommsen's theory. The demonstrative force of the argument advanced by Mommsen, that the *ludi* are not to be found on the oldest ferial calendar, depends on the dating of this calendar. Believing the calendar to be part of the twelve tables, Mommsen dated its codification to c. 450 B.C. In that case the *ludi*, because they are not mentioned, would not have become *feriae statae* until after this date. However, there is one circumstance which completely overthrows this argumentation: the festival of the *Trias Capitolina* with the *epulum Iovis*, with which the *ludi* are directly associated, is not mentioned in the oldest calendar either. There are two possibilities: 1. the calendar was recorded before 509 B.C., the year of the founding of the Capitoline temple and its cult; 2. the recording took place after 509 B.C., e.g. at the time of the *Decemviri*, c. 450, but after a *feriale* dating from the regal period, at best adjusted as to small details. Mommsen [2] elsewhere defends the latter possibility, and even goes so far as to attribute the old ferial calendar to Numa because the rite of the *Tigillum Sororium*, which dates from the time of Tullus Hostilius, is not indicated. Most of the scholars who have been engaged on the dating of the calendar share Mommsen's view

---

[1] It should be noted that the term *ludi triumphales* is not mentioned in classical literature. The games subsequently given this name are a reminiscence of the victory of Constantine over Licinius in 323 A.D. The games which, since the second century B.C., were with an increasing frequency vowed by generals at their own initiative, were not given this title either, nor were they connected with a triumph; cf. Piganiol o.c. 82 f.

[2] C.I.L. I, 1863, 361 ff.

on this subject, be it with variations [1]. Wissowa [2] dates the *feriale* after the Quirinal's becoming part of Rome, but prior to the reign of Servius Tullius (or, as he puts it later on [3], prior to the Tarquinii), because the cult of Diana on the *Aventinus*, established by Servius, and the cult of the *Trias Capitolina* are not mentioned. This view is also found in Warde Fowler [4]. For later scholars, too, the founding of the temple of Iuppiter O.M. in 509 B.C. remains the most important datum with respect to the dating of the calendar [5]. Nilsson [6] advances the theory that in this year the pre-Julian calendar was created by the Etruscan king, who at the same time introduced the *idus* and the *kalendae*. According to Nilsson this is proved by the fact that this calendar, unlike the older *feriale* of the pre-Etruscan period, did know about the Capitoline Iuppiter and Iuno, who, as he assumes, were connected with *idus* and *kalendae*. Quite rightly his theory has been sharply criticized by Agnes Kirsopp Michels [7], who points out that the Iuppiter and the Iuno of the *idus* and the *kalendae* were not identical with the gods of the Capitol, who were introduced at a later time. Moreover, it won't do to connect the calendar with the founding of the Capitoline temple if its cult itself is not mentioned on the calendar.

The same may be argued against the theories, which go partly back to Nilsson, of Hanell [8] and Gjerstad [9], whose well-known views about the dating of the end of the period of the kings are not, for that matter, relevant to this problem. The opinion of Agnes Kirsopp Michels that the big letters of the calendar do not indicate the age of the festivals, as is generally assumed since Mommsen, but their importance, should, in my view, be rejected, if only for the fact that the festival of Iuppiter O.M., one of the major, if not the most important of all festivals of the Roman calendar[10] is not stated.

---

[1] A survey of the theories is found in Agnes Kirsopp Michels, The calendar of the Roman Republic, Princeton, 1967, 207 ff.

[2] *De feriis anni Romanorum vetustissimi observationes selectae*, 1891 = Gesamm. Abh., 1904, VII, 154 ff.

[3] R.u.K., 1902, 27 ff.   [4] Roman Festivals, 1899, 15; 338.

[5] Altheim, R.R.G., 1931, 1, 26 ff.; Latte, R.R.G., 2; Dumézil, Religion romaine archaïque, 1966, 535.

[6] Strena Philologica, Uppsala, 1922, 131 ff. = Opuscula selecta, Lund, 1952, 2, 979 ff.

[7] o.c. 214; cf. A. Brelich, Vesta, 19 ff.

[8] Das altrömische eponyme Amt. Skrifter Utgivna av Svenska Institutet i Rom, Lund 1946, 95 ff.

[9] Acta archaeologica, 32, 1961, 193 ff.

[10] Even though the author makes important statements about the cha-

Summarizing, we may state that, whatever date is assumed for the recording of the oldest calendar, it is evident from the absence of the dates of a number of important festivals, including that of Iuppiter O.M. and the *ludi Romani* combined with it, that its codification was based on a *feriale* from the pre-Etruscan regal period. The absence of the *ludi* does, therefore, in no way prove that they were originally *feriae conceptivae*. Putting it yet more strongly, even if the festival of Iuppiter O.M. on the *idus* of September had been listed, we would in all probability not have found the *ludi* mentioned, since, as was pointed out by Warde Fowler [1], not counting a few primitive-Roman games, such as the *Consualia* and *Equirria*, *ludi* were never included in the calendar, because they were merely an appendage to a cultic festival and did not themselves form the religious centre.

Mommsen's interpretation of the historical data concerning the origin of the games was discussed by Piganiol. His argumentation may be summarized as follows [2].

There are three authors who have supplied information on the problem: Cicero, Livy and Dionysius. Livy explicitly states that Tarquin established games which from then on were held annually. The first time he refers to these *ludi Romani* again is in his report on the year 322 B.C. Before that there are six references to *ludi magni = ludi votivi*. This is understandable: votive games are material for the historian, annual games, as a rule, are not. Livy records the first *ludi magni = votivi* after the institution of the *ludi Romani* by Tarquin, for the year 491 B.C. [3], in connection with the *instauratio* made necessary by the sacrilegious *praesultator*. Cicero's view is in full agreement with Livy's. In De republica, 2, 20, 35, he says about Tarquin: *eundem primum ludos maximos, qui Romani dicti sunt, fecisse accepimus*. He does not, it is true, refer to the annual recurrence of the games—*ludi Romani* are, however, in his time the annual games—but this may be deduced from another passage

---

racter of festival days that were recorded (p. 132 f.), I cannot follow her in her theory. Why would "obscure" ceremonies as an *Agonium*, *Regifugium*, *Robigalia* and so many other, clearly "old-fashioned" festivals be recorded, unless they belonged to an ancient stage ?

[1] o.c. 115; see also A. Kirsopp Michels, o.c. 136.

[2] I chiefly follow Piganiol's argumentation, o.c. 75 ff. here, and indicate whenever I do not.

[3] Piganiol is, in my view, wrong here in thinking that Livy takes these games to be *ludi annui*. *Ludi magni* in Livy always stand for *ludi votivi*. This was already pointed out by Weissenborn-Müller *ad loc*.

(de div. I, 26, 55), in which, after the example of Coelius Anti-
pater, he writes:....*cum bello Latino ludi votivi maximi primum
fierent*....(n.b. not called *Romani*!). Since Cicero connects the
instauratio with them, only the games of Postumius can be meant
here. Like Livy, therefore, Cicero knows two kinds of games: the
ludi annui, generally called *Romani*, instituted by Tarquin, and the
ludi votivi, commonly called *magni* or *maximi*, vowed for the first time
by the dictator Postumius.

    From this tradition Dionysius' view differs on one point. He, too,
knows about the votive games of Postumius (6, 10), but regards
them as the first of a series of annual games: οὓς ἄξει ὁ 'Ρωμαίων
δῆμος ἀνὰ πᾶν ἔτος. In his sources, however, he comes across older
annual games. Instead of concluding that Postumius' games were
obviously not held annually, he sticks to his view and from sheer
necessity calls the older *ludi annui* "*feriae Latinae*" (6, 95). Since,
however, he says that these games were established by Tarquin
and that the second day was added after the fall of the kings [1]—
which is also reported by other authors about the *ludi Romani*, but
nowhere about the much older *feriae Latinae*—his mistake is abundantly obvious. The oldest games are those of Tarquin and are held
annually, the younger games are those of Postumius and are *ludi
votivi*. The fact that these games became so famous that Fabius
Pictor pretends still to be able to describe them, constitutes one
more proof of the non-recurrent, votive character of the *ludi* of
Postumius.

    Tradition thus corroborates what we already found on the
strength of theoretical considerations: the *ludi Romani*, instituted
by Tarquin, were *ab origine* annual games and, partly in view of their
being recurrent, cannot be directly connected with the triumph [2].
Side-by-side with them *ludi votivi* were held at irregular intervals.
The first of these were ascribed to Postumius. They may have been
planned on a larger scale than the annual games, and were for this
reason called *magni* or *maximi* [3].

---

    [1] The confusion about the addition of the third day does not concern
our problem. See Mommsen, o.c. 48 n. 12.

    [2] It is less important now that Livy connects the origin of these games
with a *votum* made by Tarquin during a war. It is possible that the *votum*
was to the effect that the games were to be repeated annually. Much more
probable is, however, that the *votum* is a reconstruction on the part of historiographers, who, given the example of the *ludi votivi*, could not imagine
any other origin of games.

    [3] The view of Mommsen that the *ludi magni* were given this name to distin-

For the name *ludi Romani*, meanwhile, a different explanation has to be sought. Here it is not the magnitude that is emphasized, as it is in the *ludi magni*, but the nationality. If we are looking for a festival outside Rome of which the *ludi Romani* might form a counterpart, we need not go far. From of old there was an annual celebration of the *feriae Latinae*, of which the *mons Albanus*, sanctuary of Iuppiter Latiaris, was the centre. Several scholars [1] have suggested that Rome, which became increasingly powerful, wanted to consolidate its position by instituting games of its own, which, by way of contrast to the *feriae Latinae*, were given the name *ludi Romani*. Although the problem of the relations between Rome and Latium during the Etruscan period is a highly complicated one—we shall have to return to this subject [2]—, this suggestion is attractive. It is supported by the fact that the *ludi Romani* were centred in the cult of Iuppiter O.M., himself the counterpart of Iuppiter Latiaris [3], by their being instituted during the Etruscan period, the period during which Rome first attempts to assume a prominent position within or against the Latin league [4], and by their being connected, according to at least one traditional source, with a war of Rome against the Latini. Since the *feriae Latinae* were held annually, it is to be assumed that their counterpart, the *ludi Romani*, were also, right from the outset, held every year.

3. *The pompa triumphalis and the pompa funebris; the relation between triumph and funus*

Among the features the triumphal and funeral rites have in common, the use of the red colour has attracted the widest attention. As early as 1906 von Duhn, as we have seen [5], compared the red colour he found on urns, coffins, skeletons, particularly

---

guish them from the smaller, ancient, agrarian games, such as the *Equirria* and the *Consualia*, is less probable, because it does not explain the identity of *ludi magni* and *ludi votivi*.

[1] W. Warde Fowler, Religious Experience, 238; Piganiol, Jeux, 90; R. Bloch, Tite-Live et les premiers siècles de Rome, 81 f.; and others.

[2] *Vide infra* p. 279 ff., where literature is cited.

[3] Wissowa, R.u.K.[2] 125. In this connection it is of great significance that Iuppiter O.M. had a pre-eminently political function, which C. Koch (Der römische Iuppiter, 1937, 126) traces back to an Etruscan pattern.

[4] G. de Sanctis, Storia dei Romani, II, 1907, 90 ff.; A. Heuss, Römische Geschichte, 1960, 11. Alföldi, Early Rome and the Latins, 1965, 318 ff., does not believe in a "grande Roma dei Tarquinii", but see the criticism of Momigliano, J.R.S. 57, 1967, 212.

[5] *Vide supra* p. 79.

skulls, in pre-Indo-European tombs in Italy, with the red lead of the triumphator. In both cases he supposed the red colour to express "pulsierendes, kraftvolles Leben", be it that the red colour of the triumphator was applied in imitation of that of the statue of Iuppiter. Bömer [1] tentatively compares the red colour of the triumphator with the masks of the *maiores* in the funeral procession. There are more parallels. It has been pointed out that some "triumphal archs" are sepulchral monuments [2], and there have been scholars who thought they recognized the *arcus triumphalis* in the symbolism of death of, particularly Etruscan, graves [3]. Not so long ago R. Heidenreich [4] in a paper "Tod und Triumph in der römischen Kunst" drew attention to the correspondence between the representations of the *pompa triumphalis* and the *pompa funebris*. In both cases the central figure—the triumphator or the deceased—distinguishes himself in a very special manner from the other persons depicted. He enumerates elements which *funus* and triumph have in common, such as trumpets, lictors, and torch-bearers, but adds: "Aber dies sind schliesslich Dinge, die auch bei anderen festlichen Gelegenheiten möglich wären" (335). Of greater significance is, in his view, that gladiators were killed at the *funus* and prisoners of war at the triumph, and that in both cases we may speak of an apotheosis: the deceased will from now on belong to the *di parentes*, the triumphator is, for one day, Iuppiter. It goes without saying that the apotheosis of the emperor most clearly shows the two facets of death and triumph.

Heidenreich does not make use of a paper in which these and other parallels between triumph and *funus* are listed, and in which the conclusion is drawn that there exists a "vasta corrispondenza fra l'ideologia trionfale e funeraria". Also elsewhere this paper "Trionfo e morte" by A. Brelich [5] is rarely referred to. The reason why I wish to subject it to a critical examination here, lies not so much in the importance of the paper as such, as in that of the subject: when literature is again and again found to contain suggestions concerning a correspondence between triumph and *funus*, based now on the red colour they have in common, now on the

---

[1] Gnomon, 21, 1949, 354 f.

[2] K. Lehmann-Hartleben, Bull. Comun., 62, 1934, 111; Kähler, R.E. 2e Reihe, 7, 1939, 408, 413, s.v. Triumphbogen.

[3] K. Lehmann-Hartleben, o.c. fig. 14.

[4] Gymnasium, 58, 1951, 326 ff.

[5] S.M.S.R. 14, 1938, 189 ff.

arcus, then again on the similarity of the *pompae*, the best plan is to collect all points of resemblance and to try and find out what they signify. The question is whether the two ceremonies do indeed show a "vasta corrispondenza." In order to ascertain this we closely follow Brelich's paper.

After having stated that a similarity between *funus* and triumph was already noticed in antiquity—*funus triumpho simillimum* is found in Seneca [1]—Brelich presents the following series of elements they have in common: [2]

1. Music and great pomp.
2. The wearing of wreaths by the deceased and his relatives on the one hand, by the triumphator and his military suite on the other.
3. Torches and other illumination.
4. Special points of resemblance between *funus imperatorium* and triumph:
   A. Caesar's funeral pile was erected on the *campus Martius*, the former cemetery of Rome, at the same time starting-place of the triumphal procession.
   B. Proposal to cremate Caesar in the *cella* of the Capitoline temple.
   C. Boards indicating the victories are carried in the triumph as well as in the *pompa funebris*.
   D. The *pompa funebris* sometimes went past the Porta Triumphalis.
   E. The element of satire is encountered in the triumph as well as in the imperial funeral procession.
5. In Etruscan paintings and sculpture the deceased is often represented on a carriage drawn by two or four horses, followed by a group of people. Its meaning is disputed; it is considered a funeral procession by some, and a triumph by others.
6. In both cases there is a meal at the end of the ceremony.
7. Both the triumph and the funeral were followed by games.
8. The arch plays an important part in the symbolism of death. But the *arcus triumphalis* also figures in it. Some *arcus*, even, were erected exclusively in remembrance of a person who died, and not on the occasion of a triumph.

---

[1] Consol. ad Marc. 3, 1.
[2] For testimonia the reader is referred to his paper.

9. The *insignia triumphalia* correspond with features of the funeral rites: the *quadriga*, the *corona Etrusca*, the red lead, the *bulla*, the *phallus* are all found again in pictures or in reality in, particularly Etruscan, tombs.

10. During the imperial period the emperor who died, or a member of the imperial family, was often represented as a triumphator.

Against the method of Brelich—and others who work along the same lines—two fundamental objections may be raised, which, if true, rob a large part of his arguments of all conclusive force. The first objection is that a not inconsiderable number of his examples are not confined to *funus* or triumph, but cover a much wider field, in many instances are, in fact, so ubiquitous that their absence from *funus* and/or triumph would be most unusual. Their presence, on the other hand, is so natural that they cannot possibly be used to demonstrate a resemblance, let alone kinship, between the two ceremonies. Inaccuracies in the data supplied by Brelich further detract from the value of his argumentation.

This first objection cannot be illustrated better than by pointing to the frequent use of the *corona* in Greece and Rome. About the use of the wreath whole volumes have been written [1], and it is difficult to find ancient sacral ceremonies in which it was not employed. Such cases are, however, known to us: the Roman funeral, at which deceased did wear a wreath, but the relatives did not, as far as we know! [2] A similarity between the two ceremonies would, moreover, be worth considering only if the same kind of wreath as worn at the triumph, viz. the laurel-wreath was worn at the *funus*.

The torch, too, played an important part in Greek and Roman cults, particularly in *pompae* [3]. In his phenomenology of the *pompa*, Eitrem also discussed the torch [4]. He explains the frequent use of torches from the fact that some important cults, the mysteries in particular, were performed during the night [5]. The torch, found with

---

[1] J. Köchling, *De coronarum apud antiquos vi atque usu.* (R.V.V. 14) 1913/14. K. Baus, Der Kranz in Antike und Christentum, Bonn, 1940. L. Deubner, Die Bedeutung des Kranzes im klassischen Altertum, A.R.W. 30, 1933, 70 ff.

[2] Köchling, o.c. 18; I. Scott Ryberg, M.A.A.R. 22, 1955, 10 n. 21.

[3] e.g. at the wedding: Prop. 4, 11, 46: *inter utramque facem.*

[4] Beiträge III, cap. 4, 98.

[5] cf. Nilsson, Gött. Gel. Anzeiger, 1916, 48 ff.

remarkable frequency in Dionysiac *pompae*, develops into a standard feature of the *pompa* generally. It is possible that the torch was, as an element of the *pompa*, introduced into Rome either via Etruria or via Hellenism, but that its use in the *funus* was originally Roman. The presence of the torch does, therefore, not warrant any conclusions as to a relationship between triumph and *funus*, not even if the torch had been attested as a standard feature of both. But even this is not the case. The only testimonium for the torch in the triumph given by Brelich is Suetonius, Div. Iul. 37, 2 which describes the five-fold triumph of Caesar. It reads: *Gallici triumphi die Velabrum praetervehens paene curru excussus est, axe diffracto, ascenditque Capitolium ad lumina, quadraginta elephantis dextra atque sinistra lychnuchos gestantibus.* Surely this can mean nothing more than that it was foreseen that the procession was going to be a very lenghty affair, and that lights had been provided in advance, because the triumph, which had started *die*, might end some time during the night. This, however, is a unique, practical measure, which has nothing to do with the triumph as such [1].

A meal concluded, and still concludes, nearly every major event in family and public life: a *nuptialis cena* [2] is, of course, just as common as is a *silicernium* or a *cena triumphalis*, whilst during the games, during which there was a political truce, strangers were *invitati hospitaliter per domos* [3]. Open tables for strangers were also set out during *lectisternia* [4]. There is on the whole nothing mysterious about these meals. They serve to celebrate something, e.g. a return from foreign parts, or the temporary or permanent admission of a stranger into a community not his own. The Romans had a special name for this meal: *cena adventicia* [5]. If one insists on cataloguing, one might class the *cena triumphalis* in this category. The *silicernium*, of which neither the meaning of the word [6], nor the precise dating within the

---

[1] The two remaining places to which Ehlers, o.c. col. 503, refers in this connection, are: Val. Max. 3, 6, 4 and Flor. Epit. 2, 2, 10. They both concern the exceptional instance of Duillius, the first who was awarded a *triumphus navalis*, and who from then on had the privilege of having himself accompanied after the evening-meal by a torch-bearer and a flute-player.

[2] Suet. Caligula, 25.

[3] Liv. 1, 9, 9.

[4] Liv. 5, 13, 7.

[5] Philarg. ad Verg. Ecl. 5, 74; Suet. Vit. 13.

[6] Walde-Hofmann, L.E.W.³, s.v. *Silicernium*.

complex of the funeral rites[1] are known to us, differs fundamentally
from the group described above. Here we do not have the celebration of a festival, the admission into a community, but, on the
contrary, a last greeting, a farewell, at which, according to most
scholars, the deceased, who is considered to be present, shares one
last meal with his relatives and is in this way reconciled and rendered
harmless[2]. This is also indicated by a statement made by Paulus ex
Festo[3]: *silicernium* . . . . *quo fletu familia purgabatur*. This implies
that the triumphal meal and the *silicernium* form about the sharpest
contrast imaginable, with, perhaps, one exception, which I shall
discuss now.

Both triumph and *funus* are followed by *ludi*, according to Brelich. This is also observed by Heidenreich[4]. I hope I have proved
that the *ludi circenses* did not belong to the triumphal ceremony
originally. Even if they did, there would not be any justification in
comparing the *ludi circenses* with the *ludi funebres*. The latter are
even given this name erroneously. Their name was *munus*, and a
terminological distinction between them and the public games was
maintained into the imperial period[5]. Their characteristic feature,
the fights of the gladiators, which were introduced into Rome in
264 B.C., and were not until 105 B.C. for the first time held as a
non-private undertaking, was never incorporated into the official
state-games. Even if, therefore, the *ludi* had constituted one of the
characteristics of the triumph, any comparison between them and
the *munera*, which are of a completely different nature, would have
been out of place.

The enormous and widely-ranging significance of the symbolism
of the door or the gate will have to be dealt with in the next chapter
in connection with the Porta Triumphalis. The *arcus* as an honour
for the dead is indeed demonstrable. The monuments of the Sergii
at Pola and of the Gavii at Verona, which are mentioned as examples,
however, date from the Augustan or an even later period[6] and

---

[1] Latte, R.R.G. 102.

[2] About the funeral repast see i.a.: A. de Marchi, Il culto privato di Roma
antica, Milano, 1896, II, 145; H. Blümner, Die römischen Privataltertümer[3],
München, 1911, 509 ff.; F. Cumont, After life in Roman paganism, London,
1923, 54 ff.; Klauser, Die Cathedra im Totenkult, 1927, 33 ff.; Bömer,
Ahnenkult und Ahnenglaube im alten Rom, 1943, 32.

[3] 377 (L).

[4] o.c. 337.

[5] Wissowa, R.u.K.[2] 465; Piganiol, Jeux, 126 ff.; Latte, R.R.G. 155 f.

[6] Kähler, l.c. col. 408 and 413.

have possibly been inspired by the ideology of the triumph, which during this very period assumes a peculiar from, about which a few remarks will be made further on. The pictures of *arcus*-shaped gates in Etruscan sepulchral monuments have been discussed in a study by G. A. Mansuelli [1]. A fresco in the Tomba del Cardinale [2] shows several representations of a gate-like, detached structure, which obviously symbolizes the passage from life to death, the *leti ianua* [3] so often depicted. Unlike Brelich, Mansuelli does not see in this *"arcus"* the link between the ideologies of death and triumph, but a purely formal correspondence between the Roman *arcus*, which came from Etruria as a *fornix*, and the purely Etruscan version of it, depicted on the fresco. Any judgment about the possibility of an independent development of the originally Etruscan *fornix* in Etruria and Rome I gladly leave to the specialists [4]. I do venture to point out, however, that a detached *arcus* depicted once, as against the *porta* or *ianua* depicted innumerable times, should not be over-emphasized. In my view it is merely a *porta* drawn in outline, which was represented as a detached structure with a view to making its function more obvious. The whole question will, for that matter, cease to be of any significance, once we know what the next chapter will show us, viz. that in origin the *arcus* had nothing whatever to do with the triumph, and that we do not know what the Porta Triumphalis, which does prove to be closely linked up with the triumph, looked like.

The elements enumerated under nr. 9 hardly require any further discussion. The phallos is widely used as an *apotropaeum*, the *bulla* (*aurum Etruscum*) is, as an *apotropaeum*, given to the triumphator as well as to the young sons of the patricians [5]. The presents the dead are given to take with them in their graves, are, moreover, as a

---

[1] S.E. 23, 1954, 433 ff.

[2] Reproductions in Weege, Etruskische Malerei, 1927, fig. 29-34.

[3] Lucret. 5, 373, quoted by Brelich.

[4] However, I cannot help making one objection, viz. against the interpretation of the tomb of *Arnθ Velimna* (picture: Giglioli, Arte etrusca, tav. 417, 2). Mansuelli discerns in it the *arcus* in its function of support of a statue or a group of statues, in this case the deceased. The gate depicted is in my view merely a consistent simplification and formalization of the gate of death so often depicted on *sarcophagi* (Giglioli, Arte etrusca, tav. 407, 2; 411, 2 and 4). Gates of this type are neither *fornix*-shaped, nor is their function that of a support. Cf. further K. Lehmann-Hartleben, Bull. Comun. 62, 1934, fig. 14 (an *arcus*-shaped passage to death) and fig. 19 (a real *ianua* with two folding-doors).

[5] Plin. n.h. 33, 10; Macrob. Sat. 1, 6, 9; Liv. 26, 36, 5.

rule objects belonging to life, so that there is no connection between the *bulla* and death, any more than between the food, jewels, implements, etc. presented to the dead, and death. The same applies to the *corona Etrusca*. The red colour was already dealt with in the preceding.

We may, therefore, conclude that the points of resemblance between triumph and *funus* discussed so far—points nrs. 2, 3, 6, 7, 8, 9 —are either based on incorrect data, or cover a much wider field, so that they do not prove anything with respect to a relationship between triumph and *funus*.

A second, and, in my opinion, more serious methodical error Brelich commits when, without taking into account place or time of origin of the various rites, he uses all their aspects indiscriminately to prove his point, irrespective of whether they were attested for the regal period, the Etruscan part of it, the republic or the principate. A clear illustration of this is found in his treatment of the *funus imperatorium*, in which he discovers elements pre-eminently related to the triumph. I wish to state at once that he is undoubtedly right here, but also that this does not warrant any conclusions as to a relationship between the ideologies of death and triumph in earlier periods. The fact is that it is abundantly clear that the *funus imperatorium* took over a number of the features of the triumph. It will appear, however, that the element they have in common should not be looked for in the substantivum *funus*, but in the adjectivum *imperatorium*.

We have seen that the magistrate had the right to wear the insignia of his office during his last journey, and that the former triumphator was at the *funus* clothed in the triumphal robes. It requires no further elucidation that the triumphal aspect of the *funus imperatorium* is merely a continuation of this old-Roman tradition, whose privileges meant little more than what we nowadays mean by "rendering the funeral honours". What is remarkable, however, is that, at the end of the republic and in the early imperial period, the triumph sets its mark much more deeply on the *funus* than it did before. The passage through the Porta Triumphalis is a novelty and, as far as we know, took place only at the *funus* of Augustus [1]; another novum was that the funeral-procession of Augustus was preceded by people carrying boards indicating the

---

[1] Tac. Ann. 1, 8; Suet. Aug. 100; Cass. Dio, 56, 42.

names of the peoples that had been subjugated [1]. However, the
funus imperatorium was characterized not only by triumphal elements, but also by other *honores*, which were also permitted for the
first time. One of these was that the *tituli legum legatarum* were also
carried in the funeral procession of Augustus [2]. Although, therefore,
the practice of wearing the *insignia triumphalia* was already an-
chored in old-Roman customs, it is obvious that the great emphasis
they were given in the *funus imperatorium* has to be explained in some
other way. A first explanation may be found in the Hellenistic
ceremonial funeral.

The practice of giving great men a pompous funeral, which already existed before this period, really began to flourish during
Hellenism. Pfister [3] collected the data concerned in his "Reliquienkult". Particularly at the *translatio* of a hero or prince who died
outside his native town, the transport was accompanied with great
pomp. From the abundant material I only choose a few examples.
Plutarch (Pelop. 33) describes the *translatio* of the dead body of
Pelopidas: ἐκ δὲ τῶν πόλεων .... παρῆσαν αἵ τε ἀρχαὶ καὶ μετ'
αὐτῶν ἔφηβοι καὶ παῖδες καὶ ἱερεῖς πρὸς τὴν ὑποδοχὴν τοῦ σώματος,
τρόπαια καὶ στεφάνους καὶ πανοπλίας χρυσᾶς ἐπιφέροντες. The same
author (Demetr. 53) calls the *translatio* of the bones of Demetrius
Poliorketes a τραγικήν τινα καὶ θεατρικὴν διάθεσιν. The Sicyonians
brought the remains of Aratos back to their town ὑπὸ παιάνων καὶ
χορῶν (Plut. Aratos 53). Of special interest to us is the statement made
by Plutarch (Philop. 21) that the Arcadians carried the body of
Philopoimen ἐπινίκιον πομπήν τινα ἅμα ταῖς ταφαῖς μίξαντες to
Megalopolis. The fact that not only the *translatio*, but also the
ordinary funeral of princes was accompanied with processions and
pomp is demonstrated by, e.g. descriptions of the funeral of Dionysius of Syracuse in Plutarch (Pelop. 34) and Timaeus in Athenaeus
(5, 206 E). Pfister rightly puts the Roman funerals on a level with
these Hellenic-Hellenistic examples. The event to which Seneca [4]
referred by the words *funus triumpho simillimum*, is the *translatio*
of the body of Drusus from Germania to Rome, which corresponded

---

[1] Tac. Ann. 1, 8.

[2] *ibid.*

[3] F. Pfister, Der Reliquienkult im Altertum. (R.V.V. 5) 1909/12, 433 ff.

[4] Consol. ad Marc. 3, 1. To my knowledge this comparison is unique
and applies only to this *translatio*. Brelich's remark, "Una rassomiglianza
fra il corteo trionfale e funebre fu intuita anche dagli antichi stessi", is,
therefore, an illicit generalization.

in every respect with, e.g. the *translatio* of Philopoimen, in which the triumphal aspect is also stressed.

Similar *translationes* are known of Augustus [1], Germanicus [2], Septimius Severus [3] and Constantius [4]. Thus we see that at least part of these elements by which the *funus imperatorium* distinguishes itself from the earlier funeral procession—pomp, veneration and elevation of the dead, aspects of a triumphal march—went through their preparatory stages in Hellenism. There is, however, an additional, and more important cause of the increasing number of triumphal elements in the *funus*.

The apotheosis of the emperor is, as it were, the effect of his achievements during his life-time. "Originairement l'*imperator* romain.... n'est que candidat à l'apothéose et son règne constitue l'examen de ses capacités" [5]. To the fact that these achievements, the *"felicitas"*, had to be apparent primarily from victories in war, testify not only, e.g. the statue of Caesar with the inscription "to the invincible god" [6], but chiefly the poets of the Augustan era, who, when describing the exploits of Augustus, never tire of comparing these with the great triumphs of Iuppiter [7], a comparison which is all the more remarkable if we realize that the triumphator in his triumph represented Iuppiter. Without going so far as Mrs. Arthur Strong, who speaks of "the temporary deification of the triumphator" [8], one has to admit that—in the words of Mrs. Ross Taylor quoted above—"the triumph....was the closest thing in Roman state ceremony to deification" [9]. In this case it is perfectly understandable that the elements of the triumph were allotted such an important place in the *funus* of the emperors: in the first place it was by showing the victories of the emperor that the apotheosis, which was supposed to take place immediately after the

---

[1] Cass. Dio, 56, 31, 2.

[2] Tac. Ann. 3, 2.

[3] Script. hist. aug. Severus 24, 2.

[4] Amm. Marc. 21, 16, 20 ff.

[5] L. Cerfaux et J. Tondriau, Le culte des souverains dans la civilisation gréco-romaine, Tournai, 1957, 311.

[6] Cass. Dio, 43, 45, 3.

[7] Hor. od. 1, 12; 2, 12; 3, 5; Prop. 2, 1, 17 ff.; Ovid, Trist. 2, 331 ff.; Manil. Astr. 1, 40 ff.; 799 ff. About this subject: Margaret M. Ward, The association of Augustus with Iuppiter. S.M.S.R. 9, 1933, 203 ff.

[8] Mrs. Arthur Strong, Apotheosis and Afterlife, 64.

[9] Lily Ross Taylor, The divinity of the Roman emperor, 57. Cerfaux and Tondriau (o.c. 274) rightly consider the triumph as one of the elements which have prepared the way for the apotheosis in Rome.

cremation, was justified, whilst in the second place the triumphal
garb and all its paraphernalia constituted the *insigne* most befitting
a future deity [1].

In a later work "Die geheime Schutzgottheit von Rom" [2] Brelich
(p. 50) says that he might be reproached with using data which are
of little importance, and "Nicht nur das, sondern mit überraschender
Vernachlässigung des historischen Kriteriums werden an Alter und
Herkunft verschiedenartigste Nachrichten verwandt". For a few
subtle remarks about this kind of method and its theoretical
foundation I may refer to Rose's review of this work [3]. In any case
we do find that Brelich employed this method at a much earlier occasion, when he set out to use the triumphal aspect of the imperial
funus in order to prove a general relationship between the ideologies
of triumph and death.

Of the points now left there is one requiring our special attention,
because it has so far been used to prove three entirely different
theories: the representations referred to under nr. 5 of a deceased man
standing on a chariot in a *pompa*. Müller-Deecke [4] considered them
to be pictures of the triumph, and used them to prove that the
triumph had come from Etruria. Wallisch [5] thinks that they can
only represent the journey to the hereafter, and it is precisely on
the absence of pictures of triumphs in Etruscan tombs that he bases
his conclusion that the triumph had not come from Etruria. Finally,
according to Brelich, this uncertainty testifies to a relationship
between triumph and *funus*. Now it was already pointed out by
Mrs. Arthur Strong [6] that a similar picture can be observed on the
sarcophagus of Hagia Triada, which can hardly be associated with
a triumph, whilst also Cumont [7] drew attention to the fact that not
only in Etruria and Rome, but also in Greece and elsewhere the

---

[1] With this ideology the *arcus triumphalis* now also fits in as a memorial
for the dead. As we have seen, this is also a late phenomenon. Lehmann-
Hartleben, o.c. 119 rightly says about this: "Invece si tratta qui di un
sicurissimo trasferimento di riti trionfali a quelli della consecrazione".

[2] Albae Vigilae, N.F. 6, 1949.

[3] Gnomon, 21, 1949, 367.

[4] Die Etrusker, 2, 199; 1, 346 f.; further B. Nogara, Gli Etruschi e la
loro civiltà, Milano, 1933, 240.

[5] Philol. 98, 1954/55, 246 f.

[6] o.c. 167.

[7] After life in Roman paganism, 1923, 148 ff. Cf. A. Dieterich, Eine
Mithrasliturgie[3], Berlin, 1923, 183 f.; L. Deubner, Röm. Mitt., 27, 1912,
11 ff.

dead are often represented as travellers, on foot, on board a ship, and very frequently on a carriage. In view of all this, it is at present generally agreed that these scenes depict the journey to the underworld [1], which, for that matter, does not imply that Wallisch's theory should be right, or that now the last word about these representations should have been said. Conclusions concerning the *pompa* on funeral urns have in the past too frequently been based on one representation, or on a very small number of them [2]. Owing to the fortunate circumstance that a complete list with illustrations of the so-called magistrates' *pompae* on Etruscan urns, sarcophagi and frescoes was published recently, we are now in a position to form our judgment on the basis of the complete material. In this matter we let ourselves be guided by the editor, R. Lambrechts [3].

The *pompae* depicted are fairly stereotyped as to form and composition. The sarcophagi show a simpler representation than do the urns (nearly all of which come from Volaterra), because the material of the urns admits of more detail. All works are from the third century B.C. or later. They show:

1. In front (usually two) *cornicines*. Sometimes they are found at the end of the procession.
2. Two (sometimes more) lictors with *fasces* without axes on their shoulders, sometimes carrying an additional rod.
3. A two-wheeled chariot drawn on the sarcophagi by two, on the urns by four horses. Behind the horses we often see a winged demon—of whose body only the upper part is visible—rising, or, in his place, Charun with the hammer, who sometimes leads the horses by the reins. In many cases we see behind the horses, instead of the daemon, a man on horseback ("avant-coureur", Lambrechts, "battistrada", Körte) who raises his hand in a gesture of salutation.
4. On the chariot the deceased in *toga* and *tunica*, sometimes wearing a wreath, sometimes *capite velato*. Among the forty reliefs known to us, Körte [4] saw one on which the deceased carried a "corto scettro (*scipio*), distintivo della sua dignità"

---

[1] See i.a. Giglioli, Arte etrusca, tav. 396-402; A. Grenier, Les religions étrusque et romaine, 58 f.

[2] Particularly on an urn in Volaterra, a picture of which is to be found in G. Körte, Rilievi III, tav. 85, 3.

[3] R. Lambrechts, Essai sur les magistratures des républiques étrusques, Bruxelles, 1959.

[4] Rilievi III, 84, 1.

in his right hand. This hand, and what it held, have unfortunately, disappeared [1].

5. The chariot is followed by one or more *apparitores* with a *tabula*
or *pugillares*.

6. An *apparitor* with a bag for hand-luggage.

7. Occasionally a person carrying the *sella currulis*.

A variation of the *pompa* here described is found in a similar procession, in which, however, the deceased goes on foot. Lambrechts [2]
holds the view that these reliefs depict episodes from the official
career of the magistrate. If titles have been inscribed, *zilaθ* always
figures among them, which means that the magistrate depicted is
one of the highest magistrates of the Etruscan city-states. The
pompa bears an unmistakably funerary character: the daemon or
Charun accompany the deceased on his way to death. The *apparitor*
with the *mantica* indicates that the scene is that of a journey.
Cornicines and lictors with the *fasces* are standard constituents of
the *pompa funebris*, also in Rome. Lambrechts nevertheless remarks: "le défunt, magistrat suprême ou non, entre aux enfers,
mais il y entre en grande pompe, comme triomphe un magistrat
suprême" (188) [3]. Does this mean that the procession depicted is
a *pompa triumphalis* after all? What is there to indicate this? The
wreath? But this may be the funeral wreath. Besides, it is by no
means found on all reliefs. The *scipio* in the right hand? The only
picture showing this is lost. As far as I can see it, there is only one
argument left: the deceased is represented as standing on a *biga* or
quadriga. Even if it is pointed out that this may have been intended
to enliven the scene, just as the deceased was in the Roman funeral
procession also represented in the form of a seated or standing wax
statue, it is possible to assume that the whole scene must have been
based on reality and that it actually shows an episode from the life of
the magistrate. The *tabellarius*, for instance, indicates this. But
the *pompa* cannot possibly depict a *pompa triumphalis*. What sense
would in that case the *pugillarius* make, or the *sella currulis*, or
the dais shown a few times with on it the *sella currulis* obviously intended for the magistrate? [4] The decisive argument, however, is

---

[1] Lambrechts, o.c. 168 and pl. XXXIV.

[2] o.c. 187.

[3] A similar ambiguity is also found in the view of H. H. Scullard, Cities
of Etruria and Rome, London, 1967, 228; I. Scott Ryberg, o.c. 16 f.

[4] Lambrechts, o.c. pl. XXXVII, XXXVIII.

that there were in Etruria in the third century B.C.—let alone in later times—no longer any occasions for the supreme magistrate of the city-states to triumph, since Rome was in control. In accordance with this we do not find any references to triumphs held in Etruria during this period. If then we may see a high light in the life of the deceased, it would seem to me that, in addition to the *funus* and the triumph, there is yet a third possibility: that we should recognize elements in it of a kind of *pompa* by which the magistrate's installation is accompanied. The new functionary may have had the right to drive a *quadriga* on that day. In the *zila θ meχl rasnal* Lambrechts sees the representative of a state, who was sent to the central meeting *ad fanum Voltumnae*[1] there to stand for the office of *Praetor Etruriae*. This was done annually, also under the Roman rule until at least under Constantine. Games formed part of the ceremony. Perhaps the reliefs show a *pompa* as it took place after the election of the new leader of the Etruscan confederation. To this suggestion we shall have to return later.

With respect to a final point, the music, we may be brief. It is noteworthy that trumpets were sounded in both the *pompa triumphalis* and the *pompa funebris*. The trumpet is, according to both Greeks and Romans, an invention of the Tyrrhenians or Etruscans, and was, as Müller-Deecke [2] made clear by means of a large number of testimonia, brought from Lydia to Italy by the Tyrrheni, or Pelasgi, as they were also called. One more indication, therefore, that Etruria developed a type of *pompa* of its own with characteristic features, which are found again in the various Roman *pompae*, without this proving any relationship between the ceremonies to which the *pompae* belong. Together with the Etruscan *pompa* the trumpet, the imitation of the central figure—triumphator, leader of games or deceased—, the satire, etc. came to Rome. The deification, which is to be observed in both the triumph and the *funus*, is also due to Etruscan influence, as was already found in the preceding chapter [3]. There is, however, one essential difference: the triumphator for one day acts the part of, or becomes one particular god, viz. Iuppiter, whereas the deceased will permanently belong to the *di parentes*.

---

[1] About this ceremony and its meaning *vide infra*. p. 275 ff.
[2] Die Etrusker, 2, 206 ff., where the reader may find the testimonia.
[3] See above. p. 90.

Summarizing the results of the investigations dealt with in the present section we find in the first place that no essential relationship or kinship between *funus* and triumph exists. There is no doubt that there are points of resemblance between the two ceremonies, but these are to be attributed to quite different causes:

1. some concern objects or usages belonging to religious ceremonies generally;
2. others belong to the standing equipment of the *pompa* generally;
3. in the case in which we do in fact find elements of the triumph in the funeral-ritual, viz. in the *funus imperatorium*, a distinct historical development may be observed. For reasons which are readily understood, and of which the introduction of the idea of the apotheosis is the principal one, aspects of the triumph were grafted upon the *funus*. This convergence did not set in until towards the end of the republic.

4. *Conclusion*

In the present chapter we dealt with two theories, that of Mommsen and that of Brelich, who have both developed ideas which, up till the present, keep re-appearing in scientific literature. The fact that we have opposed both views, and have tried to prove them incorrect, does not mean that the relation between the various *pompae* and ceremonies in general, and to our subject in particular, has become a matter of no importance. The influence of the triumph on the *funus imperatorium* is demonstrable and significant, but its implications, such as the ideology of emperorship, the cult of the ruler, apotheosis, etc. are beyond the scope of our study. Other, original connections between *funus* and triumph are non-existent. Of greater, or even vital importance to our subject is the relation between *pompa circensis* and *pompa triumphalis*. We have, indeed, rejected Mommsen's view on this relation, but this does not mean that we have closed our eyes to the remarkable similarities between these two *pompae*. One point of similarity, the most significant one, we have so far deliberately left undiscussed: the fact that the magistrate presiding over the games wore the triumphal robes. It was pointed out that, if Mommsen's theory would prove incorrect, a new explanation would have to be sought for this remarkable phenomenon. This implies that I, too, am of the opinion that there is a relationship between triumph and *ludi circenses*, only that it is unlike the one Mommsen assumed to exist. Since the figure of the magistrate who led the *ludi Romani* will occupy our attention later on, I shall, by way of conclusion, here summarize the considerations which induced Mommsen to decide that he wore the triumphal robes [1]; a fact which has not been explicitly recorded.

It is certain that the triumphal robes were worn during the *ludi Apollinares*, instituted in 208 B.C., and they are referred to several times [2] as the attire of the magistrate leading the games, from then on usually the *praetor*. For the *ludi Augustales* the *tribuni plebis* are permitted *ut per circum triumphali veste uterentur: curru vehi haud permissum* [3]. Dionysius of Hal. 6, 95, reports that the *aediles plebis* during the games wore the triumphal garb. Here the *ludi plebei* must be meant [4]. But if all these lower-grade officials had, or were at a certain moment given, the right to wear the triumphal *ornatus* when leading games, this right has, *a fortiori*, to be assumed for the magistrate leading the *ludi Romani*, the games whose *pompa* was the example for all other games [5]. The reason for this not having been explicitly recorded is that only new privileges were worth reporting, the age-old ones being considered common knowledge. When Livy, 5, 41 in his report on the year 390 B.C. says about the triumphal *ornatus: quae augustissima vestis est tensas ducentibus triumphantibusve*, the *tensas ducens* primarily refers to the leader of the *pompa circensis* of the *ludi Romani*. It is impossible to see how a privilege accorded to the *praetor* could be denied the leader of the *ludi Romani*—a consul or, in his place, a *praetor*, or, if the latter is also absent, a *dictator* especially appointed for the purpose [6]—.It is equally impossible to see where the idea of giving the *praetor* the triumphal garb to wear during the *ludi Apollinares* had come from if it had not had some precedent. Mommsen rightly postulated that it followed from this that the magistrates leading the *ludi Romani* also wore the triumphal garb. I do not know of any scholar who doubts this.

---

[1] Staatsrecht I³, 412 f.

[2] Juven. 10, 36; 11, 195; Plin. n.h. 34, 20; Martial, 8, 33, 1.

[3] Tac. Ann. 1, 15.

[4] Piganiol thought that the *aediles plebis* were the original leaders of the *ludi Romani*, which had substituted older plebeian *ludi* in honour of Liber. His theory is completely unacceptable. On the basis of testimonia mentioned below it is proved that the *ludi Romani* had to be led by a *magistratus cum imperio*. The *aedilis* was the steward at the games, not the leader who rode in the procession.

[5] Wissowa, R.u.K.² 452.

[6] Consul: Liv. 45, 1; Dictator in the absence of praetor: Liv. 8, 40 2.

On one point I should like to go further than Mommsen. He hesitates at the question whether the magistrate of the *ludi Romani* rode in a chariot, and is inclined to answer it in the negative. Riding in a chariot was obviously considered a very special privilege: the *tribuni plebis* were denied this privilege at the *ludi Augustales*, and about the right of the *praetor* to ride in a *biga* during the *ludi Apollinares* so much fuss was made [1] "dass es damit nicht recht zu vereinigen ist, wenn auch der Consul bei den römischen Spielen die Pompa zu Wagen in den Circus führt" [2]. There is, however, a strong tradition which does allot the magistrate a chariot during the *ludi Romani*. Dionysius, 5, 57, reports that in 500 B.C. one of the consuls fell from the "sacred chariot" during the circus-procession of the *ludi Romani* and died. The report does not make the impression of being based on fantasy, even though we do not find it in Livy. Elsewhere [3], too, it is reported that the magistrate "drives" as far as the *carceres*, gives the starting-signal there, and subsequently drives his chariot back to the stand of the spectators. In my view it is not necessary to mistrust these reports just because the allotting of a *biga* to the *praetor* of the *ludi Apollinares* caused a sensation. On the contrary, the two facts can very well go together: the right to ride in a chariot in the *pompa* was so strictly reserved to the magistrate as the leader of the most sacred ancient state-games of Rome, the *ludi Romani*, that an extension of this right to the *ludi Apollinares* was bound to cause a sensation. Pliny, n.h. 34, 20, *Non vetus et bigarum celebratio in iis qui praetura functi curru vecti essent per circum...*, does not contradict this, if it is realized that the task of leading the games was particularly after the institution of the *ludi Apollinares* entrusted to the *praetores*.

This chapter is therefore concluded, not with a new certainty, but with a new question: why did the magistrate as leader of the *ludi Romani* wear the triumphal robes? This question will be dealt with in the second part of this study.

---

[1] See testimonia p. 130 n. 2.
[2] Mommsen, o.c. 394, n. 4.
[3] Liv. 45, 1, 6.

CHAPTER FOUR

THE PORTA TRIUMPHALIS

the gates wide open stood,
That with extended wings a bannered host,
Under spread ensigns marching, might pass through
With horse and chariots ranked in loose array.

Milton

1. *Introduction*

In ancient literature the Porta Triumphalis is mentioned only a few times. Cicero [1] remarks that it is all the same to him through which gate his opponent Piso returned to the city, *modo ne triumphali. quae porta Macedonicis semper consulibus ante te patuit: tu inventus es qui consulari imperio praeditus ex Macedonia non triumphares.* Tacitus [2] and Suetonius [3] mention a proposal to make the funeral-procession of Augustus pass through the Porta Triumphalis. The inference that this gate was situated on or near the *Campus Martius*, since Augustus was buried there, is confirmed by a final testimonium in Flavius Iosephus [4], from whose report on the triumph of Vespasian and Titus it can be deduced that the Porta Triumphalis was somewhere near the *Circus Flaminius*. It is the only report which tells us at least something about what took place during the passage through the Porta Triumphalis: (Οὐεσπασιανὸς) πρὸς δὲ τὴν πύλην αὐτὸς ἀνεχώρει τὴν ἀπὸ τοῦ πέμπεσθαι δι᾽ αὐτῆς αἰεὶ τοὺς θριάμβους τῆς προσηγορίας ἀπ᾽ αὐτῶν τετευχυῖαν. ἐνθαῦτα τροφῆς προαπεγεύοντο καὶ τὰς θριαμβικὰς ἐσθῆτας ἀμφιασάμενοι τοῖς τε παριδρυμένοις τῇ πύλῃ θύσαντες θεοῖς ἔπεμπον τὸν θρίαμβον διὰ τῶν θεάτρων διεξελαύνοντες.

This exhausts the data [5] and opens the door for guesses and theories about the exact place, form and function of the Porta Triumphalis [6]. "There are advocates for every possible form and

---

[1] In Pis. 23, 55.

[2] Ann. 1, 8.

[3] Aug. 100; cf. Cass. Dio, 56, 42.

[4] Bell. Iudic. 7, 5, 4 (123) ff.

[5] Late and of little value is Schol. Suet. 227: *Porta triumphalis media fuisse videtur inter Portam Flumentanam et Catulariam.* Whether the gate that was too narrow for the elephants' *quadriga* of Pompey (Plin. n.h. 8, 4; Plut. Pomp. 14, 3), was the Porta Triumphalis, is not known.

[6] A bibliography up to 1933 is found in H. Petrikovits, Jahresh. Oesterr.

location of the Porta Triumphalis'', Mrs. Adams Holland [1] remarks. As far as place is concerned, it has been suggested [2] that any gate-like construction, e.g. an arch of an aquaduct, or a triumphal arch erected for only one occasion, could serve as a Porta Triumphalis, so that it is impossible to indicate one fixed location. This, however, is contradictory to literary tradition [3]. On the other hand, it is also impossible for the gate ever to have formed part of a town-wall of Rome, as might be inferred from the testimonia in Cicero and Flavius Iosephus—but these also allow of a different interpretation— and from the use of the terms *porta*, πύλη [4], because in that case the Porta Triumphalis must be allotted a place which is excluded by literary sources. The location suggested by von Gerkan [5], for example, in the town-wall near the *Circus Maximus*, is in flat contradiction to the reports of Flavius Iosephus and Suetonius [6] on the triumphs of Vespasian and Caesar respectively. On the basis of our literary testimonia E. Makin [7] had already before that made it clear that the Porta Triumphalis must have been situated near the *Porticus Octavia* and the temple of Bellona, outside the walls, therefore, as a detached structure.

The view that the Porta Triumphalis was a detached gate was also held by von Domaszewski [8]. Followed by Noack [9], he assumed that the *Ianus Quirinus* on the forum, through which the army went to war, was originally also used as the gate through which the army returned home, and as such had a lustrative function. After the lustration rites had been removed to the *Campus Martius*, the Porta Triumphalis was supposed to have taken over this function there.

Arch. Inst. Wien, 28, 1933, 196. For later literature see the works mentioned below in the text.

[1] Louise Adams Holland, Ianus and the Bridge. American academy in Rome. Papers and monographs, 21, 1961, 89 n. 56.

[2] L. Morpurgo. La porta trionfale e la via dei trionfi. Bull. Com. 36, 1908, 108 ff., who, however, wrongly refers to the entry of Nero, which was not a triumph.

[3] See Kähler, R.E. 2e Reihe 7, 1939, 375, s.v. Triumphbogen.

[4] M. P. Nilsson, Corolla Archaeologica Gustavo Adolpho dedicata, 1932, 134.

[5] Röm. Mitt. 46, 1931, 181.

[6] Div. Iul. 37.

[7] The triumphal route with particular reference to the Flavian triumph. J.R.S. 11, 1921, 30 ff.

[8] Die Triumphstrasse auf dem Marsfelde. A.R.W. 12, 1909, 67 ff.

[9] Triumph und Triumphbogen. Vorträge der Bibliothek Warburg. 1925/26, 147 ff.

A variation on this theory will be found in Wagenvoort [1], when, in the next section, the function of the triumphal gate will be dealt with in more detail.

The fact that a gate with some special ritual function did not have to form part of a wall, is for Rome demonstrated by two structures, often compared with the Porta Triumphalis, which never formed part of the walls of Rome: the *Ianus* gate and the *Tigillum Sororium*[2]. Nor have these structures ever been moved. This makes it improbable that the Porta Triumphalis at one time formed part of the wall and was, later on, moved to a place outside the walls. Besides, I fail to see how this could be done without the lustrative action being lost, or why, if this function had passed into oblivion, a removal was necessary at all.

The starting-point for an inquiry into the meaning of the Porta Triumphalis is, therefore, to us, as to many before us, the knowledge that this structure, which during the period of the Flavii stood isolated, did not in earlier times form part of the walls of Rome either. It is possible that the gate stood on the *Petronia amnis*, as was suggested by von Domaszewski [3], and that there, according to a theory of Petrikovits [4], it marked the end of the *pomerium*, which he considers to lie outside the walls. This does not tell us anything about its function, however.

There is still greater uncertainty about the form of the *porta* than about its place. This problem is inextricably interwoven with the vexed question of the origin of the so-called *arcus triumphalis* and its relation to the Porta Triumphalis. For those who held the view that the triumphal arch had come from the Hellenistic Orient or from Greece, as Gräf [5], Löwy [6] and Nilsson [7], this problem did not exist. It did not arise until it was recognized that we should see a typically Roman type of structure in the *arcus*. This view, which at present is generally accepted, was defended by Noack [8], Weickert [9],

---

[1] Roman Dynamism, 154 ff.

[2] See L. A. Holland, o.c. 88 ff.

[3] o.c. 67 ff.

[4] o.c. 191. In this case the Porta Triumphalis should have followed the extension of the *pomerium*.

[5] In Baumeister, Denkmäler des klassischen Altertums III, 1865, s.v. Triumphbogen.

[6] Festschr. Otto Hirschfeld, 1903, 423 ff.

[7] B.C.H. 49, 1925, 143 ff.; modified view in: Corolla Arch. 1932, 132 ff.

[8] o.c. 147 ff.

[9] Review of Noack's work in Gnomon, 5, 1929, 24 ff.

Weigand [1], Petrikovits, Kähler [2], Picard [3], and others. The columns supporting the architrave, which formed the *trait d'union* with Hellenistic structures, are, as was demonstrated by Noack, a later addition to the purely Roman *arcus*. This, however, makes it attractive to look upon the *arcus* as an imitation of the Porta Triumphalis, as was already proposed by von Domaszewski [4] and Rostovtzeff [5]. In a lengthy paper Noack deals with this relation and, after an inquiry into form and function of the Porta Triumphalis, comes to the conclusion that it served as the model for the *arcus triumphalis*, since it is only in this way that its arch-shaped construction can be explained. The fact that the oldest triumphal arches known to us do not in any way reflect the function of the Porta Triumphalis is explained by Noack by his assumption that these *arcus* were, of course, not the first in history, and that their meaning gradually changed.

In my view, this argumentation does not stand up against the battery of weighty counter-arguments put into the field by Weickert[6] in his review of Noack's paper. It appears highly improbable that the triumphal arch was connected with the Porta Triumphalis, or even with the triumph at all, if the following arguments are considered: The triumphal arch is not mentioned in any of the descriptions of triumphs before the period of the emperors. About the oldest *arcus* we have statements which explicitly testify to their not having been built on the occasion of triumphs: in 196 B.C. L. Stertinius erected three arches from the money of the spoils gained in Spain, *ne temptata quidem triumphi spe* [7]; in 190 B.C. P. Cornelius Scipio built an arch *priusquam proficisceretur* [8]. Like many others this arch did not stand across, but beside the road [9], which eliminates any resemblance to a gate, a difference also expressed in the names: *arcus*, formerly *fornix*, and *porta* are two different things. Pliny[10], the only author giving his view on the function of the *arcus* says: *columnarum ratio erat attolli super ceteros mor-*

---

1 Wiener Jahrb. f. Kunstgesch. 5, 1928, 71 ff.
2 o.c.
3 G. C. Picard, Les trophées romains, Paris, 1957, 122 n. 6.
4 o.c. 73.
5 Röm. Mitt. 26, 1911, 132 n. 1.
6 o.c., particularly p. 25 f.
7 Liv. 33, 27, 4.
8 Liv. 37, 3, 7.
9 *ibidem*: *adversus viam*.
10 N.h. 34, 27.

tales, quod et arcus significant novicio inventu. This defines its function: like the *columna*, the *arcus* was meant to support a statue or a
group of statues—as already did the *arcus* of Stertinius and Scipio[1]—
and as such the arch is to Pliny a recent invention. This does not add
to the probability of a long development preceding the *arcus* of the
beginning of the second century B.C. Finally, the name *arcus triumphalis* dates from a very late time [2], and also during the imperial
period there is no question of an exclusive connection between *arcus*
and triumph. The *arcus* was an arch of honour in the widest sense,
it served to support *signa* as well as to keep alive the memory of an
important event—not nearly always a victory—or a person—not
nearly always a triumphator.

Kähler [3], who accepts these counter-arguments, adds that they
are not refuted by pointing to hypothetical pictures of the Porta
Triumphalis which are arch-shaped. Some scholars [4] thought they
discovered the Porta Triumphalis in *arcus*-shaped structures depicted
on coins from the time of Domitian and later, and on reliefs which
had formed part of the arches of Titus, M. Aurelius (later on attached to the arch of Constantine), Traian and Hadrian, and on the
reliefs showing the *adventus Augusti* of the arch of Constantine. The
arch erected by Domitian in particular, supporting two elephant-
quadrigae, which, too, is still visible on coins of M. Aurelius, is by
Kähler considered a Porta Triumphalis restored by Domitian after
the great fire. It was for this reason that Martial [5] could refer to it as
a *porta ... digna triumphis* and *aditus* to Rome; and it was also
for this reason that it was not destroyed after the *damnatio memoriae*
of Domitian. However, this does not prove anything with respect
to an original connection between *porta* and *arcus*, because in the
first century A.D. more structures adopt the arched shape, whilst,
in addition, it is possible that by this time the arch, which was
gradually turning into *arcus triumphalis* exerted its influence on the
shape of the restored Porta Triumphalis. Instead of a divergence of

---

[1] Liv. l.c. The Greek translation is ἀψὶς τροπαιοφόρος: i.a. Cass. Dio,
49, 15.
[2] For the first time in the third century A.D. in Africa: see Kähler, o.c.
464.
[3] o.c. 491.
[4] A. Philippi, Ueber die römische Triumphalreliefe. Abh. philol. hist.
Classe d. Sächs. Ges. d. Wiss. 6, 1872, 301; Morpurgo, o.c., on p. 140 ff. of
which all relevant pictures may be found; Kähler, o.c. 376 f., to which the
reader is referred for additional literature and references to pictures.
[5] 8, 65.

the third/second century B.C. a convergence in the first century A.D.!

I am quite aware of the fact that this summary survey fails to do justice to the complicated problem of the *arcus* and its origin, and that my choice in favour of a non-relatedness of *arcus* and *porta* is inevitably a subjective one, because complete certainty cannot be obtained. I leave the investigations on this matter all the more readily to the archaeologists because the present results of their research may not be expected to be of any help to our inquiry into the function of the Porta Triumphalis. If the oldest *arcus* known to us were supports of *signa*, not passages, they have, for that reason, ceased to be of any significance to our study, even if the *arcus* had been modelled after the Porta Triumphalis as far as outward appearance is concerned. That the Porta Triumphalis was arch-shaped is not sensational, that it was so from the outset, is unproved and unprovable, that it was a detached structure, is certain. If we want to discover the function of the Porta Triumphalis we have to proceed along a different road, a road by which many proceeded us, and along which we can follow our predecessors for quite a distance, but not all the way.

2. *The theories*

Ancient sources do not furnish an explanation of the meaning of the passage through the Porta Triumphalis. In Cicero's time it obviously meant no more than an honour forming part of the triumph, which itself was by then looked upon as nothing but an honorary distinction. Modern scholars, however, discovered in the original meaning of this passage a magico-religious aspect, of which parallels were found in ethnological literature [1]. In the seventh volume of the

---

[1] There is a very extensive literature about the ritual passage and the sacral meaning of gate or door. Some of the important works are: H. C. Trumbull, The threshold covenant, New York, 1896; W. Crooke, The lifting of the bride. Folk-Lore, 13, 1902, 238 ff.; A. van Gennep, Les rites de passage, Paris, 1909; E. Samter, Geburt, Hochzeit und Tod, 1911, 140 ff.; M. B. Ogle, The house-door in religion and folklore. A.J.P. 32, 1911, 251 ff.; Mc. Culloch in Hastings, Encycl. of relig. and ethics, 4, 1911, 846 ff., s.v. *Door*; J. G. Frazer, The golden Bough, index s.v. *Door*, and see below; S. Eitrem, Beiträge zur griechischen Religionsgeschichte, II. Kathartisches und Rituelles, 1, Rundgang und Durchqueren, in Videnskap. Selsk. Skrifter II, Hist. Fil. KL., 1917, 2 ff.; O. Huth, Die Kulttore der Indogermanen. A.R.W. 34, 1937, 371 ff.; S. Eitrem, A purificatory rite and some allied "rites de passage". Symbol. Osloens. 25, 1947, 36 ff.; see further literature cited in the text.

Golden Bough [1] Frazer collected a large number of rites which centred in the passage through a natural or constructed gate. The examples make it clear that such a passage was meant to free people from certain taints, or, animistically, from hostile spirits. On the basis of this knowledge, Frazer gave a similar explanation for three similar customs in Rome: the passage under the *Tigillum Sororium* and under the *iugum*—"it may have been the angry ghosts of slaughtered Romans from whom the enemy's soldiers were believed to be delivered" [2]—and the passage through the Porta Triumphalis, which "may have been for the victors what the yoke was for the vanquished, a barrier to protect them against the pursuit of the spirits of the slain" [3]. Already before that, Warde Fowler had interconnected the three rites [4]: what applied to Horatius, who, after murdering his sister, had to pass under the *tigillum*—"Horatius was undoubtedly *sacer*, i.e. taboo, in an infectious condition, dangerous to society" [5]—also held good for the returning army and its commander: "The army was guilty of bloodshed and had been moving in places where there were strange beings, human and spiritual, with whom it would be unsafe to come into contact" [6]. The passage aimed at lifting this taboo, at delivering from these taints. The vanquished enemy army was forced to pass under the yoke because "they had to be brought out of one status into another; they must not be any longer the same beings they were before the surrender" [7]. This explanation of the three customs is, in different formulations, but with the same fundamental idea, found again and again in later literature. Deubner [8] says about the Porta Triumphalis: "der Durchzug durch das Tor sollte bewirken, dass der ganze Unsegen des Krieges dahinter zurückblieb", and about the *sub iugum missio*: "man glaubte, der Feind müsste auf diese Weise alles zurücklassen was den Sieger irgendwie schaden könne" [9]. Noack [10] thinks that the

---

[1] J. G. Frazer, The golden Bough VII³, 1919= Balder the beautiful, II, 169 ff.

[2] o.c. 194.

[3] *ibid.* 195.

[4] Roman essays and interpretations, 1920, 70 ff. (= Class. Rev. 27, 1913, 48 ff.).

[5] o.c. 72.

[6] o.c. 74.

[7] o.c. 75.

[8] Die Römer, in: Chantepie de la Saussaye, Lehrbuch der Religionsgeschichte, II⁴, 1925, 426.

[9] *ibid.*   [10] o.c. 154.

Porta Triumphalis renders the commander and the army harmless, Petrikovits [1] looks upon the *porta* as a boundary between two sacral provinces, *domi* and *militiae*, F. Muller [2] explains the *porta* as a boundary between the realms of death and life, Dumézil [3] speaks, in connection with the *Tigillum Sororium*, of a *furor*, which Horatius had to get rid of by the passage before entering the city.

The most recent detailed study on this subject was written by H. Wagenvoort [4]. To the three 'rites de passage' just mentioned, he adds two more: the rite *sub iugum intrare* at the installation of a priest in North Africa, described by Nock [5], and the passage through the *Ianus* gate, which, up till then, had only by O. Huth [6] been viewed in this light. Of greater significance is the fact that Wagenvoort has attempted to create order in the chaos of the terminology used, by his introduction of the concept *mana*. He holds the view that in each of the cases referred to the passage through the gate served as a means to affect the *mana* of the person passing. In his opinion Warde Fowler's explanation of the *iugum* is not incorrect, "but seen from the conqueror's standpoint, the action is a *piatio*, having the object of depriving unworthy bearers of their *mana*.. For this is the real function of the gate: it draws *mana*—either good or bad—from him who passes underneath it" [7]. In his discussion of the *Tigillum Sororium* Wagenvoort stresses the fact that Livy characterizes the sacred act connected with it as a *piatio* and compares it with the *sub iugum missio*. His explanation reads as follows[8]: "The criminal's *mana* must be diverted, which here is effected by *transitus* which often takes the place of *contactus* respectively *contagio*: hence, the gate". Wagenvoort shares Huth's view that the *Ianus* was the gate through which the army in ancient times marched out and after the war returned into the city. "Now, marching out for war is a momentous start needing a 'threshold rite', not as a symbol but for increasing the strength of the men marching to war,

---

[1] o.c. 191.

[2] Studia ad Terrae Matris cultum pertinentia, IX, De triumphi origine atque ratione. Mnemos. 3e ser. 2, 1935, 197 ff.

[3] Horace et les Curiaces⁴, Paris, 1942, 100 ff. He does not connect it with the *iugum* or the Porta Triumphalis.

[4] Imperium, Amsterdam, 1941, translated and extended: Roman Dynamism, Oxford, 1947, 154 ff.

[5] Class. Quart. 20, 1926, 107 ff.

[6] Ianus, 1932, 56 ff.

[7] o.c. 155.

[8] o.c. 157.

for transference of warrior-*mana* (.....) Ianus (.....) imparts the particular strength of which the warrior stands in need, and he takes it away at their return"[1]. Finally, the Porta Triumphalis is given the following explanation: "The victorious army, and particularly the *imperator*, are laden with the *mana* from the blood of thousands slain in battle ...."[2] "This *mana*, then, has to be drained off, the army and its commander must be 'expiated', else the citizens would stand in danger of *'contagio usurpans'* .... Evidently, the passing through the *'ianus geminus'* was not considered a sure enough means of prevention and an additional gate, the Porta Triumphalis, was erected"[3].

Wagenvoort has in this way finally reduced the rites of passage of Rome, which had been bracketed together before, to one denominator. Now that we undertake the task of evaluating the theories described above—to which we are primarily incited by the fact that the rites show not only similarities, but also differences, which are at least as noteworthy—our criticism will obviously first be levelled at the last-mentioned theory, which, to an far greater extent than the preceding ones, attributed one fundamental pattern to all these rites.

3. *Criticism*

In the introduction to his book Wagenvoort quotes with approval a warning given by an authoritative scholar[4], not to identify notions such as *mana, orenda, tondi, wakanda*, which in our eyes appear similar. Still greater risks are attached to the search for such notions in a civilization which was lost so many centuries ago as that of Rome. Wagenvoort responds to this by the words: "...my researches have convinced me that between the Austronesian 'mana' and the Roman notion which I am going to define, there exists such a profound analogy that an identification seems justified, although we shall have to be careful not to draw hasty conclusions".

By his brilliant argumentation Wagenvoort has convinced many, including the present author, of the rightness of his view[5]. I shall on

---

[1] o.c. 160.

[2] o.c. 164.

[3] o.c. 168.

[4] E. W. Mayer, cited by K. Beth, Religion und Magie bei den Naturvölkern[2], 1924, 250.

[5] Cf. Bömer, Gnomon, 21, 1949, 354; K. Marót, Zum römischen Managlauben. Capita duo, Budapest, 1943/44; the criticism of Dumézil, L'héritage

many occasions have to make use of his results. This does not alter the fact that certain details have been criticized [1] and that I am of the opinion that, particularly in the matter of the interpretation of the passage-ritual, the author has failed to meet the standard of caution he himself imposed. On the authority of the expert in this field, F. R. Lehmann, Wagenvoort defines the *mana* of the warrior as follows [2]: "In the brave warrior *mana* manifests itself in strength and courage, especially in fortune and success. This success, or generally speaking the result or effect, is a determining factor in the mana-concept: "A thing is *mana* when it works, it is not *mana* if it does not work, said a native of the Fiji islands" [3]. It will be noted that the explanation of the first passage-rite, the *sub iugum missio*, the purpose of which was supposed to be that of "depriving unworthy bearers of their *mana*", is already in flat contradiction to this definition. Strictly speaking, the phrase "unworthy bearer of *mana*" is itself a *contradictio in terminis*, for, to quote Lehmann himself when he speaks of the warrior: [4] "nur im Erfolg liegt der Beweis seiner ausserordentlichen Kraft" and "Ein solcher Manakrieger ist also ein Mann, der bereit ist, das Tollste zu wagen, was unter gewöhnlichen Umständen und nach menschlicher Berechnung fehlschlagen müsste, *dem es aber glückt*." The winner has given proof of having *mana*, the loser has given proof of not having *mana*. No *mana* can, by whatever rite, be taken from a person who does not possess *mana*.

Wagenvoort tried to forestall these and similar arguments by saying, in reaction to the condition made by van der Leeuw, that it should be clearly indicated whether *mana* was used in the original, ethnological meaning, or as a general notion of "power", that this is difficult, if not impossible in view of the nature of our material. [5]

---

indo-européen à Rome, Paris, 1949, 49 ff.; La religion romaine archaïque, 33 ff., and elsewhere, levelled at Rose and Wagenvoort, is highly subjective and does not affect the essence of the theory of dynamism; see: P. de Francisci, Primordia civitatis, 220 n. 63. H. J. Rose in a paper: Mana in Greece and Rome. Harv. Theol. Rev. 42, 1949, 155 ff., takes all of his Roman material from Wagenvoort's book.

[1] See particularly Bömer in the paper referred to in the preceding note.

[2] o.c. 9.

[3] This formulation is encountered repeatedly in ethnological literature and in studies on religious history. It might be called the minimum definition of *mana*.

[4] F. R. Lehmann, Mana, Leipzig, 1922, 9.

[5] o.c. 131.

One may be content with this, provided one realizes the consequences of such a point of view. If one does not strictly adhere to the Austronesian concept of *mana*, one, on the one hand, loses the right of applying all kinds of typical characteristics of the original concept to the general notion of power, whereas, on the other, one runs the risk of broadening the concept *mana* to such an extent that it may without harm, but also, what is more important, without advantage be used in explaining the most widely different usages. In a case like this, one should remember Nilsson's warning [1] "dass ein Schlüssel, der alle Schlösser öffnet, ein falscher Schlüssel ist". Wagenvoort's treatment of the Roman passage-rites forms, in my opinion, a case in point. The *ianus geminus* served the purpose of imparting *mana* to the warriors leaving for war, the *iugum*, on the other hand, that of draining *mana* away, not, however, as we saw, from typical bearers of *mana*, but from men who had given proof of not possessing any. For the returning army the *Ianus* gate in turn served the purpose of draining away *mana*. For a triumphing army and its commander it was, however, too weak, and was for this reason replaced by the Porta Triumphalis, which was to drain away *mana* from the triumphing commander, who, strangely enough, had, according to Wagenvoort, covered his face with blood in order to increase his *mana* or to suggest its presence [2]!

When I conclude from the clearly arbitrary character of this explanation that the *mana*-notion is here taken so widely that Wagenvoort's interpretation does not constitute a real improvement

---

[1] M. P. Nilsson, Primitive Religion, 1911, 2. Warde Fowler, Religious Experience, 19, also warns: the theories of Mannhardt, Robertson Smith, Usener, Frazer, "have been of the greatest value to anthropological research; but when they are applied to the explanation of Roman practices we should be instantly on our guard, ready indeed to welcome any glint of light that we may get from them, but most carefully critical and even suspicious of their application to other phenomena than those which originally suggested them."

[2] That it is impossible to reduce all passing-rites to one denominator is demonstrated by a peculiar Hittite custom to march an army which lost a battle, between the two halves of a man, a goat, a dog and a pig that have been cut in two, and subsequently through a gate made of wood. On the one hand this usage reminds us of the *sub iugum missio*—but here it is the country's own defeated army which had to gain, not lose, power by the *transitus*—, on the other hand it cannot be compared with the passage through the Porta Triumphalis, because this was reserved for a victorious army. O. Masson, who discusses the Hittite rite (R.H.R. 69, 1950, 5 ff.) explains it, in view of numerous comparable ceremonies, as a purification or lustration. See further p. 144 n. 3.

on the earlier theories, which spoke of taint, infectious condition, taboo, *furor*, etc., I realize that I use what I hope are logical arguments. Even if I were, not unjustly, reminded that primitive man thinks 'prelogically', 'alogically' or 'otherlogically' [1], a re-consideration of Wagenvoort's arguments would be useful only if even one testimonium had been supplied which would prove that a gate or passage *as such* could in ancient Rome indeed function as a giver or taker of *mana*. To my knowledge there is no such testimonium. What is far more important, however, is that the ethnological examples Wagenvoort refers to, also fail to prove that a gate or passage supplied or drained away *mana*. I shall start from these examples and, after a glance at the ethnological literature, return to Rome.

In order to demonstrate that the *transitus* can increase *mana*, Wagenvoort cites a report in which a cowardly Maori is said to crawl between the legs of the chief of the tribe so as to acquire *mana* [2]. In order to prove that a gate may take away *mana*, he cites Kruyt [3], who reports that, when a rice-jar breaks during an expedition, the Toradjahs from the isle of Celebes neutralize the magic that has been freed in the following way: "before setting out again the next day two sticks are stuck in the ground on the path-way they intend to go, in such fashion that the upper ends cross each other. Then they tie a hair pulled from the head to an alang-alang blade which is then fixed to one of the sticks mentioned before. Now all members of the party pass underneath the fork formed by the sticks. The hair of the head is apparently left behind to receive the harmful magic staying behind in the sticks. So the men pass under the sticks, but the evil is arrested".

If the conclusion drawn from the latter instance is: "In other words, in this case bad *mana* is drained off by an improvised gate", and in the former the author speaks of the supplying of *mana* by a gate, it is clear that an important aspect of the matter is lost sight of: in the above examples the nature of the gate or passage is far

---

[1] This term was introduced by J. Winthuis, Einführung in die Vorstellungswelt primitiver Völker, 1931, 83.

[2] This story is found in Lehmann, o.c. 34. A similar one is told by Frazer, Golden Bough, II, Taboo and the Perils of the Soul, 1920, 168. A warrior who just won a victory, washes himself in the river. All the boys of the tribe swim through between his legs: "This is supposed to impart courage and strength to them."

[3] o.c. 155.

from arbitrary. In the former case the gate is formed by the chief, or, elsewhere, by 'a victorious warrior'; in the latter great emphasis is laid on the hair of the head. But that means that it is not the passage itself that matters, but the thing under which a man passes. The warrior imparts his *mana*, the hair—whose magic significance requires no further elucidation—drains away the *mana*, or rather, as Kruyt expresses it, "the harmful magic", through *contactus*, in this case = *transitus*. [1]

A study of the ethnological literature shows that these findings are universally applicable. Whatever the object of the passage —healing, increased fertility, speeding up a confinement, clearing of taints, release from evil spirits—the reports practically always explicitly mention the special material or the special shape of the passage. [2] Very often this passage is a hole in the ground, in a rock or a tree, which by its unusual shape has attracted the attention and is considered to be magically active; a constructed gate is, as a rule, made of branches or twigs, i.e. of living wood. Another passage often encountered is that between the two halves of an animal that has been cut up, etc. [3] The passage is not infrequently preceded by ritual ablutions and/or undressing.

These rites may be divided into two groups. There is one group of rites by which people seek "to interpose a barrier between themselves and the ghost", as Frazer puts it, in which phrase the word "ghost" may, as circumstances require it, be replaced by taint, *mana, funus, miasma*, etc. The material of the gate should possess sufficient magic power. If it does not, as, e.g. may be the case with the ordinary house-door, an active agent is added. Green leaves, a wreath, a horse-shoe, owls or bats nailed down alive are examples still generally met with.

---

[1] The classing of the *transitus* with the rites of *contactus* is important. It is to be regretted that Wagenvoort did not, on the basis of this theory, ascertain for the Roman material what the objects were with which man had to come into contact through *transitus*.

[2] To be consulted, in addition to the literature already mentioned, particularly: Bächtold-Stäubli, Handwörterbuch des deutschen Aberglaubens, 2, 1929/30, 477 ff., s.v. Durchkriechen.

[3] *Vide supra* p. 142 n. 2; further: Robertson Smith, The religion of the Semites², 1894, 480; Frazer, Folk-Lore in the Old Testament, I, 1919, 408; Eitrem, Symbol. Osl. 25, 1947, 36 ff.; *idem*, Beiträge zur griechischen Religionsgeschichte, II, Kathartisches und Rituelles, 1, Rundgang und durchqueren, in Videnskap. Selsk. Skrifter, 2, Hist. Fil. Kl., 1917, 2; M.P. Nilsson, Griech. Feste, 404; F. Schwenn, Die Menschenopfer bei den Griechen und Römern. R.V.V., 15, 1915, 80.

The second group consists of rites which are expected to have a beneficial or strengthening effect. Here, too, the material is of great significance, as appears from the example of the chief who himself constitutes the gate. Here the *transitus* is another form of *contactus*. As is clear from the wreath on the door, it is in many cases impossible to make a sharp distinction between the apotropaeic-cathartic rites and those aiming at an increase in strength [1]. In the presence of blessing, evil is absent; where illness is driven away, the strength of health is invoked. The distinction is, therefore, primarily a systematical one. What matters is, that in both groups the passage is merely the means by which the material is enabled to work its magic. The difference with direct contact may be that the purification or blessing is imagined as being made permanent by the passage through a gate. And this brings us to quite a different function of the gate.

In addition to the two groups just described, there is a third group of passing-rites differing fundamentally from the first two, a group whose discovery may be ascribed to van Gennep [2], who called them *'rites de passage'* in his book named after them. Van Gennep showed that the transition from one phase of life to the next, from one social position to another, was to primitive man symbolized, or realized rather, by rites which *in concreto* gave expression to this transition. He distinguishes 'rites de séparation', 'rites de marge', and 'rites d'aggrégation', which symbolize the renouncing of the old situation, the stage in between the old situation and the new, and the entering upon the new phase respectively. Of great importance is van Gennep's demonstrating that many rites too lightly termed lustration-rites, were in fact *rites de passage* (as defined by van Gennep), and thus were not meant to avert evil influences and to attract beneficial ones, but solely to concretize

---

[1] Virtually all scholars agree that the material is so confused that no absolutely certain analysis or system is possible. On the other hand, we do have a large number of reports in which people performing a rite give an explanation which holds good in their time. It is, for example, possible that a *ritus* which is originally dynamistic, is later on interpreted animistically. Applying this to the problem which concerns us, viz. that of the meaning of the passage through the Porta Triumphalis, we may find it impossible to trace its original purpose. This, however, does not imply that we have to discontinue our investigation, since a possibly later interpretation which is perhaps still discernible may, in view of the development of the triumph, be of far greater importance to us than the original one.

[2] A. van Gennep, Les rites de passage, Paris, 1909.

the transition from one stage of life to the next. Although not denying that "rites de fécondation, rites de protection et de défense, rites de propitiation etc..... qui ont un but spécial et actuel, se juxtaposent aux rites de passage ou s'y combinent, et de manière parfois si intime qu'on ne sait si tel rite de détail est, par exemple, un rite de protection ou un rite de séparation" [1], he has nevertheless proved in the course of a brilliant argumentation that rites such as baptism and circumcision do not have a cathartic meaning, but are to be looked upon purely as the concrete representation of the leave-taking from the old situation. Passing through a gate, in particular, has, as a *rite de passage*, an object of its own. There is an "identification du passage à travers les diverses situations sociales au passage matériel, à l'entrée dans un village ou une maison, au passage d'une chambre à l'autre, ou à travers des rues et des places. C'est pourquoi, si souvent, passer d'un âge, d'une classe, etc. à d'autres, s'exprime rituellement par le passage sous un portique ou par une ouverture des portes" [2].

I have deliberately given a short summary of van Gennep's argumentation here, because, however well-known his work may be, it is found again and again that the essence of his argumentation is wrongly defined or misunderstood. It is often thought that the passing-rites as described in Frazer, are fundamentally identical with the *rites de passage* as interpreted by van Gennep. Nothing is less true. In the former the *transitus* is the *means*, the material of which the gate was made up being of major importance, in the latter the passage itself is the *object*; as symbol and realization of a change in social or religious life. In her well-known book "Ianus and the Bridge" Louise Adams Holland remarks [3]: "One obstacle to the interpretation of the *Tigillum*'s purpose lies in the unnecessary assumption that all gate-shaped structures have the same function". We have seen that ethnology puts her completely in the right. If, therefore, we want to ascertain the function of one or more passing-rites in Rome, our first task will be that of finding out whether these rites differ among themselves, and whether these differences are of such significance that they warrant a classification of these rites.

In dealing with the *sub iugum missio* so much emphasis was, on the whole, laid on the *transitus* itself, that two important elements

---

[1] o.c. 15.

[2] o.c. 275.

[3] p. 88, in connection with the *Tigillum Sororium*.

of the ritual were either overlooked or neglected: the material of which the *iugum* was made, and the outward appearance of the defeated who were forced to pass under the yoke. The construction of the yoke was described by Livy [1]: *Tribus hastis iugum fit, humi fixis duabus superque eas transversa una deligata.* Although it is in principle possible that the *hastae* were used because they were literally on hand on the battle-field, it would nevertheless appear that the building material was chosen deliberately, in view of the special significance of the *hasta* in Roman and other religions. Among the places in which the pre-eminently magic power of the lance is described, one is of great interest to us. Pliny somewhere states [2]: *Ferunt difficiles partus statim solvi, cum quis tectum in quo sit gravida, transmiserit lapide vel missili ex his qui tria animalia singulis ictibus interfecerint, hominem, aprum, ursum. Probabilius id facit hasta velitaris evulsa corpori hominis, si terram non attigerit.* What idea ancient man formed of the magic of the lance, if he visualized it at all, is of less interest to us than is the fact that the lance performs its magic action not only when touched, as it is known to do, e.g. in the Roman wedding, but also when flying across. This datum is, I think, highly illuminating when we try to explain the expression *sub iugum mittere*, which, on closer examination, is rather peculiar. The verbum *submittere/subire* is, first of all, not usual in the meaning of "(cause to) pass through a gate", whilst, in the second place, *iugum* is nowhere found to denote a gate-like structure. *Iugum* is "a yoke for oxen, a collar for horses, a beam, lath or rail fastened in a horizontal direction to perpendicular poles or posts, a crossbeam" [3]. If we know that the *sub iugum missio* does not denote the passing through a gate, but essentially a "passing under something", the meaning becomes at once clear. The lance is obviously meant to work its magic, just as does the *hasta super tectum missa*, by being situated over the victim. We find another example of this in Rome: the sale of the war-booty *sub hasta*, of which the meaning was originally the same as that in the two usages mentioned above. We see, therefore, that it was not the *transitus* which was of primary importance, but the fact that it—or, more accurately, the action of *subire*—was the means by which the *hasta* was made to

---

[1] Liv. 3, 28, 11.
[2] Plin. n.h. 28, 33, quoted by Wagenvoort, o.c. 182.
[3] Lewis and Short, s.v. *Iugum*.

function [1]. The ultimate object may have been that of absorbing the power of the enemy and rendering it harmless, as is generally thought. The term *mana* had better not be used in this connection. This object of rendering the enemy harmless is, however, achieved in yet another manner. In his reports on the *sub iugum missio* Livy hardly ever fails to describe the outward appearance of the victims. They are *inermes nudique* (3, 23, 5), *inermes cum singulis vestimentis* (9, 4, 3), *nudi* (10, 36, 14), *prope seminudi* (9, 6,1). The stress Livy puts on this aspect is certain to have a meaning. Livy, no doubt, wanted to describe the tragic elements of the situation in the live-liest possible manner, but this does not alter the fact that the (partial) undressing and the taking away of the arms at one time had some purpose. What purpose can this have been other than that of symbolizing the total enervation of the enemy? Without arms, even without clothes, he has lost his identity and his power.

This shows that in the rite of the *sub iugum missio* the enemy is not made harmless by the *transitus*, as was often stated, but primarily by two elements: the magic power of the *hasta* and the undressing and disarming of the enemy. The *transitus* is not the object, but the means.

When we now consider the much-disputed question of the *Tigillum Sororium* [2], we notice—in spite of the arguments of Mrs. Adams Holland [3]—that the *Tigillum* is no more a gate than is the

---

[1] Cf. Petrikovits, o.c. 189; comparable in Rome is the taboo which forbids the *flamen Dialis* to pass underneath a vine tendril. A parallel, mentioned by Latte, after Halliday, Folklore, 35, 1924, 93, is found in the custom that a stranger visiting the Khan of the Tartars has to pass under two tied-up spears with a view to leaving evil taints behind.

[2] In addition to the literature mentioned above, see about the *Tigillum Sororium*: M. Cary and A. D. Nock, Class. Quart. 21, 1927, 122 ff.; Latte, R.R.G. 133; R. Schilling, Mél. d'Arch. et d'Hist. 72, 1960, 102 ff.; J. Gagé, Hommages W. Déonna, 255; R. M. Ogilvie, Comm. Livy, ad 1, 24, 1; 1, 26, 13, who follows Dumézil, Horace et les Curiaces.; S. Eitrem, Symb. Osl. 25, 1947, 40, has the improbable theory that the *Tigillum* interconnects two *vici*.

[3] Ianus and the Bridge, 77 ff. The remark on p. 78 n. 4 "*Tigillum* is extended to mean the whole monument, as *iugum* often means the whole gate-shaped structure, . . .", is made none the more probable by the reference to Varro, r.r. 1, 8, 1. Varro states there: *Quibus stat rectis vinea, dicuntur pedimenta; quae transversa iunguntur, iuga.* When, a little further on, he refers to a *genus iugorum* consisting of *restes*, it is clear that Varro, as is general in Latin, takes *iugum* as a horizontal connection between two points. W. Otto in R.E. Supp. 3, 1178 ff., and Rhein. Mus. 64, 1909, 466, already pointed to this characteristic of the *Tigillum Sororium*, and the counter-

iugum, with which it has often been compared. Livy [1] compares the *Tigillum* with the *iugum,* and Dionysius [2] also connects the two structures. Most important of all, however, is the name: a *tigillum* being a "kleiner Balken" [3]. The *tigillum,* therefore, is not a gate any more than is the *iugum;* it is a cross-beam and is also defined as such in Livy [4], who speaks of *transmisso per viam tigillo.* Dionysius is even clearer. In what is obviously an eye-witness report, he refers to a ξύλον, which has been imbedded in the walls of a street: δυσὶ τοῖς ἄντικρυς ἀλλήλων τοίχοις ἐνηρμοσμένον [5]. From a much later date we have a statement in Auctor. Vir. Ill 4, 9: *ubi patris lacrimis condonatus (Horatius) ab eo expiandi gratia sub tigillum missus, quod nunc quoque viae superpositum sororium appellatur.* Even at that time the *tigillum* was evidently still visible as a beam under which people passed. When we now find that Festus [6] describes the *Tigillum Sororium* as *duo tigilla tertio superiecto,* I cannot share Mrs. Adams Holland's view in considering this testimonium more reliable than the three previous ones, which described the *tigillum* as still existing. It seems more probable that Festus, misled by the comparison with the *iugum,* concluded that the *Tigillum Sororium* was constructed on similar lines. The conclusion we have reached, however, is that the similarity between *tigillum* and *iugum,* which does in fact exist, is not based on their both being gate-shaped, but on their both being fundamentally a horizontal lath or beam.

As regards the meaning of the *Tigillum Sororium* opinions differ. Mrs. Adams Holland considers it to be a primitive *Ianus* arch, and as such originally a bridge, H. J. Rose [7] connects *sororium* with *sororiare,* of which Festus [8] says: *sororiare mammae dicuntur puellarum, cum primum tumescunt,* and thinks that the *Tigillum* had a function in an initiation-rite of the *gens Horatia.* In my view both theories, which cannot be discussed at any greater length here, take insufficient account of the ancient characterization of the rite,

---

argument of Mrs. Adams Holland, who wants to demonstrate a Ianus-shape for the *Tigillum,* is not convincing.

[1] I, 26, 13.
[2] 3, 22.
[3] Walde-Hofmann, L.E.W.[3], s.v. *Tigillum.*
[4] I, 26.
[5] l.c.
[6] 380 (L), s.v. *Sororium Tigillum.*
[7] Mnem. 53, 1925, 409; Class. Quart. 28, 1934, 156, followed by Latte, R.R.G. 133.
[8] 380 (L), s.v. *Sororiare.*

which is so generally described as an *expiatio*, that I should not like to consider this characterization as a later interpretation. Here I prefer to follow Wagenvoort, who holds the view that the rite is first and foremost an *expiatio*, even though the expiation-rite proper is, according to Livy, performed by *sacra piacularia*, and the passage *sub tigillum* is an extra [1].

The main characteristics of the *iugum* and the *Tigillum Sororium* may now be summarized as follows:

1. Both are basically not gates, but cross-beams or laths. The construction of the *Tigillum* shows that the material of the piers was unimportant.

2. As may be expected in view of point 1, *composita* with *sub-*, not with *trans-*, are used to denote the passing under the structure.

3. The rite of *mittere sub iugum, sub Tigillum*, was accompanied by other rites, disarming and undressing in the former, *piacularia sacra* in the latter case.

4. The object of the rites has thus implicitly or explicitly been stated. The *sub iugum missio* is not only by the stripping, but also by the use of the *hasta*, explained as a rite by which the enemy is rendered harmless. The *Tigillum Sororium*, which, as is indicated by the name, was made of wood, and, according to Livy [2] *hodie quoque publice semper refectum manet*, in other words, was not replaced by a more durable stone structure, probably had a magic power similar to that of the *hasta*, and is, at any rate, characterized as a means towards *expiatio*.

In view of these facts we can class these two rites with the first two groups of passing-rites described in ethnological literature. In doing so we merely indicate the type, without giving an explanation of the rites individually. It is quite impossible to reduce the many aims of the rites of this type to one denominator, such as the affecting of *mana*, even though what is called averting illness or demons in one culture or period, may be looked upon as increasing *mana* in the next. [3]

---

[1] This is emphasized by Petrikovits, o.c. 190, who looks upon the passage under the *Tigillum* as a rite which is required to come back within the range of the city gods.

[2] I, 26, 13.

[3] In my view Wagenvoort, o.c. 156 n. 2, goes much too far when he thinks that Livy makes a mistake when he describes Horatius as passing *capite*

Having thus characterized two Roman passing-rites, we shall now examine the nature of a third, the passage through the Porta Triumphalis, and first of all try to ascertain whether typologically it belongs to the same group as those described above, or is to be classed in a different category.

4. An attempt at a new interpretation of the Porta Triumphalis

If we compare the characteristics of the rites described in the preceding section with those of the Porta Triumphalis, they are found to differ in every respect. These differences are briefly stated here. Some of them will be dealt with in more detail.

1. As is apparent from its name, the Porta Triumphalis is a gate. The following points show that the Romans considered it as such.

2. To denote the passing through this gate no *composita* with *sub-* are used, but the simple *ablativus* in Latin, the preposition διά in Greek.

3. No attendant rites, such as *piacularia sacra*, are known to exist [1].

4. No data have come down to us about either the material or the shape of the Porta Triumphalis. This cannot be said of *iugum* and *Tigillum Sororium*, which were obviously worth noticing. Of great significance is the fact that *iugum* and *Tigillum* are repeatedly compared in ancient literature as to

---

adoperto under the *Tigillum*, since, according to Wagenvoort, the contact between the *Tigillum* and the *piandus* would be realized better by his passing *capite aperto*.

[1] I share the view of Ehlers, o.c. 502, that a statement of Servius, ad Aen. 9, 624, that no bull must be sacrificed to Iuppiter, *nisi cum triumphi nomine Suovetaurium fiebat: quod tamen ideo admissum est, quia non tantum Iovi sed et aliis diis, qui bello praesunt, sacrificatur*, is corrupt, as it is contrary to his own, correct explanation *de albis tauris* (ad Georg. 2, 146). *Suove-taurilia* are always associated with Mars, who has nothing to do with the triumph. Wissowa, R.u.K.[2] 415 n. 1, thinks that they have been confused with the *suovetaurilia* of the *spolia opima* (for which see below). It is possible that there is yet a greater misunderstanding involved: in Macrobius, sat. 3, 10, in which Vergil's reference in Aen. 3, 21, to a bull-sacrifice to Iuppiter is discussed, one of those taking part in the discussion reproaches the poet with not knowing the religious rules: Ateius Capito in the first book of *De iure sacrificiorum* having given the rule: *itaque Iovi tauro, verre, ariete immolari non licet*. It is worth noticing that the animals mentioned here precisely make up a *suovetaurilium*. By a misunderstanding Servius might in this way have given this *suovetaurilium* a place in the triumph, where its sacrificing should have been permitted, not to Iuppiter, but to other war-gods.

shape and function, but that the Porta Triumphalis is never referred to in this connection. Nor is any mention made of a special purpose of the passage.

As the name and its original meaning were found to be of great use in defining the function of both *iugum* and *Tigillum*, we shall here, too, start by giving our attention to practically the only thing we know: the name Porta Triumphalis.

Although the term *porta* is frequently found to denote: "gate, entrance, passage, door, etc." [1], it first of all means "city-gate". It is, as we have seen, very unlikely that the Porta Triumphalis ever formed part of the walls of Rome, but this does not alter the fact that the name *porta* indicates that, concretely or symbolically, it must have given admittance to the city or the city-area. It means yet another thing: a *porta* which gives admittance to the city, must have doors which can be closed, certainly so if it served some special ritual purpose. Mrs. Adams Holland [2] very rightly points out: "The Porta Triumphalis may in time have become a permanent fixture, ready for repeated uses, but, if so, must have been blocked in some way to prevent passage between the proper occasions". By way of parallel she refers to the "jubilee door" of St. Peter's, which is blocked in between the ceremonies in which it functions [3]. The conclusion that the Porta Triumphalis could indeed be opened and closed might also be drawn from Cicero's use of the term *patuit*, but this term admits of a different interpretation. This is all we can learn from the term *porta*, and it is very little indeed. However, we have one more datum, the epithet *triumphalis*, which, although it is neglected by nearly everyone, in my opinion forms the key to the solution of our questions.

Against the generally accepted view that the Porta Triumphalis had an apotropaeic-lustrative function, an important argument was put forward by C. Weickert [4]. He posed the obvious question of why a defeated army did not need the purification a victorious army apparently required, both armies having been in contact with the enemy, death and blood. So far this question has not been satis-

---

[1] Lewis and Short, s.v. *Porta*.

[2] o.c. 90 n. 61.

[3] Cf. the Golden Gate at Jerusalem, which opens only to the great prophet who is to come, and the main door of the iconostasis in the Byzantine church, used only by the priest at a few crucial moments during the service.

[4] o.c. 25.

factorily answered. A remark such as: "ursprünglich muss der Durchzug für jedes Heer gegolten haben, gleich ob es siegreich oder geschlagen zurückkehrte" [1], apart from being purely hypothetical, is in flat contradiction with the only datum we have: the name Porta Triumphalis. This name being given, we have to take it as our starting-point, and should abstain from making convenient suggestions which implicitly deny the close connection between the Porta and the triumph. We have seen that Wagenvoort gave this connection its due by pointing out that this passing-rite had to be performed by a victor, because he, more than anyone else, was loaded with the *mana* of the defeated enemies, which was dangerous and for this reason had to be drained off before his entry into the city. However, we had to object to this view on account of an internal contradiction to the datum that the triumphator had covered his face with the blood—according to Wagenvoort the *mana*—of the slain enemies, and because of the too wide interpretation of the concept *mana*, which proves everything, and, therefore, nothing. However, the differences we discovered between *iugum* and *Tigillum* on the one hand, and Porta Triumphalis on the other, warrant the adding of one more argument. After Wagenvoort had arrived at the following definition [2]: "*Piatio, expiatio* is the lifting of the violation of a taboo, the redressing of the *mana*-balance; *piaculum* is the means for this lifting, sometimes the violation itself", he was fully justified, provided this definition should be right, to connect the passage under the *Tigillum* with a restoring of the *mana*-balance. The *ritus* is expressly defined as an *expiatio*, it is combined with *piacularia sacra* and concerns a "*mana*-bearer". With far less justification can the *iugum* be connected with such a restoration of the *mana*-balance, not only because the defeated enemy has ceased to be a *mana*-bearer, but also because the rite is nowhere defined as an (*ex*-)-*piatio*. For the reason stated in the preceding section, the *sub iugum missio* may nevertheless be compared with the *piatio* by means of the *Tigillum*. This does not in any way hold for the Porta Triumphalis, which lacks everything that could possibly make the others into a *piaculum*. It is not referred to as such, it lacks "magic" elements such as *hasta* or *piacularia sacra*, it apparently differs fundamentally from the other structures as to style of building, and it is never compared with them.

---

[1] Ehlers, o.c. 496, referring to M. P. Nilsson, Corolla Archaeol. 1932, 133.
[2] o.c. 147.

Having found that Wagenvoort rightly connected the Porta Triumphalis with the victory, I think we should go one step further and ascertain that the Porta was not open to all victorious armies, but only to the army which *triumphans intravit*. All scholars who have studied the problems concerning this *porta*, have taken it for granted that they were dealing with a primitive-Roman phenomenon, and for this reason tried to connect it with other Roman rites such as the *sub iugum missio*. If, however, we see that the triumph is essentially an Etruscan phenomenon, which was introduced into Rome at the time of the Tarquinii [1], the obvious consequence is that the Porta Triumphalis belonging to it may also be assumed to be of Etruscan origin. The Tarquinii built the temple on the Capitol, with which the triumph was closely associated. Why don't we assume that they also built the Porta Triumphalis—or at least the first Porta Triumphalis—since we know that the Etruscans had strict ritual regulations concerning the construction of temples and gates? [2] If this assumption is right, it also becomes clear why the Porta on the one hand, and the *iugum* and *Tigillum* on the other, show such fundamental differences, also, and particularly so, as far as outward appearance is concerned, as is indicated by their names: in contradistinction to the two last-mentioned structures, the first passage was not a primitive-Roman phenomenon. To its explanation, therefore, the Roman passing-rites need not be any more relevant than are comparable rites in other, also non-Etruscan cultures.

Although this means that we have lost Roman rites as direct comparative material, we have, on the other hand, gained benefits which more than counterbalance this loss. Instead of trying to show the highest possible degree of correspondence between three passing-rites attested for Rome by making light of distinct differences or ignoring them altogether, we can now, starting from what we know, look for parallels which may offer an explanation. So far we have found the following: The triumph is the entry of a victor, originally the victorious king, who for this occasion represents the god Iuppiter. This entry takes place through a special gate, which is opened for this ceremony only, and is not used at any other time. If we succeed

---

[1] *Vide supra* p. 89ff.

[2] In this connection one may think of the Etruscan rites concerning the founding of the city, dealt with in detail by Müller-Deecke, o.c. II, 146 ff.; about the Etruscans' obligation to construct three sacred gates, see the same work, p. 150.

in uniting these elements into one whole, our task has been completed as far as the Etruscan part of the triumph is concerned.
However, it is far from likely that some other culture will be found
to have a ceremony which consists of exactly the same elements as
were described above. Such a parallel would, no doubt, have been
noted before. There are ceremonies to be found, however, which are
clearly made up of elements also encountered in the triumph, and
which together may finally produce a complete picture of the original meaning of the triumphal entry. In this chapter I wish to draw
attention to only one of the combinations possible, viz. that of the
victor and the special entry. I think that outside Rome and Italy a
striking parallel may be found, which can explain at least one aspect
of the triumphal ceremony: the Greek εἰσέλασις.

In addition to many other distinctions, the winner of unspecified
games in Greece [1] was granted a peculiar privilege: he was allowed
to enter his native town through a gap in the town-wall, made for
the occasion. The only clear testimonium about the subject is to be
found in Plutarch [2], and reads as follows: καὶ γὰρ ὁπλίτης ἐπὶ πᾶσιν
εἰσάγεται, μαρτυρούμενος ὅτι τοῦτο τὸ τέλος ἐστὶ τῆς σωμασκίας καὶ
τῆς ἁμίλλης καὶ τὸ τοῖς νικηφόροις εἰσελαύνουσι τῶν τειχῶν ἐφίεσθαι
μέρος διελεῖν καὶ καταβαλεῖν, τοιαύτην ἔχει διάνοιαν ὡς οὐ μέγα πόλει
τειχῶν ὄφελος ἄνδρας ἐχούσῃ μάχεσθαι δυναμένους καὶ νικᾶν. From a few
remarks in Pliny's letters [3] we further know that this usage still
existed at the time of Trajanus, and we also know that Nero was
accorded a similar honour when, after his return from Greece, he
made his entry into Naples. He held similar entries into Antium,
Alba and Rome [4]. Pfister already said about these [5]: "Diese Ein-
holungen des Siegers sind die Vorfahren der späteren Triumphe".
J. Gagé [6] recently devoted an exceedingly ingenious paper to the

---

[1] Originally these may have been the Olympic games. Later on, however,
special ἀγῶνες εἰσελαστικοί are mentioned. There are scholars who think
that the εἰσέλασις only dates from the time of the emperors (G. Caspar,
in Daremberg-Saglio, IV, 1, 190 f., s.v. *Olympia*; J. G. Frazer, Ovid, Fasti,
4, p. 316 n. 6). I find it impossible to believe that such a remarkable custom
arose out of nothingness during the imperial period, and I think that such
a distinct connection can be demonstrated with other usages which are
linked up with the old Greek games, that the εἰσέλασις, too, must have
been old-Greek. Cf. Suet. Nero 25: *ut mos hieronicarum est.*
[2] Quaest. Conviv. 2, 5, 2.
[3] Epist. 10, 118 (from Pliny), 119 (from Traian).
[4] Suet. Nero 25; Cass. Dio 63, 19.
[5] R.E. 11, 1922, 2127, s.v. Kultus.
[6] Fornix Ratumenus, L'entrée "isélastique" étrusque et la "porta trium-

connection between the εἰσέλασις and the Roman passage through the Porta Triumphalis. Against his theory, that the Porta Triumphalis was originally a real city-gate, that it was normally walled up, and broken open for the triumph, so many objections are to be raised, both with respect to its argumentation and its conclusions, that I cannot follow the learned author here [1]. The comparison between the εἰσέλασις and the triumph, nevertheless, facilitates the search for the function of the latter, and in my opinion Gagé's paper points the right way. In both rites two elements are of paramount significance: the victor and the special entry. If an explanation had been given for this curious Greek custom, we might try and find out

phalis" de Rome. Bulletin de la Faculté des Lettres de Strasbourg, 31, 1952, 163 ff.

[1] Gagé's argumentation may be summarized as follows: the very ancient gate called Ratumen(n)a is, as legend has it, named after an Etruscan charioteer who, after having won a victory in the games at Veii, was taken to Rome by his bolting four-in-hand, which threw him off at the gate of this name; the horses running on as far as the Capitol (Festus, 340(L); Plin. n.h. 8, 65, 161; Solin. 45, 15). This is connected with another story, that the *quadriga* which by order of Rome was made by Veientan artisans, in the oven grew to such an extent that it could be removed only, according to Plutarch, Poplic. 13: τὴν ὀροφὴν ἀποσκευασαμένων τῆς καμίνου καὶ τῶν τοίχων περιαιρεθέντων. These two legends, which are also connected by others (*vide infra*), are by Gagé considered together to show the theme of what the Greeks called an εἰσέλασις, as he thinks that *fornax* (oven) has been confused with *fornix* (*arcus*, arch). What in the legend is said about the oven which had to be broken open, would in reality apply to the *arcus triumphalis* —according to Gagé originally identical with the *fornix Ratumena*—, which, just like the wall in the Greek usage, was broken open for the entry of the victor, i.c. the triumphator, and subsequently bricked up again. My first objection is against this. The term *fornix Ratumenus* was introduced by Gagé himself; in literature we only find *porta Ratumena*. Now we saw that a *porta* and an arch are two different things, whilst, in addition, the connection between the *porta* and the *arcus triumphalis* is, on the basis of sound arguments, even considered non-existent. But if the *porta Ratumena* neither was a *fornix*, nor was called by that name, no confusion with *fornax* was possible. To this may be added that we know nothing about a usage postulated by Gagé of breaking open and walling up the Porta Triumphalis, a usage which might be expected to have been recorded if it had existed. I do believe that the Porta Triumphalis had doors which were opened only for the triumph, but this has nothing to do with the breaking open of a *fornix* or *fornax*. Finally, what is most heavily stressed in the story of the expanding *quadriga* is that the four-in-hand is a *pignus imperii*. Power and mastery are consequent upon its presence. It is for this reason that Veii tried to keep it, and it is for this reason that the *quadriga*, once it had come to Rome, was put on top of the temple of the Capitol, painted red, just like the statue of Iuppiter itself (*vide supra*, Chapter II). No source fails to report that the *quadriga* entered Rome *excusso auriga*, which is in flat contradiction to what might be expected of an εἰσέλασις.

in how far this explanation also held good for the triumph. However, I did not find such an explanation either in Gagé's paper or
anywhere else [1], so that our first task will be that of looking for a
solution ourselves.

To do so, I start from a few other privileges the ὀλυμπιονίκαι were
granted on their return to their native town. In Athens they were
given five hundred drachms [2], free meals during their life-time in the
prytaneum [3], the *prohedria* at the games [4].

That these privileges were more than mere marks of honour is
apparent from a few other reports about victories and winners of
games. The winner's wreath was at his return dedicated [5] to the city-
god. Diodorus Siculus [6] tells us a well-known story, which is relevant
here: In a war between Sybaris and Croton the army of the Cro-
tonians is commanded, not by the head of the state or by a general,
but by Milo, who as an athlete had six times been a winner in the
Olympic games. Why was he given the command, and why, stranger
still, did he, as we are told by Diodorus, put the Olympic laurel
wreath on his head when going to war? The answer is not difficult
to give. If anywhere, the concept *mana* is appropriate here. We have
already seen that the person who once performed a remarkable feat—
which need not be a military one—had given proof of having more
power than his fellow-men. This power is exactly what the Austrones-
ians call *mana*: the magic quality which makes one man superior
to another. *Mana*, once having manifested itself, may do so again [7].
The fact that the *mana*-bearer who had given proof of his superiority
by his victories in the games, also took the lead in battle, and did
so with on his head the wreath of the victory, means, therefore, that
the man who had won once was expected to do so again. This idea
of "once a victor, always a victor" is convincingly expressed in a

---

[1] J. Hubaux, Ratumena. Bull. de la Classe des Lettres et des Sciences
morales et politiques de l'Acad. Royale de Belgique. 5 sér. 36, 1950, 341 ff.
and further literature referred to in the text.

[2] Diog. Laert. 1, 55; Plut. Sol. 23.

[3] Plato, Apol. 36 E; Plut. Arist. 27.

[4] Xenophanes in Athen. 10, 6.

[5] See Stengel, Die griechischen Kultusaltertümer[2], 1898, 186.

[6] Diod. Sic. 12, 9.

[7] Ethnological literature gives plenty of examples. As far as Rome is
concerned, the *equus October* will be remembered, i.e. the *winning* horse,
which evidently possessed so much *mana* that its blood, sprinkled on the
hearth of the *regia*, strengthened the state. See p. 373f.

usage recorded by Plutarch [1]. He reports that Spartan winners of the Panhellenic games had the right to fight in a war in the front rank, side-by-side with the king. A wrestler from Sparta who had refused a prize in money, had, with a smile, replied to the question of what he had gained by his victory: πρὸ τοῦ βασιλέως τεταγμένος μαχοῦμαι τοῖς πολεμίοις. This clearly shows the same fundamental thought: in virtue of their *mana* the ἱερονίκαι fight side-by-side with the king, himself *mana*-bearer *par excellence*.

This also makes it clear why the winner of the games had the right to have himself proclaimed a citizen of another town [2]. "Welche Stadt hätte es sich nicht zur Ehre angerechnet, ihm das Bürgerrecht zu schenken..." is Stengel's [3] explanation of this privilege. This may indeed hold good for later times, but originally this usage must have been based on some other consideration. The notion "profit" is more appropriate here than that of "honour": the winner of the games constituted a highly valuable possession for his town. As a winner he personified the power of his town, as a *mana*-bearer he *brought* and *embodied* luck and good fortune to his town and his fellow-citizens, not merely in military matters, but in all provinces of life, as is still observed in the Homeric kingship [4], and will later on be observed again in the Hellenistic king—σωτήρ, be it that the latter, as a result of age-long philosophical and theological evolution, was "theologically" different from the former type. Examples [5] show that towns tried to win such a *mana*-bearer over by means of marks of honour and gifts, since they expected him to use his *mana* for the benefit of the state, as Milo did in Croton and the Spartan winners for their town. Once we see this, we are able, I think, to understand the curious entry called εἰσέλασις.

For this entry part of the wall was, as we know, knocked down. Once the ἱερονίκης is inside the town, the wall is restored to its

---

[1] Plut. Lyc. 22.

[2] Paus. 6, 13, 1; 18, 4.

[3] o.c. 185.

[4] Od. 19, 109 ff., about which Nilsson, Homer and Mycenae, London, 1933, 220: "at the bottom there is the old primitive conception of the power of the king to influence the course of nature and the luck of his people."

[5] In this connection Gagé rightly points to the legend of the wooden horse in which Troy is predicted prosperity and luck once it has taken the horse within its walls. The breaking out of the gate indicates an εἰσέλασις! The Veientan *quadriga*, once it had come within the walls of Rome, also was a *pignus imperii*, the presence of which ensured the city's good fortune.

original condition [1]. This last addition appears to me to be the key to the secret, rather than the knocking down of the wall, which is given so much emphasis. In view of the great trouble to which the town went in order to keep or procure the winner, I think his entry must be seen in the same light. A summing up of what took place during his entry will at once yield the explanation: the victor enters the town, not via an existing gate—which is used by everyone and continues to function in this way—but via a gap in the wall that did not exist beforehand, and which, *after the entry will disappear again*. In other words: the town makes it impossible for his valuable honorary citizen and bringer of good luck to disappear again, removing all traces of the passage through which he entered. The good fortune the victor brought to the town is in this way to be retained. This kind of pious fraud is encountered in innumerable customs which aim at making it impossible for unwanted persons, powers or demons to return after they have been driven away. In many cultures the dead are laid out with their feet towards the door so as to prevent their return. But just as frequently we find that part of the wall is taken down for a funeral, and restored after the dead body has been taken away. Up to this day there are, in the Netherlands, houses to be found with a special door, which is used only when a dead body is carried out to funeral, and which is not opened for any other purpose [2]. Of this carrying-out of the dead body we find the exact counterpart in the εἰσέλασις of the victor in Greece. In Hellas itself there are, in fact, usages which, much more strongly than do parallels from other cultures, show that we are on the right

---

[1] The explanation of Plutarch is clearly a rationalization, even though he was well aware of the value the winner represented to his city.

[2] When Wagenvoort, o.c. 153, wonders whether the original motive might not have been that of preventing the door from being polluted by the passage of the deceased, and from polluting other persons passing in turn, he does indeed supply an example, but against it tells a large group of similar customs whose motive was indubitably to prevent the deceased from coming back. In most cases it appears superfluous and wrong to assume that this was a later animistic interpretation of an older dynamistic rite. Of only one interpretation, for example, allows the usage O. Huth observed in parts of Germany and Switzerland, of providing the house and the stable with two doors, which in due time are opened to enable the "Wilde Heer", the army of the demons, to pass through. If the house or the stable had only one door, the spirits would not be able to leave, and would, consequently, remain inside the house, to the great detriment of its inhabitants. (O. Huth, Durchzug des wilden Heeres. A.R.W. 32, 1935, 206). See for examples and their current explanations: Van Gennep, o.c. 224.

track. First of all we find in many Greek towns the driving-out of the
pharmakos, usually on the *Thargelia* [1]. This widely-discussed rite
is characterized by the taking around of a person singled out as the
scape-goat, for which purpose it was usual to choose a man who was so
poor that he had nothing to lose, or a criminal. This *pharmakos* was
subsequently taken outside the walls and either killed or, after his
death *in effigie*—e.g. by a jump into the sea—chased outside the
boundaries of the town-area. Against my view that these ἀποπομπαί
and the εἰσέλασις are exponents of one and the same way of reasoning,
it might be objected that in the last-mentioned instance it could
safely be assumed that the *pharmakos*, and with him the evil, would
stay away after his removal, but that, on the other hand, the continued presence of the ἱερονίκης, and with him the good fortune,
was not ensured by the closing of the wall: apart from the fact that
there were gates through which he could leave the city, it was
hardly to be imagined that he would have to spend the rest of his
life within the town-walls. Now I can point out that such possibilities
are apparently not consciously realized in the way of thinking which
gives rise to rites of this nature [2]: the possibility for the spirit of the
dead man to return through the main door when he finds the
passage through which he left the house closed, is simply not
considered. However, I am glad to be able to refer to a custom in
Hellas which proves this theoretical, general argumentation *in
concreto*, and which, in addition, shows an even closer parallel with
the εἰσέλασις than does the ἀποπομπή of the *pharmakos*. The custom
in question is called ἐξέλασις. With a description of it Jane Harrison
opens her last important work "Epilegomena to the Study of Greek
Religion" [3], and in her words it reads: "The little township of
Chaeronea in Boeotia, Plutarch's birthplace, saw enacted year by

---

[1] For Athens: Deubner, Attische Feste, 179 ff.; for the rest of Greece and
colonies (Massilia!): Nilsson, Griech. Feste, 105 ff.; for ethnological parallels
see the literature cited by Nilsson, G.G.R. I², 108 f.; particularly, of course,
J. G. Frazer, The golden Bough, IX, The Scapegoat.

[2] Recently I found in the "Life of Benvenuto Cellini" a parallel which,
I think, proves this. Mention is made of a convent "delle Murate" ("of the
immured"). It owes this name to the rite of initiation of the new nuns.
On this occasion, a part of the wall was broken down, the nuns entered
through the gap, after which the wall was repaired. The Dutch commen-
tator adds: "This is merely a symbolic action, since the convent has a normal
entrance."

[3] Published in 1921. The custom is described by Plutarch, Quaest. Conviv.
6, 8.

year a strange and very ancient ceremonial. It was called 'The driving out of Famine' (καλεῖται δὲ βουλίμου ἐξέλασις). A household slave was driven out of doors with rods of *agnus castus*, a willow-like plant, and over him were pronounced the words 'out with Famine, in with Health and Wealth'. The Archon for the year performed the ceremony at the Common-Hearth which was in intent the Town-Hall of the community and each householder performed it separately for his own house". It will be conceded that the slaves may be expected to return to their homes after having acquitted themselves of their tasks, since otherwise people could hardly afford such a rite every year. Just as here the slave, and with him famine, is driven out of doors, after which the slave can come back without harming the effect of this magic action, "health and wealth" are fetched into the town by the entry of the victor, and kept inside it by closing the gap in the wall [1].

Whether or not the victor subsequently leaves the town through some other gate is immaterial. It is true, of course, that the blessing is linked up more closely with the person of the *mana*-bearer than is hunger with the person of the slave, and that the rite of the ἐξέλασις may in this respect be considered more of a symbolic action than the εἰσέλασις. But as so often, it is difficult here to make a clear distinction between symbolism and reality [2]. Besides, since the intention is obvious, it is unnecessary to quarrel over the name by which it is called.

When we now return to Rome, I think that a comparison of the Greek custom just described with the triumphal entry into Rome is not only obvious, but also furnishes a more acceptable explanation of the passage through the Porta Triumphalis than was suggested so far. In both instances we have a victor returning to his native town. This return is attended with impressive ceremonies. Both in Hellas and in Rome the victor drives a *quadriga*. In both cases the entry is effected by means of a special entry-rite. I hold the view

---

[1] Cf. the Athenian custom to dig up the bones of a murderer whose guilt became known, and remove them outside the city. A murderer who was caught, was also driven away, for which the term ἄγος ἐλαύνειν or μίασμα ἐλαύνειν is used. Arist. Ath. Pol. 1; Soph. Oed. Rex 95 ff. and Jebb's note. In Rome Camillus was exiled because, according to Appian. Ital. 2, 8, he was responsible for harmful *prodigia*. Bayet, Liv. V, p. 145: "La cité expulse un porteur de peste, un maudit".

[2] About this problem: W. B. Kristensen, Symbool en werkelijkheid. de Gids, 1931, later on included in the collection with the same title published in 1954.

that the object the Greeks had in mind when they arranged an entry through a gap in the wall which was closed afterwards, was realized by the Romans by means of an extra gate. The entry through this gate, which was subsequently closed and not re-opened until the celebration of the next triumph, had to ensure the continued presence of the *mana*-bearer and of the blessing he brought upon the city [1].

I deliberately used the term "entry-rite"—not *rite de passage*— here, for, though the rite is not comparable with the passage *sub iugum* or *sub tigillum*, it is, strictly speaking, not a *rite de passage*, as defined by van Gennep, either. On the one hand, the rite is not connected with any apotropaeic or lustrative object, on the other, it does not symbolize a "passage à travers les diverses situations sociales". When van Gennep [2] himself allotted the Porta Triumphalis a place in his system—he speaks of "l'arc de triomphe"—, he could only do so because he explained it as the means to bring the triumphator back from the enemy world outside into the world of Rome. However, the problem of the classification has lost its importance for us.

I do not for one moment deny that the explanation given here is a hypothetical one, but may point out that the same may be said of all other theories. The advantage of my suggestion—Gagé

---

[1] Once one is inside, the wall of the city or the house forms a magic circle. This holds particularly for Rome, where Remus was killed by Romulus because the former, by jumping over the wall, had broken the magic of the wall, and where it was thought that the *virgines Vestales* could, by exorcism, keep slaves that had fled from leaving as long as they still were inside the city (Plin. n.h. 28, 13). A same thought underlies the regulation that a Roman soldier was forbidden, on the penalty of death, to enter the army camp in an other way than through the gates (Zonaras, 7, 3). In Greece we find stories related to the Remus legend. Mythologically: Poimander accidently killed his son when he aimed at the architect of his house who had jumped over the wall of the house; under similar circumstances Oineus killed Toxeus (Apollod. 1, 8, 1). Historically: Miltiades is punished by illness because he jumped over a wall of a sanctuary on Paros (Herod. 6, 134). On the magic of the circle in city walls: W. F. Jackson Knight, Cumaean Gates, 1936, 97; *idem*, Vergil's Troy, 1932, 105 ff.; F. Muller, Mnem. 3ser. 2, 1935, 182 ff. A report mentioned by Wagenvoort about a tribal chief on the Marquesas isles, who refused to enter a European settlement through the gate, but preferred to climb over the wall, finds its explanation, contrary to the suggestion made by Wagenvoort, o.c. 154, in my view, in the way of thinking just described: by climbing over the wall the chief breaks its magic, and thus ensures his way back; the gate might be closed after he had passed through it.

[2] o.c. 28.

preceded me, I gladly repeat this, be it without giving an interpretation of the data—is that it avoids all the objections that can be raised against the lustration-theories, and is based solely on a comparison between comparable quantities, which cannot possibly be said of Porta Triumphalis, *iugum* and *Tigillum*. Our theory will have a claim to probability if the combination of the elements of the triumph—*victor*, king, god, entry—, maybe two by two, are found to occur elsewhere, and if it can be demonstrated that the entry-rite in such instances has a meaning which is similar to the Greek εἰσέλασις. The fact that the figure of the triumphator was according to the Roman way of thinking a *mana*-bearer *par excellence*—we shall return to this aspect later—will also be important in connection with the explanation suggested.

One important argument in favour of a correspondence between εἰσέλασις and triumph I shall give here by way of conclusion. The Greek called the ceremony εἰσέλασις, by which it is characterized. As far as Rome is concerned, however, we do not learn much from the word *triumphus*. If, however, we search the literary sources for the most commonly used term for "to triumph", we do not find *triumphare*, but nearly always *triumphans urbem inire, in urbem redire, regredi*. In the first ten books of Livy alone, these expressions are found some twenty times. If the passage through the Porta Triumphalis were nothing but a lustration-ritual, it would be difficult to understand why so much stress was laid on the entry into the town. Also the formula by which commanders on coming home requested a triumph: *ut sibi triumphanti urbem inire liceret* [1], proves that the entry itself was looked upon as being a matter of vital importance. This again makes it clear that the passage through the Porta was not an accidental purification-rite, but rather constituted the centre of the ceremony, as in the Greek εἰσέλασις [2].

The triumph was, of course, more than merely the entry. However, it will now suffice to state that the second part of the theory: "sakralrechtlich bedeutet die Feier auf dem Capitol die Einlösung der beim Auszug in den Krieg gegebenen Gelübde, rituell dient die Prozession der Reinigung des Heeres vom Unsegen des Krieges" [3], has to be rejected. The first part of it will be discussed in the next chapter.

---

[1] For testimonia and a discussion of this formula see Chapter V.

[2] For the making of the triumphal entry the Greek term is εἰσελαύνω: e.g. Plut. Marc. 8.

[3] Ehlers o.c. 495.

CHAPTER FIVE

THE *IUS TRIUMPHANDI*

How could . . .
Prerogative of age, crowns, sceptres, laurels,
but by degree, stand in authentic place?
Shakespeare

1. *Introduction*

The triumph, which was introduced into Rome in the period of
the kings, was, as a ceremony, taken over by the republic, during
which it changed its character, gradually developing, or perhaps
degenerating rather, into a personal homage to the victorious
general [1]. The change from the monarchy to a diarchy entailed
juridical problems for the triumph.Whereas during the monarchical
period there was only one candidate for the triumph, it was possible
for two persons simultaneously to claim this honour during the later
republic [2]. Which of two consuls who together had gained a victory
was entitled to a triumph? And if a praetor had won a victory, was
it to him that the triumph was to be awarded or to the consul
under whose *auspicia* the battle had taken place and whose *imperium* was greater? What conditions did the victory have to
meet to justify a triumph, and who was to decide this? Rome would
not have been Rome if it had not developed an elaborate casuistry
in this field.

About this subject we know a good deal thanks to compilers such
as Valerius Maximus, who wrote a *caput de iure triumphandi* [3],
Aulus Gellius and Pliny, whilst also Dionysius and Plutarch, and
particularly Livy supply valuable information.

[1] About this development i.a.: A. Bruhl, Mél. Éc. Rome, 46, 1929, 77 ff.;
J. Gagé, Rev. Hist. 171, 1933, 1 ff.; R. Payne, The Roman Triumph,
London, 1962.

[2] To our argumentation it is irrelevant whether one holds the view that
the monarchy of the kings is immediately followed by a diarchy, as do Mommsen and Rosenberg, and, in a more modern form, Bernardi and Voci, or
first inserts a monarchical period into the republic, as do, among others,
de Francisci, Mazzarino, de Martino. Nor is it relevant to us what date is
taken for the transition from one form of government to the other. Surveys
of the theories are found, i.a. in E. Stuart Staveley, Historia, 5, 1956, 90 ff.;
A. J. Toynbee, Hannibal's Legacy, I, London, 1965, 557 ff.; cf. Ernst Meyer,
Staat², 476 n. 1.

[3] Valer. Max. 2, 8.

It is consequently not so much the incompleteness of the data which gives rise to our difficulties, as the fact that it is impossible to find out for certain which of the conditions are original—i.e. dating from the beginning of the republic—and which later additions. To this general rule there are a few exceptions, such as the condition that the victory should not have been won in a slave-war[1], of which we know that it cannot date from before the first century B.C. Even more frustrating is the fact that we are nowhere told the primary qualification the would-be triumphator had to meet. We do know, as we shall see, that the holding of *imperium* and *auspicium* form the principal qualifications, but if we try to ascertain which of these two ranked first, we are up against great difficulties. Here, as in nearly all other aspects of the triumph, opinions differ: Mommsen[2] holds the view that *imperium* (*maius*) takes priority, whereas Laqueur[3] puts the greatest emphasis on the *auspicium*, by which, as he argues, he shifts the accent from the political to the sacral-religious field. Since this problem has extremely important consequences, we shall in this chapter mainly deal with this controversy.

This really brings our study for the first time *intra pomerium*. The name of the triumph, the figure of the triumphator, the relationship with the *ludi Romani* and the Porta Triumphalis have each time taken us outside Rome's boundaries, either to Hellas or to Etruria. But jurisprudence and law are specific products of the Roman mind. Investigations in this field may help us in our search for the meaning the Romans attributed to the triumph.

However, before dealing with the qualifications the *victor* had to meet, we shall first give a survey of the conditions the *victory* had to satisfy.

The Romans distinguished three kinds of victorious processions: the triumph, the *ovatio*, and the *triumphus in monte Albano*. Of these three the last will have to remain undiscussed in this chapter. Held for the first time in 231 B.C. by C. Papirius Maso[4], and lacking the most important feature of the real triumph—the entry into Rome—, it was a substitute triumph for the general who had been refused a real triumph. On the *mons Albanus* could he make the

---

[1] Aul. Gell. 5, 6, 21.
[2] Staatsrecht I³, 126 ff.
[3] Hermes, 44, 1909, 215 ff.
[4] Val. Max. 3, 6, 5; Plin. n.h. 15, 126.

sacrifice which at the normal triumph was made on the Capitol.
The *triumphus in monte Albano* was indeed considered valid in the
sense that it was recorded in the *fasti triumphales*, but its late creation makes it to us, in this chapter at least, unimportant [1].

Much more interesting is the *ovatio* [2], which in all probability dates
back to the beginning of the republic. According to tradition [3],
P. Postumius held an *ovatio* as early as 503 B.C. Its importance lies
chiefly in the fact that its differences with the real triumph show us
the essential features of the latter ceremony, as regards external
apparatus as well as juridical conditions.

The general who was allowed an *ovatio* (*minor triumphus* [4],
ἐλάττων θρίαμβος[5]) made his entry into the city not on the *currus
triumphalis*, but on foot or on horseback [6], he did not wear the
ornatus triumphalis, but the *praetexta*, he did not carry a sceptre [7],
his wreath was not made of laurel-leaves, but of myrtle [8], he needed
not be accompanied by his soldiers, no trumpets were sounded but
flutes were played [9]). It is not possible to explain all of these differences. Suffice it to state that the *ovatio* lacks precisely those elements which make the triumph into the triumph: the *currus*, the
ornatus, the sceptre, the laurel-wreath, and, as appears from the
name, also the cry, *ovare* probably having come from **euaio*, "to
call *eua*"[10]. The sacrifice on the Capitolinus, on the other hand, is
common to the triumph and the *ovatio*.

When is an *ovatio* awarded instead of a triumph? On this subject we
have a statement by Gellius[11]: *ovandi ac non triumphandi causa est,
cum* (1) *aut bella non rite indicta neque cum iusto hoste gesta sunt,*

---

[1] Interesting is a remark made by H. A. Goell, *De triumphi Romani
origine, permissu, apparatu, via*, Schleizae, 1854, 4, that Papirius had been
pontifex and probably knew of an older form of the triumph on the Alban
mount from the *libri pontificales*.
[2] See the excellent paper of G. Rohde, R.E. 18, 1942, 1890 ff., s.v. *Ovatio*;
Mommsen, Staatsrecht I[3], 126 ff.; Cagnat in Daremberg-Saglio, 5, 1919,
491; Barini, Triumphalia, 11 ff.
[3] *Fasti triumphales*; Dion. Hal. 5, 47, 2; Plin. n.h. 15, 125.
[4] Plin. n.h. 15, 19; Serv. ad Aen. 4, 543.
[5] Dion. Hal. 8, 67, 10.
[6] Val. Max. 2, 8, 7; Suet. Tiber. 9, 2; Dion. Hal. 5, 47, 3; Aul. Gell. 5, 6, 27.
[7] Dion. Hal. 5, 47, 3.
[8] Aul. Gell. 5, 6, 21; Plin. n.h. 15, 125; Plut. Marcell. 22, 2.
[9] Plut. l.c.
[10] Rohde, o.c. 1891; Ernout-Meillet, Dictionnaire Étymologique, 684;
Walde-Hofmann, L.E.W.[3], s.v. *ovo*.
[11] Aul. Gell. 5, 6, 21 ff.; cf. Paul ex Festo 213 (L); Plut. Marcell. 22, 5;
Plin. n.h. 15, 125.

(2) *aut hostium nomen humile et non idoneum est, ut servorum pirata-rumque*, (3) *aut deditione repente facta inpulverea, ut dici solet, in-cruentaque victoria obvenit*. Of an *ovatio* of the first type no example is to be found among the thirty *ovationes* known to us [1], the second condition cannot be old, as we already noted, but the third motive may from of old have played a part, even though it is not to be assumed that the proviso for the holding of a triumph that 5000 enemy be killed [2] is an ancient one. The regulations concerning triumph and *ovatio* clearly underwent a development, since initially the condition of the *iustum bellum* held for the *ovatio* no less than it did for the triumph [3]. This was apparently changed in later years In my opinion Rohde [4] is right when he states: "Vielmehr ergibt sich als Funktion der *ovatio* ganz allgemein dies, dass durch das Vorhandensein dieser Form der Siegesfeier dem Senate ermöglicht wurde, Erfolge zu belohnen, die aus irgendeinem Grunde nicht triumphwürdig schienen, ohne dass dabei, wenigstens zu Anfang, bestimmte Grundsätze massgebend wären". In one or two instances we can still observe that an argument for refusing the triumph gradually turns into a norm. In 211 B.C. Marcellus is refused the triumph because of the *exercitus non deportatus* [5]. This argument is here used for the first time, but shortly afterwards the triumph is on three occasions (in 191, 185 and 182 B.C.) refused for the same reason [6]. The *ovatio* was awarded when the victory did not warrant a triumph. It was also resorted to when two equally meritorious commanders competed for the triumph on the strength of a victory they had won together, since it was unusual for two commanders to be given a triumph for one and the same victory [7]. In this case one was awarded

---

[1] Rohde, o.c. 1893.

[2] Val. Max. 2, 8, 1; Liv. 40, 38; Cic. in Pison. 26, 62.

[3] Val. Max. 2, 8, 7.

[4] o.c. 1893.

[5] Liv. 26, 21.

[6] On triumph and *ovatio* during this period see: Ursula Schlag, *Regnum in senatu*. Das Wirken römischer Staatsmänner von 200 bis 191 v. C., Stuttgart, 1968, 17-70.

[7] Weissenborn-Müller ad Liv. 28, 9, 9, give a few examples of a combined triumph, but they are far from certain. In 411 a.u.c. there are indeed two consuls triumphing over the Samnites, but in virtue of two different victories; in 425 a.u.c. the *fasti* mention two *triumphatores*, but Livy knows of only one. About the year 432 a.u.c. tradition is highly confused. With reference to this war Livy even speaks of a falsification of history (8, 40) and reports (8, 39, 16): *Hoc bellum a consulibus bellatum quidam auctores sunt, eosque de Samnitibus triumphasse*. It need not be a matter of one and

a triumph, the other an *ovatio*, as according to Rohde, was recorded six times: for the years 503, 487, 462, 390, 360 and 207 B.C.

On the basis of these and similar data Mommsen in his "Römisches Staatsrecht"[1] systematically arranged the conditions a commander had to meet in order to be entitled to a triumph. In view of the criticism passed on it by later scholars we have to give Mommsen's survey *in extenso* here.

2. *The views of Mommsen*

The right to a triumph, just like that to the title of *imperator*, belongs to the magistrate who at the time of the victory holds the highest, fully valid[2] *imperium*. This means that in principle only the highest magistrate can triumph[3].

Excluded from the triumph are therefore:

A. The magistrate who has resigned office. A *vir privatus* cannot triumph.

B. The person who did not have the highest command during the victory. The dictator takes precedence over the consul[4], the consul over the praetor[5]. If the victory is won by two consuls, the triumph is awarded to the one, who according to the *turnus*, had the *imperium* and the *auspicium* during the battle[6].

C. The magistrate who, though being the highest official, holds a magistracy extraordinary, as the *tribuni militum consulari potestate*[7].

D. The magistrate who remains in function after the expiration of his term of office. If he retains his *imperium* by prorogation,

---

the same battle. For this year the *fasti triumphales*, in fact, report: *L. Fulvius ... de Samnitibus*; *Q. Fabius ... de Samnitibus et Apuleis*. Plin. n.h. 7, 136, refers only to the triumph of Fulvius. The year 500 a.u.c. shows the only double triumph before the second century B.C. It is worth noticing that the two generals do not triumph on the same day. The triumph of Marius and Catulus (Plut. Mar. 27, 9; 44, 8 and Cic. Tusc. 5, 19, 56) is too late to serve as a criterion. Marius made more changes in the usages connected with the triumph!

[1] Staatsrecht I³, 126 ff.

[2] The *lex curiata* is a *conditio sine qua non* for the triumph: Cic. ad Att. 4, 16, 12. On this subject see p. 319-349.

[3] Liv. 28, 38, 4; 31, 20, 3. Cf. Val. Max. 2, 7, 8; Appian. Hisp. 38.

[4] This happened i.a. in 494 B.C. (Liv. 2, 31) and in 431 B.C. (Liv. 4, 29, 4).

[5] This applies, e.g. to the victory of 241 B.C. (Val. Max. 2, 8, 2).

[6] Liv. 28, 9, 10.

[7] Zonaras, 7, 18, confirmed by the *fasti triumphales*.

it is, in principle, still impossible for him to triumph because the *imperium* of the promagistrate becomes ineffective when he crosses the *pomerium*. This rule was, however, never enforced [1]. In practice the *imperium* of these officials was extended to the end of the day of the triumph [2].

E. The magistrate who has handed over the command and consequently cannot take his troops to Rome [3].

F. The deputy of the commander who is absent, and the second in command of the commander who is present [4], because the triumph depends, not on the military success, but on the right of the office, and both fight *alienis auspiciis*.

G. The promagistrate whose *imperium* is purely extra-urban, as P. Scipio, who, without having held an office, was given *imperium* as a *privatus*. He was, in 206 B.C., for this reason refused the triumph [5].

The triumph is the only occasion at which the magistrate can *intra pomerium* exercise the same authority as if he were in the field of battle (*militiae*). It seems probable that in view of this the right of provocation was suspended for this day, whilst *inside* the city the *fasces cum securibus* were carried, the axes by which in olden times distinguished prisoners of war were killed [6]. In ancient times, Mommsen states in conclusion, the commander was perfectly free to triumph. Not until later did the senate assume the right to decide in this matter, whilst also the people, through the *tribuni plebis*, could mark their approval or disapproval.

A study of Mommsen's systematic arrangement of the facts shows that to him the holding of the *imperium maius* was the fundamental condition for the triumph. Apparently with good reason: all the conditions we noted may be derived from this basic requirement. We should, therefore, not hesitate to accept this datum as the basis for our argumentation, and to consider its consequences, if Laqueur, in a paper published in 1909 [7], had not arrived at quite a different conclusion. The title of his treatise reads: "Über das Wesen des

---

[1] Oldest example of a triumph of a promagistrate: Liv. 8, 26, 7.

[2] Liv. 26, 21; 45, 35.

[3] Liv. 31, 49, 10; 28, 9, 10; 26, 21; 45, 38, 13.

[4] Cass. Dio, 43, 42; 48, 41; 48, 42; 49, 21; 51, 21; 24, 25.

[5] Liv. 28, 38, 4; cf. 31, 20, 3; 32, 7, 4; Cic. de imperio Cn. Pompei, 21, 62. Pompey is the first to triumph as a private citizen.

[6] Liv. epit. 11; 26, 13, 15.

[7] R. Laqueur, Hermes, 44, 1909, 215 ff.

römischen Triumphs". The author appears to be of the opinion that
an inquiry into its juridical aspects can provide the key to the essence
of the triumph. Many have not only—rightly—applauded this fundamental thesis, but have also taken over Laqueur's conclusion. The
last-mentioned fact is surprising because Beseler [1] in the same
volume of *Hermes* in which Laqueur's paper appeared, published a
reaction which virtually tears Laqueur's argumentation to shreds.
The fact that this criticism was neglected becomes understandable—
if not forgivable—when it is found that Beseler in a particularly
forbidding jargon advances arguments which on account of their
strictly juridical character are, for the outsider, difficult to evaluate,
whilst, in addition, his argumentation is occasionally directed too
much *ad hominem*. This does not alter the fact that, in my view,
many of his arguments are sound and deserve more attention than
they were given. On the other hand, I do not always agree with
Beseler, and think that the criticism of Laqueur's theory should in
many instances follow a different course.

When in the next section Laqueur's theory is discussed, we adopt
a method which may not be the most attractive one for the reader:
brief summaries of sections of Laqueur's argumentation will each
be followed by criticism. It was not only Laqueur's step-by-step-
method of argumentation, in which the conclusion of one section
forms the starting-point for the next, which made us follow this
method; it was particularly the fact that each of these sections is in
itself significant in the interpretation of the triumph which made us
decide to evaluate each of them individually. Every time Beseler is
followed in this respect, this is indicated in a foot-note.

3. *The theory of Laqueur, viewed critically*

I A. The triumph as a homage to the gods according to
     Laqueur

In more than one place Livy gives the formulation of the request
for a triumph a commander addressed to the senate [2]. In a few instances we find a two-fold request, such as: *ut pro re publica fortiter feliciterque administrata et dis immortalibus haberetur honos
et ipsis triumphantibus urbem inire liceret...* [3]. That this for-

---

[1] G. Beseler, Triumph und Votum, Hermes, 44, 1909, 352 ff.

[2] Liv. 28, 9, 7; 38, 44, 9; 39, 4, 2; cf. 37, 59, 1.

[3] Liv. 28, 9, 7, where two consuls simultaneously ask for a triumph;
further: Liv. 38, 44, 9; 39, 4, 2.

mula does not refer to two different ceremonies but to one and the same ceremony, is proved by Livy, 37, 59, 1, *Merito ergo et dis immortalibus quantus maximus poterat habitus est honos ....et imperatori triumphus est decretus.* When now Livy goes on to say: *triumphavit mense intercalario...*, it is clear, according to Laqueur, that *honos* and *triumphus* both refer to one ceremony. When further on Livy, 45, 39, 10, says: *dis quoque enim, non solum hominibus debetur triumphus*, it follows from this: "Also muss der Triumph eine sakrale Institution sein " (216). Also in the well-known speech of Manlius [1] the speaker puts the honour of the gods on a level with his own honour. If the senate were to refuse a triumph, he argues, this would be an insult not only to the commander, but also to the gods. A final consequence is found in Livy, 41, 6, 4, in which a triumph is requested in the simple formulation: *ut dis immortalibus haberetur honos.*

At first sight this argumentation seems to be unsettled by another place in Livy. Referring to a similar two-fold request as mentioned above, Livy, 28, 9, 9, says: *et supplicatione amborum nomine et triumpho utrique decreto...* In this case the *honos deorum* would have to be the *supplicatio*, so that the double request would indeed refer to two different ceremonies: the *supplicatio* for the gods and the triumph for the commander. This *supplicatio* has, however, already taken place [2], so that there was no longer any need to ask for it. Now Laqueur thinks that *supplicatio* in the last-mentioned text does not have its technical meaning of "thanksgiving-feast", but gives expression to that part of the triumph which may be looked upon as *honos deorum*: the sacrifice on the Capitol. He does concede that the official *supplicatio* and the triumph are related. The formula *ut dis haberetur honos* we encountered in the request for a triumph, is also found in the request for a *supplicatio* [3]. Also as regards the argumentation of the request the same formulation is used in both cases: *quod bene ac feliciter rem publicam administrarit.* [4]

Laqueur concludes from all this that at the time of Livy the triumph combined two aspects: the sacral one—thanking the gods—, and the secular one—paying tribute to the commander—. Originally, however, the triumph must have been purely sacral.

---

[1] Liv. 38, 48, 13 ff.
[2] Liv. 27, 51, 8 ff.
[3] e.g. Liv. 39, 38, 5; 41, 17, 3.
[4] e.g. 38, 48, 14.

I B. Criticism

When I shall now attempt to prove that the argumentation presented above is unsound, I do not in any way wish to deny that the triumph was a sacral institution—the triumphator impersonating Iuppiter and the sacrifice on the Capitol alone testify to this—, but I do wish to deny that its sacral nature is proved by Laqueur's argumentation. The main object, however, is to make clear that it is definitely not the triumph that is meant by the *honos deorum* in the formulae quoted above.

When a general had won a victory, he at once sent a laurelled letter about it to Rome [1]. In this letter he could ask for a thanksgiving-feast, a *supplicatio "suo nomine"*, which feast could be celebrated immediately, i.e. in the absence of the general. This thanksgiving-feast for the gods, purely religious in origin, has been attested 65 times for the republic [2], and was, according to Cicero [3], refused only twice. The stereotyped, often attested formulation of a request for a *supplicatio* is: *ut dis immortalibus haberetur honos* [4].

Another privilege the commander could be granted was the triumph, a ceremony which required the presence of the commander in Rome, because, in the most literal sense of the word, he himself played the leading part in it. The general often asked in one letter for both the *supplicatio* and the triumph. L. Halkin [5] calculated that of the 65 *supplicationes* only ten were not combined with a triumph. In a letter to Cicero, Cato [6] writes: *quodsi triumphi praerogativam putas supplicationem.... neque supplicationem sequitur semper triumphus.* Although, therefore, the *supplicatio*—often held before the return of the general—was very often followed by the triumph, this was not a hard and fast rule. Even though in the long run practically the same conditions held for both ceremonies, there were originally differences, also as far as the conditions were concerned:

---

[1] The data now following have been taken from L. Halkin, La supplication d'action de grâces chez les Romains. Bibliothèque de la Faculté de Philosophie et Lettres de l'Université de Liège, Fasc. 128, 1953, 87 ff.

[2] L. Halkin, o.c. 16-76.

[3] Cic. de prov. cons. 7, 15; in Pis. 92; de off. II, 50; ad Quint. fr. 2, 6, 1; It is known to have happened in more instances, however. See Halkin, o.c. 94 f.

[4] I here mention only those testimonia of which there is not the slightest doubt that they refer to the *supplicatio*: Liv. 26, 21, 3; 39, 38, 5; 41, 17, 3; 42, 9, 3; 37, 59, 1; 35, 8, 3.

[5] o.c. 111.

[6] In Cicero, ad Fam. 15, 5, 2.

in 209 B.C. Scipio was not allowed a triumph because he had not held a magistracy, but a *supplicatio nomine eius* did take place [1].

If, therefore, there were two ceremonies a general could ask for, of which one—the *supplicatio*—was, and was called, purely a homage to the gods, whilst the other was the triumph, it is obvious that the two-fold question: *ut dis immortalibus honos haberetur et sibi triumphanti urbem inire liceret*, refers to two different ceremonies. There are plenty of texts which make this abundantly clear. Livy, 26, 21 reports that Marcellus asks for the triumph: *id non impetravit.* This leaves the problem whether it is fitting *cuius nomine absentis ob res prospere ductu eius gestas supplicatio decreta foret et dis immortalibus habitus honos, ei praesenti negare triumphum*... More clearly the difference between the two ceremonies cannot be illustrated. Neither is there any doubt as to Livy, 33, 22, 5, where the *tribuni plebis* decide that the consul C. Cornelius has performed such feats of arms *ut non magis de triumpho eius quam de honore diis immortalibus habendo dubitari possit.* Exactly the same state of affairs is found in a text Laqueur quotes in support of his thesis [2]. First a request: *ut dis immortalibus haberetur honos et ipsis triumphantibus urbem inire liceret.* After this the decision: *et supplicatione amborum nomine et triumpho utrique decreto.* That it is not one single ceremony that is referred to is proved not only by "*et*" used twice, but chiefly by the contrast between *amborum nomine* (collectively)—*nomine eius* is, moreover, the stereotyped formulation in a *supplicatio* —and *utrique* (for each separately)[3]. It will be obvious now that also in the other texts brought forward by Laqueur *honos deorum* is always the *supplicatio* and not the triumph. Weissenborn-Müller have so little doubt about this that they assumed, in the only place in which a phrase *postulandos honores meritos, ut diis immortalibus haberetur honos* [4], is followed by the statement that the triumph did

---

[1] Liv. 27, 7, 4.

[2] Liv. 28, 9, 9.

[3] Thus Beseler, o.c. 353. The double *supplicatio* which Laqueur considers impossible is not difficult to explain. Ad Liv. 28, 9, 9, Weissenborn-Müller point out that there are more instances in which a victory was twice celebrated by a thanksgiving-festival, each of which is called *supplicatio*: the first after the news of the victory has been received, the second at the return of the general. Examples are: Liv. 37, 52, 2, and 37, 59, 1. The distinction: *habitus est honos ... decretus triumphus* also, for that matter, indicates two separate ceremonies.

[4] Liv. 41, 6, 4.

indeed take place [1], "dass die Worte umgestellt und lückenhaft sind", because, as is generally known, *honos deorum* is never found in the formula used for the triumph, but always in the formula for the *supplicatio* [2].

This leaves the text: *dis quoque enim, non solum hominibus debetur triumphus* [3]. First of all it should be noted that this sentence was taken from a long speech, in which a consul defends the right of his friend L. Aemilius Paullus to the triumph, and to this end uses all, particularly rhetoric means. The plural *dis* shows how closely we have to guard against taking such texts literally: the triumph was held, not for the gods generally, but purely and solely for Iuppiter. All the same the triumph does indeed have an aspect of homage to the gods: what else is the sacrifice on the Capitol? What I object to is the identification defended by Laqueur, of the *honos deorum* with the triumph, and the consequences this entails. One of these consequences is that a conception which considers the triumph primarily a homage to the gods, pushes the man who should be in the centre, the triumphator, more and more into the background, which, as will be seen, has proved fatal to the investigations on the triumph.

Finally, one question appears justified: If the triumph had indeed been fundamentally a thanksgiving-feast for the gods on the occasion of a victory, why was it so often preceded by the *supplicatio*, which decidedly bore the character of a thanksgiving-feast? Neither Laqueur nor any of his followers provide an answer to this question.

II A. The relation between triumph and *auspicium* according to the ancient texts quoted by Laqueur

According to Mommsen, *imperium* ranked highest among the conditions for the triumph. If, however, the triumph is a sacral institution, the first requisite must have been, according to Laqueur, not *imperium*, but *auspicium*. In view of the fact that the holder of the *imperium* at the same time had *auspicium*, it is, in principle,

---

[1] It appears certain that the text is corrupt. See Weissenborn-Müller *ad loc.*

[2] The *supplicatio* by itself is never asked for, the triumph by itself is, the term *honos deorum* never being used: Liv. 10, 37, 6; 26, 21, 2; 31, 47, 7; 31, 20, 1; 33, 22, 1; 36, 39, 5; 42, 21, 7; 39, 29, 4.

[3] Liv. 45, 39, 10, and other similar texts; Liv. 38, 48, 14. The characteristic thing is that these instances concern a speech.

impossible to ascertain on the strength of which of the two he performs a certain act. In some texts, however, the *auspicium* is found to be emphasized when a triumph was involved.

1. In Livy 28, 9, 10, there are two candidates for the triumph, one of whom is chosen *quoniam* ..... *eo die, quo pugnatum foret, eius forte auspicium fuisset.*

2. In Livy 34, 10,5, the triumph is refused *quod alieno auspicio... pugnasset.*

3. Livy 31, 48, 6: *nihil praeter res gestas et an in magistratu suisque auspiciis gessisset, censebant spectare senatum debere.*

By the *auspicium*—here in the sense of the observation of the flight of the birds [1]—the consul, on entering upon his office, places the year that is to come under the protection of the gods. If he goes to war, another *auspicium* is needed, which holds especially for this war and no longer; on the day of the battle one more *auspicium* is required which is valid for that day only. It is in connection with this that twice a triumph was refused on the grounds that the victory was won *in aliena provincia* [2], and, it is added in both instances, *et alieno auspicio.* A magistrate's *auspicium* is in fact, according to Laqueur, valid only in his own province.

II B. Criticism

The thesis with which Laqueur starts is incorrect. According to him the *auspicium* is characteristic of sacral acts, the *imperium* of profane ones. Nothing is less true. First of all it has, to the present day, remained a point of controversy whether the *auspicium* and the *imperium* may be distinguished as the exponents of the sacral and the temporal power, respectively, of the magistrate. There is no agreement about the interrelation of the two concepts in the recurrent formula *imperium auspiciumque* [3]. One question one is faced with immediately is: did the magistrate hold the *auspicium* in virtue

---

[1] Laqueur does not always clearly distinguish between the meanings of "the competence to observe the flight of the birds", and "the observation of the flight of the birds".

[2] Liv. 28, 9, 10; 34, 10, 5.

[3] Since the problem will be broached in the second part of our study, I here merely quote the, in my view, correct definition of Beseler, o.c. 353: "*Auspicium* ist weder der Inbegriff des magistratischen sacralrechtlichen Könnens, noch die Grundkraft, aus der dieses gesamte Können abflösse, sondern die Befähigung des Magistrates zu dem specialen Sacralacte der Auspication."

of his *imperium* or was it the other way round? Or were both granted independently of each other, if there was any granting at all? This is not the place to go into these highly intricate problems. What can be stated with certainty, however, is that an act does not become sacral because it takes place *auspicato*. It is typical of the Romans that they did not start an action of any significance until after they had consulted the auspices, in accordance with the rule: *ut nihil belli domique nisi auspicato gereretur* [1]. Whatever the nature of the action, the only thing the gods are asked by means of the *auspicatio* is whether it may be carried out *hic et nunc*. The nature of the action is not affected in any way by the *auspicatio*. Appointing magistrates, convening the senate, going to war, are all profane events, which nevertheless take place *auspicato* [2]. While, on the one hand, we see that an *auspicatio* does not give an act a sacral character, it is clear that, the other way round, there is no justification whatever for the thesis that a sacral act, because of its sacral nature, should be determined by the *auspicium*.

Besides, the places in Livy which are supposed to prove this view, present a picture which is quite different from the one outlined by Laqueur. To demonstrate this I start from a text that was not quoted by Laqueur, but which is of vital importance to our problem.

Livy, 40, 52, 5, reports that L. Aemilius Regillus fastens a *tabula* to a temple which, among other things, reads that a victory was won *"auspicio, imperio, felicitate, ductuque eius"*. In this case we are so fortunate as to be able to prove the authenticity of this formulation—which, for that matter, is also clear from the archaic context —because we find practically the same formulation in the well-known *titulus Mummianus* [3]:

> *ductu auspicio imperioque eius Achaia capta*
> *Corinto deleto Romam redieit triumphans*
> *ob hasce res bene gestas quod in bello voverat*
> *hanc aedem et signu Herculis Victoris*
> *imperator dedicat* [4].

Since these are the oldest formulae we know, which, moreover, are couched in an official style, we have to assume that they contain the oldest conditions a victory has to fulfil. An interpretation of

---

[1] Liv. 1, 36, 6; cf. 6, 41, 4.

[2] Wissowa, R.E. 2, 1896, 2585, s.v. *Auspicium*.   [3] C.I.L. I, 541.

[4] A *tabula* of T. Sempronius Gracchus only reads *imperio auspicioque* (Liv. 41, 28, 8).

this formula [1] and an exposition about the meaning of the four terms, *ductus, auspicium, imperium* and *felicitas* would be premature and defeat the object of this chapter. We shall have to return to these much-discussed concepts later on. What is important for the present is that the formula places four (or three) qualities or circumstances side by side as being of equal value, and does not give priority to one of them.

The texts quoted above date from about the same period as that in which Plautus wrote his works. In this writer [2] we once more find the complete formulation as shown on the *titulus Mummianus*, in a passage in which a request for a triumph is parodied: *ut gesserit rem publicam ductu imperio auspicio suo*. Here, too, *felicitas* is not included. It has in such a formula been recorded only once, viz. in the place in Livy referred to above [3], perhaps because *felicitas*, unlike the others, is not a strictly constitutional condition. More clearly than any theoretical exposition could do it, Plautus illustrates the development of this formula: what in verse 196 is called *ductu, imperio, auspicio*, reads in verse 192 *imperio atque auspicio*, and in verse 657 *auspicio atque ductu*. It shows that the tendency to simplify and vary the unmanagable, clumsy formula in a literary work already existed in Plautus' time. This development continued, with the result that Livy, in texts which deal with the command during the war, uses *imperio auspicioque* [4], *ductu auspicioque* [5], or *auspicio* [6] by itself, *ductu* [7] by itself, or *imperio* [8] by itself.

We have now found two things which are of importance:

1. The texts show that the terms *auspicium* and *imperium*, either in combination or by themselves, do not differ in Livy as to meaning, but simply denote "the supreme command" [9]. It is

---

[1] This formula has been discussed by M. A. Levi in Rendic. Ist. Lomb. 71, 1938, 109 ff., to whose view we shall return later.

[2] Amphitruo, 196. See: L. Halkin, La parodie d'une demande de triomphe dans l'Amphitryon de Plaute, Bruxelles, 1948.

[3] The formula one does meet frequently in the request of a triumph is: *re bene feliciterque gesta*.

[4] Liv. 41, 28, 8; 22, 30, 4; 28, 27, 4; 28, 27, 5; 29, 27, 4; 27, 44, 4; cf. schol. Veron. Aen. 10, 241 reconstr. Mommsen.

[5] Liv. 28, 16, 14; 3, 42, 2; 3, 17, 2; 28, 12, 12; 5, 46, 6; 8, 33, 22; 8, 31, 1.

[6] Liv. 4, 20, 6; 21, 40, 3.

[7] Liv. 3, 61, 12.

[8] Liv. 29, 27, 2.

[9] Lewis and Short, s.v. *auspicium*; cf. Ernst Meyer, Staat[2], 125: "so dass der Ausdruck 'unter den Auspizien' den Besitz des Oberkommandos bedeutete."

possible that a distinction is made between *imperium-auspicium* on the one hand, and *ductus* on the other, as is apparent from a text in Suetonius:[1] *domuit partim ductu, partim auspiciis suis Cantabriam*, or in Curtius:[2] *alia ductu meo, alia imperio auspicioque perdomui* ..... *Ductus* here denotes the personal strategic command, *imperium auspiciumque* the supreme command; in later times these were not necessarily in one hand. It is not true that a distinction is made in such texts between *auspicium* with a sacral meaning and *imperium* with a secular meaning.

2. The terms *ductu*, *auspicio* and *imperio* are encountered times without number when it is reported under whose command a war was conducted, a victory won, a defeat(!) suffered, etc. etc. The triumph is only one of the many aspects of war in which the question of the command is discussed. Now it is found that the term *auspicio* is used more frequently than are either *ductu* or *imperio* when the supreme command is referred to. In view of this phenomenon, for which Beseler gives a very plausible reason, which will be discussed later, the fact that the term *auspicio* is also the one used most often in connection with the triumph—provided it were true—does not warrant any conclusion as to a special relation between *auspicium* and triumph. This would be permissible only if the use of the term *auspicio* were restricted to the triumph, whilst the other terms or combinations were applied to all other aspects of war.

Finally, I disagree with Laqueur that, in the three places he mentions in Livy, *auspicio* should have the emphasis he attributes to it, since in all three instances another argument is added which is to prevent the triumph. The texts are highly illustrative of the vagueness of the argumentation by which it was attempted to refuse a request for a triumph at a time when regulations on the subject had not yet been laid down. In Livy 34, 10, 5, the reason for the refusal is: *quod alieno auspicio et in aliena provincia pugnasset.* Laqueur considers *et* in this sentence as being used explicatively, for "seine Auspicien (viz. of the proconsul) gelten nur für seinen Amtsbezirk" (222). The situation, however, is slightly different. M. Helvetius, whose *ovatio* is discussed here, has handed over his task to a successor. At the moment he won his victory in the *provincia* of the consul Cato, on his march back to Rome, he was,

---

[1] Suet. Aug. 21.
[2] Curtius, 6, 3, 2.

therefore, without *imperium* [1], because his term had expired, and without *provincia*. The fact that a commander's *auspicium* is not valid in someone else's province, as Laqueur assumes, has nothing to do with this case. But this assumption is not correct, either, as is clearly demonstrated by a second testimonium. In Livy 28, 9, 10, which deals with the question of which of two magistrates of equal rank who together have won a victory, is to be allowed a triumph, one is granted the triumph for not one, but three reasons: *quoniam et in provincia M. Livi res gesta esset, et eo die, quo pugnatum foret, eius forte auspicium fuisset, et exercitus Livianus deductus Romam venisset, Neronis deduci de provincia non potuisset.....* From this text we learn two things. The first is that *in aliena provincia* is not the same as *alienis auspiciis*. On the contrary, *et....et* and *forte* prove that the consuls also maintain the *turnus* in the *provincia* of one of them. The second is that here, again, the question concerning the *auspicium* is only one out of several. Of equal importance are the questions in whose province the victory was won, and whose army was marched back to Rome. Worth noticing in this connection is that in the oldest example of the refusal of a triumph after a victory the candidate had won in someone else's *provincia*, neither the term *provincia*, nor that of *auspicium* is mentioned: consul Postumius is not allowed to triumph in 294 B.C.[2]

1. *quod tardius ab urbe exisset*

2. *quod iniussu senatus ex Samnio in Etruriam transisset.*

Finally, in the last testimonium, Livy, 31, 48, 6, the question asked is: *an in magistratu suisque auspiciis gessisset*, which implies at least *suo imperio*. In view of this, I am of the opinion that these three texts, as well as others, each time present variations on the theme *ductu auspicio imperioque*.

This leaves the question of why it is that, of the two equivalent notions *auspicium imperiumque* it is preferably *auspicium* which is used when enquiries are made concerning the supreme command. A plausible answer to this question was given by Beseler. He represented the course of events as follows [3]: The question invariably

---

[1] Weissenborn-Müller *ad loc.*: "als er das *imperium* bereits nicht mehr hatte". In later times the promagistrate retains the *imperium* until he is back in Rome, but this, as Mommsen points out, is only formally so (Staatsrecht I[3], 641), and his *imperium* is, in any case, inferior to that of his successor. (Rosenberg, R.E. 9, 1916, 1209, s.v. *Imperium*).

[2] Liv. 10, 37, 7.

[3] o.c. 355.

asked was: "Who held the supreme command?" Answer: "The person holding the highest *imperium*". Question: "How can such a person be recognized if there are two holders of *imperium* of equal rank?". Answer: "The person having the highest *imperium* is the one who on the decisive day had observed the *auspicia*; this is the visible indication that, according to the *turnus*, he had the supreme command on this particular day".

If we have now demonstrated that (1) a possible connection between *auspicium* and triumph in no way proves that the triumph is a sacral ceremony, and that, the other way round, it is incorrect to state that the triumph, because it is a sacral ceremony, must of necessity be connected with the *auspicium*, and with the *auspicium* alone, (2) *auspicio*, whether or not combined with *imperio* and/or *ductu* in Livy means no more than "under the supreme command of", (3) the question concerning the *auspicium* is by no means specific of the triumph, but is connected with every event in which the command has to be established, even a defeat; this does not mean that we deny that the *auspicium* was one of the series of conditions to be fulfilled in the triumph. According to the oldest authentic texts it was asked *cuius ductu, imperio auspicioque* the victory had been won. We would be guilty of the same mistake with which we reproach Laqueur, if, instead of *auspicium* we were to pronounce *imperium* to be the one and only condition for the triumph. Mommsen in his systematic arrangement also leaves room for the *auspicium*. The combination *imperium auspiciumque* is such a closely-knit one that very strong arguments will be needed to grant either of the two priority over the other. Laqueur's arguments fall short of this requirement. On the other hand, I do believe that an inquiry into another question, viz. "What was essential to the *entry* of the triumphator into Rome?", as well as into the problem linked up with it, concerning the *lex curiata de imperio*, will enable us to make a more clear-cut definition of the parts here played by the notions of *auspicium* and *imperium*, side-by-side and opposite each other. This, however, is a subject for later discussion.

That in the matter of the *ius triumphandi, imperium* and *auspicium* are fully equivalent notions cannot be demonstrated any better than by means of the following quotation from Valerius Maximus, 2, 8, 2, in which a praetor, Q. Valerius, claims the right to a triumph for a victory he personally won in the absence of the supreme commander, the consul Lutatius:

itaque iudex inter eos convenit Atilius Calatinus, apud quem Valerius in hunc modum egit, consulem ea pugna in lectica claudum iacuisse, se autem omnibus imperatoriis partibus functum. tunc Calatinus, prius quam Lutatius causam suam ordiretur, 'quaero' inquit 'Valeri, a te, si dimicandum necne esset contrariis inter vos sententiis dissedissetis, utrum quod consul an quod praetor imperasset maius habiturum fuerit momentum?' respondit Valerius non facere se controversiam quin priores partes consulis essent futurae. 'age deinde' inquit Calatinus, 'si diversa auspicia accepissetis, cuius magis auspicio staretur?' 'item' respondit Valerius 'consulis'. 'iam hercules' inquit 'cum de imperio et auspicio inter vos disceptationem susceperim, et tu utroque adversarium tuum superiorem fuisse fatearis, nihil est quod ulterius dubitem'.

III. A. Laqueur's explanation of the relation between *auspicium* and triumph

The interrelation of *auspicium* and triumph finds its explanation in the fact that the *auspicium* at the departure from Rome was linked up with the *votum*, of which the triumph was the redemption. Before going to war the magistrate made a vow on the Capitol: *pro incolumitate exercitus*, or, *pro imperio suo communique re publica*. What he promised in return is not recorded anywhere, but we may assume that it was the spoils or part of them. The triumph was a ceremony by which this vow was redeemed, as Livy, 45, 39, 11, illustrates: *victor perpetrato bello eodem in Capitolium triumphans ad eosdem deos, quibus vota nuncupavit, merita dona portans redit.* Similar descriptions are found a few more times in Livy.[1] The connection between *votum* and triumph is also confirmed in another manner: it is only at these ceremonies that the general and his *lictores* wear the war-dress (*paludamentum*) within the town-walls. The *votum* is made after the *auspicatio* has been performed: Livy, 21, 63, 9: *ne auspicato profectus in Capitolium ad vota nuncupanda paludatus inde cum lictoribus in provinciam iret.* "Das auspicium garantirt den gewünschten Verlauf eines Unternehmens" (226). Not until after the *auspicium* has proved favourable can the *votum* be made. "So ist factisch das votum an das vorausgehende auspicium geknüpft, und daraus ergiebt sich die rechtliche Consequenz, dass

---

[1] Liv. 42, 49, 6; 38, 48, 16.

nur wer das Recht des öffentlichen auspiciums hat ein votum im Sinne des Staates anstellen kann; da wir nun aber im Triumph die Vollendung des sollennen votums erkannten, so folgt mit logischer Notwendigkeit: das Recht des auspiciums ist Voraussetzung des Triumphs (226).

III B. Criticism

Starting with the statement mentioned last we have to point out that it is not confirmed anywhere in literary tradition. In all instances in which the question is asked of who has the right to vow or devote, we find descriptions in which exactly the term *auspicium* is lacking. I here quote a few:

> Livy, 22, 10, 10:
> *Veneri Erucinae aedem Q. Fabius Maximus dictator vovit, quia ita ex fatalibus libris editum erat, ut is voveret, cuius maximum imperium in civitate esset.*
> Cicero, nat. deor. 2, 10:
> *..... ut quidam imperatores etiam se ipsos ..... devoverent.*
> Livy, 8, 10, 11:
> *licere consuli dictatorique et praetori .... civem devovere.*
> Macrobius, Sat. 3, 9, 9:
> *dictatores imperatoresque soli possunt devovere.*

What mattered to the Roman was evidently that the *votum* was pronounced by the magistrate, the terms *imperium/imperator* being given special emphasis[1]. It is true that this magistrate had *auspicium* in virtue of his office, and it may even be said, as it is done by Laqueur, that there existed a factual connection between *auspicium* and *votum* [2], since before the campaign first the *auspicatio* was performed and after that the *votum* pronounced [3]. Here one is faced with a peculiarity, however, which seems to have escaped Laqueur. If, in accordance with Laqueur's theory, the *auspicium* guarantees the course of events desired, what is the point of making a *votum* for the same purpose? This question should be put to all those who think the *auspicium* is more than asking the gods for their approval

---

[1] Mommsen, Staatsrecht I³, 244: "Aber auch die sonstigen Gelübde werden von Rechts wegen von den Magistraten mit Imperium geleistet". See testimonia quoted there.

[2] See Beseler's strictly juridical refutation of this thesis of Laqueur, o.c. 358 f.

[3] Liv. 21, 63, 9.

that an action might be carried out *hic et nunc* [1]. The meaning of the *auspicium* will, however, be discussed later. Another inaccuracy needs correcting: at the triumph the general does not wear the *paludamentum*, but the *tunica* and *toga*, a pre-eminently civilian attire!

Of greater importance is the following. Laqueur looks upon the triumph as a *voti solutio*. He is not alone in that opinion. His critic, Beseler, fully agrees with him here [2]: "Der *triumphus* ist eine *voti solutio*". Ehlers also thinks [3]: "sakralrechtlich bedeutet die Feier auf dem Capitol die Einlösung der beim Auszug in den Krieg gegebenen Gelübde".

Now I also think that the idea of the *voti solutio* may have played a part in the triumph, but at the same time I believe that the great emphasis which was laid on this aspect of the triumph as if it were the root-idea of the ceremony, has formed a serious obstacle in the way of the solution of the question "what did the triumph stand for?". For, the view that the *voti solutio* is its essential meaning is unacceptable if the following is considered.

Before going to war the commander makes a vow. What he vows is not recorded, but I am ready to assume, as Laqueur does, that it was part of the war-booty, particularly sacrificial animals bought with the money seized. Not a single text gives cause for the—indeed naive—assumption that the commander vows the gods a triumph with everything attached to it. This would be impossible anyway, because the general has to redeem his *votum* after having returned from his victory. If the triumph itself were the *voti solutio*, or if it were inextricably linked up with it, it would have been impossible for the triumph ever to have been refused once it had been established—by the senate—that the gods had fulfilled their part of the agreement. Not redeeming an official state *votum* is in a case like this inconceivable in Rome. "Wie man sich bei Verweigerung des T. dieser Verpflichtung entledigte, steht nicht fest", Ehlers [4] frankly admits. Since the triumph *in monte Albano* is too young to serve as a solution, we may assume that in cases such as these the *ovatio* was resorted to, which, as we know from tradition, was held as early

---

[1] e.g. A. Hägerström, Das magistratische Ius in seinem Zusammenhang mit dem römischen Sakralrechte. Uppsala Universitets Årsskrift, 1929; Levi, o.c. 105 ff., and many others.

[2] o.c. 352.

[3] R.E., s.v. *Triumphus*, 495.

[4] *ibid.* 496.

as 503 B.C. This enabled the general to redeem his *votum* without holding a triumph. It was already argued above that those features which raise the triumph above the *ovatio* are the essential characteristics of the triumph. The sacrifice on the Capitol, which, for the time being, I do not deny the character of a *voti solutio*, is not the essential characteristic of the triumph, as it also formed part of the *ovatio*. In this connection it may be pointed out that the *votum* could be redeemed, not only without a triumph, but even without an *ovatio*, as is seen from a passage from the *monumentum Ancyranum*[1]: *Cum deinde pluris triumphos mihi senatus decrevisset eis supersedi. Item saepe laurus deposui in Capitolio votis quae quoque bello nuncupaveram solutis.*

Of the texts Laqueur used to prove his thesis "triumph = *voti solutio*", only one is, on closer inspection, worth considering [2]. And it is precisely this text which pleads in favour of our argumentation rather than Laqueur's hypothesis. Aemilius Paullus has requested a triumph, *quem.... senatus iustum esse iudicaverat*, against which, in other words, no objection could be raised on grounds of political or sacral law. This leaves only the *rogatio ad plebem, ut ei quo die urbem triumphans inveheretur, imperium esset.* This, now, the soldiers try to sabotage because of their dissatisfaction with their general. For the defence of Aemilius Paullus the consul M. Servilius now makes a long speech, in which he first of all argues that the triumph is just as much an honour for the soldiers as it is for the commander. After a whole series of arguments the triumph is at the end of the speech also defined as an honour for the gods in the following words: *cui sortito provinciam, cui proficiscenti praesagientibus animis victoriam triumphumque destinavimus, ei victori triumphum negaturi sumus? et quidem non tantum eum sed deos etiam suo honore fraudaturi? dis quoque enim, non solum hominibus, debetur triumphus. maiores vestri omnium magnarum rerum et principia exorsi ab dis sunt et finem eum statuerunt. consul proficiscens praetorve paludatis*

---

[1] Mon. Ancyr. 1, 22. According to this text the laurel branch/wreath does not form part of the *votum*. Differently Ovid, Tristia, 4, 2, 56: *et dabitur merito laurea vota Iovi*, which may be a poetic licence. Another example of the redemption of a *votum* without a triumph is given by Liv. 28, 38, 8, who reports that Scipio, who is not allowed a triumph, is permitted to redeem a *votum* of one hundred cattle on the Capitol. Inez Scott Ryberg, M.A.A.R. 22, 1955, 141, very rightly states: "Whether or not the honour of a triumph was granted to the commander on his return, his vows were paid."

[2] Viz. Liv. 45, 39. In Liv. 38, 48, 16, by *honos deorum* the *supplicatio* is meant, in Liv. 42, 49, 6, no *vota* are mentioned at all.

lictoribus in provinciam et ad bellum vota in Capitolio nuncupat; victor perpetrato bello eodem in Capitolium triumphans ad eosdem deos, quibus vota nuncupavit, merita dona portans redit. pars non minima triumphi est victimae praecedentes, ut appareat dis grates agentem imperatorem ob rem publicam bene gestam redire.

Here it is made abundantly clear that the triumph itself cannot be a *voti solutio* because, as was already argued above, if it were, it could never be refused after being approved by the senate. The fact that a speech is required to defend the triumph is ample proof that the ceremony may not be looked upon as being fundamentally a debt-redemption to the gods. Worth noticing is that Servilius, or Livy, rather, does not succinctly state "the triumph is a *voti solutio*", which would have made the whole speech superfluous, but, starting from the outward aspects of the triumph, concludes upon a connection between *votum* and triumph—"*appareat*" is revealing here—, an argumentation Laqueur appropriates. However, a rhetoric passage in Livy is not to be used as documentary evidence in a matter of religious history, but should rather be evaluated as a theory.

In view of this, I think the triumph cannot possibly itself have been a *voti solutio*. The fact that vows could be redeemed by means of an *ovatio*, and even without ceremony at all, proves this. The texts, moreover, prove exactly the opposite of what Laqueur deduces from them. We have already seen before that there is one highly characteristic difference between *votum* and triumph: a *votum* may be redeemed by someone other than the *vovens*, the triumph may only be held by the victor himself. Finally, one more question: how are all features of the triumph, the *apparatus* of the triumphator in particular, to be explained if the triumph is fundamentally a *voti solutio*? An "explanation" which does not take these characteristic features into account, does not deserve this name [1].

4. A comparison between the views of Mommsen and Laqueur

At the conclusion of his paper Laqueur goes through Mommsen's list of conditions to be fulfilled in a triumph with a view to ascertaining whether they bear out his theories concerning a relationship between triumph and *auspicium*. He thinks he can indeed prove

---

[1] This was already pointed out by F. Muller in Mnemos. 3 ser. 2, 1935, 189.

that in all these conditions *auspicium*, rather than *imperium*, is the determining factor.

According to Laqueur the magistrate could not triumph after having resigned his office because the triumph should take place, to use Mommsen's own words, "in der Continuität derselben Kriegsauspicien"; the victory had to be won in the magistrate's own province because his *auspicium* was valid only there; whilst a general who held his power by proxy could not triumph because only the magistrate, and not his deputy, had the right of *auspicium*.

These points (items A, B and F of the system of Mommsen mentioned above) do not require any further discussion. In the preceding section it became clear that the chief emphasis might in these cases just as well—if not better—be laid on *imperium*. No proof can be furnished for the justness of either view. Mommsen is for this reason more guarded in his formulation than is Laqueur, and does not *a limine* exclude the influence of the *auspicium*, which is very difficult to separate from the *imperium* of a magistrate. The meaning of the "Continuität derselben Kriegsauspicien" awaits further discussion.

Of greater interest are other issues, which will be found to take us *in medias res*, and which have to be examined in greater detail.

The *tribuni militum consulari potestate* (Mommsen's item C) never triumphed; not, as was Mommsen's idea, because their office was an exceptional one[1], but, according to Laqueur, because this office was open to the *plebs*, who were denied the *auspicia maiora*.

Laqueur here starts from an assumption which did not find supporters, either in his own time or at present [2], and which is indeed extremely improbable. That the *tribuni milit. cons. pot.* lacked certain privileges of the consuls, including the right to the triumph, is true, but that they were denied the *auspicium* is impossible. How is one to imagine that the highest authorities of the state—according to many, as apparent from their names, elected especially with a view to impending wars[3]—lacked the right as representatives of the state to observe the *auspicia*? About the competency of the

---

[1] Beseler, o.c. 361, who rightly adds that the reference to the *triumviri* of four centuries later lacks all demonstrative force.

[2] See also: E. S. Staveley, J.R.S. 43, 1953, 30 ff.; F. Adcock, J.R.S. 47, 1957, 9 ff.; R. Sealey, Latomus, 18, 1959, 521 ff.; A. Boddington, Historia, 8, 1959, 356 ff.; J. Bayet, Tite-Live, IV, 1954, 132 ff.; P. de Francisci, Primordia Civitatis, 697.

[3] See literature above, in note 2.

trib. mil. cons. pot. Mommsen [1] already pointed out: "sie ist der consularischen gleich", from which he inferred that it included the right of *auspicium*. This view still is the generally accepted one. I here quote one from the many [2]: "*trib. mil. cons. pot.* erano *tribuni militum* cui era riconosciuto l'*auspicium imperiumque* consolare".

If we assume this, the question remains of why these *tribuni militum* could not triumph. The only way which, in my opinion, leads to the correct explanation is the one which starts from what we know for certain about this office: its title. The terms *tribuni militum pro consulibus* [3], *tribuni militum consulari potestate* [4] and *tribuni militum consulari imperio* [5] are found in turn. Nobody has, as far as I know, been struck by the similarity between this title and that of another official who was also denied the right to a triumph: the *privatus cum imperio*, also called *pro consule*.

Officials of this category (Mommsen G) were also refused the triumph, according to Laqueur, because they did not have *auspicium*, as a result of which they were unable to observe the *auspicia* on the Capitolium before marching out of town. If this was indeed the case we might expect to find this reason for refusing the triumph mentioned in the texts. What we find, however, is quite a different reason:

> Liv. 28, 38, 4, about Scipio:
> *magis temptata est spes triumphi quam petita pertinaciter quia neminem ad eam diem triumphasse, qui sine magistratu res gessisset, constabat.*
> Val. Max. 2, 8, 5:
> ..... *ut P. Scipioni ..... M. Marcello ..... triumphus non decerneretur, quod ad eas res gerendas sine ullo erant missi magistratu.*
> Liv. 31, 20, 3, about L. Cornelius Lentulus:
> *res triumpho dignas esse censebat senatus, sed exemplum a maioribus non accepisse, ut, qui neque dictator neque consul neque praetor res gessisset, triumpharet.*

According to these texts the real issue is that of having a magistracy, which covers more than just having *auspicium*. Furthermore, if

---

[1] Staatsrecht II³, 188.
[2] P. de Francisci, Primordia Civitatis, 697.
[3] Aul. Gell. 14, 7, 5; Liv. 4, 7, 1; Dion. Hal. 11, 62.
[4] The most usual, often attested title.
[5] Bronze table of Claudius at Lyon; Aul. Gell. 17, 21, 19; cf. Liv. 4, 7, 2.

the *privati cum imperio* did not have *auspicium*, how could Livy[1]
say several times about Scipio that the war in Spain was conducted
auspicio ductuque eius? It proves that Scipio did have *auspicium*,
for, although it is true, as we already pointed out in connection with
Laqueur's theories, that the expression *auspicio eius* in Livy means
no more than "under his supreme command", it would never have
been used if Livy knew that Scipio did not have *auspicium*.

Here again, we have to start from what we know for certain: the
privati cum imperio, in spite of having *imperium* as well as *auspicium*,
could not triumph because they were not, and had not been magistrates—dictators, consuls, praetors. Their position is fully determined by their title. In contradistinction to the normal magistrate,
who held his *imperium* in virtue of his office, the *privatus cum imperio* was granted his *imperium* in a special manner.

When we now return to the *tribuni militum consulari potestate*—
or *consulari imperio*—,we find that these officials, too, were denied
the right to a triumph, and also that there is a striking correspondence between their title and that of the *privati cum imperio*. Here
we have to do with magistrates, not with *privati*, but nevertheless
with magistrates whose *imperium* was not automatically, in virtue
of their function, attached to their office, as it was in the case of
dictators, consuls and praetors. Their *imperium* was added to a
function which itself did not carry *imperium*.

Wouldn't it be logical to infer from this that their being denied the
triumph was, just as in the case of the *privati cum imperio*, linked
up with the nature of their function? The reason Mommsen[2]
states for their not being allowed to triumph, is that the *tribunus
milit. cons. pot.* "abweichend von der streng verfassungsmässigen
Ordnung bestellt wird". This is indeed, as Beseler[3] also grants
Laqueur, too abstract to serve as an explanation. I should prefer
to formulate the reason as follows: that the *tribuni milit. cons. pot.*—
and similarly the *privati cum imperio*—did not hold an office which
by nature carried *imperium*. But this too, of course, requires further
explanation and elaboration. What exactly was the difference with
the normal magistrate? Why was this difference so fundamental
that the one official was, and the other was not allowed a triumph?

---

[1] Liv. 28, 16, 14; 28, 38, 1.
[2] Staatsrecht I³, 128.
[3] o.c. 361.

If, according to J. Bayet [1], the *tribuni milit. cons. pot.* had an "imperium reduit"—and I think this suggestion is worth considering—, what then was the difference between this *imperium* and the *imperium* of the consul? We shall have to return to these and similar questions. For the moment it suffices to state that the fact that the *trib. mil. cons. pot.* as well as the *privati cum imperio* were refused the triumph is linked up with the nature of their functions: the former had a special magistracy, the latter had no magistracy all. Both categories were granted the *imperium* by way of extra.

This leaves item D on Mommsen's list. According to Mommsen the *prorogatio imperii* would, strictly speaking, stand in the way of a triumph, since the promagistrate lost his *imperium* inside the city. In practice, however, promagistrates did get permission to triumph, the first *prorogatio imperii* already being combined with a triumph: Liv. 8, 26, 7 (326 B.C.) *duo singularia haec ei viro primum contigere, prorogatio imperii, non ante in ullo facta, et acto honore triumphus.*

Laqueur thinks that the triumph of the promagistrate—which Mommsen had to regard as an exception to the rules he drew up—fits in very well with his own theory, since the promagistrate had in his *votum* promised to dedicate part of the war booty to the god. This vow he had to, and was able to keep. There is no reason for denying him the triumph. At first sight this argumentation appears sound, but on closer inspection it proves untenable [2].

First of all I have to point out that the *votum* could, if necessary, be redeemed by someone other than the *vovens*, so that the vow did not bind the magistrate personally, nor did it force him to celebrate a triumph. Of far greater importance is the following. In order to enable the promagistrate to triumph he had to be given the *imperium* on the day of his triumph. The formula reads: *ut tribuni plebis rogationem ad plebem ferrent, ut ei quo die in urbem triumphans inveheretur, imperium esset* [3].

To the supporters of Mommsen's theory there is nothing unusual in such a measure, because "die Feier den Besitz des Imperium fordert", even though this does not *explain* the connection between

---

[1] Tite-Live, IV, 132 ff.

[2] For a convincing refutation of this part of Laqueur's argumentation see Beseler, o.c. 360.

[3] Liv. 26, 21, 5; 45, 35, 4; cf. 26, 9, 10.

imperium and triumph. Instead of being an argument against Momm-sen's theory, this granting of *imperium* corroborates it.

To Laqueur's theory, on the other hand, the granting of *imperium* on the day of the triumph is the finishing stroke. He tries to minimize the significance of this measure: "das für den Augenblick des Triumphzuges verliehene Imperium ist nichts als eine Verwaltungs-massregel, welche mit dem Triumph nur insofern zu tun hat, als sie die factische Durchführung ermöglicht" (228). He considers the triumph to mark the end of the campaign, at which the commander, for this reason, wears the war-dress, as he did at the *votum* [1]. The inadequacy of this explanation for the granting of the *imperium* is clear here, and will become even more obvious in the course of our argumentation.

Before we proceed two remarks have to be made:

1. So far we have only dealt with *auspicium* or *imperium* held at the moment of the victory. What we are now concerned with is the part played by *imperium* or *auspicium* at the entry of the general into Rome. A first datum is that the promagistrate was allowed to keep the *imperium* also inside the city.

2. The part the *auspicium*, or the validity of the war *auspicia* observed, play in the triumph, has nothing to do with the granting of this special *imperium*. This will be readily understood if the following is considered. There is no certainty as regards the validity of the *auspicia belli* inside the city [2]. If it is assumed that the *auspicia belli* lose their validity at the moment the *pomerium* is crossed, this process will not be affected in any way by a granting of *imperium*. If, on the other hand, the *auspicia belli* retain their validity at the return of the magistrate or promagistrate, the granting of *imperium* bears no relation to the *auspicium* either.

So much is certain, therefore: the granting of *imperium* has nothing to do with the validity of the *auspicia belli*, which, ac-cording to Mommsen and Laqueur have to retain their validity until after the sacrificing on the Capitolium has taken place.

This brings us to the second important datum concerning the entry of the triumphator. The general who aspires to a triumph does

---

[1] This is incorrect, as was already pointed out above.

[2] What does become clear from statements in Varro, l.l. 5, 43, and Gellius, 13, 14, 1, is that the *pomerium* constitutes the *finis urbani auspicii*, but Wissowa, R.E. 2, 1896, 2584, s.v. *Auspicium*, points out: "Eine dem Gegen-satz von *imperium domi* und *imperium militiae* entsprechende Scheidung von *auspicia urbana* und *auspicia bellica* wird nicht bezeugt."

on no account enter the city before the day of the triumph [1]. The reason why the negotiations with the senate are held outside the city, the reason why some people, such as Cicero, voluntarily exiled themselves from Rome for months on end, was that the claims on a triumph became null and void at the crossing of the *pomerium*. Why was this custom observed? It is to explain this that Mommsen speaks of "die Continuität derselben Kriegsauspicien", for, if the magistrate were to cross the *pomerium*, the special war-auspices lose their validity, according to Mommsen. However, he adds, these *auspicia* could be renewed, and it was on the strength of such a renewal that in 20 A.D. Drusus, after already having been inside the city, held an *ovatio* [2]. This, in fact, forms a direct refutation of his arguments. Moreover, if the war *auspicia* become null and void by the crossing of the *pomerium*, I fail to see how this fact could be altered by postponing the entry until the day of the triumph. Neither the senate, nor the people, nor the granting of an *imperium* can affect the validity of the *auspicia*, not even on the day of the triumphal procession.

What we really *know* is that the promagistrate was, on the day of the triumph, granted the *imperium* even inside the city, and that the candidate for the triumph did not cross the *pomerium* prior to the day of the triumph. What is more obvious than putting these facts together and looking upon them as a unity? For an explanation of this interrelation we shall have to await a later moment. For the time being we state that the candidate for the triumph is obviously not allowed to cross the *pomerium* prior to the day on which he is officially granted the *imperium* by the people.

Up till the present it was assumed that the *imperium* was granted only to the promagistrates because they did not have *imperium intra pomerium*. However, it is found that not only promagistrates, but also magistrates remain outside the city until the day of their triumph. This rule was already noted by Mommsen [3]. If this usage is indeed connected with the granting of *imperium*, the obvious conclusion is that the regular magistrates were also granted the *imperium* on the day of the triumph. But—this question presents itself at once—why should *imperium* be granted to a magistrate who

---

[1] Mommsen, Staatsrecht I³, 127, n. 2, and places mentioned there.
[2] *ibid.*
[3] *ibid.*

held *imperium* inside the city too? If one refers to *imperium domi*, as Laqueur does, it is impossible to anwer this question. If it is recognized, however, that it is the *imperium militiae* with which we have to do here, it becomes at once clear that in that case also the normal magistrate had to be granted *imperium*. Inside the city even he did not hold the *imperium militiae*. Again it is Mommsen to whose acuteness we are greatly indebted in this matter. He saw [1] that the triumph is the only instance in which a commander functions as a general within the walls of Rome, that on this occasion the axes were carried along in the *fasces* [2], that soldiers marched in formation, that prisoners of war—among whom there might be citizens of Rome—were killed without trial: all characteristics of the military *imperium*. Mommsen even suggested that the usage of the magistrate staying outside the walls prior to the triumph, was connected with this [3]. I share this view and I think that a distinct *trait d'union* between the two data may be indicated, viz. the fact that the *pomerium* forms the boundary between the *imperium domi* and the *imperium militiae*. The crossing of the *pomerium* forms the pivot around which all juridical usages connected with the triumph revolve. Within this *pomerium* only the *imperium domi* was operative. On the day of the triumph, however, the triumphator had, with the people's consent, the *imperium militiae*. This fact seems to me to be the central one, which requires an explanation. In any case it has now become clear why a general could at all times triumph on the *mons Albanus* "*iure consularis imperii*" [4] and "*sine publica auctori-*

---

[1] Staatsrecht I³, 132.

[2] This is not only to be inferred from the similarity between triumph and *processus consularis*, but is also known from art: the axes are visible on the representation of a triumph of Tiberius on a silver goblet of the Boscoreale. See Inez Scott Ryberg, o.c. fig. 77 c; cf. fig. 81 e, 87 and comments on p. 142 n. 7.

[3] Mommsen, Staatsrecht I³, 132, n. 3. Mommsen does not believe that the regular magistrates also required a *privilegium*, granted by the people: "Die Exemption des Triumphaltags von den sonst für die Amtführung *domi* geltenden Regeln muss gleich bei der Scheidung der beiden Amtsgebiete hinzugefügt worden sein." Beseler, o.c. 360 n. 1, in this connection speaks of the "*ipso iure* vorhandene triumphale *imperium* des Magistrates". This is possible, but it is also possible, and in my view more probable, that the normal magistrate, too, needed the people's permission to retain his full military *imperium* in the city. Also E. Pais, Fasti Triumphales Populi Romani I, 1920, XXXI, thinks that the commander held the military *imperium* in the city on the day of his triumph.

[4] Liv. 33, 23, 3.

tate" [1]. The fundamental difference is that during this triumph the *pomerium* was not crossed, which meant that there was no need for an *imperium* granted by the people.

5. *Summary and conclusion*

An investigation concerning the most important conditions the victorious general had to meet in order to qualify for a triumph showed that the ultimate choice lay between *imperium* and *auspicium*. Mommsen took *imperium*, Laqueur *auspicium* to be the primary condition. For two reasons we found it necessary to follow Laqueur's argumentation closely. In the first place because his theory—often mentioned, rarely read—is by nearly everyone who has studied the triumph referred to as the generally accepted explanation of the sacral aspects of the triumph; secondly because the scholar who considers the *auspicium* as being the primary condition for the triumph has made a decisive choice as far as the interpretation of the triumphal ceremony is concerned. His view cannot differ to any material extent from opinions such as the following: "er (viz. the general) triumphierte als Sieger durch das Innehaben der höchsten, an Iupiter O.M. geknüpften Auspiziën. Oder er triumphierte als derjenige, bei dem die Kraft Iupiters in ihrer allerhöchsten Potenz als Siegeskraft vorhanden war". (Hägerström [2])

"Tale è la facoltà mediatrice rappresentata dalle conseguenze della auspicazione, che il generale vittorioso può agire come un simulacro vivente della divinità stessa nella pompa trionfale". (Levi [3])

"La République romaine avait eu sa théologie du triomphe, fondée sur le droit des auspices...... Elle avait admis le général vainqueur à l'honneur d'une sorte de divination temporaire, à condition que toutes les règles eussent été observées, qu'il eût détenu les auspices souverains attachés à l'*imperium maius*." (J. Gagé [4])

"Durch sein (viz. Iuppiter's) augurales fiat wird er Schöpfer und Führer des Reiches, ihm gelten in erster Linie das *auspicium*, wodurch jedes *imperium* göttliche Autorisation erhält, besonders aber der Dienst der Fetialen und der Triumph..... Der Triumph

---

[1] Liv. 42, 21, 7.
[2] A. Hägerström, o.c. 58.
[3] M. A. Levi, o.c. 111.
[4] La Théologie de la Victoire impériale. R.H. 171, 1933, 2.

ist die Entfaltung der Glorie des sieggekrönten Feldherrn, in welchem sich Iuppiter selbst manifestiert''. (Wallisch[1])

Serious objections against these views, which will have to be dealt with later, are, among other things, that the term *auspicium* is given the meaning of "blessing", "increase in strength" etc., a meaning which, as we shall see, is incorrect; that the connection between *auspicium* and triumph defended in the texts mentioned does not in fact *explain* anything, least of all why the triumphator manifests himself in the shape of Iuppiter; furthermore—but we found this in many instances—that here, again, other aspects of the triumph (its name, its connection with the *ludi Romani*) are neglected.

In our inquiry we found:

I.   Laqueur's view that the triumph is referred to as an *honor deorum* is based on his confusing the triumph with the *supplicatio*.

II. From the incontestable datum that the triumph was originally a sacral ceremony it may not be inferred that the *auspicium* forms its primary condition. The testimonia furnished by Laqueur disprove his view instead of corroborating it.

III. The current view that the triumph is essentially a *voti solutio* is untenable. The theory that the sacrifice on the Capitol stands for the redemption of a *votum* is acceptable, although it has not been proved. This sacrifice could, however, just as well be made in an *ovatio* and even without any ceremony of this kind at all. The interesting and problematic features of the triumph are, therefore, precisely those by which it distinguishes itself from the *ovatio* and the *voti solutio*.

IV. Various data indicate that, in connection with the triumph, the holding of the *imperium* is of great importance, particularly the fact that the triumphator held the *imperium militiae* inside the city on the day of his triumph. What was the reason for this? Why were the *tribuni mil. cons. pot.* and the *privati cum imperio* not allowed to triumph? In what respect does their *imperium* differ from that of the magistrate? These are the data and the questions on which our later discussion of the *interpretatio Romana* of the triumph has to be based.

---

[1] Wallisch, o.c. 250.

To conclude: Our defending the point of view of Mommsen against that of Laqueur does not mean that we look upon the *imperium* as being the one and only condition for the triumph. Just as *imperium auspiciumque* is a set phrase, neither of whose components may arbitrarily be neglected, we think that all the constituents of the oldest triumph-formula we know *auspicio, imperio, ductu, felicitate* merit our attention.

We shall give them that attention in the last two chapters of this study.

SUMMARY OF THE CONCLUSIONS OF THE FIRST FIVE CHAPTERS. METHOD OF FURTHER INVESTIGATION

The cheer *triumpe*, which gave the triumph its name, was originally an exlamation by which a god of the "dying and rising" type was summoned to epiphany. The call, which in the Greek θρίαμβε as well as in the *triumpe* of the *carmen arvale* retained its original function, can be traced back to a pre-Greek language, and reached Rome via Etruria. The old meaning of the exclamation is still discernible in the triumph, since there is no doubt that the triumphator at one time acted the part of the great god Iuppiter. His insignia, the meaning of which was either not understood or deliberately not acknowledged by the Romans, unequivocally testify to this. The god Iuppiter, therefore, manifested himself very concretely, during a sacral ceremony, in the person of the triumphator, summoned and accompanied by the exclamation *triumpe*. By this it is not denied that the triumphal garb goes back to the royal robes. This is also true, and here, again, our attention is directed towards Etruria, because it was by Etruscan kings that the triumphal ceremony was introduced into Rome. The problems are now focussed on the following question: what is the meaning of a ceremony in which the (Etruscan) king impersonates the supreme god manifesting himself, whilst at the same time he is by his insignia characterized as the king?

There is another ceremony, which was also derived from Etruria, in which the magistrate wears the *ornatus Iovis*: the *ludi Romani*. The *pompa circensis*, which characterizes this ceremony, also has elements in common with the *pompa triumphalis*. The view that the *ludi* were originally attached to the triumph and thus formed part of the triumphal ceremony had to be rejected. This means that one of the few aspects of the triumph which are generally regarded as having been satisfactorily explained, viz. its connection with the *ludi Romani*, has once again become a problem.

The cry *triumpe*, the figure of the triumphator-king and the *ludi Romani* all point to Etruria. This cannot be said with certainty about the Porta Triumphalis, the detached gate through which the victorious general and his army passed. Our inquiry revealed that the current interpretation of this passage as a lustration-rite, a *piatio* or a draining-away of *mana*, was not based on conclusive arguments. According to our interpretation the Porta Triumphalis emphatically determined the character of the entry of the triumphator into the city or the city-area. In addition to symbolizing and realizing his entry, it ensured that the triumphator remained inside the city and was thus kept for Rome.

The specifically Roman stipulation which required of the triumphator that he should have *imperium auspiciumque* gave rise to the question which of the two concepts was the more important in connection with the triumph. Laqueur's one-sided emphasis on *auspicium* and the consequences of this view proved incorrect. At the entry into the city not *auspicium*, but *imperium* constituted the essential factor.

These are the data on which we have to base our further inquiry. The nature of these data necessitates a caesura. From now on we can no longer refer to *the* triumph, but we shall have to distinguish between an Etruscan and a Roman triumph. *Triumpe*, the figure of the triumphator-king and the *ludi Romani* have a non-Roman origin. The obvious thing to do is to try and find an explanation for these elements collectively. Unfortunately, Etruria offers too few clues for us to start our inquiry through this channel. We shall have to proceed *per analogiam* and, by starting from the most noticeable facet, viz. that of the king acting the part of the supreme god in a sacral ceremony, have to investigate whether there are comparable ceremonies in other cultures and, if so, try and discover their meaning. Because we now enter a field which was *terra incognita* not only to me, but, as I found, to many experts on Greek and Roman religion, I think I owe it to the reader to provide so much information that he himself can evaluate the theories we shall encounter, and the way in which we shall use them. Chapter VI contains a description of what other cultures have to offer with respect to the problem on which we are engaged. An endeavour to interpret the elements which together make up the Etruscan triumph, on the basis of the knowledge gathered in this way, forms the subject of Chapter VII, dealing with the pre-Roman elements of the triumph.

The last two chapters are devoted to the *interpretatio Romana* of the triumphal ceremony. As our starting-point we take the only certain specifically Roman aspect of the triumph: the juridical condition of the holding of *imperium auspiciumque*, a subject introduced and elicited by our argumentation in the fifth chapter.

The fact is that the rejection of Laqueur's theory is merely a first step on the thorny path leading through the domain of these primitive-Roman concepts. The question concerning the priority of either *auspicium* or *imperium* in the conditions for the triumph was only tentatively broached; a more thorough inquiry is called for in this study, although it will be clear to anyone at all familiar with the subject that we shall of necessity have to confine ourselves to one aspect of the extremely intricate complex of problems. It will be found that in our case this does not present difficulties. There is an ancient Roman usage, the *lex curiata de imperio*, which gave rise to a similar difference of opinion as was observed in connection with the triumph. Here, too, the point at issue is the relation of *auspicium* and *imperium*. An inquiry into this *lex* will add to our insight into several points.

The results of the problems discussed in Chapter VIII will enable us via an interpretation of the most extensive triumphal formula we know, viz. *auspicio, imperio, felicitate, ductu*, to arrive at an explanation of the essential meaning of the Roman triumph. The interpretation of the passage through the Porta Triumphalis given in Chapter IV will here prove to be of direct use.

PART TWO

SYNTHESIS

Die Synthese nimmt die gewonnenen Einzelergebnisse zusammen und gelangt so zu einem Vollbilde. Sie ist unentbehrlich, rückt vieles einzelne erst in das rechte Licht und kann sagen, dass die analytische Forschung nur Vorarbeiten für sie liefert. Aber sie reizt zu neuer Forschung, und je stärker sie es tut, um so eher genügt sie nicht mehr. Eine neue wird nötig, und so geht es weiter, solange Leben in der Wissenschaft ist.

U. von Wilamowitz-Moellendorff.

CHAPTER SIX

GODS, KINGS AND THE NEW YEAR FESTIVAL

Salve, laeta dies, meliorque revertere semper.
Ovid

1. *Introduction*

Now that, pursuing the method outlined in the conclusion of
Part I, we attempt to trace outside Rome ritual ceremonies in
which, just as in the triumph and the *ludi Romani,* a king in the
shape of a god, or at any rate wearing a god's insignia, takes part
in such a way that not the king is deified, but that a well-known
deity manifests [1] himself in the person of the king, we have an extensive literature at our disposal. It is true that our inquiry is confined to one aspect of what is known as "divine kingship", but this
does not alter the fact that works about this comprehensive subject
first of all had to show us the way and provide us with material
for the study of our special problem. I consider myself excused from
giving a survey of the many works written about divine kingship [2]:
others have done this better than I possibly could [3]. Furthermore,

---

[1] This difference has important implications. If the king is deified, one
may rightly speak of a "divine king". In the other case, the king plays a
part, and, together with the part, lays aside the divinity.

[2] Particularly after the publication of Frazer's The golden Bough, the
subject has continuously engaged the attention of the students of the
science of religion. In 1955 a congress was held in Rome on the subject
"la Regalità Sacra". The papers have been collected in "The sacral Kingship". Studies in the history of religions. (Supplements to Numen, Leiden,
1959). Some important works of the last few decennia are: H. Frankfort,
Kingship and the Gods, Chicago, 1948; J. de Fraine, L'aspect religieux de
la royauté israélite. L'institution monarchique dans l'A.T. et dans les textes
mésopotamiens (Analecta Biblica, 3), Rome, 1954. A good survey of the
"état des questions" with very extensive bibliography, focussed on the
Hellenistic-Roman ideology of the ruler in: L. Cerfaux et J. Tondriau,
Le culte des souverains dans la civilisation gréco-romaine. Bibliothèque
de Théologie, sér. III, vol. 5, Tournai, 1957. For further literature, particularly on the Myth and Ritual theory, *vide infra.*

[3] Cerfaux et Tondriau, o.c. 10 ff.; C. M. Edsman, Zum sakralen Königtum
in der Forschung der letzten hundert Jahre, in: The sacral Kingship, 3 ff.;
the contributions of Hooke and Brandon to: Myth, Ritual and Kingship,

our first object is a phenomenological comparison of an Etrusco-Roman rite with ceremonies in other Mediterranean cultures, in which facts rather than the speculations of the experts have to tell their story.

In looking for these facts we shall continuously encounter studies written by scholars who on account of their common interest are sometimes collectively referred to as the "Myth and Ritual school" [1]. There is no doubt that the science of religion has made great progress as a result of the investigations made by these scholars. The discovery of a complex of myth and rite, drama and kingship has thrown a new light on each of these facets. It is equally certain, however, that the enthusiasm about this discovery has occasionally led to theories which lost all contact with actual facts, and which have rightly given occasion to critcism [2]. In view of this state of

edited by S. H. Hooke, Oxford, 1958, 1 ff. and 261 ff.; see the enormous bibliographical lists in I. Engnell, Studies in Divine Kingship in the ancient Near East, Uppsala, 1943, 223 ff.; Th. H. Gaster, Thespis. Ritual, Myth and Drama in the ancient Near East[2], New York, 1961, 473 ff.

[1] I mention only a few of the most outstanding representatives of this school, which has a predecessor (for Frazer, the Panbabylonists and Mowinckel, see below) in A. M. Hocart with his books: Kingship, London, 1927, and: Kings and Councelors, Cairo, 1936. In 1933 appeared: Myth and Ritual. Essays on the myth and ritual of the Hebrews in relation to the culture pattern of the ancient Near East, a collection of papers written by various scholars, and edited by S. H. Hooke. A second collection followed in 1935: The Labyrinth. After these works, the majority of which were written by British scholars, a doctoral thesis of I. Engnell, who is looked upon as a representative of what is called the Uppsala school, was published in 1943: Studies in Divine Kingship in the ancient Near East, which includes a discussion of the Ras Shamra texts. Another representative of the Uppsala school is G. Widengren, one of whose publications is: Sakrales Königtum im A. T. und im Judentum. Franz Delitzsch-Vorlesungen 1952. E. O. James, who as early as 1933 wrote Christian Myth and Ritual, published a number of popularizing works on the subject, i.a.: Myth and Ritual in the ancient Near East, London 1958. In the same year Hooke published a new collection of studies, entitled: Myth, Ritual and Kingship, Oxford, an important work because it gives the critics an opportunity to say their opinions, and contains reactions to former criticism. We should finally mention: Th. H. Gaster, Thespis. Ritual, Myth, and Drama in the ancient Near East[2], New York, 1961.

[2] Criticism given by, i.a. N. Snaith, The Jewish New Year Festival. Its Origin and Developments, London, 1947; H. Frankfort, Kingship and the Gods, passim; id. The Problem of Similarity in ancient Near Eastern Religions, Frazer Lecture 1951; de Fraine, o.c. 27 ff. The critics do not always state precisely at whom their criticism is levelled. Terms such as "Myth and Ritual theorists" are, if one raises objections, too vague, because the various scholars belonging to this school obviously hold different views. Some of them, in fact, emphatically deny that they belong to any school

affairs the student who, without knowing the languages concerned, enters the field of theses and antitheses of specialists, would at first sight appear to be guilty of *hybris*. Although it is, of course, necessary constantly to realize the dangers involved, the risk in our case is less great than it would seem to be.

First of all it is found that the specialists of the Myth and Ritual school themselves are by no means always familiar with all the languages of the cultures whose myth and ritual elements they endeavour to demonstrate, not to mention the fact that some languages are highly lacunary and in many cases are preserved uncomprehended in clay tablets, such as Hittite and Ugaritic. This fact and the disagreement on the interpretation of texts which are relevant to our investigations have given rise to an extensive literature the outsider can make use of. The greatest common factor of the views of the most prominent experts is, I think, a firm enough basis for inquiry. Added to this is the fact that there exists a *communis opinio* among both the supporters and the opponents of the Myth and Ritual theory about the aspects of the ceremonies that are essential to our investigation. I finally wish to stress once again that what matters to us are the material and the facts, and that we shall try, wherever an interpretation is unavoidable, to choose to the best of our ability between probable and improbable. In doing so we shall on several occasions take the side of the opposition, of Frankfort in particular, rather than that of the Myth and Ritual school itself. To start with, I shall here give a brief description of this new trend in the science of religious history.

In the discussions about the divine kingship in the Mediterranean cultures a remarkable Babylonian festival has long since been allotted a prominent place, a place it still occupies. The data available are considered to warrant the conclusion that during this festival, called *Akitu* [1], the king acted the part of the city-god Marduk in a drama which had as its subject the fall (disappearance) and the resurrection (return) of the god, after an ultimate victory over the forces of Chaos (the monster Tiamat). On the basis of his evolutionist view Frazer [2] gave an interpretation of this and similar

---

(e.g. A. R. Johnson, who did contribute to the collection Labyrinth). For an answer to the criticism see: Hooke, M.R.K. 1 ff.

[1] Discussion and literature see p. 220 ff.

[2] The dying God, 1920, 111. Also elsewhere he writes about this festival: The Scapegoat, 1920, 354 ff.

festivals: "Wherever sacred dramas of this sort were acted as magical rites for the regulation of the seasons, it would be natural that the chief part should be played by the king, at first in his character of head magician, and afterwards as representative and embodiment of the beneficent god who vanquishes the powers of evil". He considers it possible that originally the old king, who since his magic power was exhausted after a year, "was inexorably put to death", in the annual drama played the part of the evil, "the dragon", as "the representative of the old order, the old year", who was overcome by his successor, the new king, acting the part of the victorious god.

A different explanation is furnished by the Panbabylonists, and by A. Jeremias in particular. In his opinion, what is essential is not the death of the magic year-king, even though he, too, assumes that a king had to die every year, but the death of the year-god, as was already postulated by Mannhardt [1]. The basic principle from which Jeremias [2] started was that in the way of thinking of the Babylonians "alles irdische Sein und Geschehen einem himmlischen Sein und Geschehen entspricht", so that the king does indeed play an important part in the annual drama, but only as "Abbild des himmlischen Königs", or, ultimately "als Inkarnation der Gottheit". This puts the myth as the pattern for the New Year drama in the full light. Building on this basis, scholars, the majority of whom were English or Swedish, have sifted the many data about the *Akitu* festival, separating the non-essential from the essential, and pieced the essentialia together into a fundamental scheme, a pattern. After that they tried to discover whether a corresponding complex of myth and rite in a similar pattern existed also among other peoples.

As far as Israel was concerned they had a predecessor in S. Mowinckel [3], who in his sensational Psalmenstudien, particularly in the second volume "Das Thronsbesteigungsfest Jahwäs und der Ursprung der Eschatologie", on the basis of a comparison between psalms and Babylonian and Egyptian literary and ritual texts,

---

[1] Wald- und Feldkulte, I-II, *passim*.
[2] A. Jeremias, Handbuch der altorientalischen Geisteskultur[2], Leipzig, 1929, 171.
[3] S. Mowinckel, Psalmenstudien, I-VI, 1922-1924. He, too, already had a predecessor in H. Gunkel, who in a series of studies had drawn attention to the ritual-liturgic aspect of the kings' psalms. In 1926 his great work, Die Psalmen, appeared.

thought he recognized a New Year festival in Israel, in which Yahweh's victory over the forces of chaos were celebrated in a new enthronement, in which the king was the incarnation of the god. It goes without saying that this theory met with strong resistance, in which scientific and emotional motives intermingle. There is no denying that, however attractive some of Mowinckel's theses may be, a large part of the material he uses allows of a different interpretation [1]. It is just as obvious that the Myth and Ritual school, many representatives of which included the Israelite kingship in their considerations, were up against a similar criticism, as is the fact that precisely for this reason the Israelite material is useless for our purpose.

The same holds for the Ugaritic and Hittite material, to which the theories were also applied and which, as we shall see in passing, shows very interesting analogies, but which, on account of the obscurity and scarcity of the texts, cannot serve as our starting-point. However, there are two festivals about which we know enough to warrant a careful description, and which have both been the subject of many studies: the Egyptian *Heb sed* and the Babylonian *Akitu* festival.

This does not imply that we know everything about these festivals, or that the scholars agree on all details: our object does not require this. We looked for ceremonies in which the king in some way or other plays the part of the god; and we found that in the festivals referred to, or in the examples to which they go back, he does. If others have already pointed to parallels between these festivals, this may in a later stage help us to find an interpretation. Our first task, however, is that of giving the reader a description of the δρώμενα, in order that he may himself evaluate the conclusions drawn.

2. *Egyptian and Near Eastern festivals*

A. Egypt

The fact that the Egyptian king was considered divine is found in every work about Egyptian religion or kingship [2], and may be counted among those facts that are positively certain. After a pre-

---

[1] See the dispassionate criticism of C. R. North, The religious aspects of Hebrew Kingship. Zeitschrift für die Alttestamentische Wissenschaft, 50, 1932, 8 ff. and the literature referred to above.

[2] G. A. Wainwright, The Sky-Religion in Egypt, Cambridge, 1938, 14; A. Moret, Du caractère religieux de la royauté pharaonique, Paris, 1902,

dynastic period, during which the gods, as legend has it, themselves reigned as kings, the pharaoh took over the task of the gods
after the unification of Upper and Lower Egypt by the legendary
king Menes. The legend that Horus himself had effectuated the
unity of the realm is indicative of the close relationship between
Horus and the ruling king [1]. The king bears the name of Horus [2],
and, what is more, in the eyes of the Egyptians he was the god,
without any restriction [3]. Since the pharaoh was given the name of
Horus on his accession, it may be concluded that the ceremony of
the enthronization implied the identification of king and god [4].
This conclusion, which is corroborated by many other data, is of

---

passim; Cerfaux et Tondriau, o.c. 81; C. J. Gadd, Ideas of divine rule in
the ancient East. The Schweich Lectures of the British Academy 1945,
London, 1948, 33; J. Vandier, La religion égyptienne². Mana I, 1, Paris
1949, 140; Engnell, o.c. 4; Frankfort, Kingship and the Gods, 5; H. W.
Fairman in M.R.K. 75; S. Morentz, Ägyptische Religion, Stuttgart, 1960, 35;
H. Jacobsohn, Die dogmatische Stellung des Königs in der Theologie der
alten Ägypter, Hamburg, 1939, 46 ff. This view has of late been made
slightly less absolute without being really affected by: G. Posener, De la
divinité du Pharaon. Cahiers de la Société asiatique, 15, Paris, 1960, and
H. Goedicke, Die Stellung des Königs im A.R. Ägyptische Abh. 2, Wiesbaden, 1960, 40 ff.
    [1] Particularly: S. A. B. Mercer, Horus, Royal God of Egypt, Grafton,
1942.
    [2] K. Sethe, Urgeschichte und älteste Religion der Ägypter, Leipzig,
1930, § 128 f., traces the identification of the king and Horus back to a historical victory of Menes, who wanted to give Horus the honour of this victory
by assuming his name. This historical explanation was opposed by H. Kees,
Der Götterglaube im alten Ägypten, Leipzig, 1941, 41 n. 3; 195; 412. In
any case, we see that in an important text quoted by Frankfort, o.c. 26,
the part of Menes, the unificator, is played by Horus. It is not only in the
field of the Egyptian religion that sacral customs are interpreted historically
as well as mythically. The same phenomenon is observed in the Canaanite,
the Israelite and the Greek religions. Fierce opposition against historical
interpretations: Engnell, o.c. *passim*; for a combination see Frankfort,
o.c. 9; we postpone our judgment until after the discussion of the Dionysiac
cult.
    [3] The possibility that this function was first held by the god Re, and that
it was later on taken over by Horus (Vandier, o.c. 43), may be left out of
consideration here, as may the representation of the king as the son of Re
(Morentz, o.c. 36).
    [4] Fairman, o.c. 77. A representation that is found is that the pharaoh
was born from a marriage between a god (Amon) and a mortal woman,
the queen, but "le couronnement était ce moment où toutes les promesses
du jour de la naissance se réalisent pour le pharaon." (Moret, o.c. 76).
Frankfort, o.c. 5, therefore states: "His coronation was not an apotheosis
but an epiphany". Cf. Bonnet, Reallexikon der ägyptischen Religionsgeschichte, Berlin, 1952, 396.

fundamental significance. In view of the fact that it is precisely this ceremony which in the most important royal feast, the *Heb sed*, is repeated periodically, we shall begin by saying a few words about the accession proper.

In one of the recent publications on this subject H. W. Fairman [1] points out that a distinction should be made between the assumption of the government (accession) and the coronation. The former, a purely practical affair, coincided with the dying day of the old king; for the latter ceremony with its strongly religious accents, a suitable date had to be awaited, viz..... "the beginning of one of the decisive moments in the calendar, the beginning of one of the three seasons, the most favoured date being the first day of the first month of winter" [2]. It is assumed that during the period between accession and coronation the new king made the tour of the cities of Egypt referred to in the famous mystery-papyrus of the enthronization of Sesostris I (c. 1960 B.C.) [3].

The papyrus presents pictures of a sacred mystery play in which the coronation-rites [4]—the funeral of the old king and his resurrection in the person of the new king, the investiture and the installation, the celebration of a feast by a banquet, the progress in a barge by the new king, magic rites, sacrifices—are enacted by the king and fellow-actors. The remarkable thing, however, is that in the accompanying text these rites are given a mythical foundation, and are thus given a mythical-religious meaning which transcends by far the practical ritual object. The new king is identified with Horus and the old king with Osiris, who has been killed by the god Set; a ritual fight that is enacted represents the fight between Horus and Set; the raising of the *djed*-column (a rite we shall

---

[1] o.c. 78. See also Frankfort, o.c. 102.

[2] Fairman, o.c. 78. Since Egypt had more than one calendrical system, and the festivals, moreover, depended on the rise and the fall of the river Nile, it is impossible to give a fixed date for this day, which is generally taken as New Year's Day. For Hatshepsut the coronation on New Year's Day has been attested. In other instances, when the coronation took place on a different date, the coronation day was taken as the first day of the new year (Morentz, o.c. 39).

[3] Edited by K. Sethe, Dramatische Texte zu altägyptischen Mysterienspielen, Leipzig, 1928, 83 ff. See: Frankfort, o.c. 123 ff.; Gaster, Thespis[2], 377 ff.

[4] Fairman, o.c. 81 f., following Helck, Orientalia, 23, 1954, 383 ff., connects the papyrus rather with ceremonies which take place on the eve of the *Sed* festival, which also testifies to the interrelation between this festival and the coronation.

discuss later) is the resurrection of Osiris in the person of his son Horus, etc.[1] Thus we see that in this coronation-mystery play time and eternity overlap; the ritual performance is given its profound meaning because it actualizes the myth and thus adds a religious dimension to the coronation. This overlapping of myth and rite is found not only in this dramatic papyrus, but also in pictures and descriptions of the real coronation[2]. There, too, the actions take place on two levels: a human and a divine one.

When we assemble the none too numerous data concerning the coronation rites [3], of which especially the pictures showing the coronation ceremonies of queen Hatshepsut are a rich source, the following scene may be visualized: the ceremony starts with a purification with water, which, as is shown by the picture—the water is represented by two streams of *anch*-characters [4]—and the text—"je t'ai purifié avec la vie et la force, pourque tu rajeunisses" [5] —was to endow the pharaoh with divine life. The new king is now given his names. "Horus" he is called, and "Lord of the two Crowns", "King of South and North". As is apparent from pictures dating from the time of Horemheb and Ramses II the gods are present at this ceremony and at the subsequent ones, "c'est-à-dire de statues divines présentées par des prêtres, leurs interprètes" [6]. It is also from their hands that the king receives the double crown, whilst Horus himself puts on the royal diadem. The king, led by Horus, the old god of the Nile Valley, and Set, god of Upper Egypt, sits down first on the throne of the Southern kingdom to receive the white crown, and, after that, on the throne of the North to receive the red crown. In addition he is given the symbols of his power, the crook, the flail and the sceptre.

Preceded by standards with the symbols of the gods the king

---

[1] Frankfort, o.c. 128. See also p. 212.

[2] A royal drama which is akin to the one discussed above, is the Memphitic drama (Sethe, Dramatische Texte 1 ff.), for which see: Frankfort, o.c. 24 ff.; Gaster, o.c. 399; James, o.c. 149.

[3] Our starting-point is A. Moret, Du caractère religieux de la royauté pharaonique, Paris, 1902, 75 ff., with corrections by later scholars: Frankfort, o.c. 105 ff.; Bonnet, o.c. 395 ff.; James, o.c. 89 ff.; C. J. Bleeker, Egyptian Festivals. Enactments of religious Renewal. in: Studies in the History of Religions, Supplements to Numen 13, Leiden, 1967, 94 f., 109 f.

[4] Picture in Moret, pl. II, p. 108/109.

[5] Moret, o.c. pl. II, text. Cf. W. B. Kristensen, Het leven uit de dood, Haarlem, 1926, 40; A. H. Gardiner, J.E.A. 36, 1949/50, 3 ff.

[6] Moret, o.c. 85.

goes to the place where Horus and Set [1] symbolically unite the two parts of the kingdom under the throne. The words spoken by Horus: "je lie les deux terres sous toi, à tes pieds, Horus maître du palais" (= king) illustrate a situation which to us is difficult to imagine: Horus addresses his earthly incarnation.

Now follows the curious ceremony of the "procession round the walls" [2]. The scanty reports on this rite afford only a very hazy picture of it. It is assumed that it symbolizes the taking possession of the temple of Horus and Set, i.e. of the two kingdoms which together form Egypt [3]. A feast during which a sacrifice is made to the gods, and at which often the basis is laid for a new temple, concludes the ceremony.

Some δρώμενα thus unite in the coronation ritual into a complex of myth and rite which, with minor modifications, is also found in other cultures. On the day of the coronation the divinity of the pharaoh became apparent, his identification with Horus was effectuated. Moreover, the country was united under his rule. "It is evident . . . that to the Egyptian the death of a king meant the temporary disruption of the union of the Two Lands, and that one of the main purposes of the coronation was to restore that unity and to ensure that the new king became a god", as it was formulated by Fairman [4]. That the enthronization was also looked upon as a victory over mythical or historical enemies [5] is confirmed by another ceremony, which took place every year on New Year's day: the coronation of the sacred falcon, bird of Horus [6]. The falcon underwent a complete investiture, and was offered pieces of meat, symbols of the annihilated enemies of Horus and the king.

After a number of years, often thirty [7], the coronation cere-

---

[1] In Abydos the two gods are Horus and Thot.

[2] The translations vary: Moret, 96, translates: "faire le tour derrière le mur", Naville, Recueil de travaux, 21, p. 114: "faire le tour du mur du Nord", Fairman, 79: "circumambulation of the walls". See for a different explanation: Helck, o.c. 408.

[3] Moret, o.c. 98, sees in the rite an imitation of the victorious sun; Fairman, o.c. 79, considers it the taking possession of the kingdom; Frankfort, o.c. 104, writes: ". . . the most important ceremonies repeated the celebrations with which Menes had established his sovereignty over the Two Lands.

[4] o.c. 78.

[5] Bonnet, o.c. 398 f.

[6] To this rite Fairman, o.c. 80, has called attention in this connection.

[7] The period of thirty years is often mentioned, but other periods are also

mony[1] was repeated during a festival which was called *Heb sed* after the royal robe or diadem[2]. The meaning of this highly important and pre-eminently royal festival [3], which goes back to the first dynasty, is described in a text from Abydos, in which it is said of the king: "Tu renais en renouvelant les fêtes *Sed*" [4]. On this explanation nearly all scholars agree: "It was a true renewal of kingly potency, a rejuvenation of rulership" [5]. Clearly defined by its characteristic elements as a solemn repetition of the coronation festival, the *Heb sed*, which legend ascribes to Menes, the unificator, was by preference held on the first day of the winter season, which was taken as New Year's Day [6].

Unless an entirely new temple was built for the purpose [7], the ceremony took place in a hall especially constructed for it. After a ritual purification the gods from the whole of Egypt come to this festival, represented by their symbols [8]. They are welcomed with offerings by the pharaoh, after which a procession of king, statues of the gods, and dignitaries takes place. Now the king is given a special cloak, of which it is at present thought that it gave its name to the festival, after which the most important rite is performed. Led by the wolf-god Upuaut [9], the king sits down alternately, on the throne of the Northern and on that of the Southern land. This ceremony of the double throne, which also characterized the

---

attested. See Fairman, o.c. 83; Moret, o.c. 256 ff.; Griffith, J.E.A. 5, 1918, 61; *idem*, J.E.A. 21, 1935, 148; Frankfort, o.c. 366 n. 2.

[1] The daily rituals the pharaoh had to perform in order to maintain his kingship, cannot be dealt with in detail here. See A. Moret, Le rituel du culte divin journalier en Égypte d'après les papyrus de Berlin et les textes du temple de Séth I à Abydos, Paris, 1902.

[2] It was formerly thought that the diadem was called *sed* (Moret); at present this name is given to the typical festive cloak the king wears during this festival (Bleeker, o.c. 101; Bonnet, o.c. 158).

[3] It would be superfluous to give a detailed bibliography. The reader will find one up to 1943 in Engnell, o.c. 200, special note 4; later literature in the works cited of Frankfort, Fairman, James, Gaster and Bleeker.

[4] Moret, o.c. 256.

[5] Frankfort, o.c. 79; also Fairman, o.c. 84; W. Helck, R.E. 2e Reihe 8, 1958, 901: "Jubiläumfest, durch das die Kraft des Königs neu gestärkt werden sollte."

[6] See particularly: B. van der Walle, La Nouvelle Clio, 6, 1954, 283 ff.

[7] The close relation between *Sed* festival and the building of temples has been dealt with by G. D. Hornblower, Journal of the Manchester Egyptian and Oriental Society, 17, 1932, 21 ff.

[8] Pictures in Moret, o.c. 236 f.

[9] Wolf-god or dog-god. The Egyptians did not sharply distinguish between these animals. Cf. Herodotus, 2, 122.

coronation, occupies such a central place in the *Heb sed* that the picture of the double throne has become the hieroglyphic for the *Sed* festival.[1]

A peculiar part of the festival, which is probably a parallel of the procession round the walls of the coronation festival, is an action sometimes referred to as "the crossing of the field" [2]. Dancing or in a quick run the king, adorned alternately with the crowns of northern and southern Egypt [3], crosses a field (= Egypt) in the direction of each of the four winds, and by doing so "would dedicate it, and, therewith, Egypt to the gods and at the same time assert his legitimate power over the land" [4]. In pictures the king is seen to offer his insignia to the god Upuaut, an understandable gesture, for, as H. Kees puts it in his monograph on the dance of the pharaoh [5]: "Der König übergibt den Göttern das gleiche, was sie ihm zum Danke dafür wieder versprechen". Upuaut has every reason to be here, as he is the king's precursor, and enables him to rule by vanquishing his enemies. In pictures he is shown defeating the enemies of the god Osiris in order to help him ascend the throne. In conformity with this we often find the representation of the king killing his enemies [6], which is closely linked up with the *Heb sed* and goes back to the most ancient times.

This leads Kees to the following interesting interpretation [7]: "Upuaut ist also der eigentliche Königsgott der Zeit des siegenden oberägyptischen Reiches. Sein hervorragender Platz beim Sedfest ist darnach nur natürlich, sollte doch dieses Fest nach seiner wahrscheinlichsten Erklärung eine Verherrlichung der königlichen Macht über alle Länder sein, an dem alle Völker Tribut bringen...., ein grosser Triumph des Königs entstanden aus dem wirklichen Siegesfest über das unterworfene Unterägypten". Although this view, which assumes a historical development, has not remained

---

[1] Bleeker, o.c. 98; H. Kees, Der Opfertanz des ägyptischen Königs. Diss. Münich, 1912, 167.

[2] Fairman, o.c. 84; Moret still looked upon this dance as belonging to the founding of the temple. This point of view has now been abandoned.

[3] Good pictures in Kees, o.c.

[4] Frankfort, 86. Helck, R.E., l.c. speaks of "Besitzergreifungslauf". Vikentiev, Bulletin de l'institut d'Égypte, 37, 1, 1954/55, 277, considers it a reflection of a historic victory over the Libyans.

[5] o.c. 15.

[6] Kees, o.c. 136 and 169. Pictures in Moret, o.c. 264, with a wrong interpretation; Vikentiev, o.c. 275 ff.; Bleeker, o.c. 92; Frankfort, o.c. fig. 3.

[7] o.c. 188 f.

unopposed, it still finds supporters [1]. In any case it emphasizes once more the triumphal character of the *Heb sed* [2].

Finally, we have to mention a rite which formed part of the *Sed* festival [3], as well as being performed during—or immediately before—the coronation-ceremony, but which was also celebrated each year as a calendrical ritual. The raising of the *djed* column took place every year on New Year's Eve [4]. Texts and pictures show beyond any doubt that this action symbolizes the resurrection of Osiris, or, more accurately, his resurrection in death, Osiris being the king of the realm of the dead, the realm, according to the well-known phrase of Kristensen [5], of "spontaneous life". Kristensen [6] also furnishes the most plausible explanation of the connection between the erection of the *djed* column, the coronation and the *Sed* festival. On the day after the funeral and the resuscitation of Osiris the god arises in the shape of Horus, his son, incarnated in the new king. This explanation also leaves room for the view found, amongst others, in Frankfort [7], that Osiris personifies the old king who has died, and Horus, his son, the new king, an identification realized not only at the coronation, but also periodically in the *Sed* festival. In this way it is not only by its date, but also by a common mythical-ritual element that the *Sed* festival—and the coronation— are connected with the New Year festival. An important phenomenon is further that during the "mourning and rejoicing festival" at the turn of the year two groups of people performed a ritual fight, in which the enemies of the god Osiris were defeated [8]. We shall repeatedly encounter sham fights of this kind, sometimes in the form of *agones*, under similar conditions.

---

[1] J. Vandier, o.c. 201, thinks that Upuaut was "une divinité guerrière qui a conduit à la victoire les antiques souverains d'Hierakonpolis. L'épisode ... n'aurait été à l'origine qu'un hommage rendu par les rois hiérakonpolitains au dieu qui leur avait donné la victoire." Cf. Bonnet, o.c. 159.

[2] W. Kaiser, Z.Ä. S. 91, 1964, 89 ff., interprets the famous palette of Narmer as representing a triumph on the occasion of a *Sed* festival.

[3] In the tomb of Kheruef at Thebes. See Bleeker, o.c. 102.

[4] About this rite see H. Bergema, De Boom des Levens in schrift en historie, Amsterdam, 1938, 367 ff.; Kristensen, o.c. 96, 104; James, o.c. 61; Kees, o.c. 163 f.; Mercer, Religion of ancient Egypt, London, 1949, 122; Engnell, o.c. 10; Frankfort, o.c. *index*, s.v.; specially about this: B. van der Walle, o.c.

[5] o.c. *passim*.

[6] o.c. 32 f. Cf. *idem*, Verzamelde Bijdragen, 77.

[7] o.c. 110 ff.

[8] Kristensen, Het Leven uit de Dood, 132 f.; Bergema, o.c. 371 n. 385; Engnell, o.c. 11; James, o.c. 50.

The description here given and a first interpretation represent the view of the majority of the experts. Some of them have, of course, proceeded in different directions. Moret [1], for instance, has on the basis of the data given above, and following in Frazer's steps, defined the *Heb sed* as being originally a ritual murder of the old king, who after a period of thirty years had become feeble, was no longer capable of fulfilling his magical function, and was therefore replaced by a young, new king—all this chiefly in view of the identification of the king with Osiris. Objections against this theory were raised in various quarters [2]. It was rightly pointed out that originally Osiris as the king-god cannot have had the meaning he acquired in later times.

Bleeker, who recently devoted a study to the *Heb sed* [3], deviates in the opposite direction from what might be considered the *communis opinio*. His criticism is not only directed at Frazerian theories such as those referred to above, but also at the generally accepted view that the *Heb sed* is a repetition of the coronation ceremony. After comparing and critically sifting the material on the *Heb sed* [4], Bleeker considers the following to be the essential characteristics of this festival: the dualism of the two series of ritual acts, one for northern and one for southern Egypt; the clothing in the *Heb sed* cloak, maintained unchanged for more than fifteen centuries; the ceremony of the double throne. All other elements, the ritual dance, the raising of the *djed* column, the ritual fight, are not characteristic of the *Sed* festival because they are not shown in *all* three relevant pictures of the *Sed* festival. What is left is not sufficient to justify a

---

[1] Le mise à mort du dieu en Égypte, 1927, and other works; cf. Wainwright, o.c. 5; P. Munro, Z.Ä.S. 86, 1961, 61 ff.

[2] During the *Sed* festival the pharaoh decidedly did not represent Osiris, as Mercer, The Religion of ancient Egypt, 122, still thinks. See *contra*: J. G. Griffith, J.E.A. 41, 1955, 127 f. Frazer, Osiris, Attis, Adonis, 153 ff., had already stated that the king was at the *Sed* festival identified with the dead Osiris, and was subsequently re-born. Gardener, J.E.A. 2, 1915, 124, however, pointed out that it was Horus, and not Osiris, who manifested himself in the person of the king. See also Jacobsohn, o.c. 12. Cf. Engnell, o.c. 11: "There is, however, no distinct difference between the resurrection of Osiris, the dead king and that of Horus, the living one". Cf. Erman, Die Religion der Ägypter, ihr Werden und Vergehen in vier Jahrtausenden, Berlin, 1934, 184 f.

[3] o.c. 96 ff.

[4] He deals with the three most complete series of pictures: of Neuserre in the temple of Re at Abu Gurab; of Amenhotep III in the tomb of Kheruef at Thebes; of Osorkon in the festival hall of the temple at Bubastis.

comparison with the coronation rites. Nevertheless Bleeker, too, looks upon the *Sed* festival as "intended to renew the king's office" [1], but in his opinion this renewal does not concern the kingship, but the priesthood of the king. The *sed* cloak is, in his view, a priestly vestment, not a royal robe.

We unfortunately lack the space to deal with each of Bleeker's arguments separately. Even a non-Egyptologist is able to understand .... and to refute them. Only a few remarks will have to suffice to demonstrate that Bleeker's views will not hold against the generally accepted ones described above. The scene of the double throne on which the king is depicted twice, once wearing the crown of the North and once that of the South, the symbol of the *Sed* festival, indicates a royal, not a priestly office [2]. The dance around the field is not shown in all *sed* pictures, but it is found in the oldest one referred to by Bleeker, that of the *Sed* festival of Neuserre. The *circumambulatio* of oxen and donkeys round the walls, which is depicted in the more recent picture of the *Sed* festival of Amenhotep III, like the king's dance around the field, is strongly reminiscent of the procession around the wall of the coronation ceremony. The fact that the *Sed* festival was not always celebrated on I Tybi does not plead against a connection with the coronation, which, as we know, was not always celebrated on this date either, but itself by definition ushered in a new year. It does have to be conceded—but this was done before—that in all probability Osiris and the *djed* column not until later assumed a regular function in the *sed* rites [3], just as they did in the coronation ceremony. This, however, does not eliminate this element as the *trait d'union* between the two ceremonies. Besides, the incorporation of the Osiris myth, his resurrection in the *djed* column, the sham fights in both ceremonies, prove that both the coronation and the *Sed* festival bore a character in which the idea of death and resurrection, finishing the old and making a new start, was basically present. Finally, I fail to see how the irregularity in the celebration of the *Sed* festival can

---

[1] o.c. 115.

[2] As also Bleeker himself writes in an earlier study, Die Geburt eines Gottes. Eine Studie über den ägyptischen Gott Min und sein Fest. Supplements to Numen 3, Leiden, 1956, p. 92: ,,Der Ritus der Thronbesteigung, der so charakteristisch ist dass das sogenannte Determinativ von ḥb śd eine Doppelhalle (...) mit einem Königssessel abbildet, den der Pharao respektive besteigt um über das ganze Land Fürst zu werden."

[3] See p. 213 n. 2.

be explained by defining the festival as a re-investiture of a priest [1].

One argument remains: the main reason why the *Sed* festival cannot be the repetition of the coronation should be that another festival, which was celebrated annually, already had this function: the feast in honour of the god Min. "An annual renewal of the royal dignity is incompatible with an analogous ritual of no fixed date...." (112) However, we shall see further on that such a combination does prove possible, and that particularly the celebration of more than one New Year festival within one year is the rule rather than being exceptional, as, for that matter, Bleeker himself points out (113).

It is too early yet to draw conclusions; comparisons with other festivals, notably with the Babylonian *Akitu* festival, may prove helpful, and will perhaps show us which are the essential and which the secundary elements, which typically Egyptian and which general aspects. The festival dealt with above was one which, repeated periodically, imitated the coronation ceremony in every detail. It aimed at rejuvenating the king, at renewing the identification with Horus and at ensuring the unity of the realm under the pharaoh. This typically triumphal feast was attended by the gods, represented by statues or symbols. As a typical New Year festival it was preceded by a ceremony on New Year's Eve, in which the death and the resurrection in death of the god Osiris was celebrated, among other things by a sham fight.

B. Mesopotamia

The problems around the nature of the kingship in Mesopotamia [2] are much more complicated than those concerning the Egyptian kingship. Not only are we here confronted with a development of millennia—we also were in Egypt—, but this development was far

---

[1] In ancient cultures the investiture of a king was far more prominent than the investiture of a priest, provided it should be possible to distinguish between the kingly and the priestly functions of the ruler, as it is done by Bleeker. That the *Sed* cloak should be a priest's garment is a hypothesis which is not made credible.

[2] H. Frankfort, Kingship and the Gods, Chicago, 1948, 215 ff.; S. Smith, The practice of kingship in early Semitic kingdoms, in M.R.K. 26 ff.; E. O. James, Myth and Ritual in the ancient Near East, London, 1958, 96; C. J. Gadd, Ideas of divine rule in the ancient East, 1948, 37; R. Labat, Le caractère religieux de la royauté assyro-babylonienne, Paris, 1939. See further the works mentioned below.

from gradual in Mesopotamia. Various peoples in turn exercised political power and cultural influence, and therefore we must not expect to find one invariable view on the Mesopotamian kingship. The experts do, however, on the whole agree on the fundamental difference between the Egyptian kingship and that of Mesopotamia.

In the country between the rivers there is no continuous tradition which assigns a divine status to the king [1]. There are no indications for a divine kingship during the Sumerian period. This has been connected with the original function of the king (*lugal*), who from of old appears to have been elected "democratically" for the sole purpose of commanding the army during the war. As soon as the war was over, he resigned [2]. It is assumed that, with the steadily increasing frequency of the wars, the kingship gradually became of longer duration, and coincided with the function of priest of the city-god, thus uniting priesthood and political power [3].

Certain is that the Akkadians, who in c. 2350 B.C. [4] took over the government from the Sumerians, show higher pretensions. Sargon of Akkad assumed the title of "Ruler of the Four Quarters" [5], a title the Sumerians reserved for their gods, and Naram-Sin undoubtedly claimed divine status. He had his name preceded by the determinativum of god, as did other kings of this period [6], and on a stele built on the occasion of a victory, he is unmistakably represented as a god with the horned helmet [7], a unique phenomenon in Mesopotamia.

The signs of a deification of the king, still to be observed during the Sumerian restoration, disappeared again during the period of the first Babylonian dynasty; most conspicuous is the complete absence of divine characteristics in Hammurabi. Nor were the Assyrian kings looked upon as being divine [8], although the priest-

---

[1] See for the development Labat, o.c. 1 ff.; Frankfort, o.c. 215 ff.

[2] Frankfort, o.c. 219, Smith, o.c. 26 and others compare this with Marduk being elected champion of the gods in the Epic of Creation.

[3] The development of the various functions and titles forms an intricate and vexed problem, into which I do not wish to enter. See Frankfort, o.c. 215; D. O. Edzard in Fischer Weltgeschichte, 2, Die altorientalischen Reiche I, 1965, 73 ff.; W. W. Hallo, Early Mesopotamian Royal Titles. A philological and historical analysis, New Haven, 1957.

[4] Edzard, o.c. 92.

[5] Labat, o.c. 6; Frankfort, o.c. 228.

[6] Frankfort, o.c. 224 f.

[7] Labat, o.c. 8, fig. 1; Frankfort, o.c. 225 and fig. 43.

[8] Labat, o.c. 15 ff.

hood was one of their major functions. When, therefore, during the Assyrian period the claimant to the throne is carried to the temple, there to receive the *insignia regalia*, and is preceded by a priest who in a loud voice cries: "Assur is king, Assur is king" [1], this is decidedly not to be taken, as is done by Engnell [2], as an identification of the king and the god Assur, and to be used as an argument by which to prove a divine kingship for Assyria. Frankfort [3] understandably points out the absurdity of a deification prior to the coronation proper and thinks: "This phrase emphasized that the new ruler— as yet uncrowned, and hence not "king" in the fullest sense of the word —was on his way to the god who was the depositary of kingship in Assyria".

All in all it may be concluded that, in spite of the fact that some kings put the determinativum of god before their names, and in spite of the picture of the deified Naram-Sin, or, rather, precisely because of the rarity of these instances, it is clear that in Mesopotamia the king did not at all times *qualitate qua* have a divine status.

This does not alter the fact that his function as the intermediary between gods and humans was so important that in times of imminent danger, portending the anger of the gods, a deputy-king was appointed [4], in order that the real king remain unharmed. The deputy-king was for some time given the dignity of the kingship, and was killed afterwards—in one instance we are told after a period of one hundred days [5]—with a view to averting the danger from the real king. Since this institution is bound to have been of a non-periodical nature, it cannot be historically connected with a well-known festival in which it is also a deputy-king who plays the leading part, the *Sacaea* [6]. This festival, which, according to Greek sources [7], was celebrated in Babylonia but was of Persian origin,

---

[1] K. F. Müller, Das assyrische Ritual. Mitt. der vorderasiatisch-ägyptischen Gesellschaft, 41, 3, 1937.

[2] I. Engnell, Studies in divine Kingship in the ancient Near East, Uppsala, 1943, 17.

[3] o.c. 246.

[4] About the deputy-kingship see: Labat, o.c. 353 ff.; Gaster, Thespis, 69 n. 4 and 105 n. 67; W. von Soden, Z.A. 43, 1936, 255 ff.; H. M. Kümmel, Ersatzrituale für den hethitischen König. Studien zu den Bogazköy-texten, Wiesbaden, 1967, 169 ff.

[5] Labat, o.c. 358.

[6] Frankfort, o.c. 400 n. 11.

[7] Berossos in Athenaeus, 14, 639 C and Dio Chrysostomos, Orat. 4, 66, where one reads that the festival is a Persian one, just as in Strabo, 11, 8, 4 f.

was characterized by elation and disguise and a reversal of the social ranks: the masters served their slaves. A criminal was for a period of five days granted all the king's rights, even the free access to his harem, and was given the title of *Zoganes*. He was killed afterwards.

There is more justification in drawing a parallel between the *Sacaea* festival, which—if one compares it with, e.g. the Roman *Saturnalia* [1]—shows all the features of a celebration of the turn of the year, and the *Akitu* festival, which in later times became the real Babylonian New Year festival. Frazer [2] attempted to prove that both festivals were identical, but concedes that the different dates of the festivals plead against his view. Many [3] have followed him completely or partly, and have attempted to find solutions for other problems attaching to this theory—how, for example, a Persian festival is to be reconciled to a Babylonian origin [4]—. Some difficulties, however, remain. The most important of these is that no deputy-kingship during the *Akitu* festival has been attested [5], nor has any mention been made in this connection of rowdiness or a reversal of the social roles [6]. The safest plan, therefore, is to follow Labat when he concludes: "d'une part, il est certain que l'usage des substituts royaux était familier aux Akkadiens et que le roi renouvelait son pouvoir chaque année aux fêtes du Nouvel An; mais, d'autre part rien ne prouve qu'il y ait un lien quelconque entre ces deux coutumes".

It is for two reasons that I refer to this problem. The first is that the problem of the *Sacaea* takes us to our subject proper: the func-

---

[1] The parallel with the *Saturnalia* has been drawn before, i.a. by: S. Langdon, The Babylonian and Persian Sacaea. Journal of the royal Asiatic Society of Great Britain and Ireland, 1924, 65 ff.; F. Böhl, Mimus en Drama op het Babylonisch Nieuwjaarsfeest. In: Stemmen des Tijds, 10, 1920/21, 42 ff.

[2] G.B. The dying God, 111; The Scapegoat, 354 ff.

[3] See i.a. Langdon, o.c.; Gadd, o.c. 96; Labat, o.c. 95 ff.; Frankfort, 409 n. 14.

[4] See Labat, o.c. 101, who, following others, regards the names *Sacaea* and *Zoganes* as Akkadian, and who rightly points out that to Dio Chrys. all inhabitants of the empire of Alexander were "Persians"; cf. von Soden, Z.A. 43, 1936, 255 ff.

[5] A possibility pointed out by Frankfort, o.c. 409 n. 14, that a criminal who was beheaded on the *Akitu* festival was a deputy-king, is too hypothetical to be of any value. The text from which this datum was taken, cannot with certainty be connected with the *Akitu* festival. *Vide infra* p. 226. ff.

[6] Labat, o.c. 102.

tion of the king in the New Year rites; the second is that it may serve as a warning. It is not only in connection with the subject of the *Sacaea* that the abundant literature often contains theories which, although attractive at first sight, on closer inspection are found to be based on hypotheses, uncertain explanations of texts of doubtful identification, etc. This does not render the theories impossible, but it does rob them of evidence. The same phenomenon is repeatedly encountered in connection with our subject proper. In a brief description of the rituals the king had to perform on New Year's Day I shall try, to the best of my ability, to indicate what has been attested as certain, and what, on the basis of combination and interpretation, is assumed to be possible, c.q. probable.

One of the ceremonies in which the king played an important part was that of the sacred marriage of the city god or goddess [1]. This ἱερὸς γάμος has been attested for several cities, mainly from the Isin-Larsan period, but it goes back to the Sumerian period. It took place in the temple of the goddess, who there awaited her bridegroom, as it has been described in hymns [2]. A hymn presenting a detailed description of the ceremony of king Iddan-Dagan reports that the *conubium* gives to the city: "l'abondance et la plénitude et lui assure la nourriture et toutes choses favorables" [3]. The obvious conclusion to be drawn from this is that the sacred marriage served here, as it does elsewhere, to further the fertility of the land.

This hymn [4] is addressed to the goddess Inanna, and describes her marriage to the god Tammuz [5]. It is of great importance to us for two reasons: first of all it is stated unequivocally that the marriage took place on New Year's Day, the day further being characterized as "the day of fixing the fates" [6]. The act of the "fixing of the fates" for the year to come is one we shall meet with again in the later

---

[1] Literature about this subject is very comprehensive. For a good survey see: E. D. van Buren, The sacred marriage in early times in Mesopotamia, Orientalia, 13, 1944, 2 ff.; further, Frankfort, o.c. 295 ff.; Labat, o.c. 161 ff.; critical considerations of S. Smith in M.R.K. 22 ff.

[2] S. N. Kramer, The Sumerian sacred marriage texts. Proc. Am. Phil. Soc. 107, 6, 1963, 485 ff.; W. H. Ph. Römer, Sumerische 'Königshymnen' der Isin-Zeit, diss. Utrecht, 1965; cf. J. van Dijk, Bibl. Or. 11, 1954, 83 ff.

[3] Labat, o.c. 163.

[4] See Römer, o.c. 128 ff., 143 ff.

[5] Also in the text of Shulgi dealt with by van Dijk, Tammuz is the bridegroom.

[6] Römer, o.c. 147. Van Dijk (84) gives as characteristics "que la fête était à la nouvelle lune du nouvel an; qu'alors le mariage sacré était célébré; qu'à cette occasion le sort était fixé."

New-Babylonian *Akitu* festival as one of its major characteristics. The other important fact is that, although we know that in some cities the king as a priest performed significant tasks at the sacred marriage, he occupies a most remarkable position here. There is no doubt that in this hymn the name of the king Iddan-Dagan is mentioned in the place in which we expect the name of the god. It is certain, as the hymn describes very realistically, that the king acted the part of the god in the sacred marriage [1]. Whether the part of the goddess is played by a priestess is not certain [2]. The priestess is often called the "lady" or "spouse" of the god, and this might be the explanation of the sacral temple prostitution recorded by Herodotus [3]. It is obvious that the sacred marriage has to be explained within the framework of the myth of Tammuz, the god who has disappeared, is looked for, and returns to unite with the goddess who is at the same time his mother (or sister) and his bride [4]. It is possible that the coming of the god was already in early times looked upon as a triumph of the local god over hostile powers. Labat (164) thinks he recognizes a representation of this kind in an inscription of the king of Ur, Ibi-Sin. Games are also referred to in connection with the sacred marriage [5].

What is the connection between this New Year ceremony [6] and the festival which under the name *Akitu* is certain to have existed from the Sumerian period and which during the New-Babylonian period—from which our only clear text dates—was celebrated as a New Year festival in the first month of the year? [7] There are certain

---

[1] Also in the hymn of Shulgi. See Labat, o.c. 250; Frankfort, o.c. 296; Smith, o.c. 51.

[2] Labat, o.c. 250, considers this representation possible.

[3] I, 199.

[4] About Tammuz as a dying and rising god see E. Dhorme, Les religions de Babylonie et d'Assyrie, Mana II, Paris, 1945, 115 ff. and literature on p. 134; A. Moortgat, Tammuz. Der Unsterblichkeitsglaube in der altorientalischen Bildkunst, 1948.

[5] See Römer, o.c. 202, n. 14; Moortgat, o.c. 50 f.

[6] This does not mean that the sacred marriage always coincides with the calendrical New Year's Day. In A. Falkenstein, Festschrift J. Friedrich, Heidelberg, 1959, 155, one reads: "Dieses Fest, das dort in den 8 Monat fällt, ist das Neujahrsfest . . .".

[7] On the dating of the *Akitu* festival in the first millennium B.C. in Nisan, the first month of the year, see Falkenstein, o.c. 165. He thinks that, in spite of greatly different datings in Assyrian cities, the festival was originally celebrated in the beginning of autumn, and that a second festival was held in the spring, both around the *equinox*, "zur kultischen Einleitung des landwirtschaftlichen Jahres."

links between the two festivals: we saw that the "fixing of the fates" figured in both feasts. But there is more. It is certain that in Babylon a sacred marriage was celebrated in combination with the *Akitu* festival: there is a text [1] which reports that feasts were organized for Marduk in the *Akitu*-House, after which the god "hastened toward his marriage". This marriage, therefore, did not take place in the *Akitu*-House, but in the temple of Babylon. In addition we find that the processions of barges and chariots, which are characteristic of the *Akitu* festival, are also mentioned in the ritual of the sacred marriage of Shulgi [2]. This shows that there are sufficiently strong arguments for a relationship between the two festivals, although they are too weak for an identification.

About the *Akitu* festival [3] we know that for two millenia it was celebrated in various cities. On the basis of an inquiry into the data Falkenstein [4] has listed the characteristics of the festival and of the Festival-House of the same name in which it was celebrated:

"1. Das akitu-Haus liegt im Weichbild der Stadt, ausserhalb der Stadtmauern...

2. Das Festhaus liegt an oder in der Nähe eines Kanals.

3. Zum akitu-Fest gehört eine Prozession, bei der die Götterstatuen zum Teil zu Schiff von ihrem Stadttempel zum Festhaus zurück gebracht wurden.

4. Von allem Anfang an ist anscheinend die Teilnahme des Königs am kultischen Geschehen beim akitu-Fest verpflichtend gewesen.

---

[1] Falkenstein, o.c. 163; Pallis, The Babylonian Akitu Festival, Copenhagen, 1926, 198; Smith, o.c. 40 n. 1. W. G. Lambert, J.S.S. 13, 1968, 104 ff., must have overlooked this text when he says that he is unable to find "a scrap of evidence" for the theory that "Marduk is involved in a sacred marriage in the course of the New Year festival."

[2] van Dijk, o.c. 87.

[3] Some literature on this widely-discussed subject: H. Zimmern, Berichte über die Verhandlungen der sächsischen Gesellschaft der Wissenschaften, Ph.-Hist, Kl. 58, 1906, 126 ff.; *ibid.* 70, 1918, 1 ff.; Der alte Orient, 25, 1926, 1 ff.; A. J. Wensinck, Acta orientalia, 1, 1923, 158 ff.; S. Langdon, The Babylonian Epic of Creation, Oxford, 1923; S. A. Pallis, o.c.; F. Böhl, Nieuwjaarsfeest en Koningsdag in Babylon en in Israel, Groningen, 1927; G. Furlani, La religione babilonese e assira, Bologna, 2, 1929, 218 ff.; R. Labat, o.c. 160 ff.; Engnell, o.c. 33 ff.; Frankfort, o.c. 313 ff.; E. Dhorme, Les religions de Babylone et d'Assyrie, Mana II, Paris, 1945, 242 f.; 255; Reallexikon der Assyriologie, III, Berlin, 1957, 40 ff.

[4] o.c. 165.

5. Das akitu-Fest war ein Freudenfest, an dem auch die Masse der Bevölkerung teilnehmen konnte.
6. Das akitu-Fest ist auch in der Spätzeit, in der es die grösste Verbreitung hatte, nicht in allen Städten (......) gefeiert worden".

This characterizes the festival as a feast of the gods in which also human beings, notably the king, were allowed to take part. A famous text dating back to the sixth century B.C. [1], but of a much older origin, gives us a description of what took place on the human level during this event.

On the second of Nisan, we read, the priest of Marduk gets up before sunrise, washes himself and says a prayer to the god. On the third of Nisan an artisan is instructed to make two statues—of which a detailed description is given—, which will be beheaded on the sixth of Nisan. In a prayer said on the fourth of Nisan, Marduk is said to "determine the destinies of the gods"; according to this prayer, he gives the sacred sceptre to the king, whilst the goddess Beltu (= Sarpanitu) is requested to "determine the king's fate" [2]. On the fourth day the poem of creation "Enuma elish" is recited in full. On the fifth day Marduk is in a prayer begged for mercy. The temple is rubbed with parts of a newly killed sheep, and in this way purified. The carrion is then thrown into the river. During the period in which the god Nabu is in the city (5 to 12 Nisan) the persons who have performed this purification have to stay outside the city.

Now a meal is put on a table in the temple of Marduk, in front of the statue of the god. Nabu, the son of Marduk, arrives by boat. For him, too, a meal is dished up. The king is brought into the temple, the high priest divests him of his *insignia regalia*, sceptre, ring, sword and crown, and puts these in front of Marduk. The king kneels before the statue of the god, the priest pulls his ear, the king professes his innocence to the god [3]. The priest promises that the god will answer his prayer, that he will make the kingship

[1] F. Thureau-Dangin, Rituels Accadiens, Paris, 1921, 127 ff.
[2] Here we see a clear parallel with the marriage hymns referred to above. Beltu is the spouse of Marduk, with whom he is to unite in a sacred marriage like Tammuz and Inanna. Also in the hymns the goddess determines the king's fate.
[3] On the rite of the confession of guilt: R. Pettazoni, La confessione dei peccati, Bologna, I, II, III, 1929/1936.

flourish, and that he will destroy the enemies. The king is subsequently given back his insignia. The priest slaps his cheek. If the king produces tears, this is held to be a favourable omen. The priest finally ties up forty reeds, lays the bundle into a pit, pours cream, honey and oil over it, and puts a white bull beside the pit. King and priest together say the prayer: "O divine bull, brilliant light... bull of Anu".

Here the text breaks off, so that we have to piece together the rest of the festival, which lasted until the 11th of Nisan, with the aid of data derived from other sources. From an inscription of Nebuchadnezzar [1] we learn that on the 8th and 11th of Nisan Marduk and the gods are in the "Chamber of Destinies" in the temple inside the city. An inscription of Nabonid [2] tells us that the procession to the *Akitu*-House outside the city took place on the 10th of Nisan. Assyrian texts[3] make it clear that the kings had to be present at the festival to "take the hands of Marduk", which means that they had to head the procession with Marduk and the other gods towards the *Akitu*-House. Assurbanipal[4] describes how he makes prisoners of war draw Marduk's chariot. Nabonid offers the gods not only valuables, but also prisoners of war. This military aspect is explained by what we read in another text [5]: "All the gods who go with Marduk to the House of Prayer—it looks like a king with the assembled host". The comparison is a stringent one and presents us with a first clue for an interpretation of the festival.

An important feature of the festival is the recitation of the *Enuma elish*. This epic [6] describes how the united gods get involved in a fight with the monster of the primeval flood and chaos, Tiamat, how Marduk is chosen as the supreme commander of the gods, how he defeats Tiamat, splits up her body and from its parts creates the entire cosmos, heaven and earth. The gods finally build the temple Esagila, the celestial model of the Babylonian temple, vest Marduk with royal power and celebrate a great feast accompanied by a

---

[1] Pallis, o.c. 124; Langdon, Die neubabylonischen Königsinschriften, Leipzig, 1912, 127.

[2] Falkenstein, o.c. 161; Pallis, o.c. 124.

[3] See for the various texts: Falkenstein, o.c. 162; Labat, o.c. 173 f.

[4] Labat, o.c. 172.

[5] Frankfort, o.c. 327, after Proceedings of the Society of Biblical Archaeology, 30, p. 62.

[6] Editions: S. Langdon, o.c.; A. Heidel, The Babylonian Genesis. The Story of the Creation[2], Chicago, 1942; Pritchard, Ancient Near Eastern Texts, 1950, 60 ff.

banquet. The prominent place occupied by the *Enuma elish* in the New Year festival on the one hand, and the characteristic festive procession of the *Akitu* festival of the gods on the other, lead to the conclusion that this procession is nothing but the visible realization of the triumphal march of Marduk at the head of the gods to the Festival-House after the victory over Tiamat (= chaos). The new creation of the myth is in this way actualized in the New Year ceremony. That this view is the correct one is demonstrated by various additional data. An epitheton of Marduk is: "The Lord who sits in the midst of Tiamat at the *Akitu*-festival" [1]. In the inscription of Nebuchadnezzar already mentioned, the A*kitu*-House is called: "The temple of the sacrifices of the exalted New Year's festival of the Enlil of the gods, Marduk; the dwelling of the joy and exultation of the gods of the Upper-and Netherworlds". Frankfort [2], to whom I owe these data, points out that it is precisely these gods who in the *Enuma elish* are described as the gods who rejoice in Marduk's victory. The clearest evidence, however, is supplied by a text of Sennacherib, which describes the doors of the *Akitu*-House of Assur [3]: "A figure of Assur [4], going to battle against Tiamat, carrying the bow, on his chariot holding the "weapon of the storm", and Amurru, who goes with him as charioteer, according to the command revealed by Shamash and Adad in omens at the sacrifice, I engraved upon the gate, (besides) the gods who march in front and the gods who march behind him, those who ride in chariots and those who go on foot .... (and) Tiamat and the creatures (that were) in her".

Now that a parallelism between the sacral acts and the epic of the creation has become apparent, it has also become possible to interpret the ritual with the *insignia regalia*. The acts signify a temporary abdication of the throne, a cessation of the regal power at the transition from the old period to a new one. The beginning of the year is characterized by a new investiture: the kingship is offered anew. But this is exactly what is also said about Marduk in the

---

[1] Frankfort, o.c. 329; cf. E. Ebeling, Tod und Leben nach den Vorstellungen der Babylonier, I, Berlin, 1931, 24: "Das heisst soviel dass er von ihr verschlungen, dass er tot ist. Hiernach hat es also neben dem Enuma eliš-Mythus einen anderen gegeben der zunächst der Tiamat im Kampfe den Sieg zuschreibt."

[2] Frankfort, o.c. 329.

[3] Translation of Frankfort, o.c. 327.

[4] This god occupies Marduk's place in Assyria.

Enuma elish. Once again, therefore, we see a mythical subject being ritually actualized. However, how far does this actualization go? Does the king also play the part of the god, as he did in the sacred marriage? As far as the Babylonian festival proper is concerned, we know nothing about this for certain, but the city of Assur provides a curious datum; on the tablet describing the doors of the *Akitu*-House we find the marginal note [1]: "The victorious prince, standing in Assur's chariot; Tiamat and the creatures of her inside". It has been concluded [2] that Sennacherib himself personified the god Assur in the procession of the gods during the *Akitu* festival, which seems to be confirmed by the last sentence of the text, in which the names are given of the gods depicted. The first names on the list are: "Statue of Assur, going into battle against Tiamat, statue of Sennacherib, king of Assyria" [3].

The drawing of conclusions as to the *Akitu* festival in Babylon from the above data as such is not permissible, nor is it necessary for our purpose. We have seen that in the New-Babylonian empire there was a festival which was celebrated in the first days of the first month of the year, Nisan; that during this festival the king was re-invested, as a result of which his kingship was renewed, and that this was parallelled in the epic of creation in Marduk's acceptance of the kingship. We further saw that the procession of the gods towards the Festival-House had a mythical prototype and that the king played a major part in it, at the least that of the master of ceremonies in Babylon, very probably as the personification of the victorious god in Assur. We saw that the king of the Sumerian period acted the part of the god in the sacred marriage, and that this ceremony bore just as much the character of a New Year festival as did the attested *Akitu* festival, at which the kingship of the king and Marduk, the world and the cosmos were created anew as a result of a victory over chaos, the monster Tiamat. This

---

[1] Meissner und Rost, Die Bauinschriften Sanheribs, Leipzig, 1893, 103, read: [ana]ku kašidu ina narkabti Aššur šaknu: ,,Ich bin, der auf dem Wagen Assurs erobernd einherzieht." The addition is uncertain, but, in view of the construction, it cannot be Assur himself who is meant by the victor, nor can it be the insignificant charioteer Amurru.

[2] Frankfort, o.c. 327; Labat, o.c. 244 ff.; and others.

[3] Frankfort, o.c. 327; Meissner und Rost, o.c. 101. Cf. further a commentary-text, published by Ebeling, o.c. 33, in which the king is equated with Ninurta, who is often identified with Marduk or Nabu in Assyria.

result, which is accepted by even the most sceptical scholars [1], is sufficient for our purpose. By way of addition, however, and as an introduction to the next section, we have to mention a text which in the opinion of many [2] contains a direct comment on the rites of the *Akitu* festival, and, viewed in this light, carries us considerably further towards their interpretation, though we should bear in mind that some scholars consider it useless, partly owing to its being mutilated [3].

A *genre* peculiar to Babylonian literature is that of commentaries in which a ritual act is given a mythological explanation. The commentaries are often of a magico-exorcistic nature. The mythical parallel obviously serves to heighten the magic value. Both Zimmern [4], who was the first to connect one of these commentaries [5] with the *Akitu* festival, and, later, Pallis [6] have made it clear that, although this text also explains an action by a mythical parallel, it should not be put on a level with others of the kind, but that it served a cultic purpose.

However fragmentary this text may be, it yet shows traces of a myth in which Marduk is represented, not as the victorious, but as a suffering god [7]. We learn that he is kept a prisoner, beaten and wounded; his clothes are blood-stained. This imprisonment disrupts the order of everyday life in the city: "(they) run about the streets, they seek Marduk: Where is he held captive?" [8]. Women (or Belet Babili herself) pray to Sin and Shamash [9] "Erhalte doch Bel am

---

[1] Smith, o.c. 40 f.; Dhorme, o.c. 242 ff.; 255. Cf. Reallexikon der Assyriologie, III, 40.

[2] i.a. Zimmern, Engnell, Wensinck, Langdon, Pallis, Hooke, Gadd, James, Labat, Frankfort, Pettazoni, in the works mentioned.

[3] Thus Dhorme, o.c.; cf. Smith, o.c. 40 f.

[4] In the works mentioned.

[5] V A T 9555, supplemented by V A T 9538; see Pallis, o.c. 221 ff.

[6] Pallis, o.c. 221 f.

[7] W. von Soden, Z.A. (N.F.) 17, 1955, 130 ff. gives quite a different interpretation of the texts. He regards them as a propaganda of Senacherib in favour of the god Assur against Marduk. In his view, the texts describe Marduk's captivity as a punishment of the gods, because he had resisted Assur's supreme authority. Von Soden points out that no mention is made of Marduk's death. But in the Ugaritic epic, too, Baal's captivity is identical with death, and also in von Soden's translation (line 11) one reads: "Das Tor . . . durch das sie geht (viz. Belet Babili) ist das Grabestor; sie geht, sucht ihn." Strabo's statement about the existence of a tomb of Marduk is, in my view, not to be dismissed as evidence.

[8] Pallis, o.c. 222; Frankfort, o.c. 323.

[9] I now follow von Soden's translation.

Leben". Nabu comes, "für das Wohlergehen seines Vaters, der festgehalten ist, kommt er". Previously we saw that every year on the 6th of Nisan, during the *Akitu* festival, Nabu comes to Babylon to visit his father. We also read: *"Enuma elish* das gesprochen wird, das sie vor Bel im Nisan singen, betrifft den, der gefangen ist". The text further refers to fights in the city; a criminal is beheaded, his head is hung on the statue of Belet Babili. For whatever purpose the text may have been used, it shows that a myth of the suffering Marduk must have existed [1], which is confirmed by Strabo [2], who knows that ὁ τοῦ Βήλου τάφος is to be found in Babylon. Even the most critical study that I have read about the *Akitu* festival, the one by S. Smith [3], comes to the conclusion that this is the minimum to be inferred from this text. Whether we should follow his conclusion that Marduk, who is bound to have been a sun-god originally, has retained the characteristics of a year-god of the "dying and rising" type, or has derived these characteristics from Tammuz, as is thought by other scholars [4], is a question we need not go into here.

Most of the scholars who have written about this subject, first of all Zimmern, go further and see in the cultic actions of the text parts of the *Akitu* festival. According to this interpretation the suffering god is personified by the king during his humiliation. In this way the New Year festival could dramatize in full the sufferings and the triumph of Marduk as described in the myth. This view is, however, opposed [5], and we are not qualified to evaluate the arguments. One thing is certain: the *Akitu* festival is first and foremost a feast of joy for the victorious god Marduk, who goes to his Festival House at the head of the procession of gods: a new era sets in, a new year is started, the destinies for the year to come have been determined, the kingship has been renewed.

Finally, a brief remark about the term New Year festival. We already saw that in spite of the fact that the sacred marriage bore the character of a New Year festival, its celebration did not necessarily

---

[1] As also Böhl insists, although he was the first to discover parodistic features in the text: F. de Liagre Böhl, Christus und die Religionen der Erde, II, Wien, 1951, 477.

[2] 16, 1, 5.

[3] o.c. 41.

[4] See: Frankfort, o.c. 285 ff.; Böhl in: De Godsdiensten der Wereld, ed. by van der Leeuw, I, Amsterdam, 1940, 133.

[5] Dhorme, o.c. 255; sceptical: Smith, o.c. 41.

have to coincide with the calendrical New Year. The same holds for
the *Akitu* festivals, which were by no means always held in the
month of Nisan as they were during the New-Babylonian period.
For earlier periods the sixth/seventh month is often mentioned,
slightly less frequently the twelfth/first month of the calendrical
year [1]. Falkenstein [2] assumes that the festival was originally held
at the beginning of autumn, around the autumnal equinox, just as
in Israel, too, the New Year festival was celebrated in the month of
Teshrit, in autumn. In some cities two *Akitu* festivals were held [3],
in Ur and Erech, for example, one around the autumnal equinox
in Teshrit, the other six months later around the vernal equinox in
Nisan. The shifting of the civil New Year to the spring resulted in
Nisan becoming the month of the *Akitu* festival [4]. The celebration of
more than one New Year festival is in no way unusual: "The new
year is equivalent to the new harvest, the new supplies of food, which
through the raising of the taboo are made accessible. Where there
are several fruits, which ripen at different times, there may be
several new year festivals", says a specialist in this field, M. P.
Nilsson [5]. This is one explanation. Another one is this: the solar
year has certain intersections, viz. the vernal equinox, the summer
solstice, the autumnal equinox, the winter solstice, all moments of
standstill, of turning round, of making a new start. That in Rome
the new year began on the first of March because the beginning of a
month was the most suitable day on which to open the official year,
that the original celebrations of the turn of the year took place
around the ides of March (vernal equinox), that another celebration
of New Year's Eve may be recognized in the *Saturnalia* of Decem-
ber (winter solstice), and the later official year began on January 1[6],
are all of them illustrations of the phenomenon also observed in
Mesopotamia: that of celebrating several New Year festivals within
one calendrical year.

---

[1] Falkenstein, o.c. 152 and 173 n. 29. See about the shifting of one month
and intercalation: Smith, o.c. 33 ff.

[2] o.c. 166.

[3] About this double celebration: Frankfort, o.c. 314; Langdon, Epic of
Creation, 28; Labat, o.c. 161. On the date of the Israelite New Year festival:
Wensinck and Snaith in the works mentioned.

[4] Falkenstein, o.c. 166.

[5] Primitive Timereckoning, Lund, 1920, 270; cf. Gaster, Thespis, 47.

[6] "Ausser dem vom offiziellen Kalender geweihten 1 März haben in Rom
mehrere Tage des Jahres den Charakter der Jahreswende ... An allen diesen

C. The character of the New Year festival

In our search for ceremonies in which the king acts the part of a god, we have come across several festivals that meet this condition. Of two of the best-known I gave fairly extensive descriptions with a view to enabling us to evaluate the theory which attributes one basic pattern to these and similar festivals. As was already stated in the introduction, there is a trend in the science of religious history [1] which, in view of the remarkable similarities in e.g. the *Heb sed* and the *Akitu* festival, sees in these festivals the isolated remnants of what was once a universally celebrated New Year festival.

It is chiefly the close intermingling of myth and rite which has attracted attention, and which has given rise to the formation of a "Myth and Ritual" pattern, which in Egypt and Mesopotamia as well as in many cultures of the Near East is supposed to constitute the basis of a New Year festival, in which the king in particular played an important part. Every time a myth of a vanquished and triumphantly returning god is parallelled by a series of ritual acts— some even speak of a ritual drama—in which the scheme of the myth is made visible in a concrete form. By his abdication from the throne (atonement), re-investiture and re-enthronization the king represents the mythical death and return of the great deity. While the myth constitutes the crystallization of a cosmic standstill followed by a re-creation of nature and cosmos, this *kenosis* and *plerosis* [2] are on the human level accompanied and enacted by a ritual renewal of kingship and regal power. The day of this new beginning is, or is taken as, New Year's Day.

The pattern of what took place during these New Year festivals was already outlined by Hooke [3] in 1933, and is found again, unchanged or with only minor variations, in many later works on this subject. It reads:

a) The dramatic representation of the death and resurrection of the god.

b) The recitation or symbolic representation of the myth of creation.

Tagen kann das Jahr von irgendeinem Gesichtspunkt aus beginnen." A. Brelich, Vesta. Albae Vigiliae, N.F. 7, 33.

[1] See the literature referred to on p. 202.

[2] Gaster, Thespis, 26.

[3] Myth and Ritual, London, 1933, 8.

c) The ritual combat, in which the triumph of the god over his enemies was depicted.
d) The sacred marriage.
e) The triumphal procession, in which the king played the part of the god, followed by a train of lesser gods or visiting deities.

It is understandable that this scheme, which is supposed to serve as the pattern of *the* New Year festival in many Near Eastern cultures, was criticized. A comparison with our data about the *Sed* festival [1] and the New Year festivals in Mesopotamia [2] will at once show that neither the Babylonian, nor the Egyptian festivals combine *all* the elements postulated by Hooke. If, in addition, New Year festivals of other cultures are compared, as was done by the critics, it is found that none of these show a complete pattern either.

For the defense of their pattern Hooke and his supporters advance two arguments which should refute these objections. The first is the scarcity of our data about the New Year festivals in Near Eastern cultures. In view of this, it is simply not to be expected that we shall come across a complete pattern anywhere.

In some cases, as in that of the Ugaritic material [3], only the myth is left of the supposed "Myth and Ritual" complex. The poem about Baal's combat with Mot, the god of the underworld, his defeat, manifested in the dying vegetation in the hot summer, the search of his beloved Anat, his ultimate victory and enthronization as king, presents us with the typical scheme of the myth of the "dying and rising" god of the Tammuz type. That, however, the myth "is based on the traditional ritual drama of the autumn festival" [4], is indeed plausible, but has not been proved. Nor is the part played by the king in the recitation and/or enacting of the myth at all clear [5].

We sometimes have to search for the ritual-liturgical details in literary forms which, as a result of changes in religious conceptions,

---

[1] The sacred marriage does not seem to have figured either in the Egyptian festival of the renewal of kingship or during the annual New Year festival.

[2] For the Babylonian *Akitu* festival, for example, a ritual combat cannot be demonstrated with certainty.

[3] The best-known myths: that of Baal, that of Aqhat, "the Poem of the gracious Gods", have been discussed and interpreted within the framework of the Myth and Ritual theory. See: Engnell, o.c. 97 ff.; James, o.c. 45; 58; 97; 122 ff.; Gaster, o.c. 114 ff.; 316 ff.; 406 ff.; an important and critical survey of what has been published on the subject is given by R. de Langhe in: M.R.K. 122 ff.

[4] Gaster, o.c. 129.

[5] Guarded: James, o.c. 98; de Langhe, o.c. 139.

by migration and derivation, have completely lost their original character. A case in point is Israel [1], where psalms and historical books show elements of a liturgy of the New Year ceremonies which goes back to Canaanite cults, of which, for example, Widengren [2] after a thorough study drew up the following scheme:

1. Der Kampf gegen die Chaosmächte.
2. Sterben und Auferstehen des Gottes.
3. Hieros Gamos.
4. Inthronisation des Gottes auf dem Götterberg im Norden.

The king is here, too, supposed to have played the part of the god.

The accusation that the scholars of the "Myth and Ritual" school have "recklessly imposed" [3] their pattern on Israel's religion is an exaggeration, although it has to be admitted that in collecting and systematically arranging the disparate material they have occasionally neglected the specific qualities of the Yahwistic religion. Several of Mowinckel's earlier theories in which he had discovered the elements of a "Myth and Ritual" New Year ceremony, he himself has in later works [4] either taken back or formulated differently. Especially the change from the cyclical to the historical way of thought, and the eschatology and Messianic expectations connected with it, are characteristic of Israel. It is interesting to see which elements Johnson [5], who is fully alive to these typical features of the religion of Israel, still recognizes as belonging to a pattern of the Israelite New Year festival, which is celebrated in autumn:

a) The celebration of Yahweh's original triumph..... and His enthronement as King in the assembly of the gods.
b) A dramatic representation of the dawn of the great eschatological "Day", when Yahweh will finally triumph over the rebellious gods and nations of the earth.
c) The corresponding dramatic representation of the descent

---

[1] The literature is very comprehensive. In addition to the works referred to above of Mowinckel, North, Snaith, de Fraine, Widengren, I mention: A. R. Johnson, Sacral Kingship in ancient Israel, Cardiff, 1955; idem, Hebrew Conceptions of Kingship, in M.R.K. 204 ff.; G. Widengren, Early Hebrew Myths and their Interpretation, in M.R.K. 149 ff.

[2] Sakrales Königtum, 62.

[3] H. Frankfort, The problem of similarity in ancient Near Eastern religions, Frazer Lectures, 1951, 8. See the defence of Hooke in M.R.K. 4 ff.

[4] See Johnson in M.R.K. 233 n. 7, where additional literature is referred to.

[5] M.R.K. 235.

of the true Messiah to the Underworld and his ultimate
deliverance by Yahweh from the forces of darkness and death.

d) A triumphal procession in which the Ark, as the symbol of
Yahweh's presence, and the king, who in this dramatic
ritual has proved to be the true Messiah and the accepted
"Son" of Yahweh, proceed to the Temple for the final act of
enthronement which is to mark the beginning of this new era.

But, he adds: "this is no cultic act of a magico-religious kind, it is
worship . . . .".

Finally, *in Hittite texts*, both mythical and ritual elements are
found which by their nature would fit very well into a New Year
festival [1]. Unfortunately it cannot be proved that they all belonged
to one and the same ceremony. It is certain that during the Purulli
festival [2], which was celebrated in the spring, a myth was recited,
of which two versions have come down to us. It deals with the
combat of the Weather-god with the dragon Illuyankas, and calls
the Babylonian *Enuma elish* to mind. The ritual of a procession of
gods and the enthronization of the supreme god, which is described
in the same text, stamps the *Purulli* festival as a New Year ceremony
of the types defined above. We do not know, however, what the
connection is between this festival and another myth [3] which by its
subject—the disappearance and return of the vegetation-god
Telepinu—belongs in the same typological category. A ritual combat [4], of which the text gives us an accurate description, would also
fit in well with this festival, but such a relation cannot be proved.
A fragment has, however, been found which appears to confirm
the existence of a New Year festival of the type we described, in
which also the king and queen are referred to. I here present the
text as translated by O. R. Gurney, as well as the comment of this
cautious scholar [5]: "For the weather-god the mighty festival of the
beginning of the year, (the festival) of heaven and earth, has
arrived. All the gods have gathered and come to the house of the
weather-god. If any god has sorrow (?) in his soul, let him dispel the

---

[1] Literature in Engnell, o.c. special note 9, p. 202; Gaster, o.c. 111 f.
Discussion of the relevant texts: Engnell, o.c. 52 ff.; Gaster, o.c. 245 ff.;
O. R. Gurney, in M.R.K. 105 ff.; James, o.c. 192 ff.

[2] Literature in Gaster, o.c. 111.

[3] Gaster, o.c. 112.

[4] Gaster, *ibid*. On this subject particularly A. Lesky, A.R.W. 24, 1926,
73 ff.

[5] M.R.K. 108.

evil sorrow (?) from his soul. At this festival eat ye and drink and be satisfied! Pronounce ye the life of the king and the queen! Pronounce ye (the life) of heaven and earth! " Gurney: "This is an obvious allusion to an assembly of the gods for the purpose of "fixing the fates", the scene is laid in heaven, as at the end of the third tablet of the Epic of Creation, but the inference that such a gathering of gods was actually enacted in ritual form, as in the Babylonian festival, can hardly be evaded".

The Israelitic, Ugaritic and other Semitic, as well as the Hittite material [1] being so lacunary and disparate, one must regretfully conclude that, even if a pattern of New Year festivals had existed everywhere, it cannot and will not be recovered anywhere complete and unmutilated.

Hooke and his supporters have given yet another reason why the pattern they drew up has hardly anywhere emerged completely, by pointing to the phenomenon of "disintegration" [2]. As a result of migration and transmission some of the elements of the original pattern were lost. The sacred marriage, for example, which forms part of the New Year festival in Mesopotamia but does not occur in Egypt, is supposed to have been lost as a result of "disintegration".

It is on this point that I fully agree with the critics [3], since here the weak side of the "Myth and Ritual" theory reveals itself: if all differences between comparable religious ceremonies are explained as being due to the disintegration of a hypothetical common original pattern, one wonders how much value there is to be attached to this original pattern, which was apparently constructed into the least common multiple of elements of New Year festivals.

There is no doubt that the New Year festivals in many cultures show remarkable similarities, both as to the ideology on which they were based, and as regards their form, but it is equally certain that

---

[1] From the nature of things it is impossible here to give a survey of all the festivals in which "myth and ritual" features have been recognized. Interesting is the Attis cult, in which the elements looked for are found in large numbers: death and resurrection of the god, accompanied by mourning and jubilation of his followers, celebration of his festival around the vernal equinox, saturnalian rowdiness, masquerade, *hieros gamos*, etc. About this subject: A. Hepding, Attis, Giessen, 1903; Gaster, o.c. 68 ff. See for a picture of the triumphal procession of the reunited gods, which is often represented: H. Haas, Bilderatlas zur Religionsgeschichte, 1926, 9-11, abb. 138, 139.

[2] See the works referred to by Engnell, o.c. 1.

[3] Notably Frankfort, The problem of similarity.

each people has worded or depicted these fundamental thoughts in its own way. That the sacred marriage is characteristic of the New Year festival is true, but the postulate that for this reason it must at one time have formed part of all New Year festivals of the Near East is quite unwarranted.

The first scholar who in his study of the kingship in general, and of its coronation rites in particular, noticed a parallelism between myth and rite was A. M. Hocart in his book "Kingship" [1]. The pattern of these coronation ceremonies he reconstructed from data of a large number of peoples and cultures, consisted of no fewer than 26 (!) elements, (obviously) marked a to z. The majority of these have only sporadically been demonstrated. Found very frequently is: "the theory that (a) the king dies; is reborn; as god; (e) the king must fight a ritual combat by arms, or by ceremonies, and come out victorious; (i) the king is invested with special garments".

It is precisely this combination of (temporal) deification, victory and investiture which is found not only in the coronation rites of many peoples, but which, as we have seen, is periodically renewed in two cultures. One may rightly object to "patternism", but will nevertheless have to concede that the parallels between the two festivals we described and others recorded in the works of the "Myth and Ritual" specialists, cannot be attributed to chance.

We have looked for ceremonies in which the king acted the part of the god. The ceremonies which fulfil this condition appear to be related, to belong to one type. They are New Year festivals, festivals at which nature and cosmos are given a new beginning, after a temporary standstill [2]. The king is re-invested, the kingship is re-affirmed; but the same is done on the divine level: the divine king also assumes the new kingship in the myth. This parallelism between mythical and ritual renewal is characteristic of these New Year festivals. But parallelism is a term that has too narrow a meaning in this connection: the world of the gods and the world of man overlap at this decisive turn of the year. The king assumes the shape of the king-god; the gods reveal themselves in a procession and go to a Festival-House or temple to celebrate the victory of their king

---

[1] London, 1927.
[2] See about this New Year complex in numerous cultures M. Eliade, Traité d'histoire des religions[2], Paris, 1964, 335 ff. and Le mythe de l'éternel retour, Paris, 1949, chap. II.

over the mythical opponent. The New Year festival is a feast of renewal and joy, of "recreation" in the true sense of the word [1]. The opponent has been overcome—mock fights and games have actualized this ritual [2]—,the great god has triumphantly returned [3] after combat, danger, often imprisonment or death [4]. The king makes this triumph manifest.

These festivals are not confined to the Near East. We shall in Greece find a complex of myth and ritual which corresponds with the Near Eastern one in practically every respect. The way across Greece will ultimately lead us back to where we started from: Rome.

3. Dionysos, the king and the New Year festival in Hellas

When we now turn to Greece to try and find out whether myth or *cultus* in that country show elements which proved characteristic of the New Year festival, our attention is automatically directed to the god Dionysos. In the first chapter of our study he was found to be the very god who manifested himself. We also recognized in *triumpe* the call θρίαμβε, which caused and accompanied his epiphany. The *pompa triumphalis* shows points of resemblance with the Dionysiac *pompa*, even though the Roman procession was not directly derived from Greece. Added to this is the fact that Dionysos was in later times depicted as the triumphator *par excellence* [5], and even as the inventor of the triumph. These three elements: call, πομπή and *"Dionysos triumphans"*, I shall in this section try to show as the constituent parts of a complex of myth and rite as discussed in the previous sections.

Not only does our own inquiry point to the god Dionysos; studies by others also make it clear that an investigation on 'Myth and Ritual" elements in Greece should start from Dionysos. Long before

---

[1] The reunion of the two kingdoms under the throne of the pharaoh, carried out by Horus, is just as much a re-creation as Marduk's act of creation in the Enuma elish.

[2] See about the universality of these sham fights and their meaning p. 262f.

[3] There is no justification for looking upon the death of the god as a standard element of the New Year ceremonies, as do the "patternists". It may be commemorated immediately before the beginning of the New Year, but also a long time before that. Essential is the return after a period of absence.

[4] That in Egypt Horus rises in life and Osiris in death, is a typically Egyptian interpretation and representation of the basic theme of the dying and rising of the god.

[5] Arrian. Anab. 6, 28, 2; Macrob. Sat. 1, 19, 4; Q. Curtius, 3, 12, 18; Plin. n.h. 7, 191; Sol. 52, 5; Diod. 3, 65, 8.

the coming into being of a "Myth and Ritual school" scholars such as Miss Harrison, Cornford, Murray [1] have drawn attention to the unity in the pattern of myth and rite which was characteristic of the Dionysos-religion. The Myth and Ritual specialists on the whole confined themselves to references and parallels when the Dionysiac religion could be used to explain Near Eastern usages [2]. The lines converge in Th. H. Gaster's book "Thespis. Ritual, Myth, and Drama in the ancient Near East" [3], as is apparent from the title and from the fact that the introduction to the first edition was written by Murray.

The work was, of course, criticized. In a paper "Myth and Ritual in early Greece" [4], A. N. Marlow investigates "what evidence, if any, is provided by the literature and beliefs of early Greece for the myth of a sacral kingship, a ritual combat, a sacred marriage and a ritual death and rebirth" (374), and arrives at a negative conclusion. The greater part of his argumentation does not have any bearing on our subject. Interesting, however, is his reference to the part the Athenian βασίλιννα played at the *Anthesteria*: "She had to take part in a remarkable sacred marriage with Dionysos at the *Anthesteria*, but whatever significance there may have been in this was the wrong way round for the Myth and Ritual theorists" (393). This curiously negative judgment on the interpretation of a ceremony in which in the view of many [5] the king himself played the part of Dionysos, is based on the statement that "the βασιλεύς was merely a magistrate annually elected, and no special significance was attached to his office", the inadequacy of which is obvious. Marlow's paper, which does not require a detailed discussion here, once more makes it necessary to stress that the existence or non-existence of a divine or even sacral [6] kingship as an argument in favour of or against the presence of a Myth and Ritual pattern is completely futile and irrelevant. It was precisely for this reason that we called attention to the fact that the renewal of the kingship

---

[1] In the works to be referred to on p. 247.

[2] S. Smith in M.R.K. refers a few times to the Dionysiac cult and to the function of the king in it. Cf. E. O. James, o.c. 74; 175.

[3] New York, 1st ed. 1950; 2nd. ed. 1961.

[4] Bulletin of the John Rylands Library, 43, 1960/61, 373 ff. Cf. H. J. Rose, Myth and Ritual in classical Civilisation. Mnemosyne, 4 ser. 3, 1950, 281 ff.

[5] Deubner, Attische Feste, 109 and others. See p. 247.

[6] Marlow's paper is occasionally rather obscure, because the author did not clearly define these two terms and apparently considers them identical.

in ritual and myth at the New Year festival was encountered in both Egypt and Mesopotamia with their fundamentally different types of kingship. References to Rose [1], who denies the existence of a divine kingship in Greece, or to the more recent views on the divine status of the Mycenaean kingship of, for example, Marinatos[2], Palmer [3] and Walcot [4] are, therefore, beside the point.

Finally, when we concentrate on Dionysos we may let ourselves be guided by the knowledge that there is no Greek god who so fully conforms to the type of the Asiatic "dying and rising" god as he does. It is true that several scholars, in reacting to the generalizations of, e.g. Frazer [5], who equated Dionysos with Osiris, Attis, and Adonis, have strongly emphasized the specific characteristics of Dionysos [6]. They have every right to do so, provided they do not deny others the right to study the common characteristics of these gods, their myths and their cults. It may even be said that the typically Dionysiac features show to full advantage only when viewed in contrast: the unique and personal features of the *species* are most clearly outlined against the background of the *genus* to which the *species* belongs or from which it evolved. There is, for that matter, hardly a handbook or a study on Dionysos to be found in which the resemblance, relationship or kinship between Dionysos and the "dying and rising gods" of Asia Minor are not at least recognized.

The fact that the mythical and ritual elements in the Dionysiac cult are closely interwoven makes it extremely hard to separate these elements. For methodical reasons I shall nevertheless do so, and begin by describing the myth of Dionysos' disappearance and death, followed by his return and epiphany. In order to support my views, I shall repeatedly have to refer to cultic acts. After this we shall deal with the ritual of the return of the god, as we know it

---

[1] The evidence for divine kings in Greece, in: La regalità sacra, 371 ff.

[2] S. N. Marinatos, Studies presented to D. M. Robinson, I, St. Louis, Miss. 1951, 126 ff.

[3] L. R. Palmer, Transactions of the Philol. Soc., 1954, 35 ff.

[4] P. Walcot, Studi Micenei ed Egeo- Anatolici, 2, 1967, 53.

[5] Spirits of the Corn and of the Wild I, 1 ff. See further *index*, s.v. *Dionysos*.

[6] Here we think of W. F. Otto, Dionysos; H. Jeanmaire, Dionysos. Histoire du culte de Bacchus, Paris, 1951, particularly p. 322 ff.; K. Kerényi, Der frühe Dionysos, Eitrem-Vorlesungen, 1960, Oslo-Bergen, 1961, to mention only a few. For the relationship between Dionysos and "child-gods" of the Ploutos type see: Ch. Picard, Les religions préhelleniques, Mana 2, Paris, 1948, 114 and literature on p. 136.

from the Athenian *Anthesteria,* and conclude by directing our attention to a development of this ritual as it is observed in Hellenism.

A. The myth

In the first chapter we have seen a few examples of the god's epiphany, after he had been summoned by his followers. The disappearance of the god is already mentioned by Homer [1]. He describes it as the flight from the Thracian king Lycurgus, who pursues the god and his maenads. The god, here depicted as a child, seeks his escape by jumping into the sea. According to a legend from the Argolis [2], Perseus overcomes the god and throws him into the lake of Lerna. The mitigated form of these myths does not prevent us from discovering their original meaning. The disappearance of the god stood for his death. In Delphi his tomb was shown [3]. When Firmicus Maternus [4] reports that, according to a legend Dionysos (Liber) was torn to pieces and devoured by the Titans, but revived by Zeus, it may be argued that this story must refer to the Cretan Zagreus, rather than to the Thracian-Phrygian Dionysos [5], but other myths and rites, which will be discussed presently, also mention the σπαραγμός and the ὠμοφαγία in the Dionysiac cult [6]. The question whether Zagreus and Dionysos were related [7] or identical [8] cannot and need not be dealt with here. The tearing-up of a living bull on Crete is the ritual version of the myth handed down by Firmicus Maternus [9]. This, too, points to Dionysos, who, partic-

---

[1] Z 130 ff.

[2] Scholion T. Ilias XIV, 319.

[3] Philochoros, Jacoby, F. Gr. H. no 328, 7.

[4] De errore prof. rel. 6, 1 ff.

[5] W. K. C. Guthrie, Orpheus and Greek Religion, 109 ff.

[6] Paus. 8, 37, 5, reports that the Titans worked Dionysos' suffering. Not until Nonnos is the Dionysos who has been torn to pieces by the Titans called Zagreus. See Nilsson, G.G.R. I², 686 n. 1. About the position of this myth in the Orphic mysteries: Nilsson, Harv. Theol. Rev. 28, 1935, 221 = Opuscula Selecta II, 1952, 628 ff. Cf. H. J. Rose, The ancient Grief, in: Greek Poetry and Life. Essays presented to Gilbert Murray, Oxford, 1936, 79 ff.

[7] i.a. Guthrie, The Greeks and their Gods, 46, about Zeus Kretagenès (= Zagreus) and Dionysos: "Both were gods of the same type."

[8] Otto, o.c. 177: "Zagreus bedeutet 'grosser Jäger' . . . und das ist ja der Dionysos." About Zagreus see: V. Machioro, Zagreus. Studi intorno all' Orfismo, Firenze, 1930.

[9] Firmicus Maternus, De errore, 6, 5, p. 84 of the edition of A. Pastorino, Firenze, 1956. In the extensive note literature is cited about the omophagy

ularly when depicted as a suffering god, is by preference represented as a bull [1]. In some places the god is called back from death by *epitheta* which suppose his assuming the shape of a bull: in Elis [2] a chorus of sixteen women called him: βοέῳ ποδὶ θύων, ἄξιε ταῦρε, whilst the god was addressed as βουγένης [3] when ritually summoned from the lake of Lerna. The drowning of a lamb as a sacrifice for the πυλάοχος defines his ἄνοδος as a resurrection from the realm of the dead, which is also shown in pictures [4], and which fully corresponds with the more frequently encountered ἄνοδος of Erechtheus and Persephone [5]. Small wonder, therefore, that the god is occasionally identified with Hades [6]. The 53rd Orphic hymn explicitly states that Dionysos during his absence sleeps in the house of Persephone. The Delphic *Thuiades* arouse the small Dionysos Liknites from his sleep [7].

It seems strange that, in spite of these examples of Dionysos' epiphany, in each of which the resurrection from the realm of the dead is, either explicitly or implicitly, described in a myth or a cult, his well-known return across the sea, which will be discussed later on, is explained historically by a number of scholars [8]. They argue that Dionysos is originally a non-Greek god, whose cradle should be looked for in either Thracia or Phrygia/Lydia [9]. From Thracia he

---

of the bull. The thesis of Jeanmaire, o.c. 387 f. that Dionysos, even Zagreus, was only later introduced in a myth in which the central theme is that of the submersion in a vessel of boiling water, merely aims at recognizing here, too, an initiation rite, and has to be rejected.

[1] Plut. de Iside et Osiride, 35; Quaest. Graec. 36; Orphic hymns 30, 4; 45, 1; 52, 2. Eurip. Bacchae, 920 ff.; Schol. Lycophr. Alex. 1237. See J. Harrison, Prolegomena, 430 ff.; Otto, o.c. 153 ff., 179; O. Gruppe, Griechische Mythologie und Religionsgeschichte, 1906, 1425; H. Grégoire, in Mélanges Ch. Picard, I, 1949, 401 ff.; J. Tondriau, in Mélanges H. Grégoire, IV, 1952, 444 f.; Guthrie, The Greeks and their Gods, 50.

[2] Plut. Quaest. Graec. 36.

[3] Plut. De Iside et Osiride, 35.

[4] Pictures in J. Harrison, Prolegomena, 404 f.

[5] J. Harrison, o.c. 277 ff.

[6] Heraklitos, frg. 15: ὡυτὸς δὲ Ἀίδης καὶ Διόνυσος ... Aeschylus, frg. 228, calls Dionysos son of Hades.

[7] Plut. De Iside et Osiride, 35.

[8] O. Kern, R.E. 5, 1905, 1020, and Religion der Griechen I, 232. Deubner, Attische Feste, 111, and Archaeol. Jahrb. 42, 1927, 172 ff.; Nilsson, Archaeol. Jahrb. 31, 1916, 323 ff.= Opusc. I, 188 ff.; less clearly in G.G.R. I², 582: "... muss dieser Dionysos über das Meer gekommen sein; Dionysos hat denn auch wirklich Beziehungen zum Meer."

[9] Nilsson has, as is generally known, combined these possibilities in: M.M.R. 492 ff.; G.G.R. I², 578 f.: one Dionysos had come from Thracia

may have reached Greece overland, from Lydia he must have come by sea. The Athenian Anthesterian procession, in which Dionysos is brought into the city on the *carrus navalis*, is the annual commemoration of the arrival of the god which at one time took place. I agree with W. Otto, who has opposed this view [1]. Surely the facts which show that according to the Homeric Lycurgus-episode the god jumps into the sea, that according to another legend [2] Dionysos together with his mother is washed ashore from the sea, that in the absence of a sea a lake (Lerna) forms the god's temporary place of abode, can all mean only one thing, viz. that the sea or the "watery element" forms a refuge for the god, as does the earth in other myths. "Wenn er also am Festtage auf einem Schiff seinen Einzug hielt, so bedeutet das nichts anderes als seine Epiphanie aus dem Meere" [3]. How else could the Ionian cities in Asia Minor celebrate an entry by boat which is similar to the Athenian one, if it signified the commemoration of Dionysos' historic arrival from Asia Minor? [4]

I further agree with Otto and other scholars [5] that the stories about Dionysos' arrival and the resistance it encounters—of which the Pentheus legend is the best-known—contain a mythical gist (his annual arrival, defeat, rebirth and victory) rather than a historical one [6]. One basic theme is present in legends from the most widely separated regions: the arrival of the god and his maenads, the opposition of the king against his cult, which occasionally results in flight and disappearance, and always in the temporary humiliation

---

and another from Lydia. Contested by H. Jeanmaire, o.c. 76. According to him Dionysos came from Asia Minor to Thracia and Greece, but had there "prédécesseurs qui avaient des traits communs avec le dieu qu'il avait été chez quelques uns des voisins des Hellènes." (23)

[1] o.c. 61 ff. He is followed by Jeanmaire, o.c. 49, and others.

[2] Paus. 3, 24, 3.

[3] Otto, o.c. 62.

[4] Detailed argumentation to be found in Otto, o.c. I do not agree with his view that Dionysos is also originally a Greek god. ("undoubtedly wrong", Guthrie, o.c. 146). The fact that the name of Dionysos is found on two Pylos tablets does not make Dionysos a "Greek" god. See, i.a.: Monique Gérard-Rousseau, Les mentions religieuses dans les tablettes mycéniennes, Roma, 1968, 74 ff.

[5] Otto, o.c. 71 ff.; Bather, J.H.S. 14, 1894, 244 ff.; E. R. Dodds, Euripides, Bacchae, 1953, p. XXIV; L. R. Farnell, Cults of the Greek States, V, 1909, 171; Guthrie, o.c. 172.

[6] This is the interpretation of the Pentheus legend defended by von Wilamowitz, Glaube der Hellenen, II, 66; Nilsson, History of Greek Religion, 206 ff.; and many others.

of the god, finally his victory and the punishment imposed on the mortal.

The Thracian Lycurgus, who according to Homer is struck with blindness, according to others, having lost his mind[1], is imprisoned in a grotto[2], or quartered by horses[3], is comparable with his brother Boutes, also a Thracian king, who chases the maenads into the sea and, having lost his mind by way of punishment, drowns himself[4]. In the Boeotian Orchomenos the daughters of king Minyas resist the Dionysiac orgies. Having been driven to frenzy, they lacerate the son of one of them, Leucippe, and disappear into the mountains[5]. Practically the same story is told about the three daughters of king Proiteus of Argos[6]. The daughters of Eleuther, the founder of Eleutherae, on the boundary between Attica and Boeotia are punished with madness because they mock Dionysos, who is clothed in the skin of a black goat[7]. In principle these myths might relate to the historical arrival of Dionysos, even though in that case there are many elements which cannot be explained. This view, however, becomes highly improbable when we see that the *ritus* contains exactly the same elements as were found in the myth.

Plutarch[8] reports that once a year, during the *Agrionia* in Boeotia, the priest of Dionysos with drawn sword pursued the daughters of the family of the Minyades, and was permitted to kill whomever he overtook. During Plutarch's lifetime this was in fact done once. "Dieser Brauch (. . . .) ersetzt offenbar ein altes Menschenopfer", Kern[9] remarks in this connection. The same may be assumed to apply to the following custom[10]: every year the inhabitants of Potniae sacrifice a goat, which, as is stated explicitly, replaces a more ancient human sacrifice to Dionysos. What had happened was that the inhabitants, having become drunk at a festival of Dionysos, had once killed the god's priest. Afflicted by a mysterious disease they consulted the oracle at Delphi; the oracle ordered them to sacrifice a child every year. This child was later replaced

---

[1] Apollod. Bibl. 3, 5, 1; Hygin. Fab. 132.
[2] Sophocl. Antig. 955 ff.
[3] Apollod. l.c. Cf. Servius ad Aen. 3, 14.
[4] Diod. 5, 50.
[5] Plut. Quaest. Graec. 38.
[6] Apollod. 2, 2, 2.
[7] Suda, s.v. μέλαν.
[8] Plut. Quaest. Graec. 38.
[9] R.E. 5, 1905. 1017, s.v. *Dionysos.*
[10] Paus. 9, 8, 2.

by a goat. The *ritus* here confirms what we had already gathered from the *mythos*: originally death is not the punishment imposed on the god's antagonists on his arrival. This explanation bears just as aetiological a stamp as does the tradition that the reason why the goat was sacrificed to Dionysos was that it damaged the vines [1]. The sacrifice of the goat and the human being was *interpreted* as a punishment [2].

That even at present this interpretation is often followed is all the more amazing because the human sacrifice in the Dionysiac cult is by no means confined to the examples referred to above: besides, its real meaning is easily discernible. On Chios and Tenedos σπαραγμός of a human being took place in honour of Dionysos Omadios [3]. A similar *ritus* is by Clemens [4] located on Lesbos. Both the nature of the sacrifice and the name of the god are significant. Like the child in the legend of the Minyades, king Lycurgus and Pentheus, the victims die a characteristic ritual death, in fact exactly the kind of death Dionysos himself, as Zagreus, meets. The obvious conclusion that this constitutes an example of a far-reaching identification of man and god—"the rending and eating of God in the shape of man" [5]—is very aptly confirmed by a peculiar custom found on Tenedos [6]. In honour of Dionysos Ἀνθρωπορραίστης a newly born calf, which had been dressed up in *cothurni*, and whose mother was cared for as if she were a woman in childbed, was killed with an axe. The person who performed this sacrifice was chased away by the throwing of stones. Deubner [7], Nilsson [8] and others agree that here without doubt it is the god himself who is killed in the shape of the calf. "Soweit mag die alte Ansicht, die dieses Kalb als einen Ersatz für ein Menschenopfer betrachtete, berechtigt sein", Nilsson adds, whose view is corroborated by the parallel development in Potniae just dealt with. But if this is the case, there is no longer any reason to speak of a sacramental sacrifice in connection with

---

[1] Leonidas, Anth. Pal. 9, 99. Vergil. Georg. 2, 380 and elsewhere.

[2] Very clearly also in Servius ad Aen. 3, 14, where Lycurgus cuts off the vine tendrils of Dionysos: *quapropter per furorem a diis immissum ipse sibi crura succidit.*

[3] Porphyr. De abstin. 2, 55; See: F. Schwenn, Die Menschenopfer bei den Griechen und Römern, R.V.V. 15, 1915, 71 f.

[4] Clemens, Protrept. 3, 42.

[5] Dodds, o.c. XVI.

[6] Aelian. Hist. anim. 12, 34.

[7] Deubner, Attische Feste, 173.

[8] Nilsson, G.G.R. I², 156; Griech. Feste, 308.

Chios and Tenedos, and, on the other hand, to interpret the death of a child or a king in other legends as belonging within a historical framework of resistance and punishment!   I can do no better than quote the objective judgment of Guthrie [1]: "It is obvious that the stories which we have been considering, in so far as they concern Dionysos at all, are projections of the pattern of Dionysiac ritual. No attempt to see in them memories of historical opposition to the cult in Greece can deny this fundamental fact. The phenomena of god-inflicted mania, that is, *enthusiasmos*, and of *sparagmos*, are monotonously repeated. Even the idea of opposition, with which the stories regularly start, was probably inherent in the ritual and comes into the myths primarily from that source and only secondarily, if at all, from the fact of historical opposition to his cult in Greece".

The legend of Pentheus, the show-piece of the historical school, presents a number of elements which can be explained only if we assume that the king was originally the protagonist in a cultic drama, of which the *Bacchae* of Euripides depicts his Dionysiac death by σπαραγμός as well as a few other aspects. Pentheus lets himself be persuaded to dress up as a maenad [2] or —what comes to the same thing—as Dionysos himself [3], adorns himself with the μίτρα [4], is carried through the city as an object of ridicule, is put high on a pine-tree [5], thrashed with branches of pine-trees and oaks, and torn to pieces by the furious maenads. The triumphant procession to the city, which bears an agonistic character and ends in the head of Pentheus being attached to the front of the palace as a trophy, is given a gruesome emphasis by the fact that it is the mother Agave who calls the booty: her "γέρας" [6]. In her exaltation, however, she fails to see what it is she is carrying, and thinks—and this is significant—that she has killed a bullock [7], the very animal in whose shape Dionysos manifests himself by preference.

---

[1] The Greeks and their Gods, 172.

[2] On this subject especially: Clara Gallini, S.M.S.R. 34, 1963, 211 ff., who considers the disguising a means of controlling the irrational and emotional elements in the Dionysiac orgies.

[3] Dodds, o.c. commentary on verse 854 f.

[4] Dionysos is χρυσομίτρης (Sophocles, O.T. 209).

[5] The pine-tree was the tree of Dionysos. Cf. the name δενδρίτης and the pine-cone, one of the insignia of the god.

[6] Eurip. Bacchae, 1179.

[7] *ibid.* 1185. Later writers also know the motif: Oppian. Cyneg. 4, 304, where Pentheus is transformed into a bull, the maenads into panthers which

In the complex of these elements, which the historical explanation is forced to ignore or to belittle as an invention of Euripides [1], A. G. Bather [2] thought he discovered a spring-vegetation ritual. He concludes that "the death of Pentheus corresponds most closely to the spring folk-custom of carrying out Death, and further that the bringing-home of his head by Agave answers similarly to the bringing-home of the Maypole" [3]. In support of his theory he refers to examples from ethnology. If he were right, we would here have to do with a predeistic *ritus*, subsequently incorporated in the cult of Dionysos. It is, however, not our task to decide whether or not Bather is right; we are primarily interested in the religious stage, of which the *Bacchae* presents a clear picture, in which man, in this case the king, in every respect and unmistakably represents the anthropomorphic god, be it with theriomorphic reminiscences, also, and even particularly so, in his death. *Cur rapitur sacerdos Cereris, si non tale Ceres passa est?* Tertullian asks [4]. The same question is, *mutatis mutandis*, justified here, and the conclusion is that the king— "king of the people, and, as such, the representative and embodiment of the god" [5]—acts the part of Dionysos [6] in a ritual drama, and dies a death the myth described as characteristic of Dionysos [7]. The fact that Pentheus is closely related to the "suffering" Dionysos, is proved by Pausianas' statement that the Thebans had to worship the tree from which Pentheus had been hanged ἴσα τῷ θεῷ, and that the two sacred idols of Dionysos at Corinth were allegedly made from its wood [8].

The question whether originally an actual ritual killing of the

---

lacerate the bull; Val. Flacc. 3, 266; Schol. Persius, 1, 100: *Pentheum . . . quem mater . . . sub imagine vituli trucidavit.*; Tzetzes, Chil. 6, 577.

[1] Thus Nilsson, G.G.R. I², 612 n. 3; Griech. Feste, 274 n. 3.

[2] J.H.S. 14, 1894, 244 ff.

[3] o.c. 259. H. Jeanmaire, o.c. 21, in this connection speaks of an "arrachage rituel de l'arbre."

[4] ad Nat. 2, 7.

[5] Bather, o.c. 258.

[6] It is, perhaps, not superfluous to point out that this does not imply any statement on the origin of tragedy generally. The theories of Murray in J. Harrison's Themis, 341 ff., and Cornford, The Origin of Attic Comedy, 1914, and J.-P. Guépin, The tragic Paradox. Myth and Ritual in Greek Tragedy, Diss., Amsterdam, 1968, are outside the scope of this study.

[7] Farnell, Cults, V, 167 ff.

[8] Paus. 2, 2, 6. On this subject: Farnell, l.c.; Altheim, Terra Mater, 81. Cf. Bayet, Critique, 80, 1954, 24.

(year) king took place [1], which was later on replaced by the sacrifice of a bull [2], we may leave undiscussed. For our investigation it suffices to know that the Pentheus legend contains traces of a ritual drama in which the king is identified with Dionysos by his dying the Dionysiac death. This has thrown light upon one of the *epitheta* of "dying and rising god". That the king in some way or other acted the part of the dying Dionysos has come down to us only in myths, or, if one will, in legends—the distinction is difficult to make when a god and a human being figure together—. In the *ritus* now to be discussed the aspect of the "rising god" will come to the fore, whilst the king in his cultic role will now also become visible historically. The question is whether the *Anthesteria*, during which this rite was performed, bore the character of a New Year festival.

B. The rite

The best study on the much-discussed Athenian *Anthesteria* was written by Deubner [3], and we shall mainly follow this author. The character of this spring festival celebrated in 11, 12 and 13 of *Anthesterion* lent itself admirably to being associated with Dionysos. The first of the three days, called *Pithoigia*, *Choes* and *Chutroi* respectively, was the day on which the new wine-casks were opened, the second that of the drinking-feast. With the third day, on which, as on All Soul's Day, the dead were entertained, Dionysos, in spite of the theories, probably never had anything to do [4]. The god was later introduced into a spring festival of long standing, "und zwar nicht als Herr der Seelen, sondern als Frühlings- und Weingott" [5].

---

[1] This, as is known, was the conclusion of many who followed in the footsteps of Frazer.

[2] There is no doubt whatever that the bull as a sacrificial animal occupied an important place in the New Year rites. See: Engnell, o.c. index, s.v. *Bull*, and below p. 252. It is, therefore, not without significance that, on the one hand, Lycurgus chases Dionysos and the maenads with a βούπληξ, and, on the other, his brother, about whom an almost identical story is told, is called Boutes. A group of priests of Dionysos called themselves βούκολοι. (Guthrie, Orpheus, 260.). Cf. Bayet, o.c. 26: "Le mythe de Lycurgue, coursant le dieu et ses bacchantes déguise sans doute la poursuite de l'animal sacrificiel substituée à la chasse primitive."

[3] Attische Feste, 93 ff.; further Nilsson, G.G.R. I², 582 ff., 594 ff; *idem*, Archaeol. Jahrb. 31, 1916, 309 ff. For the archaeological data see: G. van Hoorn, Choes und Anthesterien, Leiden, 1951.

[4] Nilsson, G.G.R. I², 596 f. against the well-known views of E. Rohde, Psyche.

[5] Nilsson, l.c.

On the second day of the festival Dionysos, seated on the *carrus navalis*, made his entry into the city. In this way the return of the god from overseas was celebrated [1]. Paintings on vases show us that there was a festive procession, headed by *kanephoroi*, a youth with a *thymiaterion*, men with the sacrificial bull, and after them the *carrus navalis*, drawn by satyrs, on which Dionysos is seated in divine repose, surrounded by flute-playing satyrs, and finally a boy who holds the ἄφλαστον attached to the ship. There is no doubt that in this πομπή the ἄμαξαι were driven along which, according to Harpokration [2] were filled with revellers who mocked each other, and which by Dionysius [3] are called πομπευταί. Entries like these are known from all over the Ionian region. In Smyrna [4] priests of Dionysos draw the *carrus navalis* into the city in the month of *Anthesterion*. In Ephesos, Priene and Milete the καταγώγια [5] attested there may be taken to denote a festival of the same kind. There, too, coarse jests figured largely.

In Athens the procession headed for the Limnaion, the sanctuary of Dionysos, which was open only once a year, on this day, where the wife of the (ἄρχων) βασιλεύς, the βασίλιννα, together with fourteen women called γεραραί or γεραιραί made ἄρρητα ἱερά on fourteen altars [6].

After this a ἱερὸς γάμος took place of Dionysos and the βασίλιννα in the βουκολεῖον [7], the old office of the βασιλεύς [8]. Of what occurred there no reports have come down to us. Pictures on vases lead to the assumption that Dionysos was in the *Anthesteria* and, therefore, also at the ἱερὸς γάμος represented by a human being [9]. The parts of

---

[1] Described in detail, with illustrations, by A. Frickenhaus, Archaeol. Jahrb. 27, 1912, 61 ff. His conclusion that the procession took place at the great *Dionysia*, has been conclusively confuted by Nilsson, Archaeol. Jahrb. 31, 1916, 323 ff. and Deubner, Archaeol. Jahrb. 42, 1927, 172; Attische Feste 102.

[2] Harpocr. πομπείας καὶ πομπεύειν. Phot. τὰ ἐκ τῶν ἀμαξῶν.

[3] 7, 72, 11, where he draws the parallel with the Roman triumph.

[4] Nilsson, Griech. Feste, 268; Deubner, Attische Feste, 102; Usener, Sintfluthsagen, 115 ff.

[5] Deubner, Attische Feste, 103 f.

[6] Hesych., s.v. γεραραί.

[7] About the reminiscences of the tauromorphous Dionysos aroused by this name: Guthrie, The Greeks and their Gods, 177; Tondriau, o.c. 449.

[8] Aristot. Athen. Pol. 3, 5.

[9] Deubner, Attische Feste, 108; Jeanmaire, o.c. 51; Pfuhl, *De Atheniensium pompis sacris*, Berolini, 1900, 73; Nilsson, München. Sitz. Ber. 1930, 4, 7.

the satyrs are bound to have been acted by men. From a later period we know of a ceremony in which Dionysos and the satyrs were represented by men [1], which, as is generally known, was not unusual in Greece [2]. A ceremony such as the ἱερὸς γάμος, moreover, goes back to a time in which, as Pfuhl [3] rightly points out, anthropomorphic statues of gods were as yet non-existent. Farnell [4], followed by many others, already went a step further by making the highly plausible suggestion that, if the god in his sacred marriage with the βασίλιννα was represented by a human being, this person could be none other than the βασιλεύς, later on the ἄρχων βασιλεύς.

These are the aspects of the *Anthesteria* which to us are the most important ones. After finding the myth of the god and the drama of the dying king in the Pentheus legend, we have now come across their ritual complement in the Athenian spring-festival. The cyclus of the annually returning god, played by the king who unites with the queen in a sacred marriage, can now hardly be detached from those elements of the New Year festival we encountered before. I may add that, although the ἱερὸς γάμος is often found in the myths, the only example of a ritual nature in Greece is the one mentioned by us [5].

The last question to which we intended to find an answer ("were the *Anthesteria* a typical New Year celebration?") has long since been asked and answered in the affirmative by Miss Harrison. In her "Prolegomena to the study of Greek Religion" [6] she had already called attention to the relationship between the lustration rites of the *Anthesteria* and the Roman February customs nearly coinciding with them. In her book "Themis" the author of the chapter "The Origin of the Olympic Games", F. M. Cornford [7], counts the Attic *Anthesteria* among "those old spring festivals of the New Year, at which the resurrection of life in nature was symbolized in various

---

[1] Schol. Aristid. p. 22, 20, Dindorff. ἐν γὰρ ταῖς . . . πομπαῖς ὁ μὲν Διονύσου, ὁ δὲ Σατύρου, ὁ δὲ Βάκχου ἀνελάμβανε σχῆμα. See Deubner, Attische Feste, 107, n. 7.

[2] For material see: de Visser, Die nicht menschengestaltlichen Götter der Griechen, 41, and *supra* p. 85 f.

[3] o.c. 70; Deubner, Attische Feste, 116 f.

[4] Cults, 5, 217; Deubner, Attische Feste, 109.

[5] Nilsson, G.G.R. I², 121. Cf. A. Klinz, Ἱερὸς γάμος, Diss. Halle, 1933.

[6] P. 49. That occasionally she tries to prove too much does not, in my view, affect the essentials of her argumentation.

[7] Themis, 212 ff.

ways" [1]. Apart from the date [2], which nearly coincided with that of the Roman New Year, arguments in favour of this view are particularly the characteristic combination of flowering and death within one festival, as is found in many other cultures. Among the Persians and the Romans this festival was celebrated, as Nilsson points out [3], just as among the Greeks in February/March. But there is a more direct indication. Plutarch [4] reports that the *Pithoigia* in Thebes were celebrated on the 6th of *Prostaterios* and that sacrifices were then made to the ᾽Αγαθὸς Δαίμων. In this deity Miss Harrison [5] sees a form of the ᾽Ενιαυτὸς Δαίμων as the bestower of fertility. More important than this theory is the fact that an ᾽Ενιαυτός really takes part in a Dionysiac procession of a later period, the famous triumphal procession of Ptolemaios Philadelphos [6]. Part of the description of this *pompa* given by Kallixenos of Rhodos was preserved [7]; the following phrase is significant for us:..... ἐβάδιζεν ἀνὴρ μείζων <ἢ> τετράπηχυς φέρων χρυσοῦν ᾽Αμαλθείας κέρας, ὃς προσηγορεύετο ᾽Ενιαυτός.

Here we clearly see the year-demon as the giver of the rich harvest [8], as ᾽Αγαθὸς Δαίμων in short, in a procession which, as Frickenhaus [9] already saw, resembles the Athenian Anthesterian

---

[1] o.c. 254.

[2] Plutarch, Sulla 14, reports that Athens was taken on the *kalendae martiae*, a day which, according to him, about coincided with the first day of the month of *Anthesterion*, on which the Athenians commemorated the primeval flood. Since it is certain that this commemoration took place on the *Chutroi* (13 *Anthest.*), Nilsson, G.G.R. I², 596, assumes that Plutarch makes a mistake, and that the *kalendae* of March coincided, in Sulla's time at least, with 13 *Anthesterion*.

[3] G.G.R. I², 596. About the regaling of the dead on New Year festivals see: Gaster, Thespis, 44 ff.

[4] Quaest. Symp. 8, 3 f.; 3, 7, 1.

[5] Themis 277 ff. Ganschinietz, R.E. Supp. III, 1918, 41, s.v. *Agathodaimon*, connects this with the benediction said before drinking to the ἀγαθὸς δαίμων, but there is no doubt about this deity being associated with the chthonic powers of fertility. See Nilsson, G.G.R. I², *index* s.v.

[6] Held in 274 B.C. according to the dating of E. R. Bevan, Egypt under the Ptolemaic Dynasty, London, 1927, 127.

[7] In Athenaeus, 5, 198, A-C. A monograph on the subject: Perdrizet, Rev. Ét. Anc. 12, 1910, 200 ff.

[8] Elsewhere Athenaeus (11, 25) refers to a "horn of Amaltheia and Eniautos". The *Agathos Daimon* is also depicted with a *cornucopia* (Ganschinietz, o.c. 57).

[9] o.c. 75. As has been stated already, he sees in the Athenian procession a *pompa* of the *Dionysia*, but this does not in any way detract from the value of the rest of his argumentation.

pompa down to its details. However, our conclusion that the *An-thesteria* cannot be denied the character of a New Year festival of this kind is corroborated by yet another datum. The *Pithoigia* differed from the other festivals of the Athenian calendar by the fact that on this day slaves participated as free men in the festivities [1], and it is this element which is characteristic of all sorts of feasts around the turn of the year. The *Saturnalia* are the best-known example, but the releasing of a criminal during the Jewish *Pascha*, and of the slave-king at the *Sacaea* belong in the same category. It is, moreover, reported that in the καταγώγια mentioned in the Acta S. Timothei [2], whose character is clearly defined as Dionysiac [3] by the use of masks and *phalloi*, street fights take place, the "sham fights" which are typical of New Year festivals [4]. Finally, when Usener [5] recognizes in the carnival customs of Shrove-Tuesday in Italy and Germany—the New Year's Eve of the Christians [6]—the ship-procession of Dionysos, we no longer have any hesitation in considering the *Anthesteria*, which Jeanmaire [7] calls "le début de printemps", Nilsson [8] a "Frühlingsfest" and of which Deubner [9] says: "Es herrscht die Empfindung eines Einschnitts (....). Mann fängt neu an...", to be a New Year festival of the type met with in the cultures of the Near East.[10]

---

[1] This also took place during the *Panathenaea*, but that festival had just as much the character of an "Einschnitt" (Deubner) as had the *Anthesteria*.

[2] Usener, Progr., Bonn, 1877; Nilsson, Griech. Feste, 416 n. 5.

[3] Thus Nilsson in Archaeol. Jahrb. 31, 1916, 315, after Maas, Orpheus, 56 n. 61.

[4] See below p. 262 f.

[5] Sintfluthsagen, 119 f., with a derivation of Carnival from *carrus navalis*. Differently Deubner, Attische Feste, 102 n. 3, who derives the word from *carne levare*.

[6] Prince or king of Carnival = king of *Saturnalia*. About the Old Year character of carnival and Shrove-Tuesday see Usener, A.R.W. 7, 1904, 309 ff.

[7] o.c. 48.

[8] G.G.R. I², 582.

[9] Attische Feste, 121. He, too, compares the *Anthesteria* with Roman festivals: "hier feierte man das Totenfest der *Feralia* im Februar vor dem alten Jahresbeginn, und die um die Wintersonnenwende begangenen *Larentalia* gleichen Charakters verdanken ihre kalendarische Einordnung wohl dem Gedanken, dass auch jener Zeitpunkt des Jahres einen stärkeren Einschnitt bedeute".

[10] In my view, it is not by accident that the motif of the primeval flood, which plays a very important part in the new year myth of Babylon and Israel—the victory over the deluge is the beginning of a new creation—is found again in the *Anthesteria*, since the *Chutroi* were the day on which the

In the knowledge that in Hellas distinct traces of "Myth and Ritual" elements are to be observed in the cult of Dionysos, particularly in the New Year festival of the *Anthesteria*, we finally wish to trace the development of an ideological aspect of it, which was rudimentally present from the beginning, and which subsequently became the central motif of a ceremony first observed during Hellenism, viz. the idea of the victory.

C. History

In the preceding sections we saw that in Egypt, Babylonia and other Mediterranean cultures the feast of the enthronization of the king, as well as its periodical renewal on New Year's Day, was accompanied by myths and rites which centred round the victory of god and king over an opponent. This explains the exuberant rejoicing during these festivals. Not only has the god or the king returned from death or captivity, but, in addition, the opponent has been defeated. There is scarcely a scholar to be found who has failed to point out this fundamental idea, which, as we saw, was already put into words in antiquity. It is, therefore, not by accident that the same idea is found again in the Dionysiac religion. Here, too, the god overcomes his adversary after an initial defeat. Καλλίνικος he is called in Euripides [1]. His victories over Lycurgus, Boutes, Triton, Tyrrhenian pirates and the Titans [2] formed the motifs of many myths and legends. In a painting on a vase the god is, at his ἄνοδος from the earth, welcomed by a winged Nike [3]. Macrobius [4] knows about a Bacchus Ἐνυάλιος, whilst among the Spartans a

---

end of the deluge was commemorated. Also elsewhere Dionysos is connected with the Deucaliontic deluge. Lucian, de dea Syria, 28, 29, disputes a legend which says that the phallic monuments in the court of the temple of the Syrian goddess Astargatis at Hierapolis, which were dedicated to Dionysos, were built in memory of the deluge of Deucalion. If Usener, Sintfluthsagen, 51 ff., is right in his conclusion from a learned argumentation that Δευκαλίων, older Δεύκαλος, means "Zeusknäblein", we are also along this way brought back to Dionysos, whose name, according to Kretschmer, Aus der Anomia, 17 f. means "Sohn des Zeus". That Deucalion, according to the *marmor Parium*, ep. 2-4, after his rescue built the temple of the Olympic Zeus at Athens also reminds us of Near Eastern creation and New Year myths, in which the god is also offered a temple after the victory over the flood.

[1] Bacchae, 1147, 1161.

[2] The testimonia concerning the first three victories will be found above. The Triton story in Paus. 9, 20, 3; the Tyrrhenian pirates: Homer. Hymn to Dionysos, 1 ff.; the Titans: Eurip. Cyclops, 1 ff.

[3] Picture in J. Harrison, Prolegomena, 405.

[4] Macrob. Sat. 1, 19, 1.

statue of Dionysos carries a lance, and not the thyrsos staff. Attention has on many occasions been called to this aspect of the Dionysiac theology [1].

However, we should beware of turning Dionysos into a war god. For indeed, according to Euripides [2], Ἀρεώς τε μοῖραν μεταλαβὼν ἔχει τινα, but this is explained in the following verses: στρατὸν γὰρ ἐν ὅπλοις ὄντα κἀπὶ τάξεσιν φόβος διεπτόησε πρὶν λόγχης θιγεῖν· μανία δὲ καὶ τοῦτ' ἐστὶ Διονύσου πάρα. Dionysos is not the god of war, not even of victory, even though he was later on typified as such [3]; he is the *victorious god*, whose weapon is not the lance or the sword, but trance and μανία. In this way he has, according to Euripides [4], subjected Lydia, Phrygia, Persia, Bactria, Arabia, in short the whole of Asia known at the time, and established his τελεταί there. The peculiar part is that, unlike comparable gods in the Near East, Dionysos does not defeat a mythical, divine opponent, but that he overpowers human beings—Pentheus, Lycurgus, Boutes—and subjects continents. This replacing of a mythical-cyclical pattern by a historical view, is in my opinion, to be held partly [5] responsible for the identification of Hellenistic kings with the god.

The victorious campaign of Dionysos was, according to the biographers of Alexander the Great, deliberately imitated by the Macedonian [6]. The pattern of Dionysos' campaign is to the last detail found back in the description of Alexander's triumphal expedition to India. Did Alexander see himself as a second Dionysos, νέος Διόνυσος? A. D. Nock [7] denies this and argues that Alexander not only did not identify himself with Dionysos, but did not even attempt to imitate his triumphal tour. The reports in question are projections of Ptolemaic ideas, of kings who did proclaim themselves νέος Διόνυσος. We need not pass judgment in a matter in

---

[1] Farnell, Cults, 5, 308 f.; Otto, o.c. 183; Kern, R.E. 5, 1905, 1038, s.v. *Dionysos*; Jeanmaire, o.c. 356, and others.

[2] Eur. Bacchae, 302.

[3] Macrob. Sat. 1, 19, 3.

[4] Bacchae, 13 ff.

[5] There are more causes: i.a. the idea that Dionysos was the last man to have become a god; of great influence was also the fact that there were societies of worshippers of Dionysos, which made great propaganda for the god.

[6] See for testimonies and discussion: Cerfaux et Tondriau, o.c. 148 ff.

[7] A. D. Nock, Notes on Ruler-Cult. J.H.S. 48, 1928, 21 ff. About Neos Dionysos see J. Tondriau, Les Études Class. 15, 1947, 100 ff.; *idem*, Mélanges H. Grégoire = Annuaire de l'Institut de Philologie et d'Histoire Orientales et Slaves, 12, 1952, 441 ff., especially 453 f.

which Bevan, Hogarth, Mederer, Nestle, Robinson, Tarn and Wilcken take the side of Nock against Beloch, Berve, Ferguson, Miss Taylor, Vallois [1], who follow Radet [2], who holds the view that Alexander did pose as Neos Dionysos during the campaign.

What concerns us is that it is certain that some of the *diadochi* identified themselves with the god. Tondriau [3] mentions as unquestionable examples: Antigonos Monophthalmos, Ptolemaios IV Philopator, Ptolemaios XII Auletes, and especially Antiochos VI Epiphanes, Antiochos XII Epiphanes, both of whom by their names revealed the assimilation with the god who manifested himself; further Attalos I, who is called "son of the bull", and even ταυρόκερως, exactly like Dionysos [4], Mithradates VI Eupator, and the Romans Marius, Cn. Pompeius, M. Antonius. Of the instances which are as good as certain, mention should be made of Demetrios Poliorketes, as he is depicted with small horns, a fairly sure sign of his identification with Dionysos [5]. Tondriau rightly calls Dionysos a "dieu royal". In connection with our study it is significant that he recognizes the king-god particularly in the tauromorphic Dionysos, since, as he demonstrated, the bull was in many cultures the symbol of "la force fécondante royale" (449). Against this background the sacred marriage in the βουκολεῖον at Athens, but also the stories of Minos, the Minotauros, Pasiphae and the nine-yearly renewal of the Cretan kingship acquire a more distinct meaning [6].

Whether Ptolemaios Philadelphos identified himself with Dionysos we do not know [7], but in his great *pompa* Alexander and Ptolemaios I are represented as *Theoi Soteres*, whilst the *pompa* itself is a distinct glorification and imitation of Dionysos' Indian triumph, held on the occasion of a victory of Philadelphos [8]. This

[1] These names are mentioned by Cerfaux et Tondriau, o.c. 145 f.

[2] G. Radet, Alexandre le Grand, Paris, 1933.

[3] Mél. H. Grégoire, *cit.* 453 ff., where the testimonia and the most important literature are found.

[4] Paus. 10, 15, 3; Suda, s.v. *Attalos*.

[5] Ch. Picard, Rev. Arch. 22, 1944, particularly p. 11, 12, 15 n. 1. Another possibility is that they are the horns of Amon.

[6] Tondriau, o.c. 449 ff.; cf. Picard, Les religions préhelléniques, Paris, 1948, 199, 320, 326.

[7] P. Perdrizet, Ann. Sev. Ant. Ég. 9, 1908, 245. "Ptolemée Philadelphe eût l'illusion d'être un nouveau Dionysos quand il conduisait dans Alexandrie cette pompe immense . . .", but Tondriau, o.c. 457 n.1, points out that there is no proof for this. Cf. Taeger, Charisma, I, 289.

[8] On this subject Taeger, Charisma I, 290 ff.; Jeanmaire, o.c. 365; H.

marks the end of a development we can now survey. At the beginning we find the myth of the victory and the return of the god Dionysos, after he had for a time disappeared in the depths of the earth, the sea, death. In Athens this return is celebrated annually with a ritual in which the βασιλεύς acts the part of the god during his return and the sacred marriage with the βασίλιννα. As early as the fifth century B. C. Dionysos in Euripides is the triumphant god *par excellence*; he triumphs over man and world. This view provides an opening to history which was lacking in the Asiatic myths. This gave rise to the possibility that Alexander, either by his contemporaries or by later generations, was identified with Dionysos, not as at Athens as the principal actor in a cyclical ritual, but in the historical event of a campaign imitating the triumph of Dionysos. Thus the great triumphal *pompa* of Philadelphos was no longer part of a cyclical ritual, but a historical-political manifestation of a personal victory. From now on man, elevated to divine status, occupies the central position, as may still be observed at the entry of Antony as Dionysos at Ephese [1], and no longer the god who is made visible by man, as at the *Anthesteria*.

In this way, finally, it becomes clear how Dionysos in his triumphal entry, accompanied by a great *pompa*, could be characterized as the inventor of the triumph. The ancient interpreters are right. Both in the periodical New Year festival and in the Hellenistic *pompa* he is the triumphator [2]. The *trait d'union* between the two is the term θρίαμβος. Derived from the exclamation by which the god was invited to manifest himself, and which we probably also hear in the meaning "ἴαμβος = satire", in the *Anthesteria*, the appellativum has in later times been identified with the Roman *triumphus*. However, this could only be done because also in the Greek term the meaning of triumphing was discernible. This change in meaning

---

Volkmann, R.E. 23, 1959, 1579/80, s.v. *Ptolemaia*; idem, ibid., col. 1652, s.v. *Ptolemaios*; Börner, R.E. 21, 1952, 1954, s.v. *Pompa*.

[1] Plut. Anton. 24.

[2] Jeanmaire, o.c. 356, formulates it as follows: "Alexandre aurait célébré le premier de ces triomphes que renouvelleront effectivement les cortèges qui se dérouleront plus tard, à l'occasion des fêtes de Dionysos, dans les capitales hellénistiques. Les épiphanies de Dionysos, ses catagôgia, qui, ainsi qu'on l'a vu, donnaient lieu à processions et à mascarades, avaient toujours revêtu un certain caractère triomphal... Il est caractéristique de l'ère des grandes entreprises militaires que fut l'époque hellénistique que l'idée de solennités de ce genre ait de plus en plus évoqué celle de réjouissances à l'occasion d'une victoire."

is perfectly parallelled in the Latin *"triumpe—triumphus"*, in which, as we have seen, also a call developed into a triumphal cheer, and in this way the appellativum *triumphus* developed into triumphal procession.

Are also in Italy the ceremonies which are characterized by *triumpe* and *triumphus* respectively of a different nature? Can here, too, a development be demonstrated as in Hellas and in Hellenism? These questions will occupy our attention in the next chapter.

CHAPTER SEVEN

AN ETRUSCAN NEW YEAR FESTIVAL IN ROME

τίς ἂν θεὸν οὐκ ἐθέλοντα
ὀφθαλμοῖσιν ἴδοιτ' ἢ ἔνθ' ἢ ἔνθα κιόντα;

Homer

1. *The ludi Romani as a New Year festival*

After a long detour we are now returning to Rome. The remarkable phenomenon of the magistrate—originally the king—acting the part of Iuppiter in two different ceremonies induced us to investigate whether it had parallels among other peoples. We have found that it had, and that it was a universal constituent of New Year ceremonies, whose characteristics and meaning we described. In the Near East, but also in Greece we saw the king as the central figure in a ritual which at the beginning of the new year renewed the kingship. This ritual was in each case found to have a distinct mythical parallel in the myth of the god who, after an initial defeat, ultimately triumphs and returns as king and ruler.

When, in the present chapter, we raise the question whether perhaps in Rome, too, the identification *rex*-Iuppiter formed part of a similar New Year ritual, we should before all consider a circumstance which at first sight forms an insuperable obstacle to such a hypothesis, viz. the fact that, unlike the Greek, the Roman religion did not have any myths, as was first ascertained by Wissowa [1] and subsequently confirmed by innumerable other scholars. In the absence of myths there is, of course, no question of a "Myth and Ritual" unity [2]. When I nevertheless insist that the investigation suggested is useful and legitimate, I do not refer to the views of scholars such as Otto, Altheim, Koch and Brelich, who, each in his own way, defend the presence of myths, or at least a mythical way of thought, in the oldest Roman religion [3]. It suffices to point out

---

[1] Already in Marquardt, Röm. Staatsverwaltung, III², 1885, 2.

[2] See: H. J. Rose, Myth and Ritual in classical Civilization. Mnemos. 4e ser. 3, 1950, 281 ff.

[3] W. Otto, Wiener Stud. 34, 1912, 318 ff.; 35, 1913, 62 ff.; 40, 1918, 325 ff. Altheim, i.a. in Röm. Religionsgeschichte, I, 1951, 124; C. Koch, Gestirnverehrung im alten Italien, Frankfurt, 1933; Der römische Iuppiter, Frankfurt, 1937; A. Brelich, i.a. in Die geheime Schutzgottheit von Rom. Albae Vigiliae, N.F. 6, 1949.

that both the triumph and the *ludi Romani* are of Etruscan origin, as we partly have seen and partly will find, and that in Etruria traces of myths are clearly demonstrable. And even if the presence in Etruria of a nature-myth of the type found in Asia Minor has not been attested, it is still possible that the rite contains fossilized remnants of what at one time was a mythic-ritual δρώμενον, as is so often observed in folk-lore.

For these reasons I think I am fully justified in trying to discover whether in Rome (and/or Etruria) the identification of the king and the supreme god, as found in the triumph and in the *ludi Romani*, formed part of a New Year ceremony. We first turn to the *ludi Romani*, which, unlike the triumph, were, as an annual ceremony, included in the Roman ferial calendar.

There is no doubt about the *ludi Romani* having come from Etruria [1]. Parts of the *apparatus* of the circus-games point that way: the *metae*, marking the start and the finish of the race-course, are to the last detail identical with Etruscan funeral monuments; [2] the *falae*, wooden scaffoldings on which seven eggs were put to indicate the number of rounds to be run, are Etruscan [3], as is the symbolism of the eggs itself. Whether or not the variation in the spelling of *tensa/thensa*—the chariots in which the *exuviae deorum* were transported—points to an Etruscan origin, as Koch [4] thinks, is not for us to decide. Pictures of games found in Etruscan tombs, notably in the *tomba* Stackelberg [5], speak a clear language: games of the type of the *ludi Romani* were highly popular in Etruria, and Livy says about them [6]: *ludicrum fuit, equi pugilesque ex Etruria maxime*

---

[1] Müller-Deecke, Die Etrusker, II², 214 ff.; Wissowa, R.u.K.² 452 n. 6; Habel, R.E. Suppl. V, 1931, col. 609, s.v. *Ludi publici*; J. Toutain, Daremberg-Saglio III, 1904, 1370, s.v. *Ludi*; Piganiol, Jeux, 8; 30. Altheim, Griech. Götter, 85; Koch, Gestirnverehrung, 31; Heurgon, La vie quotidienne chez les Étrusques, 241 ff.; Gjerstad in: Les origines de la république romaine. Entretiens Hardt, 13, 1966, 13.

[2] C. C. van Essen, Over de symboliek der Romeinsche circusspelen. Bulletin van de Vereeniging tot Bevordering der Kennis van de Antieke Beschaving, 19, 1944, 34, where pictures; Bussemaker and Saglio in Daremberg-Saglio, I, 1887, 1190, s.v. *Circus*.

[3] Paul. ex Festo 78 (L): *Falae dictae ab altitudine, a falado, quod apud Etruscos significat caelum*. Walde-Hofmann, L.E.W.³, s.v. *fala*; Koch, Gestirnverehrung, 45.

[4] Koch, Gestirnverehrung, 31; *idem*, R.E. 2e Reihe, V, 533 ff., s.v. *Tensa*; contra: Walde-Hofmann, L.E.W.³, s.v. *Tensa*.

[5] F. Weege, Arch. Jahrb. 31, 1916, 106; Piganiol, Jeux, 1 ff.

[6] Livy, I, 35, 9.

acciti. Finally, the setting and pageantry of the *pompa circensis* has long since been connected with Etruria [1].

Tradition fully corroborates all this. Not only did the *apparatus* of the games come from Etruria, the games themselves were, as was explicitly stated by Livy [2] and Dionysius [3], introduced by the Etruscan Tarquinius Priscus. Another argument is the fact that the date of the *ludi*—originally September 13,—coincides with the consecration day of the temple of the Trias Capitolina, the founding of which is also attributed to Tarquin [4], and which shows decidedly Etruscan influences [5].

All this does not by any means deny that Rome originally had primitively-Roman games before the Etruscans extended their rule over Rome. The location of the *ara Consi* in the Murcia valley, the place of the later *Circus Maximus*, and the mule races round this altar on the *Consualia* are already ample proof to the contrary [6]. Yet it is abundantly clear that with the *ludi Romani* a new type of games was introduced, which, like the temple on the Capitol and the cult of Iuppiter O.M., bears a strongly political character [7], and the origin of which has to be looked for in Etruria.

When we now raise the question whether these *ludi Romani* had the character of a New Year festival, we shall for the time being leave aside the theories, ancient and modern, about the meaning of the games, and the problem of the calendrical position of the *idus septembres*, and begin by discussing some external analogies between the *ludi Romani* and the New Year festivals described in the preceding chapter.

---

[1] Müller-Deecke, Die Etrusker, II, 198 ff.

[2] Livy, 1, 35, 7.

[3] Dion. Hal. 6, 95. About the confusion of the *feriae Latinae* and the *ludi Romani* see above p. 114.

[4] According to Livy, 1, 55, 1, in such a manner that *Tarquinios ambos patrem vovisse, filium perfecisse*. As is generally known, the acts of the last Tarquin were by the annalists, notably by Fabius Pictor, distributed over the two Tarquinii. See: A. Schwegler, Römische Geschichte, I, 1853, 668 ff.

[5] H. J. Rose, S.M.S.R. 4, 1928, 165; Latte, R.R.G. 150; M. Pallottino, La Scuola di Vulca, Roma, 1945.

[6] Wissowa, R.u.K.[2] 451, distinguishes sacerdotal games—*Consualia, Equirria*, etc.—, which, as legend has it, can be traced back to Romulus and Numa, from magistrates' games, of which Tarquin is said to have been the founder.

[7] Once and for all stated clearly by Wissowa, R.u.K. first edit., 110. For the development of the political Iuppiter see: Koch, Der römische Iuppiter.

Our starting-point was the king appearing in the shape of the supreme god. The representation of the god by the king at the New Year festival in various cultures enables us to elaborate the comparison. We have seen that the god of the New Year festival was often the highest god, that he was placed at the head of the gods, or was regarded as the model for human kingship. This also applies to Iuppiter. The fact that he was in later literature the king of the gods, after the example of Zeus, should not carry weight. His title of *optimus maximus*, however, reflects his complete independence and superiority [1], so that it has been assumed that his old title was *rex* [2], just as there was also a Iuno *regina*. In the *pompa deorum*, which will be discussed presently we see him as the first among the gods. In the second chapter we saw that the *toga picta* and the *tunica palmata*, besides being *ornatus Iovis*, also constituted the official robes of the Etrusco-Roman kings. If it could indeed be made plausible that the *ludi Romani* formed part of a New Year festival, this "coincidence" would at once be explained: the New Year festival was, as we know, characterized by a renewal of the kingship by means of a re-investiture of the king, and at the same time by the epiphany of the great god in the shape of the king!

One of the most characteristic components of the *ludi Romani* was the *pompa deorum*, which we find described in Dionysius [3] and Ovid [4], and which was typified by Seneca [5] as a particularly boring item of the programme. We learn that statues of gods are carried along [6], which, after a round of honour through the circus, are placed on the *pulvinar* [7], in order that this *daemonum concilium* [8]

---

[1] See: Radke, Die Götter Altitaliens, 159.

[2] Radke, o.c. and Gymnasium, 66, 1959, 324 ff.; R. Combès, Imperator, index, s.v. *Iuppiter rex*; Dumézil, La religion romaine archaïque, 183 f.; cf. Latte, R.R.G. 151 n. 1.

[3] Dion. Hal. 7, 70 ff., who here follows Fabius Pictor. On the subject: Piganiol, Jeux, 25 f.; Latte, R.R.G. 248; de Francisci, Primordia Civitatis, 306 f.

[4] Ovid. Amor. 3, 2, 43 ff.

[5] Seneca, Controv. 1.

[6] On *fercula* (Macrob. sat. 1, 23, 13), which were carried on the shoulders, not, as Latte, R.R.G. 249, thinks, on *tensae*. Cf. Dion. Hal. 7, 72, 13.

[7] Festus, 500 (L). These *pulvinaria* F. Messerschmidt, S.E. 3, 1929, 519, thinks he recognizes in Etruscan pictures.

[8] Tertull. de spect. 8, 5.

could rejoice in the sight of the games organized in its honour [1]. Dionysius and Ovid are no longer in a position to tell us how this procession was originally composed. Their description, even though Dionysius goes back to Fabius Pictor, presents the *pompa* as it was after the Greek influence had begun to make itself felt [2]. New deities were continually added to the procession of the gods, until finally, starting with Caesar [3], the statues of the emperors [4] were also given a place in the procession.

There is no doubt, however, that we are here dealing with an Etruscan component of an Etruscan ceremony, since it is as good as certain that the Romans, at the time when the games were introduced, did not yet have anthropomorphic statues of gods[5]. The first of these, that of Iuppiter—and perhaps also those of Iuno and Minerva—was not introduced until the period of the Tarquinii, and was, like the temple itself, made by Etruscan artisans. The procession of gods, on the other hand, is such an essential part of the *ludi Romani* [6] and other games whose *pompae* were modelled after that of the oldest state games [7], that a later derivation from Greece is quite out of the question here; the more so because, according to Nilsson[8], this type of procession, in which the gods were invited to attend games, was not found in Hellas. The *epulum Iovis* [9], which was held on the thirteenth of September and may therefore be assumed to have been an important event ever since the foundation of the temple and the *ludi*, Wissowa[10] also distinguishes from the *Graecus ritus* of the later *lectisternia*, even though it was later given a Greek form.

---

[1] According to the interpretation of Labeo in Arnob. adv. gent. 7, 33. Cf. Liv. 7, 2: *caelestis irae placamina.*

[2] Piganiol, Jeux, 25; Latte, R.R.G. 249.

[3] Suet. Caesar, 76; Cic. ad Att. 13, 44, 1; Cass. Dio, 43, 45.

[4] Suet. Tit. 2; Tac. ann. 2, 43.

[5] Varro in Augustin. civ. dei, 4, 31; cf. Latte, R.R.G. 150 n. 1.

[6] Wissowa, R.u.K.² 452.

[7] A *pompa* is reported to belong to the following games: *ludi Romani, ludi Apollinares, ludi Megalenses, ludi Augustales.* See testimonies in Friedländer, in Marquardt, Röm. Staatsverwaltung, III², 508.

[8] Nilsson, Die Prozessionstypen im griechischen Kult. Archaeol. Jahrb. 31, 1916, 309 ff.

[9] The thesis of Mommsen that the *epulum* originally belonged to the *ludi plebei* and was not until later taken over by the *ludi Romani*, has rightly been refuted by Wissowa, R.u.K.², 127 n.11. and Kroll, R.E.9, 1916, 2013, s.v. *Iovis epulum.* Cf. Latte, R.R.G. 377; 251; Dumézil, o.c. 541 f.; 199.

[10] R.u.K.², 422.

If, therefore, the procession of the gods is indeed Etruscan, it is perhaps possible to find the solution of a peculiar problem: what are we to understand by the *exuviae deorum* which were carried along in the *pompa circensis* in separate chariots, called *tensae*? About this question Bouché-Leclercq [1] made a number of statements which are worth remembering. His argumentation may briefly be summarized as follows: during the *lectisternia* statues of gods are placed on the *pulvinaria*. We do not know what these statues looked like in the oldest times, but Livy [2] describes them as *capita deorum*. Through Festus [3] we know that *capita deorum appellabantur fasciculi facti ex verbenis*. They were called *struppi*, also according to Festus [4]: *struppi vocabantur in pulvinaribus fasciculi de verbenis facti, qui pro deorum capitibus ponebantur*. We further know that in later times the emperors in the *pompa circensis* were also represented by this kind of *struppi*, in the form of *coronae*, of which we have pictures [5]. Now Bouché-Leclercq thinks that these *struppi* should be seen as "mannequins" [6], primitive effigies made of twigs, and that the *tensae* transported the attributes, particularly the garments by which the effigy had to be given the character of a certain god. A comparison with the *argei* comes to mind immediately. I think these assumptions closely approach the true facts, but wish to point out that they still fail to explain why the *exuviae* had to be transported separately.

I imagine the following development. Together with the founding of the temple and the introduction of the statues of the Trias Capitolina under the Tarquinii, the *epulum Iovis* was also instituted [7] as the centre of the ceremonies marking the thirteenth of September. Valerius Max. 2, 1, 2, probably describes the original situation when he says: *Iovis epulo ipse in lectulum Iuno et Minerva in sellas ad*

---

[1] Daremberg-Saglio, III, 1904, 1010 ff. s.v. *Lectisternium*.

[2] Liv. 40, 59.

[3] Paul. ex Festo 56 (L).

[4] Festus 473 (L). What Ateius Philologus in Festus, 410 (L), thinks he knows about these *struppi* is already a late interpretation. Cf. Wagenvoort, Roman Dynamism, 21 f.

[5] See: L. Ross Taylor, Class. Phil. 30, 1935, 122 ff.; A. L. Abaecherli, *ibid.* 131 ff.

[6] This is also the view of Grenier, Les religions étrusque et romaine, 73; cf. de Francisci, Primordia Civitatis, 306: "sorta di fetici". But see Latte, R.R.G. 244 n. 1.

[7] This is, therefore, an Etruscan rite, which is not connected with the *daps*, with which *Iuppiter dapalis* was presented in the *spring*, in accordance with an old-Roman custom (Cato, agr. 132).

cenam invitabantur. To this banquet and the subsequent *pompa* more gods were invited, of whom, however, there were no statues, so that *verbenae* had to be resorted to, bundled into *struppi*, which may have been given a more or less human shape. As up till then people had contented themselves with these *"simulacra"* [1], the practice of putting *capita deorum* ("masques" according to Bouché-Leclercq) = *struppi*, on the *pulvinaria*, during the *lectisternia* as well as during the *ludi*, continued to be observed, the number of anthropomorphic statues meanwhile increasing steadily. Now I presume that, whereas the statues were carried on *fercula* on the shoulders, these *struppi* were transported in the *tensae* and, because they were taken as *coronae* on account of the shape of the wicker-work, were called *exuviae*. The argument that the *exuviae* are not to be taken as merely the robes and attributes of the statues of the gods, is proved in the first place by the fact that the *exuviae Iovis* were worn by the magistrate leading the games, whilst the exceptional sacredness of the *tensae*—they had to be drawn [2] by free-born *pueri patrimi et matrimi* [3]—forms an additional indication that the contents were more than merely the attributes of gods.

Of course, all this is no more than a hypothesis. We shall now return to the proven facts. The first of these is that the word *struppus*, whose association with the *tensae* I presume, but whose connection with the *pulvinar in circo* is certain, once again points towards Etruria, since *struppus* is a corruption, via Etruscan, of the Greek στρόφος [4]. Once again the Etruscan influence in one of the elements of *ludi* and *circus* is apparent.

I know of no processions of gods in Etruria. Yet it was found that socles discovered in Vei showed holes which made it possible for the statues to be transported by means of poles [5]. According to Livy [6], it was by means of such *adminicula* that the statue of Iuno,

---

[1] Cf. Serv. ad Aen. 2, 225: *Antiqui felicium arborum ramos, cortice detracto, in effigies deorum formabant.*

[2] According to Val. Max. 1, 1, 16 and Lactantius, 2, 16, 16, the defeat near Cannae was due to the fact that a young man of non-free birth had touched the *exuviae Iovis*.

[3] Cic. de har. resp. 23.

[4] Walde-Hofmann, L.E.W.[3], s.v. *Stroppus*. In favour of this also pleads that there was in the region of the Faliscans, who were subjected to strong Etruscan influences, a festival called *Struppearia*. (Festus 410 (L)).

[5] E. Stefani, Notizie degli Scavi, 1946, 36 f.; M. Renard, Latomus, 8, 1949, 19 ff.

[6] Liv. 5, 22, 6. Ogilvie *ad loc.* "Etruscan cult-images were designed to be carried."

after her evocation, was transported from Vei to Rome. Hubaux [1], to whom I owe these data, in this connection speaks of "transporter" generally. I venture to suppose that the structure in question was not intended merely for the transportation from workshop to temple—let alone for a possible *evocatio*—but precisely with a view to a procession of the type of the *pompa circensis*.

We have thus found a number of noticeable parallels between the New Year festivals and the rites around the thirteenth of September at Rome. On the *idus septembres* the gods assemble in the temple on the Capitol in order to join the Trias Capitolina in a banquet: the *epulum Iovis*. We learn that the senate, too, partakes of a banquet on the Capitol on this day [2]. It is highly probable that the *pompa deorum* takes place on the 15th of September [3]. In the temple on the Capitol the magistrate, in ancient times the king, is given the *ornatus Iovis*, his wreath and sceptre; the procession subsequently moves off—the leader of the games in the *quadriga* at the head, followed by the statues of the gods and the *tensae*—and reaches the Circus Maximus via Velabrum and forum Boarium.

The parallels with, e.g. the Babylonian *Akitu* festival described in the preceding chapter, are striking. There, too, the gods assemble, are carried in a procession—the characteristic feature of this ceremony [4]—and gather for a banquet. There, too, the king receives his *insignia* from the hands of the god (Marduk) and rides, in Babylon as the master of ceremonies, in Assur probably as the representative of the great god, at the head of the procession of the gods. It is not the correspondence between the various components, but the strong resemblance between the complexes of the ritual which convinces us that we have to do with similar ceremonies, the more so because—it may be repeated—none of the phenomena discussed so far can be explained as being in any way inherent to the ancient Roman religion. The characteristics now to be discussed confirm this conviction even further.

First of all there is the agonistic aspect of the *ludi*. The oldest components, the competitions of *equi* and *pugiles*, who had been

---

[1] J. Hubaux, Rome et Véies, 171.

[2] Aul. Gell. 12, 8, 2; Liv. 38, 57, 5; Cass. Dio, 39, 30, 4; 48, 52, 2.

[3] Seperated from the *epulum*, therefore, by the day of the *equorum probatio*. Wissowa, R.u.K.[2] 453 f.

[4] The procession as the characteristic feature of this festival: E. Dhorme, Les religions de Babylone et d'Assyrie, 243; Labat, Royauté, 170; Lexikon der Assyriologie, III, 42.

sent for from Etruria [1], have always remained the most important items. The *pugiles* originally fought each other in two groups (*catervae*) [2]. When in 167 B.C. the Romans for the first time saw the Greek *chorus* in the circus, they asked them to split up into two groups and to combat as *catervarii* [3]. A programme of games at Pompei still distinguishes between *pugiles catervarii* and the *pyctae* in the Greek manner [4]. Not only did we already encounter these combats between two groups as part of the Near Eastern New Year festival, but also elsewhere the ritual combat is in many cultures so closely linked with the transition from the old year to the new [5], that the combat of the *catervarii* during the *ludi Romani* may with proper justification be interpreted as a New Year ceremony of the same type. We may perhaps see a formalization of this type of combat in the weapon dances of the pyrrhics or *ludiones* of the *pompa circensis*, a "*bellicrepa saltatio*", which, as legend has it, goes back to Romulus [6].

Livy [7] gives us a description of the acts of these *ludiones*, which also included a sword-fight. It is worth noticing that the weapon-dance of the Kouretes on Crete, with which this item is typologically comparable, accompanied a New Year rite, as is apparent from the song:

Ἰώ, μέγιστε κοῦρε, χαῖρε μοι, Κρόνιε,
παγκρατὲς γάνους, βέβακες δαιμόνων
ἀγώμενος· Δίκταν ἐς ἐνιαυτὸν ἔρπε.... [8]

Here Zeus is invoked to manifest himself and to settle on Dicte for the year to come. He appears at the head of the procession of demons [9].

---

[1] Liv. I, 35, 9.

[2] See: Piganiol, Jeux, 20.

[3] Polyb. 30, 22.

[4] C.I.L. X, 1074. Piganiol, Jeux, 20 n. 2.

[5] See i.a. Gaster, Thespis, 37 f. and 55 n. 135 and 147. Mannhardt, Wald- und Feldkulte, I, 549 ff.; Usener, A.R.W. 7, 1904, 283 ff.

[6] Paul. ex Festo, 31 (L).

[7] Liv. 44, 9, 3.

[8] See: J. Harrison, Themis, I ff. The weapon-dance of the *Salii* is also much more than a ritual marking of the beginning and the end of the war season, as Wissowa, R.u.K.[2]555, and Latte, R.R.G. 115, think. Kristensen, Symbool en Werkelijkheid, 206, holds the view that it symbolizes the yearly casting out of death, and Balkestein, Mars, 20, via a different way arrives at a similar conclusion: "the victory over death and the rise of life from the nether world." Further literature to be found there.

[9] Plato also depicts him like that, Phaedrus, 246 E: ὁ μὲν δὴ μέγας ἡγεμὼν

Another item of the *ludi* to which we have to call attention is the distribution of food, often in the form of fruit, nuts, etc. It is a well-known fact that during the imperial period these distributions, both in the circus and in the amphitheatre, assumed fantastic proportions and degenerated into orgies [1]. It is certain, however, that the simpler version of the scattering of fruit etc., occurred in the days of the republic [2] and is sure to have been a primitive usage, even though it cannot be demonstrated with certainty that it went back to the *ludi Romani*. Now, the scattering of fruit and corn is a widely-practiced custom which is meant to symbolize or sympathetically to induce the abundance of the period to come, and is chiefly found as part of the coronation ritual and the New Year festival. Gaster [3] provides examples of Hittite and African installation rites which include the scattering, and also points to David's distribution of cakes of bread and raisins [4], which is interpreted as a New Year installation-rite. The distribution of grain by the king at the Delphic feast *Charila* [5] and the burying of an effigy during that feast was, already a long time ago, compared by Usener [6] with usages such as that of "burying Lent", "segare la vecchia", etc., and interpreted as the removal and destruction of a period that has come to an end. That also at the *ludi saeculares* such distributions constituted a regular item on the programme [7] may be explained from this angle: the *ludi saeculares*, too, marked the beginning of a new period [8].

Interesting to us are also the reports about huge, terrifying effigies being carried in the *pompa*. Three of them are referred to by

---

ἐν οὐρανῷ Ζεὺς ... πρῶτος πορεύεται ... τῷ δὲ ἔπεται στρατιὰ θεῶν τε καὶ δαιμόνων ... θείου χοροῦ.

[1] See testimonies and description in Friedländer in Marquardt, Röm. Staatsverwaltung, III², 495 f.

[2] Cic. de off. 2, 16, 55.

[3] Thespis, 380.

[4] 2 Sam. 6, 19 = 1 Chron. 16, 3.

[5] See Nilsson, Griech. Feste, 466 f.; J. Harrison, Prolegomena, 106 f.

[6] Italische Mythen. Rhein. Mus. 30, 1875, 182 ff. Cf. Mannhardt, Antike Wald- und Feldkulte, 298.

[7] Piganiol, Jeux, 92 ff. Cf. I. B. Pighi, De ludis saecularibus², Amsterdam, 1965, 281 ff. The Roman New Year festival of the period of the emperors was characterized by people giving each other palm-branches, figs, honey and often presents in money. See: Ovid, Fasti, 1, 185 ff. and the explanation of Bömer *ad loc*. Thus also Nilsson, A.R.W. 19, 1916/19, 52 ff. See for examples from other countries the same work, p. 115 n. 2.

[8] See: Wagenvoort, Studies in Roman literature, culture and religion, Leiden, 1956, 193 ff.

name: Manducus, Citeria and Petreia. The scarce testimonia read as follows:

I. *Manduci effigies in pompa antiquorum inter ceteras ridiculas formidolosasque ire solebat magnis malis ac late dehiscens et ingentem sonitum dentibus faciens, de qua Plautus ait: "quid si ad ludos me pro manduco locem? Quapropter? Clare crepito dentibus"* (Paul. ex Festo 115 (L)).

II. *Citeria appellabatur effigies quaedam arguta et loquax ridiculi gratia, quae in pompa vehi solita sit. Cato in Marcum Caecilium (6): 'Quid ego cum illo dissertem amplius, quem ego denique credo in pompa vectitatum ire ludis pro Citeria, atque cum spectatoribus sermocinaturum".* (Fest. 52 (L)).

III. *Petreia vocabatur, quae pompam praecedens in colonis aut municipiis imitabatur anum ebriam, ab agri vitio, scilicet petris, appellatam.* (Paul. ex Festo 281 (L)).

In spite of Diehl's [1] contesting it, these testimonia show indisputably that these figures formed part of the *pompa*, notably of the *pompa circensis* [2], whilst any connection with the *Atellana*, defended by Diehl, is fully out of the question here [3]. The Oscan farce also included such clownish figures: Bucco, Maccus, Pappus, Dossenus[4]. The latter figures are referred to only in connection with the *Atellana*, the former three only in connection with *pompa*, *ludus* and *circus* [5]. A gloss of Placidus, quoted by Diehl [6], once more

---

[1] R.E. 14, 1930, 1044 ff., s.v. *Manducus*. See also Bömer, R.E. 21, 1952, 1987, s.v. *Pompa*.

[2] This is also the opinion of Latte, R.R.G. 249, and Piganiol, Jeux, 26. A different opinion is held by J. G. Préaux, Hommages Grenier, Coll. Latomus, 58, 1962, vol. III, 1282 ff., who thinks rather of the *Compitalia*. Cf., however, a testimonium of Placidus quoted by Diehl: *manducum ligneam hominis figuram ingentem, quae solet circensibus malas movere quasi manducando.*

[3] J. G. Préaux, o.c. 1290: "Le masque appelé *manducus* est d'abord un mannequin faisant partie d'un cortège parodique organisé à l'occasion de jeux."

[4] The most recent publication on this subject: A. de Lorenzi, Pulcinella. Ricerche sull' atellana, Napoli, 1957. Cf. Heurgon, La Capoue préromaine, 436 f.

[5] Varro, l.l. 7, 95, forms the only exception: *dictum mandier a mandendo, unde manducari, a quo et in Atellanis +ad obsenum + vocant Manducum.* In spite of the argumentation of Préaux, o.c. 1282 f., I think that the conjecture of Müller, *"Dossenum"*, should be retained. It is clear that the figure of Dossenus found in the Atellana, is also called Manducus. But that does not mean that Manducus had his origin in the *Atellana*.

[6] o.c. col. 1044.

confirms this: *manducum ligneam hominis figuram ingentem, quae solet circensibus malas movere, quasi manducando*. That these gigantic, moveable effigies, carried along in a procession, are the direct precursors of the figures in the carnival processions which up to this day are highly popular in many parts of Europe, needs no further elaboration [1]. It once again characterizes the *pompa circensis* as a component of a New Year festival, for, as we saw, the carnival also accompanies the transition from the old year to the new by saturnalian wantonness.

It is not certain whether we may, with Frazer [2], recognize in the two figures Ovid [3] saw in a *pompa* held on the occasion of the real Roman New Year festival, the festival in honour of Anna Perenna on the *idus martiae*—"*senem potum pota trahebat anus*"—, Mamurius Veturius and Anna Perenna, respectively, and subsequently identify or compare the *anus ebria* (Petreia) of the *pompa circensis* with the *anus pota* of the March festival. From our point of view it is, in any case, highly significant that the September rites took place exactly six months after the primitive-Roman New Year festival [4], both of them ceremonies around an equinox.

Now that we have seen that the complex of the September rites on the one hand shows characteristics generally found in New Year ceremonies, and on the other hand includes customs which particularly resemble specifically Near Eastern New Year rites, the time has come to review the theories about the meaning of games in general and of the *ludi Romani* in particular. On the latter subject few studies have appeared, and this is not surprising. The very

---

[1] Thus Bömer, o.c. col. 1987. One of the peculiar features of the New Year festivals of the imperial period is that men disguised themselves as animals, women, but also as gods, which gave rise to coarse jests. Petrus Chrysologus, Calender homily no. 155 (Migne, 52, 609 ff.). A homily ascribed to Severianus mentions the gods Saturnus, Iuppiter, Hercules, Diana, and Vulcanus as being represented by humans. Joh. Chrysost. (Migne, 48, 953) also knows of such a procession of gods on New Year's Day. See: Nilsson, A.R.W. 19, 1916/19, 82. Cf. the description of the procession of Isis in Apuleius, Metam. 11, 8, which, too, was characterized by disguising.

[2] Comm. Ovid, Fasti, 3, 541. He follows here a theory of Alton, Hermathena, 42, 1920, 100 ff. Cf. Class. Quart. 15, 1921, 51. Bömer, Ovid, Fasti, *ad loc.* does not consider the proposal impossible.

[3] Fasti, 3, 541 f.

[4] Wagenvoort in a highly illuminating paper (Studies, 226) suggested that the rites of the first of March were, under Etruscan influence, shifted to the *idus*. I cannot deal in more detail here with either the March rites or with the very striking parallelism with the October rites, during which, just as in March, an old man is made an object of ridicule.

large number of scholars who accept Mommsen's theory that the *ludi* originally formed part of the triumph, will also be inclined to be satisfied with the explanation following from this, viz. that the *ludi* originally stood for the redemption of the *votum* the commander had made at his departure from Rome: a thanksgiving-festival for the gods[1]. Only those who reject Mommsen's interpretation may be expected to advance theories about the origin and meaning of the *ludi Romani* as an autonomous phenomenon.

Piganiol[2] has made such an inquiry and, after dealing with various games, arrived at the following conclusion [3]: "l'office principal des jeux est d'assurer l'entretien d'une force qui menace de décliner ou qui déjà décline, d'une force à laquelle est liée la vie (ou la survie) d'un homme, d'une groupe ou de la nature". As Piganiol wanted his definition to cover all games, including the *munera*, it inevitably became vague. The idea, however, of the restoration or renewal of a situation approaching its end, which in his opinion underlies the *ludi*, is in a great many instances found expressed more concretely, both in ancient times and in modern theories. Tertullian[4] already held the view that the games, notably the *quadriga*-races, reflected the combat between summer and winter. The comparison of the red and the white party of the *aurigae* with summer and winter respectively, is found again and again in ancient literature [5]. The same idea lies at the basis of the theory of Cornford[6]

---

[1] The games have by many scholars been explained as an entertainment for the gods. This view was held already in antiquity: Cic. in Verrem, 5, 14, 36; Liv. 7, 2; Arnob. adv. gentes, 7, 33; Rohde, Psyche[2], I, 20; Frazer, G.B., The Scapegoat, 65.

[2] Jeux, 137 ff.

[3] *ibid.* 149.

[4] De spect. 9, 5. He probably borrows from Varro. See: J. H. Waszink, Varro, Livy and Tertullian on the History of Roman dramatic Art. Vig. Christ. 2, 1948, 224 ff.

[5] Cassiod. Var. 3, 51, 5: *colores autem in vicem temporum quadrifaria divisione funduntur.* Coripp. Laud. Iust. 1, 317 ff.: *tempora continui signantes quattuor anni, in quorum speciem signis numerisque modisque, aurigas totidem, totidem posuere colores*; *ibid.* 1, 320 ff: *et fecere duas studia in contraria partes, ut sunt aestivis brumalia frigora flammis.* Isidor. 18, 36, 1: *quadrigam ideo Soli iungunt, quia per quattuor tempora annus vertitur vere, aestate, autumno et hieme.* See: F. Soveri, *De ludorum memoria praecipue Tertullianea capita selecta*, Helsingforsiae, 1912, and note of E. Castorina to Tertull. de spect. 9, 5, p. 206 f.; Zacher, Globus, 31, 266; Farnell, Cults, 5, 235.

[6] Cornford, The origin of the Olympic games, in J. Harrison, Themis, 212; cf. G. Murray, Excursus on the ritual forms preserved in Greek tragedy, *ibid.* 341.

about the origin of the Olympic games, viz. that they represented the conflict between the daemons of the old and the new year. Cook [1] thinks that in Olympia Zeus incarnated himself in the victor of the games, and that this victor became the king, the year-king in the Frazerian sense.

Van Essen, who wrote a paper about the *ludi Romani* [2], draws comparisons with Etruria and Hellas, and recognizes in the *ludi Romani* features of a cult of the dead, a fertility-rite which at the same time is a commemoration of those killed in battle—on this point his theory follows Mommsen—and finally states [3]: "This commemoration formed a conclusion and, hence, also a beginning". According to van Essen, the chariots in the circus were the chariots "of Sun and Moon and they adjured the light dying in autumn to come back to life and to cause the new crop, i.e. the new life, to germinate". In this connection he quotes a statement of F. Muller [4]: "riding in circus is ending and beginning anew, dying and being reborn", and points out the significance of the *idus septembres* as a starting-date.

Now it may be argued at once that each of these theories may be, and partly has been, criticized [5]. I for one find it impossible to follow van Essen when he uses the purely Roman *ara Consi* to explain the essentially Etruscan games, or when he connects the *metae* as a funerary monument with the commemoration of the dead during the triumphal ceremony. In this case van Essen is too hasty in unifying fundamentally different constituents. A similar objection might be raised against the views of Usener, Mannhardt, and others, who think that all games or *agones* should be looked upon as New Year ceremonies. Is it really possible to reduce the annual games and the funerary games to a common denominator? Only if one follows Kristensen, who considers the explanation of Usener too narrow, and states [6]: "The basic idea must have been

---

[1] A. B. Cook, The European Sky-god, Folk-Lore, 1904. *Contra*: Gardiner, Ann. British School Ath. 22, 1916/17, 85.

[2] Over de symboliek der Romeinsche circusspelen. Bulletin van de Vereeniging tot Bevordering der Kennis van de Antieke Beschaving 19, 1944, 30 ff.

[3] o.c. 35 and 36.

[4] F. Muller, Reveil van Augustus, rect. rede Univ. Leiden, 8, II, 1940, 28.

[5] See the crushing criticism of H. J. Rose on some parts of the book of Piganiol in Class. Rev. 1923, 134.

[6] "Over de godsdienstige betekenis van enkele oude wedstrijden en spelen", in Symbool en Werkelijkheid, 208.

broader: not the victory over winter, but over death explains this widely varied application of one and the same custom". Here he comes very close to Piganiol's definition. However, the views of Cornford, Cook, Usener and other scholars of the ethnological school should not be dismissed entirely because they have in part proved erroneous. Games are a remarkable element of New Year customs, and in fact often symbolize the struggle between summer and winter, between the old year and the new, etc. However, each ceremony attended by games should be investigated separately, in order to find whether or not it is to be looked upon as a New Year festival. If the *ludi Romani* are subjected to this treatment, it will be found that Latte's conclusion: [1] "So bleibt ein Vorstadium der *Ludi Romani* blosse Vermutung" is too pessimistic.

The fact is that we are so fortunate as to have at our disposal the results of a special inquiry on the character of the *ludi Romani*, made by C. Koch [2]. He started from exclusively Italic data, which included Etruscan ones, and via a strictly consistent argumentation arrived at a conclusion which scarcely differed from the earlier interpretations of the *ludi*. His conclusion was that Sol and Luna play an important, even a principal, part in the circus [3], whereas Iuppiter O.M. is the focus of the rites of the *idus septembres*. Koch's suggestion concerning an explanation of this coincidence will prove useful later. At this moment it is important that from the fact that Sol and Luna play major parts in the *ludi circenses*, it follows that these *ludi* are directly related to the "*annus vertens*", of which the sun and the moon are the visible representatives. It is highly to be regretted that the study announced by Koch [4] about the spaces of time of *annus* and *mensis* created by the sun and the moon, and their significance in Roman religion was never published [5]. What has become clear, however, is that the theory so often advanced that games symbolized the beginning of a new year, the *quadriga* circling round the *spina* like the sun completing the annual cycle [6],

---

[1] R.R.G. 250.

[2] C. Koch, Gestirnverehrung, 41 ff.; the paper by W. Quinn Schofield "Sol in the Circus Maximus" in Hommages à M. Renard, II, 639 ff. (Coll. Latom. 102, Bruxelles, 1969), in which the works of Koch are not even mentioned, did not present anything new.

[3] The testimonia are to be found in Koch, o.c. 41.

[4] o.c. 55 n. 2.

[5] See about Sol in Italy: Altheim, Neue Jahrbücher, 1932, 142 ff.

[6] See: Brelich, Vesta, 90 f.

has been made very plausible as far as the *ludi Romani* are concerned, as a result of their connection with Sol and Luna.

That the characterization of the *ludi Romani* as a New Year rite is not merely a theory based on numerous arguments, but also a fact which can be proved on historic grounds, will be shown in the next section.

2. *The rites of the idus septembres, their calendrical meaning, their origin*

The *ludi Romani*, which in the course of time extended over an ever-increasing number of days, centred round the *idus septembres*, the day of the *epulum Iovis*, at the same time *dies natalis* of the temple of Iuppiter O.M., the day regarded as the beginning of the republic since, according to tradition, one of the consuls of the first year after the expulsion of Tarquin, M. Horatius, dedicated the temple [1]. From these data it may be inferred that the thirteenth of September had the character of an incision, a conclusion further corroborated by the fact that the *mola salsa* prepared by the *virgines Vestales*—who were entrusted, to use Koch's words [2], with "die Sorge um die Kontinuität der *salus publica*"—was, apart from the *Lupercalia* and the *Vestalia*, used only on this date [3].

Dionysius, 5, 1, reports that the first consuls entered upon their office in the first year of the 68th olympiad, under the archonship of Isagoras, τεττάρων μηνῶν εἰς τὸν ἐνιαυτὸν ἐκεῖνον ὑπολειπομένων. In his "Römische Chronologie" [4] Mommsen has quite convincingly argued that this installation took place on the *idus septembres*, because Dionysius by ἐνιαυτός obviously meant the New Year's Day of his time, January 1st. A number of arguments, for which I refer to Mommsen's study, subsequently prove that from the possibilities left, *kalendae* or *idus septembres*, the latter should be chosen. The conclusion that the thirteenth of September was "Anfangstag des bürgerlichen Jahres" [5] in the first years of the republic is now generally accepted [6].

---

[1] Polyb. 3, 22, 1; Liv. 2, 8, 6; Plut. Publ. 14; Dion. Hal. 5, 35, 3.

[2] R.E. 2e Reihe, 8, 1958, 1771, s.v. *Vesta*.

[3] Serv. ad Ecloga 8, 82.

[4] Mommsen, Die römische Chronologie bis auf Caesar, 1859, 86 ff.

[5] Wissowa, R.u.K.[1] 111.

[6] Ph. E. Huschke, Das alte römische Jahr und seine Tage, Breslau, 1869, 70; Müller-Deecke, Die Etrusker, II, 308; Van Essen, o.c. 35; Thulin, R.E. 10, 1919, 1136, s.v. *Iuppiter*; R. Werner, Der Beginn der römischen Republik, 29; Dumézil, La religion romaine archaïque, 285.

It is one more proof of Mommsen's integrity that he declined to use a datum which would splendidly have confirmed his theory. Livy, in a well-known, widely-discussed pericope [1], says:

lex vetusta est, priscis litteris verbisque scripta, ut qui praetor maximus sit, idibus septembribus clavum pangat; fixa fuit dextro lateri aedis Iovis optimi maximi ex qua parte Minervae templum est. eum clavum, quia rarae per ea tempora litterae erant, notam numeri annorum fuisse ferunt. [2]

In Festus [3] we read:

clavus annalis appellabatur, qui figebatur in parietibus sacrarum aedium per annos singulos, ut per eos numerus colligeretur annorum.

As Mommsen thought [4] that he had to infer from other texts that the *clavus* was driven in every *saeculum*, he found it impossible to assume the existence of a "year-nail".

The only argument really worth mentioning in favour of this hypothesis—viz. that the *fasti Capitolini* mention a *dictator clavi figendi causa* in the years 363 B.C. and 263 B.C., with an interval, therefore, of a *saeculum* of 100 years—loses its demonstrative force when we find that also in 331 [5] and 313 B.C. [6] a *dictator clavi figendi causa* was appointed. There is, moreover, not a single instance in literature in which the *clavus* is connected with the *saeculum*. Finally, it would seem extremely improbable that the series of *ludi saeculares*, started, according to Varro [7], in 249 B.C., had been superimposed on a *saeculum*-chronology indicated as late as 263 B.C. by the driving in of a nail, without this discrepancy having drawn attention. To my knowledge there is no longer anyone who, with Mommsen, denies that a nail was driven in every year [8].

---

[1] Liv. 7, 3.

[2] Heurgon, Entretiens Hardt, 13, 1966, 105, thinks that Livy's informant Cincius himself read the law on the Capitol; thus also Momigliano, Bull. Com. 58, 1930, 38.

[3] Festus 49 (L).

[4] Chronologie[1], 176 ff.

[5] Liv. 8, 18.

[6] Liv. 9, 28, 6; Fasti Capitol. 441/313; Diodor. Sic. 19, 102. De Francisci, Primordia Civitatis, 302, rightly points out that we have to distinguish two different rites: the annual and the irregular *clavi fixatio*; thus also Hanell, Das altrömische eponyme Amt, 125 ff.; Momigliano, o.c. 39; Werner, Der Beginn der römischen Republik, 26 ff.

[7] In Censorinus 17, 8 ff.

[8] Mommsen was explicitly opposed by: G. F. Unger, Philol. 32, 1879,

For a detailed critical discussion of the problems involved I refer to Hanell's book "Das altrömische eponyme Amt" [1], whose conclusions I fully endorse in so far as they concern the *ritus* of the *clavus annalis*. Briefly summarized they are the following: Wherever Livy states the reason for the driving-in of a *clavus*, this reason is an epidemic or some other imminent danger, from which it may be concluded that this *ritus* was of an expiatory nature. Livy, 8, 18, 12, in fact refers to a *piaculum*. The warding-off of danger or disease by pinning it down by means of a nail is a practice which is widely followed [2]. Side by side with this irregular *clavi fixatio* there had been since olden times the *clavus annalis*. The best proof that the *clavus annalis* goes back to the earliest period of the republic is a reference to a *praetor maximus*, by which undoubtedly the highest magistrate is meant. This dates the reference to a time when the highest magistrates were not yet called *consules*, and a government made up of two *collegae* of equal rank did not yet exist. Hanell now concludes: "Für diese frühe Zeit müssen wir uns also eine Nageleinschlagung als jährlich wiederkehrende Zeremonie denken. Sie fand am 13 September statt, an dem Tag, an dem der kapitolinische Tempel eingeweiht wurde, dem ursprünglichen *Neujahrstag des kapitolinischen Jahres*. Die Nageleinschlagung muss also ein *Neujahrsritus* gewesen sein und hatte aller Wahrscheinlichkeit nach eine magisch-apotropeische Bedeutung". (137)

In the first place we have, on the basis of phenomenological considerations, come to the conclusion that there is every reason to assign the character of a New Year ceremony to the *ludi Romani* and the rites connected with them. We have further seen that this theory is often defended for games in general, and that it was confirmed for Rome by the place of Sol and Luna in the circus. Finally, we have found proof for our thesis in the historic data concerning the *idus septembres*. On this day the magistrates of the initial period of the republic entered upon their office, the day was taken as the *dies natalis* of the temple of the state-god Iuppiter, on this day the

---

531 ff.; W. Soltau, Die römischen Amtsjahre, 51 ff.; L. Holzapfel, Römische Chronologie, 13 ff. See the survey of the counter-arguments in Werner, o.c. 30 ff.

[1] In addition to the scholars referred to on p. 271 n. 6 the following share his view: R. Bloch, Tite Live et les premiers siècles de Rome, 78 ff.; Alföldi, Early Rome and the Latins, 78 ff., 325; Turchi, La religione di Roma antica, 98.

[2] For literature see below p. 274.

clavus annalis was driven into the wall of the *cella* of Minerva. There is no room for any doubt: for some time, notably in the beginning of the republic, the *idus septembres* were taken as the calendrical New Year's Day, and the celebration of this day took place in a New Year festival of the type described in the preceding chapter[1]. And now the problems really begin: how is the presence of a mythical-ritual complex, the origin of which we have found in Egypt, Mesopotamia and other Near Eastern countries, to be explained in Rome?

Since we have repeatedly pointed out that it is certain that the *ludi Romani* with their *apparatus*, the *pompa*, the temple, the statues of the gods, were derived from Etruria, it may be expected that the answer to this question will also be found in Etruscan culture. When, immediately after the end of the regal period, the Roman magistrate entered upon his office on September 13th in a ceremony attended by games, at which the official wore the royal purple which is at the same time *ornatus Iovis*, this procedure was not invented in the republic, but was taken over from the period of the kings, notably from the Etruscan kings. It is probable, therefore, that the investiture of the magistrate on the *idus septembres* goes back to an Etruscan ritual.

The usage of the *clavus annalis* as part of the rites of the 13th of September will be found to settle this issue. But not only that: it also enables us topographically to define the origin of the *ludi* as a New Year festival, to make it credible that they also had the character of a New Year ceremony in Etruria, and finally to establish another link between the *ludi* and one of the components of the Babylonian New Year festival.

Further to the pericope quoted above, Livy, 7, 3, 7, reports: *Volsiniis quoque clavos indices numeri annorum fixos in templo Nortiae, Etruscae deae, comparere diligens talium monumentorum auctor Cincius adfirmat.* This is a highly significant statement. We learn

---

[1] Hubaux, Rome et Véies, 153 ff., discovered a few remarkable texts of Byzantine scholars, including Cedrenus in which Februarius, who undoubtedly "ait été un symbole de la fin de l'année", is beaten and expelled in the month of Sextilis. Hubaux tries to explain how these two months of February and Sextilis were confused, but the story tells us that the expulsion of Februarius took place during the winter. There is, therefore, no confusion possible, but the month of Sextilis is in these sources equated with February, the final month of the year in the oldest Roman calendar. But if February is the sixth month of the year, September must, at one time, have been the first. Unfortunately we do not know from what sources the Byzantines took the story of Februarius.

from it that the *clavi fixatio*, like most of the rites round the *idus septembres*, was an Etruscan usage, associated with the goddess Nortia, taking place in or near Volsinii.

Of the goddess Nortia, who, it seems, was worshipped only at Volsinii [1], very little is known [2], but that little is enough to characterize her, with Wissowa [3], as a "Schicksalsgöttin". A scholion on Iuvenal Sat. 10, 74, says about Nortia: *Fortunam vult intellegi*, and Martianus Capella 1, 88, says: *alii Sortem asserunt Nemesimque nonnulli Tychenque quam plures aut Nortiam*. Now that the character of the goddess has thus been defined, it is no longer possible to isolate the *clavi fixatio* from this "Schicksal"-character. Although, as we saw, such a practice of nailing down is widely followed as a *defixio* to ward off disaster and epidemics [4], it is no less common as "Symbol der Schicksalfestigung" [5]. The remedy originally applied at irregular intervals in case of emergencies, is converted into an annual preventive *ritus*, a development also observed in purification rites and the *votum*. By means of the *clavi fixatio* the fate of people and country is determined and fixed for the year to come. This implies, however, that in Etruria we have tracked down a rite which had precisely the same object as had the Mesopotamian custom of "fixing the fates" on New Year's Day [6]. To the points of contact between the Etrusco-Roman 13 September-rites and the Near Eastern New Year usages a highly remarkable one is thus added [7]. Was the *clavi fixatio* at Volsinii part of a more comprehensive annual ceremony? I think this can indeed be made plausible.

---

[1] As the special goddess of Volsinii she is referred to in Tertull. Apolog. 24; ad nation. 2, 8; as patroness of Seianus, who had come from Volsinii, in Iuven. 10, 74.

[2] About Nortia: Bernert, R.E.17, 1936, 1048; Deecke in Roscher Lexikon, III, 457; Wissowa, R.u.K.² 50 n. 2; 288; L. Ross Taylor, Local Cults in Etruria, 154 ff.; Latte, R.R.G. 154; Radke, Die Götter Altitaliens, 232.

[3] R.u.K.² 288; the same view is held by nearly all of the scholars referred to in note 2.

[4] R. Wünsch, *Defixionum tabellae Atticae*, Einleitung; Handwörterb. des deutschen Aberglaubens, I, 957, 1337; v. Premerstein, R.E. 4, 1900, 2 ff., s.v. *Clavus*; Frazer, G. B. Scapegoat, 59 ff.

[5] Wissowa, R.u.K.² 288. Cf. Horat. carm. 1, 35, 18; 3, 24, 5. Bernert, o.c., compares the expression *clavo trabali fixum* and points to the goddess Necessitas, servant of Fortuna, who is depicted with hammer and nails.

[6] For a possible Hittite parallel, the *Parcae* and the "tablets of destiny" see Gaster, Thespis, 288.

[7] About derivation or migration of particularly the mantic art from Babylonia and Asia Minor see R. Pettazzoni, S.E. 1, 1927, 195 ff.; G. Furlani, S.E. 10, 1936, 153 ff. Cf. Grenier, Les religions étrusque et romaine, 30.

In or near Volsinii another very important politico-religious ceremony took place: the annual national meeting of the Etruscan confederation. It is true that Livy sets this meeting *ad fanum Voltumnae*,
without giving any further indications as to the place [1], but on the
one hand we know that Voltumna is identical with Vertumnus, of
whom Propertius reports that he had come from Volsinii [2], and on
the other hand it was recorded in an edict of Constantine [3] that
national-Etruscan games were held at Volsinii as late as the fourth
century A.D.

This *principum Etruriae concilium* [4] met annually [5] on a date
unknown to us. In addition meetings were held at irregular intervals, e.g. when a war threatened [6]. The object of the annual meeting
was the election of what in the republican period is called the
sacerdos of the Etruscan confederation [7]. Since, according to Livy [8],
it was the king of Vei who once competed for this office, the ambiguous nature of this function is at once clear. Here we see in one
person two spheres overlapping: the religious and the political.
During the royal period the twelve cities of the confederation elected
one supreme king [9], who, by having twelve lictors carrying *fasces* [10],
one on behalf of each city, united the authority in one hand. The
sacerdos is the republican successor of this supreme king. Rosenberg[11] has rightly identified this sacerdos with the *zilaθ meχl rasnal*
we encounter on Etruscan inscriptions. The latter, in his turn, is
supposed to be identical with the official who in inscriptions from
the second to the fourth century A.D. is called *praetor Etruriae* or
praetor Etruriae XV populorum. Although Mazzarino[12] and Alföldi[13]

[1] Liv. 4, 23, 5; 4, 25, 7; 4, 61, 2; 5, 17, 6; 6, 2, 2.
[2] *Vide infra* p. 277.
[3] C.I.L. XI, 5265.
[4] Liv. 10, 16, 3 and 6, 2, 2. See about these *concilia*: J. Heurgon, Historia,
6, 1957, 86 ff.; Werner, o.c. 406 ff.; F. Altheim, Der Ursprung der Etrusker,
Baden-Baden, 1950, 65 ff.; M. Pallottino, Die Etrusker, 113 f.; Müller-
Deecke, Die Etrusker, I, 329 ff.; R. A. Fell, S.E. 2, 1928, 135 ff.
[5] Liv. 4, 25, 6.
[6] Liv. 10, 16, 3; 4, 23, 5; 4, 61, 2.
[7] Liv. 5, 1, 5.
[8] *ibid.*
[9] Liv. 1, 8, 3: *ex duodecim populis communiter creato rege*. Serv. ad Aen.
8, 475.
[10] Serv. ad Aen. 8, 475; Liv. 1, 8, 2.
[11] Der Staat der alten Italiker, 62.
[12] Dalla Monarchia allo Stato Repubblicano, 99; 239 n. 91.
[13] Early Rome and the Latins, 42; thus also Werner, o.c. 407.

among others follow him in this view, we learn from a study by Heurgon [1] that matters are more complicated. However, this issue need not concern us here. For us it suffices to know that during the regal period a supreme king, during the republican period a *zilaθ-sacerdos*, was elected annually, that his function continued to exist far into the period of the emperors, and that his election was followed by an investiture during which the insignia, notably the *fasces*, were bestowed upon him.

Games constituted the religious centre of the *concilium*. During the period of Constantine they had the form of a *spectaculum tam scenicorum quam gladiatorii muneris* [2], at which, according to the edict, the *sacerdos* had to be present. An annual fair was also held on the occasion [3].

In this way we find a number of ceremonies at Volsinii uniting into a whole—it seems only natural that the *clavus annalis* was fixed during the *concilium*—which so closely corresponds to the rites round the *idus septembres* at Rome that coincidence is out of the question. In both instances we see the *clavi fixatio*, one of the best arguments for the theory that the ceremonies bore the character of a New Year ritual, in both cases a leading functionary enters upon his one-year period of office, in both instances this magistrate is the leader of the annual games which form the religious centre of the complex. In both instances the festival is combined with an annual fair [4]. Müller-Deecke [5] have suggested that the *idus septembres*, the date of the *clavi fixatio* at Rome, was, for this reason, the first day of the Etruscan year. We do not know whether it was, but Pallottino [6] appears to think along the same lines when he tentatively translates the stem *cel-* of the Etruscan name of the month of September by "Kardinalpunkt".

Before trying to explain the correspondence between the two festivals, we shall first direct our attention toward the character

---

[1] Historia 6, 1957, 91 ff. See also slightly different Pallottino, Die Etrusker, 114; L. Pareti, La disunione politica degli Etruschi e i suoi riflessi storici e archeologici. Rendic. Pont. Accad. Arch. 7, 1929-30, 91 ff. Cf. the recent study of B. Liou, *Praetores Etruriae XV Populorum*. Latomus, Bruxelles, 1969, who adheres the view of Rosenberg.

[2] Edict of Constantine, C.I.L. XI, 5265.

[3] Liv. 4, 23 f.; Müller-Deecke, Die Etrusker, I, 287.

[4] For *ludi Romani* and the market see Wissowa, R.u.K.[2] 454.

[5] o.c. II, 308.

[6] Die Etrusker, 246.

of the deity at whose sanctuary the *concilium Etruriae* was held, viz. Voltumna.

In literature the name Voltumna [1] is only found in Livy [2], viz. in the phrase *ad fanum Voltumnae*, which does not give us any clue as to the nature of the deity. Fortunately, however, it is as good as certain that the Roman deity Vertumnus/Vortumnus goes back to the deity of the *fanum Voltumnae* [3], since Vertumnus had come from Volsinii [4], the city of Voltumna. About Vertumnus we also know little, but at any rate we know more about him than about his Etruscan counterpart. Propertius [5] gives three explanations of the name of the god, all variations on the basic theme: the stem *vert-* "turn".

1. When the Tiber had flooded, the god "turned" the water [6].
2. The god is given the fruit of the *annus vertens* [7].
3. (the correct explanation, according to Propertius) The god could change into any shape [8], a datum Ovid, of course, used in his Metamorphoses.

A fourth explanation was added in later times: the god is *praeses vertendarum rerum, hoc est emendarum ac vendendarum* [9].

Now it goes without saying that the care we have to excercise when dealing with etymologies from ancient times is more than ever called for when the name of an Etruscan god is connected with the stem of a Latin verb. If Schulze[10] is right in considering Voltumna a gentile god, any relationship with the verb *vertere* is fully out of the

---

[1] The literature of the relation between Voltumna and Vertumnus and the character of these gods is extensive: W. Schulze, Z.G.L.N. 252, 272; Wissowa, R.u.K.[2] 287 f.; Herbig, Mitt. d. Schles. Ges. f. Volkskunde, 23, 1922, 13 ff.; L. Ross Taylor, Local Cults in Etruria, 152 ff.; R. Pettazzoni, S.M.S.R. 4, 1928, 207 ff.; Altheim, Griech. Götter, 8 ff., 159; Heurgon, R.E.L. 14, 1936, 109 ff.; La Capoue préromaine, 71 ff.; Devoto, S.E. 14, 1940, 275; A. J. Pfiffig, Gymnasium, 68, 1961, 55 ff.; Eisenhut R.E. 2e Reihe, 8, 1958, 1669, s.v. *Vertumnus*; Radke, Die Götter Altitaliens, 317, 347; Alföldi, Early Rome and the Latins, 204; Latte, R.R.G. 191.

[2] Liv. 4, 23, 5; 4, 25, 7; 4, 61, 2; 5, 17, 6; 6, 2, 2.

[3] Thus most of the scholars referred to in note 1.

[4] Prop. 4, 2, 3.

[5] Prop. 4, 2.

[6] Thus also Serv. ad Aen. 8, 90; Ovid, Fasti 6, 409; see Bömer *ad loc.*

[7] Thus also Columella, de r.r. 10, 308 ff.

[8] Ovid, Metam. 14, 642 ff.; Tibull. 4, 2, 13; Horat. sat. 2, 7, 14.

[9] Porph. Hor. epist. 1, 20, 1; Ps. Asconius ad Cic. in Verrem p. 199; Colum. de r.r. 10, 308.

[10] Z.G.L.N. 252, 272.

question. In spite of this, the connection Vertumnus-*vertere* has been defended by many distinguished scholars, especially in the second explanation given by Propertius. Preller-Jordan [1], for example, think "Vertumnus speciell der Fruchtgott des *annus vertens*. So ist er zunächst sowohl ein Gott des Frühlings, als der des fruchtbaren Herbstes, ganz besonders aber dieses letzteren...", and Wissowa [2]: "Vertreter des *annus vertens*". Warde Fowler [3] defends this view linguistically as well: "But his name, like Picumnus, is beyond doubt Latin, and may be supposed to indicate the turn or change in the year at the fruit-season; and if he really was an immigrant, which is possible, his original cult in Etruria was not Etruscan proper but old-Italian".

This remark by Warde Fowler was linguistically elaborated and made credible by Devoto [4]. He pointed out that words with a formans *mn/mno* may with equal justification be attributed to the Etruscan and to the Latin language. Gentile names such as Velimna, Recimna, etc. are typical of Etruria and find parallels in pre-Indo-European names such as Σέδαμνος, 'Ρίθυμνος etc. But also in Indo-European there is a formans *meno/mono/mno*, which indicates the participium medium, and which has survived in Latin in, e.g. *alumnus*. Vertumnus, according to Devoto, belongs to this type. This implies that the name is neither originally Etruscan, nor Latin, but proto-Latin. "Vertumno è entrato così in etrusco, come attributo di una divinità connessa con l'anno che volge, allo stesso modo che il protolatino *leudho-*, non il latino *liber*, è entrato in etrusco prima che Roma esistesse, e vi ha fatto nascere *lautn liberto*". (277)

It is rather curious that, after this very sound argumentation, Devoto fails to connect Vertumnus with Voltumna. Here he follows Schulze and connects Voltumna, a "dea Etrusca", with a nominal component Volta, although the identification of Vertumnus and Voltumna has been widely accepted and though it is quite possible that protolatin *Vortumno-* evolved in Etruscan, with the characteristic confusion of *r* and *l*, into Voltumna [5].

---

[1] Römische Mythologie, I, 452.

[2] R.u.K.[2] 287.

[3] Roman Festivals, 201; cf. Eisenhut, R.E. *cit.* 1685.

[4] S.E. 14, 1940, 275 ff.

[5] Voltumna is also taken to be a female god by: Altheim, Ursprung der Etrusker, 66. On this question see Herbig, o.c. 13 ff. and Eisenhut, R.E. 2e Reihe, 9, 1961, 852 f., s.v. *Voltumna*.

From the above it is clear that we find ourselves in good company when we think that we may see the god of the *annus vertens* in the god Voltumna/Vertumnus. Also along these lines, therefore, we arrive at a confirmation of the theory that the ceremonies *ad fanum Voltumnae* formed a New Year ceremony. But how are we to explain that in Volsinii the fairly obscure deity Voltumna, but in Rome Iuppiter himself formed the centre of the ceremony? The solution is supplied by Varro [1], who says about Vertumnus that he was *deus Etruriae princeps*. Attempts have been made to deny the truth of this statement [2], and the most improbable explanations [3] have been suggested although in fact Pettazzoni [4] provided a simple answer to the question whether Tinia (Iuppiter) or Voltumna (Vertumnus) was the *deus Etruriae princeps*. He holds the opinion that Tinia and Vertumnus are identical in the sense that "Voltumna (Vertumnus) sia stato in origine una divinità niente affatto gentilizia, e precisamente sia stato lo stesso Tinia in un aspetto particolare, forse una forma locale, Volsiniense di Tinia, e precisamente Tinia nella funzione speciale di protettore della nazione e confederazione etrusca..." [5].

Here we have Voltumna, the central god of the Etruscan annual games, as a variation of Tinia/Iuppiter, god of the Etrusco-Roman *ludi Romani* [6]. The final question is how the correspondence between the two annual ceremonies is to be explained.

That the Etruscans during the period of their supremacy over Latium and Rome decisively influenced the form and organization of the Latin confederation has often been argued and expounded [7].

---

[1] Varro, l.l. 5, 46.

[2] C. Clemen, Religion der Etrusker, 1936, 22, whose argumentation I cannot endorse.

[3] Radke, Die Götter Altitaliens, 319 f., wants to explain *princeps* as meaning the first of the array of gods, just as Ianus is the first, but not the most important, of the array of Roman gods. But this was decidedly not the meaning of the word in the phrase *deus Etruriae princeps*.

[4] S.M.S.R. 4, 1928, 207 ff.

[5] o.c. 212. Although we shall see that Voltumna is more than that, I largely agree with the Italian scholar.

[6] Is it by coincidence that, according to Fulgentius, serm. ant. 11, p. 115, 5, (Helm.) Vertumnus is, together with Priapos and Epona, reckoned among the Semones to whom in Rome, in the *carmen arvale*, the invocation *triumpe* was addressed?

[7] See i.a. Altheim, Der Ursprung der Etrusker, 60 ff.; Heurgon, Historia, 6, 1957, 87; Werner, o.c. 399 n. 1; Rosenberg, Der Staat der alten Italiker, 76 f.; Alföldi, Early Rome and the Latins, 26 ff.; 177 ff.; *idem*, Gymnasium, 70, 1963, 385 ff.; R. Bloch, Rev. Hist. Rel. 159, 1961, 141 ff.

It was during this period that, according to reports of Livy, 1, 45, 2 and Dionysius, 4, 26, 3, Servius Tullius founded the temple of Diana on the Aventine as the symbol of and the stimulus for Rome's growing power in the Latin confederation, and made this temple the centre of the Latin confederation [1]. This new confederation, according to Altheim [2], was modelled after the Etruscan confederation of twelve cities. The purpose of the meetings at the temple of Diana was chiefly political, whilst the meetings *ad caput aquae Ferentinae*, at the foot of the *mons Albanus*, were intended only for the mobilization of the army and for the holding of markets and political discussions [3]. Of quite a different, chiefly ritual nature were the meetings of the Latini on the *mons Albanus*, place of worship of Iuppiter Latiaris.

Both the institution of these *feriae Latinae* and the building of the sanctuary of Iuppiter Latiaris are ascribed to Tarquinius Superbus[4]. There is, however, no doubt that these meetings were of an older, pre-Etruscan origin, as notably Alföldi [5] has stressed. Several elements of the *ritus* are of great antiquity. The sacred mountain was sprinkled with milk to enhance fecundity [6]. A banquet took place to which each city had to contribute [7]. The climax was the killing of a white bull[8], of whose meat each of the thirty cities was given a part (*carnem petere*) [9]. The character of such ceremonies is well-known. It is a "Kommunionsmahl"[10], of which Alföldi says: "They were in their most primitive forms the participation of a social group in the vital forces of the zoomorphic ancestor by absorbing some part of his body, and renewing thereby the ties of relationship"[11].

---

[1] See Werner, o.c. 397 ff. Alföldi, o.c. 318 ff., believes neither in a "grande Roma dei Tarquinii", nor in a temple-founding by Servius Tullius. For a refutation of his view see A. Momigliano, Rendic. Acc. Lincei, 1962, 387, and J.R.S. 57, 1967, 215.

[2] o.c. 63 ff.

[3] Alföldi, o.c. 34 f.

[4] Dion. Hal. 4, 49, 2; 6, 95, 3; Auct. de viris ill. 8, 2; Schol. Bob. in Cic. pro Planc. 23.

[5] o.c. 19 ff.

[6] Cic. de divin. 1, 11, 18.

[7] Dion. Hal. 4, 49, 1 ff.

[8] Liv. 41, 16, 1 f.; Arnob. 2, 68.

[9] Cic. pro Planc. 9, 23 and Schol. Bob. *ad loc.*; Varro l.l. 6, 25; Dion. Hal. 4, 49, 2; Plin. n.h. 3, 5, 69; Serv. Aen. 1, 211.

[10] G. van der Leeuw, Phänomenologie der Religion², 1956, 404.

[11] Alföldi, o.c. 22. See on this subject: Robertson Smith, Lectures on the Religion of the Semites, Edinburgh, 1889, 236 ff.

He draws parallels with, for example, the rending of the bull or other animals in the Dionysiac cult.

In later times the *feriae Latinae* were not held on a fixed date. They were *conceptivae*. After Rome had definitely assumed the leadership of the Latin confederation, the consuls had the duty of proclaiming this festival immediately after their installation, and to celebrate it before performing any other official act [1].

With Alföldi we find that the *feriae Latinae* on the *mons Albanus* indeed constituted a primitive federal festival, in which the unity of the *nomen Latinum* was expressed by the joint worship of Iuppiter Latiaris. Etruscan influence is apparent from the reports which attributed the establishing of the *feriae* and the building of the temple to Tarquin [2], although in fact it was only a renewal and re-organization, not a new creation that took place [3]. The Etruscan influence is apparent from yet another phenomenon, which forms the real reason why, side by side with the Etruscan *concilium ad fanum Voltumnae* and the ceremonies around the *idus septembres* at Rome, we here discuss the *feriae Latinae*, which at first sight do not quite belong in the same category: the triumph *in monte Albano*.

In the fifth chapter we saw that the general who was refused a triumph in Rome, could triumph on the *mons Albanus*, and that, as tradition has it, this was done for the first time by C. Papirius Maso in 231 B.C. Aust [4] demonstrated that in its external characteristics this triumph was not or hardly distinguishable from the real triumph. It should not be assumed that this triumph was a *creatio ex nihilo*. As early as 1854 H. A. Goell suggested that Papirius Maso, who had been *pontifex*, knew of an older form of triumph on the Alban mountain from the *libri pontificales*. That there was in ancient times a *ritus* of this kind within the Latin confederation may be as-

---

[1] See Alföldi, o.c. 32 f.; Werner, o.c. 399 ff.; the state-sacrifice in the old federal city of Lavinium had the same priority. It is highly significant that precisely here F. Castagnoli (Bull. Com. 77, 1959/60, 3) found 13 altars, of which one is older than the other twelve, which are from the sixth century. B. C. Momigliano, J.R.S. 57, 1967, 215, connects this number with a confederation of twelve members, such as the Etruscan one, and supposes a reformation of the Latin federation after the Etruscan pattern. It is possible, then, that the kings of Rome assumed the twelve lictors with the *fasces* as a token of the rule of Rome over Latium.

[2] The remnants of the temple do indeed date from this time: Wissowa, R.u.K.[2] 40.

[3] Werner, o.c. 400 n. 4. Altheim's argumentation that the *Latiar* was founded by the Etruscan kings of Rome is untenable.

[4] Roscher Lexik. II, 694, s.v. *Iuppiter*.

sumed with a high degree of safety [1]. M. Radin [2] went even further:
in an ingenious paper, entitled "Imperium", which contains many
useful ideas, even though, in my opinion, the trend of the argument
as a whole is not sound, he argued that the *triumphus in monte Albano* was originally an installation rite. The newly appointed leader
of the Latin federation "was clothed in the embroidered robe of
Iuppiter; his face was painted red; a wreath was placed upon his
head, he took in his hand the symbols of the god, the eagle with
outstretched wings.... So equipped he was paraded through the
various cities of Latium over the hills and valleys between Praeneste
and Alba until the procession ended at the federal shrine on the
Alban Mount" (26).

There is no need to repeat the whole of the argumentation which
led Radin to this point of view. I think nothing corroborates his
suggestion more strongly than does a datum that he does not use,
but which has come to our knowledge: the fact that the *ludi Romani*,
during which the magistrates wore the *ornatus Iovis* = triumphal
robes, formed a New Year installation ritual. The cult of Iuppiter
O.M., of which the *ludi Romani* formed part, shows—it has already
been pointed out several times—a close resemblance to the cult of
Iuppiter Latiaris [3], and, as we have seen [4], it has often been suggested that Rome during the Tarquinian period deliberately instituted the *ludi Romani* and the cult of Iuppiter O.M. in competition with the *feriae Latinae* and Iuppiter Latiaris.

Viewed in the light of our conclusions concerning the striking
correspondence between the *ludi Romani* and the annual Etruscan
festival *ad fanum Voltumnae*, this theory may perhaps be slightly
modified. If the *feriae Latinae* also form a parallel of the Etruscan

---

[1] Wissowa, R.u.K.[2] 125; E. Pais, Fasti Triumphales Populi Romani, I,
1920, XX f. See the discussion between Hanell, Alföldi, Gjerstad, Heurgon
and Waszink in Entretiens Hardt, 13, 1966, 31 ff.; further: G. de Sanctis,
Storia dei Romani III, 1, 1916, 283 and particularly II, 1907, 100; Combès,
Imperator, 68.

[2] Studi Riccobono, II, Palermo, 1936, 21 ff.

[3] See literature above Chapter III, p. 115; further Werner, o.c. 400 n. 4;
Wissowa, R.u.K.[2] 40. A parallel is seen in the sacrifice of the white bull
on the *mons Albanus* (Arnob. 2, 68) and in Rome at the installation of the
consuls (Mommsen, Staatsrecht I[3], 616). During the *feriae Latinae* chariot-
races were held on the Capitolinus (Plin. n.h. 27, 45); further the triumph.
There are, of course, differences as well; see about these Brelich, Vesta
82; Koch, Der römische Iuppiter, 127.

[4] Above p. 115. n. 1.

festival, as Werner [1] and others have pointed out, it has to be concluded on the basis of the above argumentation that in the period of the Etruscan domination both the *feriae Latinae* and the *ludi Romani*, independently of each other, acquired the outward appearance described in later literature: the *feriae Latinae* were recreated, the *ludi Romani* were created. Like the *concilium* at Volsinii, the former was a federal festival, at which at one time a supreme commander of the Latins was elected and/or installed; during the republican period, immediately after the expulsion of the kings, the latter was the installation festival of the magistrates, the beginning of the new year. What the Latin and the Roman festivals have in common is that the installation ceremony was, as it were, repeated after a victory, in the triumph. It may, therefore, safely be assumed that the Etruscans, who, as tradition has it, created the triumph, also celebrated a similar triumph-ceremony either *ad fanum Voltumnae* or locally. This matter will be discussed in the next section.

Only one question remains: what was the function of the *ludi Romani* during the period of the kings, when there was no *annual* installation of a magistrate, i.c. the king? About the official installation rites of the Roman kings we know next to nothing. However, Vergil probably was not far from the truth in Aeneis 7, 170 ff, which were probably inspired by the installation of the magistrate:

> *Tectum augustum, ingens, centum sublime columnis,*
> *Urbe fuit summa, Laurentis regia Pici,*
> *Horrendum silvis et religione parentum.*
> *Hic sceptra accipere et primos attollere fasces*
> *Regibus omen erat, hoc illis curia templum,*
> *Hae sacris sedes epulis; ....*

In this description of Laurentan conditions the poet had in mind, not the Roman temple of Apollo, the Palatium or the Curia [2], but the Capitolium [3]. It is quite possible that, like the magistrates in

---

[1] o.c. 399 n. 1. Cf. Combès, Imperator, 34, "Si la cérémonie du triomphe existe à la fois à Rome, à Préneste (a thesis of Radin, which is not accepted by Combès) et sur les Monts Albains, c'est que les trois cités ont été également soumises aux Étrusques; il n'est pas nécessaire de supposer qu'il y a eu influence ou concurrence entre elles."

[2] For the various views see the well-known commentaries.

[3] Thus also Bömer ad Ovid, Fasti I, 81.

later times, the Etruscan kings of Rome were installed in the temple of the great god. In view of the fact that the *ludi Romani*, which reflect this installation rite, were already held annually during the royal period, we cannot but conclude that during that period the investiture and installation were repeated annually in the New Year ceremony in which the king represented the supreme god, as kings have been found to have done in Near Eastern cultures. Once we have seen this, the transition from kingship to annual magistracy becomes less abrupt than is assumed. The New Year festival of the re-investiture of the king impersonating Iuppiter develops into an investiture ceremony of the annual magistrate. But for the time being the *ludi Romani* and the September-rites remain what they also were during the period of the kings: a New Year festival.

3. *The origin of the triumph*

So far we have been concerned with the ceremonial of the *ludi Romani*, and have attempted to discover its original meaning. That we have not until now inquired into the original meaning of the triumph is due to the fact that, unlike the *ludi*, the triumph was not celebrated on a fixed date. If either of the two ceremonies is comparable with New Year festivals of other cultures, priority should be given to the *feriae statae*.

Mommsen has described the *ludi Romani* as being a part of the triumph, which, after having detached itself, assumed an existence of its own as *feriae annuae*. We have contested this view without, however, denying the existence of a relation between the *ludi Romani* and the triumph. Both by tradition said to have been introduced by Tarquinius Priscus, both centred round the temple on the Capitolinus, they have one feature in common which precludes independence: the king/magistrate wearing the robes of Iuppiter. If the *ludi* are not to be derived from the triumph, it is still possible that the triumph evolved from the ceremony of the *ludi Romani* or, rather, from the Etruscan preliminary stage of them, or was at any rate conceived after this example. I think I can make it credible that this was in fact what happened.

No indisputable testimony of the Etruscan triumph exists. The nature of the processions depicted on funeral urns and sarcophagi cannot be ascertained. It is, as we have seen, improbable that they were triumphal processions [1]. Neither has the word *triumpe* so far been found in the Etruscan vocabulary, which may be due to the exclamatory character of the term, which only in Latin developed into an appellativum. Heurgon [2] has made a very attractive conjecture in an *elogium* found at Tarquinia of an Etruscan magistrate who was the first to cross the sea with an army. Heurgon reads the last two lines of the *elogium* as follows:

> *aqu[ila cum corona]*
> *aurea ob vi[ctoriam donatus]*

This would give us the Etruscan equivalent of the Roman triumph. However attractive this conjecture may be, it does not, of course, prove anything.

I nevertheless am of the opinion that in our inquiry into the existence of an Etruscan triumph we need not exclusively rely on the reports of ancient historians and on linguistic arguments already discussed in the preceding chapters. Rather than direct archaeological or historical indications I think that, in the present case, legend will help us out. In one of the rare legends dealing with the oldest history of Rome, Latium and Etruria, a vague reminiscence of an Etruscan triumphal rite which included the identification of the victorious king with the god Iuppiter, is discernible—in an age during which such an idea was alien and abhorrent to the Romans. I refer to the legend of Mezentius, the *contemptor deum* [3]. About the deeds of this king of Caere which earned him this title several reports have come down to us [4]. In exchange for his aid in the war he is reported to have claimed the entire vintage of either the Rutulians or the Latins in case of a victory. This made the Latins promise Iuppiter their wine if he agreed to take their side. This is the reason why on the *Vinalia rustica* the first wine was still dedicated to Iuppiter [5].

---

[1] I consider it more probable that these pictures show the annual investiture, which was accompanied by games.

[2] Mél. d'Arch. et d'Hist. 63, 1951, 119 ff.

[3] Cf. Aen. 8, 7; 7, 648. About Mezentius: Wörner, Roscher Lexik. II, 2943 ff.; Marbach, R.E. 15, 1932, 1511 ff. Alföldi, Early Rome and the Latins, 209 n. 1 and 210 mentions the later literature.

[4] The main sources have been cited by Alföldi, o.c. 209 f.

[5] On Iuppiter and the *Vinalia* i.a. Bömer, Rhein. Mus. N.F. 90, 1941, 30 ff.; Dumézil, Latomus 20, 1961, 524 ff.; *idem*, R.E.L. 39, 1961, 261 ff.; Latte, R.R.G. 74 ff.

At first sight the explanation seems simple: the legend may be a reminiscence of an Etruscan domination of Latium, which was obliged to pay a tribute in kind, *in casu* wine. This datum is then supposed to serve as an *aition* for the *Vinalia rustica* and the curious connection between Iuppiter and the new wine. Alföldi [1] was the last to defend this view. On closer investigation, however, such a historical explanation is contestable for more than one reason, particularly when we read the oldest testimony of this legend carefully. By way of explanation of Vergil's expression *Mezentius contemptor deum*, Macrobius [2] writes as follows: *Veram huius contumacissimi nominis causam in primo libro originum Catonis diligens lector inveniet. ait enim Mezentium Rutulis imperasse, ut sibi offerrent quas dis primitias offerebant, et Latinos omnes similes imperii metu ita vovisse: Iuppiter, si tibi magis cordi est nos ea tibi dare potius quam Mezentio, uti nos victores facias.*

This oldest testimony throws quite a different light on the matter. In the original version Mezentius apparently did not claim the entire vintage, but emphatically its *primitiae*, the part usually reserved for the gods, *in casu* for Iuppiter. Rather than referring to a tribute imposed on Latium, the legend describes the pretension of an Etruscan king who as a reward for a victory demanded the same rights as the supreme god, and in this way put himself on a level with Iuppiter. Following Macrobius one thus finds a natural explanation of the phrase *contemptor deum*, which Vergil himself tried to explain in a different way.

In many respects the legend is comparable with that of Salmoneus [3], who by throwing a thunderbolt imitated Zeus, even pretended to be Zeus [4]. He is called ὑβριστὴς καὶ ἀσεβής [5]; he demanded that sacrifices be made to him instead of to Zeus [6]. There is more to this legend than merely a reminiscence of the magic "rainmaker" as many see Salmoneus [7].

---

[1] o.c. 209 ff.

[2] Sat. 3, 5, 10.

[3] The data in Nawrath, R.E. 2e Reihe, I, 1920, 1989 f.; Ilberg, Roscher Lexik. IV, 290 ff.; cf. J. Harrison, Themis, 79 ff.; O. Weinreich, Menekrates Zeus und Salmoneus, 82 ff.; Frazer, G.B. I³, 1, 247 ff.

[4] Apollod. Bibl. 1, 9, 7.

[5] Diod. Sic. 4, 68, 2.

[6] Apollod. l.c.

[7] Nilsson, G.G.R. I², 117; Nawrath, o.c. 1990; Ilberg, o.c. 293; J. Harrison, Themis, 79.

Of course, the imitation of thunder and lightning is a well-known action in rain magic. Even in historic times the inhabitants of Krannon in Thessalia still observed the practice of moving a bronze carriage to and fro in order that the resulting thunder-like noise might cause rain [1]. But this proves that the action of rainmaking was not in itself looked upon as *hubris*. The Salmoneus figure should therefore be considered rather a "Gottkönig", as Weinreich calls him [2], of the pre-Greek period. Now the peculiar thing is that Vergil represents this Salmoneus on his chariot as a kind of triumphing *victor*: Aen, 6, 587.

> *Quattuor hic invectus equis et lampada quassans*
> *Per Graium populos mediaeque per Elidis urbem*
> *Ibat ovans, divum sibi poscebat honorem,*
> *Demens! qui nimbos et non imitabile fulmen*
> *Aere et cornipedum pulsu simularet equorum.*

On a crater from the fifth century he also appears to be depicted as a *victor*, this time of the Olympic games [3].

Both in the story of Salmoneus and in the Mezentius legend, therefore, we find traces of an identification of a man with the supreme god, an identification which by the cultures which came into contact with it, was disapproved of and qualified as *hybris* or *dementia*. I think that the pretension of Mezentius, who on the occasion of a victory claimed the honour of Iuppiter for himself, forms the first indication of the Romans becoming familiar with the triumph [4]. In this connection it is significant that Mezentius is sometimes called king of Caere, [5] but at other times king of the Etrus-

---

[1] Antigon. of Karyst. Hist. mirab. 15.

[2] o.c. 86 n. 22.

[3] See picture and discussion: J. Harrison, Themis, 80; A. B. Cook, Class. Rev. 17, 1903, 275.

[4] In his method of torture Mezentius resembles another presumptuous man who imitated Zeus, viz. Klearchos of Heraklea, of whom it is reported that he had his captives tortured in an atrocious manner during his "triumph" already discussed. In view of the above data, Frazer, Comm. Ovid, Fasti III, p. 401, sees a god-king in Mezentius. I do not want to go as far as this. But it can hardly be a matter of coincidence that Latinus, whose deification and triumph are depicted on the *cista Pasinati*, is *Iuppiter factus Latiaris* in the combat against precisely this Mezentius (Festus 212 (L)). What the Etruscan king was denied, fell to the share of the Latin: a triumph in the highest sense of the word, identification with the highest god!

[5] Festus 212 (L); Liv. 1, 2, 3; see Alföldi, o.c. 209 n. 1.

cans [1]. This can mean only one thing, viz. that he was the supreme king elected *ad fanum Voltumnae*.

If my point of view is right, it once more confirms the Etruscan origin of the triumph, but does not as yet explain the relation between the Etrusco-Roman New Year rites of the *concilium Etruriae* and the *ludi Romani* on the one hand, and the celebrations on the occasion of a victory in the form of the triumph on the other. To solve this question we once again, in the absence of Italic data, have to proceed *per analogiam*. We shall then find that our detailed discussion of the New Year ceremonies of cultures around the Mediterranean and their development, particularly in Hellenism, will prove useful.

In his "Kingship", the book we have already referred to several times, Hocart demonstrated that the enthronization of a king was universally celebrated as a feast of victory. In the preceding chapter we saw that the same holds for the New Year festivals which reaffirm the king's authority by a renewed investiture, and restore cosmic order. In the Dionysiac cult we have traced the development of a similar annual ritual feast of renewal in which the god, represented by the βασιλεύς, entered the city triumphantly, to the triumphal procession of the Hellenistic kings which was connected with a military victory, and for which the way had been paved by the myth of Dionysos *triumphans* and the historical data about Alexander's Dionysiac triumphal tour. This development forms an example of a universal process, which M. Eliade [2] has defined as follows: "Mais, on le verra, cette victoire du dieu sur le Dragon doit être symboliquement répétée chaque année, car chaque année le monde doit être créé à nouveau. De même la victoire des dieux contre les forces des Ténèbres, de la Mort et du Chaos se répète à chaque victoire de la cité contre les envahisseurs" [3].

Just as in Hellas and in Hellenism there are in Rome two different ceremonies in which the king/magistrate plays the part of the god, in this case the part of Iuppiter. In the ceremony of the *ludi Romani* we have recognized a New Year festival, which as such is comparable with the Dionysiac *Anthesteria*; in the triumph—others, notably

---

[1] Plin. n.h. 14, 88; Plut. Quaest. Rom. 45; Dion. Hal. 1, 65, 1 ff.

[2] M. Eliade, Le sacré et le profane, Paris, 1965, 45. The subject he deals with is that of the mythical dragon, the shape in which many cultures represent the divine opponent who threatens to destroy the cosmos.

[3] The behaviour of, e.g., Klearchos of Herakleia may be interpreted in this way.

Wallisch [1], have already pointed this out—we can see a parallel of the Hellenistic Dionysiac *pompa* by which a victory was celebrated. The *ludi Romani* and the attendant rites, as well as the triumph have come from Etruria. As far as the *ludi Romani* are concerned, we have in the *concilium ad fanum Voltumnae* found their Etruscan preliminary stage; an Etruscan precursor of the Roman triumph has not been attested with certainty, but has to be postulated on the basis of historic and linguistic data.

Between the pairs:

1. *Anthesteria*—Hellenistic Dionysiac *pompa*,
2. *Ludi Romani*—Roman triumph, and
3. *Concilium ad fanum Voltumnae*—Etruscan triumph

the name Θρίαμβε, Θρίαμβος/triumpe, triumphus forms the *trait d'union*. We have seen that the development of Θρίαμβε to *triumpe* must have taken place via Etruscan. Neither a derivation in Hellenistic times (Wallisch), nor a direct introduction of a Greek ceremony into sixth-century Rome (Durante) is possible. I think that in this chapter I have furnished an extra-linguistic proof of this by demonstrating the relationship between the Etruscan and Roman ceremonies.

In this way we have found a relation between Greek, Etruscan and Roman ritual which years ago was outlined by C. Koch [2], to whose suggestion, however, nobody paid any attention [3]. Partly because the remaining problems are also implicitly to be found in Koch's view I here quote the entire passage in question [4]:

> "Nun ist sicher, wenn auch im einzelnen noch undurchsichtig, dass zwischen dem griechischen Dionysoskult dieser archaïschen Zeit und dem Iuppiterdienst der tarquinischen Dynastie Roms, aus dem das Triumphritual der römischen Republik hervorgegangen ist, ein historischer Zusammenhang bestanden haben muss. Denn *triumphus* ist nichts anderes als die italische Umbildung des hellenisch-dionysischen Kultwortes Θρίαμβος, und mit dem Worte muss auch die Sache auf Altgriechenland zurückgehen. Die Folgerung ist unausweichlich, dass einstmals Dionysos die Stelle eingenommen hat, die in historischer Zeit Iuppiter als Gott des Triumphes einnahm.

---

[1] See above p. 90 n. 3.

[2] Gottheit und Mensch im Wandel der römischen Staatsform. Das neue Bild der Antike, 2, 1942, 134 ff. = Religio, 94 ff.

[3] Critical i.a. J. Bayet, Gnomon, 33, 1961, 524: "Il paraîtra audacieux de supposer une origine dionysiaque au rite jovien du triomphe."

[4] Religio, 95 f.

> Der Triumphator der historischen Zeit trägt die Insignien und den
> Ornat Iuppiters, wenn er in die Stadt seinen Einzug nimmt.
> Beachtet man lediglich die Umstände seines äusseren Auftretens, so
> könnte man glauben, leibhaftig eine Gottheit vor sich zu haben.
> Die Gestalt des in Athen alljährlich zur heiligen Hochzeit ein-
> ziehenden Gottes Dionysos kann sich im Äusseren nicht wesentlich
> von ihm unterschieden haben. Ist die soeben gezogene Folgerung
> richtig, dass Dionysos die Rolle Iuppiters in der vorgeschichtlichen
> Urform des italischen Triumphes spielte, so stehen wir vor der
> Gegebenheit sogar eines ursprünglich sachlichen Zusammenhanges
> zwischen der Gestalt des Triumphators und der des kommenden
> Gottes Dionysos....."

It will be seen that here an outline based on surmise was given
of what I have tried to map out in the present study. Several connections which Koch thought he could discern, have, I hope, been
demonstrated or clarified by our investigation of the data. One
important question, however, still remains: how are we to explain
that in Greece Dionysos, in Rome Iuppiter is the central god? And,
in this connection, how are we to imagine that the Greek ceremony
reached Rome?

Beginning with the second question, I must reject the most
obvious hypothesis, viz. that the Greek Dionysos-ceremony was
taken over by Etruria, there assumed a different character, and was
subsequently introduced into Rome. Several arguments tell against
this hypothesis.

1. Our investigation has made it clear that it is not one, but two
ceremonies we are dealing with: a New Year festival (*Anthesteria*,
ludi Romani) and the celebration of a victory (Hellenistic *pompa*,
triumph). The fact that during the regal period the triumph already existed as an autonomous victory-rite makes it impossible
for this ceremony to have been taken over from Greece, as the
Greek "triumph" is not found prior to Hellenism. Even so it might
be possible that the New Year ceremony of the *Anthesteria* had
been directly derived from Hellas, and that in Etruria it had developed into the triumph. Against this theory, however, tells the following
circumstance:

2. The Greek Dionysos, once he has arrived in Etruria, never
belies his Greek origin in pictures, in spite of his Etruscan name of
Fufluns. Either by his attributes or by the setting of the scene he is
always clearly recognizable as the Greek Dionysos [1]. That this

---

[1] Bruhl, Liber Pater, 70 ff., makes this clear.

Hellenic god should have been confused or identified with a Iuppiter type is most improbable [1], and contrary to the archaeological data. Nor is it to be assumed that the Etruscans deliberately substituted Dionysos by Iuppiter/Tinia in a Dionysiac ritual, in view of the great popularity of Dionysos in Etruria [2]. To this the following consideration should be added:

3. The resemblance between the Dionysiac *pompa* of the *Anthesteria* and the Etrusco-Roman *pompa* of the circus on the one hand, and the triumph on the other, should not be exaggerated. The procession of the statues of the gods lends to the circus procession its peculiar character, the triumphal *pompa* has only the name—or rather the exclamation—in common with the Dionysiac procession, and perhaps also the satirical songs. The *phallos* which played a part in both *pompae* has so widely been used apotropaeically that it should not be looked upon simply as a relic of the Dionysiac cult.

4. The god playing the principal part in the Etruscan annual festival was Voltumna, whose title of *deus Etruriae princeps* identified him with Tinia.

5. A development of a New Year festival into the celebration of a victory, as we have traced it in Hellas, and as we also suppose it to have existed in Etruria, can take place only on condition that the New Year festival in its deepest, original meaning is understood by the people celebrating it. Only then can the fundamental meaning of, e.g., the exclamation *triumpe* be felt in such a way that the aspect of the victory can develop and become increasingly significant. But so deeply ingrained can be only a festival which either germinated within a people or was taken over from a neighbouring people after centuries of close association and thorough cultural influencing. One wonders whether the cultural contacts between the Greek colonies in Italy and their Etruscan neighbours satisfy these conditions.

I think a solution presents itself if we do not ask how Tinia/Iuppiter could take over the function of Dionysos in the ceremonies described in Etruria, but try to find out in which area a deity existed who showed features of Dionysos as well as aspects of Iuppiter, and who lived among one people as the supreme god, and

---

[1] It is true that the Etruscan Fufluns, with whom Dionysos was identified, has connections with Tinia, but these are to be traced to the Etruscan, not to the Greek Dionysos figure. See below p. 293 ff.

[2] See Bruhl, o.c. 70 ff.

among another people as the divine son. Here the conclusion of the
first chapter of this study will show us the way.

There we defended the possibility that a P.I. *thriambe* developed
into Greek θρίαμβε, and independently from this, into Etruscan
triumpe. We also found that this cry functioned as an invocation by
which a god was invited to manifest himself. The god in question
belonged to the "dying and rising" type, but was not necessarily
Dionysos. This is proved by gods such as Sabazios and Iakchos,
whose names developed from exclamations, and who were later
equated with Dionysos without being originally identical.

It is certain that in Asia Minor and Crete gods were worshipped
who belonged to this type and who—in later times—were called
Zeus [1]. The best-known example is the Ζεὺς Κρεταγένης, whose
annual birth was celebrated in cult and myth, and of whom Nilsson,
who is very cautious on this point, concedes [2]: "Dies Zeuskind ist
der ἐνιαυτὸς δαίμων Miss Harrisons". Now this child-Zeus cannot be
separated from the Cretan Dionysos-Zagreus [3]. Such a kinship
between Zeus and Dionysos is so common in Asia Minor—an
inscription even refers to a Zeus Bakchos [4]—that Cook, the unequalled expert on the Zeus cult, concludes on the strength of a very
large amount of material [5]: "The plain fact is that to the Phrygians
Zeus and Dionysos were but different aspects of the selfsame god",
and before Cook the great authority on Phrygian culture, Sir. W. M.
Ramsay, had already said about Zeus and Dionysos [6]: "the character
and personality of the God-father and God-son pass into one
another in such a way in the divine tale or drama, that no clear line
can be drawn to separate them" [7]. Hence it would appear that the
etymological explanation of the name Dionysos as Zeus-son or
child-Zeus is most probable. This means that, if anywhere, it will
have to be in Asia Minor that we shall have to look for the solution

---

[1] See: C. Picard, Les religions préhelléniques, 1948, 217 ff., with extensive
bibliography.

[2] G.G.R. I², 311.

[3] Cook, Zeus, I, 645; cf. J. Harrison, Themis, 1 ff.; R. F. Willets, Cretan
Cults and Festivals, London, 1962, 144; 202 ff.; Guthrie, Orpheus², 112 f.;
see the critical review of W. Fauth, R.E. 2e Reihe, 9, 1967, 2227 ff., s.v.
Zagreus.

[4] C.I.G. III, 3538.

[5] A. B. Cook, Zeus, II, 287.

[6] The Cities and Bishoprics of Phrygia, I, 140.

[7] Cf. W. B. Kristensen, Symbool en Werkelijkheid, 145; O. Kern, R.E.,
5, 1905, 1036, s.v. *Dionysos*.

to the problem of how the Dionysos of the Greek *Anthesteria* can return as Iuppiter in Etruria and Rome, because, in the opinion of the large majority of the experts, Asia Minor was the country from which the Etruscans, or at least the culture-bearing top-layer of this people had come.

I hold the view that the Etruscans brought the New Year festival with them from Asia Minor, together with the god who formed the centre of it, a god whom the Greeks called Dionysos, the Etruscans Tinia (or by an Italic name Voltumna), a figure of the "dying and rising" type, who was invoked by the cry *thriambe* and who on New Year's Day was represented by the king. Data from various sources appear to bear out the fundamental kinship between the great god Tinia/Voltumna and the later Greek Dionysos.

An inscription from Magnesia on the Maeander in Asia Minor [1] describes the festival in honour of Zeus Sosipolis. Preceded by the *stephanophoros* and the priestess of Artemis Leukophryene and other dignitaries, as well as by two choruses of youths and girls whose parents are both alive, the beautifully robed *xoana* of the twelve gods are carried to their altars on the market-place, where in a wooden hut (θόλος) they are offered a meal on beds (στρωμναί). A bull selected the year before and fattened for the purpose, is killed. Its meat is distributed among those taking part in the procession. About this bull Nilsson says [2]: "Unter den von der Religionswissenschaft herausgearbeiteten Typen sieht dieser Stier wirklich dem Jahrkönig Frazers oder noch besser dem ἐνιαυτὸς δαίμων Miss Harrisons ähnlich, d.h. einer Verkörperung der sich jährlich erneuernden Vegetation". As Miss Harrison [3], already observed, the bull was originally not a sacrifice to Zeus, but "a communal meal... In him is concentrated as it were the life of the year; he is the incarnate ideal of the year..... The bull is Sosipolis, Saviour of the city, in the making" [4]. The communal eating of an animal, particularly a bull, is pre-eminently typical of the Dionysiac cult, but a similar meal occurred in the cult of Iuppiter Latiaris. Following

---

[1] Sylloge, 589, 41; Kern, Inschriften von Magnesia nr. 98; on this subject: Nilsson, Griech. Feste, 23 ff.; G.G.R. I², 154 f.; von Wilamowitz, Glaube der Hellenen II, 347; J. Harrison, Themis, 151 ff.

[2] G.G.R. I², 154.

[3] Themis 154.

[4] This is, among other things, apparent from the prayer that is said for the welfare of country, city, fruit and cattle.

others, Altheim [1] has demonstrated the striking resemblance between
the confederation of the twelve cities of Etruria and that of Ionia.
Is the communal meal on the *mons Albanus*, in which we have observed Etruscan influences, also a ritual introduced from Ionia via
Etruria? Are the twelve altars found near Lanuvium significant
in this connection? But let us leave those questions aside.

The Zeus Sosipolis, the ἐνιαυτὸς δαίμων of Magnesia, is there depicted in the shape of an adult man [2]. The same Sosipolis is found
again in Olympia, where in the Altis there was a sanctuary for
Eileithuia and Sosipolis [3]. But this Sosipolis is represented as a baby.
At an invasion of the Arcadians he is said to have put the enemy to
flight by changing into a serpent. Not far from Olympia, in Elis
itself, Sosipolis shared a sanctuary with Tuche [4]. There he was represented as a boy, wearing a star-covered cloak, and holding the
cornucopia, the horn of Amaltheia with the fruit of the year, in his
hand [5]. C. Robert [6] has forcibly argued that in Sosipolis we should
recognize the Cretan Zeus type. We do indeed have a clear example
of a year-god here, who is represented as a baby, a child or a man,
a bearer of plenty like the *eniautos daimon* in the Hellenistic *pompa*
with the *cornucopia*. The Sosipolis of Magnesia was in later times
assimilated to Zeus, but those of Olympia and Elis may with
equal justification be called Dionysos, an example of the divergence
of two lines both starting from one figure of a year-god.

Worthy of notice is the *parhedria* of the Sosipolis of Elis with
Tuche, personification of fate. In this connection it is significant
that Eileithuia, the goddess sharing Sosipolis' cult in Olympia, is
also very often depicted as a goddess of fate [7]. Not only has the

---

[1] Der Ursprung der Etrusker, *passim*, particularly 68 ff. See objections
in Werner, Der Beginn der römischen Republik, 402 n. 4, but approval
of Heurgon, Historia, 6, 1957, 91 ff. and Alföldi, Early Rome and the Latins,
26, (with literature), who, in contradistinction to Altheim is of the opinion
that the Etruscans brought this form of confederation of cities with them
from their Asia Minor country of origin. Cf. Pallottino, Die Etrusker, 113.

[2] O. Kern, Arch. Anz. 1897, 80; Nilsson, Griech. Feste, 24.

[3] Paus. 6, 20, 2. About this: Cornford in J. Harrison, Themis, 239 ff.;
Nilsson, G.G.R. I², 415.

[4] Paus. 6, 25, 4.

[5] On Dionysos in the star-covered cloak: Eisler, Weltenmantel, 72, 74 f.

[6] Mitt. d. Arch. Inst. Ath. 18, 1893, 37 ff.

[7] See i.a. P. Baur, Eileithuia, Inaugural-Dissertation, Heidelberg, 1901,
462; 472 ff.; 509. Paus. 8, 21, 3, calls her εὔλινος, the "well-spinning". Birth-
goddesses are in antiquity often taken as goddesses of destiny: Pind. Nem.
7, 1; Ol. 6, 41; Plato, Symp. 206 D. For Roman material see L. L. Tels-

combination of Tuche or 'Αγαθὴ Τύχη with 'Αγαθὸς Δαίμων often
been attested [1], so that Sosipolis is to be equated with the "Αγαθὸς
Δαίμων as the giver of an abundance of fruit [2], an identification for
which there are more arguments to be found, but we have also come
across such a combination in Etruria: side by side with the year-god
Vertumnus, giver of abundant quantities of fruit [3], there was the
goddess Nortia, goddess of fate [4]. This is not meant to imply that the
goddess Tuche was from of old worshipped as a personal goddess [5],
or that the combination Tuche/Sosipolis was inherited by the
Etruscans as the couple Nortia/Voltumna. What it does imply,
however, is that the similarity between the combinations constitutes
one more indication that Vertumnus, like Sosipolis, was a year-god,
sometimes represented as a youth, then again as an adult. Is it a
coincidence that a *theoxenion*, such as that of the twelve gods at
Magnesia, is found again in Rome at the September rites? This
type of banquet of the gods, later on cast in the purely Greek mould
of the *lectisternium*, probably came to Rome from Etruria [6]. At any
rate it may be said that the resemblance between Voltumna and the
pre-Greek Zeus/Dionysos type has become apparent. Others have
carried out investigations along these lines, and these may now
enable us to make further progress.

    C. Koch [7] has pointed out the significance of the connection
between Iuppiter and Sol in the circus. Iuppiter is the central god
of the *ludi Romani*, but Sol has an altar *in circo*. The fact that both
gods are given the predicate *indiges* is indicative of a relationship,

---

de Jong, Sur quelques divinités romaines de la naissance et de la profétie.
Diss. Leiden, 1959.

  [1] Ganschinietz, R.E. Supp. 3, 1918, 45/46; s.v. *Agathodaimon*; Nilsson,
G.G.R. II², 215.

  [2] J. Harrison, Themis, 282 ff.

  [3] Prop. 5, 2, 11 ff.

  [4] In this connection it is interesting to note that the temple of the Etruscan
goddess Uni at Pyrgi, who on the gold *lamellae* found there is identified with
the Phoenician Astarte, is in literature referred to as temple of Eileithuia
(Pallottino, Die Etrusker, 98). One should further compare the still mysterious Fortuna of Praeneste, nurse of the young Iuppiter. S. Ferri, S.E.
24, 1955/56, 107, discovered in Etruria a mother-goddess in the shape of a
kourotrophos, who is given the names of Aphrodite, Ino, Leukothea, Eileithuia, Fortuna, and who is recognizable in the Veientan Iuno Regina. He
shows that this type is akin to the Asia Minor Ino-mother-goddess.

  [5] For the development of Tuche see Nilsson, G.G.R. II², 200 ff.

  [6] J. Gagé, L'Apollon romain, 1955, 168 ff.; Dumézil, La religion romaine
archaïque, 541.

  [7] Gestirnverehrung, 49 ff.

which, however, has not yet been explained [1]. Koch further showed that on Etruscan mirrors the personal sun-god is depicted in a typically Dionysiac setting, surrounded by ivy and dolphins or placed beside Dionysos [2]. The picture of a sun-ship [3] is equally reminiscent of Dionysos and his return by boat [4]. Indeed the connection between the sun and Dionysos, which appears to be confirmed by a priestly title *maru paχaθuras caθsc* [5], in which *paχa* is the god Bakchos and *caθa* the Etruscan sun-god, is also found in Greece [6].

Whereas in Etruria we find a relationship between Dionysos and the sun-god on the one hand, we see that, on the other hand, Tinia has distinct points of contact with Sol/Usil. The Agram mummy-text [7] speaks of Θ*esan Tins* "dawn of Tinia", and on mirror [8] Tinia is depicted in a situation in which, on another mirror [9], we see Usil. These data, which I owe to Koch, form an indicium that the Etruscan Iuppiter had Dionysiac features. That Tinia might rightly be called a Zeus Bakchos is apparent from pictures in which Tinia is now shown as a bearded man, then again as a beardless, sometimes ivy-wreathed youth [10]. This fact, and the explanation of Paulus ex Festo [11] of Tinia as *vasa vinaria* gave Schwenk [12] the idea that Tina was Zeus/Iuppiter, and Tinia his son Dionysos. This theory is untenable [13], but this does not alter the fact that the Etruscan Tinia has features which in Greece belong to Dionysos [14].

In view of all this it is not to be wondered at that the combination

---

[1] In the work referred to, Koch demonstrated that both Iuppiter and Sol were looked upon as the progenitors (*indiges*) of the Latin people, but, as he admits himself, he did not succeed in ascertaining the relationship between the two gods.

[2] Gerhard-Körte, Etruskische Spiegel, V, 158 a; Gerhard, Etruskische Spiegel, CCXCII.

[3] Gerhard-Körte, Etrusk. Spiegel, V, 159, unique for Italy.

[4] Also interpreted as a sun-ship by H. Usener, Sintfluthsagen, 130 ff.

[5] On a *sarcophagus* from Toscanella, Koch, o.c. 60.

[6] S. Wide, Lakonische Kulte, 1893, 161.

[7] V, 19-20.

[8] Gerhard, Etr. Spiegel, CCCXCVI.

[9] *Ibid.* LXXVI. On the young Tinia as a god of light: Thulin, Der etruskische Disciplin, I, 40 f.

[10] Gerhard, Etrusk. Spiegel, 74, 75, 82, 181, 284, 396; Daremberg-Saglio, III, 708, fig. 4234.

[11] 501 (L).

[12] Mythologie der Römer, 455.

[13] See i.a. Aust, Roscher Lex. II, 627, s.v. *Iuppiter.*

[14] Aust, o.c. 628.

Iuppiter-Sol, which formed the introduction to this discussion is found precisely there where the Etruscan New Year festival received its Roman form: in the Circus Maximus, place of the *ludi Romani*. It is most remarkable that the Dionysiac character of the Etruscan Iuppiter is revealed to us in a picture of the *cista Pasinati* [1]. There we see Pater Latinus, whose identification with Sol indiges on the one hand, and with Iuppiter indiges on the other, was demonstrated by Koch, standing on the weapons of his slain enemies, in the company of Aeneas. He wears the robes of Iuppiter and a laurel wreath. The whole situation stamps the picture as a triumphal scene. However, Latinus shows one unmistakably Dionysiac characteristic: he wears a wreath of ivy leaves round his neck. Unlike Alföldi [2] I do not regard this as an "additional feature of the Lavinian cult", but rather as a reminiscence of the Dionysiac aspect of Iuppiter, in particular of Iuppiter indiges as a triumphator, whose relationship with Sol indiges may be traced back to Etruria.

Finally, we also find lines running from the Etruscan Dionysos, Fufluns, to Vertumnus, in whom we recognized an aspect of Tinia. On a mirror from Orvieto [3] Fufluns appears beside the Italic goddess Vesuna. In the *tabulae Iguvinae* this goddess is described as the companion of Pomonus publicus [4], who has his counterpart in the Roman goddess Pomona. About this Pomona, Ovid, Metamorphoses 14, 623 ff. tells us that she was involved in a love-affair with Vertumnus. The least to be inferred from this is that Fufluns, Pomonus and Vertumnus belonged in one and the same category [5], which was already obvious for Pomonus and Vertumnus as gods of fruit. Voltumna, as *deus Etruriae princeps* has further been equated with Catha by i.a. Thulin [6], Bayet [7], Bruhl [8] and Grenier [9], because this god was the first mentioned on the lead tablet of Magliano. This Catha is beyond doubt a name for the sun-god[10]. His name is found

---

[1] Picture in Alföldi, Early Rome and the Latins, pl. XVII.

[2] o.c. 257.

[3] Gerhard-Körte, Etruskische Spiegel, V, 35.

[4] *Puemunos Puprikos*, see: Radke, Die Götter Altitaliens, s.v. *Pomona*.

[5] Bruhl, Liber Pater, 74 f.

[6] Die Götter des Martianus Capella und der Bronzeleber von Piacenza. R.V.V. III, 1906, 49 ff.

[7] Herclé, Étude critique des principaux monuments relatifs à l'Hercule étrusque, Paris, 1926, 240 ff.

[8] Liber Pater, 74 ff.

[9] Les religions étrusque et romaine, 45.

[10] See literature referred to in the preceding notes.

next to that of Fufluns on the bronze liver of Piacenza. Also along these lines the scholars just referred to arrived at an equation of Fufluns and Vertumnus. And again we can extend this equation to Tinia because he, too, was found to be akin to the sun-god and sometimes to be identified with him.

There are, therefore, indications, however vague and lacunary they may occasionally be, that a pre-Greek deity of the "dying and rising" type, sometimes represented as a child, sometimes as a youth or a grown man, and, as a result called Dionysos one time and Zeus another time, can be found again in Etruria in the figure of Tinia/Voltumna. One of the main arguments in favour of the thesis that the deity and his New Year festival were indeed brought along by the Etruscans from Asia Minor still must be dealt with briefly.

We have interpreted the *concilium ad fanum Voltumnae* as a New Year ceremony in which, among other things, the investiture of the new supreme king was celebrated. His insignia included the *fasces cum securibus*, twelve in number, one for each city of the confederation. In Rome these *fasces* became the symbol of the supreme state authority, the symbol of the *imperium* [1]. However, there is no longer any doubt at present that originally they had a deeper meaning and were rooted in religion. Archaeological findings have shown that in Etruria the axe was not of the single-edged type as later on in Rome, but of the double-edged kind [2]. Such a *bipennis* and the *fasces* going with it happen to have been preserved in Vetulonia. Now this double axe is the symbol of the royal power, not only in Etruria, but also, as we learn from Plutarch [3], in Lydia. In the same passage he moreover mentions the Zeus Labrandeus of Asia Minor, who, standing on a bull, holds the *labrys* in his hand [4]. The Hittite god of lightning, who lived on in Iuppiter Dolichenus, also carried the double axe. We shall here pass over the contested issue of whether the double-edged axe originally symbolized the

---

[1] See i.a. A. M. Colini, Il fascio littorio, 1932. P. de Francisci, S.E. 24, 1955/56, 34; W. B. Kristensen, Verzamelde Bijdragen, 151 ff.; K. H. Vogel, Z.S.S. Rom. Abt. 67, 1950, 62 ff.; Ch. Picard, Les religions préhelléniques, 99.

[2] See Pallottino, Die Etrusker, 118.

[3] Quaest. Graec. 45. About the double-edged axe: Halliday *ad loc.*; H. G. Buchholz, Zur Herkunft der kretischen Doppelaxt. Geschichte und auswärtige Beziehungen eines minoïschen Kultsymbols, 1959.

[4] On the deities with the double axe: Cook, Zeus, II, 559 ff.

lightning [1], or developed from a cult-object into the attribute of a god [2]. It is certain that the double-edged axe was primarily considered the property of the gods [3]. And once again the experts find that the god who is depicted with this attribute, often standing on a bull, is either a Dionysos-like Zeus or a Zeus-like Dionysos [4]. Here, too, it is impossible to make a clear distinction. When this *bipennis*, property of "Zeus Bakchos", carried as symbol of sacred power by Lydian kings, is encountered again as the symbol of the royal authority of the Etruscan kings [5], particularly of the supreme king of the federation of cities, this may be considered an important indication of the Asia Minor origin of the entire underlying ideology [6], and of the ceremony of investiture in which the *bipennis* played a part.

In conclusion I wish to point out the fact that the oldest triumphal ceremony outside Rome, which in every respect corresponds with the Etrusco-Roman ceremony, viz. the triumph of Klearchos of Heraklea, took place in Asia Minor in the fourth century B.C. Just as impossible as it is that Rome at that time took over this ceremony from Asia Minor, or that, inversely, Heraklea derived it from Rome, just as probable it is that the Hellenistic Dionysiac *pompa* and the Etrusco-Roman triumph are both final products of a development which had its origin in a dramatic-victorious New Year festival, which is to be located in Asia Minor. The fact that Klearchos in the *pompa* of Heraklea did not act the part of Dionysos, but that of the son of Zeus, yet had himself preceded by the *insigne* of the supreme god himself, the eagle, forms the link which closes the chain of our argumentation. Here we see in a ceremony held on the occasion of a victory the divine son with the attributes of the divine father, the νέος Διόνυσος of the Hellenistic *pompa* with the insignia of the Iuppiter of the Etrusco-Roman triumph, in short, "Zeus Bakchos" represented by the king in the god's native country.

---

[1] This is the current interpretation; see Nilsson, G.G.R. I², 276 f.; Chr. Blinkenberg, The thunder-weapon in religion and folk-lore, Cambridge, 1911.

[2] Thus Nilsson himself, l.c.

[3] Nilsson, l.c.

[4] Cook, Zeus, II, 663 "It matters little, therefore, whether we assert that among the Tenedians the 'Minoan' axe passed into the hands of a Dionysiac Zeus or into those of a Zeuslike Dionysos." Cf. Kristensen, Symbool en Werkelijkheid, 145.

[5] This relation i.a. in P. Ducati, Le problème étrusque, Paris, 1938, 152; Cook, Zeus, II, 633.

[6] On the divine majesty of Etruscan kings as a legacy from Asia Minor: Latte, G.G.N. NF. Fachgruppe I, 1, 1934-36, 73; Taeger, Charisma, II, 13.

4. *Conclusion*

In 1928 M. Hocart [1] classed the Roman triumph with the coronation-rites, drawing attention to the striking resemblance between some of the components of the triumph and the coronation-ritual of peoples of the Middle and Far East. This theory did not meet with appreciation, nor did it become at all well-known. It is, in fact, not tenable as such. Many components of the triumph are wrongly interpreted, many of its aspects are left unexplained in his theory, and the triumph is the celebration of a victory, not a coronation. In spite of all this Hocart has indicated the direction in which we were to look for an explanation of the triumph, for his book prepared the way for the subsequent studies on the New Year festival as the festival of the renewal of cosmos and kingship. And these studies have in turn been our guides in our inquiry into the origin of the triumph.

What we have found is that the triumph developed after the example of a New Year festival in which the appearance of the reborn or returning god was accompanied with, sometimes identical with the annual investiture of the king. The development from a cyclic annual festival to a political-historical celebration of a victory is clearly traceable in Greece and the Hellenistic eastern Mediterranean area. A similar development took place in Etruria. The Etruscans brought the New Year festival with them from Asia Minor and gave Rome two ceremonies: the *ludi Romani* as the festival of the New Year, the triumph as the festival of the victory. During this period the cry *triumpe* still had its original meaning of a call to epiphany, as is apparent from the *carmen arvale*.

Only along this way is it possible to explain the data supplied by the first three chapters of this study: 1. the Dionysiac call to epiphany *triumpe*, introduced via Etruria; 2. the identification of the Roman victorious general and of the magistrate leading the games with the god Iuppiter; 3. the typological and historic relation between the *ludi Romani* and the triumph.

I should like to add here that no more was done in the two preceding chapters than to make an attempt at presenting a total picture of the origin of the triumph by starting from these three major data. In this respect it is a first attempt. That it will also be the last, is neither to be expected, nor to be hoped. One single ar-

---

[1] Kingship, 86.

chaeological find, one new fragment of a text may change the picture
radically. At this moment, however, and with the knowledge now
at our disposal I see no possibility other than the one here defended to
piece together all the relevant data on the triumph in such a manner
that the facts are mutually in harmony.

Naturally it is quite impossible to deal more thoroughly with all
the problems that have an indirect bearing on the large complex
of ideas on triumph and victory in the present study. Neither is it
possible definitely to smooth away all the inequalities my theory
shares with earlier ones. To give only one example: the cry *triumpe*
has not been attested for the *ludi*, but it has been certified for the
triumph. How can this be explained if it is assumed that *triumpe*
was originally a call to epiphany which functioned in the New Year
festival? The numerous followers of Mommsen's theory should obviously be asked a similar question: what happened to the call if
the *ludi Romani* developed from the triumph? I consider it probable
that the meaning of cry of victory which, as we saw, was discernible
from the outset, became increasingly predominant, with the result
that the original meaning became gradually obsolete, and the cry
no longer fitted in with a ceremony which at first sight had nothing
to do with a victory. A similar, be it less radical, development may
be observed in the verb *ovare*. Our cry "hurrah, hurray" has also
completely lost its original meaning of "hurry" and has turned into
a shout of joy [1].

The beginning of a new year or of a new period, accession to an
office, installation or re-installation, victory over the opponent,
are three aspects of human life which hope and expectation have
often woven into one pattern. Highly remarkable is, for example,
what Q. Curtius (Alex. 3, 3) writes about the manner in which
Darius goes to war: *Magos trecenti et sexaginta quinque iuvenes
sequebantur puniceis amiculis velati, diebus totius anni pares numero:
quippe Persis quoque in totidem dies discriptus est annus. Currum
deinde Iovi sacratum albentes vehebant equi: hos eximiae magnitudinis
equus, quem Solis appellabant sequebatur.* [2] The association of year and

---

[1] The cry "Hoschia-nna", addressed to God or king, at one time meant
"do help", but later on became a benediction. Th. Klausen, Reallex. Ant.
u. Christ. I, 218, s.v. *Akklamation*.

[2] This reminds one of Camillus on his triumphal chariot drawn by white
horses, which are at one time said to belong to Iuppiter, another to Sol.
Hubaux, Rome et Véies, 60 ff., has calculated that his triumph took place
a *magnus annus* after the founding of the city.

victory is difficult to understand here. Italy furnishes clearer examples: The day on which the emperor assumes the government is *annus novus, initium saeculi felicissimi* [1]. Even the day of the arrival of the emperor at the city was by some cities made into *initium anni* [2]. A good example of the association of the notions of victory and new beginning is also provided by the lamps that during the period of the emperors used to be given as presents on New Year's Day. Very often they show pictures of either Fortuna or Victoria [3].

In view of these facts it is not to be expected that the close association which at one time existed between the triumph and the New Year festival of the *ludi Romani* was quite lost in later times. In fact, it will be observed that the ways along which these two ceremonies developed after having started at the same point during the royal period, converged again during the imperial period.

The ceremony of the installation of the consuls during the republic is roughly known to us [4]. After an *auspicatio* the new consul is given his official robes. Preceded by the lictors with the *fasces* and accompanied by his friends, he goes to the Capitol. There he sits down on the *sella curulis*, and sacrifices white oxen by way of redemption of the *votum* of his predecessors. After that he holds the first session of the senate. This session takes place in the temple itself and is devoted to religious matters. During the period of the emperors this ceremony was given a new —or actually a very ancient —aspect [5]: the *processus consularis*, the solemn procession in which the consul showed himself for the first time in office on the first of January, the New Year's Day of the calendrical and official year, was in every respect remodelled after the example of the triumphal *pompa* from at least the time of Domitianus. The new consul wears

---

[1] Seneca, Apocoloc, 1, 1.

[2] Suet. Aug. 59; the meaning of the *adventus* of gods and princes will have to be discussed later on.

[3] Nilsson, A.R.W. 19, 1916-1919, 65. About Victoria on New Year lamps: T. Hölscher, Victoria Romana, Mainz am Rhein, 1967, 109, 111 f.

[4] See for description and testimonia: Mommsen, Staatsrecht, I³, 615 ff.; cf. Wissowa, R.u.K.² 126; Dumézil, La religion romaine archaïque, 285.

[5] All data in Mommsen, Staatsrecht, I³, 414 ff.; further G. Bloch, Daremberg-Saglio I, 1470 ff.; Alföldi, Die Ausgestaltung des monarchischen Zeremoniels am römischen Kaiserhofe, Rhein. Mus. 49, 1934, 93 ff. Hölscher, Victoria Romana, 85, makes a comparison with the triumph of Marius, which he celebrated on the first day of his second year as a consul (Plut. Mar. 12, 2).

the purple, characteristic of the triumphator, he stands on a triumphal chariot, the *fasces cum securibus* are carried along.

Mommsen [1] explains this new custom as an imitation of the triumphal robes the consuls wore at the consular games, and assumes that the *processus consularis* goes back to the example of the *pompa circensis* [2]. There is, however, one feature directly calling the triumph to mind: the *fasces* of the new consuls are adorned with laurel. Martial, 10, 10, addresses the consul Paulus: *laurigeris annum qui fascibus intras* [3]. Some centuries later Lydus [4] again described this procession. He makes special mention of laurel-branches [5], which, according to him, are used for the driving-away of demons. But what is most remarkable is that he calls the procession of the consul *"ovatio"*! The New Year festival of the imperial period, the day of the new accession to office, has thus acquired the features of those ceremonies which themselves, centuries before, had developed from a New Year festival: the *ludi Romani* and the triumph.

---

[1] o.c. 416.

[2] H. Stern, Le calendrier de 354, Paris, 1953, 158 ff., thinks that the *quadriga* and other *triumphalia* cannot be demonstrated for the *processus consularis*, and that the pictures show the consul in the *pompa circensis*. This view, however, does not stand against the testimonia advanced by Mommsen and Alföldi.

[3] See further Mommsen, o.c. 415.

[4] De mens, 3, 3 f.

[5] Here we probably have a blending of two originally different customs: the laurel-wreath and laurel-branches of the triumph, and the laurel-leaves used on varous high-days: at the wedding (Iuven. 12, 91); generally at festivals (Martial. 3, 58, 23; Tertull. de idol. 15) and, therefore, also at the New Year festival. See: Nilsson, A.R.W. 19, 1916/19, 61 f.

CHAPTER EIGHT

IMPERIUM AND AUSPICIUM

Οἶμαι δ' ἂν αὐτὸν εἰπεῖν πρὸς τὴν Τύχην τοῖς κατ-
ορθώμασιν αὐτὴν ἐπιγράφουσαν, ''μή μου διάβαλλε
τὴν ἀρετήν''.

Plutarch

1. Introduction. The bearer of the spolia opima

In this chapter and in the next we shall consider the question of what the triumph was to the Romans. The ceremony was taken as the highest honour that could be bestowed on a mortal, and was as one of the most typical exponents of the Roman politico-religious system incorporated into the symbolism of the ideology of emperor-ship [1]. What was the meaning of this ceremony, whose importance induced some generals to send fraudulent reports on their victories to the senate [2], and others to stay outside the walls of Rome for months until the day of the triumph [3]? There is no doubt that the triumph was considered the highest honour Rome could confer [4]. But just as we saw that in Etruria the ceremony had a different, deeper meaning, in which the god and the king—ἓν διὰ δυοῖν—played their parts in a New Year festival, we have to assume that the triumph was to the Romans of the early republic more than just a mark of honour. Anyone wanting immediate proof of this thesis should consider that the Romans could not possibly *honoris causa* keep up a ceremony which, more than any other, presumed the ideology of kingship. They could do so only on the basis of deeper, notably religious, motives, just as in the case of the *rex sacrorum*, who only in his capacity of priest was allowed, but also obliged, to retain a place in the body politic. The insignia of meritorious soldiers, the

---

[1] A. Alföldi, Insignien, *passim*, especially 28 ff.

[2] Liv. 33, 22, 9; Val. Max. 2, 8, 1; one of the works of Cato is even entitled: *De falsis pugnis.* (Gell. 10, 3, 17).

[3] The well-known example is that of Cicero after his return from Cilicia. C. Pomptinus waited for six years (Cic. ad Quint. fratr. 3, 6, 4; ad Att. 4, 18, 4; Cass. Dio, 39, 65). Lucullus waited for three years. (Vell. Paterc. 2, 34; Eutrop. 6, 10, 2).

[4] Liv. 30, 15, 12: *neque magnificentius quicquam triumpho apud Romanos . . . esse.*

hasta pura, the medal, particularly the various wreaths [1], were originally—there is not the slightest doubt about this—not marks of distinction, but talismans with magic effects, either blessing, cathartic or apotropaeic [2]. That the Roman meaning of the triumph will also have to be looked for in this direction will be apparent from the typically Roman aspect: the juridical conditions the triumphator had to satisfy.

On the other hand there is no doubt that the Etruscan triumph, once it had been introduced into Rome and was kept up by the republic, underwent a fundamental change of meaning. One has to grant Warde Fowler and Deubner that the scene of a man acting the part of a god, a deification, is incompatible with the truly Roman religion as we know it from the republican period [3]. There is historic proof of this, as we saw: when Camillus [4] put greys before his triumphal chariot, he aroused fierce protests, because this was looked upon as *hybris* against the gods. Only Iuppiter or the sun-god were entitled to a chariot drawn by greys. In keeping with this, no allusion is found before the time of Caesar to an identification of the triumphator with Iuppiter. In the seemingly irreconcilable contradiction between this fact and the equally certain one that at some time in history the triumphator *was* the representative of Iuppiter, as is apparent from his insignia, lies the *fons et origo malorum*. The difficulties remain unsolved until one realizes that what is not possible in a Roman ceremony, is not only possible, but even probable in an Etruscan one. The Etruscan triumph was adopted by Rome, but it was given a different meaning. The question

---

[1] Marquardt, Röm. Staatsverwaltung II², 1884, 573 ff.

[2] On the meaning of the wreath: L. Deubner, A.R.W. 30, 1933, 70 ff. On the magic function of the *dona militaria* generally: Anita Büttner, Bonner Jahrb. 157, 1957, 160 ff., who concludes: "Man verwendete sie als Amulette die den Träger vor Übel und bösen Geistern schützen, ihm Kraft verleihen und ihn unter den besonderen Schutz der Götter stellen sollten."

[3] Cf. the translation of θεόφιν μήστωρ ἀτάλαντος by: *vir summus adprimus* by Livius Andronicus, observed by F. Leo, Geschichte der römischen Litteratur I, 74. Burck, Gymnasium, 58, 1951, 168 n. 11: "Wenn diese Vorstellung dort (viz. in Etruria) wirklich heimisch war und mit der Herrschaft der Etrusker — wie viele andere Institutionen auch—in Rom eingezogen sein sollte, so dürfte sie von den Römern bei der Feier ihrer Triumphe in einen anderen funktionalen Zusammenhang gerückt worden sein und eine ähnlich tiefgreifende Umdeutung erfahren haben wie die meisten etruskischen oder griechischen Gottheiten bei ihrer Übernahme durch die Römer." Cf. C. J. Classen, Gymnasium, 70, 1963, 312 ff.

[4] Diod. Sic. 14, 117, 6; Liv. 5, 23, 5; 5, 28, 1; Plut. Camill. 7, 1; Cass. Dio 52, 13, 3; de vir. ill. 23, 4.

now to be asked is: "Which religious motives were powerful enough to ensure the continued observance of a characteristically royal ceremony in a strongly anti-royalist polity?"

To answer this question we can only to a limited extent make use of our findings in the first part of this study. The results of Chapters I, II and III all relate to the Etruscan triumph and have been incorporated into the preceding chapter. We are not sure whether the Porta Triumphalis is Roman or Etruscan. Our interpretation may at best be used to prove the sum, not as a datum. This leaves Chapter V, in which purely Roman concepts were discussed. Our conclusion was that the triumphator had to have *imperium auspiciumque*, in which *imperium* stands for the highest *imperium*. We have opposed a one-sided emphasis on *auspicium*. That the *imperium* was just as important, if not more so, was, among other things, apparent from the fact that the triumphator, on the day of his entry, held the *imperium militare* in the city.

If this appears a meagre basis for an investigation into the meaning of the Roman triumph, it should be borne in mind that, as far as Roman political life is concerned, the importance of the term *imperium auspiciumque* is not surpassed by any other. We can be certain that we have in the relation between triumph and *imperium auspiciumque* encountered a purely Roman aspect. This makes it necessary for us to investigate the meaning of this relation and of each of its components.

There is, however, yet another way to approach our problem, which will prove to lead to the same end. We have tried to solve the question of the original meaning of the Etruscan triumph by comparing it with a few typologically similar ceremonies. Since neither Rome nor Etruria offered anything of the kind, we had to go beyond the boundaries of Italy. We intend to follow a similar method now, but this time we need not leave Rome: there was in Rome a ceremony which is in many ways comparable with the triumph, which bears a primitive-Roman signature and of which Plutarchus [1] says: ἡ μὲν οὖν πομπὴ τῶν αὖθις θριάμβων ἀρχὴν καὶ ζῆλον παρέσχε. The ceremony I refer to is that of carrying the *spolia opima* into the city.

The proper meaning of *spolia opima* [2] is the armour captured by

---

[1] Rom. 16, 6.

[2] On the *spolia opima*: G. A. B. Hertzberg, Philol. 1, 1846, 331 ff.; Marquardt, Röm. Staatsverwaltung II, 560 ff.; F. Lammert, R.E. 2e Reihe,

the Roman commander from the enemy general. Liv. 4, 20, 6: *quod ea rite opima spolia habentur quae dux duci detraxit, nec ducem novimus, nisi cuius auspicio bellum geritur.* Roman tradition mentions three examples: Romulus [1] captured the armour of the king of the Caeninenses, A. Cornelius Cossus [2] in 437 B.C. that of Lars Tolumnius, M. Claudius Marcellus [3] in 222 B.C. that of Viridomarus, prince of the Insubres.

Difficulties of a historic nature are encountered in the tradition concerning Cossus. Livy [4] knows of a tradition which says that Cossus was tribunus militaris. He himself, however, after a lengthy excursus, comes to the conclusion that Cossus was a consul, as the emperor Augustus, who read the inscription on these *spolia* in the temple of Iuppiter Feretrius, testified. In this matter, however, Augustus' honesty is questioned [5]. The fact was that he was looking for an argument by which he could forbid M. Lic. Crassus, who had killed king Deldo of the Bastarnes with his own hands, to consecrate the *spolia opima* to Iuppiter Feretrius. He used the argument that Crassus had not fought *auspiciis suis*, but could do so only if Cossus *had* killed his opponent *auspiciis suis*, i.e. as a *consul* (or as *trib. mil. c.p.*). Elsewhere, too, we come across discrepancies between the testimonia concerning Cossus' function. Festus, 204 (L.), calls him *consul*, Servius ad Aen. 6, 481, *tribunus militaris*, to which Servius auctus adds *consulari potestate*; Valer. Max. 3, 2, 4, and Auctores de vir. ill. 25, refer to him as *magister equitum*. The definition of the *spolia opima* changes accordingly, and this is what is of interest to us. Festus reports: *M. Varro ait opima spolia esse etiam, si manipularis miles detraxerit dummodo duci hostium.* And he quotes a *"Lex Numae"* [6] handed down by Varro, in which a distinction is made between *spolia opima prima, secunda, tertia*, the first of which

---

3, 1929, 1845, s.v. *Spolia opima*; E. Norden, Aeneis VI, p. 340; G. C. Picard, Les trophées romains, *index*, s.v. *spolia opima*.

[1] Liv. 1, 10, 4 ff.; Plut. Rom. 16; Serv. ad Aen. 6, 859; Prop. 5, 10, 1 ff.; C.I.L. X, 809.

[2] Liv. 4, 19, 5; 4, 20, 2 f.; Plut. Rom. 16; Serv. ad Aen. 6, 841; Prop. 5, 10, 17 f.; Festus, s.v. *opima spolia*, 204 (L).

[3] Fasti triumphales ad ann. 532; Plut. Marc. 8; Serv. ad Aen. 6, 856; Liv. epit. 20; Val. Max. 3, 2, 5; Prop. 1, 1, 41; Sil. Ital. 1, 133; 3, 587; 12, 280.

[4] Liv. 4, 19, 5 ff.

[5] On this matter see: H. Dessau, Hermes, 41, 1906, 148; G. C. Picard, o.c. 245. Hanell, Das altrömische eponyme Amt, 200, thinks that Cossus was tribunus militum cons. pot., but nevertheless bore the title of consul.

[6] About the value of this *lex regia* see G. C. Picard, o.c. 131.

are to be consecrated to Iuppiter Feretrius, the second to Mars at
the *ara Martis*, the third to Ianus Quirinus. He unfortunately fails
to add what exactly is meant by this difference in ranks. Plutarch [1],
who is also familiar with this *lex Numae* and its classification of the
spolia, does not supply this information either. The only explanation
from antiquity (Serv. Aen. 6, 859) is decidedly incorrect, since
Servius, who on this subject follows in the footsteps of Vergil,
thinks that the three kinds of *spolia* refer to the three different
spolia captured in the course of history. He believes that Romulus
dedicated the *prima spolia* to Iuppiter Feretrius, Cossus the *secunda*
to Mars, and Marcellus the *tertia* to Quirinus.

The problem of the function of Cossus should be disconnected
from that of the three kinds of *spolia opima*. It is certain that Cossus
consecrated the *spolia* to Iuppiter Feretrius. This was exclusively
the right of the *dux* (Livy), the στρατηγός (Plutarch), who fights
suis auspiciis, and was for this reason αὐτοκράτωρ στρατηγός (Cassius
Dio 51, 24)[2]. Cossus must consequently have been consul or tribunus
militum consulari potestate.

With respect to the second problem Hertzberg[3] has endeavoured
to prove that only the *spolia prima* were the *spolia opima* proper,
quae dux duci detraxit, and that the others were given this name
owing to a loose application of the term. In this matter he opposes
Perizonius [4], who defended Varro's view, according to which the
armour captured by a private soldier from an enemy commander
was also called *spolia opima*. Hertzberg, however, is up against an
important testimonium, viz. the so-called *lex Numae*, which may
indeed not go back to Numa, but which makes a very archaic impression all the same. The classing of the *spolia* is therefore at
present taken seriously, and interpreted as meaning that the *spolia
prima* were captured by the supreme commander, the *secunda* by an
officer, and the *tertia* by a private soldier [5]. This interpretation is in

---

[1] Marc. 8.

[2] It is significant that αὐτοκράτωρ is the Greek translation of *imperator*.

[3] Philol. 1, 1846, 331 ff.

[4] Animadv. hist. VII, 236 ff.

[5] Yet a different conclusion is reached by Norden, ad Aen. VI, p. 340:
"die drei ersten Soldaten, die je einen Feind spoliïerten, brachten die drei
Spolien der Reihe nach dem Iupiter Feretrius, dem Mars und dem Quirinus
dar." However, this view is untenable: for practical reasons—how could it
be decided in the turmoil of battle who captured the first armour?—, and
for historical reasons—a far greater number of dedications to Iuppiter Fere-

agreement with statements of Florus[1], Valerius Max.[2] and Cassius Dio[3], that there have been Romans who did capture the *spolia opima*, but were not allowed to consecrate them to Iuppiter Feretrius, because they were not supreme commanders. The following consideration leads to the same conclusion. The *spolia opima* are the armour of the enemy commander. One cannot imagine a single reason why these *spolia* should be less *"opima"*[4] when captured by a lower-ranking soldier. There is, however, a very good reason why only the *dux* is allowed to consecrate these *spolia* to Iuppiter Feretrius. And here we are coming to the crux of the matter.

Unlike the Greeks and the Germans, the Romans shrank from the enemy armour they had captured. It was, loaded as it was with enemy power, dangerous and not to be brought within the walls of Rome. Because it was burned it was said to be consecrated to Vulcanus[5] (sometimes also to Lua[6]).But Reinach[7] and particularly W. Warde Fowler[8] pointed out that these arms were originally *sacra* without any further definition, as is also found in the XII tables (8, 21). They were taboo, no more to be handled by humans, and released for destruction. Apart from the *spolia opima* there was to this rule one exception: the *spolia provocatoria*[9]. The winner of a single combat which followed a challenge was allowed to take the *spolia* of his defeated opponent home[10]. Does this imply that these *spolia* were not taboo? They were to all outsiders, but evidently not to the person who, by his victory, had proved himself to be stronger —"to possess more *mana*"—than his opponent, and who for this reason no longer had anything to fear from the—to him—harmless *spolia*. This is fully in agreement with the meaning of taboo laws among primitive peoples. The taboo which held good for the or-

---

trius would have come to our knowledge—. This theory is, moreover, contrary to the phrase of Varro: *dummodo duci hostium.*

[1] Flor. 1, 33, 11.

[2] Val. Max. 3, 2, 6.

[3] Cass. Dio, 51, 24.

[4] For the meaning of *opimus* see below p. 311.

[5] Liv. 8, 10, 13; 23, 46, 5; 30, 6, 9; 41, 12, 6.

[6] Liv. 45, 33, 2; 8, 1, 6.

[7] S. Reinach, Cultes, Mythes et Religions, III, Paris, 1908, 223 ff.

[8] W. Warde Fowler, The Death of Turnus, Oxford, 1919, 155.

[9] See: Marquardt, o.c. II, 560 f. and F. Lammert, R.E. 2e Reihe, 3, 1929, 1843 ff. s.v. *Spolia.*

[10] Gell. 2, 11; Plin. n.h. 7, 102. Cf. Liv. 10, 79; 23, 23, 6; 38, 43, 11.

dinary man did not hold good for the chief, etc. The most famous example of the capturing of *spolia provocatoria* is that of Horatius [1]. He brings the *spolia* inside the city and piles them up into the *"pila Horatia"*. I think it may safely be assumed that the expiatory sacrifice which father Horatius makes at the public cost [2], is linked up with this action rather than with the murder of his daughter fabled in connection with the *Tigillum sororium*. For, even though the victorious Horatius himself might not suffer any harm as a result of his owning the *spolia*, the taboo which prohibited the bringing of enemy arms into the city had been violated. This had to be put right by means of a *piaculum*, according to the view of Latte [3]: "Piacularopfer.... dienen der Lösung eines Tabu das wegen einer Befleckung, einer Unterlassung oder eines Verstosses gegen Satze des *ius sacrum* auf jemand liegt". It happened more often that the risk of violating a taboo weighed less heavily than did the advantage or the necessity which gave rise to it. A case in point is the cutting-down of part of a sacred wood [4].

The interpretation of the *piaculum* of Horatius given here is a hypothetical one, but in the case of the *spolia opima* we are on firmer ground. Here, too, a taboo was violated, [5] and now we may certainly speak of a *piaculum*, as the *lex Numae* explicitly states: *cuius auspicio capta, dis piaculum dato*. To the question why the *spolia opima* (*prima*) may be carried into the city, whereas the *secunda* and *tertia* have to be left outside the city, *ad aram Martis* and near the gate (Ianus Quirinus), respectively, a similar answer can be given as in the case of the *spolia provocatoria*. Latte [6] says about this: "Der gemeine Soldat, der über geringere "Macht" ver-

---

[1] Liv. I, 24 ff.

[2] See above p. 150.

[3] R.E. 9, 1916, 1118, s.v. *Immolatio*.

[4] Cato, agr. 139; Acta fratr. arv. Hentzen, 20.

[5] It is possible that the regulation that the person who has seized the *spolia opima* has to give 300, 200, 100 *aeris*, respectively (*C qui ceperit ex aere dato*, Festus, l.c., but the text is corrupt), is to be looked upon as a kind of *multa*, as in C.I.L. I², 366, XI, 4766: *Honce loucom ne quis violatod . . seiquis scies violasit dolo malo, Iovei bovid piaclum datod et a(sses) CCC moltai suntod*. This text also refers to a *piaculum* as well as to a sum of money which has to be presented on top of that. Plut. Marcell. 8, however, takes it as meaning that the person who captured the spolia is *given* the amount. This is also the view of, i.a. Dumézil, La religion romaine archaïque, 171.

[6] R.R.G. 205; cf. *idem*, R.E. 9, 1916, 1119, s.v. *Immolatio*: the commander has to offer a *piaculum* "wohl weil die geweihten Waffen des feindlichen Führers *funesta* sind."

fügt als der führende Offizier, muss die von feindlicher Magie er-
füllte Rüstung am Tor zurücklassen....."

The positive reason for the taking along of the *spolia opima*, instead of burning them together with the rest of the armour captured,
is to be sought in the magic power this commander's armour still
possessed. In addition to hostile and dangerous magic, of which only
the victor had nothing to fear, these *spolia opima* possessed energy
which might be useful to the possessor, i.e. Iuppiter Feretrius and
through him Rome itself [1]. This theoretical explanation is confirmed
by the name: *spolia opima*. The most recent thorough etymological
and semantic discussion of the word *opimus* is to be found in Miss
P. H. N. G. Stehouwer's doctoral thesis "Étude sur Ops et Consus"[2].
She rejects the etymologies of Walde-Hofmann, from **opipimus*,
"Fülle-strotzend", and of Brugmann[3], from **opimnos*, and follows
Hirt[4], who compares *patrimus* and *matrimus*, in which the *-i* may
be long. *Opimus* then means "possessing *ops* = energy". The use of
the words with stem *op*-lies indeed chiefly in the field of dynamism.
This is shown by, e.g. *opimae victimae*, which particularly refers to
lambs, to which the current translation of "fat" is hardly applicable.
They are sacrificial animals with a special "force, intensité" (p. 83),
and this also holds good for the *spolia* which are called *opima*.[5] Because
they are *opima*, "full of power", they are brought inside the walls of
Rome[6], attached as a trophy to an oak-trunk[7] carried by the victor;
because they belonged to the enemy, they must not be touched by

---

[1] Cf. what Jane Harrison says about the sacred shield of the Mycenaeans
in Themis, 86: "The shield on the altar is sacred because it is a shield, a
tool, a defensive weapon, part of man's personality, charged with magical
force, spreading the contagion of its *mana* by its very presence." L. Lévy-
Bruhl, Les fonctions mentales, Paris, 1918, 282, gives as reason for the
bringing of captured weapons back home by primitive man: "de rendre
sa supériorité durable par la possession de trophées."

[2] Diss. Utrecht, 1956, 78 ff.

[3] I.F. 16, 504.

[4] I.F. 31, 5.

[5] No more then we believed on the authority of Wagenvoort that the
colour of the red lead on the face of the triumphator symbolized blood, we
follow Miss Stehouwer when she thinks that the *spolia* owe their power to
the blood of the slain possessor.

[6] The mere term *spolia opima* is an argument against the theory of G.
Dumézil, Horace et les Curiaces, Paris, 1942, that these weapons embody
the *furor Martis* of the returning warriors, and that the dangerous *furor*
should be rendered harmless by the consecration of these *spolia*.

[7] About the connection between *spolia opima* and the τρόπαιον see: G. C.
Picard, o.c. 124 f.; 131 ff.

anyone else, they are taboo. This, in my opinion, is the answer to Plutarch's question [1] why of all votive offerings only the *opima spolia* were never repaired and were doomed to waste away, and not Rose's explanation [2] that, just as the *spolia* corroded, the enemy would also perish. The process of corrosion of the *spolia* can scarcely have made any visible headway in the course of a lifetime, if Augustus could still see the armour of Lars Tolumnius (end 5th century B.C.) complete with inscription. The typically ambivalent attitude with respect to the *spolia opima*—bearers of energy, but at the same time a source of danger—is not unusual in primitive thought. Wagenvoort mentions a few examples of both aspects [3].

Our knowledge concerning the *spolia opima* now enables us to compare a typically Roman rite of victory with an originally Etruscan one. For, that the ceremony of the *spolia opima* is primitive Roman, is apparent from the name and the typically Roman dynamistic sphere in which it belongs [4]. This ceremony may be termed a "triomphe romain antérieur à l'établissement par les Tarquins du culte capitolin" [5], provided the difference is not lost sight of. Next to the *victor* it was particularly the *spolia opima* offered to Iuppiter Feretrius on which the ancient Roman triumphal procession centred. In the later triumph only the victorious commander was left, for the spoils he captured were indeed often spectacular, but did not, or not in the first place, consist of armour. There was, therefore, no need for the triumphator to make an expiatory offering. Instead of the *spolia opima* he gave his laurel-wreath to Iuppiter O.M. Here, too, lies a difference: Iuppiter Feretrius, the god protecting the oath and the law, particularly the law of war and peace, is in the later triumph replaced by the state-god Iuppiter O.M.

The parallels between the two ceremonies are nevertheless striking. Both are fundamentally the entry of a *victor* into the city.

---

[1] Quaest. Rom. 37.

[2] The Roman Questions of Plutarch, 186, after Jevons, Plut. Rom. Qu. LXXXI.

[3] Roman Dynamism, 75 n. 3.

[4] Cf. Latte, R.R.G. 126: "Aber die Institution der *spolia opima*, die noch Einzelkämpfe und unmittelbare Beteiligung der Führer am Kampf voraussetzt, scheint sehr alt: sie passt weder zur Phalanx noch zu der späteren Manipeltaktik."

[5] G. C. Picard, o.c. 133. Cf. W. Warde Fowler, Class. Rev. 30, 1916, 153: "A trace of the older form of triumph, or rather the native germ of the later practice, survives in the account given by Livy 1, 10, of the deposition of spoils by Romulus on the oak of Iuppiter Feretrius."

In either case it is toward Iuppiter that the procession is directed, and in both instances an ox is sacrificed to this god. By far the most important phenomenon is, however, that the triumphal formula *auspicio, imperio, felicitate, ductu*, we encountered earlier on, is, as far as its contents are concerned, found again in the conditions the person carrying the *spolia opima* had to meet. The victory had to be won under his *auspicia* and his *imperium*, he must have been the *dux*; the proof of his *felicitas* he carried on his shoulders.

This is what we have gained from our discussion of the *spolia opima*. This primitive Roman "triumphal march" is, in the first place, characterized by a dynamistic sphere, which is highly significant in connection with our inquiry on the Roman meaning of the triumph; in the second place, our attention is once more directed towards the concepts *imperium auspiciumque*. The meaning of this complex will be discussed in the next section.

2. *Imperium auspiciumque*

When the author of a nearly 500 page specialistic study about the title "Imperator", R. Combès [1], has to abandon the idea of presenting a survey of the numerous theories on the meaning of the concept *imperium*, and of considering his position in respect of them, and when the extensive work of P. Catalano, "Contributi allo studio del diritto augurale" [2], by its mere title indicates that the last word has not yet been spoken about the meaning and development of the concept *auspicium*, the writer of a book about the triumph, who finds an unavoidable complex of problems about *imperium auspicium QUE* in his way, feels his heart sinking. If the conflicting points of view centred on one controversial issue, the present writer might, with or without motivation, take one of the sides. However, the situation is not like that at all. In these extremely complex problems no two scholars are found to agree in every respect, and there are many points of controversy.

If, for the moment, we confine ourselves to the concept *imperium* [3], we find, i.a. the following views opposing each other:

---

[1] R. Combès, Imperator. Recherches sur l'emploi et la signification du titre d'Imperator dans la Rome républicaine, Paris, 1966, 36 ff.

[2] Vol. I, Torino, 1960.

[3] Surveys of the state of affairs are found in: R. Monier, Iura, 4, 1953, 90 ff.; E. S. Staveley, Historia, 5, 1956, 74 ff.; P. Catalano, o.c. 395-412; 532-549; Literature in Ernst Meyer, Röm. Staat und Staatsgedanke[2], 502 n. 6.

The view that *imperium* originally expressed the unrestricted power of the king in matters military as well as civilian, elaborated by Rubino [1], Mommsen [2], Leifer [3], and still, be it with variations, defended by Ernst Meyer [4], P. de Francisci [5] and others, is contested by Heuss [6], who is of the opinion that the oldest meaning of *imperium* was "military supreme command". The principal arguments on which his view is based, are the common parlance, which assigns a chiefly military meaning to *imperare* and *imperator* [7], and the *"lex curiata de imperio"*, which had to grant the magistrate this *imperium*, and which almost certainly refers to the military *imperium* [8]. The oldest magistrates had, according to Heuss, a much more restricted competency than Mommsen tries to make us believe. Only gradually did the *imperium* become what it is by tradition said to be: sovereign power. Very soon, however, c. 300 B.C., it was restrained by the right of *provocatio* [9].

A few modern scholars are inclined with Heuss to see in the oldest *imperium* a military concept[10], without, however, denying the oldest magistrates the collective royal competency; only, the term *imperium* did not cover this sovereign power[11]. Among these scholars a new difference of opinion arises. Voci[12] thinks that the notion *imperium* as the highest commanding authority has been imported from Etruria. Servius Tullius and his successors reigned over Rome in virtue of their supreme command of the new army

---

[1] Rubino, Untersuchungen über römische Verfassung und Geschichte, 1839.

[2] Römisches Staatsrecht I.

[3] Die Einheit des Gewaltgedankens im römischen Staatsrecht, 1914.

[4] Römischer Staat und Staatsgedanke², 117, and see literature on p. 502 n. 6.

[5] P. de Francisci, Studi Albertario I, 1953, 399 f.; *idem*, Arcana imperii, III, 1, 31 f.; on many points, however, he differs from the current views.

[6] Z.S.S. Rom. Abt. 64, 1944, 57 ff.

[7] The basic meaning of *praetor* was also "Heerführer".

[8] For the testimonia concerning this *lex* see below p. 319-326.

[9] P. de Francisci, Studi Albertario, I, 397 ff., has contested this theory in detail. Cf. H. Rudolph, Neue Jahrb. 114, 1939, 145 ff.; M. Kaser, Das altrömische Ius, 349 ff.; Ernst Meyer, Staat², 502 n. 6.

[10] In addition to those referred to in the text, the following scholars join Heuss: Alföldi, Der frührömische Reiteradel und seine Ehrenabzeichen, Baden, 1952, 86; Bernardi, Athenaeum, 30, 1952, 37; Arangio-Ruiz, Storia del diritto romano, Napoli, 1957, 16; Mazzarino, Dalla Monarchia allo Stato repubblicano, Catania, 1945, 206 ff. Catalano, Diritto augurale I, 534.

[11] See: S. S. Staveley, Historia, 5, 1965, 109 f.

[12] P. Voci, Studi Albertario, II, 1953, 23 ff.

of hoplites. The general regal power proper Voci calls *auctoritas* [1]. Coli [2], on the other hand, makes a distinction between *potestas* as the absolute power of the Roman king over his practically rightless subjects, and *imperium* as the supreme command of the leader of the Latin federation over fundamentally independent *socii* [3].

A comparable difference of opinion also exists among those who look upon *imperium* as the original expression of the regal sovereign power. Here the view of Rosenberg [4] and others who consider *imperium* a Roman form of Etruscan despotism, is fiercely contested by de Francisci [5], who does not believe in either the Etruscan origin, or the despotic, absolutist meaning of *imperium* as it is described by tradition [6]. He opens a door to quite a different approach to the problem of *imperium*.

The above-mentioned, mutually conflicting theories have all of them one feature in common: they are based on the assumption that already during the regal period, and certainly during the early republic, *imperium* had a clearly defined, constitutional meaning, even though there is no agreement on the meaning itself. A primitive, magico-religious fundamental meaning or implication is either neglected or explicitly dismissed as being not to the point [7].

---

[1] Thus also Mazzarino, o.c. 42.

[2] U. Coli, Regnum, S.D.H.I. 17, 1951, (reprint 1961) 153 ff.

[3] Concurring i.a. Staveley, Historia, 5, 1956, 111; also Radin, Studi Riccobono II, 1936, 21 ff., had already explained *imperium* as the command over the army of the Latin allies. Thorough criticism of Coli's theses given by de Francisci, Rivista Italiana per le Scienze Giuridiche, ser. III, 6/7, 1952/53, 423 ff. Disagreeing also: Heuss, o.c. 57 n. 1; E. Meyer, Staat, 502 n. 6.

[4] Rosenberg, Der Staat der alten Italiker, 1913, 65. Also some of the scholars mentioned above regard *imperium* as an Etruscan heritage: i.a. Voci, o.c. 67 f.; Mazzarino, o.c. 208 ff.; Coli, o.c. 145 ff.

[5] S.E. 24, 1955/56, 19 ff.

[6] He has convinced me, but, in my opinion, goes too far when he also wishes to deny the Etruscan origin of the *insignia regia* or the *insignia imperii*. Heuss had already quite rightly pointed out (o.c. 61) that the Etruscan origin of the *fasces* does not by any means prove that the idea of *imperium* had also come from Etruria. On this subject: K. H. Vogel, Z.S.S. Rom. Abt. 67, 1950, 62 ff.; E. Meyer, Staat², 472 n. 32.

[7] I quote a few characteristic statements:
Heuss, o.c. 57 n. 1, about the theory of Hägerström (see below): "wie viele Ergebnisse der vergleichenden Religionswissenschaft kann sich auch diese Erklärung nur auf eine Entwicklungsstufe beziehen, von der wir historisch keinerlei Anschauung haben und die, geschichtlich gemessen, weit vor der Begründung des römischen Staates liegen muss."
Voci, o.c. 80 n. 62, on the theory of Wagenvoort: "Elementi magici possono

Now P. de Francisci has in a series of papers [1] drawn attention to this more primitive meaning of *imperium*. In this matter he could refer to Hägerström [2] and Wagenvoort [3] as his predecessors.

Between the views of the representatives of the religious interpretation, however, there is just as much fundamental disagreement as between the juridical-historic interpretations. Hägerström thinks he discovers in the magisterial *ius*, which he equates with *iustum imperium*, a primitive *mana*-notion. He postulates that the *imperium* which the magistrate has been granted by his election in the *comitia centuriata*, is not yet active. It still has to be "aktualisiert", made *iustum*. This, he thinks, is done by the *lex curiata de imperio*, by which the people transfers the *auspicia* to the magistrate. The magistrate's *potestas* (= *iustum imperium*) is "eines von den durch die Wahl empfangenen Auspizien abhängiges überlegenes Können", a "durch die Übertragung der Auspizien konstituierte Kraft" (p. 11). That it is indeed, according to Hägerström, the relationship with the gods or the divine, as effectuated by the holding of the *auspicia*, which gives the *magistratus iure creatus* his personal *mana*, is clearly apparent from his statement about the triumphator quoted before: "....er triumphierte als Sieger durch das Innehaben der höchsten, an Iupiter O.M. geknüpften Auspizien. Oder er triumphierte als derjenige, bei dem die Kraft Iupiters in ihrer allerhöchsten Potenz als Siegeskraft vorhanden war...."(p. 58) [4].

---

esistere come scorie di un passato oramai superato, ma la loro esistenza come fossili, o il ricordo, che si conserva di loro, non possono indurre a considerarli elementi vitali."

Combès, Imperator, 37: "Relever dans cette notion (viz. *imperium*), comme le fait P. de Francisci, tout ce qui peut se rattacher à une mentalité primitive, c'est expliquer ces restes fossilisés, mais non pas éclaircir l'essentiel. Rome a certainement connu un stade "prélogique"; . . . Mais elle l'a dépassé et refoulé en même temps qu'elle mettait au premier plan de ses institutions la cérémonie des auspices, dans laquelle l'intention essentielle est de consulter la volonté des dieux, sans aucun souci de la contraindre par des procédés magiques."

[1] Stud. Etr. 24, 1955/56, 38; Primordia Civitatis, 367 ff.; and elsewhere.

[2] A. Hägerström, Das magistratische Ius in seinem Zusammenhang mit dem römischen Sakralrechte. Uppsala Universitets Årsskrift, 1929. Iuridiska Fakultetens Minnesskrift 8.

[3] Roman Dynamism, Oxford, 1948.

[4] For criticism on the work of Hägerström see: H. Kunkel, Z.S.S. Rom. Abt. 49, 1929, 479 ff.; P. de Francisci, Primordia Civitatis, 363; Studi Albertario, I, 403 n. 4.

In this respect Wagenvoort, whose related theories have become much more widely known than those of Hägerström [1], differs fundamentally from the Swedish scholar. In his book "Roman Dynamism" Wagenvoort investigates the *mana*-notion in usage and language of the Romans. He defines *imperium* as "chief's *mana*" [2]. This charismatic power, which enables the commander to inspire his soldiers—*imperare* is, according to Wagenvoort, "to call to life in"[3]—is not granted by gods, least of all by means of the *auspicia*. To denote an increase in strength the term *augurium*, not that of *auspicium* should be used. The *augur*, however, himself had the power of increasing, he was, as is apparent from his name, the one who increases [4].

De Francisci takes up an intermediate position with respect to the theories just referred to. *Imperium* is originally "una potenza personale carismatica che conduce al successo" [5], in which he largely accepts the argumentation of Wagenvoort, with the exception of his etymology. However, he recognizes more terms denoting the charismatic royal power: *potestas*, which, as far as the regal period is concerned, is often used in the texts in a meaning which is indistinguishable from *imperium*; [6] *vis*, etc. Originally this *imperium* was vested in the person and could not be transferred, either by the *patres*, or by the people in the *comitia curiata*. The old-Roman king was a "ductor, al quale ci si sottomette per la fiducia nella sua forza, nel suo coraggio, nella sua potenza magica personale" [7]. In a later stage his place is taken by the "*rex inauguratus*: un capo che è tale perchè Iupiter, con l'*augurium* favorevole, ha attestato l'esistenza in lui delle qualità necessarie per esercitare funzioni di direzioni e di comando" [8]. The *inauguratio* by the god, therefore, changed *im-*

---

[1] Since he does not mention Hägerström, the Dutch scholar obviously arrived independently at his related views on *mana* in Roman religion.

[2] Here he has unquestionably made a better choice than did Hägerström with *ius*, since, wherever Hägerström discovers a *mana*-component in the concept of *imperium iustum*, it lies concealed in *imperium*, not in *iustum*!

[3] This etymology was proposed by F. Muller in "Augustus". Mededelingen. Kon. Ak. v. Wet. afd. Lett. 63 A no. 11, Amsterdam, 1927, 53 ff.; cf. *idem*, Altitalisches Wörterbuch, 1926, 163: < in-parare, "zur Erzeugung nötigen".

[4] For positive and negative criticism see below p. 375 n. 3.

[5] Primordia Civitatis, 370.

[6] The testimonia for *potestas regia* are found in Coli, Regnum 99 n. 1; for royal *imperium*: de Francisci, S.E. 24, 1955/56, 40 n. 105; Primordia Civitatis, 393 n. 149.

[7] S.E. 24, 1955/56, 38.

[8] *ibid.*

perium from a personal-concrete quality to an impersonal-abstract concept.

When we now survey this small selection of contradictory views, we find that the theory which attempts to furnish a well-founded explanation of the interrelation of *auspicium* and *imperium*, viz. that of Hägerström, starts from the *lex curiata de imperio*, by means of which, according to Hägerström, the *auspicia* are transferred to the new magistrate. In virtue of these *auspicia* the magistrate has an *imperium iustum*. The same *lex curiata de imperio* was, however, as we saw, interpreted in quite a different way by Heuss: [1] it granted the magistrate the *imperium* and *through it* the right to observe the *auspicia*.

This *lex curiata*, therefore, presents exactly the same problems as did the triumph: what was essential (or which of the two had priority): *imperium* or *auspicium*?. From a closer study of the relevant literature it is apparent that nowhere does the question become as acute as in connection with the triumph and the *lex curiata de imperio* [2].

This observation supplies us with the first reason to confine our inquiry to the connection between *auspicium* and *imperium* in the application of this *lex curiata*. But it is not the only reason. We also found that the interpretation of this remarkable *lex* engaged the attention of both the student of the history of law and the expert on religion and sacral law [3]. And such a common field of interest is exactly what we are looking for: in Chapter V we have as strictly as possible confined ourselves to the field of legal history and sacral law, whereas the introductory section of the present chapter led us in the direction of religious history, notably toward the phase of dynamism.

However, there is in addition quite a different reason which induces us to make such an inquiry: Cicero [4] reports that the wish of Pomptinus to triumph is crossed by Cato and others: *"negant enim*

---

[1] o.c. 70 ff.

[2] The views of the scholars about *auspicium*, *imperium* and *lex curiata* will, in so far as they are relevant to our subject, be discussed in the next section.

[3] This applies only to Hägerström. Wagenvoort does not mention the *lex curiata*, de Francisci not only denies any connection between *auspicium* and *lex curiata* (Studi Albertario, I, 407), but holds the view that the *lex curiata* does not have the purpose of granting *imperium* either (Primordia Civitatis, 383).

[4] ad Att. 4, 16, 12.

latum de imperio". Without *lex curiata de imperio*, therefore, no triumph! When, finally, we remember that the *vir privatus cum imperio*, such as Scipio, was not allowed to triumph, this at once gives rise to the question whether this was perhaps connected with the unusual way in which he had been granted the *imperium*. Had in his case the *lex curiata* not been pronounced? The answer given to this question by, for example, Combès [1] is: "Les simples particuliers que Rome place à la tête de ses troupes en leur accordant l'*imperium*, ne peuvent pas être investis par la loi curiate, puisqu'ils ne remplissent aucune magistrature curule: ils n'ont pas légalement le droit d'auspices...".

There are, therefore, plenty of reasons to discuss the *lex curiata* and to try to use it as a basis on which we can tentatively define the relation *imperium auspiciumque*. It will be found that the results of this inquiry will also in other respects benefit the subject which primarily concerns us: the Roman meaning of the triumph.

3. The lex curiata de imperio: the theories

The highest Roman magistrates were not given their authority until after a twofold ceremony. The election proper took place in the *comitia centuriata*. After this, however, the newly elected magistrate had to propose in the *comitia curiata* a *lex* [2], which was in some way connected with his *imperium* and was therefore called: *lex curiata de imperio* [3].

Cicero reports that legend has it that the kings, starting with Numa, already subjected themselves to such a *lex curiata*.

> I. *Qui (viz. Numa) ut huc venit, quamquam populus curiatis eum comitiis regem esse iusserat, tamen ipse de suo imperio curiatam legem tulit* [4].

From this it follows that, provided the kings were elected—but this is a moot point [5]—the *comitia curiata* had two tasks during the

---

[1] Imperator, 394.

[2] The testimonia concerning the *lex curiata* collected and discussed in Mommsen, Röm. Staatsrecht I³, 609 ff. For older literature see Liebenam, R.E. 4, 1901, 1826, s.v. *Curiata lex*.; F. Leifer, Die Einheit des Gewaltgedankens im röm. Staatsrecht, 1909, 149 ff.

[3] This combination is found only in the phrase *legem curiatam de imperio (suo) ferre*.

[4] Cic. de rep. 2, 13; also for the other kings: de rep. 2, 17; 2, 18; 2, 20; 2, 21.

[5] Ernst Meyer, Staat,² 470 n. 29; de Francisci, Relazioni del X⁰ Congresso Internazionale di Scienze storiche II, Firenze, 1955, lit. p. 63-126.

regal period: electing the king, or, as Cicero expresses it in the above quotation, giving the instruction to be king, and ratifying the *lex curiata*. Cicero explains this curious double ceremony as the opportunity given to the people of going back on the choice after the election of the magistrate.

> II. *Maiores de singulis magistratibus bis vos sententiam ferre voluerunt: nam cum centuriata lex censoribus ferebatur, cum curiata ceteris patriciis magistratibus, tum iterum de iisdem iudicabatur, ut esset reprehendendi potestas, si populum beneficii sui poeniteret* [1].

There is no doubt in anyone's mind that this explanation is "blosse Konstruktion" [2]. It merely testifies to the fact that the original meaning of the ceremony was no longer known to Cicero. Cicero and Livy, meanwhile, do not leave room for any doubt about the *lex curiata* being connected with the *imperium*.

> III. *ei* (viz. a dictator) *legem curiatam de imperio ferenti triste omen diem diffidit* [3]. See also quotation I.

It is also certain that, at Cicero's time at any rate, the *lex curiata* was *a conditio sine qua non* for the obtaining of the offical powers.

> IV. *Hic autem tribunus plebis, quia videbat, potestatem neminem iniussu populi aut plebis posse habere, curiatis ea comitiis, quae vos non sinitis, confirmavit; tributa, quae vestra erant, sustulit* [4].

> V. *Vidit et perspexit, sine curiata lege Decemviros habere potestatem non posse* [5].

About the meaning, as well as about the time of origin of the *lex* widely different views are held, as is to be expected. Heuss [6] states: "dass wir über die *lex curiata* selbst eben nichts wissen". The following selection of views about the *lex curiata* may illustrate this disagreement, and at the same time serve as an introduction to our further inquiry.

Rubino [7] assumes that the *lex* was needed because the people in

---

[1] Cic. de leg. agr. 2, 11, 26.
[2] A. Heuss, Z.S.S. Rom. Abt. 64, 1944, 73 n. 40, with literature.
[3] Liv. 9, 38, 15.
[4] Cic. de leg. agr. 2, 11, 27.
[5] *idem*, 2, 11, 28.
[6] o.c. 79 n. 48.
[7] J. Rubino, Untersuchungen über römische Verfassung und Geschichte, 1839, 376.

the *comitia centuriata* had made the promise to grant the new magistrate *imperium* not to the magistrate himself, but to his predecessor.

Mommsen [1] sees in the *lex curiata* an "Act, durch den die Gemeinde sich ausdrücklich verpflichtet dem Imperium oder der Potestas des neu eintretenden Beamten innerhalb der Competenz desselben zu gehorchen", and compares the ceremony with the modern "Huldigung" [2].

Nissen [3] believes that the king/magistrate through the *lex* obtained the *imperium militiae*, whilst the *imperium domi* had already been granted by the election preceding it [4].

Heuss [5] closely approaches this view. He thinks that the *lex curiata* granted the king the *imperium*, and was kept up during the republic as a relic. We saw, however, that according to Heuss there was originally only one *imperium*: the *imperium militiae*, denoting the military command. That this was the case, he infers from the fact that there *was* a *lex curiata*, whose special purpose it was—and this is the essential part of his theory—to confer the military command.

VI. *consuli si legem curiatam non habet, attingere rem militarem non licet* [6].

VII. *comitia curiata quae rem militarem continent* [7].

VIII. *dictator postero die auspiciis repetitis pertulit legem; et profectus cum legionibus....* [8].

Latte [9] compares the ceremony with the *coniuratio* known from later times, which establishes a "Treuverhältnis" between general and army, king and people. He looks for parallels in Italy and elsewhere and finds these, i.a. among the Samnite *milites sacrati* (Liv. 9, 40, 9), who pledged themselves to obedience by a *lex*

---

[1] Röm. Staatsrecht I³, 609.

[2] *ibid.* 611 n. 4.

[3] Ad. Nissen, Beiträge zum römischen Staatsrecht, 78 and 89.

[4] Thus also Karlowa, Römische Rechtsgeschichte I, Leipzig, 1885, 83 f. and 130, contested by Hägerström, o.c. 21.

[5] o.c. 77 ff. Cf. Bernardi, Athenaeum, 30, 1952, 207 and Hanell, Das altrömische eponyme Amt, 1946, 196 ff.

[6] Cic. de leg. agr. 2, 30.

[7] Liv. 5, 52, 16.

[8] Liv. 3, 39, 1.

[9] K. Latte, Zwei Exkurse zum römischen Staatsrecht, I, *Lex curiata* und *coniuratio*. G.G.N. N.F. Fachgr. 1, Band 1, 1934-36, 59 ff.

sacrata (Liv. 4, 26, 3), which shows the same etymological meaning of "Bindung" as the *lex curiata*. "In allen Fällen gelobt die Gemeinde oder der Heerbann dem bereits bestimmten Führer, seine Rechte anzuerkennen" (66). During the regal period this custom only made sense, according to Latte, if the kingship was hereditary, because a later pledge of loyalty would be superfluous if the king had been elected.

Von Lübtow[1] holds yet another view, because in his opinion the kingship had a charismatic character[2]. "Erschien jemand als König charismatisch qualifiziert..... so gingen nach dem Willen der Götter das *imperium* und das *auspicium* von selbst auf ihn über". In such a situation there is no room for the *lex curiata*. It only became necessary during the republic, because the rule was then transferred from a king with automatic *imperium* to a praetor, who up till then had never had *imperium*. The people's assembly "wurde gefragt, ob sie es wolle und für recht halte, dass das *imperium* an Stelle des Königs (oder des *interrex*) bei dem ernannten *praetor maximus* sei"[3].

Ernst Meyer[4] sees in the *lex* a "Gehorsamsverpflichtung des Volkes gegenüber den nicht von ihm selber gewählten König".

Voci[5] speaks of "un solenne impegno di obbedienza da parte dei cittadini". De Francisci[6] remarks: "Mentre i *comitia centuriata* procedono alla *creatio*, i *comitia curiata* sono convocati dal "magistrato creatus" (e quindi già investito di *auspicium imperiumque*) perchè si vincolino all'obbedienza verso di lui".

From the above one thing becomes abundantly clear, viz. how dangerous it is to determine the nature of the Roman kingship on the basis of an explanation of the *lex curiata*, or, the other way round, to explain the *lex curiata* on the basis of a supposed character of the

---

[1] U. von Lübtow, Z.S.S. Rom. Abt. 69, 1952, 154 ff. Thus already Leifer, Die Einheit des Gewaltgedankens, 147 ff.

[2] p. 162 ff. Here he follows i.a. Altheim, R.R.G. I, 1931, 66; C. Koch, Das neue Bild der Antike 2, 1942, 133 ff.; M. Weber, Wirtschaft und Gesellschaft, Tübingen, 1921, 763 ff.

[3] o.c. 158. Werner, Der Beginn der römischen Republik, 252, also believes in the existence of a *praetor maximus* with *imperium* side by side with the king.

[4] Röm. Staat und Staatsgedanke[2], 25.

[5] Studi Albertario, II, 73. Cf. J. Gaudemet, Institution de l'Antiquité, Paris, 1967, 337: "Une promesse solennelle d'obéissance."

[6] Studi Albertario I, 408.

regnum. In Latte's view the kingship had to be hereditary, because the *lex curiata*, as he interprets it, does not fit in with the elected king. Von Lübtow, on the other hand, thinks that the *lex curiata* did not come into being until the beginning of the republic, because in his view the kingship was charismatic. Others see no objection in combining a hereditary kingship with the *lex curiata*. The fact that the ceremony of the *lex curiata* dates back to the regal period, is doubted by nobody except by von Lübtow. His theory that the *lex curiata* as well as the *interregnum* (!) dates from the republic is, however, too improbable to merit any further discussion [1].

The abundance of theories about the meaning of the *lex curiata* discussed so far may be divided into two large groups. The first is the one in which the view is held that the *lex curiata* granted the *imperium* [2], in which connection some refer to the *imperium militiae*, others to the total *imperium*. The second group is convinced that the *lex curiata* implied not a granting, but an acknowledgment of the *imperium*. The terms used here, "Huldigung, Treuverhältnis, Gehorsamsverpflichtung, impegno di obbedienza", are not fundamentally different. What all the above theories have in common, however, is that they directly connect the *lex curiata* with the *imperium*.

With respect to the following statements of scholars who hold the view that not the *imperium*, but the *auspicium* played the principal part in the ceremony of the *lex curiata*, I wish to point out beforehand that the majority of these opinions are not based on a careful investigation of the testimonia concerning the *lex curiata*. In many cases they are extensions of the general views of these scholars about the relationship between gods and men in Roman religion, and about the influence of *auspicium* on the actions of the magistrates. The theories of those few who do advance arguments for their views, will be dealt with in more detail. First a few brief summaries.

After Hägerström, whose views were already briefly described, it was particularly Levi who stressed the significance of the *auspicium* in political life, and consequently also in the ceremony of the *lex*

---

[1] The *interregnum* is also looked upon as a republican institute by E. Friezer, Mnem. 12, 1959, 308 ff. Disagreeing Ernst Meyer, Staat², 471 n. 21.

[2] Thus, e.g. also Werner, o.c. 252; M. Kaser, Römische Rechtsgeschichte², 1967, 43.

curiata. He says [1]: "....l'*auspicium* appare la condizione perchè si possa avere l'*imperium*" and: "Il diritto dei magistrati, cioè la loro *potestas*, deriva quindi dagli *auspicia* e si manifesta nell' *imperium*" [2].

Particularly in French circles great emphasis is always laid on the significance of the *auspicium*, often under the influence of the "Théologie de la victoire", as designed by J. Gagé [3]. The triumph is, according to Gagé, based on the right of the *auspicia*. The victorious general had a right to the triumph "à condition que toutes les règles eussent été observées, qu'il eût détenu les auspices souverains attachés à l'*imperium maius*...." J. Bayet [4] goes even further. With approval he cites Hägerström and concludes: "C'est donc l'investiture *auspicato* par les comices curiates (*lex curiata de imperio*), qui, en donnant au magistrat le droit d'auspices, crée sa mystérieuse puissance ("mana")" [5].

A. Magdelain [6] in so many words says what is implied by many, that the action of the *auspicatio* during the *comitia curiata* results in "une investiture sacrale qui confère l'impérium et l'auspicium", for "c'est de Iupiter que vient tout pouvoir".

Also according to Combès [7] the commander owes his victory, among other things, to the "auspices qu'il avait pris avant chaque action importante" [8]. Now the right to observe the *auspicia maiora* was conferred by the *lex curiata* [9].

We here see again and again how closely the views about the triumphal laws are linked up with the views on the *auspicium* and its function in the *lex curiata*.

Altheim[10] thinks that the *lex curiata* conferred the *ius auspicii*, not upon the *magistratus maiores*, however, but upon the *minores*.

---

[1] Rendic. dell Ist. Lomb. Classe di Lett. II della ser. III, 1938, 107.

[2] *ibid.* 105. He elaborated his views in an appendix "*Auspicium e imperium*" to his book Il tempo di Augusto, Firenze, 1945, 435 ff.

[3] Rev. Hist. 171, 1933, 1 ff.

[4] Tite-Live, III, Budé, 1954, 120 n. 5.

[5] In the text on p. 120, however, he makes the right to observe the *auspicia maiora* dependent from the bearing of the *imperium*!

[6] Rev. Hist. de Droit franc. et étranger, 42, 1964, 202. Elsewhere (Mél. Bayet, Coll. Latomus, 70, 1964, 443) he says about the *auspicium*: "charisme royal ... republicanisé au profit exclusif de la magistrature."

[7] Imperator, 48.

[8] But also to the *votum*. Combès concedes that the *auspicium* did not itself ensure the victory. This was done by the *votum* and the sacrifice, p. 410.

[9] *ibid.* 46; 390.

[10] Röm. Geschichte, II, Frankfurt, 1953, 86.

He refers to a very well-known, certainly corrupt, text of Gellius, 13, 15, 4 [1].

IX. *minoribus creatis magistratibus tributis comitiis magistratus, sed iustus curiata datur lege; maiores centuriatis comitiis fiunt.*

For a refutation of this theory, which is accepted by nobody but Catalano, I refer to a paper by E. S. Staveley: "The Constitution of the Roman Republic (1940-1954)" [2]. This scholar concludes his section about the *lex curiata* as follows: "Its purpose, then, can only have been to afford popular recognition of the right of the newly elected magistrate to take auspices in an official as opposed to a private capacity, and thus formally to confirm his *auspicia* as *auspicia publica* or *auspicia populi Romani*" (89). His argumentation, as well as that of Catalano, who takes up a similar, be it not identical standpoint [3], will be discussed now that we turn our attention to the argumentation and sources Hägerström and his followers use to prove their views.

Hägerström's starting-point is a text which is found quoted again and again by others in this connection, viz. Cicero, de leg. agr. 2, 11, 27.

X. *Nunc, Quirites, prima illa comitia tenetis centuriata et tributa; curiata tantum auspiciorum causa remanserunt,*

which a little further on (2, 12, 31) is varied thus:

XI. *Sint igitur X viri neque veris comitiis, hoc est, populi suffragiis, neque illis ad speciem atque ad usurpationem vetustatis per XXX lictores auspiciorum causa adumbratis constituti.*

Starting from the thesis that the *auspicia* here referred to must be those of the newly elected magistrate, Hägerström wonders what the aim of the ceremony was. The answer was that the ceremony aimed at "Uebertragung der Auspizien an den Gewählten" (19). In this way, therefore, the new magistrate receives the *ius auspicii* from the people, as a result of which his *imperium* becomes *"iustum"*.

---

[1] A plausible reconstruction of this text is given by von Lübtow, o.c. 171: *minoribus creatis magistratibus tributis comitiis magistratus iustus est. maiores centuriatis comitiis fiunt, sed iustus magistratus datur lege curiata, censor lege centuriata.* The attempts made by Catalano, Diritto augurale, I, 470 n. 104, to save the text of Gellius by resorting to Tac. ann. 11, 22, as was also done already by Altheim, failed.

[2] Historia, 5, 1956, 84 ff.

[3] P. Catalano, Contributi allo Studio del Diritto augurale I, Torino, 1960, particularly 469 ff.

Holding the *auspicia* is, as such, the condition for the "Ueberlegenes Können", the "Kraft" of the magistrate [1]. Catalano holds more or less the same view. He stresses that by *auspicia* is not in the first place meant the *ius auspicandi*, but that they are the expression and projection of the magisterial competency "è il potere di comando sui cittadini" [2]. The Italian scholar also holds the view that the *lex curiata* was the means by which the people granted the newly elected magistrate the *auspicia populi*, not, however, as a "trasferimento", but as a "conferimento" [3]. In how far Staveley deviates from this view is shown by the formulation quoted above: according to him the people acknowledged the *ius auspicii* the magistrate already possessed through his *creatio*, and thus converted his *auspicia* into *auspicia publica* or *auspicia populi Romani*.

That the people indeed held *auspicia*, which it transferred to the magistrate, or which formed the basis for the *auspicia magistratum*, is demonstrated by two texts, which are quoted again and again:

XII. Cicero, de divin. 2, 36, 76:
> *Solebat ex me Deiotarus percontari nostri augurii disciplinam, ego ex illo sui ..... Atque ille iis semper utebatur, nos nisi dum a populo auspicia accepta habemus quam multum iis utimur?*

XIII. Livy, 7, 6, 10:
> *irent, crearent consules ex plebe, transferrent auspicia, quo nefas esset.....*

The last four quotations form the real basis for the theory which takes the *auspicium* as the first and most important component of the combination *imperium auspiciumque*, also, and even particularly so, in the ceremony of the *lex curiata*. All other texts brought up in this connection are capable of various explanations [4]. It is unnecessary to discuss all indirect arguments, it is impossible within the framework of the present study to argue with Catalano, whose interpretation of the *lex curiata* can be understood only as part of his general views about *auspicium*. I have to confine myself here to the remark that I cannot follow the Italian scholar either in his interpretation of the concept *auspicium* with the strong accent

---

[1] See quotations above p. 316.
[2] o.c. 457, where he refers to the *auspicia patrum*. Cf. p. 486: "Nell' *auspicium* il potere politico si esprime religiosamente, ma il potere auspicale si definisce solo attraverso i concreti poteri politici."
[3] 488-500; 506.
[4] The most interesting will be discussed below.

on its aspect of power [1], or in his view on the nature of the old-Roman kingship [2], or in his ideas about the *populus* as the holder of *auspicium* and *imperium* [3]. Without agreeing with him in every respect, I follow de Francisci [4] on all these points, and I do not in any way consider the essentials of his argumentation refuted by Catalano's reactions [5].

In a few brief points I shall here criticize the concrete arguments as described above, as well as a few matters resulting from or connected with them.

1. First of all a few remarks in connection with the texts X and XI. Together they form the only testimonium which as the reason for the *lex curiata* mentions: *auspicia*. But how exactly has the relation been formulated and what is meant by *auspicia*? A thorough study of this text within its context shows that Hägerström and his epigones have, to say the least, read more into it than it contains.

Cicero opposes the tribunus plebis P. Rullus, who wants to create a college of X *viri* with practically unrestricted power, and to ratify it by means of the *lex curiata*. Cicero first explains the *lex curiata* as the *reprehendendi potestas* given to the people (test. II). This was the old function of the *comitia curiata*. Test. X now follows immediately, and its formulation should be noted: *Nunc . . . . . curiata tantum auspiciorum causa remanserunt.* Testimonium XI repeats this and proves that only the lictors were left to represent the *curiae*. Cicero knows, therefore, that the *lex curiata* formerly had a wider scope—even though his interpretation of *reprehendendi potestas* is incorrect—, of which by now only the *auspicia* have remained. This wider scope concerned the *potestas magistratus*, as Cicero himself tells us in the context (test. IV, V), which even in his time could not yet be granted *iniussu populi aut plebis*, and which still was in an undefined manner linked up with the *lex curiata*. From the many examples from this pericope which unequivocally demonstrate this connection, I here quote one more: de leg. ag. 2, 11, 29: *Quid postea,*

---

[1] Catalano, o.c. *passim*, especially 440 ff.

[2] o.c. 395 ff.

[3] o.c. 463 ff. Cf. the reviews of F. de Visscher, L'Antiqu. Class. 31, 1962, 480; H. Lévy-Bruhl, R.E.L. 39, 1961, 443; D. Sabbatucci, S.M.S.R. 32, 1961, 155 ff., all of whom make the objection that Catalano views the matter too rationalistically, and that he pays too much attention to the aspects of legal history and too little to the religious aspects of the subject.

[4] See the works mentioned above, particularly Primordia Civitatis.

[5] Catalano, o.c. 168-189; 488-502.

si ea (viz. *lex curiata*) *lata non erit? Attendite ingenium* (viz. *Rulli*).
*Tum ii decemviri, inquit, eodem iure sint, quo qui optima lege. Si hoc
fieri potest, ut in hac civitate, quae longe iure libertatis ceteris civi-
tatibus antecellit, quisquam nullis comitiis imperium aut potesta-
tem assequi possit: quid attinet tertio capite legem curiatam ferre
iubere, quoniam quarto permittas, ut sine lege curiata idem iuris
habeant, quod haberent, si optima lege a populo essent creati?"*

It is abundantly clear that, even though the *comitia curiata* had
in Cicero's time remained merely *auspiciorum causa*, the magistrate
still needed the *lex* to obtain his *imperium* or *potestas*. The expression
lex curiata auspiciorum causa Catalano uses[1], is therefore an un-
permitted brachylogy, which tries to conceal the fact that the *lex
curiata* originally covered rather more than *auspicia*.

As far as the last-mentioned term *auspicia* is concerned, Hägerström and his followers think that it means the transferring or
granting of the *auspicia* to the magistrate. Here, however, the wish
seems to me to be father to the thought: *auspicium/auspicia* is
used in various meanings, the most important of which are "the
right to observe the flight of birds", "the observation of birds" and
"auspices, omen" [2].

No more than the sentences: *in terris dictum templum locus....
auspicii causa quibusdam conceptis verbis finitus* [3]; or *augures
Romani ad auspicia primum pararunt pullos....* [4]; or *refriva faba
ad sacrificium referri solet domum ex segete auspicii causa"* [5], leave
room for any doubt as to the meaning of *auspicium/auspicia*, can,
in my view, the meaning of *auspicia* be questioned in the text of
Cicero: the *comitia curiata* were maintained only to observe the
auspices, for the sake of the observance of the flight of the birds!
For, that an *auspicatio* took place during these *comitia curiata* is
known to us from other texts [6]. And that this practice was enforced
even when the proper meaning of the *lex* had fallen into oblivion is
understandable for Rome. The explanation *auspiciorum causa* as

---

[1] o.c. 506.
[2] See thesaurus s.v. *auspicium*. In the meaning *"auctoritas, potestas"* the
ablativus is so overwhelmingly more frequent than the other cases that
this meaning can only have developed from the expression *auspicio imperioque*.
[3] Varro, l.l. 7, 8.
[4] Varro, re rust. 3, 3, 5.
[5] Fest. 277 (L); Plin. n.h. 18, 119.
[6] Liv. 9, 38, 15; 9, 39, 1.

"for the sake of granting the *auspicia* to the new magistrate" can be read in this text only by the person who sets out to do so, [1] and who, in addition, is prepared to twist the meaning accordingly.

2. It is impossible to see why the *lex curiata*, if it was to grant the *auspicium*, was given the predicate *de imperio*, or, in other words, why a magistrate had to *legem curiatam de imperio ferre* [2] in order to obtain the *auspicia*. Why do we never find the term *legem curiatam de auspicio ferre*, which in that case would be expected, the more so if not merely holders of *imperium*, but all magistrates, as Catalano suggests, were bound to the *lex curiata*? The explanation given by, for example, Staveley, is clearly a last resource: "It remains, of course, an indisputed fact that all those in whose favour a *lex curiata* (...) was carried were holders of *imperium*; and it is possibly this which led the ancients to associate the curiate law with the *imperium*, and even to speak as if it referred specifically to the power of military command" (88)[3].

We conclude that so far no proof has been furnished for the thesis that the *comitia curiata* granted or acknowledged the *auspicium* of the newly elected magistrates, and that, on the other hand, the attested relation between *lex curiata* and *imperium* stands unimpaired.

3. The view that the *populus*, assembled in *comitia curiata* or *centuriata*, could confer the *auspicia* upon the magistrate has to be rejected. Of the two texts by means of which Hägerström wants to

---

[1] It would be just as difficult to imagine that a hypothetical sentence *nunc tantum comitia curiata imperii causa remanserunt* should mean "now the *comitia curiata* have been kept up only for the sake of the granting of *imperium*".

[2] This expression is to be found in two writers, viz. Cicero and Livy (Testim. I and III, cf. Cic. ad Att. 4, 16, 12; ad fam. 1, 9, 25.). For a refutation of the view that the *lex curiata* also applied to the *magistratus minores* (Catalano and Altheim), I refer to the conclusive arguments of Latte, Heuss, von Lübtow and Staveley in the papers on the *lex curiata* mentioned. See also de Francisci, Primordia Civitatis, 581 ff. With respect to the *lex curiata* mentioned by Tacitus, ann. 11, 22, I go further than Staveley, who only points to Tacitus' unreliability in this field (o.c. 86). In my opinion it cannot be inferred from the text at all that a *lex curiata* was ever required for quaestors. That, strictly speaking, the term *lex curiata de imperio* is not correct, as Cancelli, Studi sui censores e sull' arbitratus della lex contractus, Milano, 1957, 16 f., argues, I have already indicated above, p. 319 n. 3.

[3] And this in spite of the fact that it was precisely Staveley who pointed out that the censors, who also had to submit a *lex* (a *lex centuriata*), did not hold *imperium*.

prove this thesis, and which are also found in Catalano, one (test. XIII) is quite useless in this connection. It does not state that the people has conferred its or the *auspicia* upon the consul [1]. Livy has the patricians say that the people, by its wrong decision, has transferred the *auspicia* from the hands of the *magistratus patricii* (*"ubi fas esset"*) to magistrates of plebeian origin (*"quo nefas esset"*). The election of plebeians to the office of magistrate has had the result that, together with all other competencies, they have gained possession of the *auspicia*.

The other text is explicit: Cicero says that *nos* (Roman magistrates) *a populo auspicia accepta habemus*. Now besides being the only instance in ancient literature in which the matter is represented in this way, this statement is contradictory to everything we know about the holding of *auspicium*. The *plebs*, which not only in Cicero's time, but also during the early republic, formed a constituent part of the assembly, [2] both in the *comitia centuriata* and in the *comitia curiata*, did not hold *auspicia* [3], as is, e.g. apparent from the absence of the *ius auspicii* in the purely plebeian offices. The presentation of facts as given by Cicero is, therefore, juridically impossible [4]. But this does not deny the expression's ideological right to exist in the first century B.C. It can even be clearly indicated how the idea of the *auspicia a populo accepta* developed. *Auspicia publica* is the expression for the *auspicia* the magistrate observes in the interest and on behalf of state and people [5]. *Auspicia populi Romani* is a variation of this expression [6]. The fact that this expression may be interpreted as *auspicia a populo accepta* is easy to understand, particularly where the post-Gracchic period is concerned, in which the idea that the *imperium* belonged to the people also gained ground, as M. I. Henderson [7] has demonstrated. But juridically the existence of *auspicia populi* is impossible for the oldest time.

---

[1] How could they, if Livy just a little earlier (6, 41, 4) makes Appius Claudius argue with respect to the same question that the plebeians did not have the *auspicium* either as *privati* or as magistrates?

[2] Catalano also concedes this, 485, n. 142.

[3] Liv. 4, 6, 1; 4, 2, 5; 6, 41, 4 ff.; 10, 8, 9; Ernst Meyer, Staat², 124.

[4] Staveley also admits this, o.c. 89.

[5] See Catalano, o.c. 450 ff.

[6] This is beyond doubt in places such as Cic. dom. 14, 38; nat. deor. 2, 4, 11. See Catalano, 450 ff.

[7] *Potestas regia*, J.R.S. 47, 1957, 82 ff.

Catalano, who defends the thesis that the *populus* has *auspicia* [1]
(and *imperium*), also—as might be expected—gets into serious difficulties on other points. The problem of the presence of plebeians
without *auspicium* in the *comitia* which had to confer *auspicia*, he
solves by saying that the number of plebeians was so small that
they could not affect the outcome, and could therefore not do any
harm [2]. In order to make plausible that the *rex* was given not only
the *auspicia* of the people, but also the *auspicia* of the *patres* by his
succession as well as through the *creatio* by the *interrex* [3], he has to
assume that the *patres* conferred the *auspicia domi*, the *comitia
curiata* the *auspicia militiae* [4]—a distinction by no means made
apparent by the texts he quotes [5]. But in the absence of king or
patrician magistrates *auspicia ad patres redeunt*. There is no text recording the returning of the *auspicia* (*militaria*) "*ad populum*" [6].

---

[1] He refers to two texts: Liv. 30, 14, 8, *Syphax populi Romani auspiciis
victus captusque est*, and Liv. 29, 27, 2 f., *Divi Divaeque, qui maria terrasque
colitis, vos precor quaesoque, uti quae in meo imperio gesta sunt geruntur
postque gerentur, ea mihi populo plebique Romanae sociis nominique Latino,
qui populi Romani quique meam sectam imperium auspiciumque terra marique
amnibusque sequuntur bene verruncent eaque vos omnia bene iuvetis, bonis
auctibus auxitis* ... With Weissenborn-Müller it can be remarked that,
in the first text, *auspicia populi Romani* is a stately definition of *auspicia
magistratuum*, and it may be posed that in the second text the term *imperium
auspiciumque populi Romani* can be used because the *imperium auspiciumque*
of Scipio is also mentioned. But there is a more important consideration.
In a passage of Gellius, 4, 18, 3, *Hannibalem Poenum, imperio vestro ini-
micissimum, magno proelio vici* ... (which Catalano uses for his theory
concerning the existence of an *imperium populi*, and for which I refer the
reader to the paper of M. I. Henderson cited), just as in the other two passages from Livy quoted, it is Scipio Africanus Maior who is talking. Now it
has been repeatedly pointed out that Scipio was the first person in Roman
history in whom an "idéologie du chef divin" (Cerfaux et Tondriau, Le
culte des souverains, 273) became manifest. Also via the title of *imperator*
he tried to establish a special tie with the Roman people (on this subject
see below p. 340 ff.). In view of this, I think that the texts quoted reflect a
very personal allusion to the relationship between Scipio and "his" people,
in the sense that he was the first to look upon his *auspicium imperiumque*
as the real property of the *populus Romanus*. See further on Scipio's ambi-
tions: Combès, Imperator, *index* s.v. and the literature below p. 341 n. 1.

[2] o.c. 485 n. 142.

[3] 487 and elsewhere.

[4] i.a. 431 f.; 482.

[5] 431 n. 147. There are *auspicia urbana* (Varro l.l. 5, 143), but there is
no difference between *auspicia domi* and *auspicia militiae*. Wissowa, R.E.
2, 1896, 2582, s.v. *Auspicium*.

[6] The explanation he gives (485 n. 69a and 70) is improbable to say the
least.

Why do in 443 B.C. the censors have to submit to a *lex centuriata*, with the same object as the *magistratus maiores*, if, as appears certain, they did not hold the *auspicia militiae*?

The fact that the magistrates convened the *comitia curiata* proves that they already held the *auspicium*. Catalano also concedes this [1]. According to his view on *auspicium* this may be explained as follows: "i magistrati, siccome avevano certi poteri prima della *lex curiata*, dovevano già trovare la proiezione di essi sul piano del diritto augurale". (482). In this way everything can be explained, except why a *magistratus creatus*, who in virtue of his *auspicia maxima* convened the *comitia curiata*, was once again given these *auspicia* by these *comitia*.

4. We saw that the majority of the defenders of the *auspicium*-theory implicitly or explicitly state that the new magistrate obtains his *potestas*, *imperium* (*iustum*), *ius* or "Kraft" by holding the *auspicia*, either because he can now establish relations with the gods and influence their activities (Hägerström), or because the *auspicia* themselves constitute a divine blessing or guarantee (Levi, Bayet, Magdelain, Cancelli). Cancelli formulates this as follows [2]: "il massimo potere per il governo della *civitas*, l'*imperium*, deriva ed è implicito negli *auspicia maxima*".

The very many texts in which *auspicia* means "supreme command" [3], do not, of course, prove this. This meaning *auspicia* acquired through combinations such as *imperio auspicioque*. Under war conditions *auspicium* is the visible indication of the presence of *imperium*. In this sense we can accept Catalano's formulation [4]: "Questo significato pregnante di *auspicium* esprime una compenetrazione del potere auspicale con il potere umano (*di cui è proiezione*) . . . . . .".

There is, however, one text from which it might be deduced that *auspicium* imparts *imperium*: Servius ad Aen. 4, 102 [5] *Paribusque regamus auspiciis: aequali potestate: et ab eo quod praecedit id quod sequitur. Dictum est a comitiis, in quibus iisdem auspiciis creati, licet non simul crearentur, parem tamen habeant honorem propter eadem auspicia*. Servius indeed argues here that magistrates who

---

[1]   481 f.

[2]   o.c. 29.

[3]   Catalano, o.c. 438 f.

[4]   o.c. 443. This scholar does not establish a similar causal connection between *auspicium* and *imperium*.

[5]   Quoted by Hägerström, o.c. 10 n. 1.

were elected under the same *auspicia*, have for this reason the same *potestas* or *honor*.

The first thing to be noticed is that, if this explication is accepted as proof, it fells at one blow the main thesis of Hägerström and others, that the *comitia curiata* conferred the *auspicia* and, consequently, the magisterial power. For, the Servius-text refers to the *creatio* in the *comitia centuriata*, the elections proper, which preceded the *comitia curiata*. The *auspicia* of the magistrate who directed *these* elections (i.c. a consul or dictator) determined, or even, according to Servius (in Hägerström's interpretation) conferred the *potestas*. But in that case there is no longer any point in such a conferment by a *lex curiata*, and that, according to Hägerström, was precisely the function of this *lex*.

However, the explanation has obviously been invented by Servius himself, for matters are more complicated than he presents them. In order to see this, we can start from a second text Hägerström quotes in support of his thesis, this time that of an expert: the famous statement of the augur M. Messala in Gellius 13, 15, 4: *Patriciorum auspicia in duas sunt divisa potestates. Maxima sunt consulum, praetorum, censorum. Neque tamen eorum omnium inter se eadem aut eiusdem potestatis, ideo quod conlegae non sunt censores consulum aut praetorum, praetores consulum sunt.* In this text *potestas* is no more than the power, the rank of the *auspicia* themselves, Hägerström admits. But a little further on Gellius writes: *Maiora autem dicuntur auspicia habere, quia eorum auspicia magis rata sunt quam aliorum*, in which the political influence of the *auspicia* is already given more emphasis, in such a way that, as a result of the difference in *auspicia* of the magistrates, *ideo illi minores, hi maiores magistratus appellantur*.

If Hägerström is right, and the *auspicium* does impart the political power, the *imperium iustum*, it follows that magistrates who were elected *iisdem auspiciis* must also share *idem imperium*. If we investigate this as far as consuls and praetors are concerned, it is found that they are elected *iisdem auspiciis*, in *comitia* led by a consul, and that in addition their own *auspicia* have the same power, since *praetores consulesque inter se et vitiant et obtinent* and: *Sed et conlegam esse praetorem consuli docet, quod eodem auspicio creantur.* This is confirmed by many other texts, e.g. Liv. 8, 32, 3: *praetores isdem auspiciis quibus consules creati.* If Hägerström's theory were right, consuls and praetors would also have the same *imperium*.

This, however, is by no means the case. If this still requires proof, we cannot do better than quote another part of Messala's argumentation, which is not found in Hägerström [1]: *Praetor etsi conlega consulis est, neque praetorem neque consulem iure rogare potest.. quia imperium minus praetor, maius habet consul, et a minore imperio maius aut maior a minore conlega rogari non potest.* Servius ad Aen. 4, 103 also says: *potest imperium par non esse, cum auspicium par sit.*

It is understandable that Hägerström does not quote this phrase, for, contrary to his theory, it is found that in elections it is not the (degree of) *auspicium*, but the (degree of) *imperium* which was the primary qualification. And this holds good for many texts, in which the authority of the magistrate is in each instance determined by the degree of his *imperium*, which Hägerström invariably tries to explain as a degree of *auspicium* [2]. Catalano [3] saw this. His view, however, that a connection between *auspicium* and *potestas* does exist, but that the *auspicium* does not determine the *imperium* of the magistrate, lies, partly owing to the vagueness of the concept *potestas* [4], outside the scope of the problem which concerns us.

We saw that there is not a single indication corroborating the thesis that the holding of *auspicium* implies or entails the holding of *imperium*. Whether or not the reverse is the case, as some scholars think [5], need not be decided here [6]. My opinion is that neither the one, nor the other holds good, and that those who decide in favour of one of the two possibilities, are considering too much as a juridical

---

[1] Gell. 13, 15, 4; exactly the same in Cicero ad Att. 9, 9, 3.

[2] For example when he uses Liv. 8, 3, 4, *religio incessit ab eis, quorum imminutum imperium esset, comitia haberi* for his theory. Also when he says about the expression *vis imperii* of the *praetor maximus*, used in Festus 152 (L): "Die grössere oder geringere *vis imperii* muss dann eine grössere oder geringere Auspizienkraft bedeuten." (p. 15). Cf. Val. Max. 2, 8, 2, where *auspicium* is considered to be fully independent of *imperium*.

[3] o.c. 447 f.

[4] On p. 446, he promises to return to these problems in the second volume of his study.

[5] e.g. Nocera, Il fondamento del potere dei magistrati. Ann. Facoltà di Perugia, ser. 7, 2, 1946, 177: "La inscindibilità del binomio *imperium auspiciumque* vale solo nel senzo che colui il quale ha *l'imperium* ha pure l'*auspicium* ma non viceversa." R. G. Austin, Aeneidos liber quartus, Oxford, 1963, ad Aen. IV, 102: "the commander-in-chief alone had authority to take the *auspicia* in virtue of his *imperium*."

[6] In texts referring to the change of supreme command the terms *imperium* or *summa imperii* are used: Liv. 4, 46; 22, 41; 3, 70; Polyb. 3, 110, 4, in this connection speaks of ἀρχή.

system something which in fact, certainly in origin, was a *"mos"*, which was not subject to rigid regulations [1].

5. That the *auspicatio* is not to be looked upon as a blessing or a guarantee of the gods, is easily demonstrated both for the *auspicium* which is observed when a general goes to war, and for the *auspicatio* during the *comitia curiata* initiating the year of office.

The general who, when going to war, failed to observe the *auspicia*, made a serious mistake, which might result in defeat. The behaviour, the defeat and the punishment of P. Claudius Pulcher in 249 B.C. constitutes the well-known example. If, on the other hand, the *auspicatio* was held, and the auspices proved favourable, this did not in any way imply that the victory was ensured or that the favour of the gods supported the Romans. Anyone witnessing a Roman defeat after favourable auspices must have realized this.

And this realization is clearly demonstrated by the fact that a *votum* and/or a sacrifice was made after the *auspicatio* [2]. If the favourable outcome of the *auspicia* themselves ensured blessing or success, a subsequent attempt to win the favour of the gods would be quite superfluous. Latte [3] has repeatedly stressed that the notion *fas* does not mean, positively, that an act should be carried out, but, negatively, that there is no objection to the act taking place *hic et nunc*. If an *auspicium* is unfavourable, this does not mean that the action will not take place at all, but that it will be started on some other day [4]. Coli [5] has concisely and clearly put it this way: "Gli auspici, che il console prendeva prima di partire per la guerra, non avevano altro scopo che di accertare se gli dei gradivano che la partenza avesse luogo in quel giorno".

Another argument showing that there is no question of the *auspicium* having a benedictive or strengthening effect, is the fact that another term existed which both etymologically and as regards usage denoted "increase", viz. *augurium*. The exact meaning of this term—magic or religious—need not be discussed here [6]. There is no

---

[1] Thus also E. S. Staveley, Historia, 12, 1963, 463 n. 21.

[2] Liv. 9, 14, 4; 38, 26, 1; cf. 36, 1, 2; 21, 63, 7 ff.; 22, 1, 6 ff.

[3] R.R.G. 38; Z.S.S. Rom. Abt. 67, 1950, 55. See also C. A. Peeters, Fas en Nefas, Diss. Utrecht, 1945.

[4] *Alia die* is the terminus technicus: Cic. Phil. 2, 33; de leg. 2, 12, 31.

[5] Regnum, 94 n. 46, with reference to Varro in Gell. 3, 2, 10; Macrob. sat. 1, 3, 7; Censor, 23, 3 f.; Plut. Quaest. Rom. 84. Thus also Combès, Imperator, 410; Catalano, o.c. 42 ff.

[6] In the controversy between Wagenvoort, Roman Dynamism, 37 ff. and de Francisci, Primordia Civitatis, 431 ff. and 511 ff. on the one hand, and

denying that there was originally a wide difference between *auspicium* and *augurium*. No text shows this more clearly than Livy, 1, 18, 6ff. It has as its subject the inauguration of Numa, described after the ceremonies which in historic times accompanied the accession to priestly office. The augur takes his place beside the king: *tum lituo in laevam manum translato dextra in caput Numae imposita precatus est: Iuppiter pater, si est fas hunc Numam Pompilium, cuius ego caput teneo, regem Romae esse, uti tu signa nobis certa adclarassis inter eos fines, quos feci*. This passage is significant for two reasons. In the first place, it confirms what was said just now, viz. that the *auspicium* itself may not be looked upon as a strength-giving rite, but merely as a sign that there are no objections against performing such a rite (*fas!*). For, and this is the second point, in addition to the permission of the gods yet another rite was required, carried out by the augur, "the one who increases", who obviously through *contactus*, by laying his hand upon the king's head, had to impart the *augurium* (the increase in strength) [1].

A second function of the *auspicatio* is also apparent from this passage. What is important here is not the determining of the right day, but of the right person. This meaning, which we shall encounter in the *lex curiata*, will have to remain undiscussed here. But just as in the case of the first function, its meaning is of a purely divinatory nature, as we shall see further on [2].

6. Finally, we are not dissuaded by E. S. Staveley from our rejection of the theories just dealt with. In a paper [3] about the questions: "was there or was there not a necessary connection between the *lex curiata* and the *imperium*?", and "was the *lex* in any way concerned with the conferment of the *ius auspicii*?", he answers the former question in the negative, the latter in the af-

---

Catalano, o.c. 27; 96 ff.; 158 ff.; 340 ff.; 347; 354 ff. on the other, I take the side of the first two scholars. Their views are followed in the text.

[1] He acted as an intermediary with the purpose "di trasfondere nel soggetto una certa quantità di energia, di incrementarne la personalità". (de Francisci, Primordia Civitatis, 432). This should be an originally magic rite. Thus also J. Heurgon, Rome et la Méditerranée occidentale jusqu'aux guerres puniques. Nouvelle Clio, Paris, 1962, 202.

[2] Precisely about this *auspicatio* on the occasion of the ceremony of the *lex curiata* C. Gioffredi, Iura, 9, 1958, 28, says: "È quindi da concludere che il magistrato non riceve una investitura dagli dei: i riti dell' auspicazione non acquisiscono in lui nè gli conferiscono alcuna capacità mistica."

[3] E. S. Staveley, The constitution of the Roman republic (1940-1954) 2. The *lex curiata*. Historia, 5, 1956, 84 ff.

firmative. He bases his conclusions on the datum of Cicero, which had been almost completely neglected up till then, that the election of censors was not followed by a *lex curiata*, but by a *lex centuriata* (test. II). This *lex*, Staveley argues, must have had a function which for the consuls was incorporated in the *lex curiata*. This cannot have had anything to do with *imperium*, as censors did not hold *imperium*. The fact that all those requiring the *lex curiata* were holders of *imperium* has given the *lex* its name *"de imperio"*. Since, however, the censors had the *auspicia maxima* in common with the *magistratus maiores*, Staveley thinks that the ceremony either served to make the *auspicia* "greater", or that it was required just because their *auspicia* were *maxima*.

In this way Staveley explains the statement made by Appius Claudius[1], consul of 54 B.C., that the *lex curiata* was not a *conditio sine qua non* for the governorship of a province. For, according to Staveley, he had *imperium* but not *auspicium*. The fact that Pomptinus was refused a triumph because he had not submitted a *lex curiata*[2], was, according to Staveley, also due to Pomptinus' lacking the *auspicium* required for a triumph. Since, as Coli has argued [3], the *rex*, in virtue of his inauguration, need not observe the *auspicia*, it follows that the *lex* was required only for magistrates and was therefore not introduced until the beginning of the republic.

This theory appears attractive, not least because Staveley does not go nearly as far as did his predecessors. Nevertheless I think that it is not acceptable, in the first place because a large part of our above objections apply here as well. Moreover, the instances of Appius Claudius and Pomptinus, dating from after the Sullan reformations, do not have conclusive force. Appius Claudius was, for that matter, far less sure of his ground than is Staveley, because, in spite of his statement [4] *legem curiatam consuli ferre opus esse, necesse non esse*, he nevertheless tried to procure a falsified *lex curiata* by bribing augurs, *qui se affuisse dicerent, cum lex curiata ferretur, quae lata non esset*[5]. In addition, the following difficulty should be considered. If the *lex curiata* had been instituted in 509 B.C. with a view to granting or ratifying the *auspicia maxima* required by the

---

[1] Cic. ad fam. 1, 9, 25; cf. ad Quint. fratr. 3, 2, 3.
[2] Cic. ad Att. 4, 16, 12.
[3] Regnum, 98.
[4] Cic. ad fam. 1, 9, 25.
[5] Cic. ad Att. 4, 18, 2.

22

magistrates, it is difficult to see why in 443 B.C., when, according to Staveley, the meaning of the *lex* was still generally known, the censor has to be granted the same *auspicia maxima* by the *comitia centuriata*, wheras in 367 B.C. the third praetor again received the *auspicia* via a *lex curiata*.

Staveley's great argument, however, is that the censor did not hold *imperium* and that consequently the *lex centuriata* could not be a *lex de imperio* any more than the *lex curiata*, which served as a model. This fact, which since Mommsen was not questioned by anyone, was convincingly refuted by a pupil of de Francisci [1]. According to him, the censor, at any rate the censor of the oldest period, did hold *imperium*, and he can prove this by means of texts which give an impression of authenticity, or demonstrably belong to ancient literature.

In a fragment from the *tabulae censoriae* quoted by Varro [2], the action by which the censor convenes the people is indicated by the term *imperare*, which elsewhere is used only for magistrates *cum imperio*, such as consuls [3] and praetors, but not, for example, for quaestors. Far more significant even is Livy, 26, 10, 9, in which a resolution of the senate is referred to, issued on the day when Hannibal stood *ad portas*: *placuit omnes qui dictatores, consules censoresve fuissent cum imperio esse*. Livy, 34, 44, 5, further says: *(censores). . . . ludis Romanis aedilibus curulibus imperarunt ut loca senatoria secernerent a populo*. The phrase *imperare tributum* [4] is used for censors.

To this we may add the following. Although a censor never commanded an army, he did have the right to convene the *exercitus urbanus* (*imperare*!) on the campus Martius, i.e. *extra pomerium*.

Varro l.l. 6, 93: *censor, consul, dictator, interrex potest* (viz. *exercitum urbanum convocare*) *quod censor exercitum centuriato constituit quinquennalem, cum lustrare et in urbem ad vexillum ducere debet*. Also in other respects the censor has a great deal in common with the magistrates *cum imperio* [5]. Elected in the same *comitia* (*centuriata*) led by a consul, he, too, used the *sella curulis* and the *toga praetexta*. Of special importance to us is the fact that, although

---

[1] F. Cancelli, Studi sui censores e sull' arbitratus della lex contractus, Milano, 1957, I, 1 ff.

[2] Varro, l.l. 6, 86.

[3] *ibid.* 6, 88.

[4] Varro, l. l. 5, 181. Cf. Gell. 10, 23, 4.

[5] See Mommsen, Röm. Staatsrecht, II³, 354 f.

he could not triumph, he was the only person, apart from the *magistratus cum imperio*, who was buried in triumphal robes [1].

All this does not mean, however, that the censor, together with his *imperium* (= competence to *imperare*) should also in other respects have the same powers as the *praetores* (= consules). This difference as to function and authority, which may have been the cause of the difference between the *lex curiata* and the *lex centuriata*, proves that *imperium* during the first century of the republic did not as yet have a clearly defined meaning, a fact that Cancelli [2] and de Francisci [3] have strongly emphasized.

This brings us to the conclusion of my criticism on the theories which primarily connect the *lex curiata* with the *auspicium*. Our inquiry, which covered only the main arguments and the most important testimonia, led to the following conclusions:

I. The phrase *legem de imperio ferre* proves that the people, in some way or other, had to pronounce on the *imperium* of king or magistrate.

II. The ceremony did not confer or ratify the *auspicia*. An *auspicatio* did take place.

III. The *auspicium* could not be conferred by the people; the *auspicium* was neither condition, nor cause of the holding of *imperium*; the *auspicatio* was neither "blessing" nor an "increase of strength".

These conclusions form the starting-point for our own inquiry concerning the meaning and function of the *lex curiata*. We add two data, which are generally accepted as correct:

IV. The ceremony goes back to the royal period.

V. The *lex curiata* specially, although not exclusively, concerned the *res militaris* [4].

---

[1] The difference and the similarity are even more striking if it is borne in mind that the censor was not allowed to triumph, whereas the *magistratus* was only carried to the grave in the triumphal robes if he had once received the honour of a triumph.

[2] o.c. 25 ff.

[3] Primordia Civitatis, 397. Cf. Gioffredi, Iura, 9, 1958, 29. The place allotted to the *censor* on the lists of magistrates after *dictator*, *consul* and *praetor*, but before *aedilis* and *quaestor* is symptomatic of the hesitation of tradition as to the value of the rank of the *censor*. See Mommsen, Röm. Staatsrecht, I³, 562.

[4] Besides by the testimonia mentioned before, this is also proved by the fact that the interrex did not require a *lex curiata* (Cic. de leg. agr. 2, 10, 26)

4. *An attempt at a new interpretation of the lex curiata*

In several instances scholars have tried to explain the *lex curiata* by comparing it with ceremonies found among other peoples. Mommsen refers to the "Huldigung" and Latte to the *coniuratio* he found among Italic peoples, but also outside Italy, in Macedonia and in Germania. These comparisons may prove helpful, but the first question to be asked is whether the ceremony can be explained within the framework of the culture in which it had its place. In my opinion this is in this case possible, because a few purely Roman customs have been handed down which on closer inspection are found to resemble the ceremony of the *lex curiata* so closely, that they may be assumed to be related.

When the question is asked whether, apart from the *lex curiata*, there is evidence of a custom in Rome in which the people pronounced judgment upon the *imperium* of its superior, the first that comes to mind is the well-known, widely-discussed custom of what is nowadays called: the acclamation as *imperator*, but for which ancient authors do not use the term *acclamare* [1], but *appellare imperatorem* or *(con)salutare imperatorem* [2].

In the past it was assumed that every holder of *imperium* was, *qualitate qua*, *imperator* [3]. Later studies of Momigliano, Levi, Wagenvoort, Kienast and Combès [4], however, pointed out that in this case a curious phenomenon was left unexplained: the *appellatio imperatoria* did not take place immediately after the election to the magistracy or at the installation, but was deferred until after a victory in war. The term *imperator* had indeed from of old been in general use to denote the commander, but it was not an official title, as was demonstrated by thorough investigations of Combès [5]. The *appellatio imperatoria* gave the title *imperator* its special significance, and it is this title, conferred after a victory, which developed into the title of the emperor. After being attested for the first time for P. Cornelius Scipio on the occasion of his victory in Spain in 210 B.C., the *appellatio* is found to have become more and more frequent in the second century B.C. Caesar bore the title per-

---

and, on the other hand, never exercised *imperium militare*. (De Francisci, Primordia Civitatis, 393; Catalano, o.c. 459 n. 76; 476.)

[1] A few times *conclamare*: Tac. ann. 3, 74; cf. Caesar, b.c. 3, 71.
[2] Testimonia in Combès, o.c. 90 n. 50.
[3] Mommsen, Röm. Staatsrecht, I³, 123 ff.
[4] These studies will be discussed below.
[5] Imperator, 9-27.

manently, Octavianus bore it as a first name. The last commander who was awarded an *appellatio imperatoria,* was Iunius Blaesus in 22 A.D. From then on the title was reserved for emperors [1].

A survey of the various interpretations of this custom will be given after the new interpretation I myself want to suggest. A confrontation between the old and the new theories will show in how far they differ and agree.

The *appellatio imperatoria* is by no means the only example of an acclamation in Rome. In his book "Regnum" [2], Coli has collected a number of places in which similar spontaneous acclamations in connection with the *rex* are referred to; not, however, after a victory, but at his accession.

Livy, I, 7, 1: *nuntiato augurio, utrumque regem sua multitudo consalutaverat.*

Livy, I, 6, 2: *cum avum regem salutassent...*

Livy, I, 47, 3: *te regem appello.*

Livy, I, 48, 5: *regem prima (Tullia) appellavit.*

Schol. Bob. in Vat. 23: *ita ipsos reges appellatos...*

That it is certain that we here have a *terminus technicus* is proved by the fact that, in foreign affairs, *regem appellare* denotes the recognition of a foreign prince [3]. It should be noted that for this ceremony the same terms are used as in the acclamation of the commander: *appellare* and *salutare.* What was the meaning of this custom? Coli [4] says: "Quando il sovrano, *declaratus rex,* discendeva dall'altura, la moltitudine lo chiamava col nome di *rex* e questa acclamazione, che rispondeva al "regem appellare" o "salutare"... costituiva certamente un elemento importante del rito: ne era il suggello finale".

In addition there is a third kind of *appellatio* or *salutatio,* which, handed down by Cincius in Festus 276 (L), referred not to the king, but to a praetor: *Praetor ad portam nunc salutatur is qui in*

---

[1] This development has been widely discussed. I.a. D. Mac. Fayden, The History of the title Imperator under the Roman Empire. Diss. Chicago, 1920; G. de Sanctis, Studi Riccobono II, 1932, 57; A. von Premerstein, Vom Werden und Wesen des Prinzipats, 1937, 245. Especially on Scipio as the first monarch and the title *imperator*: W. Schur, Scipio Africanus und die Begründung der römischen Weltherrschaft, Leipzig, 1927, 1 ff.; 24; 47 f.; J. Vogt, Hermes, 58, 1933, 85 ff.

[2] p. 93.

[3] Liv. 30, 17, 10; 31, 11, 11; 49, 9, 3; Tac. ann. 4, 26; Caes. b. G. 1, 43; Cic. de har. resp. 13, 39; and elsewhere. Cf. Combès, Imperator, 91 n. 52.

[4] Regnum, 93.

provinciam pro praetore aut pro consule exit. By way of elucidation
the passage starts by explaining that the Latin peoples, after the
destruction of Alba, had adopted the practice of *imperium communi
consilio administrare*, and goes on to say: *itaque quo anno Romanos
imperatorem* [1] *ad exercitum mittere oporteret iussu nominis Latini,
conplures nostros in Capitolio a sole oriente auspiciis operam dare
solitos. Ubi aves addixissent, militem illum, qui a communi Latio
missus esset, illum quem aves addixerant, praetorem salutare solitum,
qui eam provinciam obtineret praetoris nomine.* Coli also quotes this
text, but in another place [2], in order to corroborate his theory that
the Roman king merely held *imperium* in so far as he was in command of foreign troops. As the leader of the troops of the Latin
federation he held *imperium*, he was *imperator* and was technically
called *praetor*. I find it impossible to follow the Italian scholar on
this point [3]. At present, however, it is only important for us to
encounter a third *appellatio*, which closely resembles the *appellatio
regia*, whilst these two rites together show a resemblance to, as well
as a difference from, the *appellatio imperatoria*.

What the three ceremonies have in common is that the people,
the soldiers, shout acclamations, the *terminus technicus* of which is
appellare or *salutare*. The essential part is that the people bestow a
title upon the person in power: *rex, praetor, imperator*. The difference
between the *appellationes regia* and *praetoria* on the one hand, and
the *appellatio imperatoria* on the other, is that the former two follow
an *auspicatio*, which is to decide *which* candidate is the right one,
or *that* the candidate nominated is the right one, whereas the
appellatio imperatoria follows a victory. The *appellare regem* and
praetorem might, therefore, in fact be looked upon as a "nomination"
by the people, from which it need not follow that the people also had
the right of electing or appointing the king or the *praetor Latinus*.
"Nominating" is here to be taken in its original and literal meaning.
The *auspicatio* has decided who is the "best"; the people now acknowledges the king or the praetor as such by calling him by this

---

[1] Thus Coli, Regnum, 163; *imperatores* (mss.)

[2] *ibid.*

[3] Examples of *imperium* denoting "authority of Rome over the allies"
are few in number and do not prove anything. In later time *imperium*
could denote any official, or even private authority. One of the oldest
testimonia, Ennius: *uter esset induperator*, does not relate to the Latins
at all. See objections against Coli: Combès, Imperator, 35 f.; F. de Martino,
Iura, 4, 1953, 191; P. de Francisci, Primordia Civitatis, 403 ff.

name. The action is an *omen accipere*. The remarkable thing is that Livy expresses this very precisely (1, 6, 2): *iuvenes per mediam contionem agmine ingressi cum avum regem salutassent, secuta ex omni multitudine consentiens vox r a t u m   n o m e n   imperiumque regi efficit*. The last part of this sentence contains exactly what we expect in a nomination in the sense just described. In passing it may be pointed out here that this text diametrically opposes the theory of Hägerström, who, after rightly having argued [1] that *ratus* meant the same as *iustus*, thought that the *iustum imperium* was imparted by the *auspicium*. Livy, however, states—and this is the essence of the *appellatio regia*—that the voice of the people makes the name (*rex*, and in the same way, *praetor*) valid, and, as a result, also makes his *imperium* valid. The ambassador of the Latins acts in exactly the same manner when one of the candidates has been indicated as praetor by the *auspicia*.

If we now compare the three *appellationes*, we find that the characteristic they have in common is the acknowledging of a person in a certain capacity by the pronouncing of his "title". In two of the three instances an *auspicatio* had to prove that the person in question was worthy of this title. What did this proof consist of in the third instance, that of the *appellatio imperatoria*? The answer can be given at once: the victory and the *felicitas* which has brought about this victory. It should be fully realized that *auspicium* and *felicitas* were not the cause of the *imperium* or *potestas* held—and of the title attached to it—,but, on the contrary, just proof of their presence. The *auspicatio* and the victory thus gave occasion to the recognition and ratification through an acclamation by the people or the army of a worthiness already proved.

At this stage I list three data:

1. There were three comparable "nomination rites": the *appellationes regia, praetoria* and *imperatoria*. The first two took place immediately after the *creatio*, after the observation of the auspices, the third after a victory.

2. The first to be awarded an *appellatio imperatoria* was P. Cornelius Scipio [2].

3. P. Cornelius Scipio was also the first *privatus cum imperio*.

---

[1] o.c. 10 n. 1.

[2] Livy does not say so explicitly, but we do not know anything about an earlier *imperator sensu stricto*.

I think there must be a causal relation between these facts. It is surely asking too much to make us believe that two events such as those mentioned under 2 and 3, which both made history, were by a mere coincidence attested for the first time for one and the same person, P. Cornelius Scipio [1]. The nature of this interrelation becomes clear as follows: why was P. Scipio the first to be accorded an *appellatio imperatoria* after a victory? Because, we assume, he was the first to have won this victory as a *vir privatus cum imperio*. What was the essential difference between a normal magistrate or promagistrate and the *vir privatus cum imperio*? That the former was installed in Rome after an *auspicatio* and in a special ceremony, whereas the latter had to do without such an official installation [2]. What was this ceremony in the case of the normal magistrate *cum imperio*? The *lex curiata*, ratified by the *comitia curiata, quae rem militarem continent*! Finally: what gave the soldiers at the end of the third century B.C. the idea of proclaiming their general *imperator*? I do not agree with Wagenvoort [3], that this custom in this form and function went back to primitive times, because I consider its connection with the first *vir privatus cum imperio* too striking. On the other hand it cannot be assumed that this *ritus* came into being spontaneously, from nothingness, because the term *imperator*, be it not as the honorary title of later times, already existed.

Only one answer to the last question supplies, in my opinion, a satisfactory explanation which can be reconciled with the conclusions already drawn: in honour of their general, the *vir privatus cum imperio*, the soldiers performed a ceremony which had not been necessary for any previous commander, since up to that time such a ceremony had taken place prior to the war, along with the installation. This can mean only that the *appellatio imperatoria* was intended as a non-official conferment of a *lex curiata de imperio* upon a commander who had not proposed the *lex* officially. From this it follows that the ceremony of the *lex curiata* itself

---

[1] As is assumed only by Wagenvoort, Roman Dynamism, 61. For Levi's counter-arguments see below p. 348 n. 2.

[2] This is not so much apparent from the fact that Livy, 28, 38, does not record such an official installation after the election in the *comitia centuriata*, as from the usage that the *lex curiata* was everywhere expressly reserved for the magistracy. Combès, Imperator, 394: "Les simples particuliers que Rome place à la tête de ses troupes en leur accordant l'*imperium*, ne peuvent pas être investis par la loi curiate, puisqu'ils ne remplissent aucune magistrature curule."

[3] Roman Dynamism, 72.

must have had the character of an *appellatio imperatoria* [1], by which it is put on a level with the *appellatio regia* and *appellatio praetoria* already discussed. Cancelli [2] and de Francisci [3] are right, therefore, when they define the ceremony of the *lex curiata* as a *suffragium*, i.e. a *fragor plaudentium et acclamantium* [4].

There are several data which support our theory, or, when viewed in that light, are given a new explanation [5].

1. It would be most peculiar if a "nomination-ceremony" (*appellatio*) which during the period of the kings and the early republic was indispensable to *rex* and *praetor* as regular leaders of people and army respectively, had only survived in later times for the functions of *propraetor* and *proconsul* later to be created, as Festus says, but had disappeared without trace for the regular magistrate. If the people, as indicated by the term *lex curiata*, had to pronounce on the *imperium* of the magistrate, it follows that this ceremony should be looked upon as a legalized form of *appellatio*.

2. If in the *lex curiata de imperio* there was any "titling", this title can hardly have been any other than *imperator*, a term which was, in fact, also used prior to the *appellatio imperatoria sensu stricto*.

3. The praetor was saluted at the gate when he went to war, as were the later propraetor and proconsul. *Imperator* also had primarily a military meaning. In striking agreement with this is the fact that the *lex curiata de imperio* especially concerned the *res militaris* and, as we learn from Livy, was submitted before the departure for war. Was the *imperium* with which the *lex* was connected, the *imperium militare*?

4. *Rex, praetor* and *imperator* are all three transparent *nomina agentis*, all of which define a function—*regere, praeire, imperare*—

---

[1] D. Kienast, Z.S.S. Rom. Abt. 78, 1961, 404, who proceeds along quite different lines, has expressed this in nearly the same way: "Denn dadurch dass der römische Magistrat oder Promagistrat vom Volke in den Curiat-comitien mit dem *imperium* ausgestattet wurde, machte man ihn eben zum *imperator* . . . Der Brauch aber, erst nach einer solchen imperatorischen Akklamation (viz. the acclamation after the victory) den Imperatortitel zu führen, widerspricht geradezu dem Sinn der *lex curiata* und erweist sich schon von daher als verhältnismässig jung."

[2] o.c. 14.

[3] Primordia Civitatis, 581 f.

[4] In favour of the *suffragium*-character of the *lex curiata* tells Liv. 6, 41, 6.

[5] The etymology of the word *lex*, which, thanks to its uncertainty, has by various scholars been used for their respective theories, is left out of account here.

which only gradually assumed a political meaning, *rex* being the first in this respect, *imperator* the last.

5. Very remarkable and significant is that the *appellatio imperatoria* once again becomes during the imperial period what, in my view, it originally was. Originally acclamation and recognition of the *imperator* who was by the *auspicatio* indicated as being "the right one", it becomes via the *acclamatio* after a victory, during the principate the official means by which the soldiers can voice their views as regards the candidate elected for the emperorship. In this way *salutare imperatorem* again becomes what at one time was *salutare regem*. Finally, from the middle of the third century A.D. it assumes, as a yearly acclamation, the character of a real benediction, *"salutatio"* [1].

6. With respect to the *appellatio regia* Livy uses a terminology which closely resembles the description of the *lex curiata* known from other sources.

Liv. 1, 6, 2, *secuta ex omni multitudine consentiens vox ratum nomen imperiumque regi efficit.* The people, through its *appellatio*, ratified the name and the *imperium* of the king. Hägerström rightly equated *ratum* with *iustum*. Now Gellius, 13, 15, 4, says: *minoribus creatis magistratibus tributis comitiis magistratus, sed iustus curiata datur lege* and Liv. 22, 1, 5, about the consul Flaminius, who fails to perform his sacral consular duties, including the *lex curiata*: *quod enim illi iustum imperium, quod auspicium esse?*

7. Just as the *appellationes regia* and *praetoria* followed an *auspicatio*, the *lex curiata* was preceded by an *auspicatio*, which now acquires a distinct meaning. It is worth noticing that both Livy and Ennius, in connection with the indicating of Romulus or Remus by an *auspicium*, use the terms *imperium, imperator*.

Liv. 1, 6, 4, *ut dii.... auguriis legerent, qui nomen novae urbi daret, qui conditam imperio regeret.*

Ennius, Vahlen XLVII (77).

> *Curantes magna cum cura, tum cupientes*
> *Regni, dant operam simul auspicio augurioque.*

---

[1] About this development: L. Lesuisse, La nomination de l'empereur et le titre d'imperator. L'Antiquité Classique, 30, 1961, 415. "L'avènement de l'empereur romain est identique à une salutation impériale." (Piganiol, Jeux, 123, quoted by Combès, Imperator, 88). I think we can discern a trace of a primitive *periodical* benediction in Macrobius, Sat. 1, 15, 13: *sicut apud Tuscos Nonae plures habebantur, quod hi nono quoque die regem suum salutabant et de propriis negotiis consulebant.*

Remus auspicio se devovet atque secundam
Solus avem servat. At Romulus pulcher in alto
Quaerit Aventino, servat genus altivolantum,
Certabant urbem Romam Remoramne vocarent.
Omnibus cura viris uter esset induperator.

8. *Cum imperio esse* is preferably used to denote the extraordinary or delegated supreme command [1], as was held by Scipio. Is it possible that Paulus ex Festo 43 (L), *Cum imperio est, dicebatur apud antiquos, cui nominatim a populo dabatur imperium* had just such a case as that of Scipio in mind? In such instances the people indeed confers *nominatim*, but in a way other than by means of the *lex curiata*, the *imperium* upon the *vir privatus*. Livy, 28, 43, 11, has Scipio say: *Cum mihi . . . . . detulisset imperium populus Romanus* [2]. In this way it could be understood why Scipio was the first to establish a special relation between his *imperium* and the *imperium populi Romani*, as we saw above.

If we now confront our interpretation of the *appellatio imperatoria* with the most important views held so far, it is found that they corroborate or complement each other on various points. Momigliano [3] pointed out that the title of *imperator* was before 90 B.C. never assumed by consuls, but only by extraordinary holders of *imperium* or promagistrates [4]. His statement that only the promagistrate had in his province the disposal of the spoils of the defeated enemies [5] has proved incorrect [6]. After a victory the consul is just as much entitled to the spoils and the title of *imperator* as is the promagistrate. Vinay and Levi think that the cause is to be looked for rather in the mutually exclusive functions of consul and *imperator*. The title of *imperator* is a personal nomination, which is incompatible with the public, impersonal character of the regular magistracy. I also be-

---

[1] Mommsen, Röm. Staatsrecht, I³, 117 n. 1. *Magistratus* is in many instances even used in contrast to *imperium* in this function.

[2] Varro, l.l. 5, 16, 87, *imperator ab imperio populi, qui ei qui id attemptassent, oppressit hostes*, has nothing to do with this, because *imperium* here denotes the province of authority.

[3] Bullet. Com. 58, 1930, 42 f.

[4] L. Mummius and L. Aemilius Paullus assumed the title of *imperator* after their consular year, although their victories were won during their consular years.

[5] "Imperator cioè reggente dei popoli sottomessi" (p. 51).

[6] G. Vinay, Riv. di Filol. e di Istr. Class. Nuova ser. 10, 1932, 219 f.; M. A. Levi, Riv. di Filol. e di Istr. Class. Nuova ser. 10, 1932, 207 ff., particularly 213 ff.

lieve that the solution will indeed have to be sought along these lines, but I propose the following modification. The regular magistrate was acclaimed *imperator* before leaving for war.This *acclamatio* in the *comitia curiata* tended to fall into disuse because of its formal and impersonal character. The spontaneous *acclamatio imperatoria* after the battle took over its function, at first only for the extraordinary bearer of *imperium*. This personal acclamation came to flourish, so that in the first century B.C. even regular magistrates were acclaimed *imperator* no longer in the *comitia curiata* but after a victory. This theory is corroborated by the following fact: no more than *privati cum imperio* did promagistrates for the year after their normal term of office propose a *lex curiata de imperio* [1]. In case of the latter the validity of the *lex curiata*, once ratified, was extended. For this reason, too, it is now easy to understand why an *appellatio imperatoria* for promagistrates was, but for magistrates was not held in the second century B.C. The latter were nominated *imperatores* for the year to come by a ceremony of the *lex curiata*, whereas the former were not.

Also in our interpretation it is possible to retain nearly all of the most important results of Levi and Wagenvoort, who in the *appellatio imperatoria* see the acknowledgment of the personal *felicitas* and *virtus* of the commander. At the *appellatio imperatoria* the *felicitas*, which stamped the commander as an *imperator*, was proved by a victory, whilst in the *lex curiata* a favourable *auspicium* constituted the proof. However, as I already explained, it is not to be assumed that this *felicitas* was a gift from Iuppiter, as Levi thinks it was, or that there had been a series of *appellationes imperatoriae* before Scipio, as Wagenvoort believes [2]. Highly important and to the point is a comparison Kienast makes with the acclamation to βασιλεύς, which fell to Pyrrhus, who had been king for a long time, after his victory over Demetrius Poliorketes [3]. The βασιλεύς-title here develops from a name of office into a personal quality. After Scipio the same is found to happen to the title *imperator*. When, however, Kienast thinks that the *appellatio imperatoria* of Scipio was modelled after the example of the acclamation to βασιλεύς, he puts

---

[1] Mommsen, Röm. Staatsrecht, I[3], 613.

[2] Levi, o.c. 210 ff., already proved that Scipio was the first to receive an *appellatio*; thus also Kienast, o.c. 406.

[3] D. Kienast, Z.S.S. Rom. Abt. 78, 1961, 403 ff. Cf. A. Aymard, Rev. du Nord, 36, 1954 (Mél. L. Jacob), 121 ff.

the facts supplied by Livy [1] the wrong way about, and I stop following him [2]. Combès [3], finally, considers it possible that the *appellatio praetoria* which was discussed above, was by Scipio transferred to the province and there re-shaped into an *appellatio imperatoria*, and, further, that it was precisely the Italic allies who, unlike the Romans, having long been familiar with the term *imperator* as an official title, initiated the *appellatio*. In any case the *appellatio* signifies a personal relationship between the soldiers and the commander, who from now on is looked upon as the personal victor proper. Combès' remarks about the interpretation Scipio himself gave of the title of *imperator* do not directly concern us, since we are interested in the nature of the concepts *imperium* and *imperator*, and not in the personal interpretation a general in 210 B.C. gives of these terms [4].

With the exception of the views of Combès, the modern theories may, therefore, largely be combined with the new interpretation we gave to the usage of the *appellatio imperatoria*. Our conclusion is that it is an unofficial version of the ceremony of the *lex curiata*. The *appellatio* is determined on the one hand by the situation which constituted its background, and on the other by the comparison with the *appellationes regia* and *praetoria*. It is the acknowledgment of a personal quality of the general as the leader, whose *felicitas* has led to the victory. Like the three *appellationes*, the *lex curiata de imperio* implied, not a granting, but an acknowledgment of an *imperium* which the favourable *auspicium* had proved to be present. The *appellatio* as "entitling" was at the same time a *salutatio*, a "benediction". The act was in the literal sense of the word a "nomination".

We shall now see in how far our inquiry into the *lex curiata* and the title *imperator* is relevant to our subject proper.

5. *Conclusions*

The direct occasion of discussion of the *lex curiata* was the question of the relation between *auspicium* and *imperium*, which

---

[1] Liv. 28, 19, 4 (after the Spaniards had proclaimed Scipio king): *Tum Scipio ... sibi maximum nomen imperatoris esse dixit, quo se milites appellassent; regium nomen alibi magnum, Romae intolerabile esse.*

[2] For detailed and well-founded criticism the reader is referred to Combès, Imperator, 63 f.

[3] Imperator, 64 ff.

[4] I find it impossible to follow Combès when he thinks that Scipio used the

precisely in the triumph and the *lex curiata* constitutes the issue on which the contesting views are focused. We found that *auspicium* is in neither of the two instances to be interpreted as the blessing or the support of the gods. We also found that the significance to be attached to *auspicium* is not to be taken as having priority over that of *imperium*. In battle and war, and consequently also in the triumph-al procedure, *imperium auspiciumque* denotes the supreme command, in the sense that the observance of the auspices on the day of the battle was the visible indication of the highest *imperium*. During the ceremony of the *lex curiata* neither *auspicium* nor *imperium* was granted. The *auspicatio* there had the object of proving that the newly elected magistrate—who in virtue of the *creatio* had the *ius auspicandi*—held *imperium*, which was then acknowledged by his being proclaimed *imperator*.

In view of these facts it can no longer be maintained that extra-ordinary magistrates were refused the triumph because they did not have *auspicium*. On the contrary, the testimonia which continually refer to an absence of the regular magistracy, tell us the same things we learned from our inquiry into the *lex curiata*. Scipio was refused a triumph, not because he did not have *auspicium*, but because he *sine magistratu res gessisset*. It is now found that this may also be expressed differently. Pomptinus was in later times, as we saw, refused the triumph because he had failed to submit the *lex curiata*. It was only by the *lex curiata* that a person was made a regular magistrate, because the presence of *imperium* was confirmed by the *auspicatio* and acknowledged by the people. This state of affairs could not officially be changed for Scipio by a similar acknowledg-ment by the soldiers.

I believe that this is also the reason why *tribuni militum consulari imperio (potestate)* never triumphed. The suggestion made by Com-bès [1] that they did not have *auspicia maxima* seems highly improb-able, because patricians were also elected in this college, and other-wise the *auspicia* would have gone back *ad patres*, who could use them only via *interreges*. It appears much more likely that these extraordinary officials, who, as shown by their title, just like the

---

title of *imperator* to establish a kind of mystical relation with Iuppiter Imperator. However, I lack the space to deal with this problem in any detail.

[1] o.c. 46, against Bayet, Tite-Live IV, 145, and R. Monier, Iura, 4, 1953, 110 f.

vir privatus cum imperio, were given their *imperium* in a special manner, other than via the *lex curiata*, were for this reason not allowed to triumph.

By our inquiry the concept *imperium* and its function in the triumph have come to the fore again. In the fifth chapter we saw that the triumphator on the day of his triumph retained the *imperium* in the city, on the strength of a resolution of the people. In the present chapter we saw that only the general *cum imperio* was allowed to bring the *spolia opima* inside the city to the temple of Iuppiter Feretrius.

The *appellatio imperatoria* we included in our inquiry also shows remarkable connections with the triumph. For it is true that Scipio was, in spite of his title, refused a triumph, but in later times the *appellatio imperatoria* became, as it were, the first step on the way to the triumph [1]. The conditions applying to the victory which formed the occasion, were at that time the same for both ceremonies[2]. It is, therefore, not by chance that in the case of Scipio, the first *imperator* in the strict sense, it was proposed that his *imago* should be carried in triumphal garb from the temple of Iuppiter O.M. [3]

But if *imperium* is found to play such an important part in the ideology of the victory, in the considerations involved in the triumph and in the entry itself, we can no longer avoid the question of which *imperium* we are discussing: the political notion or the magico-religious concept, which, according to some scholars, not merely formed its foundation, but for a long time continued to function as an essential component.

This is the second instance in which the discussions about the *lex curiata* and the title of *imperator* prove useful, for, if my explanation is correct, we can give a fairly accurate answer to this question. The *appellatio imperatoria* definitely had no political meaning. The soldiers did not intend to proclaim their commander magistrate, for which *imperator* was not the right term anyway. If the soldiers acknowledged, by their acclamation, the presence of *imperium*, they acknowledged not a political notion, but a personal quality of the commander by which he distinguished himself from others. This is also conceded by Catalano [4], who distinguishes a political *imperium*

---

[1] See Combès, 78 ff.
[2] *ibid.*
[3] Liv. 38, 56, 12; Appian. hisp. 23; Val. Max. 8, 15, 1.
[4] o.c. 534 f.

and an *imperium* as a "potere personale", and thinks that the
appellatio imperatoria refers to the latter. Levi, Combès, Wagenvoort and others defend, as we saw, similar views. However, the
first two here observe for the first time the personality making its
entrance into history, Wagenvoort, on the other hand, thinks that a
primitive dynamistic concept *imperium* is here reverted to.

If the soldiers, after the victory, did indeed, by their acknowledgment of the *imperium* of their commander, applaud his personal qualities, and if on the other hand, this *appellatio* is an
imitation of the regular nominations via the *lex curiata de imperio*, it
follows that the *imperium* of the last mentioned ceremony must at
least have had a not to be underestimated aspect of personal power [1],
side by side with a possible political meaning. This is also evident
from the following: it seems hardly probable that the favourable
outcome of an *auspicatio* is to affirm the presence of a political
authority, but one can easily imagine that the *auspicatio* had to
prove that the new magistrate had the "charisma" to hold his
office. For the moment I shall leave it at this. There are more indications—Wagenvoort in particular has shown this— that in the
third century B.C. *imperium* could still be the expression of a personal charismatic power. I shall return to this matter in the last
chapter.

Finally, there is yet another ambiguity as regards the concept
imperium about which we can say a few words on the basis of our
interpretation of the *lex curiata*. The Romans distinguished between
imperium domi and *imperium militiae*. The former was subject to
restrictions, the latter expressed unlimited power, comparable to
that of a king [2]. Intercession and provocation did not apply to the
imperium militiae, only outside Rome were the axes carried in the
fasces. Together with Roman tradition Mommsen thought that this
imperium militiae was a relic of the old regal power, which the *rex*
also possessed *domi*. But, even though the king's authority is not

---

[1] I point to a very striking parallel with the ceremony of an investiture,
in which the acknowledgment of a personal authority is also expressly
asked for: on the isle of Madagascar the newly appointed king asks his
people: "Do I have, do I have, do I have "hasina"?" To which the people
answers: "You decidedly have hasina". *Hasina* is "Häuptlingsmana",
which Wagenvoort has precisely found in the original notion of *imperium*.
About this ceremony: G. van der Leeuw, Phaenomenologie der Religion[2],
Tübingen, 1956, 115; K. Beth, Religion und Magie, Berlin, 1914, 187; A.
van Gennep, Tabou et Totémisme à Madagascar, Paris, 1904, 115 ff.

[2] Cic. de rep. 1, 40, 63; de leg. 3, 3, 6; 3, 3, 8; Brut. 73, 25.

affected when he crosses the *pomerium*, he nevertheless does not do so without a ritual [1]. The procedure accompanying the later magistrates' departure for war still testify to this. In the city the *auspicia* are observed, on the Capitol the *vota* are pronounced, and after that the general and his lictors march *paludati* out of town. This *mutatio vestis* symbolizes the transition from the area *domi* to the stay *militiae*.

It is true that Alföldi [2] has denied that a qualitative distinction existed during the period of the kings between the areas separated by the *pomerium* [3], but his arguments lack conclusive force and are occasionally demonstrably wrong. The primitive prohibition to assemble the *exercitus urbanus* within the *pomerium*, he explains "weil für eine so grosse Menge drinnen überhaupt kein geeigneter Versammlungsplatz da war" (86). The formulation of this prohibition, however, points quite a different way: *centuriata comitia intra pomerium fieri nefas esse, quia exercitum extra urbem imperari oporteat, intra urbem imperari ius non sit* [4]. The use of the term *nefas* is indicative rather of a religious taboo, which is in agreement with the sacredness of walls and *pomerium*. In passing I may point out that *imperare* in this ancient regulation is a term which functions *extra pomerium*, i.e. *militiae*.

I prefer to follow Vogel,[5] who on the basis of a thorough study takes the boundary line and the distinction between the areas *domi* and *militiae* to be a primitive heritage. Even though this boundary did not in principle delimit the king's powers, the distinction was, according to Vogel, already clearly observed during the *regnum*. One of the indications was the carrying or not carrying along of the axes, which did not originally symbolize, as instruments of punishment, the absolute power of the king, but represented the *imperium militiae*. Also in Etruria the combination of *fasces* and *secures* is not a close one [6].

---

[1] For the testimonia see Mommsen, Röm. Staatsrecht, I³, 63 f.

[2] Reiteradel, 81 ff. A detailed refutation of the main theses of this work is given by Altheim, Röm. Geschichte, II, Frankfurt, 1953, 429 ff.

[3] His conclusion is quite different from that found in his well-known work: Insignien und Tracht der römischen Kaiser, 6: "Die wichtigste *mutatio vestis* im Staatsleben der Römer war mit den uralten rituellen Handlungen verknüpft, die bei der Ueberschreitung der geheiligten Stadtgrenze vorgenommen wurden."

[4] Laelius Felix in Gellius 15, 27.

[5] K. H. Vogel, *Imperium* und *Fasces*. Z.S.S. Rom. Abt. 67, 1950, 62 f.

[6] Etruscan pictures often show the *fasces* without the axe.

I cannot follow Vogel all the way. That the king never carried the axes inside the city is—Staveley [1] rightly points this out in his criticism on Vogel's views—almost certainly an incorrect representation of affairs, since the dictator during the republican period did carry the *fasces cum securibus intra pomerium*. On the other hand Staveley grants Vogel that the connection of the prohibition of wearing the axes within the walls with the *lex de provocatione* [2] is a fable of Valerius Antias. But if the *fasces cum securibus* were originally not instruments of punishment [3] and (therefore) not the symbol of the absolute power of the king over his subjects, why was it then that the carrying of the axes was reserved for the general who stayed *militiae*? Why was only the dictator allowed the use of the axes within the city? I think we can answer these questions only if, like Staveley, we take the road Heuss has indicated, and which Voci, Coli, de Martino, Alföldi, Bernardi, Gioffredi and others follow for quite a distance.

I share Heuss' view that *imperium, imperare, imperator* were originally military terms, which did not until later assume a civil-political meaning, just as *praetor, duke, duce*, etc [4]. *Imperium* is in my opinion the personal charismatic power of the *rex* as *"ductor"* [5], a power which primarily functioned *militiae*. This *imperium* was made manifest by the carrying of the *fasces cum securibus*, originally the symbol of the high majesty of the Etruscan kingship, specifically belonging to the supreme king of the Etruscan confederation, whose function was not exclusively, but to the outsider nevertheless primarily, a military one. The *fasces cum securibus* thus also to the Romans who inherited them, chiefly had a military function as the symbol of the regal power.

---

[1] Historia, 12, 1963, 458 ff., especially 465.

[2] This *lex* is, moreover, not to be dated to 509, but probably to 300 B.C. Staveley, Historia, 3, 1955, 412 ff.

[3] As Kristensen, Verzamelde Bijdragen, 149 ff. has demonstrated.

[4] For the argumentation I refer to Heuss' paper. Worth noticing is that *imperium auspiciumque*, since Mommsen, Staatsrecht I³, 76, looked upon as "Die Gewalt des Beamten . . . in ihrem höchsten und vollsten Ausdruck", is in the texts exclusively found to denote the military command. Mommsen himself says, o.c. 116, "Es beruht dies darauf, dass der militarische Ober-befehl der eigentliche Kern der obersten Beamtengewalt und formell von ihr untrennbar ist."

[5] The term was coined by de Francisci, who in his definition of *imperium* as "una potenza personale, carismatica che conduce al successo," also primarily thinks of the conduct of war.

This does not mean, however, that the axes were never carried inside the city. Their use was, however, confined to rites which marked the beginning or the end of the war, or to those situations in which it was necessary that the king also held the *imperium* inside the city, the only *imperium* then known, and later on called *imperium militiare*. The fact that the dictators carried the axes inside the city is, in my view, due to the same cause. The oldest dictators were appointed in emergencies, during which Rome itself was not rarely the scene of war. The rite originally preceding the marching out to war was the *lex curiata de imperio*. The connection between this *lex* and the military *imperium* was, on the basis of testimonia cited above, made plausible by Heuss, although it should be borne in mind that originally there was no other *imperium*. In later times, when the notion of civil *imperium* had come into being, the ceremony of the *lex curiata* no longer immediately preceded the marching out, but was celebrated right after the election. At that time it had also ceased to concern exclusively the *imperium militare* [1].

Our investigations support this view on an important point. The *lex curiata* was found to be the acknowledgment of the new functionary, not as a magistrate, but as *imperator*. And this is a military term, which retained its original function much longer than the term *imperium*. The comparison of the *lex curiata* with the *appellationes imperatoria* and *praetoria* have proved this [2].

Now this *imperium*, originally the undivided and undifferentiated, unique property of the *rex*, in which the aspect of the personal, charismatic power and that of the military background were closely linked up and continued to be discernible for a long time, an *imperium* which was acknowledged, not conferred, which was by an *auspicium* revealed, but not bestowed, is the *imperium* in virtue of which the supreme commander in a primitive triumphal procession was permitted to bring the *spolia opima* inside the walls of Rome. It is also the *imperium* the triumphator retained, on the day of his triumph, within the walls of Rome. What this means will be investigated in the last chapter.

---

[1] This also explains why the real function of the *lex curiata* fell into oblivion.

[2] It is, therefore, very well possible that the *rex* received two *appellationes:* one which appointed him *rex*, and another which appointed him *imperator* immediately before he went to war.

CHAPTER NINE

THE MEANING OF THE ROMAN TRIUMPH

ἥκω γὰρ ἱερὸς εὐσεβής τε καὶ φέρων
ὄνησιν ἀστοῖς τοῖσδε.

Sophocles

1. *Auspicio, imperio, felicitate, ductu*

Our inquiry into the meaning of the *lex curiata* revealed a meaning of *imperium* which differs from the strictly political denotation generally attributed to this term. The *imperium* which is acknowledged by the *lex curiata* was found to express the magistrate's personal qualities as a commander. This brought us very close to the interpretation Wagenvoort has given of the concept *imperium*. The "chief's *mana*" is indeed exactly this personal quality, a magic, immanent power which "works", manifesting itself in miraculous deeds, and as such is acknowledged by people who come into contact with it. Thus I hope that my inquiry, although it differs on some points from Wagenvoort's views, is yet an additional confirmation of the justness of his interpretation of *imperium*.

In the preceding chapter we saw that there is not a single indication justifying the view that *imperium* is bestowed upon man by the gods. On the contrary, *imperium* as "magic power" is immanent in a person and manifests itself. Further proof of this will be seen later on. However, I am not prepared to go to the point of stating that a magico-dynamistic power is never by a god or gods bestowed on man. The Greek term δύναμις, for example, is used for an immanent, non-imparted power, as well as for an energy conferred by gods. It is the term which in the New Testament denotes the miraculous power of Jesus and the disciples. A similar ambiguity will be encountered in the Latin term *felicitas*. Here we should reckon with the possibility of a shifting from an immanent to a transcendent notion of power. However, this does not disentitle us from continuing to use terms such as dynamism, dynamistic, etc. in the well-known meaning for such ambiguous notions as well, since, e.g. δύναμις, whatever its origin, is a "force mystérieuse et active que possèdent certains individus" [1], a power which enables its bearer to perform

---

[1] M. Eliade. Traité d'histoire des religions², Paris, 1964, 30, about *mana*.

"superhuman" deeds, a power which may be imparted to others, but which may also be dangerous for less "powerful" people. For this energy we shall from now on use the terms "power" or *dynamis*, and avoid using the term *mana*, because this term is still a subject of controversy among the scholars [1], and I am not qualified to take sides. The discussion of the concept *felicitas* will further clarify my views on the notion of *dynamis*.

The terminological problem does not apply with the same force to the concept *imperium*. Here experts on the history of law and on the history of religion held different views on the question whether *imperium* stood for a primitive notion of power at all. Many scholars, law-historians included, are prepared to concede that it did, but some of them add that this notion of power was in later times left only in a fossilized form [2]. We have seen, however, that as late as the end of the third century B.C. the *"dynamis*-component" of *imperium* still actuated a new custom, the *appellatio imperatoria*. And in this case it is as good as certain that this power was not regarded as being conferred by the gods. That *imperium* has in fact long continued to have a personal dynamistic meaning besides the political one is proved by the following data [3].

Only bearers of *imperium* could dedicate temples. [4]
Liv. 9, 46, 6... *cum more maiorum negaret nisi consulem aut imperatorem posse templum dedicare.*
It might be thought that the magistrates performed this religious act on the strength of the *auspicia maxima*. The phrase in Livy, however, points a different way. The term *imperator* in particular, "ein Magistrat, der den Oberbefehl führen kann, also ausser dem

---

[1] See i.a. Eliade, o.c. 29 ff.

[2] See the statements quoted above p. 315 n. 7. About the influence of magic and dynamism on the old-Roman system of law see P. de Francisci, Primordia Civitatis, 214 f. n. 58 and 219 n. 61 with extensive bibliography.

[3] Cf. Wagenvoort, Roman Dynamism, 14; 31 ff. and P. de Francisci, Primordia Civitatis, 367 ff.; J. Bayet, Tite-Live III, p. 121 n. 1. I omit Wagenvoort's examples of *imperare* in peasant dialect because they are not relevant to our subject. Wagenvoort's interpretation of the concept *imperium* has been accepted by many scholars. In addition to Bayet and de Francisci in the works referred to above, I mention G. van der Leeuw, De Gids, 1942, 130; A. Brelich, S.M.S.R. 21, 1947/48, 150, who is sceptical as far as the dynamistic theory is concerned, but applauds the interpretation of *imperium*; Ernst Meyer, Die Welt als Geschichte, 13, 1953, 138 f.; F. Bömer, Gnomon, 21, 1949, 354 ff.; K. Marót, Zum römischen Managlauben, Budapest, 1943/44.

[4] See Wissowa, R.E. 4, 1901, 2356 ff., s.v. *Dedicatio*.

Consul der Dictator und Prätor" [1], refers to the holder of *imperium*. This is far more obvious still from a text which has as its subject not a *dedicatio* but a temple-*votum*. Liv. 22, 10, 10, *Veneri Erucinae aedem Q. Fabius Maximus dictator vovit, quia ita ex fatalibus libris editum erat, ut is voveret, cuius maximum imperium in civitate esset.*

This makes it abundantly clear 1. that what matters is the holding of the highest *imperium*, not the highest *auspicium* [2], 2. that this *imperium* cannot possibly denote a strictly and exclusively political notion of power—not even in 217 B.C. What it does denote becomes apparent from texts dealing with the *devotio*. The *devotio*, too, was reserved to magistrates *cum imperio*. Liv. 8, 10, 11, *licere consuli dictatorique et praetori ... civem devovere.* Cic. de nat. deor. 2,10,.. *ut quidam imperatores etiam se ipsos...devovent.* Macrob. Sat. 3, 9, 7, *Dictatores imperatoresque soli possunt devovere.* Again emphasis is laid on the *imperium* through the term *imperatores*. This case does not concern a strictly religious deed such as a dedication to the gods, but a semi-magical one [3]. The commander links the fate of the enemy to his own and seeks death in battle, thus also effectuating the destruction of the enemy. The assumption that the *imperium* as the *dynamis* of the commander must render this magical deed successful, is confirmed by a legend which represents the prototype of the *devotio*, and which has as such not previously been included in the discussions on the meaning of *imperium*.

When in 362 B.C. an earthquake had resulted in an enormous hole in the *forum*, it proved impossible to fill or to close it, according to Livy, 7, 6, 2, *priusquam deum monitu quaeri coeptum, quo plurimum populus Romanus posset: id enim illi loco dicandum vates canebant, si rem publicam Romanam perpetuam esse vellent. Tum M. Curtium, iuvenem bello egregium, castigasse ferunt dubitantes, an ullum magis Romanum bonum quam arma virtusque esset? Silentio facto templa deorum immortalium, quae foro imminent, Capitoliumque intuentem et manus nunc in caelum, nunc in patentes terrae hiatus ad deos manes porrigentem se devovisse.* Varro, who presents two more versions, writes, l.l. 5, 148: *responsum deum Manium postilionem*

---

[1] Weissenborn-Müller *ad loc.*

[2] It is questionable whether the dictator's *auspicia* are superior to those of the consul. The *auspicia* of the consul and those of the *praetor* ranked equally.

[3] About the magic nature of the *devotio*: W. Warde Fowler, The religious Experience of the Roman People[2], 1922, 206; F. Deubner, A.R.W. 8, Usener-heft, 1905, 66 ff.

postulare, id est civem fortissimum eo demitti. Tum quendam Curtium virum fortem armatum ascendisse in equum et a Concordia versum cum equo eo praecipitatum.

It is immaterial here in how far the version here presented is to be considered historically "correct" [1]. What is important is the description of the *devovens*. For, whereas in the historical *devotio* only the magistrate *cum imperio* could perform this act, it is in the legendary example the *fortissimus vir*, the *vir bello egregius*, who in his *arma virtusque* possessed and sacrificed the highest good of Rome, who played the principal part. This proves that in the *imperium* of the *devovens* the qualities of the *fortis vir*, the personal quality of the *virtus*, was of paramount importance.

Finally there is one more official act which only the bearers of the highest *imperium* were allowed to perform: the *clavi fixatio*. We saw [2] that this act consisted, in the earliest period of the republic, of the annual fixing of the fate, and was carried out by the *praetor maximus*. In later times this practice became obsolete, and was performed only in emergencies, such as epidemics, with a view to warding-off imminent danger. As such it was a purely magical act. Livy, 7, 3, reports that it had to be performed by a dictator, not by consuls, *quia maius imperium erat*. "The suggestion that a dictator was sometimes exceptionally appointed to perform the rite even when the consuls were at Rome, in the belief that his superior *imperium* would produce a greater effect, is perfectly reasonable", Staveley thinks [3]. Only, we have to add, if it is recognized that the *imperium* of the dictator distinguished itself in the first place dynamistically, rather than politically, from that of the consuls and praetors, as, for example, Bayet [4] saw when he spoke of a "dictateur, dont l'*imperium*—"mana"—prime celui des consuls"[5].

The *dictator clavi figendi causa* did not fundamentally differ from the *dictator rei gerundae causa*. Merely the conditions which necessitate the temporary accepting of a monarchic bearer of the highest *imperium*, differ. However, just like the "ordinary" dictator, the *dictator clavi figendi causa* had to appoint a *magister equitum* immediately after

---

[1] Literature about the legend of Curtius is to be found in Bömer ad Ovid. Fasti 6, 403.

[2] above p. 272.

[3] Historia, 5, 1956, 97 n. 113.

[4] Tite-Live III, p. 123.

[5] This was also the reason why, in the absence of a magistrate, a dictator had to be appointed to lead the games: Liv. 8, 40, 2.

his *creatio* [1]. If then, for the dedication of a temple, or the driving-in of the *clavus* a dictator was created *quia maius imperium erat*, and this *imperium* had the desired effect not on the strength of its political, but thanks to its personal-dynamistic qualities, it is doubtful whether there was a different motive for the conferring of the *imperium maximum* to the *dictator rei gerundae causa*. In this case too, I think that, in addition to the advantage of a monarchical absolute rule, the concentration of the personal *dynamis* in one person must have constituted an additional, and perhaps the principal argument. That the concentration of power in one person is of great importance in the dynamistic way of thought, will be seen further on. This personal "power" of the dictator, characterized by the *fasces cum securibus*, later on defined as *imperium militare*, also applied inside the walls, which forms the *trait d'union* between dictator and triumphator. Why the triumphator was allowed, on the day of his triumph, to retain the *imperium* (*militare*) inside the city, is a question which can be answered after we have first briefly discussed the other primary quality of the triumphator, the *felicitas*. That in the discussion of the *imperium* of the triumphator, here, too, symbolized by the *fasces cum securibus*, we primarily think of the dynamistic notion, will be clear from what has been said in the preceding [2].

The formula *auspicio, imperio, felicitate, ductu* is in this form found only once, and not even in a triumphal formula at that, but in a *tabula* which records the dedication of a temple by the victorious L. Aemilius Regillus in the year 179 B.C. [3] Does the fact that *auspicio, imperio* and *ductu* in various combinations are sure to have belonged to the triumphal formula, warrant the assumption that *felicitas*, too, was specifically connected with the triumph? We can answer this question in the affirmative thanks to the following data.

---

[1] Liv. 7, 3, 4.

[2] Cf. Bayet, Tite-Live III, p. 120 on *imperium*: "Il désigne, semble-t-il en effet, une sorte d'efficience mystérieuse (sinon religieuse) dont est pourvu le chef en tant que tel, qui tient sa personne à l'abri des outrages, rayonne sur et par les licteurs dont il s'entoure, le rend seul habile à prendre les *auspicia maiora*, s'exprime dans ses actes par le "bonheur" (*felicitas*) qui voue l'*imperator* victorieux au "triomphe"." As further indication of a "valeur religieux" he mentions a phrase of Cicero, de har. resp. 17, 37, about the secret sacrifice to the Bona Dea: *quod fit per virgines Vestales, fit pro populo Romano, fit in ea domo, quae est in imperio; fit incredibili caeremonia.*

[3] Liv. 40, 52, 5 f.; see above p. 176 f.

Felix, felicitas, and particularly *feliciter* are terms used most frequently in connection with a prayer for victory, or when the favourable outcome of a battle is described [1]. Combinations such as *virtute et felicitate* [2] —often together with other qualities of a commander: *consilio, gravitate, constantia, fide, auctoritate* [3], etc.—, *fortiter feliciterque* [4], *imperio et felicitate* [5], most often *bene feliciterque*[6] or *feliciter* by itself [7], are the components of the formulas which are encountered again and again when a victory or a victor is denoted. Halkin [8] has shown that the formulas in which the general requested a *supplicatio* or a triumph, are exactly identical as far as these phrases are concerned. There can be no doubt that *felicitas* was a term which, although not peculiar to the triumph, yet denoted a quality a general had to possess to be allowed to triumph [9]. That this already applies to the earliest period from which we have testimonia, is beautifully shown by Cicero, de fin. 4, 22, *An senatus, cum triumphum Africano decerneret, quod eius virtute aut felicitate posset dicere, si neque virtus in ullo nisi in sapiente nec felicitas vere dici potest?*

It is generally agreed that the *senatus consultum* Cicero here quotes must have concerned the triumph of Scipio Africanus Maior in 201 B.C.[10] Erkell's view[11] that Cicero does not render the expression

---

[1] The testimonia referred to in the text and the notes were collected by, i.a. L. Halkin, La supplication d'action de grâces chez les Romains, Paris, 1953, § 10; F. Taeger, Charisma II, 22 ff.; H. Erkell, *Augustus, Felicitas, Fortuna*. Lateinische Wortstudien, Göteborg, 1952, 54 ff.; H. Wagenvoort, Mnemosyne, ser. 4, 7, 1954, 300 ff.; C. J. Classen, Gymnasium 70, 1963, 316 f.

[2] Cicero, Font. frg. 6 Clark = 9 Müller; Phil. 5, 41; 14, 11; 14, 28; 14, 37; 4, 15; Manil. 28; Domo 16; Prov. 35; Mur. 12; Liv. 8, 31, 2; 10, 24, 16; 28, 32, 11; 30, 12, 12; 38, 48, 7; 41, 16, 9; 22, 27, 4; 22, 58, 3; 30, 30, 23; 39, 32, 4.

[3] In many of the places referred to in the previous note, particularly those of Cicero.

[4] i.a. Cic. Phil. 14, 37; Mur. 28; Liv. 28, 9, 7.

[5] Cic. de leg. agr. 1, 5.

[6] Cic. Mur. 1; Phil. 5, 40; Liv. 38, 51, 7; 39, 4, 2. In prayers: Liv. 40, 46, 9; 31, 5, 2; 31, 7, 15; 31, 8, 2; 21, 17, 4; 36, 1, 1.

[7] Liv. 41, 28, 8; 35, 8, 3; 27, 7, 4; 34, 10, 3; 10, 37, 8; Sall. bell. Iug. 55, 2; Caes. bell. G. 4, 25, 3.

[8] o.c. § 10.

[9] In connection with the triumph *felix* and *feliciter* are found i.a. in Liv. 28, 9, 7; 39, 4, 2; 10, 37, 8; 34, 10, 3; 35, 8, 3; 41, 28, 8. About this relation see Erkell, o.c. 54 ff.

[10] See Wagenvoort, Mnemosyne ser. 4, 7, 1954, 307, and bibliography attached.

[11] H. Erkell, o.c. 58.

verbatim, and paraphrases the expression *fortiter feliciterque*, has been conclusively refuted by Wagenvoort [1] with the remark that Cicero, if he wants to give a definition of *felicitas*, cannot possibly quote a *senatus consultum* of 201 B.C. in which the term itself is not found. In any case Erkell also concedes that, as far as the triumph is concerned, "*bene (fortiter) ac feliciter* der gewöhnliche Ausdruck gewesen ist, und in dieser Verbindung ist *feliciter* das wichtigste Wort" (58).

But what did *felicitas* mean in this connection? Opinions differ. F. Taeger describes *virtus* and *felicitas* as "Mächte die nach echt italischer Auffassung als immanent gedacht sind" [2]. He is literally followed by A. Passerini [3], who refers to a "forza immanente, concetto puramente italico", and who proves this by, among others, the well-known story of Valeria [4], who takes some fluff from the cloak of Sulla *Felix*, and in answer to his astonished reaction says: Οὐδὲν δεινόν, αὐτόκρατορ, ἀλλὰ βούλομαι τῆς σῆς κἀγὼ μικρὸν εὐτυχίας μεταλαβεῖν.

This *felicitas* is thus characterized as a *fluidum* which through *contactus* may be transferred from the bearer of *felicitas* to someone else. M. A. Levi [5] largely follows this view, but does not disconnect *felicitas* completely from the support of the gods. In his opinion *felicitas* is the physical ability of enlisting the support of the gods without *auspicia*. *Felicitas* assumed its significance only when *privati cum imperio* (but, according to Levi, without *auspicium*) won victories as commanders, and had thus shown their ability to secure the favour of the gods without the divine guarantee of the *auspicia* [6]. Wagenvoort thinks *felicitas* should be "not regarded as 'fortune' subject to chance, but as evidence of personal excellence", and as testimonia quotes, i.a. the famous passage Cic. imp. Cn. Pomp. 28: *Ego enim sic existimo, in summo imperatore quattuor has res inesse oportere, scientiam rei militaris, virtutem, auctoritatem, felicitatem.*

In a word-study about the terms *augustus*, *felicitas* and *fortuna*, H. Erkell [7] has objected to this interpretation of the concept *felicitas*

---

[1] l.c.
[2] Phil. W. schr. 53, 1933, 932.
[3] Il concetto antico di Fortuna, Philol. 90, 1935, 90 ff.
[4] Plut. Sulla, 35, 4 f.
[5] *Auspicio, imperio, ductu, felicitate*. Rendic. Istit. Lomb. 71, 1937, 38.
[6] Erkell has rightly opposed a splitting-up of *auspicium imperiumque* as being held by the magistrate and *felicitas ductusque* as attributes of the *vir privatus*.
[7] o.c. 41 ff.

and argued that the term had the meaning "göttlicher Segen" (53). To prove this he supplied a large number of testimonia. Erkell does concede, however, that there are examples in which *felicitas* ex-presses an immanent personal quality—Publil. C. 36: *contra felicem vix deus vires habet*, and the story of Valeria and Sulla [1]—, but "Dass jemand bei einer einzigen Gelegenheit *felicitas* als ein materielles Kraftfluidum aufgefasst hat, beweist nicht, dass man nicht im grossen und ganzen *felicitas* als "göttlichen Schutz, göttlichen Segen" betrachten könnte". (44)

Exactly the reverse may, however, with equal justification be argued: that during a certain period *felicitas* was generally taken to denote the divine blessing does not imply that the—fairly numerous—testimonia for the meaning "personal excellence" cannot be relics of an older meaning, which survived in the belief of the people. Erkell's argumentation completely fails to take the factors time and evolution into account. Wagenvoort points this out in his reaction to Erkell's work [2]. That the Romans from Cicero to Augustinus regarded *felicitas* as good fortune or success bestowed by higher power in reward of *pietas* and/or *consilium*, is proved by Erkell on the basis of a large number of texts, but who questioned this anyway? The questions which remain, however, are why *felicitas* is nearly always used in connection with a military success, particularly when gained by *imperatores* [3]; how it was possible for the Roman also to attribute *felicitas* to the enemies of his people if it stood for "divine blessing" [4], and where the magic meaning of the term in Pliny [5] and Tertullian [6] has come from. These questions can be answered only if, with Wagenvoort, it is assumed that *felicitas* is originally an immanent quality, which lends its possessor success. The etymological meaning of *felix* "fertile, productive" also testifies to this [7].

Unfortunately, it cannot be ascertained whether the term *felicitas*

---

[1] See other examples in Erkell, o.c. 67 ff.; Wagenvoort, o.c. 305 f.

[2] Mnemos. ser. 4, 7, 1954, 300 ff.

[3] Erkell, o.c. 69; Wagenvoort, o.c. 303 f.

[4] Liv. 42, 12, 2; 22, 58, 3; 30, 12, 12; 30, 30, 23; Nepos, Timol. 2, 1; Cic. inv. 1, 94; ad Att. 6, 6, 3.

[5] Plin. n.h. 26, 19: *Cur Caesaris miles ad Pharsaliam famem sensit, si abundantia omnis contingere unius herbae felicitate poterat?*

[6] Tertull. anim. 50, 4: *Quaenam et ubinam felicitas aquarum, quas nec Johannes baptizator praeministravit nec Christus ipse discipulis demonstravit?* Cf. Georg. 2, 126 f.; Aen. 6, 229 ff.; 7, 750 ff.; 9, 771 ff.

[7] cf. Combès, Imperator, 213 f.

has in the triumphal formula *auspicio, imperio, felicitate, ductu* its old meaning of "magic personal excellence" or that of "blessing of the gods", which probably developed under Greek influence. Erkell fails to make me understand why *felicitas*, taken as "profanes Glück", should be "eine Lästerung" in this formula (59). That, on the other hand, *felicitas*, when taken as the blessing of the gods, should be, according to Wagenvoort (313), in relation to *ductus* "*cuculi ovum in nido aviculae cantricis*" cannot be accepted as evidence—and there is no further evidence—of the primitive meaning of the term in this formula. Equally uncertain is the meaning of *felicitas* in two other texts, the only ones Wagenvoort rightly considers to be of value, because they date from 201 B.C. and 167 B.C. The former of these is the text already quoted from Cicero de fin. 4, 22, on the *senatus consultum* concerning the triumph of Scipio, the second a quotation from a speech made by Aemilius Paullus in Valerius Maximus, 5, 10, 2: *Cum in maximo proventu felicitatis nostrae, Quirites, timerem ne quid mali fortuna moliretur, Iovem... Iunonemque.... et Minervam precatus sum ut, si quid adversi populo Romano immineret, totum in meam domum converteretur.*

From the former text we learn little beyond the fact that the combination of *felicitas* and *virtus* in the formula relating to the triumph or the victory is a very ancient one. And even if one is prepared to grant Wagenvoort that *proventus* in the latter text is bound to mean "*fructus, incrementum*", this does not prove incontestably that *felicitas* in this quotation is an immanent quality.

The oldest authentic testimonia, therefore, are unfortunately not devoid of ambiguity, and one wonders whether this is due to accident. *Felicitas* could hardly have acquired the meaning of divine blessing in the second and first century B.C. if the germs of this meaning had not been present from the outset. I wonder whether terms such as *felicitas*, which can be shown to have a religious meaning besides a primitive magic denotation, are not viewed too rationalistically if they are only ascribed one meaning in each text. It has repeatedly been pointed out that it is impossible to make a true distinction between a magico-dynamistic stage and a religious phase in the history of human belief [1]. Very often, if not always, it will be seen

---

[1] G. van der Leeuw, Phaenomenologie der Religion[2], Tübingen, 1956, 9. K. Marót, Zum römischen Managlauben, 3; M. Eliade, Traité d'histoire des religions, Paris, 1964, 1-41; Catalano, Diritto augurale, I, 118 and 172; de Francisci, Primordia Civitatis, 211; R. Schilling, Acta Class. 7,

that, during one and the same period, besides the belief in personal gods, the belief in an impersonal, magico-dynamistic power claims its rights. No religion illustrates this more clearly than the Roman one [1]. The woman who wanted to possess part of Sulla's *felicitas* did not care about the source of this *felicitas*. When Erkell, in support of his argumentation, says about relics: "sie teilen ihre Kraft durch Berührung mit, eine Kraft die letzten Endes von Gott ausgeht" (44 n. 3), this "letzten Endes" gives expression to a reflection which may be important in connection with the study of religious history, but which need not be assumed to be present in the mind of the believer who expects to be cured or strengthened by touching the sacred object or the holy man. "Alles 'Krafterfüllte' kann man als 'heilig' in der vorchristlichen Bedeutung des Wortes bezeichnen: wer Heill, d.h. wirkungsvolle Kraft besitzt, ist 'heilagr'", Pfister says somewhere [2]. That this term 'heilig' [3] could also be employed in connection with the Christian worker of miracles, whose power "letzten Endes" came from God, is typical of the overlapping of the magical and religious *dynamis*. One need only to have witnessed the worship of a miracle-working icon or image of a saint in one of the Mediterranean countries, to see this confirmed even for the present day.

Now this brief survey of the various points of view was primarily intended as an introduction to a discussion of the concept *felicitas*, in which the question of whether the commander owed his *felicitas* to his own excellence or to the favour of the gods does not constitute the main issue. We identify ourselves with the soldiers who proclaimed their general *imperator* because of his manifest *felicitas*, and with the people of Rome who gave this *felix imperator* a triumphal reception. To these people the commander was the bearer of *felicitas*, no matter where his good fortune had come from. Everything centred in this *felix vir*, both in the *appellatio imperatoria* and in the triumphal procession, and it is our task to try and find out what this bearer of good fortune meant to people and city. Was he also

---

1964, 44 ff., demonstrates on the basis of two Roman festivals that in Rome: "magic and religion often coexist and can be distinguished by analysis alone" (45).

[1] See the paper of R. Schilling referred to in the preceding note.

[2] Gymnasium, 67, 1960, 475. Cf. Wagenvoort, Roman Dynamism, 25.

[3] The remarkable thing is that, just as in the case of *felicitas*, there is a controversy among Germanists about the question whether "Heill" is an immanent, or a god-given force; see Erkell, o.c. 48 ff.

a *bringer* of good fortune? In the fourth chapter of this study we saw that the results of our inquiry pointed that way. We shall elaborate this suggestion here.

To this end we have to start from a meaning of *felix* which was observed, without its importance being realized. First of all, however, I shall summarize the data concerning the stem *felic-* which were found by the above-mentioned scholars, and which are now generally considered certain.

1. *Felicitas* primarily means "success" or "good luck" in war, particularly in connection with the *imperator*.
2. It is very frequently combined with *virtus*.
3. The original meaning of *felix* is "fertile", "bearing fruit". This meaning also survives in later literature [1].

Besides "successful", "fortunate", *felix* also means "bringing good luck":

> Verg. Aen. I, 330:
> *Sis felix nostrumque leves, quaecumque laborem.*
> Serv. ad Aen. I, 330:
> *felix enim dicitur et qui habet felicitatem et qui facit esse felicem.*
> Macr. Sat. I, 12, 35:
> *S.C. de mense Augusto: cum* .... *hic mensis huic imperio felicissimus sit ac fuerit...*
> Liv. 3, 54, 9:
> *Ibi felici loco, ubi prima initia inchoastis libertatis vestrae, tribunos plebi creabitis.*

It probably has this meaning also in the formulas and wishes: *quod bonum faustum felix fortunatumque sit* [2], and *quod bonum fortunatum felixque salutareque siet populo Romano Quiritium* [3].

> Liv. 22, 30, 4:
> *quod tibi mihique sit felix, sub imperium auspiciumque tuum redeo...*

---

[1] Liv. 5, 24, 2; Lucr. 5, 1378; Verg. Georg. 2, 81; Horat. Ep. 2, 14, and others.

[2] Cic. div. I, 45, 102.

[3] Varro, l.l. 6, 86.

In precisely the same way we find the meaning "bringing bad luck" for *infelix* [1]. This meaning will, of course, first of all be looked upon as an extension of the fundamental meaning "bearing fruit". This is done by Wagenvoort [2], but with some reserve. He assumes that an *arbor felix* was indeed originally a tree bearing fruit, but points out that a magic meaning soon crept in, so that *felix*, in addition to its meaning of "bearing fruit" has a connotation of "working magic". Of Georg. 2, 126 f., *Media fert tristis sucos tardumque saporem felicis mali*, Servius gives two explanations: either *"felix malum"* is *malum arboris felicis*, or: *"felicis": salubris; nulla enim efficacior res est ad venena pellenda*, which last-mentioned meaning is confirmed by Oppius in Macr. Sat. 3, 19, 4. It is indeed a magically active, curative fruit which is discussed here, but also the tree itself, its branches or its leaves may, in addition to being "fruit-bearing", be "lucky" [3].

The explanation of this development in meaning is, in my opinion, to be sought in a typically dynamistic way of thinking, according to which an object, plant, animal or human being which at one time manifested its magic power, retains this "productivity" and uses it not only in the original field, but in all spheres of life, and thus, through its own *felicitas "facit esse felicem"*. In this way it can be understood that *rami felices*, originally fruit-bearing branches, via the connotation "magically active branches", are in later times generally used as "lucky, blessing branches" [4]. This last meaning is found in, i.a. Vergilius:

> Aen. 6, 229 f.:
> *Idem ter socios pura circumtulit unda*
> *spargens rore levi et ramo felicis olivae*
> *lustravitque viros*
> Aen. 7, 750 f.:
> *Quin et Marruvia venit de gente sacerdos*
> *fronde super galeam et felici comptus oliva.*

The function of *felix* is very clearly indicated in the following text.

---

[1] Verg. Aen. 2, 245; 3, 246 and elsewhere.

[2] o.c. 305 f.; 318 f.

[3] The dedication of *arbores felices* and *infelices* to the *Di superi* and the *Di inferi*, respectively, is a late development, which does not help us in our inquiry.

[4] This does not deny that *felix* was associated ultimately with generic names, particularly olive-branches, and with specific sacrificial animals.

The subject is the rebuilding of the temple of the Capitolinus by Vespasian:

Tac. Hist. 4, 53:
XI kalendas Julias serena luce spatium omne, quod templo dicabatur, evinctum vittis coronisque ingressi milites, quis fausta nomina, felicibus ramis; dein virgines Vestales cum pueris puellisque patrimis matrimisque aqua e fontibus amnibusque hausta perluere.

Just as the names were to bring good fortune by their favourable meaning, the branches had to do so by their own magic activity. In this meaning *felix* is also found in animals:

Verg. Ecl. 5, 65 = Georg. 1, 345:
terque novas circum felix eat hostia fruges.

In what way did *felicitas* originally manifest itself here? Probably just as in the case of the plants, viz. by fecundity [1]. It is possible that, just as in the *hostia opima*, the "well-fed" appearance played a part.

It is not surprising now that the human being who is characterized, *proventu felicitatis*, by "the fruit of his good fortune", may also benefit other people or society as a whole.

We should like to know in what respect the *felicissimus puer*, who, according to Servius ad Aen. 4, 167, fetched the water for the wedding-feast, differed from others. Was he *patrimus et matrimus*, as Erkell (127) supposes? It is indeed *pueri patrimi et matrimi* who are by preference used for this kind of ceremony [2], and the having of *pater* and *mater* may be looked upon as a sign of *felicitas*, also in the primitive sense. Very remarkable is Serv. Ecl. 4, 26: *nam felicitas temporum ad imperatoris pertinet laudem*, which goes back to a very old way of thinking, of which even the formulation is indicative: Cato frgm. 135 *praeclara fertur oratio de lustri felicitate. Iam tunc*

---

[1] That this is not imaginary is shown by the fact that in primitive thought "le jardin cultivé par une femme féconde produit en abondance". (Lévy-Bruhl, Les fonctions mentales dans les sociétés inférieures⁵, 1922, 348), whilst in Uganda "une femme stérile, en général, est renvoyée par son mari, parce qu'elle empêche son jardin de donner des fruits". (Lévy-Bruhl, L'expérience mystique et les symboles chez les primitifs, 1938, 253). Both places have been quoted by Wagenvoort, Roman Dynamism, 172. Cf. Servius ad Georg. 1, 345.

[2] See C. Koch, R.E. 18, 1949, 2250 ff., s.v. *Patrimi et matrimi.*

enim in illa vetere re publica ad censorum laudem pertinebat, si lus-
trum felix condidissent, si horrea messis implessit, si vindemia re-
dundaret, si oliveta larga fluxissent [1].

Small wonder, therefore, that Sulla, whose *felicitas* in war deeds
had manifested itself, was considered capable of imparting this
felicitas to others by simple touch. This was in agreement with a primitive Roman way of thought.

Now it might be thought that the retrospective and prospective
meanings of the "proved success" and "the (to be expected) imparting of good luck" could only by chance develop in this term,
owing to the unique meaning of *felix*. Nothing is less true.

Latin has an expression in which this double meaning is also
apparent, viz. *macte virtute esto*.

The expression is generally used as a congratulation for a courageous deed performed [2]. It is a felicitation, a recognition of courage.
In his discussion of this expression in his thesis about the concept
virtus [3], van Omme quotes the explanation of Pfister [4] of *mactare* =
"increase, strengthen". Both the expressions *vino deum mactare* and
hostiam deo mactare can be explained in this way. *Mactus* means
"increased, augmented". *Macte virtute esto* literally means "be increased by your manliness", a congratulation for a laudable deed.
There are, however, texts which suppose a different meaning
of the expression.

> Acc. frgm. 473 (R):
> ...*macte his armis, macte virtutei patris.*
> Pac. frgm. 146:
> *macte esto virtute, operaque omen adproba.*
> Liv. 2, 12, 14, in which Mucius Scaevola after burning his
> hand is addressed by king Porsenna as follows:
> *iuberem macte virtute esse, si pro mea patria ista virtus staret.*

Quite rightly van Omme points out (34) "that the words are indeed connected with something already performed, but at the same

---

[1] The other way round, the censor was also personally blamed for a bad
lustrum: The tribune Ti. Claudius Asellus reproaches the younger Scipio
that his *lustrum* has been *malum infelixque*. Cic. de or. 2, 268; Gell. 4, 17, 16;
Fest. 366 (L).

[2] Cic. ad Att. 12, 6, 3; Liv. 4, 14, 7; 22, 49, 9; 2, 12, 14; 7, 10, 4; 7, 36, 5;
10, 40, 11; 23, 15, 14; Verg. Aen. 9, 641.

[3] A. N. van Omme, Virtus. Een semantiese studie. Diss. Utrecht, 31 ff.

[4] R.E. 11, 1922, 2171 s.v. Kultus.

time refer to future accomplishments" [1]. Here again, therefore, we see the central theme of dynamism—once a success, always a success—clearly outlined, this time in connection with the word *virtus*, whose originally dynamistic value was demonstrated by van Omme[2], and which in formulas is often found in combination with *felicitas*. A similar ambiguity of "acknowledgment" and "expectation" is found in the double *appellatio imperatoria* as we have interpreted it. On the march out to war the acclamation was an acknowledgment of the *imperium* which the *auspicatio* had proved to be present, as well as an expectation that this *imperium* would "work" (*salutare* is very significant here); the acclamation after the battle has proved the presence of *imperium* by its effect, the *felicitas*. But this was not the end of this *felicitas*.

On the basis of what we know we may assume that the entry of the triumphator and his keeping his *imperium* on the day of his entry are linked up with the expectation people had of the *felix imperator* [3]. His *dynamis*, manifest in his *felicitas*, could also in other fields prove efficacious. If in "*mactus virtute*" besides an acknowledgment, also a hopeful expectation is expressed, this definitely applies to the man who "*redit magno mactatu' triumpho*" [4].

That in fact the winner in any field, but particularly in war, benefits his city and that this holds *a fortiori* for the triumphator, will be shown in the next section.

By way of conclusion we have to make one remark. Above we saw that *felix* is chiefly, if not exclusively, used in connection with the victorious *imperator*. The private soldier could also be *felix*, but it is as if his *felicitas*, although proved and acknowledged, was yet arrested in its further development. Although the private soldier could capture the *spolia opima* he was not allowed to bring them inside the walls. It remains exceptional for the ordinary civilian who was considered *vir fortissimus*, to perform a sacred rite (as we saw in the case of the *devotio* of Curtius) [5]. Just as in other cultures and

---

[1] I do not follow van Omme when he thinks (p. 34 f.) that the *virtus* to which the phrase refers, is embodied in the blood of the defeated opponent.

[2] Cf. Combès, Imperator, 213.

[3] A relation between *imperium* and *felicitas* becomes apparent in Liv. 22, 27, 4, where the magister equitum whose *imperium* was by the people equalized to that of the dictator, boasts *tantum suam felicitatem virtutemque enituisse*.

[4] Ennius. Ann. 301 (Vahl.). Cf. Servius auct. ad Aen. 9, 641: *mactus autem apud veteres mactatus dicebatur*.

[5] In this connection the introduction of the Magna Mater at Rome may

times it was the king who was the real *vir felix*, it was in the Roman republic for a long time the bearer of the highest *imperium* who was looked upon as such.

This is clearly indicated by the triumphal formula with the stereotyped *imperio auspicioque*. The first and most important question asked was: "Who was the highest official?" It may safely be assumed that the *imperium auspiciumque* was in the oldest times always combined with the *ductus* [1], which might have been separated later on. In that case the triumph was celebrated, not by the person who by his *ductus* had won the victory, but by the absent commander who by his *imperium auspiciumque* had furnished the inspiration for this victory! Here, too, the *felicitas* is ascribed to the magistrate in whose *imperium* was, as it were, embodied the institutionalized condition for the achieving of *felicitas*.

2. *The triumphator as the bearer of good fortune*

The victory over the enemy, the salvation from danger and distress have far and wide been looked upon as the sign of a new beginning. The victory heralds a period of happiness and prosperity. For the Israelites the victory and the deliverance (*teshua*) was followed by a period of peace (*shalom*), which signified a blessing also in the purely material presence of rain and harvest [2]. The *victor* has a power he can impart to others. The warrior who comes home after a successful campaign and washes himself in the river, imparts his strength to this water, which in turn "strengthens" the boys swimming around the warrior [3]. This power is, however, also effective in a field totally different from the one in which it first manifested itself. Radjah Sir James Brooke, the British ruler of Serawak (N. Borneo), was venerated not only as the divine liberator from the domination of the Malayans; he also made the crops grow; the water with which the women had washed his feet was preserved and divided among the settlements to ensure a rich harvest [4].

be called to mind. She had to be received by the *vir optimus*, for which the young private citizen Scipio Nasica was chosen. But here strong political motives were involved. See Th. Köves, Historia, 12, 1963, 321 ff.

[1] About *ductus* in the triumphal formula: R. Combès, Imperator, 205 f.

[2] G. van der Leeuw, Phaenomenologie der Religion², Tübingen, 1956, 112; J. Pedersen, Israel I, II, London, 1926, 332: "like victory in the court of justice, rain and fertility are included in salvation".

[3] J. G. Frazer, The golden Bough. Taboo and the perils of the soul, 168.

[4] Van der Leeuw, Phaenomenologie, 119.

The *victor qualitate qua* is the chief or the king. In him the power of victory has been acknowledged in his enthronization. In many cultures the king is also the source of welfare, growth and prosperity[1]. Scandinavian sagas speak of a "king's luck", which unites victory, invulnerability, curative powers and the power to cause good weather[2]. A Gothic definition calls the king "the one in whose good fortune a man wins victories"[3]. When the Norse king Halfdan Svarti was to be buried, all parts of the kingdom wanted their share of the "king's luck"; the body was consequently cut into four parts, which were buried in each of the four countries[4]. How long-lived such a belief can be is shown by the example of the English kings, who, as late as the 18th century, were still thought to be able to cure scrofula, "the king's disease"[5].

Neither has such a belief been alien to Hellas. The well-known passage in the Odyssey (19, 109 ff.) refers to a king who by maintaining the εὐδικία is the cause of rich harvests, thriving herds of cattle, even of rich catches of fish. "At the bottom there is the old primitive conception of the power of the king to influence the course of nature and the luck of his people", Nilsson says[6].

These examples, to which an endless number might be added, make it clear that Voltaire's well-known statement: "Le premier qui fut roi, fut un soldat heureux" is too facile. Whether such a view on the origin of the kingship may categorically be dismissed as a fabrication of "arm-chair philosophers" as is done by Frazer[7], is however, questionable. There is no denying that there are plenty of examples of warriors who, thanks to their great war-deeds, were appointed commander, chief or king. Nor did this happen only in primitive communities[8]. Terms such as *praetor, dux,* duke, *imperator, Führer* were originally military titles, and only gradually began to denote

---

[1] See i.a. F. Kampers, Vom Werdegange der abendländischen Kaisermystik, Leipzig, 1924; Frazer, The golden Bough, I, The magic art; G. van der Leeuw, Phaenomenologie, 114 ff.; La regalità sacra, Supplements to Numen, Leiden, 1959, *passim.*

[2] Van der Leeuw, o.c. 115.

[3] *ibid.*

[4] J. de Vries, Das Königtum bei den Germanen, Saeculum, 7, 1956, 295.

[5] Frazer, o.c. I, 368 ff.

[6] Homer and Mycenae, London, 1933, 220. See also H. Meltzer, Philol. 62, 1903, 481 ff.

[7] J. G. Frazer, Lectures on the early history of kingship, 1905, 36.

[8] F. Lehmann, Mana, 13: "Der Krieg hat zweifellos am meisten Anlass zur Entwicklung eines wirklichen autoritativen Häuptlingstums gegeben."

civil leadership. Such a development of leadership is not contrary
to a "magical origin of kings". The magical power of the man of
exceptional qualities becomes most clearly apparent during the
most acute crises in a people's existence: war and battle. The wan-
ing success of the prince may become manifest in bad crops [1], but
it reveals itself much more directly in a defeat. In the song of victory
accompanying the entry of Saul and David [2]: "Saul hath slain his
thousands, and David his ten thousands", a sign becomes visible
of the diminishing power of the old king and the growing success of
the man who is to become king.

These introductory remarks are necessary to make it clear that,
as soon as we broach the subject of the relation between victory,
victor and welfare, we have to do with the ideology of the ruler, and
that it is not to be expected that, apart from the king, who in virtue
of his office brings victory and blessing, we shall encounter many
examples of victors who at the same time act as the bearers of good
fortune. Yet there are some striking examples, of which a few follow
here. It goes without saying that the connection between triumph
and kingship will not be left undiscussed. This subject will concern
us in the next section.

Although different theories have been published about the *ritus*
of the *equus October*, the following data and interpretations are to be
considered certain [3]. On the fifteenth of October races were held
around the *ara Martis*, after which the right-hand horse of the
winning team was killed in honour of Mars. The explanation given
by Paulus ex Festo [4], probably in imitation of Verrius Flaccus, that
this rite took place *ob frugum eventum* may safely be assumed to be
incorrect. It is at present generally believed that this rite formed
part of the ceremonies which concluded the war season [5]. The central
figure of the god Mars and the *equi bellatores* indicate this. To us the
following is of special interest: the blood from the tail of the winning
war-horse is dripped into the hearth of the *regia* and preserved by
the *virgines Vestales* to be mixed on the *Parilia*—April 21—with the
ashes of the unborn calves of the *Fordicidia*, and subsequently

---

[1] La regalità sacra, *passim.*

[2] 1 Samuel 18, 7 and 8; cf. 1 Samuel 21, 11.

[3] Here I follow Latte, R.R.G. 119 ff. and J. Balkestein, Onderzoek naar
de oorspronkelijke zin en betekenis van de Romeinse god Mars. Diss. Leiden,
1963, 61-85, which contains an analysis of the data.

[4] 246 (L).

[5] i.a. Wissowa, R.u.K.² 145; Latte, R.R.G. 119 ff.

distributed among the people. The head of this horse, "reinforced" by a wreath of loaves, is combatted for by the inhabitants of the quarter of the *Via sacra* and those of the *Suburra*. "Das ist der Kampf um ein segenmächtiges Heiltum, wie er vielfach vorkommt.... In der gleichen Richtung weist es, wenn man das Blut, in dem die Lebenskraft am stärksten konzentriert ist, für den Herd sichert", says Latte [1]. Here we have, therefore, a first primitive Roman example of a subject which, as a result of a victory, is laden with "power" being magically active in the interest of people and city.

Remarkable is also the magic action of the *hasta caelibaris "quae in corpore gladiatoris stetisset"* [2]. Although we here have a two-fold magic action, that of the iron and that of the blood [3], it should be borne in mind that the aspect of the deadly, and therefore successful, weapon has also played a part. This also applies to the *hasta velitaris evulsa corpori hominis, si terram non attigerit*, the *sagittae corpori eductae, si terram non attigerint*, and the *lapis vel missile ex his qui tria animalia singulis ictibus interfecerint hominem, aprum, ursum*, which, according to Pliny [4], all of them facilitate a difficult confinement. The *comitialis morbus* is cured *cibo e carne ferae occisae eodem ferro quo homo interfectus est* [5]. The implement which has succesfully accomplished its task obviously has to use its proved power also in another field.

By their mere presence the *pignora imperii* ensure the continued existence and prosperity of Rome. One of these pledges was the *quadriga* which had been manufactured in a Veientan workshop and which had, on account of its miraculous growth, been recognized as a "source of power". In the preceding [6] we saw that there is a parallel story, in which Gagé saw a duplicate of the other version, which described this *quadriga* as a normal four-in-hand, which had won a race in Veii, and, after it had bolted, entered Rome via the Porta Ratumena *excusso auriga*. Just as in the rite of the *equus October* the *winning* team is here connected in a special manner with the well-being of Rome. Combat and games do not constitute any essential difference in this respect. In both instances, a man or an

---

[1] o.c. 120.

[2] Paul. ex Festo 55 (L).

[3] Bömer ad Ovid. Fasti 2, 560; Frazer *ad loc.*; H. J. Rose, Comment. on Plut. Quaest. Rom. p. 205.

[4] n.h. 28, 34.

[5] *ibid.*

[6] See above p. 561 n. 1.

animal is stronger, more powerful than the other, and this power, his *felicitas*, benefits the community to which it belongs.

In the fourth chapter we have "unmasked" the honours bestowed on the winners of the Greek *agones* as attempts to keep the winner for the city. We have also seen in what way the *felicitas* of the winner of the Olympic games was put to use in Sparta: from that time onwards he was allowed to fight side-by-side with the king. Two bearers of *dynamis*, the one in virtue of his office, the other on the strength of his proved success, here side-by-side use their personal power for the benefit of the state. Other honours, too, are in my opinion misinterpreted if they are classed with the medal and the badge. In Elis the sacrifices and gifts for Athena are carried by the winners of a beauty contest[1]. This practice is, in my view, comparable with a curious privilege that might in Rome fall to the share of people who had performed remarkable feats of war.

Pliny, n.h. 22, 6, 11, reports that a certain M. Calpurnius Flamma, who as tribunus militum had been given a *corona graminea, praeter hunc honorem adstantibus Mario et Catulo consulibus praetextatum immolasse ad tibicinem foculo posito*. A highly instructive parallel is found in the story of P. Decius Mus, also a tribunus militum, also a winner of the *corona graminea*. Livy, 7, 34 f., describes how this officer, together with a small party of soldiers, allowed himself to be surrounded in order to give the main body the opportunity to free itself from an encirclement by the Samnites, subsequently broke through this encirclement himself, and, together with the main body, defeated the enemy. By these feats he was characterized as a man of exceptional qualities and *virtus*. Livy does not tire of singing his praises. In addition to the *corona graminea* he was given one hundred cattle *virtutis causa*[2], among which there was an unusual, white one, *opimus*, with gilt horns[3]. He gave the hundred cattle to his soldiers, and, crowned with the *corona graminea*, he sacrificed the one, exceptionally beautiful animal to Mars.

The *corona graminea* was the highest mark of honour to be awarded a Roman commander. It was presented only when an entire army

---

[1] Athen. 13, 565 f. and 609 f. Cf. the stipulation that the Magna Mater had to be received in Rome by the *vir optimus*, in which connection Köves, Historia, 12, 1963, 331, points out: "Aus dem Grundwort *ops* "Macht, Reichtum" gebildet . . . bezeichnete es eine Vorzüglichkeit nicht zuletzt im Sinne einer "natürlichen", körperlichen Blüte." Cf. Marouzeau, Eranos. Acta Philol. Suecana, 54, 1956, 227 ff.

[2] Plin. n.h. 22, 5, 9.

[3] Liv. 7, 37, 1.

was by the strategy or valour of its commander saved from the direct danger of annihilation. It was the only wreath the soldiers gave to their *imperator*, the other wreaths were, the other way round, given by the commander to the meritorious soldier [1]. Although the term *imperator* may in this context have been used loosely by Pliny and Festus, it is nevertheless clear from the definition that the wreath is meant for the supreme commander. Just as in the case of the *appellatio imperatoria* the awarding of the *corona graminea* may be looked upon as an acknowledgment of his exceptional qualities and *virtus*. The reason why the two examples of tribuni militum being awarded the *corona* are so remarkable, is that in both cases an officer made a sacrifice which normally had to be performed by the commander *cum imperio*. Particularly striking is in the story of M. Calpurnius Flamma the privilege, which Pliny also considered most unusual, by which the officer made the sacrifice *praetextatus*, whilst the real bearers of *imperium*, the only persons entitled to the *praetexta* and the sacrifice, stood by and watched. Anyone considering the term "privilege" or "mark of honour" adequate in this connection, must be astonished at the banal, in this case even ridiculous, material of which the *corona graminea*, the highest honour Rome could award, was made of: grass [2].

As on so many earlier occasions I think that here again it is not a question of a privilege, but of benefit to the community. The fact that Calpurnius and Decius are allowed to perform sacrificial rites they owe to their exceptional personal *dynamis*, which for once makes them superior in success to the *magistratus cum imperio* proper. The fact that Calpurnius makes his sacrifice *praetextatus* is not an honour, but either a momentary promotion to dignitary with a view to giving the sacrifice more "poids", or a temporary granting of a *velamen*, meant as a talisman, protecting and strengthening—undoubtedly the original meaning of the *praetexta* [3], which in addition to being worn by *magistratus curules* was also the dress of young children [4]—, probably both. The *corona graminea* has to be interpreted in the same way: although taken as a mark of honour in later

---

[1] Plin. n.h. 22, 3, 7 f.; Festus 208 (L).

[2] About the strength-giving power of grass see: Wagenvoort, Roman Dynamism, 19; 28; 198.

[3] W. Warde Fowler, The toga praetexta of Roman children. Roman essays and interpretations, 42 ff.; H. J. Rose, Religion in Greece and Rome, New York, 1959, 190.

[4] Plin. n.h. 33, 1, 10; Plut. Quaest. Rom. 101.

times, it was originally a means by which to preserve and increase the proved "power" of its wearer, as was also the case with other wreaths. "Dem Zweck, die Kraft zu stärken, diente auch Kranz und wollene Binde, die der Priester trug", says Pfister [1], who assumes a similar function for the special garments worn by priests and kings. Deubner [2], too, considers this protecting, preserving function to be the original meaning of the wreath.

We find therefore that also the wearers of the *corona graminea*, men who not merely defeated the enemy, but in addition saved their own armies, and in this way manifested an exceptional *virtus*, who, as it were, had become representatives of the state by the *praetexta*, and whose power was fully protected by the *corona graminea*, performed sacrificial rites to which normally only the consul or praetor was entitled. Just as the winner of the Olympic games in Sparta used his *felicitas* to fight side-by-side with the king, we also see here the *felicitas* which has manifested itself in one field, being applied in another: the sacrifice, which, as we saw, gained in effect by the *imperium* of the magistrate-sacrificer, is here made even more efficacious by its being made by a man who for the moment is still more powerful on account of his *dynamis*. It does strike one, however, that not even Decius seems to have been allowed to sacrifice to Iuppiter because he did not have constitutional *imperium*. The parallel with the *spolia opima* is evident.

We have now seen a few examples of the manner in which the *vir felix* applied his proved *felicitas* in some other field, in the interest of fellow-citizen and native city. We also saw that only by way of exception, and in view of outstanding achievements, a private person was elevated to such an extent that he was allowed to perform a sacred rite *pro salute populi Romani* instead of the "power"-bearer *qualitate qua*, the king (priest) or, in the Roman republic, the *magistratus cum imperio*. Curtius formed an example, and so did Decius and Calpurnius, but they were still subject to restrictions. Decius, for example, was not allowed to triumph [3]. Yet Livy [4] describes his entry into the camp as a *castrensis triumphus*. Weissen-

---

[1] R.E. 11, 1922, 2133, s.v. Kultus.

[2] A.R.W. 30, 1933, 70 ff.

[3] Cf. Val. Max. 2, 8, 5, referring to Scipio and Marcellus being refused triumphs: *Sed clarissimos solidae veraeque virtutis auctores, humeris suis salutem patriae gestantes etsi coronatos intueri senatus cupiebat iustiori tamen reservandos laureae putavit.*

[4] Liv. 7, 36, 8.

born-Müller *ad loc.* rightly point out that Livy uses metaphorical language here, but the terminology remains remarkable all the same. Also in the real triumph in Rome [1], Decius marches in the procession *insignis cum laude donisque, cum incondito militari ioco haud minus tribuni celebre nomen quam consulum esset.*

How much the more may, in view of these examples, the holder of *imperium* who wins a victory be expected to be looked upon as an exceptional bearer of *dynamis*! How great will the dynamistic significance of the triumph be in comparison to the *castrensis triumphus* of an ordinary officer. In the following pages I will try to make this clear. I am not the first to hold the view that the triumph should be interpreted as a "dynamistic" phenomenon. Wagenvoort [2] preceded me here. He used two arguments to prove his thesis that the triumphator was pre-eminently the bearer of *mana*:

1. the red colour of the triumphator, which symbolized the blood of the slain enemies, and thus made the *mana* of the commander manifest;
2. the passage through the Porta Triumphalis, which had the function of draining-away this dangerous *mana*.

We found it impossible to agree with these—mutually contradictory—explanations, and defended a different interpretation. This, however, does not mean that Wagenvoort's suggestion concerning the essence of the Roman triumph was found incorrect. On the contrary, there are many data which unquestionably indicate that to the Romans the triumph was a dynamistic *ritus*, dynamistic in the sense that a man whose *felicitas* had revealed his exceptional "power", brought his good luck, embodied in his person, into Rome.

One of the main characteristics of the triumphator is his laurel-wreath [3]. The laurel-branch or wreath was, in Rome, applied in so many other fields, that, if we also take the typically Roman wreaths dealt with above, such as the *corona graminea* etc. into consideration, it may be held to be a purely Roman element. The meaning of the laurel-wreath can be inferred from another Roman usage: on the first of January the citizens of Rome presented the magistrates with laurel-leaves [4]. Deubner [5] rightly assumed that here we see a

---

[1] Liv. 7, 38, 3.
[2] Roman Dynamism, 72; 163-168.
[3] Plin. n.h. 15, 127: *laurus triumphis proprie dicatur.*
[4] Geoponica, 11, 2, 6.
[5] o.c. 72 f.

remnant of the originally blessing, strenghtening action of leaf, twig and wreath as ὑγιείας ἐργαστική[1]. When we find an ancient author[2] defining the laurel-branch or wreath as a means of driving away demons, we must assume that this is a later interpretation. With respect to the *corona laurea* Deubner curiously enough follows Festus[3], who says: *laureati milites sequebantur currum ut quasi purgati a caede humana intrarent urbem*, "um dadurch von dem Unsegen des Krieges gereinigt zu werden". (98). There is no doubt that the balance between blessing and strengthening on the one hand, and the warding-off of evil and purification on the other, is a precarious one. We have already found on various occasions that it is impossible to draw a sharp line between them, since the bringing of good luck and the warding-off of bad luck can obviously be taken as two sides of one action. Nevertheless, I find it impossible to follow Deubner when precisely in the case of the *corona laurea* he takes the purifying action as being essential, whereas in connection with other wreaths he lays more stress on the blessing they confer. In this respect he has obviously been influenced by the theory already developed in antiquity and still prevailing, that the triumph is a purification rite.

If we put the *corona laurea* on a level with the other Roman wreaths, with the wreaths the winners of the Greek *agones* received, and with the wreath the Spartans put on before the battle[4], there is, in my view, one basic explanation which holds for all of them: just as does the twig, these green wreaths symbolize the power of vegetative life, and they impart this, or rather their *felicitas*, to their wearers; in this way they enhance and protect the strength and the success of their possessors. The fact that this explanation is accepted for other wreaths, whereas for the *corona laurea* it is not, is based on the following premise: the wreath as a "source of energy" points to deeds still to be performed, as in the case of the Spartans going to war, or in that of the *verbenae* of the *fetiales*. The *victor*, however, has already accomplished his task; the wreath is no longer needed to supply energy, and consequently has a different function, e.g. a cathartic one (an argumentation which does not

---

[1] Geoponica, 11, 2, 6.
[2] Geoponica, 11, 2, 5; cf. Plin. n.h. 15, 135: *suffimentum . . . caedis hostium et purgatio.*
[3] Festus, 104 (L).
[4] Plut. Lyk. 22, 4.

account for the fact that the wreath of the Greek ὀλυμπιονίκαι can hardly have had a purifying function). This is where the misunderstanding begins, because the assumption that the *victor* has, by his victory, "seine Schuldigkeit getan", and therefore "gehen kann", to "rest on his laurels", as the saying goes, is wrong. His task, as a source of prosperity and blessing for his city and people, really begins after his exceptional qualities have manifested themselves. This explains the attempts at increasing or protecting his strength, among other things, by means of the *corona laurea*.

In the same way we can interpret the laurel-branch in the hand of the triumphator [1], and the custom of throwing flowers at the triumphal procession, which Deubner compares with the Greek usage of the φυλλοβολία, meant to enhance the magic power of the *victor*.

A successful man is from all sides threatened by "feindliche Mächte", whether demonic or divine. I share Ehlers' view [2] that the words spoken by the slave *respice post te, hominem te esse memento*, the iron ring worn by the triumphator, the phallos, the flail and the bells fastened to the chariot and the *ioci militares* are all of them apotropaeic means of warding-off *invidia*. The *bulla*, however, is, notwithstanding Macrobius [3], a heritage from the old royal insignia, which was taken over by the triumphator, although it is, of course, very possible, and even probable, that the function of the *bulla* as a *regale* was to avert evil. At present, however, we are looking for evidence of a more positive nature from which it may be inferred that the triumphator was primarily looked upon as a bearer of *dynamis*.

Evidence of this kind is found in the conditions the victory had to fulfil. As we saw, the war had to be a *iustum bellum*, conducted *cum iusto hoste*, i.e. not against slaves or pirates; an *incruenta victoria* did not give occasion to a triumph. A regulation recorded by Valerius Maximus [4] requires the death of at least five thousand of the enemy. In any case blood had to be shed [5]. Some of the conditions may date from later times, but in spite of this I think an ancient nucleus may

---

[1] Ovid, am. 1, 2, 40; trist. 4, 2, 50; Pont. 2, 1, 36.

[2] R.E. s.v. *Triumphus*, col. 507.

[3] Macrob. sat. 1, 6, 9: *bulla gestamen erat triumphantium, quam in triumpho prae se gerebant inclusis intra eam remediis, quae crederent adversus invidiam valentissima.*

[4] Val. Max. 2, 8, 1; Oros. hist. 5, 4, 7.

[5] Plin. n.h. 15, 125; Serv. ad Aen. 10, 775; 11, 6; 11, 790.

be discovered, which cannot be explained merely by pointing out that regulations were necessary to limit the number of triumphs. That the victory had to be won after bloodshed can be explained only if it is borne in mind that the number of dead determined the "strength" of the *victor* [1]. "Saul hath slain his thousands and David his ten thousands" speaks the same language as do a few traditional *carmina triumphalia*, the crude improvisations of the victorious soldiers.

> *Mille Sarmatos, mille Francos semel et semel occidimus*
> *mille, mille, mille, mille, mille Persas quaerimus* [2].

or, more remarkable still:

> *mille, mille, mille decollavimus,*
> *unus homo! mille decollavimus.*
> *Mille vivat, qui mille occidit* . . . . . [3]

A conclusive proof of the dynamistic character of the triumph can, I think, be found in the 79th of Plutarch's *Quaestiones Romanae*, which I did not find discussed in any of the studies about the triumph or components of it, although it furnishes one of the most important data. "Why", asks Plutarch, "was it permitted to take a bone of a man who had at one time triumphed, afterwards died and been cremated, and to bring it into the city and bury it there?" This question might well be asked, because, as is generally known, burials inside the city had already been forbidden by the law of the twelve tables, a prohibition that was continually renewed [4]. Plutarch himself gives the answer in the form of a question: ἢ τιμῆς ἕνεκα τοῦ τεθνηκότος; He points out that other famous figures from the history of Rome had also been awarded this honour, as, for example, Publicola and Fabricius. A mark of honour, therefore. This is also what Cicero [5] seems to think, but his formulation allows of a different, and, in our eyes more correct, interpretation: *Credo, fuisse aut eos, quibus hoc ante hanc legem virtutis causa tributum est, ut Poplicolae, ut Tuberto, quod eorum posteri iure tenuerunt,*

---

[1] Thus also Wagenvoort, Roman Dynamism, 167. Cf. Lehmann, Mana, 53, who thinks "dass eine solche Manawaffe wahrscheinlich ihr Mana durch die Anzahl der durch sie geraubten Leben gewonnen hat."

[2] W. Morel, Poet. Lat. Min. 1927, 158.

[3] *ibid.* 157.

[4] Cic. de leg. 2, 58; Serv. ad Aen. 11, 206.

[5] de leg. 2, 58.

aut eos, si qui hoc, ut C. Fabricius, virtutis causa soluti legibus consecuti sunt. Twice *virtutis causa*! Since we also know that the Vestal virgins, too, were always buried inside the city [1], the reason for these apparent privileges becomes abundantly clear: it was thought, to quote Pfister [2]: "dass eben von der Leiche solcher Männer keine Befleckung ausging, sondern vielmehr gute Kräfte von ihr ausstrahlten, *deren sich die Stadt versichern musste*".

This characterizes the triumphator as the person who by his *dynamis* represents a source of welfare to his city, whether alive or dead, just as the heroes or θεῖοι ἄνδρες of the Greeks even after their death brought good fortune and prosperity to the city possessing their relics. In a description of the victorious return of two consuls, C. Claudius and M. Livius, we read in Livy, 28, 9, 6, that the people who went out to meet them *non salutabant modo universi circumfusi, sed contingere pro se quisque victrices dextras consulum cupientes, alii gratulabantur, alii gratias agebant......* This is, of course, a case of poetic embellishment rather than of historic reality. But the touching of the hands of the *victor* must at least have been something with which Livy was familiar, just as modern man may feel the need of touching his idol. The explanation of this practice is, to use the words of the woman who touched Sulla *Felix*: "I, too, want a small share of your good fortune".

In this way it may be possible to explain another report, and to retrieve it from the realm of the myths, to which it has been consigned. We are told a few times that the triumphator offers his soldiers a meal [3] which he prepares himself. In one instance it is moreover reported that one of the ingredients is *minium* (red lead) [4]. The part played by the triumphator is in itself remarkable enough. His helping to prepare the meal is fully in keeping with his character of bringer of blessing and good luck. By means of the meal he imparts some of his *dynamis* to his soldiers and, if the item about the *minium* is authentic, it provides an insight into the *interpretatio*

---

[1] Serv. ad Aen. 11, 206. That the Vestal virgins brought the city luck has been attested several times: Cic. Font. 38; Symmachus, rel. 3, 11, 14; particularly noteworthy Plin. epist. 4, 11, 7, where a condemned *virgo Vestalis* exclaims: *me Caesar incestam putat, qua sacra faciente vicit, triumphavit.*

[2] Reliquienkult, 449.

[3] Flav. Ios. bell. Iud. 156; Plin. n.h. 33, 112; Dion. Hal. 2, 34, 2; Appian. Lib. 66.

[4] Plin. n.h. 33, 112, after Verrius Flaccus: *hac religione etiamnum addi in unguenta cenae triumphalis* (viz. *minium*), "a very odd application to make of it" (Reid, o.c. 182).

Romana of the red lead on the triumphator's face. The red lead may in this case be taken to represent to the Romans a magic agent, which for that reason could also be used in the meal as "strength-giving food", activated by the triumphator. However, the red lead has been weakly attested, and *minium* is poisonous. This detail of the triumphal meal may be assumed to be based on fiction.

The special *devotio* of the *senes* at the invasion of the Gauls in Rome [1] also becomes understandable. In 390 B.C. some *seniores* decide to "devote" themselves *pro patria Quiritibusque Romanis*. To this end they take an unusual measure: *qui eorum curules gesserant magistratus, ut in fortunae pristinae honorumque ac virtutis insignibus morerentur, quae augustissima vestis est tensas ducentibus triumphantibusve, ea vestiti medio aedium eburnis sellis sedere.* For this way of clothing Livy gives a romantic explanation, which is corroborated by the fact that the person who had once triumphed also wore his triumphal robes during his last journey. If, however, this passage of Livy is accepted as correct in broad outline, the same should be done with his report (§9), that these old men also carried the *scipio eburneus*, which belongs exclusively to the triumph, and has not been attested for the funeral. And then a different explanation presents itself. The *devotio* which was once performed by the *fortissimus vir* Curtius, is normally carried out by the magistrate *cum imperio*, who is dressed in the *praetexta* even in the turmoil of battle in which he seeks death. If the *praetexta* strengthens its wearer in the action he performs (sacrifice, *votum*, *devotio*), this will hold all the more forcibly for the *ornatus triumphalis*. It would therefore appear to me that the reason why the *seniores* wore these garments was that they would render their *devotio* in this extreme emergency more effective.[2]

One time in history, finally, we encounter a man refusing the triumph, viz. Cn. Fulvius Flaccus [3], in 211 B.C. By way of punishment he is exiled. This is inexplicable if we see in the triumph merely a honorary reward. It is fully understandable if it is seen that this *victor*, by refusing the triumph, deprives the city of the welfare and blessing it entails.

---

[1] Liv. 5, 41, 2 ff.

[2] When Wagenvoort, Roman Dynamism, 33, thinks that the *seniores* were by their *ornatus* characterized as bearers of *imperium*, this constitutes a different phrasing of the same motive.

[3] Val. Max. 2, 8, 3.

This casts a vivid light on the *entry* of the triumphator. The *victor* had to enter the city, and he had to do so, not as a private person, as Fulvius Flaccus wanted to do, but in a ceremony which precisely in the nature of its entry reveals its most fundamental aspect. The importance and the meaning of the entry as a characteristic feature of the triumph has so far been insufficiently realized. The following section will set off the *felicitas* and the *imperium* of the triumphator against the background of the triumphal entry.

3. *The entry of the bearer of good fortune*

On a few earlier occasions we have referred to the cult of the relics. The relics, as the bearers of good fortune to the city, form a good illustration of what ancient man expected of a man vested with magic power, as was the triumphator. But the comparison may be extended. When discussing the state-funerals of the Roman emperors in the third chapter, we drew the attention to the transport of relics, the *translatio cadaveris*, notably to the bringing into the city of the sacred bones. We found there that this was generally done in the form of a great festive procession, with singing and dancing. Plutarch [1] in one instance even refers to participants of the procession: ἐπινίκιον πομπήν τινα ἅμα ταῖς ταφαῖς μίξαντες, in which the phenomenological relationship with the triumphal entry at Rome is very directly expressed. Pfister [2] has concisely formulated the reason of these *translationes*, the festive entries and the funeral in the city as follows: "Von den Reliquien dieser Heroen gingen eben gute Kräfte aus". This power he calls *dynamis*. To what lengths one went to keep a holder of magic power, i.c. a saint, for one's own city, is illustrated by two examples I take from van der Leeuw [3]. When St. Francis was dying, he was brought back to Assisi. Care had to be taken, however, that Perugia was avoided, because it was feared that the saint would be seized there. On his arrival at Assisi the saint was received with jubilation, because it was hoped that he would soon die. More striking even is the story of St Romuald, whom the Catalans beseeched to stay with them. When he refused, they had him murdered so as to keep his body for their country. It is impossible to give a clearer illustration of how highly the possession of the bearer of good fortune is evaluated. Van der Leeuw states:

---

[1] Philop. 21.

[2] Reliquienkult, 532; cf. van der Leeuw, Phaenomenologie², 262 ff.

[3] o.c. 265.

"Ein Heiliger ist also zunächst eine Leiche oder ein Teil davon. Für lebendige Heilige hat die Welt keine Verwendung. Heilige sind Tote, besser noch: Totenmächtigkeit". This may hold true for the Christian faith, for ancient man it was not, or at least only partly, true. He also honoured the living saints as being what van der Leeuw himself defines as "Mächtträger".

The winner of the Greek *agones* is a man vested with this kind of power. Now a second entry-*ritus* we have encountered completes the picture of the entry of the bearer of good fortune, viz. the Greek εἰσέλασις, which we have interpreted as an entry which by its peculiar form hinted at its aim. The definitive closing of the gap in the wall by which the winner had entered was to keep him for the city and to prevent his leaving it, an idea we see again just as concretely in the treatment of the mediaeval saints. Now this εἰσέλασις was already compared with the triumph by Pfister and Gagé [1], and we have interpreted the passage through the Porta Triumphalis from this point of view. Here, again, the bearer of good fortune not only expressly had to enter the area of Rome, but here, too, he was prevented from leaving by the closing of the gate.

By its being compared with these two entry-ceremonies the triumph has been placed within the framework of a type of ceremony which has its roots in primitive thought, but which has acquired a well-defined form in Hellenism: the arrival of the σωτήρ. The meaning, the historical and religious development, and the application of the term σωτήρ has so often been investigated and discussed that a reference to some relevant literature [2], together with a brief description will suffice. The man or god who has saved people from distress is called σωτήρ [3]. The distress may be due to

---

[1] See above p. 155 f.

[2] P. Wendland, Σωτήρ. Eine religionsgeschichtliche Studie. Zeitschrift für neutestamentliche Wissenschaft, 5, 1904, 355 ff.; A. Oxé, Σωτήρ bei den Römern. Drei Skizzen zu Horaz. Wiener Stud. 48, 1930, 38 ff.; A. D. Nock, Soter and Euergetes. The Joy of Study. Papers on New Testament and related Subjects presented to Honr. F. C. Grant, New York, 1951, 127 ff.; Höfer, Roscher Lex. 4, 1236 ff., s.v. *Soteira*, and 1248 ff., s.v. *Soter*; F. Dornseiff, R.E. 3, 1927, 1213 s.v. *Soter*; H. Kasper, Griechische Soter-Vorstellungen und ihre Übernahme in das politische Leben Roms. Inaug. Diss. München, 1961. L. Bieler, Θεῖος ἀνήρ, 120 ff.; F. J. Dölger, Antike und Christentum, 6, 1950, 241 ff. More literature in Nilsson, G.G.R. II, 390 n. 4.

[3] Gelon of Syrac. in Diod. Sic. 11, 26, 6; Brasidas in Thucid. 5, 11, 1; Pelopidas in Plut. Pelop. 12; Agesilaos in Xenoph. Agesil. 11, 13; Philippus of Maced. in Demosthenes, 18, 43 and others.

enemies as well as to epidemics. Victors in war are often greeted as σωτήρ, but also Apollo and Asklepios are called σωτῆρες [1]. Particularly as the title of Hellenistic kings the term undergoes an enormous development [2]. The salvation these kings were supposed to bring, remained, however, "diesseitig", until influences from the East, and particularly those of the rising Christianity, preached in the σωτηρία of the one Σωτήρ a salvation which is not of this earth and not of this time. The name σωτήρ was in the past considered nearly exclusively reserved for gods and heroized or deified humans [3]; more recent investigations have shown that the term has only gradually assumed a religious connotation [4]. What concerns us is that the σωτήρ, who in some way or other, but generally by military action, has saved town and people from danger, is brought into the city in a specific entry [5]. Festively attired, the people go to meet him, and receive him to the accompaniment of acclamations; wreaths are presented, songs of good wishes are sung. The temples are opened, sacrifices are made. The σωτήρ himself is sometimes asked to make a sacrifice [6].

One often finds the acclamation σωτὴρ καὶ εὐεργέτης [7], but also, notably when a ruler is expelled by another, and the city has thus been "liberated", the title of σωτήρ is added to the βασιλεύς title. After the victory over the Carthaginians on the Himera in 480 B.C. Gelon of Syracuse was by the people called μιᾷ φωνῇ εὐεργέτης καὶ σωτὴρ καὶ βασιλεύς [8]. A hymn of Ion of Chios in honour of the Spartan king Archidamos [9] begins: χαιρέτω ἡμέτερος βασιλεὺς σωτήρ τε πατήρ τε. Demetrios Poliorketes, whom the Athenians honoured as a god, as σωτήρ also assumed the title βασιλεύς[10]. The entry of the σωτήρ does not, therefore, differ, neither outwardly nor intrinsically,

---

[1] See Höfer, o.c. col. 1237 ff.; Kasper, o.c. 30.
[2] See i.a. Kasper, o.c. 61 ff.
[3] Thus Wendland, Höfer, Dornseiff in the works referred to.
[4] Nock and particularly Kasper.
[5] A description of this entry with testimonia is to be found in E. Peterson, Die Einholung des Kyrios. Zeitschrift für systematische Theologie, 7, 1929, 682 ff.
[6] Attalos in Polyb. 16, 25, 3.
[7] See the paper with the same title by Nock referred to above.
[8] Diod. Sic. 11, 26, 6.
[9] frg. 2 (Diehl).
[10] Plut. Demetr. 10, 3; 13, 2; cf. Cerfaux et Tondriau, o.c. 173. Cf. further the reception of Tiberius as ἀπελεύθερος τύραννος in Magnesia (Syll.[2] 371, 17 ff.); Vitellius' entry into Cremona after his victory, regium in modum. (Tac. hist. 2, 70, 2)

from that of the king who has assumed the government and who for the first time or after a long absence enters a city [1]. His arrival is in Hellenistic times celebrated as the παρουσία of a god. The ὑπάντησις or ἀπάντησις [2] by which the people welcome him is continued in the welcoming of the Roman emperors in the special ceremony of the *adventus* in Rome or other cities [3]. The opening of the gate, the entry through the gate is throughout expressly reported [4].

The arrival of the king or *soter* is seen as the beginning of a new period of prosperity, peace and welfare [5]. The famous hymn to Demetrios Poliorketes [6] expresses this very clearly. His παρουσία is celebrated, but whereas the other gods are far away or have no ears, he is actually present, not made of wood or stone, but in the flesh. Then follows the prayer: πρῶτον μὲν εἰρήνην ποίησον, φίλτατε. κύριος γὰρ εἶ σύ. On coins on which the *adventus* of emperors is depicted [7], Felicitas is represented with the *cornucopia*, or we read in the legend: *adventui aug. felicissimo*. A marble altar at Rome bears the inscription: *adventui aug. feliciter/victoriis aug. feliciter* [8]. Above we saw that during the reign of Augustus: *Quaedam Italiae civitates diem quo primum ad se venisset, initium anni fecerunt*, just as the day on which the government was assumed was *annus novus, initium saeculi*

---

[1] On παρουσία and *adventus* of kings: Pfister, R.E. Supp. 4, 1924, 311 ff.; A. Alföldi, Die Ausgestaltung des monarchischen Zeremoniells am römischen Kaiserhofe. Rhein. Mus. 49, 1934, 88 ff.; *idem*, Hermes, 65, 1930, 369 ff.; A. Deissmann, Licht vom Osten⁴, 1923, 314 ff.; E. Peterson, o.c.; F. Hölscher, Victoria Romana, 1967, 48 ff.; Bömer, R.E. s.v. *Pompa*, col. 1973 f.; G. Koeppel, *Profectio* und *Adventus*. Diss. Köln, 1966, and G. Vanella, L'*adventus* di Vespasiano nei suoi aspetti mistico-religiosi e giuridico-costituzionali, Napoli, 1965, I was unable to consult.

[2] On this subject especially Peterson, o.c.

[3] The ceremonious entry of king or emperor is found into the Middle Ages: E. Kantorowicz, The Art Bulletin, 26, 1944, 208 ff.

[4] Hölscher, o.c. 51 f.

[5] Pfister, R.E. Suppl. 4, 1924, 311; Alföldi, Rhein. Mus. 49, 1934, 88 ff.; van der Leeuw, Phaenomenologie², 125 f.

[6] Discussed in detail by O. Weinreich, Antikes Gottmenschentum. Neue Jahrb. f. Wiss. u. Jugendbildung, 6, 1926, 647; K. Scott, A. J. P. 49, 1928, 232 ff.; V. Ehrenberg, Antike, 7, 1931, 279 ff.; Cerfaux et Tondriau, o.c. 182 ff.

[7] Testimonia in Hölscher, o.c. 58.

[8] Cf. Cicero de imp. Gn. Pomp. 13, about the cities which consider themselves fortunat ein accommodating Pompey within their walls: *hunc audiebant antea, nunc praesentem vident tanta temperantia, tanta mansuetudine, tanta humanitate, ut ei beatissimi esse videantur, apud quos ille diutissime commoretur.*

felicissimi[1]. Elsewhere, too, we find datings based on the ἐπιφάνεια or παρουσία of Roman emperors [2].

After Deissmann, Norden [3], Pfister, it was particularly Alföldi [4] who stressed the religious significance of the *adventus* of the emperors. This is to be looked upon as a continuation of the Hellenistic epiphany-processions of the king making his entry. These processions are of a strongly soteriological nature. It is true that Hölscher [5] has pointed out that, during the early imperial period, the *adventus* is decidedly not to be looked upon as the arrival of a "Weltheiland". However, from the 3rd century the *adventus* has been typified as an entry of the bearer of welfare, as is apparent from legends on coins such as *expectate veni* and from sacrifices to the returning emperor. Although there is, therefore, no direct historical development from the Hellenistic royal παρουσία to the later imperial *adventus*, they are phenomenologically very closely related. Now this *adventus* has in the late imperial period replaced the triumph and taken over its ceremonial [6], one of the indications that the triumph belongs in the category of the entries described.

The triumph was an entrance-*ritus*, not only in form but also in content. The last can be demonstrated on the basis of the best testimonia one can wish for: the stereotyped request of a general for the triumph. As we have seen [7], the general asked : *ut sibi liceret triumphanti urbem inire,* just as the current term for "to celebrate a triumph" was not *triumphare*, but *triumphans urbem inire, invehi,* etc. This makes it perfectly clear that the entry into the city was an essential element in the Roman triumph. This was also the reason why any general could, without asking permission, hold a triumph on the mons Albanus, because there the characteristic element of the entry was lacking.

Summary of what we have found:

    1. The triumphator is the *"vir felix" par excellence.*

---

[1] Cf. the enthronization of Vespasian: Plin. n.h. 33, 41: *salutaris exortus Vespasiani imperatoris*; Tac. Agric. 3, describes the beginning of Nerva's reign as *beatissimi saeculi ortus*.

[2] Pfister, R.E. l.c. 311, where the testimonia are to be found.

[3] Die Geburt des Kindes, 1930.

[4] o.c. 88 ff.; Hermes, 65, 1930, 369 ff.

[5] o.c. 48 ff.

[6] H. Stern, Le calendrier de 354, Paris, 1953, 162; M. J. Déer, Schweizer Beiträge zur allgemeinen Geschichte, 8, 1950, 51 ff.

[7] Above p. 163.

2. The *felicitas* is not only proved to be "good luck", but a "power" which retains its effect.
3. The triumphator is, in virtue of his *felicitas* considered as vested with (magic) power. His presence, even that of his bones, brought the city luck.
4. The triumph is essentialy an entrance-ceremony.

The triumph has thus been typified as a ceremony whose pattern is similar to that of the Greek-Hellenistic entry of σωτήρ and/or βασιλεύς, which in turn shows a considerable influence of the old entry of the king-saviour in Near Eastern cultures. It should be borne in mind that it is a Roman interpretation of a religious ritual imported from Etruria, in which to the Romans the triumphator is neither god nor *heros*. The "salvation" he brought is, therefore, not a metaphysical σωτηρία, but a *salus* for the city, which, though not always given concrete form, may originally have concerned especially the keeping-out of the enemy and the thriving of cattle and crops, just as *felicitas* also had a very concrete meaning originally. In spite of its Greek background, Cicero's phrase [1]: *is est nimirum soter, qui salutem dedit* also applies to the old-Roman belief.

I consider that the meaning of the *imperium militare* of the triumphator, whose personal-dynamistic aspects have now been elucidated, stands out in full relief only against the background of our present knowledge of triumph and triumphator. Since on the one hand the triumphator, because of his exceptional *dynamis*, which had become manifest by his victory, entered the city as the bearer of good fortune, and on the other hand a dictator was appointed in exceptional situations or for particularly important sacral rites, because his *imperium* (= the *imperium militare*) as "*imperium maius*" had a greater magico-dynamistic efficacy, there is hardly room for any doubt as to the original meaning of the *imperium* of the triumphator. It was this *imperium* which as *imperium militare* had two meanings: constitutionally "supreme command in the field", magico-dynamistically—the original meaning, which, however, survived long—: the "*dynamis* of the commander/chief". These two meanings can exist side by side *militiae*, but are under normal conditions not found *intra pomerium*. In very unusual situations, however, when the belief that the superior *imperium* has to perform its task inside the town came into conflict with the law which forbade the exercising

---

[1] In Verr. 2, 2, 154.

of the *imperium militare intra pomerium*, the belief and the religious necessity weighed more heavily than did the constitutional laws. This happened in two instances: at the *creatio* of a dictator and at the entry of the triumphator. By his *dynamis* and his *felicitas* the triumphator brought welfare and blessing into the city. In view of this he was not to be deprived of the *imperium* which stood for his authority as a commander as well as for his personal *dynamis* as linked up with his function and proved by his victory. The *maius imperium* had to be retained inside the city there to have its beneficial effect, just like the *imperium* of the dictator.

We may now expect that, just as the dictator was the holder of the highest *imperium* and virtually monarch, the triumphator was unequalled and unsurpassed by others. This is indeed beautifully demonstrated by a custom to which up till now little attention has been given and which, just like the funeral-privilege discussed before, is of great significance. Again Plutarch [1] is one of our sources: Διὰ τί τοὺς θριαμβεύσαντας ἑστιῶντες ἐν δημοσίῳ παρῃτοῦντο τοὺς ὑπάτους, καὶ πέμποντες παρεκάλουν μὴ ἐλθεῖν ἐπὶ τὸ δεῖπνον; As a possible answer to this question Plutarch says that the triumphator was obviously entitled to the place of honour at the table, but that he could not have this when the consuls were present, because they could claim the place of honour. Rose [2] thinks this is the correct explanation. I nevertheless think the explanation Valerius Maximus, 2, 8, 6, gives of this usage is more direct and right: *moris est ab imperatore ducturo triumphum consules invitari ad cenam, deinde rogari ut venire supersedeant, nequis eo die quo ille triumpharet maioris in eodem convivio sit imperii*. The custom evidently dates from a period when promagistrates could triumph after a victory. Staveley [3] assumes that Valerius Maximus is mistaken when he uses the term *maius imperium*, since—as Staveley rightly argues— the *consules* did not hold a *maius imperium* than the *proconsules*. The explanation of Valerius Maximus can indeed not be correct in this form. The custom does nevertheless concern the holding of *imperium* and in my view we have here another example of a conflict between religious requirements and constitutional laws.

As soon as a proconsul crossed the *pomerium* he lost his *imperium*. In exceptional cases the proconsul was given in the city an *imperium*

---

[1] Quaest. Rom. 80.

[2] The Roman Questions of Plutarch, 202.

[3] Historia, 12, 1963, 470 f.

equal to that of the consuls [1], but the triumph went even further. Here the proconsul had an *imperium* which, as *imperium militare* was "more powerful" than that of the consuls. He thus held an *"imperium maius"*, as elsewhere the *maior* consul is the person *penes quem fasces sunt.*[2] Here, I think, Valerius Maximus made his mistake. Not the consuls but the proconsul-triumphator held a *maius imperium*. In the usage by which the constitutionally highest holders of *imperium* were indeed invited, but were subsequently asked to stay away, the whole ambiguity of the concept *imperium* and the conflicts it was bound to entail, is manifested. Here the law was formally obeyed, whilst on the other hand the confrontation with a constitutional contradiction was avoided. But this was not the only reason for this curious practice. The other is that the triumphator as the holder of the highest *imperium*—more or less like the dictator—had to be a unique person, whose "power" was not equalled by anyone else. The presence of other holders of *imperium* might, to speak with Wagenvoort, cause *"contagio enervans"*, drain away "power", concretely as well as ideologically. The *imperium maius* of the triumphator, explicitly acknowledged and maintained in the city, was not to be "weakened" by the presence of other, constitutionally equal holders of *imperium*. Now we also understand why two generals with equal *imperium* never triumphed together. If both of them triumphed—which happened only very rarely—they did not do so on one day nor in one ceremony. This must be connected with the wish to concentrate the *imperium* in one person. Here again we find a parallel with the *imperium* of the dictator.

The comparison between triumphator and dictator finally holds in one more respect. We saw that in many cases the bearer of good fortune was of importance to the city only on account of his personal charismatic power. There were, however, several instances, precisely in Rome, in which the man who was vested with "power" had to enhance the effect and the success of certain, often magic or religious rites. The sacrifice made by Attalos at his *parousia* in Athens [3] does not differ in this respect from the *votum, devotio*, or *consecratio* made by the holder of *imperium*, the temple-dedication and *clavi fixatio*

---

[1] Liv. 26, 9, 10, about a proconsul: *cui ne minueretur imperium, si in urbem venisset, decernit senatus, ut Q. Fulvio par cum consulibus imperium esset.*

[2] Festus 154 (L).

[3] Polyb. 16, 25, 3.

performed by the dictator as the bearer of the highest *imperium*, the special sacrifice of the winners of the *corona graminea*, which they even made in *praetexta*. The triumphator, as the bearer of "power", brings good fortune into the city, but like the officials just referred to he has to perform a well-defined task. This task consists of the carrying-out of the rite which by many is considered the central one of the triumph: the sacrificing of an ox to Iuppiter O.M.

We have objected above [1] to the views of those who see in this sacrifice, and, hence, in the triumphal ceremony, nothing beyond the redemption of the *votum* made before marching out to war. We saw that the *votum* could also be redeemed in another way, in an *ovatio*, or even without any official ceremony. If, after the entry, the triumphal sacrifice on the Capitol formed the second highlight of the ceremony—and the attention ancient authors devote to it points that way—this is, in my opinion, to be explained by the fact that the triumphator as the bearer of exceptional "power" gave this ceremony a special significance, just as did the dictator to other sacral rites. This also means that this sacrifice was not merely a thanksgiving-sacrifice for the victory, but was at the same time looked upon as a sacrifice *pro salute rei publicae* pointing to the future, just as the sacrifice the magistrates made at their installation was not merely the redemption of the *votum* of their predecessors [2], but at the same time—and I think primarily—what the Greeks call εἰσιτήρια, a sacrifice which was to place the year to come under the protection of gods. Cass. Dio, 45, 17, reports on consul Vibius making these εἰσιτήρια.

Once we recognize this, we notice the peculiar parallelism between the tribunus militum M. Calpurnius Flamma, who "against the law" sacrificed *praetextatus* and the triumphator, who, in a still more unlawful manner, made a state-offering in a garment which to the Romans was recognizable as a *regalis habitus* [3], in a ceremony which did not deny its royal descent. To what extent the person is typified

---

[1] p. 183 ff.

[2] It is worth noticing that the places mentioning this sacrifice (Ovid. fast. 1, 79 ff.; ep. ex Ponto 4, 4, 23 ff.; 4, 9, 3 ff.; Cic. de leg. agr. 2, 93; Tertull. nat. 1, 10; Cass. Dio, 58, 8, 4) nowhere state the *voti solutio* as the reason for it. The sacrifice the censor made at the *lustrum* was also considered to further the prosperity of the period to come. This is clear from the fact that Scipio repels the accusation that his *lustrum* was unlucky by the riposte that not he, but his predecessor had made the sacrifice.

[3] Epic. Drusi, 333; Dion. Hal. 2, 34, 2; 3, 62, 2; 4, 74, 1; 5, 35, 1. Cass. Dio, 44, 6, 1; 46, 17, 5. See further about this subject above p. 83 f.

by his robes, particularly in connection with the sacrifice, is further apparent from the fact that it is decided for Caesar θύειν αὐτὸν ἀεὶ θριαμβικῶς ἠμφιεσμένον [1]. We have interpreted the *praetexta* of Calpurnius Flamma as the official indication of his temporary promotion, by which the sacrifice would gain in effectiveness. During the sacrifice he *was* a magistrate. In exactly the same way it may be said that the triumphator, during his entry and the sacrificing on the Capitol was by his insignia characterized as king. And now we have mentioned an aspect of the triumph which was already referred to in the beginning of this study and which at its conclusion merits a brief discussion.

If the Greek acclamation σωτὴρ καὶ βασιλεύς were transposed into the Roman way of thought, we have so far looked upon the triumphator as a σωτήρ. All attempts to collect the places in which the triumphator is called *servator* or *conservator urbis, patriae, Romae* [2], etc. would be made in vain. There are plenty of testimonia, but the terms are not found in the official titles and in the formulas concerning the triumph [3]. This does not imply that the "saviour" was a figure unknown to the Romans. On the contrary, they gave, as we saw, the most honorific wreaths to the Roman who had saved one fellow-citizen or a group of them. It is, therefore, not improbable that the triumphator was also looked upon as a "saviour", but the texts which call him by that name have almost certainly been influenced by the Greek-Hellenistic terminology [4]. The triumphator was, moreover, more than just a saviour, and we compared him only with the σωτήρ in connection with the definition of the entry of the bearer of good fortune.

A Roman counterpart of the acclamation βασιλεύς is, of course, not found during the republic. When the triumphator and the triumph nevertheless bear unmistakably regal characteristics, these are not incidental relics from the regal period. They testify to a deliberate keeping up of a ceremony which in fact could only be performed by a king.

There are, therefore, no objections to be raised to the view held by Deubner, Warde Fowler and Wagenvoort, in which the triumphator

---

[1] Appian, b.c. 2, 106.

[2] A good survey of the concepts *servare, servator, conservator* in Latin is given by H. Kasper, o.c. 77 ff.

[3] The oldest testimonium of *servator* is Plaut. Pseud. 873 denoting "pre-server".

[4] See Kasper, o.c. 87 ff.

is looked upon as the temporary revival of the old *rex*. Wagenvoort [1] in particular has very clearly formulated this: "When a Roman commander had shown that he had been able to inspire his troops with the greatest courage, he wore for one day the robe of him in whom anciently all *imperium*, all the chief's mana, was concentrated, *viz.*—the king". The total *imperium maius*, which, as I hope I have demonstrated, was essential to the triumphator on the day of his entry and at the sacrifice, is in fact the *imperium* of the king. That in the triumph this *imperium* had to be concentrated in one person finds its explanation here. No more than the king was the triumphator as to power—*imperium*—to be equalled by others. The Romans abolished the kingship. Important acts directly connected with the *salus publica* could, however, be performed only by the king. For this reason they created the office of the *rex sacrorum*, just as the Greeks created the ἄρχων βασιλεύς; for the same reason they kept up specifically regal ceremonies such as the triumph [2].

It should be pointed out, however, that the scholars just referred to misunderstood the original meaning of the triumph. The exclamation *triumpe* is not explained by their theory, the red lead, the expression *ornatus Iovis* and other data require an explanation, which can be found only via the Etruscan culture. The view formulated by Wagenvoort is therefore correct, but represents only part of the truth. The crux of the matter is not that the king as the holder of the highest power revived in the triumph—although he did—, but that a specifically regal ceremony was kept up during the republic. In other words, it was not the *rex*, but the *rex* as triumphator—with the insignia which were required especially for this ceremony, showing the red lead, which was used only in this ceremony, and accompanied by the exclamation *triumpe*, which was used only on this occasion—who for one day manifested himself again, embodied in the victorious commander. The Romans were no longer familiar with the original meaning of the triumph—the god manifesting himself in the figure of the king—, but they did know that it somehow or other served the continuance of the state. The sacrifice on the Capitol was made *pro rei publicae salute*. This sacrifice was made by the person who not only in a legal, but also in a dynamistic sense had proved to hold the highest *imperium*. He was allowed for one day to exchange the *praetexta* for the insignia even

---

[1] Roman Dynamism, 72.

[2] As also the leader of the games was clearly the successor of the *rex*.

the king wore only during the triumph and the old New Year festival of the *ludi Romani*. To what extent the triumph was a regal ceremony may finally be illustrated by a highly instructive legend, which may be assumed to date back to the early republic.

The legend of the praetor Genucius Cipus [1] has come down to us in several versions. Plin. 11, 123, 45, briefly mentions him as one of those who miraculously grew horns on their heads. Valerius Maximus, 5, 6, 3, gives more information: *Genucio Cipo praetori paludato portam egredienti novi atque inauditi generis prodigium incidit: namque in capite eius subito veluti cornua eruperunt, responsumque est regem eum fore, si in urbem revertisset. quod ne accideret, voluntarium ac perpetuum sibimet indixit exilium: dignam pietatem, quae, quod ad solidam gloriam attinet, septem regibus praeferatur. cuius testandae rei gratia capitis effigies aerea portae, qua excesserat, inclusa est dictaque Raudusculana: nam olim aera raudera dicebantur.*

Before looking at a still more detailed and complete report of this event, we can already at this stage state a number of facts. In the *gens Genucia* the cognomen Cipus is no longer found in later times. This forms an indication as to the time from which the story dates. This time is narrowed down by two more data: the fact that Cipus is called *praetor*, and the rejection of the kingship. In view of these data we believe that this legend may date back to the 5th century B.C. [2]. What are the main facts of this story? When marching out to war (*paludato!*), the praetor Genucius Cipus passes a gate. He grows horns on his head, which is looked upon as an *omen*, and may be compared with the flames round the head of Servius Tullius. An oracle also predicts the kingship for Genucius Cipus *if he will return into the city*. He does not do so, renounces the kingship, and, as a reward, gets his *effigies* on the Porta Raudusculana.

A version which is identical in some essentials, but which differs in one important respect, is given in Ovid, Metamorphoses, 15, 565 ff. Here it is the Etruscan seer Tages, who welcomes Cipus after the *prodigium*: *Rex, ait, o salve* (580); *namque urbe receptus rex eris* (584). Entering the city through the gate is several times explicitly mentioned as a condition of the kingship 583, 584/85, 594/95, 597, 598,

---

[1] About Cipus i.a. Wissowa, Gesammelte Abhandlungen, 135 ff.; E. W. Palm, R.H.R. 119, 1939, 82 ff.

[2] Hanell, Das altrömische eponyme Amt, 188, even sees in the Cipus-story the proof that there was a *praetor* side by side with the king during the regal period.

600, 616. Here, too, Cipus refuses and is as a reward given a piece
of land of a size he could encircle with his plough in the course of one
day. The essential difference is that Cipus grows his horns not when
marching out, but when returning from war, *after a victory: ut
victor domito veniebat ab hoste* (569). For this reason he puts a
laurel-wreath on his head, by which his horns are concealed to the
people. When he has taken off the wreath his audience does not
allow this, and *festam imposuere coronam* (615).

There are no decisive reasons why Ovid's reports should be looked
upon as the original version [1]. But it may be pointed out that the
report of Valer. Maxim. is highly condensed, and that in his version
too, war plays a part. If Ovid's version is the original one, we cannot
wish for a more beautiful illustration of a complex of ideas that has
revealed itself in the course of our investigation: the complex
in which the victorious highest magistrate, adorned with the laurel-
wreath, an official entry through a gate, and kingship connected
with it or resulting from it form a pattern: the pattern of the
triumphal procession. I do not see more than an illustration in the
Cipus legend. But we find that also to the Romans the connection
of the entry of the *victor* into the city with the figure of the *rex* was
not an unfamiliar one.

4. *Conclusion*

The development of the triumph took place in two stages, of
which the *caesura* is to be looked for in the last part of the regal period
in Rome. In the Etruscan culture a primitive New Year festival,
which had been imported from Asia Minor, and in which the king
acted the part of a god who manifested himself, developed into a
historic festival of victory. Rome inherited both ceremonies. The
festival of victory was given here a specifically Roman meaning.
The triumphator as *felix vir*, as *imperator* even inside the city vested
with the highest *imperium*, brought, by his entry, welfare and blessing
into the city. The rites he performed he carried out *pro salute rei
publicae*, he functioned as king in his greatest power.

Even though there is a great difference between the Etruscan and
the Roman triumphs, which reveals itself most clearly in the position
of the triumphator, who in the original ceremony acted the part of

---

[1] Wissowa, Ges. Abh. 134 ff. sees in the story an aetiology of the horned
head on the Porta Raudusculana. However, he, too, does not know how the
name of Genucius Cipus came to be associated with it.

Iuppiter, a representation which did not find acceptance in Rome, there are no essential changes as to the idea underlying the ceremony. For the coming of salvation and blessing, which the history-minded Roman saw represented in the entry of the triumphator, people which created myths saw in the annual rising of the god who returned from death or captivity. The epiphany of Dionysos, acted by the βασιλεύς during the *Anthesteria* at Athens, also brought prosperity, new life, a new beginning. This is the line which, without interruption, remains discernible from the earliest forms of the mythical-cyclical New Year ritual into the historical triumphal ceremony of the Romans. Here, as elsewhere, Rome rejected the myth; the pattern of the ceremony, however, remained visible in its elements: victory, new beginning, the coming of the bearer of good fortune.

When C. Julius Caesar as the first man to bear the title of *imperator*, not only *extra*, but also *intra pomerium* as "*cognomen*" [1], has himself preceded by lictors with laurel-wreaths, in 44 B.C. assumes a dictatorship which is not to be limited as to time, in the same year exchanges the *toga praetexta* for the purple triumphal robes[2], these insignia are so unequivocal that his refusal of the royal diadem with the words *Caesarem se, non regem esse* [3], even if they were sincere, yet have every appearance of hypocrisy. Here we see a king, even though he did not bear the title *rex*. The title *imperator* is to take over this function [4]. The time is also ripe for a deification of the ruler: Caesar is the first who is given unmistakably divine honours. The impulse for the coming into being of the ideology of this kind of ruler was unquestionably given by Hellenism. But its germs are to be found in a ceremony which, rooted in the sacral kingship, also according to the Romans closely linked up with the coming of a new era of prosperity, never quite denied its origin: the triumph.

---

[1] About the meaning of the title of *imperator* and the triumphal robes of Caesar see R. Combès, Imperator, 126.

[2] From then on he was allowed to wear these robes all the time: Cass. Dio 44, 4, a fact which deeply impressed his contemporaries: Cic. de div. 1, 52, 119; 2, 16, 37; Plin. n.h. 11, 37, 186; Nic. Damasc. vita Caes. 21; Cic. Phil. 2, 34, 85; Plut. Caes. 61 and Anton. 12.

[3] Suet. Div. Iul. 79, 2.

[4] About the reminiscences of the *rex* during the first century B.C. see J. Gagé, De César à Auguste. Où en est le problème des origines du principat. Rev. Hist. 177, 1936, 279 ff.; A. Alföldi, Die Geburt der kaiserlichen Bild-symbolik. Mus. Helv. 7, 1950, 1 ff.; 8, 1951, 190 ff.; 11, 1954, 134 ff.

BIBLIOGRAPHY

(For literature on special subjects, such as the *carmen arvale*, the *Porta* and *Arcus Triumphalis*, kingship, Near Eastern festivals, etc., which, as a rule, has not been included in this list, the reader is referred to the bibliographical notes in the text)

Abaecherli, A. L., *Fercula, carpenta* and *tensae* in the Roman procession. *Bollettino dell' Associazione internazionale degli Studi Mediterranei*, 6, 1935/36, 1 ff.

Alföldi, A., Der neue Weltherrscher der IV Ekloge Virgils. *Hermes*, 65, 1930, 369 ff.

——, Die Ausgestaltung des monarchischen Zeremoniells am römischen Kaiserhofe. *Rhein. Mus.* 49, 1934, 1 ff.

——, Insignien und Tracht der römischen Kaiser. *Mitteilungen des deutschen archaeologischen Instituts. Röm. Abt.* 50, 1935, 1 ff.

——, Die Geburt der kaiserlichen Bildsymbolik. *Mus. Helv.* 7, 1950, 1 ff.; 8, 1951, 190 ff.; 9, 1952, 204 ff.; 10, 1953, 103 ff.; 11, 1954, 133 ff.

——, *Der frührömische Reiteradel und seine Ehrenabzeichen*. Deutsche Beiträge zur Altertumswissenschaft, 2, Baden-Baden, 1952.

——, *Early Rome and the Latins*. Jerome Lectures, ser. 7, 1965.

Altheim, F., *Griechische Götter im alten Rom*. R.V.V. XXII, 1, Giessen, 1930.

——, *Terra Mater. Untersuchungen zur altitalischen Religionsgeschichte*, R.V.V. XXII, 2, Giessen, 1931.

——, *Römische Religionsgeschichte*. Sammlung Göschen, 1931-1933.

——, Altrömisches Königtum. *Die Welt als Geschichte*, 1, 1935, 414 ff.

——, *Italien und Rom*, Amsterdam, 1941.

——, *Der Ursprung der Etrusker*, Baden-Baden, 1950.

——, *Römische Religionsgeschichte*. Baden-Baden, 1951-1953.

——, *Römische Geschichte*, Frankfurt, 1951-1953.

——, *Römische Religionsgeschichte*. Sammlung Göschen, 2nd ed., 1956.

Balkestein, J., *Onderzoek naar de oorspronkelijke zin en betekenis van de Romeinse god Mars*. Diss. Leiden, 1963.

Barini, C., *Triumphalia. Imprese ed onori militari durante l'impero Romano*, Torino, 1952.

Baus, K., *Der Kranz in Antike und Christentum*, Bonn, 1940.

Bayet, J., *Les origines de l'Hercule romain*, Paris, 1926.

——, Le phénomène religieux dionysiaque. *Critique*, 80, 1954, 20 ff.; 81, 1954, 132 ff.

Bernardi, A., Dagli ausiliari del rex ai magistrati della res publica. *Athenaeum*, 30, 1952, 3 ff.

Beseler, G., Triumph und Votum. *Hermes*, 44, 1909, 352 ff.

Beth, K., *Religion und Magie bei den Naturvölkern*, 2nd ed., Berlin, 1924.

Bieler, L., Θεῖος ἀνήρ. *Das Bild des "göttlichen Menschen" in Spätantike und Frühchristentum*, Wien, 1935/36.

Bloch, R., *Tite-Live et les premiers siècles de Rome*, Paris, 1965.

Bömer, F., *Ahnenkult und Ahnenglaube im alten Rom*. Beihefte zum A.R.W. 1, 1943.

——, *Rom und Troia. Untersuchungen zur Frühgeschichte Roms*, Baden-Baden, 1951.

——, *P. Ovidius Naso. Die Fasten*, Heidelberg, 1958.

Boisacq, E., *Dictionnaire étymologique de la langue grecque*, 3d ed., Heidelberg-Paris, 1938.

Brandenstein, W., ἴαμβος, θρίαμβος, διθύραμβος. *I.F.* 54, 1936, 34 ff.

Brelich, A., Trionfo e morte. *S.M.S.R.* 14, 1938, 189 ff.

Bruhl, A., Les influences hellénistiques dans le triomphe romain. *Mélanges d'archéologie et d'histoire de l'école francaise de Rome*, 46, 1929, 77 ff.

——, *Liber Pater. Origine et expansion du culte dionysiaque à Rome et dans le monde romain*, Paris, 1953.

Cancelli, F., *Studi sui censores e sull' arbitratus della lex contractus*, Milano, 1957.

Catalano, P., *Contributi allo studio del diritto augurale*, I, Torino, 1960.

Cerfaux, L.-J. Tondriau, *Le culte des souverains dans la civilisation gréco-romaine*. Bibliothèque de Théologie, ser. III, 5, Paris-Tournai, 1957.

Chantraine, P., *La formation des noms en Grec ancien*, Paris, 1933.

Classen, C. J., Gottmenschentum in der römischen Republik. *Gymnasium*, 70, 1963, 312 ff.

Clemen, C., *Die Religion der Etrusker*. Untersuchungen zur allgemeinen Religionsgeschichte 7, Bonn, 1936.

Coli, U., *Regnum*. (Excerptum ex "Studia et Documenta Historiae et Iuris", XVII, 1951) Pavia, 1951.

Colini, A. M., *Il fascio littorio*, Roma, 1932.

Combès, R., *Imperator. Recherches sur l'emploi et la signification du titre d'Imperator dans la Rome républicaine*. Publications de la faculté des lettres et sciences humaines de l'université de Montpellier, XXVI, Paris, 1966.

Cook, A. B., *Zeus. A study in ancient religion*. 5 parts, Cambridge, 1914-1940.

Cumont, F., *Afterlife in Roman Paganism*, London, 1923.

Deissmann, A., *Licht vom Osten*, 4th ed., Tübingen, 1923.

Deubner, L., *Die Römer*. Chantepie de la Saussaye, Lehrbuch der Religionsgeschichte II, 4th ed., 1925.

——, *Attische Feste*, 2nd ed., Berlin, 1932.

——, Die Bedeutung des Kranzes im klassischen Altertum. *A.R.W.* 30, 1933, 70 ff.

——, Die Tracht des römischen Triumphators. *Hermes*, 69, 1934, 316 ff.

Dieterich, A., *Mutter Erde. Ein Versuch über Volksreligion*, 3d ed., Leipzig, 1925.

Dölger, F. J., *Der Heiland. Antike und Christentum. Kultur- und Religionsgeschichtliche Studien*, VI, 1950, 241 ff.

Dumézil, G., *Les mythes romains I. Horace et les Curiaces*, Paris, 1942.

——, *Maiestas* et *gravitas*. *Rev. Phil.* 26, 1952, 7 ff.; 28, 1954, 19 f.

——, Remarques sur "augur", "augustus". *Rev. Ét. Lat.* 35, 1957, 126 ff.

——, *La religion romaine archaïque, suivi d'un appendice sur la religion des Étrusques*. Bibliothèque historique. Collection "Les religions de l'humanité." Paris, 1966.

Durante, M., *Triumpe* e *triumphus*. Un capitolo del più antico culto dionisiaco latino. *Maia*, 4, 1951, 138 ff.

Eisler, R., *Weltenmantel und Himmelszelt. Religionsgeschichtliche Untersuchungen zur Urgeschichte des antiken Weltbildes*, München, 1910.

Eitrem, S., *Beiträge zur griechischen Religionsgeschichte II, Kathartisches und Rituelles. 1. Rundgang und Durchqueren*, 1917; III, 3, *Die ὀλολύγη*; III, 4, *Die Prozessionen*, 1919. (Skrifter utg. av Videnskapsselskapet i Kristiania. Hist.-Phil. Klasse.)

Eliade, M., *Traité d'histoire des religions*, 2nd ed., Paris, 1964.

Engnell, I., *Studies in divine Kingship in the ancient Near East*, Uppsala, 1943.

Ericsson, H., Sulla Felix. Eine Wortstudie. *Eranos*, 41, 1943, 77 ff.

——, Caesar und sein Glück. *Eranos*, 42, 1944, 57 ff.

Erkell, H., (= H. Ericsson) *Augustus, Felicitas, Fortuna. Lateinische Wortstudien*, Göteborg, 1952.

Ernout, A., *Philologica*, I, Paris, 1946.

——, *Aspects du vocabulaire latin*, Paris, 1954.

Ernout, A. — A. Meillet, *Dictionnaire étymologique de la langue latine*, 3d ed., Paris, 1951.

Essen, C. C. van, Over de symboliek der Romeinsche circusspelen. *Bulletin van de Vereeniging tot Bevordering der Kennis van de antieke Beschaving*, 19, 1944, 30 ff.

Farnell, L. R., *The Cults of the Greek States*, 5 parts, Oxford, 1896/1909.

Fiesel, E., *Namen des griechischen Mythos im Etruskischen*, Göttingen, 1928.

Fitzhugh, Th., *Triumpus-θρίαμβος*. The Indoeuropean or Pyrrhic Stress Accent in Antiquity. *Univ. of Verg. Bulletin of the School of Latin*, 2nd ser. 1/2, 1930.

Fowler, W. Warde, Iuppiter and the triumphator. *Class. Rev.* 30, 1916, 153 ff.

——, *Roman Essays and Interpretations*, Oxford, 1920.

——, *The religious Experience of the Roman People*, 2nd ed., London, 1922.

——, *The Roman Festivals of the period of the Republic*, 5th ed., London, 1933.

Francisci, P. de, *Arcana Imperii*, III/1, Milano, 1948.

——, Intorno alla natura e alla storia dell' *auspicium imperiumque. Studi in memoria di E. Albertario*, I, Milano, 1953, 397 ff.

——, Intorno all' origine etrusca di concetto di *imperium. S.E.* 24, 1955/56, 19 ff.

——, *Primordia Civitatis*. Pontificum Institutum utriusque Iuris, Studia et Documenta, 2, Roma, 1959.

Frankfort, H., *Kingship and the Gods. A study of ancient Near Eastern Religion as the integration of society and nature*, Chicago, 1948.

Frazer, J. G., *Lectures on the early history of Kingship*, London, 1905.

——, The golden Bough, 3rd ed., 1911-1918, London.

——, *P. Ovidii Nasonis Fastorum Libri sex*, London, 1929.

Frisk, Hj., *Griechisches etymologisches Wörterbuch*, Heidelberg, 1954-.....

Gagé, J., La théologie de la victoire impériale. *Rev. Hist.* CLXXI, 1933, 1 ff.

——, De César à Auguste. Où en est le problème des origines du principat. *Rev. Hist.* CLXXVII, 1936, 279 ff.

——, Le genre littéraire des "*res gestae*" triomphales et ses thèmes. *Rev. Ét. Lat.* 17, 1939, 33 ff.

——, "Fornix Ratumenus". L'entrée "isélastique" étrusque et la "porta Triumphalis" de Rome. *Bulletin de la Faculté des Lettres de Strasbourg*, 31, 1952, 163 ff.

——, Les clientèles triomphales de la république romaine. *Rev. Hist.* CCXVIII, 1957.

Gaster, Th. H., *Thespis. Ritual, Myth and Drama in the ancient Near East*, 2nd ed., New York, 1961.

Gennep, A. van, *Les rites de passage*, Paris, 1909.

Gioffredi, C., Sulle attribuzioni sacrali dei magistrati romani. *Iura*, 9, 1958, 22 ff.

Goell, H. A., *De triumphi Romani origine, permissu, apparatu, via*, Schleizae, 1854.

Grenier, A., *Les religions étrusque et romaine*. Mana, III, Paris, 1948.

Guardini, R., *Der Heilbringer in Mythos, Offenbarung und Politik*, Zürich, 1945.

Guthrie, W. K. C., *The Greeks and their Gods*, London, 1950.

Hägerström, A., *Das magistratische Ius in seinem Zusammenhang mit dem römischen Sakralrechte*. Uppsala Universitets Årsskrift, Juridiska Fakultetens Minnesskrift, 8, 1929.

Halkin, L., La parodie d'une demande de triomphe dans l'Amphitryon de Plaute. *L'Ant. Class.* 1948, (Misc. H. v. d. Weerd) 297 ff.

——, *La supplication d'actions de grâces chez les Romains*. Bibliothèque Fac. Philos. Univ. Liège, fasc. CXXVIII, Paris, 1953.

Hanell, K., *Das altrömische eponyme Amt*, Lund, 1946.

Harrison, J. E., *Prolegomena to the study of Greek Religion*, 3d ed., Cambridge, 1922.

——, *Themis. A study of the Social Origins of Greek Religion*, 2nd ed., Cambridge, 1927.

Heidenreich, R., Tod und Triumph in der römischen Kunst. *Gymnasium*, 58, 1951, 326 ff.

Henderson, M. J., *Potestas regia. J.R.S.* 47, 1957, 82 ff.

Hertzberg, G. A. B., *De spoliis opimis quaestio. Philol.* 1, 1846, 331 ff.

Heurgon, J., *Recherches sur l'histoire, la religion et la civilisation de Capoue préromaine des origines à la deuxième guerre punique*. Biblioth. Ec. franc. Rome, CLIV, Paris, 1942.

——, *La vie quotidienne chez les Étrusques*, Paris, 1961.

Heuss, A., Zur Entwicklung des Imperiums der römischen Oberbeamten. *Z.S.S. Rom. Abt.* 64, 1944, 57 ff.

Hocart, A. M., *Kingship*, London, 1927.

Hölscher, T., *Victoria Romana. Archäologische Untersuchungen zur Geschichte und Wesensart der römischen Siegesgöttin von den Anfängen bis zum Ende*, Mainz a. R., 1967.

Hofmann, J. B., *Etymologisches Wörterbuch des Griechischen*, München, 1950.

Holland, L. A., *Ianus and the Bridge*. Papers and Monographs of the American Academy in Rome, 21, 1961.

Hooke, S. H., *Myth and Ritual. Essays on the Myth and Ritual of the Hebrews in relation to the culture pattern of the Ancient East*, London, 1933.

——, *Myth, Ritual and Kingship. Essays on the Theory and Practice of Kingship in the Ancient Near East and in Israel*, Oxford, 1958.

Hubaux, J., *Rome et Véies. Recherches sur la chronologie légendaire du moyen âge romain*. Biblioth. Fac. Philos. Univ. Liège, fasc., CXLV, Paris, 1958.

James, E. O., *Myth and Ritual in the ancient Near East*, London, 1958.

Jeanmaire, H., *Dionysos. Histoire du culte de Bacchus*, Paris, 1951.

Kampers, F., *Vom Werdegange der abendländischen Kaisermystik*, Leipzig, 1924.

Kaser, M., *Das altrömische Ius. Studien zur Rechtsvorstellung und Rechtsgeschichte der Römer*, Göttingen, 1949.

Kasper, H., *Griechische Soter-Vorstellungen und ihre Übernahme in das politische Leben Roms*. Inaug. Diss. München, 1961.

Kern, O., *Die Religion der Griechen*, I-III, Berlin, 1926-1938.

Kienast, D., *Imperator. ZSS, Rom. Abt.* 78, 1961, 403 ff.
Kittel, G., *Theologisches Wörterbuch zum neuen Testament*, Stuttgart, 1933- . . .
Koch, C., *Gestirnverehrung im alten Italien*, Frankfurt, 1933.
———, *Der römische Iuppiter*. Frankfurter Studien zur Religion und Kultur der Antike, 14, Frankfurt, 1937.
———, *Religio. Studien zu Kult und Glauben der Römer*. Erlanger Beiträge zur Sprach- und Kunstwissenschaft, 7, Nürnberg, 1960.
Köchling, J., *De coronarum apud antiquos vi atque usu*. R.V.V. 14, 1913/14.
Kraft, K., Der goldene Kranz Caesars und der Kampf um die Entlarvung des "Tyrannen". *Jahrbuch für Numismatik und Geldgeschichte*, 3/4, 1952/53, 7 ff.
Kretschmer, P., *Sprache*, in: Gercke-Norden, *Einleitung in die Altertumswissenschaft*, I, 3rd ed., 6, 1923.
Kristensen, W. B., *Het leven uit de dood*, Haarlem, 1926.
———, *Verzamelde bijdragen tot kennis der antieke godsdiensten*, Amsterdam, 1947.
———, *Symbool en werkelijkheid*, Zeist, 1962.

Labat, R., *Le caractère religieux de la royauté assyro-babylonienne*, Paris, 1939.
Lambrechts, R., *Essai sur les magistratures de républiques étrusques*. Études de Philologie, d'Archéologie et d'Histoire anciennes publiées par l'Institut historique belge de Rome, 7, 1959.
Laqueur, R., Über das Wesen des römischen Triumphs. *Hermes*, 44, 1909, 215 ff.
Latte, K., Zwei Exkurse zum römischen Staatsrecht. *Nachrichten von der Gesellschaft der Wissenschaften zu Göttingen. Phil.-hist. Klasse. N.F. Fachgruppe* 1, 1, 1934/36, 59 ff.
———, Religiöse Begriffe im frührömischen Recht. *Z.S.S. Rom. Abt.* 67, 1950, 47 ff.
———, *Römische Religionsgeschichte*. Handbuch der Altertumswissenschaft, V, 4, 1960.
Leeuw, G. van der, *Phaenomenologie der Religion*, 2nd ed., Tübingen, 1956.
Lehmann, F. R., *Mana. Eine begriffsgeschichtliche Untersuchung auf ethnologischer Grundlage*. Diss. Leipzig, 1915.
Leifer, F., *Die Einheit des Gewaltgedankens im römischen Staatsrecht*, München, 1914.
———, *Studien zum antiken Ämterwesen, I, Zur Vorgeschichte des römischen Führeramts*, Leipzig, 1931.
Leumann, M.,-J. B. Hofmann,-F. Stolz,-J. Schmalz, *Lateinische Grammatik*, München. 5th ed., 1928.
Levi, M. A., L'appellativo *imperator*. *Rivista de Filologia e di Istruzione Class.*, 10, 1932, 207 ff.
———, *Auspicio, imperio, ductu, felicitate*. *Reale Istituto Lombardo. Rendic. Classe di Lettere*, 71 (ser III, 2), 1938, 101 ff.
Lévy-Bruhl, H., *Les fonctions mentales dans les sociétés inférieures*, 5th ed., Paris, 1922.
———, *L'expérience mystique et les symboles chez les primitifs*, Paris, 1938.
Lübtow, U. von, Die *lex curiata de imperio*. *Z.S.S. Rom. Abt.* 69, 1952, 154 ff.

Mc Fayden, D., *The History of the Title Imperator under the Roman Empire*. Diss. Chicago, 1920.

Magdelain, A., Note sur la loi curiate. *Revue historique de droit français et étranger*, 42, 1964, 198 ff.
——, *Auspicia ad patres redeunt*. *Mélanges Bayet, Latomus*, 70, 1964, 443.
Mannhardt, W., *Wald- und Feldkulte*, I, II, 2nd ed., Berlin, 1904/05.
Marót, K., *Zum römischen Managlauben*. *Capita duo*, Budapest, 1943/44.
Marquardt, J., *Römische Staatsverwaltung*, 2nd ed., Berlin, 1881/85.
Mazzarino, S., *Dalla monarchia allo stato repubblicano*, Catania, 1945.
Meyer, E., *Römischer Staat und Staatsgedanke*, 2nd ed., Zürich, 1961.
Michels, A., Kirsopp, *The Calendar of the Roman Republic*, Princeton, 1967.
Momigliano, A., Ricerche sulle magistrature romane. *Bull. Com.* 58, 1930, 42 ff.
——, An interim report on the origins of Rome. *J.R.S.* 53, 1963, 95 ff.
Mommsen, Th., *Römische Forschungen*, I, II, Berlin, 1879.
——, *Römische Geschichte*, I-III, Berlin, 1881/85.
——, *Römisches Staatsrecht*, 3rd ed., Leipzig, 1887.
Müller, K. O.,-W. Deecke, *Die Etrusker*, Stuttgart, 1877.
Muller, F., "Augustus". *Mededeelingen der Koninklijke Akademie van Wetenschappen, afd. Letterkunde*, deel 63, ser A no 11, Amsterdam, 1927.
——, *Studia ad Terrae Matris cultum pertinentia*. IX *De triumphi origine atque ratione*. *Mnemos*. 3rd ser. 2, 1935, 197 ff.

Nacinovich, M., *Carmen Arvale*, I, II, Roma, 1933/34.
Nilsson, M. P., *Griechische Feste von religiöser Bedeutung mit Ausschluss der Attischen*, Leipzig, 1906.
——, *Primitive Religion*, Tübingen, 1911.
——, Studien zur Vorgeschichte des Weihnachtfestes. *A.R.W.* 19, 1916/19, 50 ff.
——, *Primitive Time Reckoning*, Lund, 1920.
——, *Geschichte der griechischen Religion*, 2nd ed., Handbuch der Altertumswissenschaft, V, 2, 1-2, München, 1955/61.
Noack, F., Triumph und Triumphbogen. *Vorträge der Bibliothek Warburg*, 1925/26, Berlin, 1928, 147 ff.
Nock, A. D., Soter and Euergetes. *The Joy of Study. Papers on the New Testament and related Subjects presented to Honor. F. C. Grant*, New York, 1951, 127 ff.
Norden, E., *Die Geburt des Kindes. Geschichte einer religiösen Idee*, Leipzig, 1924.
——, *P. Vergilius Maro. Aeneis, Buch VI*, 3rd ed., Leipzig-Berlin, 1934.
——, *Aus altrömischen Priesterbüchern*, Lund, 1939.

Omme, A. N. van, *"Virtus". Een semantiese studie*. Diss. Utrecht, no date.
Otto, W. F., *Dionysos. Mythos und Kultus*, Frankfurt am Main, 1933.
Oxé, A., Σωτήρ bei den Römern. Drei Skizzen zu Horaz. *Wien. Stud.* 48, 1930, 38 ff.

Pais, E., *Fasti triumphales populi Romani*, Roma, 1920.
Pallottino, M., *Elementi di lingua etrusca*, Firenze, 1936.
——, *Il trionfo Romano, il Campidoglio, gli archi nella storia della civiltà*. Estratto dagli Atti del V Congresso nazionale di studi Romani. Istituto di studi Romani, 1940.
——, *Die Etrusker*, Fischer Bücherei, 1965.
Payne, R., *The Roman Triumph*, London, 1962.
Peine, S., *De ornamentis triumphalibus*. Diss. inaug., Berolini, 1885.
Peterson, E., Die Einholung des Kyrios. *Zeitschrift für systematische Theologie*, 7, 1929, 682 ff.

Petrikovits, H., Die Porta triumphalis. *Jahreshefte des Oesterreichischen Archäologischen Instituts in Wien*, 28, 1933, 187 ff.
Pfister, F., *Der Reliquienkult im Altertum*, R.V.V. 5, 1909/12.
Pfuhl, E., *De Atheniensium pompis sacris*, Berolini, 1900.
Picard, C., *Les religions préhelléniques*. Mana, 2, I, Paris, 1948.
Picard, G. C., *Les trophées romains. Contribution à l'histoire de la religion et de l'art triomphal de Rome*, Paris, 1957.
Pickard-Cambridge, A., *Dithyramb, Tragedy and Comedy*, 2nd ed., Oxford, 1962.
Piganiol, A., *Recherches sur les jeux romains. Notes d'archéologie et d'histoire religieuse*. Publications de la Faculté des Lettres de l'Université de Strasbourg, fasc. 13, Paris, 1923.
Pighi, I. B., *De ludis saecularibus*, 2nd ed., Amsterdam, 1965.
Pohlmen, E., *Der römische Triumph. Der Triumph im allgemeinen, der Triumphzug des Aemilius Paullus, Germanicus, Titus*, Gütersloh, 1891.
Preller, L., *Römische Mythologie*, 3rd ed. by H. Jordan, Berlin, 1881.
Prellwitz, W., *Etymologisches Wörterbuch der griechischen Sprache*, 2nd ed., Göttingen, 1905.

Radin, M., *Imperium. Studi in Onore di S. Riccobono*, II, Palermo, 1936, 21 ff.
Radke, G., *Die Götter Altitaliens*, Münster, 1965.
Regalità, *La regalità sacra. The sacral Kingship. Studies in the History of Religions*. Supplem. to Numen, Leiden, 1959.
Reid, J. S., Roman Ideas of Deity. *J.R.S.* 6, 1916, 177 ff.
Reinach, S., *Cultes, Mythes et Religions*, I-V, Paris, 1905/23.
Rose, H. J., *Religion in Greece and Rome*, New-York, 1959. Reprint of: *Ancient Greek Religion*, 1946, and *Ancient Roman Religion*, 1948.
——, Mana in Greece and Rome. *Harv. Theol. Rev.* 42, 1949, 155 ff.
Rosenberg, A., *Der Staat der alten Italiker. Untersuchungen über die ursprüngliche Verfassung der Latiner, Osker und Etrusker*, Berlin, 1913.
Rubino, J., *Untersuchungen über römische Verfassung und Geschichte*, Cassel, 1839.
Rudolph, H., Das Imperium der römischen Magistrate. *Neue Jahrb.* 114, 1939, 145 ff.
Ryberg, I. Scott, *Rites of the State Religion in Roman Art*. M.A.A.R. 22, 1955.

Sanctis, G. de, *Imperator. Studi in Onore di S. Riccobono*, II, Palermo, 1936, 57 ff.
Schofield, W. K. Quinn, *Ludi, Romani magnique varie appellati*. Latomus, 26, 1967, 96 ff.
——, Observations upon the *Ludi Plebei*. Latomus, 26, 1967, 677 ff.
Schwyzer, E., *Griechische Grammatik*, I, Handbuch der Altertumswissenschaft, II, 1, 1, München, 1934.
Simone, C. de, *Die griechischen Entlehnungen im Etruskischen*, I, II, Wiesbaden, 1968-1970.
Sommer, F., *Griechische Lautstudien*, Strassburg, 1905.
——, *Handbuch der lateinischen Laut- und Formenlehre*, 2nd ed., Heidelberg, 1914.
Staveley, E. S., The Constitution of the Roman Republic, 1940-1954. *Historia*, 5, 1956, 74 ff.
——, The *fasces* and *imperium maius*. *Historia*, 12, 1963, 458 ff.
Stehouwer, P. H. N. G., *Étude sur Ops et Consus*. Diss. Utrecht, 1956.

Stern, H., *Le calendrier de 354. Étude sur son texte et sur ses illustrations*, Paris, 1953.

Stolz, F.-A. Debrunner-W. P. Schmid, *Geschichte der lateinischen Sprache*, Sammlung Göschen, Berlin, 1966.

Strong, S. Arthur, *Apotheosis and After life*, London, 1915.

Sturtevant, E. H., Studies in greek Noun-formation. *Class. Rev.* 5, 1910, 326 ff.

Taeger, F., *Charisma*, I, II, Stuttgart, 1960.

Taylor, L. Ross, *Local Cults in Etruria*. Papers and Monographs of the American Academy in Rome, 2, 1923.

——, *The Divinity of the Roman Emperor*, Middleton, 1931.

Turchi, N., *La religione di Roma antica*, Bologna, 1939.

Usener, H., *Götternamen. Versuch einer Lehre von der religiösen Begriffsbildung*, Bonn, 1896.

——, *Religionsgeschichtliche Untersuchungen*, III, *Die Sintfluthsagen*, Bonn, 1899.

Vinay, G., Nota su consul e imperator. *Rivista di Filologia e di Istruzione classica*. Nuovo serie, X, 1932, 219 ff.

Voci, P., Per la definizione dell' *Imperium*. *Studi in memoria di E. Albertario*, II, Milano, 1953, 23 ff.

Vogel, K. H., *Imperium* und *Fasces*. *Z.S.S. Rom. Abt.* 67, 1950, 62 ff.

Vries, J. de, Das Königtum bei den Germanen. *Saeculum*, 7, 1956, 295 ff.

Wagenvoort, H., *Imperium. Studiën over het "Mana"-begrip in Zede en Taal der Romeinen*, Amsterdam, 1941. 2nd ed.: *Roman Dynamism*, Oxford, 1947.

——, *Felicitas imperatoria*. *Mnemos*. ser. IV, 7, 1954, 300 ff.

——, *Studies in Roman Literature, Culture and Religion*, Leiden, 1956.

Walde, A.-J. B. Hofmann, *Lateinisches etymologisches Wörterbuch*, 3rd ed., Heidelberg, 1957.

Wallisch, E., *Die Opfer der römischen Triumphe*. Diss. Tübingen, 1951.

——, Name und Herkunft des römischen Triumphes, *Philol*, 98, 1954/55, 254 ff.

Ward, M. M., The association of Augustus with Iuppiter. *S.M.S.R.* 9, 1933, 203 ff.

Weinreich, O., Antikes Gottmenschentum. *Neue Jahrb.* 6, 1926, 633 ff.

——, *Menekrates Zeus und Salmoneus. Religionsgeschichtliche Studien zur Psychopathologie des Gottmenschentums in Antike und Neuzeit*, Stuttgart, 1933.

Wendland, P., Σωτήρ. Eine religionsgeschichtliche Studie. *Zeitschr. für Neutestamentliche Wissenschaft*, 5, 1904, 355 ff.

Werner, R., *Der Beginn der römischen Republik. Historisch-chronologische Untersuchungen über die Anfangszeit der libera res publica*, München-Wien, 1963.

Wilamowitz-Moellendorff, U. von, *Der Glaube der Hellenen*, I, II, 3rd ed., Darmstadt, 1959. Unaltered reprint of the 2nd ed., 1955.

Windekens, A. J. van, *Le pélasgique. Essai sur une langue indo-européenne pré-hellénique*, Louvain, 1952.

——, Gr. θρίαμβος et lat. *triumphus*. *Orbis*, 2, 1953, 489 ff.

Wissowa, G., *Gesammelte Abhandlungen*, München, 1904.

——, *Religion und Kultus der Römer*, München, 2nd ed., 1912.

Wunderlich, E., *Die Bedeutung der roten Farbe im Kultus der Griechen und Römer*. R.V.V. 20, 1925.

INDEX